Ius Gentium: Comparati
Perspectives on Law and

Volume 68

More information about this series at http://www.springer.com/series/7888

Richard Albert · Bertil Emrah Oder
Editors

An Unamendable Constitution?

Unamendability in Constitutional
Democracies

 Springer

Editors
Richard Albert
School of Law
The University of Texas at Austin
Austin, TX, USA

Bertil Emrah Oder
Law School
Koç University
Sarıyer, Istanbul, Turkey

ISSN 1534-6781   ISSN 2214-9902 (electronic)
Ius Gentium: Comparative Perspectives on Law and Justice
ISBN 978-3-319-95140-9   ISBN 978-3-319-95141-6 (eBook)
https://doi.org/10.1007/978-3-319-95141-6

Library of Congress Control Number: 2018946670

This Springer imprint is published by the registered company Springer Nature Switzerland AG
The registered company address is: Gewerbestrasse 11, 6330 Cham, Switzerland

Acknowledgements

On a splendid summer day in June 2015, 15 scholars convened in Istanbul for a conference on one of the most provocative subjects in modern public law: unamendable constitutional provisions. The papers presented at the conference have since been revised and refined into the fascinating chapters in this volume.

We gathered on the picturesque campus of Koç University Law School, our host for this gathering in partnership with Boston College Law School. We organized this program under the auspices of the International Society of Public Law, at the time only 1-year old but today the leading learned society for the study of public law.

We thank the staff at Koç University Law School for their contributions to the success of the conference and this volume. We are particularly grateful to Esra Özcan and Zeynep Koçer for their masterful organizational work, their enthusiasm for the conference program, and also for their generosity of spirit to all conference participants.

We thank our friends at Springer for publishing our ideas in their series on *Ius Gentium: Comparative Perspectives on Law and Justice*. We thank series editors Mortimer Sellers and James Maxeiner for their excitement about our project, and we express our gratitude to Diana Nijenhuijzen, Neil Olivier, Manjula Saravanan, and Corina van der Giessen for their advice in shepherding our manuscript to publication.

Finally, we exclaim our profound appreciation for the contributors to this volume. They have been model colleagues from the very beginning of this project. They made our conference a resounding success with their careful advance preparation for our gathering, with their sustained and constructive engagement during the conference and since then in the process of editing and revising their chapters, and also with their friendliness to us and each other. We can state with no uncertainty that their chapters will enrich the study of a subject that is extraordinarily important for understanding the promise and limits of constitutionalism.

Richard Albert
Bertil Emrah Oder

Contents

Contributors

Richard Albert The University of Texas School of Law, Austin, TX, USA

Juliano Zaiden Benvindo University of Brasília, Brasília, Brazil

Chintan Chandrachud Quinn Emanuel Urquhart & Sullivan LLP, London, UK

Ignacio N. Cofone McGill University Faculty of Law, Montreal, Canada

Fruzsina Gárdos-Orosz Hungarian Academy of Sciences, Center for Social Sciences, Institute of Legal Studies, Budapest, Hungary

Gert Jan Geertjes Leiden University Law School, Leiden, The Netherlands

Ridwanul Hoque University of Dhaka, Dhaka, Bangladesh

Serkan Köybaşı Law Faculty, Bahçeşehir University, Istanbul, Turkey

Mazen Masri The City Law School, City, University of London, London, UK

Stephan Michel Institute of Law and Economics, University of Hamburg, Hamburg, Germany

Bertil Emrah Oder Koç University Law School, Istanbul, Turkey

Tarik Olcay School of Law, University of Glasgow, Glasgow, UK

Konstantinos Pilpilidis Institute of Law and Economics, University of Hamburg, Hamburg, Germany

Yaniv Roznai Radzyner School of Law, Interdisciplinary Center (IDC), Herzliya, Israel

Valentina Rita Scotti Department of Political Science, LUISS University of Rome, Rome, Italy

Jerfi Uzman Leiden University Law School, Leiden, The Netherlands

Oya Yegen Sabancı Unversity, Istanbul, Turkey

The Forms of Unamendability

Richard Albert and Bertil Emrah Oder

Abstract In this introductory chapter to our edited volume on "An Unamendable Constitution? Unamendability in Constitutional States," we explore one of the most fascinating—and controversial—developments in constitutional design in the last half-century: the rise of unamendability. Whether formal or informal, unamendability serves many purposes, and we illustrate each of them with reference to constitutions around the world. We discuss the substantive, procedural and temporal limitations on constitutional amendment, we highlight the foundational questions in modern constitutionalism raised by unamendability, and we situate each of the thirteen chapters comprising the volume within the literature on constitutional change. Our objective in this volume is to theorize the subject of unamendability and to probe deeply the uses and misuses of unamendability in constitutional design.

The late political scientist John Burgess described the amending clause as "the most important part of a constitution."[1] Formal amendment rules indeed serve fundamental functions in a constitutional democracy, notably the expression of values that define a community constituted under an authoritative charter.[2] Formal amendment rules also provide a roadmap for amending actors to alter the constitution,[3] they distinguish constitutional from ordinary law,[4] and they reflect the democratic values of participation, deliberation, and ownership.[5] At their best, they

---

[1]Burgess (1893), p. 137.
[2]Albert (2013), pp. 225, 247–257.
[3]Dixon and Holden (2012), p. 195.
[4]Sajó (1999), pp. 39–40.
[5]Rasch and Congleton (2006), pp. 319, 326, Denning and Vile (2002), p. 247, 279.

R. Albert (✉)
The University of Texas School of Law, Austin, TX, USA
e-mail: richard.albert@law.utexas.edu

B. E. Oder
Koç University Law School, Istanbul, Turkey
e-mail: boder@ku.edu.tr

© Springer International Publishing AG, part of Springer Nature 2018
R. Albert and B. E. Oder (eds.), *An Unamendable Constitution?*
Ius Gentium: Comparative Perspectives on Law and Justice 68,
https://doi.org/10.1007/978-3-319-95141-6_1

promote debate about constitutional meaning,[6] they channel popular will into institutional dialogue,[7] and they formalize the democratic right of citizens to amend their constitution.[8]

Only very few constitutions do not codify formal amendment rules.[9] Formal amendment procedures range from easy to satisfy, as in New Zealand where only a simple legislative majority is needed, to extraordinarily difficult, for instance, in the United States where national and subnational actors must agree to a change by high supermajority thresholds.[10] In the vast majority of countries, formal amendment requires procedures more onerous than the ones used in normal lawmaking. This makes constitutional amendment a unique moment in the life of a state.

1 The Duality of Formal Amendment Rules

Formal amendment rules hold the key to making or unmaking a constitution.[11] Political actors have used these rules to divest courts of their powers, to guarantee equality for all persons under law, to abolish term limits for chief executives, and to restructure legislative powers from a bicameral to a unicameral system. Whatever the content of the amendment, successfully deploying these rules confers legal authority on the change, whether the amendment enhances the constitution or destroys its core commitments.[12] Here, then, is the problem: political actors can abuse the constitution with recourse to the constitution's own formal amendment rules.[13]

This duality of formal amendment rules—their availability for both good and ill—presents a challenge for constitutionalism: the rules of change are indispensable for the functioning of constitutional democracy, yet they open the door to the demise of constitutional democracy itself. How, then, can we protect constitutional democracy from the misuse of its own devices?

Constitutional designers have turned to one solution with increasing frequency: formal unamendability. A formally unamendable provision is "impervious to the constitutional amendment procedures enshrined within a constitutional text and immune to constitutional change even by the most compelling legislative and popular majorities."[14] Constitutional designers entrench unamendable provisions

---

[6]Ku (1995), pp. 535, 571.
[7]Dellinger (1983), pp. 386, 431.
[8]Rubenfeld (2001), p. 174.
[9]Giovannoni (2003), pp. 37.
[10]Lutz (2006), p. 170.
[11]Albert (2018a).
[12]Albert (2018b), pp. 29–60.
[13]Dixon and Landau (2015), p. 606, Landau (2013), pp. 189.
[14]Albert (2010), pp. 663, 665–666.

for many different purposes but in most cases intend them "to last forever and to serve as an eternal constraint on the state and its citizens,"[15] hence the phrase *eternity clause* that some scholars have used to describe them.[16]

Formal unamendability was once rare but today it is a near-global norm in the modern era of constitutionalism. From 20% of all constitutions from 1789 to 1944, to roughly 25% from 1945 to 1988, and now to over 50% of new constitutions since 1989, formal unamendability has emerged gradually as a common feature of codified constitutions.[17] Constitutional designers entrench a variety of provisions against amendment. Germany, for example, makes human dignity unamendable.[18] The Algerian,[19] Brazilian,[20] and Ukrainian[21] Constitutions make unamendable all of their constitutional rights. The Constitution of Bosnia and Herzegovina makes unamendable the requirement that the country remains or becomes party to specific international human rights agreements.[22] In Turkey and Togo, secularism is unamendable,[23] as is theocracy in Iran and Afghanistan,[24] socialism in Cuba,[25] unitarism in Indonesia and Kazakhstan,[26] monarchism in Jordan and Kuwait,[27] republicanism in France and Haiti and Italy,[28] the separation of powers in Greece,[29] presidential term limits in El Salvador and Guatemala,[30] and political pluralism in Portugal and Romania.[31] This list of formally unamendable provisions is just a small sample of the many examples we see around the world.

Constitutional democracies sometimes recognize the existence of unamendability even where nothing is entrenched as unamendable in the constitutional text. In these jurisdictions, unamendability becomes informally entrenched as a result of a binding declaration by the authoritative interpreter of the constitution that something in the constitution is inviolable. In virtually all cases, it is a court that

---

[15]Ibid, p. 666.

[16]See, eg, Kommers (1991), pp. 837, 846, Preuss (2011), pp. 429, Zuleeg (1997), p. 505, 510.

[17]See Roznai (2017), pp. 20–21.

[18]German Basic Law, pt I, art 1(1) (1949); pt VII, art 79(3).

[19]Algeria Const, tit IV, art 178 (1996).

[20]Brazil Const, sec VIII, sub-sec II, art 60, s 4(IV) (1988).

[21]Ukraine Const, tit XIII, art 157 (1996).

[22]Bosnia & Herzegovina Const, art II(7) (1995).

[23]Togo Const, tit XIII, art 144 (1992); Turkey Const, pt I, art 4 (1982).

[24]Afghanistan Const, ch X, art 149 (2004); Iran Const, ch XIV, art 177 (1980).

[25]Cuba Const, ch XV, art 137 (1976).

[26]Indonesia Const, ch XVI, art 37, s 5 (1945); Kazakhstan Const, sec IX, art 91(2) (1995).

[27]Jordan Const, ch III, art 126 (1984); Kuwait Const, pt V, art 175 (1962).

[28]France Const, tit XVI, art 89 (1958); Haiti Const, tit XIII, art 284(4) (1987); Italy Const, tit VI, s 2, art 139 (1948).

[29]Greece Const, pt IV, sec II, art 110 (1975).

[30]El Salvadore Const, tit VI, ch II, arts 154, 248 (1983); Guatemala Const, tit IV, ch III, arts 187, 281 (1985).

[31]Portugal Const, pt IV, tit II, art 288(i) (1976); Romania Const, tit VII, art 152 (1991).

declares the existence of an informally unamendable norm. Courts thereafter acquire the power to invalidate any contrary action, law or formal amendment. These informal restrictions rest on the fusion of two roles that have traditionally been separated across time and institutions: constitutional author and constitutional interpreter.

Judges have deployed the doctrine of informal unamendability to defend their constitution from what they regard as attacks on the constitution itself.[32] The doctrine has been effective in cases where the other branches of government have laid down their arms and acquiesced to this extraordinary assertion of judicial power. The doctrine has been much less effective—destructive even—where judges have manipulated the doctrine to the advantage of political actors to whom they are partial, as we recently saw in Honduras in a glaring example of its problematic misuse.[33]

There are many more layers of complexity to the design and interpretation of unamendability, whether formal or informal. In this introduction to *An Unamendable Constitution? Unamendability in Constitutional Democracies*, we begin by classifying the forms of unamendability. We distinguish not only between formal and informal unamendability but also between substantive and procedural forms of formal and informal unamendability. We moreover add another dimension to our analysis: time. Some forms of unamendability are temporally limited and others are not temporally bound. We also raise the possibility that unamendability may reflect a hybrid form that combines substantive with procedural protections. Our discussion of the forms of unamendability leads us to our thematic overview of the major lines of inquiry that await readers in this first-of-its-kind scholarly collection on unamendability—arguably the most fascinating design feature of modern constitutions.

2   Classifying Unamendability

Unamendability comes in many forms. In an important contribution to the study of unamendability, Melissa Schwartzberg classifies unamendability along temporal and formal dimensions.[34] Schwartzberg's classification turns on two inquiries: whether entrenchment is temporally limited or unlimited, and whether it is formally

---

[32]Albert (2017), pp. 188–189.

[33]See Marsteintredet (2015). In a similar decision, the Bangladesh Supreme Court's Appellate Division has recently applied the doctrine to invalidate an original constitutional provision. For a critique of this judgment, see Hoque (2016), p. 13.

[34]Schwartzberg (2007), pp. 8–16.

specified or implicitly enforced.[35] This generates four forms of unamendability: (1) formal, time-unlimited entrenchment; (2) formal, time-limited entrenchment; (3) de facto entrenchment; and (4) implicit entrenchment.[36]

For Schwartzberg, *formal, time-unlimited* entrenchment refers to a textually entrenched constitutional provision that is not subject to a time limitation, for instance, Portugal's absolute entrenchment of republican government.[37] *Formal, time-limited* entrenchment introduces a temporal wrinkle to textual entrenchment: the absolute entrenchment of a given constitutional text expires after a predefined period of time. As an example, Schwartzberg points to the United States Constitution's temporary entrenchment of the slave trade until 1808.[38] Under Schwartzberg's classification, de facto entrenchment refers to a textual provision that is unamendable despite not being textually entrenched against formal amendment and whose "amendment is virtually impossible because of exceptionally high procedural barriers to change."[39] Finally, *implicit* entrenchment incorporates the normative view that a norm may be so fundamental to the constitutional order that its amendment would transform the regime. It also incorporates the positive view that a norm has become so deeply embedded as a matter of fact that amending it would be unimaginable.[40] These four forms of unamendability illustrate an important view of how states may entrench constitutional provisions against formal amendment.

Yet, there is another possible classification of unamendability. Instead of classifying unamendability along temporal and formal dimensions to yield four forms of unamendability, we can classify unamendability along substantive and procedural dimensions to yield as many as eight forms. The classification we propose interrogates whether entrenchment is specified in the constitutional text—it can be formal or informal—and it also examines whether the amendment restriction applies to constrain *what* may be changed or *how* something may be changed. Each of these distinctions can be further refined according to their duration, namely whether they are limited or whether they are intended to last as long as the constitution itself. We can therefore imagine four forms of substantive unamendability: formal or informal substantive unamendability with an expiration date or not. And we can likewise see four forms of procedural unamendability: formal or informal procedural unamendability with an expiration date or not. There are limits to our classification but it offers another way to understand unamendability.

---

[35]Ibid, p. 8.

[36]Ibid, pp. 8–16.

[37]Portugal Const, pt IV, tit II, arts 288(b) (1976).

[38]US Const, art. V (1789).

[39]Ibid, p. 12.

[40]Ibid, pp. 13–14.

3   Substantive Unamendability

Unamendable provisions sometimes impose substantive restrictions on what is amendable. These restrictions concern the content or subject matter of a constitutional rule. For example, a rule that divests political actors of the power to amend a provision guaranteeing republican government, secularism, or federalism represents a substantive restriction on the amending power. Each of these three examples—unamendable republicanism, secularism, and federalism—is a substantive restriction because it defines what may not be amended. Identifying what is unamendable is only part of the inquiry into substantive unamendability. We must also inquire how these substantive restrictions arise to begin with. There are two possibilities: they may be formally entrenched in the constitutional text or they may emerge informally.

Formal substantive unamendability refers to subject matter unamendability codified in the text of the constitution. For example, under the Italian and French Constitutions, respectively, "the republican form [of the state] cannot be a matter of constitutional amendment"[41] and "the republican form of government cannot be the object of an amendment."[42] This is a straightforward form of unamendability because it is written down for all to see.

Although nothing in the United States Constitution is today formally unamendable, the Constitution entrenches two expired examples of formal substantive unamendability. The United States Constitution entrenches a now-expired temporary form of formal unamendability in the following clause of its amendment rule in Article V: "Provided that no Amendment which may be made prior to the Year One thousand eight hundred and eight shall in any Manner affect the first and fourth Clauses in the Ninth Section of the first Article."[43] The first and fourth clauses of Article I, Section 9 were formally unamendable from the moment of the coming-into-force of the Constitution in 1789 until the year 1808. Article I, Section 9, Clause 1 authorizes states to move and import slaves, and Article 1, Section 9, Clause 4 guarantees that taxation would be census-based.[44] Both clauses formed part of the Constitution's institutionalized framework for the protection of slavery.[45] These two formally unamendable provisions were necessary for the slave states to approve and ratify the Constitution. The authors of the Constitution entrenched these protections as temporarily unamendable until the year 1808 with the objective of later returning to the subject in twenty years to reconsider it "with less difficulty and greater coolness."[46]

---

[41]Italy Const, tit VI, s 2, art. 139 (1948).

[42]France Const., tit. XVI, art. 89 (1958).

[43]Ibid.

[44]US Const, art I, § 9, cl 1; US Const, art I, § 9, cl 4.

[45]See Greene (2011), pp. 517, 518–19.

[46]Linder (1981), pp. 717, 721.

4   The Purposes of Formal Unamendability

These two now-expired temporarily unamendable slave trade clauses reflect one of five purposes of formal amendability: to secure a constitutional bargain.[47] Where political actors reach an impasse on a divisive question of constitutional design, they may choose to make a resolution formally unamendable only for a defined period of time or they may alternatively opt to make an enduring compromise formally unamendable, a constitutional design choice that frees them to deal with other matters of basic governmental structure and function.[48] The use of formal unamendability to secure a constitutional bargain is appropriate for temporary agreements that political actors may choose to revisit after the constitution has been given time to take root in the political culture.[49] It is not uncommon, for instance, for new constitutions to prohibit formal amendments for a fixed number of years immediately upon their ratification.[50]

Formal unamendability may also be deployed for the second purpose: to preserve a core feature of the self-identity of the state. This preservative function of unamendability privileges one or more constitutional principles, rules, values, structures, or institutions as fundamentally constitutive of the regime. Preservative unamendability reflects the judgment of the drafting generation that the unamendable feature is important at the time of the adoption of the constitution and that successor generations should respect the sacrality of both this founding judgment and the entrenched feature itself.

Constitutional states entrench many examples of preservative unamendability. For example, Brazil and Germany both make federalism unamendable as a way both to preserve a governmental structure that has historically been necessary to manage conflict and disagreement, and to recognize its centrality to political life.[51] We can likewise interpret the absolute entrenchment of an official religion, or indeed of secularism, as an expression of the importance of religion or non-religion in that constitutional regime, either as a reflection only of the views of the constitutional drafters or of the views of citizens as well. Algeria and Iran make Islam unamendable as the official state religion, whereas Portugal and Turkey establish secularism as an unamendable feature of the state.[52] Both reflect a founding value intended to be preserved.

---

[47]See Dixon and Ginsburg (2011), pp. 636, 644. One can understand unamendability in this respect as a 'gag rule' that silences debate on matters of contention. See Holmes (1993), pp. 19–58.

[48]For more on temporary unamendability in the United States and elsewhere, see Varol (2014), pp. 409, 439–448.

[49]For an analysis of the forms of temporal restrictions on formal amendment. See Albert (2014), pp. 913, 952–54.

[50]See, e.g., Cape Verde Const, pt VI, tit III, art 309(1) (1980) (prohibiting formal amendments for 5 years following ratification of the constitution).

[51]See Albert (2010), p. 679.

[52]Compare Algeria Const, tit IV, art 178(3) (1989), Iran Const, art 177 (1980), with Portugal Const, pt IV, tit II, art 288(c) (1976), Turkey Const, pt I, art 4 (1982).

   In contrast to its preservative function, formal unamendability may also be used to transform a state. This is the third purpose of unamendability. Transformational unamendability seeks to repudiate something about the past and to adopt a new operating principle that will shape and inform a new constitutional identity.[53] This is sometimes more of an aspiration than a justiciable commitment, but it reflects a value seen as important enough by the authoring generation to make it unremovable from the constitutional text. Transformational entrenchment is intended to reflect the state's commitment to pursuing the values served by the entrenched constitutional provision and to urge respect for the entrenched provision by present and future political actors, present and future citizens, as well as present and future external actors.

   Constitutional states entrench many examples of transformational unamendability. For example, under the new Bosnian and Herzegovinian Constitution, all civil and political rights are formally unamendable,[54] in contrast to the regime that predated the new constitution.[55] The Ukrainian Constitution today likewise makes all rights unamendable,[56] something that would have been unimaginable before the new constitution came into force.[57] As a final illustration, consider the Namibian Constitution, which makes rights and liberties unamendable,[58] also in contrast to its own problematic past infringements on rights.[59] These examples suggest how formal unamendability may be used to help transform a state's default posture from rights infringement to rights enforcement.[60] Although formal unamendability cannot by itself defend rights from abuse, it can express the significance that constitutional designers attribute to rights enforcement along with their hope that their successors will ultimately and durably agree.

   Fourth, formal unamendability may be a reconciliatory device. The purpose of reconciliatory unamendability is to achieve peace by absolving factions and their leaders of criminal or civil wrongdoing in an effort to move past conflict and discord. For example, reconciliatory unamendability is illustrated by a formally unamendable grant of amnesty or immunity for prior conduct leading to a coup or an attempted one. By conferring amnesty upon political actors, constitutional designers seek to avoid a contentious and potentially destabilizing criminal or civil prosecution of wrongdoers by putting prosecution off the table altogether. The goal is instead to allow opposing factions to start afresh, free from threat of legal action, and sometimes in tandem with a Truth and Reconciliation Commission to give victims the opportunity to record their memories but without the consequence of

---

[53]For useful illustrations of the use of unamendability as a transformative device in Germany, India and South Africa, see Halmai (2012), pp. 182, 183–88, 190–91.

[54]Bosnia & Herzegovina Const., art X, § 2 (1995).

[55]See Mansfield (2003), pp. 2052, 2056.

[56]Ukraine Const, tit XIII, art 157 (1996).

[57]See Rezie (1999), pp. 169, 175–81.

[58]Namibia Const, ch XIX, art 131 (1990).

[59]See Wing (1993), pp. 295, 337–44.

[60]See Albert (2010), pp. 685–87.

legal duty and violation.[61] An example of reconciliatory unamendability is the now-superseded 1999 Constitution of Niger, which entrenched an unamendable amnesty provision for those involved in two coups—on January 27, 1996 and April 9, 1999—in order to give the new constitutional settlement a chance to succeed without the looming threat of the governing party prosecuting the opposition for earlier acts.[62]

The fifth purpose of unamendability is related to each of the others: to express constitutional values. Where a constitutional text distinguishes one provision by making it immune to the formal amendment rules that ordinarily apply, the message both conveyed and perceived is that this provision is more highly valued than those not granted protection.[63] Whether or not the absolute entrenchment of a given provision is intended to be enforceable, unamendability is nevertheless an important statement about the value, either objective or subjective or both, of the provision to that constitutional community. It is the ultimate expression of importance that can be communicated by the constitutional text. For example, the Cuban Constitution's absolute entrenchment of socialism is a statement of the importance of socialism,[64] just as the Afghan Constitution's absolute entrenchment of Islam and Islamic Republicanism reflect its highest constitutional values,[65] according to the authors of these constitutions. The expressive purpose of unamendability differs from its transformational purpose, the latter entailing a temporally prior social or political referent that the unamendability seeks to repudiate. The expressive purpose need not necessarily reflect a repudiation of the past; it may instead reflect altogether new values without reference to an old or superseded constitutional order or text.

5 Informal Unamendability

In contrast to the codification of a formally unamendable rule, *informal substantive unamendability* results from an authoritative judicial interpretation by the national court of last resort. Where the power to invalidate a constitutional amendment rests with a court, the act of reversing a popular or legislative judgment to amend the constitution raises a foundational question: on what democratic basis may a court rule that a duly passed constitutional amendment is unconstitutional?[66] The Supreme Court of India wrestled with this question in a series of important judgments from 1967 to 1981. Faced with the threat of the legislature abusing its

---

[61]Ibid, pp. 693–98.

[62]Niger Const, tit XII, art 136 (1999) (superseded); Niger Const, tit XII, art 141 (1999) (superseded).

[63]See Albert (2013), p. 254.

[64]Cuba Const, s 3 (1976) (as amended in 2002).

[65]Afghanistan Const, art 149 (2003).

[66]Colón-Ríos (2013), pp. 521, 525.

textually unlimited power of formal amendment, the Court was compelled to consider whether the amendment power was indeed unlimited. The Court ultimately ruled that the amendment power was limited. The Court in turn created the "basic structure doctrine" to invalidate amendments that, in its view, are not consistent with the Constitution's framework. At the time and with a handful of exceptions, the Indian Constitution authorized the national legislature to pass amendments with a bare majority vote in each house, provided two-thirds of all members are present.[67] By comparison of other constitutional democracies, this is a relatively low threshold for constitutional amendments.[68] And since the Indian Constitution did not then, nor does it today, formally entrench anything against amendment, all constitutional provisions are susceptible to legislative change, often by simple legislative vote. This constitutional design raises the risk that political actors will treat the Constitution like a statute, making it just as easily amendable.[69]

The Court's first major pronouncement on the national legislature's implicitly limited powers of formal amendment was in fact a reversal of its prior holding nearly 20 years before that the amendment power was unlimited.[70] The Court laid the foundation for invalidating a constitutional amendment at some point in the future, holding that the amendment power could not be used to abolish or violate fundamental constitutional rights.[71] Surely sensing, however, that actually invalidating a constitutional amendment could be too bold a move too soon, the Court held that the rule applied only prospectively, not retrospectively, and that only henceforth would the national legislature's textually plenary but now actually limited power of amendment be subject to judicial review. This case was a prelude to unveiling the basic structure doctrine.

In *Kesavananda Bharati Sripadagalvaru v. Kerala*, the Court held that the amendment power could be used only as long as it did not do violence to the Constitution's basic structure.[72] The concept of the basic structure was said to include the supremacy of the constitution, the republican and democratic forms of government, the secular character of the state, and the separation of powers and federalism.[73] In asserting these elements of the basic structure doctrine, the Chief Justice wrote that "every provision of the Constitution can be amended provided in the result the basic foundation and structure of the Constitution remains the

---

[67]India Const, pt XX, art 368(2) (1950).

[68]See Lutz (2006), p. 170 (ranking the Indian Constitution as one of the least rigid in a study sample of 36 democratic constitutions).

[69]See Sajó (1999), pp. 39–40, Sullivan (1995), pp. 20, 22–23.

[70]See *Sri Sankari Prasad Singh Deo v. Union of India*, 1951 AIR 458, 1952 SCR 89, online: http://www.indiankanoon.org/doc/1706770.

[71]*Golaknath v. State of Punjab*, 1967 AIR 1643, 1967 SCR (2) 762, online: http://www.indiankanoon.org/doc/120358.

[72]1973 SCC (4) 225, online: http://www.indiankanoon.org/doc/25786.

[73]Ibid. para 316.

same."[74] It is important to stress here that the Constitution's text itself did not then, nor does it now, identify expressly what is "basic," as in foundational, to its own structure.[75] That judgment of constitutional priority finds its origin in judicial interpretation, not in popular consent-driven constitutional design.

Some years later in *Minerva Mills Ltd. v. Union of India*, the Court invoked the basic structure doctrine to invalidate amendments to India's formal amendment rules.[76] The amendments had proposed to limit the Court's power to review constitutional amendments. The amendments declared that "no amendment of this Constitution … shall be called in question in any court on any ground"[77] and that "for the removal of doubts, it is hereby declared that there shall be no limitation whatever on the constituent power of Parliament to amend by way of addition, variation or repeal the provisions of this Constitution under this article."[78] These amendments were a direct response to the Court's assertion of supremacy and just the latest move in the battle for constitutional primacy between the national legislature and the Court.

The question for the Court was not whether the legislature's amendment power was subject to implicit limits. That question had been resolved in *Kesavananda*. The question was instead whether the legislature could overrule the Court using its amendment power. The Chief Justice began from the proposition that although "Parliament is given the power to amend the Constitution," it is clear for the Court that this "power cannot be exercised so as to damage the basic features of the Constitution or so as to destroy its basic structure."[79] This cornerstone of the basic structure doctrine—that the amendment power is constrained by implication of its limited nature even where the constitutional text does not entrench any limitation on its use—has since migrated beyond India to many other countries since its articulation around half a century ago.[80]

6 Procedural Unamendability

Constitutional provisions may also be unamendable in procedural terms. Whereas substantive unamendability entrenches a constitutional provision against formal amendment by reference to the content or subject matter of the provision, procedural unamendability likewise entrenches a constitutional provision against formal

---

[74]Ibid.

[75]One could interpret India's escalating formal amendment rules as creating a hierarchy of constitutional importance. See Albert (2013).

[76]1980 AIR 1789, 1981 SCR (1) 206, SCC (2) 591, online: http://www.indiankanoon.org/doc/1939993.

[77]*Constitution (Forty-second Amendment) Act, 1976*, s 55.

[78]Ibid.

[79]*Minerva Mills* (see Footnote 76).

[80]See Roznai (2013), pp. 657, 670–711.

amendment but does so by reference to the process of formal amendment itself. Procedural unamendability may be formally entrenched or it may arise informally. These two variations may be temporary or indefinite under the existing constitution.

Formal procedural unamendability refers to procedural unamendability codified in the constitutional text. For instance, the Mexican Constitution effectively makes itself unamendable in the event of rebellion leading to its violation, suspension or replacement: "This Constitution shall not lose its force and effect even if its observance is interrupted by rebellion. In the event that a government whose principles are contrary to those that are sanctioned herein should become established as a result of a public disturbance, as soon as the people recover their liberty, its observance shall be reestablished, and those who had taken part in the government emanating from the rebellion, as well as those who cooperated with such persons, shall be judged in accordance with this Constitution and the laws that have been enacted by virtue thereof."[81] This illustrates formal procedural unamendability insofar as the restriction on formal amendment—prohibiting formal amendment in connection with rebellion—is codified in the constitutional text. Of course, the enforceability and effectiveness of this provision is another matter altogether.

The second type of procedural unamendability—informal procedural unamendability—results from the political process. Informal procedural unamendability develops where the procedures required by a formal amendment rule are so onerous that political actors cannot realistically (though they could theoretically) meet the amendment threshold. It reflects procedural unamendability arising informally from the dialogic interactions of political actors, in contrast to the textually commanded unamendability that characterizes formal procedural unamendability. The Articles of Confederation illustrate informal procedural unamendability: the 13 states could theoretically satisfy the demanding unanimity threshold for formally amending the Articles,[82] but in practice, it was not possible for them to fulfill those procedures.[83]

7 Temporal Unamendability

Temporality is best understood as a tertiary variation on unamendability. It is neither a primary category—like substantive or procedural unamendability—nor a secondary variation like formal or informal unamendability. In any given constitutional regime, the forms of unamendability may be of either temporary or

---

[81]Mexico Const, tit IX, art 136 (1917).

[82]Articles of Confederation, art 13 (1781) ("And the articles of this confederation shall be inviolably observed by every State, and the Union shall be perpetual; nor shall any alteration at any time hereafter be made in any of them, unless such alteration be agreed to in a Congress of the United Sates, and be afterwards confirmed by the legislatures of every State.").

[83]James Madison criticized the Articles of Confederation on these grounds. See Cooke (1961), pp. 258, 263.

indefinite duration. For example, formal substantive unamendability may be entrenched temporarily, as we see in the United States Constitution,[84] or indefinitely, as we see in the German Basic Law,[85] subject of course to revision, replacement or revolution.[86] Likewise, formal procedural unamendability may be entrenched temporarily or indefinitely. A constitutional text may disable its formal amendment rules on procedural grounds for the duration of the regime, which is reflected in the Mexican Constitution,[87] or for a more limited period of time, a strategy the Cape Verdean Constitution illustrates by prohibiting formal amendment for 5 years after its coming-into-force.[88]

Informal substantive and procedural unamendability may similarly be temporary or indefinite. A national high court could, for instance, interpret the constitution as anchored in inviolable unwritten principles that are immune from formal amendment—thereby entrenching informal substantive unamendability—but this decision is susceptible to refinement or reversal by a successor court. With regard to informal procedural unamendability, the political climate that gives rise to unamendability need not necessarily be permanent. It may evolve to either assuage or exacerbate the social, cultural, and economic conditions that have generated the political intractability that had given rise to informal procedural unamendability to begin with.

This classification we have proposed has an important limitation of its own. The distinction between substance and procedure is not as clear as it might seem because substantive restrictions on formal amendment are often cast in procedural terms. Consider again the Mexican Constitution, which disables its formal amendment rules as to the entire Constitution in the event of rebellion. We have characterized this as an example of formal procedural unamendability because it entrenches a textual rule invalidating formal amendments affected during rebellion and does not expressly insulate the subject matter of a constitutional provision from formal amendment. Yet, we could alternatively characterize this prohibition as an example of formal substantive unamendability insofar as its actual though implicit purpose is to protect the content of the Constitution. The substance–process divide is thus less definitive than the classification suggests.

Nonetheless, this classification is modestly useful because it complicates our understanding of unamendability. It demonstrates that unamendability may be textually entrenched or informally derived, and that it may concern the content of a constitutional rule or the process by which it may be altered. This classification moreover illustrates that a procedural limitation on formal amendment may conceal

---

[84]See US Const., art V (1789) (temporarily entrenching Article I, Section 9, Clauses 1 and 4 from formal amendment until the year 1808).

[85]See Germany Const, pt VII, art 79(3); ibid. at pt II, art 20(1) (1949) (permanently entrenching federalism against formal amendment).

[86]Unamendability of course cannot survive revolution. See Goldsworthy (2010), p. 70. Indeed, unamendability may provoke revolution. See Dicey (1915), p. 66.

[87]See Mexico Const, tit IX, art 136 (1917).

[88]See Cape Verde Const, pt VI, tit III, art 309(1) (1980).

a substantive prohibition. In addition, this classification questions whether temporality should be a dominant category in defining the forms of unamendability. The result may admittedly raise more questions than answers, but it brings us closer to understanding how unamendability becomes entrenched in a constitutional regime.

8 Foundational Questions in Modern Constitutionalism

Both formal and informal unamendability invite questions that strike at the core of constitutionalism. Unamendability in either form urges us to contemplate the relationship between the constituting powers of self-government and its constituted institutions, the relationship between constitutionalism and democracy, and the function of text in law. Are unamendable constitutional provisions undemocratic or do they reflect a deep respect for the true democratic foundations of constitutionalism? What are the functions, limits, uses, and abuses of unamendability in modern constitutions? What are the optimal conditions under which unamendable constitutional provisions, constitutions, or norms achieve the intent of their designers? What circumstances frustrate their intended purposes? These are foundational questions in constitutionalism, and now made more urgent by the prevalence of unamendability.

Despite the importance of unamendability, there remains a void in the literature. To this day, we lack a systematic and comprehensive inquiry on the subject that is attentive to the comparative, doctrinal, empirical, historical, and theoretical dimensions of unamendability. Scholarship in comparative public law tends largely to focus on the interpretation and construction of rights and liberties, the design of federalism, the allocation of powers, the tools and strategies for ensuring judicial independence, and on the forms of popular participation in constitutional-making. What makes the void all the more glaring is that unamendability engages with each of these important subjects—each one reflected in some form or implication of constitutional unamendability. To be sure, there exists important scholarship on constitutional unamendability. One of the first efforts to survey the universe of unamendability was Kemal Gözler's study of the judicial review of constitutional amendments.[89] Schwartzberg's Democracy and Legal Change is an important book that takes a historical and comparative perspective on a particular view of unamendability, namely, that it fails to satisfy the democracy principle.[90] The alternative perspective is perhaps stated most compellingly by Sudhir Krishnaswamy, whose book defends the invalidation of constitutional amendments in India.[91]

---

[89]Gözler (2008).

[90]Schwartzberg (2007), pp. 8–16.

[91]Krishnaswamy (2010).

The most recent book on the subject is the best one: Yaniv Roznai's magisterial study of unconstitutional amendments.[92]

And yet the subject of constitutional unamendability lacks a focal resource that can serve as a point of reference for scholars interested in its deepest questions, from no single national perspective or from any particular view of the merit of unamendability. This is the void we seek to fill. In June 2015, public law scholars from around the world gathered in Istanbul at Koç University for an intensive Workshop on unamendable constitutional provisions. The purpose of the gathering was to map the field of unamendability with a view to publishing a volume that would serve as a major first point of reference on the subject. The Workshop featured participants from Bangladesh, Canada, Israel, Germany, Hungary, India, Indonesia, Italy, the Netherlands, Scotland, Turkey, the United Kingdom, and the United States. These jurisdictions are some of the most important in defining the subject of unamendability. The Workshop was sponsored jointly by Koç University Law School and Boston College Law School, held under the auspices of International Society of Public Law, and convened by the Editors of this volume.

9   Examining Unamendability in Constitutional Democracies

This volume emerges from the papers, discussions, and debates featured at that Workshop. We have divided this collection into two major parts. The first comprises four chapters under the heading "The Forms and Limits of Unamendability". The chapters in this part explore and evaluate the legitimacy of unamendability in the various forms they exist in constitutional democracies. The second part investigates "Unamendability in Constitutional Democracies", with case studies of unamendability in countries across the globe, with special attention to Asia, Europe, the Middle East as well as comparative perspectives from the United States.

Part I begins with a Yaniv Roznai's chapter on "Necrocracy or Democracy? Assessing Objections to Constitutional Unamendability". Roznai begins by observing that unamendability is a growing trend in global constitutionalism. Yet, as he observes, unamendability, as a constitutional mechanism raises various challenges and objections. He identifies theoretical challenges (that it imposes the *dead hand of the past*), practical objections (that it encourages extra-constitutional change, it exerts a limited effect, and that it confers vast powers on the judiciary) as well as textual concerns (that implicit unamendability has no textual referent). He argues that we can mitigate the challenges of unamendability if we construe it as a mechanism that reserves constitutional space for "the people" in their capacity as holders of the primary constituent power to decide their own fate.

---

[92]Roznai (2017).

In his chapter on "A Constitution for Eternity: An Economic Theory of Explicit Unamendability", Konstantinos Pilpilidis takes a law-and-economics approach to unamendability. He presses the question how to justify the use of unamendability, recognizing that no constitution is ever truly eternal. Pilpilidis offers a novel typology of constitutional eternity, suggesting that the only plausible benefit of unamendability in rational choice theory is that it makes constitutional political rents redistribution proof. As is evident from Pilpilidis' chapter, the institutional economics literature offers a new perspective to assess the impact of unamendability and to evaluate rent distribution and rent extraction. To our knowledge, this is the first law-and-economics analysis into unamendability that offers a test to justify it.

In their chapter on "Conventions of Unamendability: Covert Constitutional Unamendability in (Two) Politically Enforced Constitutions", Gert Jan Geertjes and Jerfi Uzman highlight a little-noticed form of unamendability that does not emerge from the formal design of master-text constitutions but rather from constitutions like United Kingdom's. They suggest that conventions of unamendability in politically enforced constitutions can arise from judicial disobedience, and in turn approximate the kinds of unamendability we see in master-text constitutions.

Stephan Michel and Ignacio Cofone offer a counterpoint in their chapter titled "Credible Commitment or Paternalism? The Case of Unamendability". They evaluate the functional value of unamendable provisions as commitment devices and in turn present a provocative theory of paternalism in constitutional design, arguing that unamendability is problematic in the face of changing preferences over time and the risk of abuse by constitutional drafters.

The subsequent chapters comprise Part II. We begin in India, the site of the creation of the basic structure doctrine, which the Court may invoke to invalidate a duly passed constitutional amendment for violating unwritten limits to constitutional change, those limits being identified by the reviewing court itself. In his chapter on "Constitutional Falsehoods: The Fourth Judges Case and the Basic Structure Doctrine in India", Chintan Chandrachud asks what impact does India's acclaimed "basic structure" doctrine have on the text of the Constitution? He observes that constitutional theorists have long neglected this question in favour of debates surrounding the implications of the doctrine of separation of powers, popular sovereignty, and the role of the judiciary in a constitutional democracy. Over the years, the Indian Supreme Court has struck down multiple provisions of the Constitution on basic structure grounds. These provisions have formally remained part of the text, producing constitutional falsehoods—significant disjunctures between text and practice. By considerably extending the contours of the basic structure doctrine, the Indian Supreme Court's decision in the Fourth Judges Case exacerbates the potential for these falsehoods. This chapter considers how these falsehoods have arisen, the attempts to redress them, and what they mean for constitutional interpretation outside of the courts.

Mazen Masri then shifts our attention to Israel in his chapter on "Unamendability in Israel: A Critical Perspective". Israel does not have a master-text constitution but, argues Masri, it entrenches two forms of unamendability. He calls the first "concealed unamendability," which makes certain amendments impossible without a favorable political configuration in the Knesset. He refers to the second as "judicially introduced unwritten unamendability." In both cases, he argues, unamendability seeks to protect Israel's definition as a Jewish and democratic state.

In his chapter on "Eternal Provisions in the Bangladeshi Constitution: A 'Constitution Once and For All'?", Ridwanul Hoque uncovers an important development in constitutional law: unlike most jurisdictions that have adopted the basic structure as a result of judicial interpretation, Bangladesh has amended its constitution to provide that the "basic provisions of the Constitution" shall be unamendable. This raises a special problem for the basic structure doctrine because, unlike other jurisdictions, here the decision to make something unamendable is clothed in the sociological legitimacy of the constitutional amendment process itself.

In her chapter on "Unamendability as a judicial discovery? Inductive learning lessons from Hungary", Fruzsina Gardos-Orosz asks a fundamental question that constitutional designers must ask themselves today: is it possible to create a stable constitutional democracy with a completely flexible basic law that does not entrench something against amendment? Beginning with the Norwegian Constitution, which entrenched the spirit of the constitution against amendment, Gardos-Orosz proceeds to trace the rise of amendability as a "judicial discovery," developing a case study of Hungary. Gardos-Orosz seeks to justify the judge-made doctrine of unamendability in the absence of explicit eternity clauses. She conceptualizes unamendability as an implicit normative principle that can be deduced from the very nature of liberal constitutionalism.

Serkan Köybaşi brings us to Germany in his chapter on "Amending the Unamendable: The Case of Article 20 of the German Basic Law". The German Basic Law entrenches what is perhaps the most well-known eternity clause, making human dignity inviolable. Köybaşi focuses our attention on a 1968 amendment to Article 20 in the German Basic Law. Article 20 is formally unamendable and dates to the 1949 Basic Law. Köybaşi asks whether the amendment—which purports to incorporate the right to resistance into Article 20—may be properly viewed as unamendable in the same way as the amended article had itself been prior to its amendment.

What follows are a pair of inquiries into the Turkish Constitution. In "Debating Unamendability: Deadlock in Turkey's Constitution-Making Process", Oya Yegen diagnoses the challenges facing the Constitutional Conciliation Commission of Turkey in 2011, one of which was the question of unamendability. In debating the content of a new constitution for Turkey, the Commission reached an impasse on whether the new constitution should retain its current unamendable provisions or break with this tradition. With close attention to the debates in the Commission, Yegen shows that the parties held irreconcilable positions with respect to unamendability, and that this contributed to the breakdown of the negotiations on constitutional reform. And in "The Unamendability of Amendable Clauses: The Case of the Turkish Constitution", Tarik Olcay draws from Carl Schmitt's theory of constitutionalism to illustrate how and why the Turkish Constitutional Court has exercised substantive constitutional review of constitutional amendments under three different constitutional settings.

In his chapter on "The Unamendability of Amendable Clauses The Case of the Turkish Constitution", Juliano Zaiden Benvindo explores unamendability in Latin America, what he describes as a "contradictory concept" given that formal constitutional change has long been a natural feature of constitutionalism in the region. As he explains, although the amendment rate varies significantly among its countries and the pace of constitutional replacements has waned in recent years, Latin America has long been portrayed as a region where amendment or replacement is a common occurrence. Zaiden Benvindo notes, however, that the comparative constitutional literature has practically overlooked most Latin American constitutional realities, calling into question the convention view that Latin America is home to inherently unstable constitutionalism. He focuses on Brazil but draws lessons from elsewhere in the region.

The volume closes with a broader view of Europe. In "Unamendable Constitutional Provisions and the European Common Constitutional Heritage: A Comparison Among Three Waves of Constitutionalism", Valentina Rita Scotti probes the unamendable provisions in post-war Germany and Italy, in Romania and the Czech Republic after the fall of the Wall, and most recently in Morocco and Tunisia after Arab Spring. She sets out to trace the common European heritage through all cases, each occurring in a different era of constitutionalism.

10   Four Themes

There are four themes running through this volume. The first concerns the problem of dead hand control: unamendable provisions privilege the past over the present insofar as they insulate the constitutional preferences of yesterday against change by the current generation. There are three distinguishable views on the problem of dead hand control. One view is best represented in the chapters by Michel and Cofone, Masri, and Hoque, respectively. All three chapters take the position that formal unamendability is undemocratic. Michel and Cofone argue that unamendability is undemocratic because it withdraws from the present generation the free range of choice to deal with constitutional challenges that may arise—a range of choices that would be unrestricted were it not for the unamendable rules blocking certain paths to reform. Masri echoes this view: unamendability is democratically illegitimate because it ties the hands of citizens and makes permanent hierarchical societal arrangements that unamendability can create. Hoque reinforces this position with reference to Bangladesh. The Bangladeshi Constitution is today arguably entirely entrenched against amendment, the consequence being that what was once—and perhaps should have always remained—a living and breathing instrument has been fossilized into an unchangeable text, something we might even describe as permanently frozen.

Another view appears in chapters by Köybaşi and Scotti. Here, we see strong arguments in favor of unamendability for rights protection. For Köybaşi, modern constitutional democracy rejects simple majoritarianism, and if it has not yet done so it should. The core of constitutional democracy, he argues, is the principle of limitation: limits on government, limits on the exercise of official power, and limits on what simple majorities can do. The implication of Köybaşi's position is that unamendability is a profitable device where it serves this limitation principle. Scotti's own view is consistent with Köybaşi's insofar as both see the virtue of unamendability as limitation. For Scotti, unamendability can be used without democratic objection to protect human rights. She draws from the German Basic Law after the Second World War and Eastern European constitutions after communism to show the current use of unamendability as a strategy both to protect human rights and to express their importance.

Roznai's chapter illustrates a third view that we might identify as meta-democratic: unamendability is not democratic when considered at a low level of abstraction—after all, it prevents amending actors from changing the constitution —but we must regard unamendability as the very embodiment of democracy because it is intended to safeguard the people's constitution from amendments made by their representatives without the people's authorization. On this view, una-mendability does not deny the people their power of changing their constitution how they wish or indeed whenever they wish but it requires the people to mobilize as popular sovereigns to make clear that those constitutional changes are ones they recognize and accept as valid. The people's representatives cannot act in the people's name to make constitutional changes that violate the people's constitution without first securing the people's permission. In this way, an unamendable constitutional provision is democratic, Roznai argues, because it establishes the people's prefer-ences at the writing of the constitution and it prevents the people's representatives from making changes to those preferences until and unless the people agree. This approach endeavors to strike a balance between democracy and constitutionalism.

In his chapter, Zaiden Benvindo takes an altogether different view: that a court can use unamendable provisions to expand its own powers, either gradually or quickly, but in either case definitively. Zaiden Benvindo draws predominantly from Brazil but also from Colombia to suggest that courts can interpret unamendability in strategic ways to enhance their powers, to insulate themselves from coordinate branches, and to give constitutional rules new meaning. What Zaiden Benvindo therefore suggests is that unamendability can be used not to freeze the past in place but to make substantial changes to law and society through judicial interpretation.

The problem of dead hand control derives from a second theme that we might describe as the related problem of sovereignty identification. Who is sovereign and how can the sovereign exercise its powers? This question of sovereignty engages the distinction between the constituent and constituted powers; the former refers to "the people" in whom ultimate power resides and the latter refers to the branches of government given delegated authority to carry out the commands of the former. The sociological construction of constituent power was developed in the French Revolutionary era by Emmanuel Joseph Sieyès, whose writings proposed a strict division of powers between the omnipotent pouvoir constituant and the subservient pouvoir constitué.[93]

In our present context of constitutional unamendability, the debate pits those who accept the theory of constituent power versus those who reject it. Adherents of the theory argue that unamendability is a proper constraint on the constituted powers, for instance, the legislative branch, and that only the constituent power may validly exercise the power to both establish and abrogate unamendability. The contrary view rejects constituent power theory as a legal fiction that does not accurately reflect how constitutions are designed or how they are changed insofar as "the people" do not actually write or authorize constitutions, though they do of course sometimes ratify constitutions by referendum. On this view, constituent power theory is but a normative aspiration for how constitutions should be written not how they are actually written.

In their chapters, Roznai and Köybaşi root their arguments against an unlimited amendment power in constituent power theory. Constituted powers, they argue, cannot override unamendable provisions because those provisions were authorized by the constituent power, which exercised its constitution-making power to entrench those provisions to begin with. Since the constituted powers are bound to act within the parameters set by the constitution, they must respect the unamendable provisions. More controversially, the constituted powers cannot on this theory exercise their amending powers to do violence to the constitution that the constituent power has created. The constituted powers may do no more than adjust the constitution consistent with its existing framework; anything more would exceed their limited authority as constituted powers. Only the people exercising their constituent power may go further. This, at least, is the standard view in constituent power theory, a view shared by Roznai and Köybaşi.

The implication of constituent power theory is that constituted powers cannot entrench provisions against amendment because this authority belongs only to the constituent power. And yet, as Hoque explains in his chapter, the Bangladeshi legislature exercised what the dominant view defines as a constituted power to amend the Constitution to entrench a lengthy catalogue of provisions as unamendable. The question, then, is whether this eternity clause should be regarded as truly eternal since it was introduced by a constituted power and not directly authorized by the constituent power, meaning the people, in Bangladesh. Or, alternatively, whether this exercise of constituted power was an illegitimate expansion of the limited powers of the legislature.

Yegen's chapter raises another important challenge to the dominant view. Yegen brings us back to the period 2011–13, when the Constitutional Conciliation Commission of Turkey made a serious effort to change the Constitution. The Commission was an ad hoc body that did not have a legal basis either in the Constitution or in the rules of parliamentary procedure. Yet this was not the reason for its failure. In its modern history, Turkey has relied on such commissions on more

---

[93]Sieyès (2002), p. 53.

than one occasion, finding success on big packages promoting democratization and Europeanization, in sharp contrast to the failure of the 2011–13 Commission.[94] The Commission broke down in the face of disagreement about whether the body could validly exercise constituent power, in which case it would have the authority to remake the entire Constitution and reconsider the unamendable provisions entrenched in it, or whether the body was bound in what it could do as merely a constituted power, in which case the body could only amend the Constitution in line with the existing constitutional structure, meaning that the unamendable rules could not be changed. This episode suggests the inefficacy of constituent power theory. At a high level of abstraction, Yegen argues, it may be an idea arguably worth following but when we try to operationalize it, the realities of constitutional power and politics often stand in the way of realizing any promise it may have.

Indeed, Michel and Cofone suggest in their chapter that constituent power theory is just that—a theory. An unconstitutional constitutional amendment remains possible where the amending actors act in breach of the limits imposed on them by the theory. In these cases, there is no effective way to prevent an unconstitutional constitutional amendment, unless there is some entity authorized to police the exercise of the amendment power or, if no authorization is given in the text or in political practice, some entity nonetheless willing to assert the power of review.

The answer, of course, is the judiciary. Courts have increasingly exercised the power to review the constitutionality of constitutional amendments. This leads us to the third theme in this collection: the problem of judicial review. What implications do unamendability entail for courts, and how should courts adjudicate a claim of unamendability? We must approach these questions along two separate but related tracks: one where the constitution expressly entrenches a rule against amendment and another where the constitution makes nothing unamendable.

Where the constitution makes something unamendable, that unamendable provision requires interpretation, explication, and delimitation. We might argue that courts are well positioned to play this role. Indeed, the Turkish Constitutional Court has historically interpreted the Constitution's unamendable provisions in this way, as Olcay shows in his chapter. But Olcay has shown that this power entails consequences for the rest of the Constitution: the Court has interpreted the remainder in light of the formally unamendable provisions, in some cases declaring unconstitutional otherwise valid constitutional amendments for affecting in some way the unamendable matters even where there is no direct violation. This is unobjectionable where the Court is transparent in its reading of the values the Constitution requires the Court to protect, and the Court protects them in a consistent manner. But this has not always been the result in Turkey. We have seen similar slippage elsewhere around the world.

The bigger controversy arises where a constitution makes nothing expressly unamendable. We have seen courts declare that the constitution makes implicitly

---

[94]For more on the failed process in 2011–13 and comparisons with previous commissions, see Oder (2015), pp. 136–140, Oder (2012), pp. 69–98.

unamendable certain rules and principles in which judges believe the constitution is rooted. In her chapter, Gárdos-Orosz demonstrates how the Hungarian Constitutional Court has arrived at the conclusion that the Constitution incorporates implicitly unamendable values that constitutional amendments must meet in order to be valid, even if those amendments are procedurally perfect. The Court's role is to defend the "basic founding principles of the rule of law," as Gárdos-Orosz describes them. Similarly, in his chapter on India, Chandrachud traces the emergence of the basic structure doctrine from meta-principles identified by the Indian Supreme Court. Chandrachud explains that in the years since the creation of the doctrine, Indian courts have deployed the doctrine as a shield to protect the independence of the judiciary. Surely this principle is worth defending in a constitutional democracy committed to the separation of powers and liberal constitutionalism.

This is a matter of some controversy because implicit unamendability is the result of what we might describe in neutral terms as a "judicial discovery." A more skeptical description might be "judicial constitution-making"—a concept that runs contrary to our conventional Lockean understanding insofar as constitutions ought to spring from the consent of the governed. But even as a judicial discovery, the content of implicit unamendability hinges on what courts regard as fundamental in a given constitutional jurisdiction. Whether courts define the basic constitutional structure as implicitly unamendable as in India, or the spirit of the constitution as has historically been the case in Turkey or certain fundamental constitutional principles in Hungary, a common thread reappears: courts are the ones to decide what counts as a trump card.

In both of these scenarios—explicit and implicit unamendability—the focus is on courts. But in their chapter, Geertjes and Uzman show that similar forces develop in politically rather than legally enforced constitutional orders. Geertjes and Uzman draw our attention to jurisdictions like the United Kingdom or the Netherlands where they have identified a phenomenon they call "covert unamendability." Unlike in legal constitutional orders that are court-centric in their interpretation and enforcement of the constitution, in political constitutional orders like these it is Parliament that largely if not exclusively determines the content of the constitution as a final matter. Faced with a virtually omnipotent legislature, courts in these jurisdictions have been intentionally "deaf" to legislative actions that might be invalid in a legal constitutional order but that courts here cannot invalidate because of the rule of legislative primacy. What Geertjes and Uzman have observed these courts do instead is fascinating: since courts cannot strike down a parliamentary act, they interpret the legislation creatively through deafness or outright disobedience—even constitution-level legislation—to make them constitutionally benign. Geertjes and Uzman therefore make an important discovery of their own: just like legally enforced constitutional orders that have identified implicitly unamendable rules, politically enforced constitutions also recognize fundamental rules in which their regime is anchored. In both cases, the integrity of the constitutional order requires respect for these unwritten rules.

The fourth theme evident across the chapters is the problem of constitutional endurance. Constitutional democracy requires some measure of flexibility and some measure of rigidity. Striking the balance between both, however, may be elusive. On the one hand, a constitution that is too flexible undermines its role as a guarantor of predictability and stability in governance. On the other, a constitution that is too rigid risks provoking its own violation out of necessity. In our context, the question is whether unamendability enhances or hinders constitutional stability: is a constitution more or less likely to endure when its designers entrench a rule against amendment?

In his important chapter on the law-and-economics of unamendability, Pilpilidis observes that the practical realities of absolute entrenchment lead to less than optimal outcomes for a constitutional state. Faced with a formally unamendable rule that limits their range of available choices, political actors or interest groups may violate the constitution if some significant benefit would accrue to them. Unamendability, then, may induce instability in the constitutional order. Michel and Cofone marshal some data reinforcing Pilpilidis' analysis: supermajority constitutional amendment rules, they suggest, offer greater prospects for constitutional longevity than unamendability. As Roznai explains, unamendability can undermine stability not only by preventing constitutional changes but moreover by leaving political actors driven to make a prohibited change with no choice but to resort to extra-constitutional means. Here, then, is the paradox of unamendability: it may well be intended to foster stability and endurance but in reality it might provoke the demise of the very constitution it seeks to shield from change.

There is no clear answer, however, on whether unamendability enhances or hinders stability, not to mention whether this should be the ultimate constitutional value to which we aspire. Zaiden Benvindo shows us that unamendability is not necessarily a bar to constitutional change where a court sees its role as transformative and exercises its power to that end. Köybaşi finds favor in the unamendable rules in the German Basic Law for setting a clear barrier to the country's decline into dictatorship; unamendability on its own of course cannot stop a country's decent but it does establish a public benchmark that sets a standard for all to see. Gárdos-Orosz takes a similar view of unamendability, arguing that unamendable norms can serve to instill a set of shared commitments and in so doing create a more stable political culture. Yet, Scotti stresses that the opposite of unamendability—easy amendability—was one point of origin of the great horrors the world witnessed in the days of the Weimar Republic, though of course unamendability itself could not have prevented the rise to power of the Nazi regime.

11 Three Aspirations

Each of these four lines of inquiry and others apparent in this volume opens a different window into the promise and peril of unamendability. The chapters are written to be in close conversation with each other and with the larger literature on unamendability.

What results is a volume that we hope will become an early point of reference for scholars interested in learning about unamendability in all of its forms and manifestations in constitutional democracies, about whether and how we might defend unamendability both explicit and implicit, and about the possible and proper roles of courts, political actors and citizens when confronted with unamendability either at the stage of designing a constitution or subsequently when it must be interpreted by courts, executed and enforced by political actors and lived by the people.

We have three aspirations for this volume. The first is that it will be an accessible introduction to the subject of unamendability for scholars of public law interested in exploring what is to our mind the most interesting pre-commitment device in constitutional law. The second is that advanced scholars of comparative constitutionalism will find the perspectives in these pages challenging and useful to their own understanding of the stakes involved in choosing to entrench unamendability in a constitution, whether formally by design or informally by practice or interpretation. Our third aspiration relates to the construction of constitutions: we hope that constitutional designers will consider the arguments both for and against unamendability presented in this volume, and that if they ultimately opt for unamendability their choice will be the one that best aligns with the history and hopes of the people they represent. There has always been one enduring truth in constitutionalism—a truth in which all constitutions are rooted: the fountain of constitutional legitimacy is the people themselves. Whether unamendability can live up to this highest of ambitions is for constitutional designers to decide.

References

Albert R (2010) Constitutional handcuffs. Ariz State Law J 42:663, 665–66

Albert R (2013) The expressive function of constitutional amendment rules. McGill Law J 59:225, 247–57

Albert R (2014) The structure of constitutional amendment rules. Wake Forest Law Rev 49:913, 952–54

Albert R (2017) How a court becomes supreme. Maryland Law Rev 77:188–189

Albert R (2018a) Amendment and revision in the unmaking of constitution. In: Landau D, Lerner H (eds) Edward Elgar handbook on comparative constitution-making. Edward Elgar Publishing Ltd., Cheltenham, UK

Albert R (2018b) Constitutional amendment and dismemberment. Yale Int Law J 43:29–60

Burgess J (1893) Political science and comparative constitutional law, vol I. Ginn & Company, Boston, p 137

Colón-Ríos J (2013) Beyond parliamentary sovereignty and judicial supremacy: the doctrine of implicit limits to constitutional reform in Latin America. Victoria Univ Wellington Law Rev 44:521, 525

Cooke JE (ed) (1961) The Federalist. Wesleyan University Press, Hanover, New Hampshire, p 258, 263

Dellinger W (1983) The legitimacy of constitutional change: rethinking the amendment process. Harv L Rev 97:386, 431

Denning BP, Vile JR (2002) The relevance of constitutional amendments: a response to David Strauss. Tulane Law Rev 77:247, 279

Dicey AV (1915) Introduction to the study of the law of the constitution (1982), vol 66. Liberty Fund, Indianapolis

Dixon R, Ginsburg T (2011) Deciding not to decide: deferral in constitutional design. Int J Const Law 9:636, 644

Dixon R, Holden R (2012) Constitutional amendment rules: the denominator problem. In: Ginsburg T (ed) Comparative Constitutional Design. Cambridge University Press, Cambridge, p 195

Dixon R, Landau D (2015) Transnational constitutionalism and a limited doctrine of unconstitutional constitutional amendment. Int J Const Law 13:606

Giovannoni F (2003) Amendment rules in constitutions. Pub Choice 115:37

Goldsworthy J (2010) Parliamentary sovereignty. Cambridge University Press, Cambridge, p 70

Gözler K (2008) Judicial review of constitutional amendments: a comparative study. Ekin Press

Greene J (2011) Originalism's race problem. Denver Univ Law Rev 88:517, 518–19

Halmai G (2012) Unconstitutional constitutional amendments: constitutional courts as guardians of the constitution? Constellations 19:182, 183–88, 190–91

Holmes S (1993) Gag rules or the politics of omission. In: Elster J, Slagstad R (eds) Constitutionalism and democracy. Cambridge University Press, pp 19–58

Hoque R (2016) Can the court invalidate an original provision of the constitution? Asian-Pac Law Policy J 2:13

Kommers DP (1991) German constitutionalism: a prolegomenon. Emory Law J 40:837, 846

Krishnaswamy S (2010) Democracy and constitutionalism in India: a study of the basic structure doctrine. Oxford University Press

Ku R (1995) Consensus of the governed: the legitimacy of constitutional change. Fordham Law Rev 64:535, 571

Landau D (2013) Abusive constitutionalism. UC Davis Law Rev 47:189

Linder D (1981) What in the constitution cannot be amended? Ariz Law Rev 23:717, 721

Lutz DS (2006) Principles of constitutional design. Cambridge University Press, New York, NY, p 170

Mansfield AM (2003) Ethnic but equal: the quest for a new democratic order in Bosnia and Herzegovina. Columbia Law Rev 103:2052, 2056

Marsteintredet L (2015) The Honduran Supreme Court renders inapplicable unamendable constitutional provisions. Int J Const Law. Blog Online: http://www.iconnectblogcom/2015/05/Marsteintredet-on-Honduras

Oder BE (2012) Turkish constitutional transformation and the EU: Europeanisation towards constitutionalism? In: Nas C, Ozer Y (eds) Europeanisation and Turkey. Ashgate Publishing, Aldershot, pp 69–98

Oder BE (2015) The much awaited and deeply controversial constitutional process: learning from Turkey's failed process in 2013. In: Themes of conflict in middle eastern democracies: a comparative perspective from Turkey and Israel. The Van Leer Jerusalem Institute, Istanbul, pp 136–140

Preuss UK (2011) The implications of eternity clauses: the German experience. Isr Law Rev 44:429

Rasch BE, Congleton RD (2006) Amendment procedures and constitutional stability. In: Congleton RD, Swedenborg B (eds) Democratic constitutional design and public policy: analysis and evidence. MIT Press, Cambridge, Mass, p 319, 326

Rezie RCO (1999) The Ukrainian constitution: interpretation of the citizens' rights provisions. Case W Reserve J Int Law 31:169, 175–81

Roznai Y (2013) Unconstitutional constitutional amendments: the migration and success of a constitutional idea. Am J Comp Law 61:657, 670–711

Roznai Y (2017) Unconstitutional constitutional amendments: the limits of amendment powers. Oxford University Press, Oxford, pp 20–21

Rubenfeld J (2001) Freedom and time: a theory of constitutional self-government. Yale University Press, New Haven, p 174

Sajó A (1999) Limiting government: an introduction to constitutionalism. Central European University Press, Budapest, pp 39–40

Schwartzberg M (2007) Democracy and legal change. Cambridge University Press, Cambridge, pp 8–16

Sieyès EJ (2002) Qu'est-ce que le Tiers état? vol 53. Éditions du Boucher, Paris (originally published in 1789)

Sullivan KM (1995) Constitutional Amendmentitis. The Am Prospect 23:20, 22–23

Varol OO (2014) Temporary Constitutions. Calif Law Rev 102:409, 439–48

Wing AK (1993) Communitarianism versus individualism: constitutionalism in Namibia and South Africa. Wis Int Law J 11:295, 337–44

Zuleeg M (1997) What holds a nation together? Cohesion and democracy in the United States of America and in the European Union. Am J Comp Law 45:505, 510

Part I
The Legitimacy and Limits of Unamendability

Necrocracy or Democracy? Assessing Objections to Constitutional Unamendability

Yaniv Roznai

Abstract Unamendability is a growing trend in global constitutionalism. Yet, unamendability, as a constitutional mechanism, raises various challenges and objections. Mainly, by perpetuating certain constitutional rules, values and institutions, unamendability exacerbates the 'dead hand' of the past, and by restricting all constitutional possibilities available to the people to revise their constitution, unamendability is seen as undemocratic and dangerous as it encourages extra-constitutional and revolutionary means in over to modify unamendable principles. Furthermore, the judicial enforcement of unamendability grants courts vast powers over other governmental branches, turning the judiciary into the final arbitrator of society's values. This chapter identifies and analyses the main theoretical, practical and textual challenges to unamendability. It demonstrates that unamendability is a complex mechanism which ought to be applied with great care. Yet, it also argues that if the theory of unamendability is correctly construed as a mechanism which reserves a constitutional space for the decision-making of 'the people' in their capacity as holders of the primary constituent power (in contrast with the limited amendment power), this mitigates many of the challenges raised by unamendability.

An earlier version of this chapter was presented at the Koç-BC-Icon·S Workshop on Unamendable Constitutional Provisions held at Koç University Law School on 9 June 2015. I would like to thank the organisers of the workshop—Bertil Emrah Oder and Richard Albert and the participants for their valuable comments, especially to Serkan Köybaşi for his discussion. I would also like to thank Martin Loughlin, Thomas Poole, Ida Koivisto and the anonymous reviewer for useful remarks. An elaborated argument appears in Yaniv Roznai, *Unconstitutional Constitutional Amendment—The Limits of Amendment Powers* (OUP 2017).

Y. Roznai (✉)
Radzyner School of Law, Interdisciplinary Center (IDC), Herzliya, Israel
e-mail: yaniv.roznai@idc.ac.il

1   Introduction

Constitutional unamendability refers to the limitation on amending constitutional subjects (provisions, principles, rules, symbols or institutions) through the formal constitutional amendment provision.[1] In that sense, such constitutional subjects carry a certain 'supra-constitutional' status.[2] Unamendability may be explicit in the constitution, in the form of 'eternity clauses' or 'provisions of unamendability'.[3] Unamendability may also be implicit as result of courts interpretation of the constitutional text, holding that even in the absence of explicit limitations, certain constitutional principles are implicitly unamendable.[4] There is a growing trend in global constitutionalism not only to impose limitations on the constitutional amendment power but also to enforce this unamendability by means of substantive judicial review of constitutional amendments.[5]

I have argued that constitutional unamendability and its judicial enforcement rest on the fundamental distinction between *primary constituent* (constitution-making) *power* and *secondary constituent* (constitution-amending) *power*, and are in accordance with the nature and scope of amendment powers, understood as limited delegated powers. As a delegated power acting as a *secondary constituent power*, the amendment power cannot destroy the constitution and replace it with a new one since this is the role of the *primary constituent power*, conceived as the people's democratic appearance of popular sovereignty through which the people may establish and reshape the political order and its fundamental principles.[6] Of course,

---

[1]See Albert (2008), pp. 37–44. Unamendability can also be informal when the social or political climate is such that although legally permissible, it is unimaginable that political or public agreement on amending certain constitutional subjects would be achieved. See Albert (2014a), p. 181, (2014b), pp. 1029, 1043. Likewise, unamendability can be 'covert', especially in politically enforced constitutions, when there is a convention that certain constitutional arrangements shall not be abolished or significantly altered; a convention which is enforced through disobedience of governmental branches, including the courts. See Geertjes and Uzman (this volume).

[2]See Roznai (2013b), p. 557. Whereas unamendability can limit the constitutional amendment power, it cannot limit the *primary constituent power* which is unbound by prior constitutional rules. See Roznai (2017b), p. 23. This of course does not mean that the *primary constituent power* is unbound by any restrictions. See e.g., Widner and Contiades (2013), pp. 57, 58 ('Today, the prevailing view is that there are implicit substantive limits built into the concept of constituent power...').

[3]See Roznai (2015), p. 775.

[4]Roznai (2012), p. 240.

[5]See Roznai (2013c), p. 657, Roznai and Yolcu (2012), p. 175, Roznai (2014b), p. 29.

[6]Roznai (2017c), p. 5, see also Cahill (2016), pp. 245, 249–258 (argues that unamendability exists not only to defend specific content but also to defend the constituent power). A brief review of this distinction as the basis for unamendability appears in Yap (2015), pp. 114, 116–118. This distinction raises its own complications such as how do we recognise a genuine expression of *primary constituent power*? And where do we draw the line between amending a constitution and its replacement? These challenges are beyond the limited scope of this chapter which focuses on the main objections to unamendability. For an analytical description of the separation between *primary* and *secondary constituent powers* see also Köybaşi (this volume). Indeed, not everyone

if one takes the view that *primary* and *secondary constituent powers* are similar types of powers, this argument in favour of unamendability is weakened. For example, in the U.S. context, it was argued by Stephen Griffin that once the U.S. Constitution was established, the constitutional amendment procedure contains constituent power.[7] Yet, since the amendment power is merely a power established in the constitution and delegated to constitutional organs, it cannot be a genuine constituent power which carries extra-constitutional features. It is still a constituent power, in the sense that it has the capacity to create and modify constitutional norms, yet it is an inherently limited capacity. The idea that 'the people' have delegated amendment powers to constitutional organs yet in turn retain their *primary constituent power* is acceptable by some eminent American Scholars such as Akhil Reed Amar and William Harris II.[8]

Nevertheless, constitutional unamendability and its judicial enforcement raise many complications and objections on various grounds. Richard Albert, for example, argues that unamendability undermines the basic promise of democratic constitutionalism since it restricts the constitutional possibilities open to the people governed by the constitution.[9] Unamendability, he further argued, 'hijack[s] their most basic of all democratic rights'.[10] Additionally, unamendability confers upon courts vast powers in vis-à-vis other governmental branches.[11]

This chapter aims to identify the main objections to the theory of unamendability and analyse them. Section 2 analyses the theoretical challenges to unamendability: the idea that unamendability exacerbates the 'dead hand' challenge of constitutionalism by which past generations bind current and future generations; the argument that courts—as organs created by the constitution and subordinated to it—cannot decide upon the validity of constitutional norm; and finally, that unamendability and its judicial enforcement are undemocratic. Section 3 is dedicated to practical objections to unamendability: the claims that unamendability encourages extra-constitutional and forcible changes or that unamendability has a limited effect; and that from an institutional perspective, unamendability enhances judiciary's power over other governmental branches, turning it into the final arbitrator of society's values. Section 4 confronts textual challenges to unamendability, according to which the absence of explicit provisions to the contrary, the textual meaning of 'amendment' allows any change to the constitution and that in light of the maxim *expressio unius est exclusio alterius*, there should be no inference of

---

accept the distinction between primary and secondary constituent power. For example, Loughlin (2014), pp. 218, 231–232 argues that in light of the reflexive and relational nature of constituent power, this distinction is flawed. However, this is still the best explanatory theory for the constitutional phenomenon of unamendability, and therefore it is this premise for the analysis in this chapter.

[7]Griffin (2007), p. 49.

[8]See e.g., Amar (1988), pp. 1043, 1054–1058, Harris (1993), pp. 167, 193.

[9]Albert (2008), pp. 47–48.

[10]Albert (2010), pp. 663, 698.

[11]Albert (2015), p. 655.

implicit unamendability aside to those limits which are explicitly stated in the constitutional text. Section 5 concludes.

The analysis demonstrates that unamendability is a powerful mechanism which carries with it serious consequences to the constitutional order. Therefore, it should be used with great care. Nonetheless, notwithstanding these challenges, the exploration reveals that the distinction between the *primary* and *secondary constituent power*—correctly construed—manages to mitigate many of the difficulties associated with unamendability.

2 Theoretical Challenges to Unamendability

2.1 The 'Dead Hand'

Unamendability seems to pose an obstruction to what might be viewed as a healthy social development. A society ought to abide by a set of values it believes in. At the same time, it should not accept any set of values as taken for granted, but critically examine them and modify them if it believes that some are either unjustified or unsuited to the society. When society's world view of values is changed without the ability to amend the constitution accordingly, the constitution then does not protect the values that the society believes in, but simply binds the current generation to the values of past generations.[12] In what can be described as *necrocracy* rather than democracy, this is the known problem according to which present and future generations are ruled by the 'dead hand' of their ancestors.[13]

Constitutional amendment formulas are Janus-faced. They both create the 'dead hand' difficulty by requiring an often-formidable procedure for amending the constitution and simultaneously manage to relax it by allowing future generations to change the constitution.[14] By preventing current and future generations from amending certain parts of the constitution, unamendability exacerbates the 'dead hand' difficulty.[15] This is a (perhaps the) major objection to unamendability. One can only recall Art. 28 of the *French Declaration of Rights and Men and Citizens* of 24 July 1793, according to which 'A people have always the right of revising, amending and changing their Constitution. One generation cannot subject to its laws future generations'.[16]

---

[12]Sapir (2010), pp. 178–179.

[13]On this problem, see e.g. Ely (1980), p. 11, Klarman (1997), pp. 381, 382, McConnell (1998), pp. 1127–1128, Samaha (2008), p. 606.

[14]Sager (1995–1996), p. 275, Pettys (2008), pp. 313, 332.

[15]Albert (2010), p. 667.

[16]For an analytical elaboration of the people's role in the French amendment process, see Derosier (2017), p. 315.

Thomas Jefferson[17] and Thomas Paine[18] pronounced similar ideas. Therefore, the notion that a generation can perpetually tie the hands of another is understandably contentious.[19] Elisha Mulford gave an acute expression for this idea, describing an unamendable constitution as:

> The worst tyranny of time, or rather the very tyranny of time. It makes an earthly providence of a convention which has adjourned without day. It places the sceptre over a free people in the hands of dead men, and the only office left to the people is to build thrones out of the stones of their sepulchres.[20]

In light of this challenge, critics have argued that unamendability should be repealed or ignored at will, and all the more so not be judicially enforceable.[21]

The dead hand objection is significant yet it is not entirely convincing. First, even when provisions of unamendability are considered as legally binding, they can arguably be amended. How? The majority of unamendability provisions establish the unamendability of certain constitutional subjects but they are themselves not entrenched.[22] Accordingly, from a purely formalistic approach, provisions of unamendability may be amended in a *double amendment procedure*: first, repealing the provision that prohibits certain amendments (an act that is not in itself a violation of the constitution) and second, amending the previously—but no longer—unamendable principle or provision.[23] Of course, a wise constitution drafter would use a 'double entrenchment mechanism' by drafting provisions of unamendability which are self-entrenched.[24] However, even when provisions of unamendability are not self-entrenched, I have argued elsewhere, provisions of unamendability should be recognised as implicitly self-entrenched based upon the maxim 'what cannot be done directly cannot be done indirectly',[25] and since any other approach would be akin to a 'fraud of the constitution'.[26]

---

[17]In a famous correspondence between James Madison and Thomas Jefferson from 6 September 1789, Jefferson argued that constitutions should be rewritten every generation, declaring that the dead should not govern the living, since 'the earth belongs always to the living generation'. For an analysis, see Rubenfeld (1997–1998), p. 1085. In contrast, in Federalist No. 49, Madison contended that frequent 'recurrence to the people' would endanger 'the public tranquillity by interesting too strongly the public passions' and 'deprive the government of that veneration which time bestows' and on which every government depends for stability. See Hamilton et al. (1817), pp. 233, 274.

[18]Paine and Philp (1998), pp. 91–92 ('every age and generation must be as free to act for itself ... [I]t is the living, and not the dead, that are to be accommodated').

[19]Fombad (2007), pp. 27, 57–58.

[20]Mulford (1870), p. 155.

[21]See Linder (1981), p. 717.

[22]See Elster (2000), p. 102.

[23]See debate in Da Silva (2004), pp. 454, 456–458, Smith (2011), pp. 369, 375, Tribe (2000), pp. 111–114, Orfield (1942), p. 85.

[24]See e.g. Joseph and Walker (1987), pp. 155, 159.

[25]On this maxim see Singh (1966), p. 273.

[26]See Roznai (2014a), see also Mazzone (2005), pp. 1747, 1818, Klein (1999), pp. 31, 37–38, Albert (2014a), 209–215.

Second, and more importantly, unamendability does not entirely restrict future generations who may exercise their *primary constituent power* and alter even provisions of unamendability (whether self or non-self-entrenched).[27] As Vicki Jackson argues, unamendability should not be viewed as blocking all the democratic avenues, but rather merely proclaiming that one such avenue—the amendment process—is unavailable. In order to legitimately achieve the sought constitutional change, other procedures ought to be used.[28] On such a reading, the 'dead hand' argument is founded on a fallacy. The purpose of unamendability is not to empower past generations but to maintain and reform the fundamental principles and institutions in a self-conscious manner.[29] Since unamendability limits only the *secondary constituent power*, it is entirely consistent with the people's sovereignty as manifested by the *primary constituent power*, through which 'the people' can constitute a new constitutional order.[30]

Stephan Michel and Ignacio Cofone are correct in claiming that overcoming unamendability by initiating a completely new constitution-making process is problematic, since by opening the entire constitution for re-negotiation it increases costs and facilitates strategic bargaining.[31] Moreover, there is surely a great value to the continuity and maintenance of the existing constitutional order, not the least in order to preserve stability, and respect and faith in the political order, and in the supreme document which sets and regulates governmental institutions, and protects fundamental rights and principles.[32] Yet at least from a theoretical point of view, the important point is that unamendability is not inconsistent with the people's

---

[27]See Roznai (2017b).

[28]Jackson (2013), p. 47. See also Goerlich (2008), pp. 397, 404, Hutchinson and Colón-Ríos (2011), p. 43.

[29]Compare with Eisgruber (1997), pp. 1611, 1616.

[30]Mazzone (2005), p. 1843. Moreover, when considering the fact that a national constitution's median lifespan is a mere 19 years, any arguments regarding unamendability as binding future generations to the 'dead hand of the past' are relaxed. On the lifespan of constitutions, see Elkins et al. (2009), p. 129.

[31]Michel and Cofone (this volume). The authors give as an example for the high costs of constitution-making bargaining the failed constitution-making process in Turkey as described in Yegen (this volume).

[32]On the constitution as a means for ensuring respect-worthiness in the legal system, see e.g. Balkin (2003), pp. 485, 486. Of course, Balkin himself acknowledges that 'The legitimacy of the constitutional/legal system ... is not simply a matter of its current content. It is always imbricated with the past and projected toward the future. It is always premised on an interpretation of and selective identification with the past, the creation of a transtemporal "us," whom we revere and of whom our present selves are merely the latest installment'. This idea of a transtemporal people actually supports unamendability which seeks to protect a certain constitutional identity superior to the present temporary political majority. In other words, unamendability seems compatible with the transcendental understanding of primary constituent power, which aims to link diverse generations and unite the nation under common basic principles. It invites the people to see themselves as part of something greater than their individuals—having a superior unamendable constitutional identity.

sovereign power.[33] On the contrary, unamendability not only accords with the people's sovereignty, as it allows them to reform their constitution by exercising *primary constituent power*, but it is a sovereignty–reinforcement mechanism, as it creates a space of decision-making (that of the fundamental principles of the polity), which is reserved solely for 'the people'.

2.2 Logical Subordination

When unamendability is enforced by courts, this creates at least one theoretical challenge. Constitutions create courts and grant them authority. All powers possessed by constituted organs, including courts, derive explicitly or implicitly from the constitution. This postulation raises the difficulty of logical subordination: how can courts—organs created by the constitution and subordinated to its provisions—rule upon the constitution's validity? As Joseph Ingham wondered:

> If the Supreme Court, created by, and owing its authority and existence to the Constitution, should assume the power to consider the validity or invalidity of a constitutional amendment […] it would be assuming the power to nullify and destroy itself, of its own force, a power which no artificial creation can conceivably possess.[34]

The subordination difficulty rests on a fallacy. It only arises if one conceives amendment powers as equivalent to *primary constituent powers*. Indeed, if the court reviewed a provision of an original constitution that established its own authority, this might involve the logical subordination difficulty. The constitution of Bosnia and Herzegovina is an interesting case study. In two cases before the Constitutional Court, certain constitutional provisions that granted privileges for Bosnians, Serbs and Croats were challenged before the Constitutional Court for conflicting with the principle of equality. The majority of the Constitutional Court's judges held that the Court lacked the competence to decide upon the constitutionality of the constitution. Otherwise, if it decided that part of the constitution was 'unconstitutional', it would fail its duty under Art. VI(3)(a) of the Constitution to 'uphold this Constitution'.[35] This differs from the example of South Africa, in which the

---

[33]For such claims of inconsistency, see Orfield (1929–1930), pp. 550, 581, McGovney (1920), pp. 499, 511–513, Albert (2010), p. 676.

[34]Ingham (1928–1929), pp. 161, 165–166.

[35]Case No U-5/04 Request of Mr Sulejman Tihić, Decision of 31 March 2006 http://www.codices. coe.int/NXT/gateway.dll/CODICES/full/eur/bih/eng/bih-2006-1-003, Case No U-13/05, Request of Mr Sulejman Tihić, Decision of 26 May 2006 http://www.codices.coe.int/NXT/gateway.dll/ CODICES/full/eur/bih/eng/bih-2006-2-005. Accessed 14 August 2016. See Feldman (2011), pp. 117, 142–144, (2012), pp. 151, 164. Contrary to the Constitutional Court, the European Court of Human Rights held that it has the jurisdiction to decide upon the issue, and that the abovementioned constitutional provision is discriminatory and constitutes a breach of the European Convention of Human Rights. See *Sejdić and Finci v. Bosnia and Herzegovina*, App. No. 27996/ 06, Eur. Ct. H. R., Judgment of Dec. 22, 2009. See e.g., Bardutzky (2010), p. 309.

Constitutional Court declared the Constitution of 1996 to be unconstitutional.[36] In the latter case, the Interim Constitution of 1993 entrusted the constitutional assembly to work within a framework of 34 agreed-upon principles, and empowered the Constitutional Court to review the compliance of the draft Constitution with those principles. Therefore, the Court was exercising an explicit delegated authority, within its competence, in observing the constitution-making process.

However, since *primary constituent powers* and amendment powers are dissimilar, the challenge imposed by the logical subordination difficulty does not rise. An analogy from the distinction between *constituent power* and *legislative power* may elucidate this: in ordinary exercise of judicial review, the acts of the ordinary lawmaker operating under the constitution are reviewed against the background provided by the constitution-maker.[37] Similarly, a constitutional amendment adopted by the *secondary constituent power* may be reviewed against the background provided by the *primary constituent power*. Of course, this logic only applies when one accepts the distinction between constituent power and amendment power. In acknowledging the distinction between the *primary* and *secondary constituent power*, it is possible to grasp that by the exercise of the judicial review of constitutional amendments the judiciary does not act in contradiction of the constitution, but as its preserver.[38]

2.3   Undemocratic

A central objection to unamendability is that it is deemed as undemocratic. Since a self-governing people ought to be able to challenge or revise its basic commitments, the ability to amend the constitution seems an essential element of any democratic society. Unamendability positions certain rules or values not only above ordinary politics but also above constitutional politics and the popular will.[39] By not allowing majorities—even super-majorities—to modify these rules or values, and by neglecting the importance of the present political process as a basic protection for the exercise of democratic self-government, unamendability is in clear tension with democratic principles.[40] Arguably, it should be the people's decision (directly or through their representatives) whether a certain constitutional element is essential to the constitutional order or not and this decision should not be subject to judicial review.[41] Critics therefore argue that unamendability 'betrays one of democracy's

---

[36]*Re Certification of the Constitution of the Republic of South-Africa*, 1996(4) SALR 744. See Sachs (1996–1997), p. 1249.

[37]Suksi (1995), p. 6.

[38]Beaud (1994), p. 345.

[39]See e.g., Roznai and Suteu (2015), p. 542.

[40]Albert (2016), p. 13.

[41]Bernal (2013), pp. 339, 349.

most attractive legacies: the ability to modify law',[42] or 'deny citizens the democratic right to amend their own constitution and in so doing divest them for the basic sovereign rights of popular choice and continuing self-definition'.[43] Some have even gone as far as describing unamendability as a 'constitutional dictatorship' or 'a legal authoritarianism'.[44]

The question whether unamendability is 'undemocratic' involves four separate aspects.[45] The first is whether the absolute entrenchment itself of any subject (regardless of its content) is undemocratic. The second is whether the content of the protected unamendable subject is undemocratic. The third is the scope of the unamendability, and the fourth is its judicial enforcement. Any answer to these different questions depends on what one considers 'democracy'. If one considers democracy as purely procedural, i.e. simply as a system of self-government in which citizens have the ability to make majority collective decisions, then surely unamendability is 'undemocratic' by limiting that ability to some extent. But if one conceives democracy to include protection of certain basic rights and principles, this adds a substantive pre-condition for a democracy.[46] In that respect, entrenching *certain* principles and values that characterise modern democracy in the substantive sense is not necessarily undemocratic.

Therefore, as for the first aspect, the argument that *any* pre-commitments constraining the amendment power present a challenge to democracy relies on a narrow procedural view of democracy. Unamendability may accord with a broad substantive theory of democracy.[47] Moreover, there is no doubt that unamendability exacerbates the counter-majoritarian difficulty.[48] Yet, unamendability is precisely an institution that aims to neutralise the dangers of majoritarianism.[49] Unamendability could thus be viewed not as undemocratic but rather as a tool forestalling the possibility of a democracy's self-destruction.[50] Lastly, if we recognise constitutionalism as a system of 'higher law', according to which democratic majoritarianism must give way to certain commitments to principles, or as indispensable legal limits to governmental power,[51] unamendability simply takes

---

[42]Schwartzberg (2009), p. 2.

[43]Albert (2010), p. 667.

[44]Nogueira (2005), pp. 79, 84.

[45]Earlier thoughts appeared in Roznai (2013a).

[46]Dworkin (1990), pp. 14, 35, (1995), p. 2, Barak (2009), pp. 23–26, Rostow (1952), pp. 193, 195, Bishin (1977–1978), p. 1099, Michelman (1998), pp. 399, 419.

[47]Rousseau (1994), pp. 261, 273–282.

[48]Mohallem (2011), pp. 765, 766–767. Therefore, Oran Doyle argues that 'The further that a constraint moves power away from a contemporary majority, the stronger the justification that is needed'. See Doyle (2017), p. 73.

[49]Albert (2010), p. 675.

[50]Cf. Holmes (1993), pp. 195, 239. Especially in weak democracies, judicial review of constitutional amendments may strengthen democracy from collapsing into autocracy rather than be deemed undemocratic. See Issacharoff (2012), pp. 33, 45.

[51]See e.g., McIlwain (1975), p. 132.

this idea to its extreme. The recognition of the amendment power—like any other power within the constitutional scheme—as limited is an indispensable consequence of the organisation of powers within a limited government.[52]

With regard to the content of the unamendable subject, there is no categorical answer and every case must be judged on its own merits. Clearly, unamendability can protect issues that would reasonably be considered 'desirable' democratic values, such as human dignity, the democratic process or the rule of law. Other unamendable provisions, even if 'desirable' from a democratic perspective, can hardly be considered a pre-condition for democracy.[53] Unamendability can also protect 'undesirable' principles or practices, from a democratic perspective, such as the Corwin Amendment, which was proposed in 1860 and aimed to protect slavery.[54] Such an unamendable provision would be undemocratic from both the procedural and substantive notions of democracy. Unamendability which protects autocratic values or oppresses minorities is surely objectionable.[55] Unamendability can also be problematic from a democratic point of view in deeply divided societies when it entrenches a certain ethnic/religious identity which alienates minorities.[56]

With regard to the scope of unamendability, *prima facie*, the wider the scope of the unamendability—i.e. the larger number of principles, institutions or rules which are placed beyond the reach of any majority—the greater its tension with democracy.[57] Without the ability of citizens to modify society's basic values, civil motivation to participate in any decision-making process would probably deteriorate, and the public debate would be replaced by apathy. By that, unamendability risks impoverishing democratic debates.[58]

In response, it has to be noted that the mere act of unamendability of certain values might actually place them at the centre of public debate when otherwise such values might not have been even open for dispute. Moreover, unamendability creates a 'chilling effect', what Mark Tushnet describes as a 'sword of Damocles',[59] leading to hesitation before repealing an unamendable constitutional subject, thereby allowing time for political and public deliberations regarding the protected constitutional subject and placing them at the centre of the public agenda.

---

[52]Roznai (2017c), Keshavamurthy (1982), p. 89.

[53]For example, art. 288(e) Const. (1976) (Portugal) entrenches 'The rights of the workers, workers' committees, and trade unions'.

[54]See e.g., Christopher Bryant (2003), p. 501, Brandon (1995), see also Albert (2013b) (arguing that another way of reading the Corwin Amendment is not as making slavery absolutely unamendable but only as restricting congressional power).

[55]Michel and Cofone (this volume).

[56]See Masri (this volume).

[57]For example, the unamendable provision which was inserted in the Constitution of Bangladesh is extremely broad as it protects nearly third of the constitution (the preamble, all fundamental rights provisions and 'the provisions of articles relating to the basic structure') from any amendment. See Hoque (this volume).

[58]Sapir (2010), p. 79.

[59]Tushnet (2018), p. 332.

As for judicial enforcement of unamendability, surely, endowing court with the authority to declare constitutional amendments unconstitutional for violating unamendable provisions enhances the counter-majoritarian difficulty embodied in the situation of unelected and unaccountable judges who override the decisions of people's representatives.[60] How can a small, often divided, set of judges replace the democratic judgment of the people and their representatives? As Rory O'Connell correctly notes, allowing courts to review constitutional amendments might turn the 'people's guardian of the constitution against politicians' into 'a guardian of the constitution against all comers'.[61]

One possible reply is that when courts review amendments *vis-à-vis* the constitution's unamendable principles, they are not acting in a completely counter-majoritarian manner, for they have the support of the high authority of the *primary constituent power*. Judicial review thereby expresses the democratic base of the constitution, i.e. it gives expression to the will of 'the people' as a superior legal norm which conflicts with the present will of the political majority as expressed by the constitutional amending power.[62] Thus, when judges enforce unamendability, they are vindicating, not defeating, the will of the people as expressed in constitutional moments contra to the everyday political process. According to this view, judicial review of amendments articulates a different, deeper or more basic will, than the current political majority. The conflict that the court then decides is between the supra-temporal will of the people as expressed in the basic principles of the constitution, and the temporary will of the people as expressed in a constitutional amendment. Consequently, judicial enforcement of unamendability may be regarded as democratic or even majoritarian in a way, since it represent past–present–and future super-majorities. However, even if one rejects that said conception of *primary constituent power*, unamendability does not necessarily prevent the people from engaging in the political process and deliberations. The reason for this is that via the emergence of the *primary constituent power* even the most basic principles of society can be reformed. That makes the people in their *primary constituent power* capacity, not the courts, the final arbiters of society's basic values.[63]

---

[60]See generally Bickel (1962), pp. 16–23.

[61]O'Connell (1999), pp. 48, 51. Of course, at least with regard to explicit unamendable provisions, Michel Rosenfeld was right to state that 'any countermajoritarian difficulty would have to be ascribed to the constitution itself rather to judicial interpretation'. See Rosenfeld (2005), pp. 165, 186.

[62]Cf Freeman (1990–1991), pp. 327, 353–354 and echoing Hamilton (1817), pp. 418, 421.

[63]I elaborate on this point in Roznai (2017c).

3   Practical Objections to Unamendability

3.1   Revolutionary or Forcible Change

The amendment process is meant *inter alia*, to forestall, as far as possible, revolutionary upheavals. Unamendability allegedly blocks any constitutional manner to amend certain principles. It is thus potentially dangerous; citizens might find unamendability to be an intolerable obstacle to political and social change, thus resorting to a forcible revolution in order to change it.[64] Of course, the risk of forcible means as recourse exists even in the absence of unamendability; nonetheless, it seems that unamendability as a mechanism almost forces a society to recourse to revolutionary means for changing unamendable principles.[65] In other words, if courts can enforce unamendability and invalidate constitutional amendments, they might 'invalidate the last institutional route the will of the majority has to make itself heard', leaving them only with the option of revolution.[66]

It follows that in terms of constitutional dynamics, unamendability serves the exact opposite of its original purpose of preservation and stability: not only does it not prevent the changes but it invites and encourages the realisation of that change in an extra-constitutional manner.[67] 'Ulysses', in the words of Jon Elster, 'would have found the strength to break the ropes that tied him to the mast'.[68] This might be especially dangerous in weak democracies which lack established democratic traditions or have an apparent history of coups, where the temptation to use extra-constitutional measures might be irresistible.[69] This raises the inevitable question: if the change were to occur regardless of the temporary hindrance by a few judges, would it not be better to allow the change by peaceful constitutional means?[70]

This is a legitimate concern which should be a warning sign for constitutional designers to use unamendability carefully. That said, changing unamendable subject must not necessarily be done through forcible means. The idea that unamendability limits only the *secondary constituent power* and not the *primary constituent power* need not necessarily result in a call for violent (albeit inevitable extra-constitutional) changes. On the contrary, understanding a democratic

---

[64]See Fombad (2007), p. 57, Friedrich (1968), pp. 138, 143–146, Suber (1999), pp. 31–32, Tushnet (2012–2013), pp. 1983, 2007.

[65]Albert (2010), pp. 684–685.

[66]Mendes (2005), pp. 449, 461, 721.

[67]Vanossi (2000), p. 188.

[68]Elster (2000), pp. 95–6.

[69]See Friedman (2011), pp. 77, 93–96.

[70]Linder (1981), p. 723. As Tushnet (2012–2013) 2007 suggests, 'perhaps constitutional theory should treat an unconstitutional amendment as a pro tanto exercise of the right to revolution through the form of law, a form that allows fundamental change to occur without violence'; See also Tushnet (2015), pp. 639, 642–643.

constituent power simply calls for further development of how the *primary constituent power* may peacefully 'resurrect' and change even unamendable constitutional subjects.[71] This theoretical understanding—which urges the further development of the democratic exercise of *primary constituent power*—manages to relax to some extent the fear of revolutionary actions in order to overcome unamendability.

3.2 Limited Effectiveness

A related practical objection is that unamendability is ineffective. Already in 1918, Lawrence Lowell wrote that 'the device of providing that a law shall never be repealed is an old one, but I am not aware that it has ever been of any avail'.[72] Likewise, Benjamin Akzin expressed his scepticism regarding the usefulness of unamendability:

> One understands that we deal here with provisions which the respective constitution-makers hold in particular esteem and to which they would like to give added protection. But if this esteem is shared by the rest of the politically-active groups, this by itself should ensure that the standard procedure for constitutional amendments would protect them sufficiently; if, on the other hand, the demand for change were to become so strong that it could overcome these standard procedure, it is hardly imaginable that its protagonists would renounce their objectives only because the Constitution says that the provision is inviolable.[73]

Those objecting to unamendability would simply treat it as 'pointless impediments, permissibly ignored'.[74] Silvia Suteu and I have recently demonstrated how certain provisions of unamendability are especially vulnerable. In light of the Crisis in Crimea in 2014, we argued that the unamendable protection of territorial integrity faces a double threat: internal in the form of a secessionist movement and external in the shape of forceful annexation of territory, which severely curtail the preservative promise of unamendability, even when backed by a constitutional court with far-reaching powers of judicial review.[75]

It appears that the effectiveness problem of unamendability has various aspects. First, as elaborated in the previous subsection, just as 'no Constitution … can be expected to survive intact the social cataclysm involved in a true revolution',[76] unamendability cannot block extra-constitutional activity. As Hannah Arendt taught

---

[71]See, on this, Roznai (2017b); Roznai (2017a).

[72]Lawrence Lowell (1918), p. 103.

[73]Akzin (1967), pp. 1, 12.

[74]Tushnet (2012–2013), p. 2007.

[75]Roznai and Suteu (2015).

[76]Akzin (1956), pp. 313, 332. See also Vile (1990–1991), pp. 271, 295: 'No mere parchment barrier can prevent the people from exercising the right to propose a new constitution if sufficient numbers insist upon doing so and have the necessary power to back up their demands'.

us, 'in a conflict between law and power, it is seldom the law which will emerge as victory'.[77] For example, the prohibition of the 1824 Mexican Constitution on altering the form of government did not prevent a *coup d'état*, in which the conservatives came into power and in 1836 replaced the Constitution with a new one that rejected federalism.[78] In Greece, notwithstanding the unamendability protection of the democratic system of government in the 1952 Constitution, the Constitution was suspended in April 1967 by a military putsch, which established a military dictatorship that lasted until 1974.[79] The issue of unamendable provisions can thus be both a question of fact and norm.[80] As a factual matter, the ability of physical power to force prohibited changes is unquestionable. From a normative perspective, the question is whether such changes would be valid according to the standards of the constitutional order.[81]

Second, and related to the first aspect, the effectiveness of unamendability is directly linked to the effectiveness of the entire constitution. Where the constitution is mostly ignored, regarded as a mere parchment, one cannot expect unamendable provisions to be any more effective or operative than the constitution's other provisions.[82] Thus, unamendable provisions could be *de jure* valid, but *de facto* ignored. For example, returning to Greece, the 1968 dictatorial Constitution contained the unamendable provision of the previous 1952 Constitution, which protects the form of government as a royal democracy, notwithstanding the fact that in 1967 the government exiled the king from the country.[83] Likewise, the Brazilian Constitution of 1891 protected the republican form of government from amendments. This, however, did not prevent a *coup d'état* and the *de facto* dictatorial rule of President Vargas. Only in 1934 a new constitution was promulgated, which legitimised the regime while still protecting the 'republican form of government' from abolishment. In 1937, a new constitution, which transformed Vargas' presidency into a legal dictatorship, was promulgated, and only this time the Constitutional text did not include any unamendable protection of the republican form of government. After Vargas' resignation in 1945, the 1946 and 1967 Constitutions included an unamendable protection of the republican form of government, although this did not prevent the military dictatorship (1964–1988) from severely violating the right to vote, thereby suppressing the republican principle.[84]

Finally, the effectiveness of unamendability is related to its judicial enforcement. Claiming that amendment powers are limited and claiming that such limitations are

---

[77]Arendt (2006), p. 142.

[78]Roel (1968), pp. 251, 256–259, Moses (1891), pp. 1, 4.

[79]Spiliotopoulos (1983), pp. 463, 466–467.

[80]Muñiz-Fraticelli (2009), pp. 379–380.

[81]Murphy (1992), pp. 337, 348.

[82]On sham constitutions, see recently Law and Versteeg (2013), p. 863.

[83]Pilpilidis (this volume).

[84]Maia (2000), pp. 54, 60.

enforced in courts are not identical claims.[85] One may argue that although the amendment power is limited, it is not the role of courts to enforce these limitations.[86] For example, in Norway[87] and France,[88] the existence of unamendable provisions did not necessarily lead to the judicial oversight over unamendability. In these states, one may argue, unamendable provisions are merely declarative and non-justiciable, which raises questions regarding their effectiveness.[89] The same applies to implicit unamendability. In Pakistan, although the Supreme Court acknowledged a set of implicitly unamendable 'salient features' of the constitution, it used to draw a distinction between these limitations and their judicial enforcement, holding that limitations on the amendment power are to be enforced by the body politic through the ordinary mechanisms of parliamentary democracy, rather than by the judiciary.[90] It is therefore clear that the heavy criticism against unamendability (explicit or implicit) is mainly applicable when unamendability is deemed enforceable in courts or otherwise.[91]

Admittedly, there is no easy answer for these challenges. Like any other legal instruments, the effectiveness of unamendability is not absolute. No constitutional schemes—even such that expressly attempt to—can hinder for long the sway of real forces in public life.[92] Nevertheless, one has to consider the following claims:

First, the fact that unamendability can be overridden by violent and extra-constitutional means should not severely undermine its usefulness in normal times and in states where political players understand that they have to play according to the democratic rules of the game. In that respect, unamendability, as I have explained in earlier occasions, is like a lock on a door.[93] A lock cannot prevent housebreaking by a decisive burglar equipped with effective burglary tools, and even more so, the lock cannot prevent the entire door's destruction by sledgehammer or a fire. On the other hand, if we are dealing solely with honest people, there is no need for a lock since there is no fear that any of them will attempt to break into one's house. The lock's utility is in impeding and deterring those who might not overcome the temptation to exploit an easy opportunity to improve their condition at the expense of fellowmen in the absence of effective safety measures. Similarly, unamendability cannot block extra-constitutional measures and is not needed once the socio-political culture is that of binding the rules and self-restraint.

---

[85]See e.g. Wright (1994), pp. 35, 72.

[86]See e.g., Tribe (1983), pp. 433, 440–443, Ingham (1928–1929), p. 168.

[87]See e.g. Smith (2011), p. 369.

[88]See e.g. French Constitutional Council No. 2003-469DC, March 26, 2003; Wright (2005), p. 495, Baranger (2011), pp. 389, 396.

[89]Ibid., p. 398.

[90]Pakistan Lawyers Forum v. Federation of Pakistan, repored as PLD 2005 SC 719; Conrad (2003), pp. 186, 192.

[91]Vile (1995), pp. 191, 198–199.

[92]Zweig (1909), p. 324.

[93]Roznai (2017c), Roznai and Suteu (2015).

Karl Loewenstein was correct in observing that in times of crisis, unamendability is just a piece of paper which political reality could unavoidably disregard or ignore. But in normal times, unamendability can be a useful red light before certain 'unconstitutional' constitutional changes and stand firm in the normal development of political momentum.[94] Hence, unamendability should not be underestimated.

Second, whereas it is true that unamendability cannot serve as a complete bar against movements aiming to abolish the protected subjects,[95] it is not completely useless. Unamendability mandates political deliberation as to whether the amendment in question is compatible with society's basic principles or not. Gregory Fox and Georg Nolte remark that the framers of the German Basic Law believed that if an unamendable provision 'had been presented in the Weimar constitution, Hitler would have been forced to violate the constitution openly before assuming virtually dictatorial power. ... given the traditional orderly and legalistic sentiment of the German people, this might have made the difference'.[96] Hence, unamendability and its institutional enforcement may provide sufficient additional time for the people to reconsider their support for a change contrary to their fundamental values and thereby impede the triumph of the revolutionary movements.[97]

3.3   Enhancing Judiciary's Power

From an institutional perspective, enforceability of unamendability shifts the locus of constitutional change from those authorities entrusted with the amendment power towards the courts, allegedly granting them the last word on constitutional issues.[98] Courts can use unamendability as a strategic trump, applying it selectively, and overall elevating their powers *vis-à-vis* other branches.[99] This problem is accentuated with regards to implicit unamendability, where, in contrast with situations in which the textual standard provides guidance and constraints, the judiciary has sweeping power to determine the 'spirit', 'basic structure' or 'basic principles' of the constitution.[100] For example, the Indian basic structure doctrine has been heavily criticised for its open-ended nature and the wide discretion that it grants judges.[101]

Judicial enforcement of unamendability may not only lead to a power imbalance by elevating the judiciary's power *vis-à-vis* the executive and legislature branches, but

---

[94]Lowernstein (1972), pp. 180–181.
[95]Conrad (1970), pp. 380, 394.
[96]Fox and Nolte (1995), pp. 1, 19.
[97]Ackerman (1993), pp. 20–21.
[98]Schwartzberg (2009), pp. 3, 22, 184–189.
[99]Mohallem (2011), p. 781.
[100]Schwartzberg (2009), pp. 15–16, Landau (2013), p. 189.
[101]Madhava Menon (2006), pp. 59, 137, 138.

might also fracture the fragile balance of judicial review.[102] One of the arguments justifying the judicial review of ordinary legislation is that courts do not necessarily possess the last word, since unpopular judicial decisions may be overturned by constitutional amendments.[103] In the French constitutional debate, Georges Vedel famously compared constitutional amendments to the ancient institution of *'lit de justice'* by which the sovereign king could appear before the court and overturn a judicial decision. Similarly, in a sort of *lit de justice*, the people can overturn a court's ruling through constitutional amendments.[104] This democratic check would arguably disappear if courts could review constitutional amendments.[105]

Judicial enforcement of unamendability undeniably enhances the judiciary's power. Yet, the theory behind unamendability manages to moderate this concern. Again, even if courts have the power to review constitutional amendments, they do not possess final decision-making power. Recall, decisions by the *primary constituent power* are not submitted to judicial review, but rather merely those decisions adopted by the limited *secondary constituent power*.[106] Consequently, the judicial branch is not sovereign and can still be overridden by an exercise of the superior *primary constituent power*.

Moreover, the theory of unamendability calls for judicial restraint. The exercise of the extreme judicial power to declare constitutional amendments as unconstitutional should be undertaken only in the most aggravated cases and exceptional circumstances in which the constitutional change strikes at the heart of the constitution's basic principles, depriving them of their minimal conditions of existence thereby substantively replacing the constitution with a new one.[107] Of course, a review of amendments that overturn prior judicial decisions might damage the court's legitimacy[108]; therefore, courts would be inclined to restrain themselves and refrain from adjudicating the issue of amendments that overrule judicial decisions. Especially if constitutional amendments are adopted through *demanding amendment procedures* which are multistages, inclusive, participatory, deliberative and time-consuming, courts should restrain themselves when adjudicating constitutional

---

[102]Mohallem (2011), p. 766.

[103]See Dixon (2011), pp. 96, 98, Sweet (2000), p. 89, Yap (2006–2007), pp. 99, 104–105, Dellinger (1983–1984), pp. 386, 414–415, Comella (2009), pp. 104–107, Kyvig (1996), p. 106. On how constitutional amendments are used in order to nullify effects of courts' judgments in India see Chandrachud (this volume).

[104]Vedel (1992), p. 173, cited in Troper (2003), pp. 99, 113, Baranger (2011), p. 407. On 'lit de justice' see Radin (1934–1935), pp. 112, 115.

[105]Tribe (1983), pp. 442–443.

[106]Ponthoreau and Ziller (2002), pp. 119, 140.

[107]See Roznai (2014b), pp. 38–40. Cf Yap (2015), p. 132 (argues that in easily amended constitutions, 'judges may interfere with the substance of the amendment only when its passage would substantially destroy the pre-existing constitution, i.e. the constitutional change in question must be manifestly unreasonable'.).

[108]Dellinger (1983–1984), pp. 414–416.

amendments.[109] All this, however, should not exclude the recognition of the power of judicial review of amendments.

Additionally, one should not be overly petrified by the possibility of courts annulling constitutional amendments. Commonly, courts can interpret amendments, which have become part of the constitution once adopted, during their ordinary judicial review of legislation.[110] If courts have the authority to interpret the constitution, and in doing so to grant to a constitutional provision a very narrow or broad interpretation, then allowing it to invalidate an amendment is not such a radical step. True, in the case of interpretation, it would be open to another court to choose a different interpretation in the future. Nevertheless, the results of an interpretation that significantly differs from the legislative intent, or is detached from the provision's wording, could be more severe than the act of annulment.[111] As Christine Landfried remarks:

> A clear-cut invalidation of a law can give the legislature more room for political manoeuvring, in that a new law can be enacted. However, the declaration that only one particular interpretation of a law is constitutional often entails precise prescriptions and can quite easily result in law-making by the Constitutional Court.[112]

In the case of annulment, the 'ball returns to the hands' of the amending authority, which can reconstitute the amendment according to the court's decision or otherwise. In the case of interpretation, if the amending authority is not satisfied with the new meaning of the amendment, it would have to annul the amendment through the amendment process, only this time, the 'ball has left the hands' of the amending authority.[113] It is now in the public sphere shaped by the hands of the judiciary until its replacement with a new amendment.

Lastly, judicial review of amendments can be viewed as a useful mechanism for relaxing the main abovementioned challenges of unamendability as it allows courts to interpret the protected principles and give them modern meaning. What republicanism meant in France in 1791 is infinitely different from what it means nowadays,[114] and the Norwegian Constitution's spirit and principles are not

---

[109]Roznai (2017b).

[110]Baranger (2011), p. 414. Even in Hungary, where the constitution explicitly prohibits the constitutional court from conducting a substantive judicial review of amendments, the Hungarian Constitutional Court has emphasised in decision 12/2013 that as guardian of the constitution, it will continue to interpret and apply the Fundamental Law as a 'coherent system', which might lead to a 'de facto substantive review of constitutional amendments'. See Gárdos-Orosz (this volume).

[111]Otto Pfersmann describes provisions that were given a different meaning from what they actually mean (because otherwise they would be invalidated by the court) as 'norms without texts'. See Pfersmann (2009), pp. 81, 88. Of course, such application of interpretation may conflict with principles of legal certainty and separation of powers. See Tobisch (2011), pp. 424, 427.

[112]Landfried (1988), p. 154.

[113]Kyvig (2000), pp. 9, 10 (arguing that 'removing an amendment from the constitution requires the same supermajority approval as its initial adoption, thus a reversal of political sentiment of enormous magnitude').

[114]Baranger (2011), p. 421.

necessarily those of 1814, but the present ones.[115] Indeed, constitutional identity is never a static thing but can always be reinterpreted and reconstructed.[116] The courts' ability to review amendments can have important benefits in that respect. While unamendability is aimed, *inter alia*, to provide stability for society, it might cause constitutional stagnation. The ability of courts to review amendments and to interpret (and reinterpret) unamendable provisions manages simultaneously to preserve the core elements of the protected principles while allowing a certain degree of change, and in so doing eases rigidity with the changing needs of society.[117] In the same vein, albeit suffering from uncertainty, some view the vagueness of implicit unamendability as an advantage; being judicially formulated, it contains an inherent flexibility as it leaves space for subsequent judicial interpretation, clarification, and public and political dialogues and deliberations.[118]

4 Textual Challenges to Constitutional Unamendability

4.1 The Meaning of 'Amendment'

The term 'amendment', McGovney argues, encompasses as an element of euphemism, the assumption that it is an improvement. But 'beyond this euphemistic tinge, amendment as applied to alteration of laws, according to current dictionaries means alteration or change'.[119] Thus, arguably, in the absence of explicit limitations, one cannot infer legal consequences from the grammatical interpretation of the word 'amendment'. This is why Kemal Gözler claims that the amendment provision can be used in order to change several or even all of the constitution's provisions. In order to support his argument, Gözler claims that some constitutions, for example, that of Austria (Art. 44), Spain (Art. 168) and Switzerland (Art. 139), explicitly allow for their *total revision*. Moreover, in other languages, different terms than *amendment* are used: Francophile constitutions use the term *revision*, the Italian Constitution uses *revision*, the Portuguese Constitution uses *revisao*, the Spanish Constitution uses *reforma*, the German Basic Law uses *anderung* and the Turkish Constitution use *değişiklik*. These terms, Gözler claims, do not carry the exact same meaning as *amendment* which might imply limitability.[120]

These arguments carry some force, but they are not entirely convincing. First, the limited scope of amendment powers does find implicit textual support in the

---

[115]Opsahl (1991–1992), pp. 181, 185–186.

[116]See Rosenfeld (1994–1995), p. 1049, Jacobsohn (2006), pp. 361, 363, Jacobsohn (2010a), pp. 133, 335, Jacobsohn (2010b), p. 47.

[117]Gören (2009), pp. 1, 12–13.

[118]Abraham (2000), pp. 195, 204, Issacharoff (2012), p. 45, Stith (1996), pp. 65–66.

[119]McGovney (1920), p. 514. See also Orfield (1942), p. 108.

[120]Gözler (2008), pp. 69–71.

literal meaning of the term 'amendment'.[121] Literally, the Latin word *emendere* means 'to correct fault'. This, Walter Murphy reminds us, does not mean 'to deconstitute and reconstitute'.[122] Based on this textual meaning, Murphy argues that, 'amendments that would change the basic principles on which the people agreed to become a nation or overturn compromises on any principle that made the coming together possible would not be *amendments* at all, but efforts to construct a new constitution'.[123] The textual basis distinguishes between amendments and revolutionary changes to the constitution.[124] Even 'in our everyday discourse', Sotirios Barber notes, 'we distinguish amendments from fundamental changes because the word *amendment* ordinarily signifies incremental improvements or corrections of a larger whole'.[125] This textual argument is not novel[126] and was recently influential in courts decisions that recognised implicit unamendability, for example, in India[127] and Bangladesh.[128]

Second, it can be argued that in those numerous and limited cases in which constitutions allow for their *total revision*, this authorisation is an explicit permissibility given to the delegated amending authority to revise the entire document.[129] However, *this is the exception rather than the rule*. It can also be argued, following Carl Schmitt, that when constitutions allow their *total revision*, this should be regarded as allowing amendments of the *entire constitution's provisions*, but not of the state's *basic premises*.[130] Even an amendment of a single provision can be considered revolutionary, while revising the entire constitution can still maintain its basic constitutional principles. This applies with even greater force to constitutions that use the terms *revision* or *reform*, rather than *total reform*. The Latin meaning of the word *reformare* is 'to transform an already existing thing'.[131] A revision or a reform can indeed make dramatic changes, but they still cannot

---

[121]Schweber (2007), p. 137, Kay (1997), pp. 161, 163, Yap (2015), pp. 118–120.

[122]Murphy (1995), pp. 163, 177. See also Murphy (1992), p. 14.

[123]Murphy (1987), pp. 1, 12–13.

[124]Cf, Child (1926), pp. 27, 28, Machen (1909–1910), pp. 169–170, Morris (1909), pp. 82, 85, Marbury (1919–1920), pp. 223, 225, Holding (1923), pp. 481, 487, Schaffner (2005), pp. 1487, 1493, Han (2010), pp. 71, 82, Murphy (2007), p. 506.

[125]Barber (1984), p. 43.

[126]See, for example, Davis (1881), p. 197; *Livermore v. Waite*, 36 P. 424,426 (Cal. 1894); and the briefs presented before the U.S. Supreme Court against the validity of the 18th Amendment (see Dodd (1921), pp. 321, 330–332).

[127]*Kesavananda Bharati v. State of Kerala*, AIR 1973 SC 1461 (J. Khanna at 1426-7).

[128]*Anwar Hossain Chowdhury v. Bangladesh*, 41 DLR 1989 App. Div. 165 (Judge B.H. Chowdhury, para 196; Shahabuddin, J, id., at paras. 336, 417).

[129]Cf Yap (2015), p. 121 ('in such instances where the constitution explicitly authorizes the repeal of any of its provisions via the amendment process, the textual argument in favour of giving a narrow reading to the word "amend" loses its force').

[130]Schmitt (2008), p. 152.

[131]Borucka-Arctowa (1991), pp. 79, 80.

destroy the existing constitutional order and replace it with one that denies these basic values.[132]

Lastly, even in some other languages, the amending provisions carry the same meaning as *amendment*. For instance, the Israeli Basic Laws use the Hebrew term *Tikun* (תיקון), which means 'correction', and even the old Turkish version, which is still often used in the literature, uses the term *Tadilat* which originally means 'repairing.' In any event, the vast majority of national constitutions use the term *amendment* (or its equivalent).[133]

4.2 Expressio Unius Est Exclusio Alterius

The mere existence of implicit unamendability is contentious. Had a constitution's framers intended to prohibit certain amendments, one could reasonably expect them to have included a provision to that effect.[134] This problem obviously exists with regards to those constitutions that lack any unamendable provisions, and it is aggravated when the constitution contains certain unamendable provisions. According to the maxim *expressio unius est exclusio alterius*, the existence of explicit limitations provides evidence that the constitution-makers considered limits on the amendment power, that the omission of other limitations was intentional and, that therefore, implicit unamendability should be excluded.[135] Indeed, John Vile argues that this is 'perhaps the strongest argument against implicit limits on the amending process'.[136] In 1871, George Helm Yeaman attacked the notion of implicit limitations on the amendment power:

> We cannot have two constitutions, one of the letter and one of the spirit, the letter amendable and the spirit not. Letter, spirit and approved judicial construction all go to make up the constitution. That constitution by its own terms is susceptible of amendment, and the amendments, when adopted in the way pointed out, are binding and must be obeyed.[137]

This is akin to David Dow's argument that Art. V of the U.S. Constitution is exclusive and that its words 'mean what they say'.[138] Likewise, Gözler defends the approach according to which no limitations exist apart from those explicitly included in the constitution.[139]

---

[132]Murphy (1992), pp. 351–352. See also Nielsen (1979), pp. 155, 157.

[133]Dhamija (2007), p. 223.

[134]The rejection of the Indian basic structure doctrine in Singapore was based upon this argument. See *Teo Soh Lung v. The Minister for Home Affairs* [1989] 2M.L.J. 449, 456–457.

[135]See Pillsbury (1909), pp. 741, 742–743, Williams (1928), pp. 529, 544, Orfield (1942), pp. 115–116, Orfield (1929–1930), pp. 553–555; Linder (1981), p. 730, Da Silva (2004), p. 459.

[136]Vile (1985), pp. 373, 383.

[137]Yeaman (1871), pp. 710–711.

[138]Dow (1990–1991), p. 1, Dow (1995), p. 127. See also Baker (2000), pp. 1, 3.

[139]Gözler (2008), p. 102.

These arguments are important, but they are not entirely resounding. First, I share Otto Pfersmann's position that the approach taken by Gözler is too narrow. 'Many things', Pfersmann notes, 'are indirectly explicit, i.e. they are contained in the meaning of the norm-formulation, accessible though interpretation'.[140] CJ Sikri's opinion in *Kesavananda* takes a similar approach: 'in a written constitution it is rarely that everything is said expressly. Powers and limitations are implied from necessity or the scheme of the Constitution'.[141]

Second, and more importantly, any organ established within the constitutional scheme to amend the constitution cannot modify the basic principles supporting its constitutional authority; even in the absence of any explicit limitations.[142] Hence, explicit and implicit unamendability are not mutually exclusive rather they are mutually reinforcing. Explicit unamendability should be regarded as confirmation, a 'valuable indications' that the amendment power is limited, but not as an exhaustive list of limitations.[143]

Examples from comparative law strengthen this presumption. For instance, under the 1961 Turkish Constitution, the provision establishing the republican form of the state (Article 1) was explicit unamendable.[144] Even so, the Turkish Constitutional Court held in 1965 that the unamendability of the form of state implicitly extends also to the characteristics of the republic (Article 2) stating that the amendment power cannot provide for 'causing regression to the Turkish society, destroying fundamental right and freedoms and the principle of the rule of law, in a word, taking away the Essence of the 1961 Constitution'.[145] Later, the Court reaffirmed that there are certain principles which comprise the constitution's 'spirit and philosophy' and its competence to examine whether amendments do not damage the 'coherence and system of the constitution'.[146] Likewise, the Italian Constitution includes an explicit unamendability according to which 'The republican form of the state may not be changed by way of constitutional amendment'.[147] Italian scholars contend that additionally, fundamental constitutional principles such as democracy, inviolable rights and the rigidity of the constitution itself are

---

[140]Pfersmann (2012), pp. 81, 103.

[141]*Kesavananda Bharati v. State of Kerala*, AIR 1973 SC 1461, para 210.

[142]Roznai (2017c), Keshavamurthy (1982), p. 51.

[143]Conrad (1970), p. 379, Schmitt (2008), p. 152. Compare with Fleming (1994–1995), pp. 355, 366 (entrenchment of certain compromises should not deny unalienable rights held by the people).

[144]Article 9 Const. (1961) (Turkey). See Olcay (this volume).

[145]Turkish Constitutional Court, decision No 1965/40, 4 AMKD 290, 329 (26 September 1965) (obiter dicta), cited in Olcay (this volume). See also Gözler (2008), pp. 95–96, Yegen (this volume).

[146]Turkish Constitutional Court, decision No 1970/37, 9 AMKD 416, 428–429 (3 April 1971), cited in Olcay (this volume) and Gözler (2008), pp. 96–97.

[147]Art. 139 Const. (1947) (Italy).

implicitly unamendable.[148] The Italian Constitutional Court accepted this approach in its decision 1146/1988, stating that:

> The Italian Constitution contains some supreme principles that cannot be subverted or modified in their essential content [...]. Such are principles that the Constitution itself explicitly contemplates as absolute limits to the power of constitutional revision, such as the republican form [...] as well as principles that, although not expressly mentioned among those not subject to the principle of constitutional revision, are part of the supreme values on which the Italian Constitution is based.[149]

In other words, notwithstanding the explicit unamendable provision, the Constitutional Court recognised further implicit unamendability of the supreme constitutional principles.[150]

It is with this understanding that one can accept Maurice Hauriou's claim that there are always implicit supra-constitutional principles: 'not to mention the republican form of government for which there is a text, there are many other principles for which there is no need to text because of its own principles is to exist and assert without text'.[151] Even Georges Burdeau, who took a formal approach in his doctoral thesis,[152] later changed his mind to claim:

> [T]o say that the power of revision is limited, is to support, not only that it is bound by the terms of form and procedure made its exercise by the text – which is obvious – but also that it is incompetent, basically, to repeal the existing constitution and develop a new one [...] by repealing it, it would destroy the basis of its own jurisdiction.[153]

I am fully aware that an argument in favour of implicit unamendability may seem contradictory in that it both upholds and rejects the constitution; in one breath it views the constitution as so sacred that interference with its basic principles is prohibited, while in the next breath it claims that the constitution's own amendment procedure must be ignored or recognised only to a limited extent.[154] However, to demonstrate the absurdity of relying solely on explicit unamendability imagine the extreme examples of amendments providing that the constitution has no legal validity, or that the Parliament extends its term indefinitely without elections.[155] Such amendments undermine the entire legitimacy of the constitutional order. Restricting ourselves to a formalistic approach, according to which the amendment

---

[148]See in Carrozza (2007), pp. 168, 174–175, Groppi (2012), pp. 203, 210, Galizzi (2000), pp. 235, 241, Fusaro (2011), pp. 211, 215, Comella (2009), p. 107.

[149]Corte Const. judgment no. 1146 of Dec. 15, 1988, quoted in Del Duca and Del Duca (2006), pp. 799, 800–801.

[150]Escarras (1993), pp. 105, 112–116; 117, 130–138, Scotti (this volume).

[151]Hauriou (1923), p. 297 (my translation).

[152]Burdeau (1930), pp. 78–83.

[153]Burdeau (1983), pp. 231–232, quoted in Gözler (2008), p. 94 (my translation).

[154]Williams (1928), p. 543.

[155]As Black once wrote, 'these are (in part at least) cartoon illustrations. But the cartoon accurately renders the de jure picture, and seems exaggerated only because we now conceive that at least some of these actions have no appeal to anybody'. See Black (1963), pp. 957, 959.

power is solely limited by explicit limitations, would mean that such amendments would be 'constitutional' in the absence of express limitations to the contrary. Yet, it would be absurd to include in every constitution a provision stating that it is prohibited to use the amendment process to destroy the constitution itself, because it is evident that the delegated amendment power cannot destroy the fundamental political system to which it owes its existence.[156] Just as in private law, no action may be founded on illegality or immorality (*ex turpi causa non oritur action*), so too, the constitutional process cannot be used to undermine the constitutional regime itself.[157] The all-encompassing idea underlying amendment provisions in the first instance was the desire to preserve the constitution.[158] While infallibility is not an attribute of a constitution, its fundamental character and basic structure cannot be overlooked. Otherwise, the power to amend may include the power to destroy the constitution, and that would be *reductio ad absurdum*.[159] Thus, the best response to the *expressio unius est exclusio alterius* argument is that 'what is logically impossible does not need to be positively prescribed'.[160]

In reply to this 'amendophobia', the fear that the amendment power will be abused to undermine democracy or constitutionalism, Lester Orfield has argued that the possibility of abuse of power should not be the test for the power's existence. Moreover, even if an abuse of the amendment power occurs, 'it occurs at the hands of a special organization of the nation [...] so that for all practical purposes it may be said to be the people, or at least the highest agent of the people, and one exercising sovereign powers [...] it seems anomalous to speak of "abuse" by such a body'.[161] These claims should be refuted. While it is true that the mere possibility of abuse should not be the test to the mere existence of a power, it is unclear why it should not be a test for its scope, especially if ignoring limitations on scope may not only bring absurd results, but may also subvert the entire notion of constitutionalism. Furthermore, the amendment power, though an extraordinary one, is not sovereign. It is indeed different from ordinary governmental power, but it is still an *agent* of the people, an agent that is capable of abusing its power.[162] This should

---

[156]Roznai (2017c).

[157]Cf., Judge Landau opinion in Israeli Supreme Court decision *Yeredor v. Chairman, Central Election Committee for the Sixth Knesset*, 19 P.D. 365. (1965). See Guberman (1967), pp. 455, 457. On this case, see Masri (this volume) at 9–10.

[158]Harris (1993), p. 183.

[159]Iyer (2003), pp. 1, 2. As Ringera J stated in the case which adopted the basic structure doctrine in Kenya: 'Parliament has no power to and cannot in the guise or garb of amendment either change the basic features of the Constitution or abrogate and enact a new Constitution. In my humble view, a contrary interpretation would lead to a farcical and absurd spectacle'. *See Njoya & Others v. Attorney General & Others*, [2004] LLR 4788 (HCK), high Court of Kenya at Nairobu, 25 March 2004, para 61 http://www.chr.up.ac.za/index.php/browse-by-subject/336-kenya-njoya-and-others-v-attorney-general-and-others-2004-ahrlr-157-kehc-2004-.html.

[160]Da Silva (2004), p. 459.

[161]Orfield (1942), pp. 123–124.

[162]I elaborate on this in Roznai (2017c).

not be dismissed as a mere 'argument of fear'. Even those who reject the notion of implicit unamendability have to admit that the Indian basic structure doctrine was created as a response to abuse of the amendment power, and proved that unamendability may avert unauthorised usurpation of power and preserve democracy.[163] True, implicit unamendability and its judicial enforcement may be seen as 'an imperfect response to imperfections'[164]; yet it could be regarded as a necessary evil.

5 Conclusion

Unamendability may be a useful constitutional preservative mechanism. It might also be desirable from a paternalistic perspective with its expressive effects,[165] or as means for reducing wasteful spending in rent-seeking.[166] Nevertheless, as this chapter demonstrated, unamendability raises many theoretical and practical objections. Noah Webster, writing a series of articles in the *American Magazine* in 1787–1788 (as 'Giles Hickory'), criticised any attempt to create an unamendable constitution. This attempt is not only 'arrogant and impudent' since it means to 'legislate for those over whom we have as little authority as we have over a nation in Asia', but it would also be useless since 'a paper declaration is a very feeble barrier against the force of national habits, and inclinations'.[167]

Indeed, unamendability is a 'complex and potentially controversial constitutional instrument, which should be applied with care, and reserved only for the basic principles of the democratic order'.[168] Nevertheless, if the theory of unamendability is correctly construed in light of the theoretical distinction between the *primary* and *secondary constituent powers*, many of the objections to unamendability are relaxed. Most importantly, unamendability and its judicial enforcement should be regarded not as completely preventing democratic deliberation on a given 'unamendable' matter, but as making sure that certain changes take place via the proper participatory channel of higher level democratic deliberations. Understood in this way, the doctrine of constitutional unamendability can be seen as a safeguard of the people's *primary constituent power*. Unamendability is therefore not an expression

---

[163]Katz (1995–1996), pp. 251, 273, Lakshminath (1978), pp. 144, 159, Keshavamurthy (1982), p. 82, Sripati (1998), pp. 413, 480, Nahar and Dadoo (2008), pp. 559, 571.

[164]Garlicki and Garlicka (2012), p. 185.

[165]Michel and Cofone (this volume). On the expressive function of unamendability, see Albert (2013a), pp. 225, 254.

[166]Pilpilidis (this volume), p. 21.

[167]Hickory (1787–1788), pp. 138–139, 140–141, cited in Wood (1998), pp. 377, 379.

[168]'Report on Constitutional Amendment', European Commission for Democracy Through Law (Venice Commission), adopted by the Venice Commission at its 81st Plenary Session (Venice, Dec 11–12 2009) para 218 www.venice.coe.int/docs/2010/CDL-AD(2010)001-e.asp?PrintVersion=True&L=E#P768_153923. Accessed 14 August 2016.

of *necrocracy*—a government whereby the people are governed by the dead, but rather as the ultimate expression of *democracy*.

References

Abraham M (2000) In: Andenas M (ed) Judicial role in constitutional amendments in India: the basic structure doctrine, pp 195, 204

Ackerman B (1993) We the people: foundations. Harvard University Press, Cambridge, pp 20–21

Akzin B (1956) On the stability and reality of constitutions. Scripta Hierosolymitana 3:313, 332

Akzin B (1967) The place of the constitution in the modern state. Isr Law Rev 2(1):1, 12

Albert R (2008) Counterconstitutionalism. Dalhousie Law J 31:1, 37–44

Albert R (2010) Constitutional handcuffs. Ariz State Law Rev 42:663, 698

Albert R (2013a) The expressive function of constitutional amendment rules. McGill Law J 59 (2):225, 254

Albert R (2013b) The unamendable Corwin amendment (27.02.2013). Available via ICONnect. www.iconnectblog.com/2013/02/the-unamendable-corwin-amendment

Albert R (2014a) Constructive unamendability in Canada and the United States. Supreme Court Law Rev 67:181

Albert R (2014b) Constitutional disuse or desuetude. Boston Univ Law Rev 94:1029, 1043

Albert R (2015) Amending constitutional amendment rules. Int J Const Law 13(3):655

Albert R (2016) The unamendable core of the United States constitution. In: Koltay A (ed) Comparative perspectives on the fundamental freedom of expression. Wolters Kluwer, Netherlands, p 13

Amar AR (1988) Philadelphia revisited: amending the constitution outside article V. Univ Chicago Law Rev 55:1043, 1054–1058

Arendt H (2006) [1963] On revolution, rev. edn. Penguin Classics, London, p 142

Baker TE (2000) Towards a more perfect union: some thoughts on amending the constitution. Widener J Public Law 10:1, 3

Balkin JM (2003) Respect-worthy: Frank Michelman and the legitimate constitution. Tulsa Law Rev 39:485, 486

Barak A (2009) The judge in a democracy. Princeton University Press, Princeton, pp 23–26

Baranger D (2011) The language of eternity: constitutional review of the amending power in France (Or the absence thereof). Isr Law Rev 44(3):389, 396

Barber SA (1984) On what the constitution means. Johns Hopkins University Press, USA, p 43

Bardutzky S (2010) The Strasbourg court on the Dayton constitution: judgment in the case of Sejdić and Finci v. Bosnia and Herzegovina, 22 December 2009 (October 19, 2010). Eur Const Law Rev 6(2):309

Beaud O (1994) La puissance de l'état. Presses Universitaires de France, France, p 345

Bernal C (2013) Unconstitutional constitutional amendments in the case study of Colombia: an analysis of the justification and meaning of the constitutional replacement doctrine. Int J Const Law 11:339, 349

Bickel AM (1962) The least dangerous branch: the Supreme Court at the bar of politics. Bobbs-Merrill, Indianapolis, pp 16–23

Bishin WR (1977–1978) Judicial review in democratic theory. South Calif Law Rev 50:1099

Black CL Jr (1963) The proposed amendment of article V: a threatened disaster. Yale Law J 72:957, 959

Borucka-Arctowa M (1991) Innovation and tradition against the background of revolutionary changes of law—a conceptual and functional analysis. In: Bankowski Z (ed) Revolutions in law and legal thought. Aberdeen University Press, Aberdeen, pp 79, 80

Brandon M (1995) The "Original" thirteenth amendment and the limits to formal constitutional change. In: Levinson S (ed) Responding to imperfection: the theory and practice of constitutional amendment. Princeton University Press, Princeton

Burdeau G (1930) Essai d'une Théorie de la Révision des Lois Constitutionnelles en Droit Français. Thèse, Faculté de droit de Paris, pp 78–83

Burdeau G (1983) Traite de Science Politique, 3rd édn. LGDJ, pp 231–232

Cahill M (2016) Ever closer remoteness of the peoples of Europe? Limits on the power of amendment and national constituent power. Camb Law J 75(2):245, 249–258

Carrozza P (2007) In: Loughlin M, Walker N (eds) Constitutionalism's post-modern opening. pp 168, 174–175

Chandrachud C (this volume) Constitutional falsehoods: the fourth judges case and the basic structure doctrine in India

Child SR (1926) Revolutionary amendments to the constitution. Const Rev 10:27, 28

Christopher Bryant A (2003) Stopping time: the pro-slavery and "irrevocable" thirteenth amendment. Harvard J Law Pub Policy 26:501

Comella VF (2009) Constitutional courts & democratic values—a European perspective. Yale University Press, USA, pp 104–107

Conrad D (1970) Limitation of amendment procedures and the constituent power. Indian Yearb Int Aff 15–16:380, 394

Conrad D (2003) Basic structure of the constitution and constitutional principles. In: Sorabjee SJ (ed) Law and justice: an anthology. Universal Law Publishing, Uttar Pradesh, pp 186, 192

Da Silva VA (2004) A fossilised constitution? Ratio Juris 17(4):454, 456–458

Davis J (1881) The rise and fall of the confederate government. D. Appleton, USA, p 197

Del Duca LF, Del Duca P (2006) An Italian federalism? the state, its institutions and national culture as rule of law guarantor. Am J Comp Law 54:799, 800–801

Dellinger W (1983–1984) The legitimacy of constitutional change: rethinking the amendment process. Harvard Law Rev 97:386, 414–415

Derosier JP (2017) In: Albert R, Contiades X, Fotiadou A (eds) The French people's role in amending the constitution. p 315

Dhamija A (2007) Need to amend a constitution and doctrine of basic features. Wadhwa, Nagpur, p 223

Dixon R (2011) Constitutional amendment rules: a comparative perspective. In: Ginsburg T, Dixon R (eds) Comparative constitutional law. Edward Elgar Publishing, UK, pp 96, 98

Dodd WF (1921) Amending the federal constitution. Yale Law J 30(4):321, 330–332

Dow DR (1990–1991) When the words mean what we believe they say: the case of article V. Iowa Law Rev 76:1

Dow DR (1995) In: Levinson S (ed) The plain meaning of article V. p 127

Doyle O (2017) In: Albert R, Contiades X, Fotiadou A (eds) Constraints on constitutional amendment powers. p 73

Dworkin R (1990) A bill of rights for Britain. Chatto & Windus, UK, pp 14, 35

Dworkin R (1995) Constitutionalism and democracy. Eur J Philos 3(1):2

Eisgruber CL (1997) The living hand of the past: history and constitutional justice. Fordham Law Rev 65:1611, 1616

Elkins Z, Ginsburg T, Melton J (2009) The endurance of national constitutions. Cambridge University Press, Cambridge, p 129

Elster J (2000) Ulysses unbound—studies in rationality, precommitment, and constraints. Cambridge University Press, Cambridge, p 102

Ely JH (1980) Democracy and distrust: a theory of judicial review. Harvard University Press, USA, p 11

Escarras JC (1993) Presentation Du Rapport Italien De Massimo Luciani' and Massimo Luciani, 'La Revision Constituzionale in Italia' in La Revision De La Constitution. Economica, pp 105, 112–116, 117, 130–138

Feldman D (2011) "'Which in your case you have not got": constitutionalism at home and abroad'. Curr Legal Probl 64(1):117, 142–144

Feldman D (2012) The nature and effect of constitutional rights in post-conflict Bosnia and Herzegovina. In: Harvey C, Schwartz A (eds) Rights in divided societies. Hart Publishing, UK, pp 151, 164

Fleming JE (1994–1995) We the exceptional American people. Const Comment 11:355, 366

Fombad CM (2007) Limits on the power to amend constitutions: recent trends in Africa and their potential impact on constitutionalism. Univ Botswana Law J 6:27, 57–58

Fox GH, Nolte G (1995) Intolerant democracies. Harvard Int Law J 36:1, 19

Freeman S (1990–1991) Constitutional democracy and the legitimacy of judicial review. Law Philos 9(4):327, 353–354

Friedman A (2011) Dead hand constitutionalism: the danger of eternity clauses in new democracies. Mexican Law Rev 4:77, 93–96

Friedrich CJ (1968) Constitutional government and democracy—theory and practice in Europe and America, 4th edn. Blaisdell Publishing Company, New York, pp 138, 143–146

Fusaro C (2011) 'Italy'. In: Oliver D, Fusaro C (eds) How constitutions change—a comparative study. Hart Publishing, UK, pp 211, 215

Galizzi P (2000) In: Andenas M (ed) Constitutional revisions and reforms: the Italian experience. pp 235, 241

Gárdos-Orosz F (this volume) The role of non-amendable clauses in judicial review of constitutional amendments: theoretical considerations inspired by Hungarian Constitutional Court case law

Garlicki L, Garlicka ZA (2012) Review of constitutionality of unconstitutional amendments (an imperfect response to imperfections?) Anayasa Hukuku Dergisi: J Const Law 1:185

Geertjes GJ, Uzman J (this volume) Conventions of unamendability; unamendable constitutional law in politically enforced constitutions

Goerlich H (2008) Concept of special protection for certain elements and principles of the constitution against amendments and article 79(3), Basic law of Germany. NUJS Law Rev 1:397, 404

Gören Z (2009) Anayasa Koyan Erk Ve Anayasa - Değişikliklerinin Sinirlari'. İstanbul Ticaret Üniversitesi Sosyal Bilimler Dergisi 16:1, 12–13 [The constitution-making power and the limitations on constitutional amendments]. http://siyasaliletisim.org/pdf/anayasadegisikligi.pdf

Gözler K (2008) Judicial review of constitutional amendments—a comparative study. Ekin, Bursa, pp 69–71

Griffin SM (2007) Constituent power and constitutional change in American constitutionalism. In: Loughlin M, Walker N (eds) The paradox of constitutionalism. Oxford University Press, Oxford, p 49

Groppi T (2012) Constitutional revision in Italy—a marginal instrument for constitutional change. In: Contiades X (ed) Engineering constitutional change: a comparative perspective on Europe, Canada and the USA. Routledge, London, pp 203, 210

Guberman S (1967) Israel's supra-constitution. Isr Law Rev 2:455, 457

Hamilton A (1817) In: Hamilton A, Jay J, Madison J (eds) The federalist no. LXXVIII. pp 418, 421

Hamilton A, Jay J, Madison J (1817) [1788] Federalist, on the new constitution. Benjamin Warner, Philadelphia, pp 233, 274

Han WT (2010) Chain novels and amendments outside article V: a literary solution to a constitutional conundrum. Hamline Law Rev 33:71, 82

Harris WF II (1993) The interpretable constitution. Johns Hopkins University Press, USA, pp 167, 193

Hauriou M (1923) Precis de Droit Constitutionnel, 1st edn. Sirey, Paris, p 297 (my translation)

Hickory G [Webster N] (1787–1788) Government. I Am Mag 138–139, 140–141

Holding AM (1923) Perils to be apprehended from amending the constitution. Am Law Rev 57:481, 487

Holmes S (1993) Precommitment and the paradox of democracy. In: Elster J, Slagstad R (eds) Constitutionalism and democracy. Cambridge University Press, Cambridge, pp 195, 239

Hoque R (this volume) Eternal provisions in the constitution of Bangladesh: a constitution once and for all?

Hutchinson AC, Colón-Ríos J (2011) Democracy and constitutional change. Theoria 43

Ingham JF (1928–1929) Unconstitutional amendments. Dickinson Law Rev 33:161, 165–166

Issacharoff S (2012) In: Harvey C, Schwartz A (eds) Managing conflict through democracy. pp 33, 45

Iyer K (2003) A constitutional miscellany, 2nd edn. Eastern Book Company, Uttar Pradesh, pp 1, 2

Jackson V (2013) Unconstitutional constitutional amendments: a window into constitutional theory and transnational constitutionalism. In: Wallrabenstein A, Dann P, Bäuerle M (eds) Demokratie-Perspektiven Festschrift für Brun-Otto Bryde zum 70, Mohr Siebeck, Germany, p 47

Jacobsohn GJ (2006) Constitutional identity. Rev Politics 68:361, 363

Jacobsohn GJ (2010a) Constitutional identity. Harvard University Press, USA, pp 133, 335

Jacobsohn GJ (2010b) The disharmonic constitution. In: Tulis JK, Macedo S (eds) The limits of constitutional democracy. Princeton University Press, Princeton, p 47

Joseph PA, Walker GR (1987) A theory of constitutional change. Oxford J Legal Stud 7:155, 159

Katz E (1995–1996) On amending constitutions: the legality and legitimacy of constitutional entrenchment. Columbia J Law Soc Probl 29:251, 273

Kay RS (1997) Legal rhetoric and revolutionary change. Caribbean Law Rev 7:161, 163

Keshavamurthy CV (1982) Amending power under the Indian constitution—basic structure limitations. Deep & Deep, New Delhi, p 89

Klarman MJ (1997) Antifidelity. South Calif Law Rev 70:381, 382

Klein C (1999) A propos constituent power: some general views in a modern context. In: Jyränki A (ed) National constitutions in the era of integration. Kluwer Law International, pp 31, 37–38

Köybaşi S (this volume) Amending the unamendable: the case of article 20 of the German basic law

Kyvig DE (1996) Appealing Supreme Court decisions: constitutional amendments as checks on judicial review. J Supreme Court Hist 21(2):106

Kyvig DE (2000) Arranging for amendment: unintended outcome of constitutional design. In: Kyvig DE (ed) Unintended consequences of constitutional amendment. University of Georgia Press, USA, pp 9, 10

Lakshminath A (1978) Justiciability of constitutional amendments. In: Dhavan R, Jacob A (eds) Indian constitution—trends and issues. N.M. Tripathi Private Ltd., Mumbai, pp 144, 159

Landau D (2013) Abusive constitutionalism. UC Davis Law Rev 47(1):189

Landfried C (1988) Constitutional review and legislation in the federal Republic of Germany. In: Landfried C (ed) Constitutional review and legislation: an international comparison. Nomos, Germany, p 154

Law DS, Versteeg M (2013) Sham constitutions. Calif Law Rev 101(4):863

Linder D (1981) What in the constitution cannot be amended? Ariz Law Rev 23:717

Lowernstein K (1972) Constitutions, constitutional law. In: Kenig CD (ed) Marxism, communism, and western society: a comparative encyclopedia (Herder and Herder 1972), p 169

Loughlin M (2014) The concept of constituent power. Eur J Polit Theor 13(2):218, 231–232

Lowell L (1918) Greater European governments. Harvard University Press, USA, p 103

Machen AW (1909–1910) Is the fifteenth amendment void? Harvard Law Rev 23:169–170

Madhava Menon NR (2006) Basic structure: after 30 years' and R.K.P, Shankardass, 'anomalies of the 'doctrine''. In: Chopra P (ed) The Supreme Court versus the constitution: a challenge to federalism. Sage, USA, pp 59, 137, 138

Maia L (2000) The creation and amending process in the Brazilian constitution. In: Andenas M (ed) The creation and amendment of constitutional norms. BIICL, London, pp 54, 60

Marbury WL (1919–1920) The limitations upon the amending power. Harvard Law Rev 33:223, 225

Masri M (this volume) Unamendability in Israel: a critical perspective

Mazzone J (2005) Unamendments. Iowa Law Rev 90:1747, 1818

McConnell MW (1998) Textualism and the dead hand of the past. Geo Wash Law Rev 60:1127–1128

McGovney DO (1920) Is the eighteenth amendment void because of its contents? Columbia Law Rev 20:499, 511–513

McIlwain CH (1975) Constitutionalism: ancient and modern. Liberty Fund Inc., Indianapolis, p 132

Mendes CH (2005) Judicial review of constitutional amendments in the Brazilian Supreme Court. Fla J Int Law 17:449, 461, 721

Michel S, Cofone IN (this volume) Credible commitment or paternalism? the case of unamendability

Michelman FI (1998) Brennan and democracy. Calif Law Rev 86:399, 419

Mohallem MF (2011) Immutable clauses and judicial review in India, Brazil and South Africa: expanding constitutional courts' authority. Int J Hum Rights 15(5):765, 766–767

Morris JMF (1909) The fifteenth amendment to the federal constitution. North Am Rev 189:82, 85

Moses B (1891) Constitution of the United States of Mexico: antecedents. Ann Am Acad Polit Soc Sci 2:1, 4

Mulford E (1870) The nation: the foundations of civil order and political life in the United States. Hurd and Houghton, New York, p 155

Muñiz-Fraticelli VM (2009) The problem of a perpetual constitution. In: Gosseries A, Meyer L (eds) Intergenerational justice. Oxford University Press, Oxford, pp 379–380

Murphy WF (1987) Slaughter-house, civil rights, and limits on constitutional change. Am J Juris 32:1, 12–13

Murphy WF (1992) Staggering toward the new jerusalem of constitutional theory: a response to ralph F. Gaebler. Am J Juris 37:337, 348

Murphy WF (1995) In: Levinson S (ed) Merlin's memory: the past and future imperfect of the once and future polity. pp 163, 177

Murphy WF (2007) Constitutional democracy: creating and maintaining a just political order. Johns Hopkins University Press, USA, p 506

Nahar S, Dadoo A (2008) Constituent power & sovereignty: in light of amendments to the Indian constitution. NUJS Law Rev 1:559, 571

Nielsen K (1979) On the choice between reform and revolution. In: Johnson HJ, Leach JJ, Muehlmann RG (eds) Revolutions, systems, and theories—essays in political philosophy. D. Reidel Publishing Company, USA, pp 155, 157

Nogueira CG (2005) A Impossibilidade de as cláusulas pétreas vincularem as gerações futuras. Revista de Informação Legislativa 42(166):79, 84

O'Connell R (1999) Guardians of the constitution: unconstitutional constitutional norms. J Civ Liberties 4:48, 51

Olcay T (this volume) Unamendability of amendable clauses: the case of the Turkish constitution

Opsahl T (1991–1992) The reflection of social values in the constitutional history of Norway—some illustrations. Holdsworth Law Rev 15:181, 185–186

Orfield LB (1929–1930) The scope of the federal amending power. Mich Law Rev 28:550, 581

Orfield LB (1942) The amending the federal constitution. Callaghan & Company, Pennsylvania, p 85

Paine T, Philp M (1998) In: Philp M (ed) Rights of man, common sense, and other political writings. Oxford University Press, Oxford, pp 91–92

Pettys TE (2008) Popular constitutionalism and relaxing the dead hand: can the people be trusted? Wash Univ Law Rev 86:313, 332

Pfersmann O (2009) Ontological and epistemological complexity in comparative constitutional law. In: Engelbrekt AB, Nergelius J (eds) New directions in comparative law. Edward Elgar Publishing, UK, pp 81, 88

Pfersmann O (2012) Unconstitutional constitutional amendment: a normativist approach. Zeitschrift für öffentliches Recht 67:81, 103

Pillsbury AE (1909) The war amendment. North Am Rev 189:741–743

Pilpilidis K (this volume) A constitution for eternity: an economic theory of explicit unamendability

Ponthoreau MC, Ziller J (2002) The experience of the French Conseil Constitutionnel: political and social context and current legal-theoretical debates. In: Wojciech S (ed) Constitutional justice, east and west: democratic legitimacy and constitutional courts in post-communist Europe in a comparative perspective. Springer, Berlin, pp 119, 140

Radin M (1934–35) The judicial review of statutes in continental Europe. W Va Law Q 41:112, 115

Roel S (1968) History of Mexican constitutional experience: from Zitacuaro, 1811, to Queretaro, 1917. Calif W Law Rev 4(2):251, 256–259

Rosenfeld M (1994–1995) The identity of the constitutional subject. Cardozo Law Rev 16:1049

Rosenfeld M (2005) Constitutional adjudication in Europe and the United States: paradoxes and contrasts. In: European and US constitutionalism. Council of Europe, pp 165, 186 fn 80

Rostow EV (1952) The democratic character of judicial review. Harvard Law Rev 66(2):193, 195

Rousseau D (1994) The constitutional judge: master or slave of the constitution? In: Rosenfeld M (ed) Constitutionalism, identity, difference, and legitimacy: theoretical perspectives. Duke University Press, USA, pp 261, 273–282

Roznai Y (2012) The migration of the indian basic structure doctrine. In: Lokendra M (ed) Judicial activism in India—a festschrift in honour of justice V. R. Krishna Iyer. Universal Law Publishing Co., Uttar Pradesh, p 240

Roznai Y (2013a) Is judicial review of constitutional amendments undemocratic? (17.10.2013) ICONnect. http://www.iconnectblog.com/2013/10/article-review-response-carlos-bernal-pulido-and-yaniv-roznai-on-unconstitutional-constitutional-amendments

Roznai Y (2013b) The theory and practice of 'supra-constitutional' limits on constitutional amendments. ICLQ 62(3):557

Roznai Y (2013c) Unconstitutional constitutional amendments—the migration and success of a constitutional idea. Am J Com Law 61(3):657

Roznai Y (2014a) Amending "unamendable" provisions' (20 October 2014) constitution-making & constitutional change blog. http://constitutional-change.com/amending-unamendable-provisions/

Roznai Y (2014b) Legisprudence limitations on constitutional amendments? reflections on the czech constitutional court's declaration of unconstitutional constitutional act. ICL 8(1):29

Roznai Y (2015) Unamendability and the genetic code of the constitution. Eur Rev Public Law 27 (2):775

Roznai Y (2017a) 'We the people', 'oui, the people' and the collective body: perceptions of constituent power. In: Jacobsohn G, Schor M (eds) Comparative constitutional theory. Edward Elger, UK

Roznai Y (2017b) Constituent powers, amendment powers and popular sovereignty: linking unamendability and amendment procedures. In: Albert R, Contiades X, Fotiado A (eds) The foundations and traditions of constitutional amendment. Hart Publishing, UK, p 23

Roznai Y (2017c) Towards a theory of constitutional unamendability: on the nature and scope of the constitutional amendment powers. Jus Politicum – Revue de Droit Politique 18:5

Roznai Y, Suteu S (2015) Eternal territory? The crimean crisis and Ukraine's territorial integrity as an unamendable principle. German Law J 16(3):542

Roznai Y, Yolcu S (2012) An unconstitutional constitutional amendment—the Turkish perspective: a comment on the Turkish constitutional court's headscarf decision. Int J Const Law 10(1):175

Rubenfeld J (1997–1998) The moment and the millennium. George Wash Law Rev 66:1085

Sachs A (1996–1997) South Africa's unconstitutional constitution: the transition from power to lawful power. Saint Louis Univ Law J 41:1249

Sager LG (1995–1996) The dead hand and constitutional amendment. Harvard J Law Public Policy 19:275

Samaha AM (2008) Dead hand arguments and constitutional interpretation. Columbia Law Rev 108:606

Sapir G (2010) The constitutional revolution—past, present and future. Miskal, Yedioth Ahronoth Books, pp 178–179 [Heb]

Schaffner J (2005) The federal marriage amendment: to protect the sanctity of marriage or destroy constitutional democracy? Am Univ Law Rev 54:1487, 1493

Schmitt C (2008) Constitutional theory (trans: Seitrzer J). Duke University Press, Durham, p 152

Schwartzberg M (2009) Democracy and legal change, Cambridge University Press, Cambridge, p 2

Schweber H (2007) The language of liberal constitutionalism. Cambridge University Press, Cambridge, p 137

Scotti VR (this volume) Unamendable constitutional provisions and the European common constitutional heritage. A comparison among three waves of constitutionalism

Singh DK (1966) "What cannot be done directly cannot be done indirectly": its meaning and logical status in constitutionalism. Mod Law Rev 29:273

Smith E (2011) Old and protected? on the "supra-constitutional" clause in the constitution of Norway. Isr Law Rev 44(3):369, 375

Spiliotopoulos E (1983) Judicial review of legislative acts in Greece. Temp Law Q 56:463, 466–467

Sripati V (1998) Toward fifty years of constitutionalism and fundamental rights in India: looking back to see ahead (1950–2000). Am Univ Int Law Rev 14(2):413, 480

Stith R (1996) Unconstitutional constitutional amendments; The extraordinary power of Nepal's supreme court. Am UJ Intl L Pol'y 11:47

Suber P (1999) Amendment. In: Gray CB (ed) Philosophy of law: an encyclopaedia I. Garland Pub. Co, New York and London, pp 31–32

Suksi M (1995) Making a constitution: The outline of an argument. Rättsvetenskapliga Institutionen, p 6

Sweet AS (2000) Governing with judges: constitutional politics in Europe. Oxford University Press, Oxford, p 89

Tobisch K (2011) Public procurement law and effective legal protection. Vienna J Int Const Law 424, 427

Tribe LH (1983) A constitution we are amending: in defense of a restrained judicial role. Harvard Law Rev 97:433, 440–443

Tribe LH (2000) American constitutional law, 3rd edn. Foundation Press, pp 111–114

Troper M (2003) The logic of justification of judicial review. Int J Const Law 1(1) :99, 113

Tushnet M (2012–2013) Constitution-making: an introduction. Tex Law Rev 91:1983, 2007

Tushnet M (2015) Peasants with pitchforks, and toilers with twitter: constitutional revolutions and the constituent power. ICON 13(3):639, 642–643

Tushnet M (2018) Amendment theory. In: Jacobsohn G, Schor M (eds) Comparative constitutional theory. Edward Elger, UK

Vanossi JRA (2000) Teoria constitutional, 2nd edn. Depalma, p 188

Vedel G (1992) Schengen et Maastricht (à propos de la décision n°91-294 DC du Conseil constitutionnel du 25 juillet 1991). Revue Française de Droit Administratif 8(2):173

Vile JR (1985) Limitations on the constitutional amending process. Const Comment 2:373, 383

Vile JR (1990–1991) Legally amending the united states constitution: the exclusivity of article V's mechanisms. Cumberland Law Rev (1990-1991) 21:271, 295

Vile JR (1995) In: Levinson S (ed) The case against implicit limits on the constitutional amending process. pp 191, 198–199

Widner J, Contiades X (2013) Constitution-writing process. In: Tushnet M, Fleiner T, Saunders C (eds) Routledge handbook of constitutional law. Routledge, London, pp 57, 58

Williams GW (1928) What, if any, limitations are there upon the power to amend the constitution of the United States? Am Law Rev 62:529, 544

Wood GS (1998) The creation of the American Republic 1776–1787. University of North Carolina Press, USA, pp 377, 379

Wright S (1994) The constitutional implications in France of the Maastricht treaty. Tulane Eur Civ Law Forum 9:35, 72

Wright S (2005) The self-restraint of the French Conseil Constitutionnel in 2003 and 2004. Eur Pub Law 11(4):495

Yap PJ (2006–2007) Rethinking constitutional review in America and the commonwealth: judicial protection of human rights in the common law world. Georgia J Int Comp Law 35:99, 104–105

Yap PJ (2015) The conundrum of unconstitutional constitutional amendments. Global Constitutionalism 4:114, 116–118

Yeaman GH (1871) The study of government. Little, Brown and co., USA, pp 710–711

Yegen O (this volume) Debates on unamendable articles: deadlock on Turkey's constitution-making process

Zweig E (1909) Die Lehre vom Pouvoir Constituant. Tiibingen, p 324

A Constitution for Eternity:
An Economic Theory of Explicit
Unamendability

Konstantinos Pilpilidis

Abstract Although no constitution is truly eternal, the justification for heightened constitutional entrenchment remains an important problem. The paper provides a novel typology of constitutional eternity. Further, it argues that eternity clauses decrease constitutional flexibility and therefore endanger the longevity of the constitution. The importance of explicitly considering dynamic efficiency is shown and a novel justification for eternity clauses is provided based on this aspect. Since eternity clauses increase the cost of constitutional change, they are suited as barriers against the redistribution of political rents deriving from constitutional protection. The paper concludes by proposing a test of justifiability based on dynamic efficiency.

1 Introduction

All constitutional provisions are not created equal. On the contrary, as the plurality of amendment tracks within constitutions shows, there is an implicit constitutional hierarchy.[1] Various functions have been attributed to this plurality. Just to name a few, plurality creates constitutional distinction, expresses the internal hierarchy of the constitutional rules, and averts or postpones the process of political change, when needed.[2] The strictest form of amendment constraints are self-entrenched eternity clauses. By prohibiting the amendment of a provision either implicitly or explicitly, they put the entrenched provisions to the highest level of legal hierarchy.

Once eternity clauses are examined as a vehicle to understand amendment constraints, we find that the promise they carry cannot be credible from the

---

[1]For a better understanding of the concept of plurality consider the constitution of Canada, which includes four different amendment tracks. See also: Albert (2015a), p. 85.
[2]Albert (2013), p. 225, 240 f.f. A word of caution is necessary here. Specifically, as later will be made clear the functions mentioned in the text should not be interpreted as an explanation on why legal plurality exists.

K. Pilpilidis (✉)
Institute of Law and Economics, University of Hamburg, Hamburg, Germany
e-mail: konstantinos.pilpilidis@uni-hamburg.de

© Springer International Publishing AG, part of Springer Nature 2018   63
R. Albert and B. E. Oder (eds.), *An Unamendable Constitution?*
Ius Gentium: Comparative Perspectives on Law and Justice 68,
https://doi.org/10.1007/978-3-319-95141-6_3

perspective of legal philosophy. The credibility problem is founded upon the *paradox of self-amendment*.[3] Specifically, if the sovereign is omnipotent, then the formal constraint is only an unenforceable promise. Thus, as long as the governed are aware of the paradox, then the sovereign cannot reap the benefits of credible commitment from introducing eternity clauses and such rules would only exceptionally exist. However, an abundance of constitutions is found to contain eternity clauses, despite the aforementioned paradox.[4] A more plausible explanation is to consider, since unitary actors cannot benefit from eternity clauses, that these clauses must be targeted against non-unitary actors, as the ones found in modern democracies. Specifically, eternity clauses are to be interpreted as constraints intended not for the omnipotent sovereign but for tacit future sovereigns or for the organs to which the sovereign delegates powers with a constitution.[5]

Once the who-is-bound is established, we need to establish how. In order to understand the enforcement of eternity clauses by dead framers, one must go beyond the contractarian approach. Lewis distinguishes between two states: acting under a contract, where certain behavior is induced by the existence of a mechanism to enforce compliance, and acting within a convention, where the behavior is induced by a belief that others expect us to act in a certain way and, therefore, will act in a certain way themselves, i.e., complying to what is expect is necessary to reap the benefits of coordination.[6] Since the latter state can be initiated also with long-term contracts, one could make the claim that constitutions can be used as devices for steering/speeding up the creation of conventions. Hardin and Ordeshook argue that to the extent that no actor external to the constitution can exist to enforce the constitutional text, compliance to all surviving constitutions must by definition be a result of the existence of a convention and not a contract.[7]

Ordeshook calls the strength of the convention *legitimacy*.[8] According to Ordeshook, legitimacy is dependent upon the duration for which a constitution has not been violated. Legitimacy, further, is not reduced, as long as the alterations in the content of the constitution are done pursuant to the amendment rules. Under this conception of the constitution, even if the constituencies would be willing to bear the costs to change a particular provision, they still have to think whether they are

---

[3]Suber (1990).

[4]Roznai (2015), p. 775.

[5]Chapter One: Roznai, 'Necrocracy or Democracy? Assessing Objections to Formal Unamendability'; Preuss (2011), p. 429.

[6]Lewis (1969).

[7]Hardin (2013a), Ordeshook (1992), p. 137.

[8]Ordeshook (2002), p. 3. An alternative trichotomous distinction of legitimacy is proposed by Fallon (2005), p. 1787. Both definitions bear great similarities. What Ordeshook calls self-enforcing, i.e., that all citizens are better-off by having such a constitution compared to other alternatives, is mirrored to a great extent by Fallon's moral legitimacy. Moreover, Ordeshook's coordination is an alternative formulation of Fallon's legal and sociological legitimacy, i.e., the fact that people believe that the majority of others consent to it and, therefore, accept their obligation to act accordingly.

willing to accept the constitutional convention to be rendered obsolete and lose the benefits of the conventional state. In other words, eternity clauses are an instrument to extend the constitutional convention to the content of the constitution.

This interpretation, however, brings forth a new question, namely on what grounds is the present sovereign legitimized to constraint the future generations. Until today, the arguments proposed to justify differentiations in the degree of entrenchment are lacking. Theory so far tries to justify the introduction of amendment constraints by assuming a superiority of constitution-making processes in terms of the incentives they provide. This approach is driven by an idealization of constitution-making through a systematic disregard of the divergent interests within the constitutional assembly. Subsequently, the question remains unanswered as to what extent and under which circumstances should constituted powers be allowed to propose such a mechanism.

If one can accept that constitutional constraints influence the distribution of political power after their introduction, then attaining consent on their content should be costly.[9] Under the shadow of limited resources, rational constitution-makers will engrave in the constitution provisions that will allow them to extract the greatest benefits from the constituted state. Therefore, the content of the constitution can be studied as the product of bargaining for rules on how to make rules between rational and free individuals.[10] A further benefit of looking into the constitution as endogenous to the pre-constitutional status quo and the constitution-making process is that theoretical predictions can be formulated on the impact of the constitutional content.[11]

Using rational choice theory, I propose a novel justification in an effort to solve the conundrum of eternity clauses. I argue that because of the aforementioned divergent interests, manipulation of entrenchment cannot be justified with the arguments provided thus far. Heightened entrenchment can only be justified inasmuch as it averts wasteful spending of resources. Very briefly, constitutional rules have distributional effects, i.e., create winners and non-winners.[12] If non-winners can change their status by amendment, instead of focusing on production they will waste resources in achieving an amendment. Moreover, winners will have to waste resources in order to protect their constitutional endowment. By prohibiting the

---

[9]The concept of cost as understood in economics is a very broad concept and bigger than monetary/pecuniary transfers. Specifically, costs could be understood in our case as the time needed for bargaining, instead of producing, or the concessions needed to achieve agreement. This broader notion of costs as disutility will be used in the rest of the chapter.

[10]Buchanan and Tullock (1962).

[11]Voigt (2011), p. 205.

[12]Wicksell (1896) was the first to state that if we want all members of the society to be made better-off while none is made worse-off (Pareto superior constitutions), the social contract needs to be ratified with unanimity. Subsequently, the statement that constitutional rules create winners and non-winners is true as long as constitutions are not ratified with unanimity. The extent to which a smaller majority could produce a Pareto superior constitution, i.e., a constitution as if it was produced by unanimity (hypothetical consent), will be discussed later in the chapter.

shift in a specific area, we decrease these waste. In that sense, eternity clauses can be justified as a tool to revert resources from rent-seeking to productive activities.

The chapter is structured as follows: In Sect. 2, a definition for unamendability is given and a typology of eternity clauses is proposed that distinguished between the different forms of absolute entrenchment. Section 3 presents the arguments that are used in the literature to justify unamendability. Then, Sect. 4 introduces the rent-redistribution optimization framework. Lastly, the chapter concludes.

2 Delineating Eternity Clauses

Eternity clauses are provisions in the constitution that impose substantive immunities against the amendment procedure.[13] They are only by name eternal, inasmuch as they were introduced by the constituting will and the reconstitution of the constituting will, i.e., constitution-making, is required for their content to be altered.[14]

Moreover, they are also not eternal inasmuch as they are subject to imperfect enforcement. For example, the constitution of Honduras prohibited the amendment of the provision that regulates the term limits for the President (Article 374). In 2009, based on this eternity clause, the highest tribunal of Honduras with the support of the National Congress mobilized the army, in order to oust President Manuel Zelaya on the charge of proposing the amendment of the unamendable term limit clauses in the constitution.[15] On April 22, 2015, the Constitutional Chamber of the Honduran Supreme Court rendered this constraint inapplicable.[16] Despite the importance of the problem of the judiciary selectively enforcing the constitution, for the time being, I will ignore it because it does not influence the understanding of eternity clauses *in abstracto* of the chapter. After establishing a baseline definition, this section expands upon the different types of eternity clauses and their distinct characteristics.

Looking into the existing classification schemes, three contributions can be found that are specific to absolute amendment constraints.[17] First, eternity clauses may be divided according to which provision they entrench. If different characteristics of the constitution influence the life of citizens and politicians differently, then in order to understand how they will be adhered to one needs to know their

---

[13]Otherwise put [are] *impervious to the constitutional amendment procedures enshrined within a constitutional text and immune to constitutional change even by the most compelling legislative and popular majorities.* Albert (2010), p. 663, 665f.

[14]Only exceptionally eternity clauses are introduced with an amendment: Bangladesh (2011), Belgium (1984), Cambodia (1999), Colombia (1855), France (1884), Indonesia (2002), Peru (1940), Romania (2003), Guatemala (1993) (after a self-coup attempt).

[15]Ruhl (2010), p. 93.

[16]Marsteintredet (2015).

[17]For a review of the existing classifications of the amendment process in general, see: Albert (2014a), p. 913 Voigt (1999a), p. 197.

content. Friedman proposes such a division.[18] Specifically, he divides eternity clauses to entrenchments of the character of the government, the spirit or principles of the constitution and the character of the country. This categorization is nevertheless very ambiguous and arbitrary to facilitate comparative work.

Second, Schwartzberg by looking into unamendability from the perspective of the difficulty of amendment and time proposes four categories of entrenchment, namely formal, time-unlimited (eternity clauses) and time-limited (sunset clauses) entrenchment; de facto (prohibitive amendment process) entrenchment; and implicit entrenchment.[19] This categorization also suffers from inconsistencies. Specifically, the same amendment constraint could in one legislative period lead to de facto entrenchment, when in a next period due to changes in the power of the winning coalition does not.

Lastly, Albert proposed two classifications.[20] The first scheme is based on two dimensions, namely the goals of the constraint and the degree of the constraint. Like the Friedman scheme, unamendability is broken down with the use of subjective valuation into preservative entrenchment, transformational entrenchment, and reconciliatory entrenchment, according to its goals.[21] Moreover, according to an objective measure, i.e., the degree of constraint, it is divided into three stages, namely conventional, heightened, and indefinite entrenchment. The second scheme is refining the same temporal and formal characteristics of Schwartzberg, but also adds qualitative characteristics (substantive and procedural entrenchment).[22] This scheme is very precise and utilizes objective criteria, which could facilitate legal discourse. Nevertheless, it suffers from the extent of its complexity.

The merits of the scheme proposed here are multiple. It captures all absolute constraints, namely both in the *big-C,* i.e. the constitution-as-form, as well as the *small-c,* i.e., the constitution-as-a-function without increasing complexity.[23] It is based on objective criteria and not the aspirations of the framers, which are to a great extent unobservable. Lastly, despite the fact that this scheme is applied to eternity clauses, because of its generality it could be applied to all other amendment constraints.

The first criterion of Table 1 asks whether constraints in the amendment process are explicitly included in the constitutional master text. This dimension captures to a great extent the saliency of the amendment constraint. First, the writeness of formal clauses makes them significantly less volatile or interpretable in their application compared to informal constraints. Moreover, since even nonexperts can

[18]Friedman (2011), p. 77.

[19]Schwartzberg (2009).

[20]Albert (2010), p. 666.

[21]An additional goal, namely aspirational entrenchment is proposed in Roznai (2017), p. 32.

[22]Albert (2014b) 185 f.f.

[23]For the distinction between the two aspects see: Elkins et al. (2009), Chapter: Conceptualizing Constitutions. For the importance of examining both when analyzing the constitution see: Voigt (2013), p. 1.

K. Pilpilidis

Table 1 Typology of eternity clauses

	Absolute	Limited
Constitutional	True substantive	Procedural
Ultra-constitutional	Judicial/Conventional substantive	Factual

know the content of a codified constitution and perceive it as a unity, such constraints will be more costly to disregard. In that sense, it refines the formality criterion, to the extent that it is interested only in constitutional formality. The second criterion looks into whether the constraints imposed poses an absolute hurdle, i.e., a hurdle which can be overcome only with the reconstitution of the constituting will, or a limited hurdle, which is lifted after certain conditions are fulfilled. Absolute constraints make the option of a nonrevolutionary change unavailable. Subsequently, they directly increase the benefits of revolutionary change. Limited constraints, on the other hand, simply increase the cost of non-revolutionary change.[24]

On the first cell of the matrix, we find true substantive constraints. They are the *taboos* of the constitutional order. They are provisions that are absolutely entrenched themselves, i.e., insusceptible to a double amendment procedure.[25] Even though, rank-ordering the difficulty of changing constitutions is a mean task and many have given up,[26] it seems straightforward to consider self-entrenched eternity clause as the strictest conceivable constraint.

On the bottom left cell, we find ultra-constitutional substantive constraints. One vehicle to introduce unamendability is through the lack of an amendment procedure. According to contractarians, there is a distinction between those consenting and those that are enabled to act within their capacities because they acquired consent. The former is the constituting power and the latter is the constituted power.[27] In this setting, the power of the constituted actors to amend is not self-evident. On the contrary, amending the constitution is a bridge built by the constituting power to allow for adaptations by the constituted powers, i.e., it is a delegated constituting power.[28] Subsequently, the lack of an amendment procedure

---

[24]To give a numerical example, let us assume that the cost of amending with limited constraints is 10 units of effort (disutility) and the cost of revolutionary change 12 units. Let us further assume that the benefit from amending a provision is 11 units of utility. Under absolute constraints, an amendment will more likely not take place since it is irrational to pay 12 to get 10. Contrary, under limited constraints, such an amendment is more likely to take place, since the benefit covers the price.

[25]The double amendment danger is the condition where by changing amendment rules one can amend the eternal part of the constitution. If such a possibility exists, then a seemingly substantive constraint is reduced to a merely procedural constraint. For a detailed description of the double amendment danger, see also: Albert (2015b), p. 655.

[26]For example see: Ginsburg and Versteeg (2014), p. 587.

[27]Hardin (2013a), p. 51.

[28]Schmitt (2007).

is to be interpreted as no power to amend. However, legal interpretation has allowed even constitution with no amending formula,[29] to get amended. Just to give an example the British North America Act of 1867, which outlined the system of government in Canada, contained no amendment procedure. Nevertheless, it was amended at least 20 times with various acts until 1982, when an amendment procedure was introduced. In other words, the lack of a procedure only through interpretation leads to an amendment constraint. Subsequently, constitutions which include no amending power and constitutions which prohibit amendment are not to be treated the same.

Following that point, even when constitutional texts remain the same, implementation allows the *organic instrument* to be adapted to the needs of times.[30] Constitutions change also implicitly or unlawfully.[31] However, to avoid overuse of this option, framers introduce independent formal institutions that are entrusted with the task of guarding constitutionalism or allow for the emergence of political conventions.[32] Such constraints are driven by internal institutions[33] in the sense of institutional economics or the *amendment culture*.[34] Weintal based on the severity of the constraint proposed bundling absolute constraints created by the judiciary and constraints introduced by the constitution.[35] Nevertheless, besides the saliency differences mentioned above, this bundling is for another reason unfortunate. As the identity of the one introducing unamendability is different, the structure of the constraints is different. That leads to a different production mechanism for unamendability. Specifically, while constitution-making is subject to democratic participation, i.e., citizens choose the constitutional assembly ex ante, ratify in a referendum ex post or both, the other two production tracks are not. This lack of an

---

[29]Just to name the country-years in which a constitution was introduced after WWII with no amendment procedures: Hungary (1946), Nepal (1948), Bhutan (1953), Cambodia (1976), Iran (1979), Poland (1992).

[30]Schwartz (2013).

[31]Indicatively, such changes can be attained through: Authoritative interpretation of the constitution, i.e., the changes in the interpretation of the meaning without changing the text, see: Voigt (1999a); Super-statutes, i.e., statutes with increased entrenchment that extend the constitutional text, see: Eskridge and Ferejohn (2001), p. 3. Systematic manipulation of constitutional provisions, i.e., the use of systematic interpretation in order to manipulate the policy outcomes, see: Posner and Vermeule (2008), p. 991; Gap filling (incorporation) and gap creation (repudiation), see: Albert (2015c), p. 387.

[32]Ginsburg (2002), p. 49, argues further that the introduction of constitutional courts is significantly correlated with the concern of the framers that they will lose power by future majorities. For an analysis of politically introduced unamendability, see Chapter Three: JG Geertjes and J Uzman, 'Conventions of Unamendability: Unamendable Constitutional Law in Politically Enforced Constitutions'.

[33]Internal institutions are rules which are not enforced by the state but the society (ethic, customs, rules of contact, etiquette) or the individual himself (categorical imperative). For description of internal institutions see: Voigt (2013).

[34]Elkins et al. (2009).

[35]Weintal (2011), pp. 449, 456.

additional stage of popular participation makes unamendability for third parties absolute but for the actor itself volatile.[36]

Moving on to the top right cell of the matrix, we find procedural constraints. Under this category belong quasi-procedural constraints (not absolutely entrenched substantive constraints) and true procedural constraints. The former are constraints not protected against the double amendment procedure with substantive nature.[37] True procedural constraints impose barriers to change. An example of procedural unamendability is the prohibition to amend again the constitution within a certain period after an amendment (temporal) or the requirement of a certain quorum to vote on an amendment (requirements of process).

The economic literature on constitutional change claims that if the formal procedure for amendment becomes too cumbersome unconstitutional change is more likely to occur.[38] In the language of economics, there is a substitution effect. Assuming that politicians want to keep their constituencies happy by transferring rents through amendment, whether the change is done formally or informally affects the quality of the service politicians provide to their constituencies. Formal amendment is a superior good in that it satisfies the need for keeping constituencies happy in a more long-lasting way. When the price of the superior good becomes high (cost of formal amendment) or income is reduced (political support), political actors shift to the inferior good, i.e., informal change.

Finishing, on the bottom right cell lies what I will call *factual* unamendability. This protection originates from the improbability of overcoming even the simplest amendment constraints for certain provisions, due to the structure of the state and the political game.[39] Certain institutions and structures within the constitution are so entrenched in the existence of a state that they enjoy a de facto amendment-proofness. Specifically, even in the absence of formal entrenchment, such provisions will enjoy a greater longevity due to the very low factual willingness of amending them. In other words, factual unamendability could be understood as the results of the preferences of a society and the structure of the political arena. Specifically, it captures a situation where the willingness to support a topic does not meet the willingness to provide of the politicians. Either none or only marginalized minorities are willing to campaign for changing such provisions. Subsequently, this demand is not sufficient to cover the costs of a political actor forwarding such a demand. This type of unamendability is not an actual constraint in the sense that if preferences change the relevant actors would be able to change the constitution. Nevertheless, prolonged structural unamendability might open the door to conventional substantive unamendability.

---

[36]Dixon (2011) claims that only a new constitution can overcome unfavorable unamendability introduced by third actors. Contrary, as the case of India shows even non obstante clauses could suffice to undermine judicial unamendability.

[37]For example, see: Abdelaal (2016), p. 1.

[38]Gavison (2002), p. 89, Lutz (2006), Rasch and Congleton (2006), Gerken (2007), p. 925.

[39]Albert (2014a, p. 1029, 2014b).

Constitutions entrenching Islam to that respect can serve as an extreme example. The constitution of Saudi Arabia of 1992 explicitly states that the constitution of the country is the Holy Quran and the prophet's Sunnah (Article 1). One can interpret the clause such that the constitutional document is no longer a constitution, inasmuch as it is not the supreme law of the land[40] or that Article 1 is a nonbinding declaration, which has no place in the constitution. In either case, there is no explicit constraint to amend. Nevertheless, amending in discordance with such supra-constitutional rules—divine ones at that—is highly unlikely.

From the categorization, we directly see that true substantive eternity clauses bear significant comparative advantages against other forms of unamendability. First of all, they are written in a compact body of text. That means that they are on the long run protected from amendment through desuetude. Specifically, it is plausible that on the short run all political actors might agree upon breaching the social contract, for example, in times of emergency, however, unconstitutionality becomes unstable under the constant threat of a political actor invoking the eternity clauses and overturning the amendment. Moreover, citizens know their content and can form stable expectations. The textual nature of eternity clauses allows the People to directly monitor and hold accountable the politicians against violations. Of course, this effect can be muted when eternity clauses entrench *vague legal terms*, so that courts can decide the content of the constitution.[41] This is, however, another consideration which will not be touched upon by the chapter.

3 Justifying Eternity Clauses

Prima facie, substantive eternity clauses are counter-majoritarian, inasmuch as they limit the will of the People to constitutionally change the rules set by the framers. Ramseyer explaining the introduction of counter-majoritarian institutions and specifically an independent judiciary claimed that politicians driven by the fear of electoral loss want to be able to entrench their favored policies against future majorities. Subsequently, they are willing to create and tolerate an institution that restrains them, so that their opposition will also be constrained.[42]

A result of this kind of self-constraint is the constitutional crisis of the Czech Republic in 2009. In short, a constitutional-unfriendly majority—the government with the two largest parties—wanted jointly to pass an ad hoc constitutional act to activate a faster earlier-election-track. However, not all political actors were in agreement. Subsequently, the opposition invoked the eternity clauses in front of the constitutional court to avert the unconstitutionality.[43]

---

[40]For a more detailed analysis of Islamic Constitutionalism, see: Ahmed and Gouda (2015), p. 1.

[41]Albert (2013), p. 270.

[42]Ramseyer (1994), p. 721.

[43]Roznai (2014), p. 29.

Moreover, eternity clauses are also connected with another normative discussion. It has yet to be made clear, on what grounds the present sovereign is legitimized to give up something that it does not possess, namely the power of all future sovereigns to amend the constitution. Jefferson states that "the earth belongs [...] to the living".[44] The *dead hand problem*, as it is coined, is the problem that framers, who might be long dead, have set the rules by which the current generation has to live.[45]

One way to avoid the problem is to say that eternity clauses do no such thing. As became clear in the case of Crimea, an eternity clause protecting something (in the Crimean case the territorial integrity of Ukraine) is not enough to avert the fulfillment of the will of a self-determining majority (for secession).[46] Such a solution, however, is underplaying the significance of eternity clauses. If not complying with eternity clauses instigates contempt towards the entire constitution, compliance is ensured by the unwillingness to pay the cost of legal uncertainty.

In the next subsections, I will use eternity clauses as the extreme form of amendment constraint to look into the logical limits of the arguments provided so far, in order to legitimize the trade-off between flexibility and precommitment. Then, in Sect. 3.2 an alternative justification will be proposed. Specifically, it will be shown that eternity clauses can only be justified through their ability to avert rent redistribution. This will be called the rent-redistribution optimization theory.

3.1 Protective Theories

The first strand of the literature will be classified as the protective theories. This strand justifies eternity clauses through their role in protecting *exceptionally fair* rules.[47] As a mechanism for the framers to impose a rule on future majorities, the introduction of eternity clauses has been claimed to be desirable because constitutions are emplaced in times when everyone is acting in a far-sighted and selfless fashion, the so-called *constitutional moments*.[48]

The merits of having eternity clauses, under this naive conception of constitutionalism, lie in the belief that eternity clauses protect democracy from itself.

---

[44]Letter To James Madison Paris, Sep 6. 1789.

[45]McConnell (1997), p. 1127, Elster and Slagstad (1988), Eisgruber (2009), Congleton and Swedenborg (2006).

[46]Roznai and Suteu (2015), p. 542.

[47]Although fairness can take many forms, protective theories implicitly equate fairness with hypothetical consent. In this context, fair is the rule that would have been hypothetically agreed upon unanimously had all citizens been asked in a point in time, during which they are acting selflessly.

[48]The theory of constitutional moments was popularized in the work of Ackerman (1993). Although the work of Ackerman is not explicitly advocating eternity clauses, the exceptionality of constitution-making, for which it argues, has become the cornerstone of all protective theories.

During constitutional moments, individuals will introduce exceptionally fair regulation, because their myopia is lifted and they disregard their short-term benefits. In order for this far-sighted regulation to promote freedom and stability, it needs to be protected from the short-sighted majorities.[49] Constitutionalism to that extent is justified because of a time inconsistency problem. Specifically, the problem that a rule introduced today might be changed tomorrow in a moment of weakness as the preferences do not remain intertemporally the same.[50] The figures of Ulysses tying himself to the mast while in port, Peter Sober binding Peter Drunk are only a few picturesque examples used in the literature to describe this goodwill precommitment.[51]

Sadly, a look at the birth of constitutions does not seem to give evidence in favor of the existence of eye-opening inspirational precedents.[52] In addition to that, if constitutional moments induced benevolence, then selecting the members of the assembly, setting constraints and subjecting the proposal to a referendum would lead to the same text compared to a constitution written by a dictator acting under no constraint. However, procedural rules matter.[53] Moreover, empirical evidence show that also the identity of the framers matters for the constitutional proposal.[54] Subsequently, constitutions are better to be understood as the products of utility maximizing politicians, who try to influence through the clauses of the social contract the post-constitutional political game. To sum up, far-sightedness or benevolence is not a plausible justification for introducing unamendability.[55]

Even under a less naive conception of framers, a protective function for eternity clauses is hard to justify. The most influential protective theories looking into framers as self-serving individuals are the veil theories. The first to use individual decision making under risk in order to formulate theories on societal choices was Harsanyi.[56] However, Rawls was the first to coin the term *veil of ignorance* for the required oblivion in order to reach universally fair rules.[57]

Because Rawlsian ignorance, compared to Harsanyi, is normative and, therefore, has little predictive power, Brennan and Buchanan inspired by the idea of the veil proposed a different veil, namely the *veil of uncertainty*.[58] Their theory in a nutshell claims that in the state of anarchy, if individuals cannot accurately predict the

---

[49]Hayek (1960).

[50]Rubenfeld (1997), p. 1127.

[51]Elster (1984), Brewer (1968).

[52]Widner (2007), p. 1513, Russell (1993).

[53]Boudreaux and Pritchard (1993–1994), p. 111, Ginsburg et al. (2009), p. 201, Landemore and Elster (2012), Chapter Seven; Cofones and Michel (2017) Kyklos [Forthcoming].

[54]Beard (1913), McGuire (1988), pp. 483–522, McGuire and Ohsfeldt (1989).

[55]For detailed review of the shortcomings of the precommitment argumentation, see also Chapter 4: S Michel and NI Cofones, 'Credible Commitment or Paternalism? The Case of Unamendability'.

[56]Harsanyi (1953), p. 434.

[57]Rawls (1971).

[58]Brennan and Buchanan (1985), Buchanan (1987), p. 243.

distribution of political power in the ordered society, they will be able to agree upon fair rule-making processes. Moreover, they claim that the thickness of the veil can be manipulated by individuals. Applying this theory implies that the entire constitution should be bargained under the shadow of eternity.

First, by thickening the veil through expanding the time horizon of a rule (*durability*) to eternity[59] it can be made sure that the rules introduced would represent the fairest realizable rules under the current constitutional assembly. Second, since constitution-making is conducted when the veil is thicker and procedural rules are used to thicken the veil—something that is impossible for constitution amending—the initial content of the constitution should be protected from majorities acting outside the veil.

This theory is too stylized to predict the content of actual constitutions. Diverse relative preference-intensities in the post-constitutional setting, different degrees of risk affinity or different forms of uncertainty might still keep a constitutional assembly from introducing fair rules.[60] By pushing the time horizon and increasing uncertainty, parties emerge, which are unwilling to commit themselves *eternally* from their current position. Such parties might block constitutional bargaining.[61] For example, in post-conflict situations, when constitutions are mostly needed, even agreement on the interim constitution is difficult. In such circumstances, if the levels of violence are sufficiently high even a shorter time horizon, through sunset clauses, is necessary to achieve agreement.[62] Subsequently, allowing an eternal horizon to infiltrate the deliberation might sabotage constitution-making.

Even if for a minute, we forget the prohibitive costs of bargaining for an *eternal* constitution and assume that for (inexplicable) reasons the content of a constitution is indeed exceptionally fair, we cannot agree with the Lockean claim that there is a fundamental constitution, which *shall be and remain [...] forever.*[63] Although against such a claim, an abundance of arguments can be brought, I will focus on the most straightforward and undisputed, namely the fact that institutions change because of many reasons; one of them being also learning.[64] Even if the framers were indeed acting under the best conditions to introduce the fairest rules they can conceive, they are still limited by their cognitive capacities and their priors. Leaving the rational choice paradigm, Hayek claims that constitutions are not the result of rational design but the result of trial and error.[65] Even if that is not the case, still due to innovation and progress, the ideal social and moral setting for today might not

---

[59]Vanberg and Buchanan (1989), pp. 49, 54.

[60]For an extensive survey and a critical discussion of the problems of the veil, the readers are referred to: Voigt (2015).

[61]Müller (1998), p. 5.

[62]Widner (2007).

[63]Fundamental Constitution of Carolina, s 120.

[64]For evidence of such concerns in the political thinking of Madison and Hamilton see: Ostrom and Allen (2007).

[65]Hayek (1960).

remain ideal for tomorrow. According to Friedman, dead hand constitutionalism hinders such innovation in a society.[66]

To sum up, as has been made clear, entrenching with the aim to preserve benevolent regulation is at best a dubious claim. First, we cannot expect regulators to be benevolent so as to give them the power to absolutely entrench. Second, even if by a fluke framers introduce benevolent regulation, we cannot be certain that this regulation will be intertemporally optimal.

3.2 Expressive and Signaling Theories

If we cannot be certain that the constitution content is or will remain optimal, amendment procedures are needed to enable the recalibration of the *imperfect* constitution in order to avert a violent change.[67] To that extent, one can argue, that such procedures are a practical expression of humility by the framers. Although the first best would be another unamendable ideal constitution, they admit that they could only come up with and agree to a lesser constitution and therefore they allow its optimization through the amendment procedure. That failure need not be blamed on the inadequacy or the ill-nature of the framers but it can also be the result of the nonexistence of such a constitution.

Expressive theories would claim that eternity clauses are the mirror image of amendment procedures. Through them, framers express their belief that the rule need not be further improved through a process of trial and error. The rule is seen as the truest representation of the values and principles upon which the country is built and strives to function. Albert calls this function, the *expressive function* of amendment rules.[68] Expressive theories claim that unamendability is simply a mechanism for states to *narrate their collective political identity into existence.*[69]

If the sovereign gains intrinsic benefits by expressing a certain identity, eternity clauses are subsequently justified by the mere will to express this identity. To rationalize that scheme one could argue that a rational sovereign would include eternity clauses as long as the cost of rigidity is compensated by intrinsic benefits of expression. However, this argumentation tells us nothing in particular. If one argues with diverging utilities and intrinsic motivation, then the theory can be adjusted to justify anything and, therefore, justifies nothing.

One should, however, distinguish between pure expression and signaling. Although protective theories implicitly assume that the optimal constitutional setting is universal and unique, such an assumption is unrealistic. Were that the case, given sufficient time all constitutions would converge. However, they do not.

---

[66]Friedman (2011).

[67]Dellinger (1983), p. 386, Levinson (1995).

[68]Albert (2013).

[69]Eisgruber (2009), p. 11.

Voigt argues that constitutions are the product of a spontaneous process of creation and abolition of institutions.[70] Therefore, constitutions are better analyzed as a choice between the various bargaining equilibria (attainable settings) produced by an institutionally constrained process. In this context, signaling is used to make the choice of equilibrium salient to groups external to constitution-makers. The problem of signaling legal continuity under change is in nature the same as the so-called ship of Theseus puzzle, formulated by Plutarch.[71] Constitutions, as the ship of Theseus, might have almost all of its initial parts amended. By stating which amendment would constitute constitution-making, the question to when the previous constitutional setting becomes obsolete and continuity is lost can be simply answered by asking whether eternity clauses have been breached. To that extent, the unamendable part of the constitution as a supra-constitution becomes its *genetic code*.[72]

In economic theory, signaling is necessary inasmuch as hidden information could deter from utility-increasing transactions.[73] If states can signal legal continuity, despite enabling change, they gain advantages internally and externally. Externally continuity enables the accumulation and acquisition of reputation on an international level.[74] Internally, if citizens can expect legal continuity and consistency, then they will be more willing to do long-term investments. Moreover, signaling what was the minimum content for the framers bears also other informational benefits. Specifically, it enables a more fine-grained understanding of the subjective valuations and hierarchy of the constitutional provisions in constitutional showdowns.[75] Moreover, if the subjective valuations as the foundations of the constitution become superfluous and outdated due to the spontaneous evolution of informal institutions, the political actors are forced, instead of disparately patching the problems, to fix the whole.

Although signaling theories are more realistic than the benevolence theories, they themselves face various shortcomings. First, the signal from eternity clauses is a noisy signal. It signals namely legal continuity even in cases of severe change in the legal order and therefore does not suffice for the differentiation between amendments and constitution-making. Specifically, constitutions through eternity clauses create a second puzzle, the puzzle of Tib and Tibbles (also known as the Dion and Theon Puzzle).[76] The philosophical conundrum is asking which is the

---

[70]Voigt (1999b), p. 283.

[71]Here, legal continuity opposed to transition is understood as the nonrevolutionary-controlled transformation as defined in Dahrendorf (1990), p. 133.

[72]Albert (2010), Roznai (2015).

[73]Akerlof (1970), p. 488, Cho and Kreps (1987), p. 179.

[74]Downs and Jones (2002), p. S95, Guzman (2008).

[75]Albert (2013), p. 244.

[76]The puzzle was introduced in modern philosophy in Wiggins (1968), p. 90. Wiggins question is whether two entities can occupy the same space simultaneously.

initial entity that survives a reduction process, the whole (constitution) or whether by defining a separate entity from the parts (supra-constitution), we actively make the whole a supplement to the part.

Looking in Greek constitutional history for a practical example, after the military coup, the junta wanted to signal that their actions were aimed at resolving the constitutional instability. For that reason, the new dictatorial constitution—introduced in September 29, 1968—contained the eternity clauses of the 1952 constitution (Art. 108) protecting the form of government as a royal democracy (Art. 137 of 1968 Constitution). Nevertheless, the king was already ousted from the country by the regime since December 14, 1967. This behavior is at first sight paradoxical. However, looking it from a signaling perspective, the regime tried by claiming that the genetic code of the constitution was preserved to avoid paying the cost of breaking continuity.

Both expressiveness and signaling are problematic. They are rather a description than a viable criterion for the justifiability. Framers are given a free reign to choose what they consider important or what they want to signal and how. Nevertheless, without additional criteria, i.e. on what grounds is this choice made and under which constraints should it be allowed, these theories do not tell us anything on justification. Subsequently, expressiveness and signaling cannot shed light on what constitutes unjustified entrenchment.

4 Rent-Redistribution Optimization

4.1 Rent-Seeking and Rent-Extraction

In the previous section, I presented the different theories used so far to justify unamendability and their shortcomings. In this section, I look into the institutional economics literature for a novel justification for eternity clauses and restraints on the amendment process. As discussed, different informal institutions restrict the set of attainable constitutional settings.[77] Interest groups by fixing the rules gain advantages against other groups. In this section, it will be examined whether eternity clauses can mitigate the perils of allowing such advantages to be unstable (easily redistributable).

First, special advantages in themselves are not negative; namely, they ensure that there will be an investment in the production of a good from the enjoyment of which an individual cannot be excluded once that is produced (public good).[78] All regulations are connected with such advantages (rents); the question is how to make

---

[77]Voigt (1999b).
[78]Olson (1965).

the process of rent-acquisition less costly for social welfare.[79] Olson argued that the existence of rents is one of the determinants of the fail of nations.[80] Nevertheless, rents themselves are usually redistribution, i.e., the winner can compensate the loser. Subsequently, for many years, economists claimed that rents created only a negligible deadweight loss (loss in efficiency).[81] In his seminal work, however, Tullock suggested, that when measuring losses in efficiency due to rents, one must also take into consideration the unsuccessful investments to acquire rents and the distortion in the allocation of resources in maintaining rents.[82] These investments have been later coined as *rent-seeking*.[83]

Posner with a very simple model proclaimed that all rents are dissipated in rent-seeking (*full dissipation hypothesis*) and, therefore, any expenditure toward acquiring rents is socially undesirable.[84] Nevertheless, Tullock by looking into rent-seeking as a first-price all-pay auction for rents disproved that hypothesis.[85] Consequently, he implied that the goal is not to condemn all rent-seeking but to minimize the dissipation of rents.

Buchanan and Congleton looked at the problem of wasteful rent-seeking as a problem that could be mitigated by generality. By decreasing the allowed specificity of the rule a regulator can introduce, it is harder for the regulator to distribute discriminatory rents.[86] According to contest theory, another way toward reducing dissipation is the manipulation of the process of rent-seeking.[87] Eternity clauses manipulate the process by making redistribution of rents very costly. Specifically, eternity clauses appoint violation costs in terms of legitimacy (coordination losses) upon certain shifts (redistribution). Subsequently, they act as a barrier to entry (BtE) in political competition over certain matters.[88] With eternity clauses, *citizens [would] benefit [...] by avoiding a wasteful struggle over abstract rules.*[89]

In order to make the argument clear, I will use one of the simplest BtE, i.e., high sunk costs. Sunk costs are the part of the investment that cannot be retrieved, if the

---

[79]The chapter discusses a special form of rents, namely political rents. A political rent is the increase of utility of an individual due to favorable regulation (regulatory capture) without any form of improvement.

[80]Olson (1982).

[81]Harberger (1959), p. 134.

[82]Tullock (1967), p. 224.

[83]Krueger (1974), p. 291.

[84]Posner (1975), p. 807.

[85]Buchanan (1980). For an extensive and technical review of the determinants of rent dissipation, see also: Mueller (2003), Ch. 15; Leininger (1993), p. 43 Leininger and Yang (1994), p. 406, Nitzan (1994), p. 41.

[86]Buchanan and Congleton (1998).

[87]Hillman (1989).

[88]The reason I treat them as BtE and not absolute legal prohibitions is the fact that those setting the rules are the ones following them and there is no enforcing mechanism. As a result, amendment constraints introduce very different incentive structures compared to normal legal constraints.

[89]Holmes (1988).

competitor leaves the market. In political competition, most costs are non-retrievable. For example, if an interest group that has invested in lobbying "drops" the topic, then it cannot get its campaign contributions back. In order for an interest group to bring forth the amendment of an unentrenched provision, it must invest so that at least the costs of an amendment are covered. Contrary, in order to bring a change to the eternal part of a constitution, an interest group has to bear at least the cost of constitution-making. Since constitution-making is correlated with higher costs, the marginal competitors will not enter a competition on attaining the rents. On the one hand, some competitors may not be able to finance the minimum investment in absolute terms. On the other hand, the expected benefit may not be able to offset their costs, i.e., rent-seekers valuing the shift less will not enter the competition. This situation, in turn, enables the beneficiaries of the status quo to save on the investments needed to protect themselves from rent-seekers.

At this point, it needs to be reminded that the goal is not to avert all rent-seeking but to avert inefficient rent-seeking. As noted already, often public goods arise as a by-product of rent-seeking. If there is a constant threat of regulatory capture, i.e., either the regulator redistributing the rents or the executive using executive decrees to change the regulation, then the willingness of participants to invest in long-term rents will be lower. Contrary rent-seeking for short-term extractive rents is more likely.[90] Furthermore, introducing a process that is not targeted against the marginal rent seeker would be undesirable. In other words, when interest groups face significant benefits from a shift, they might still be willing to violate the constitution, if that is the only way to their preferred setting. In that sense, eternity clauses would be inducing constitutional instability.

The optimization approach proposed focuses on areas where constant renegotiation is not desirable. For example, allowing the amendment of term limits, leaves space for presidents to bargain with the rest of the political actors to prolong their term. Specifically, in order to achieve an amendment, presidents need to compensate the rest of the veto players. Subsequently, they indulge themselves in rent-seeking concessions and vote trading. If all presidents act as rent-seekers then less true policy making and more politics would be exercised.

Another side of the problem of redistributing rents is rent-extraction. In his seminal work, Stigler described the introduction of regulation as a process through which politicians gain private benefits.[91] As we have discussed, rent-seeking involves the supply of rents from politicians against a demand for regulation by the interest groups (free transaction). Rent-extraction is a practice going a step further. The term is used to describe the phenomenon of regulators using their competences, in order to secure transfers, *ego-rents*,[92] by threatening to introduce unfavorable regulation (coercive transaction).

---

[90]Olson (1993), p. 567.

[91]Stigler (1971), p. 3.

[92]The term was coined in Rogoff (1990), p. 21.

One of the effects of rent-extraction is that economic growth is harmed. The argument is very intuitive. Growth requires long-term investments. The goods or services exchanged with long-term contracts cannot be as efficiently attained on the on-spot market. Nevertheless, when citizens or potential investors perceive a danger of rent-extraction, then their willingness to undergo long-term investments is lower.[93] That is to be attributed to the fact that long-term contract have a lock-in effect. First, such contracts are usually connected with investments that require high asset-specificity.[94] However, the higher the asset-specificity, the easier it is for a regulator to extract rents. Specifically, investors that cannot shift investments toward another sector or another venture face a choice: they can pay the ego-rent and avert disadvantageous regulation, accept the disadvantageous regulation or abort the investment. If entering and exiting a market is not costless, the fear of investors that regulators will drive their costs up (or limit profits by imposing price ceilings) and force them out of the market *ceteris paribus* will avert the marginal investor from entering. Subsequently, countries that manage to reduce the fear of rent-extraction should face greater economic growth.[95]

By introducing an amendable constitution the commitment problem, i.e., that once the investment is done the constitution will not be amended, is only partially resolved. Making rents non-redistributable is a mechanism to solve the commitment problem. By crystallizing the distribution of rents in an unamendable part of the constitution introducing unfavorable regulation or reverting previously beneficial regulation is very costly. As already discussed, the marginal politician will drop out of the market (supply side). Subsequently, the threat of unfavorable regulation is less credible, if rents are protected by eternity clauses.

This conception of eternity clauses has the additional benefit of providing a plausible explanation of why—from a positive perspective—a rational assembly member would write such a constitution. The argument in favor of such choice is the following. Eternity clauses can empower politicians. Specifically, when present constituencies are called to invest, the degree to which they can be certain that returns on investment will be positive in the future is determining the size of the investment. Eternity clauses are an additional guarantee that future majorities will not be able to expropriate that returns. Subsequently, in cases where certainty is increased, the resulting increased growth will enable politicians with the same or even lower taxation to collect higher state revenues. As a result, they can implement a wider range of policies in their effort to gain votes. For that reason, also from a positive perspective, the proposed justification seems to perform well.

---

[93]North and Weingast (1989), p. 803.

[94]Asset-specificity is the characteristic that the invested asset cannot be repurposed after the investment without significant costs. An example for such an asset would a part for a unique car model. See also: Williamson (1981), p. 548.

[95]The example is chosen since it is very easy to test empirically. One could make a similar argument using fairness or democracy instead of growth. Specifically, if the law is perceived as including fair rules, allowing for a constant change of the law creates confusion on what constitutes fairness. Alternatively, if a certain setting is perceived as democratic, changing the setting might create doubts on the democratic character of the new state, i.e., whether the will of the People is respected.

4.2 Justifying Through Rent-Redistribution Optimization

By examining the justifications found in the literature, it became clear that they were only answering part of the question. That was a result of not having examined the potential costs and benefits of eternity clauses to their full extent. In order to claim that a certain legal instrument is desirable, we must not only look into what we want it to do but also in whether the goals we set are attainable with the constraints under which we are acting.

First of all, I discussed the theories arguing that eternity clauses are desirable inasmuch as they protect rules introduced by benevolence (or the least malevolence). They claimed that since constitution-making is an extraordinary moment, then we need to protect it from ordinary rule making. Although the argument seems appealing, I have shown that it is at best flawed. Framers act differently but not necessarily less self-oriented.

Then, I discussed the theories that look into the symbolic significance of eternity clauses. They claimed that such clauses are important because they serve as beacons of the state's identity. By enforcing continuity on certain aspects of the state, a state expresses and signals its will or that of the People to be a member of a group of states (democracies, social states, socialist states etc.) However, expression is the materialization of a preference for expression. Using that criterion, all eternity clauses are desirable, if one could argue in favor of any kind of a hypothetical preference for expression. Subsequently, the problem was analyzed from another perspective and an additional function for eternity clauses was presented. Specifically, it was argued that eternity clauses crystallize certain political rents and as a result minimize the social costs of redistributable rents. The benefit of this approach is that it can be operationalized. This section will give an example of such an operationalization.

Eternity clauses might actively perpetuate minor inefficiencies. Nevertheless, as shown, not changing some of the rules during the game might be one of the necessary evils for sparking long-term investments and the realization of cost-savings. Subsequently, a two-stage test is needed that balances these two aspects. This test needs further take under consideration the characteristics of the rule. Not all rules are the same. On the one hand, some rules are already entrenched through internal (informal) institutions and path dependencies. On the other hand, some rules allow for regulation with significant distributional effects that eternity clauses do not suffice to avert a change. The test proposed checks whether eternity clauses can fulfill their function in an efficient way, i.e., avert the least benefited parts of the society from indulging in rent-seeking, without unbearable costs due to rigidity.[96]

---

[96]For the avid reader, it should by now be clear that fulfilling a function in an efficient way is not synonymous to the goal being efficiency. Eternity clauses can still be used to promote fairness, if fairness would, for example, induce disenfranchised minorities to agree on accepting the constitution peacefully.

The first question asked is a question of necessity, i.e., are eternity clauses needed or lesser degrees of amendment constraint would also be enough to avert wasteful expenditure? The second question asked is a question of sufficiency, i.e., are eternity clauses sufficient or even these would be violated due to the high benefits of a shift? Specifically, as a first step, the framers should first compare the total cost of using eternity clauses with the cost of lesser entrenchment for the relevant rules. Toward that goal, it is important to take into consideration the rent differential between the winners and the non-winners in the long run. Thus, as a second step, this differential should be compared to a cut-off point, where the cost of amendment exceeds the cost of violating an eternity clause, i.e. breaking the constitution.

Similar to Buchanan and Tullock's calculus,[97] eternity clauses require a complicated interdependence calculus. One part of the calculus consists of the following consideration. On the one side, assembly members are asked to estimate the cost of a constitution delivering a weak promise for the future. These costs decrease as rigidity increases. On the other side, they need to estimate the political costs in order to come to an agreement in favor of certain provisions. These costs increase as rigidity increases. As a result, rigidity would ideally be set where the sum of these costs minimizes. However, that might not be possible.

As long as social welfare is not the same with and without eternity clauses it is important to see what are the pros and the cons of both constitutional settings. The second step of the test requires an explicit weighing of the opportunity cost of using eternity clauses instead of other lesser entrenchment. Eternity clauses impose the cost of the risk of constitutional breakdown due to the increase in rigidity. Depending on the rule being entrenched, the rent differential between the winners and the non-winners might be very high. Thus, increasing rigidity for such distributions does not increase the strength of the promise.

To put it simply, the benefits of entrenchment disappear when the rent differential exceeds the cost of drafting a new constitution. As a result, in such cases even when eternity clauses are introduced they will only be parchment barriers, which to that extent undermine the credibility of the constitution. Furthermore, drafters need to consider the risk of impeding innovation.[98] Moreover, playing the constitutional game once (one-shot game)[99] with high stakes induces the players to invest more in this single round than, if the rent could be redistributed in the future (costly constitution-making). However, as said eternity clauses benefit in the short-run

---

[97]Buchanan and Tullock (1962).

[98]For the cost of inhibiting innovation and solidifying institutions see: Acemoglu et al. (2005).

[99]One-shot games are a type of models to analyze strategic interaction in cases where the actors even if they play the game again, the payoffs are not connected to the strategy of the first game, i.e., interact as if it was the first time. Whether rent-seekers bid simultaneously or sequentially or have the chance to rebid is another aspect that could influence the dissipation of the rent but it is not discussed here since it cannot be manipulated through eternity clauses. See also: Leininger (1993).

society by facilitating positive growth due to long-term investments (reduction in rent-extraction) and the effective avoidance of wasteful spending in rent-seeking in the long run.

On the other hand, without eternity clauses, constitution-making is not as costly. In addition to that, due to constitutional flexibility, change is ceteris paribus not inhibited and mistakes on the initial text could be removed. Nevertheless, each society must weigh the potential losses due to lesser or even a negative growth and the losses due to rent-seeking expenditure. The second step tells us that only when the social welfare of the entrenched state outweighs the social welfare of the unentrenched state should eternity clauses be used.

As becomes obvious this part of the test manages to incorporate fairness considerations, without falling victim of moralism.[100] Thus, it disentangles eternity clauses from concerns of fairness. Whether a rule is considered fair or not at a specific time does indeed influence whether a rule will be included in the constitution. However, a justification is important to the extent that it allows us to formulate constraints. As long as there is no universal and abstract definition of what constitutes fairness, justifications become subjective. Nevertheless, different fairness conceptions have different distributional effects, which can be objectively observed. Subsequently, the test covers the gap for a more objective justification.

At this point, two issues need to be discussed. First, the barriers to amendment set by eternity clauses are derivative barriers. Specifically, constitutions even without eternity clauses have a lock-in effect. Path dependencies, political transaction costs or coordination benefits act as barriers against many amendments. The barriers set by eternity clauses are efficient inasmuch as these barriers are functioning. Subsequently, eternity clauses become stronger as the constitution becomes a stronger constraining device. If the constitution is a weak coordination device, including eternity clauses cannot have a significant negative impact on rent redistribution on its own. Therefore, the justifiability of eternity clauses in new constitutions or on countries with a history of weak formal institutions is at best questionable. In a worst-case scenario by reducing flexibility, the framers might condemn the constitution to failure.

Second, it is claimed that obvious inequalities and rules with strong distributive effects would not pass the test. It seems intuitive that high-rent differentials would always compensate the costs of drafting a new constitution. Nevertheless, even if we relax that assumption, a highly (economically) divided society suffers from high political instability[101] and faces a constant risk of revolution.[102] Subsequently, the benefits of entrenching a dividing social setting will have to be discounted due to the political instability. As a result, in the second step, the discounted utility of the entrenched state will only exceptionally—if ever—exceed the utility of the unentrenched state.

---

[100]In plain words, as long as "unfair" settings are connected with great rent differentials, using eternity clauses can no longer be justified.

[101]Alesina and Perotti (1996), p. 1023.

[102]Acemoglu and Robinson (2005).

5 Conclusion

To sum up, the chapter began by looking into the various typologies that amendment constraints can take. A conceptual framework was introduced and a classification scheme based on two dimensions (limitation and explicitness) was provided for future research. Then, the strands of theory justifying the introduction of amendment constraints were critically presented with eternity clauses as the vehicle. After their examination, it has been showed that all justification provided thus far fail to formulate an effective criterion for distinguishing justified against unjustified eternity clauses. The protective theories are unrealistic in their assumptions, while the symbolic value theories remain simply descriptive. As a result, the chapter proposes a novel justification of amendment constraints, i.e., through the expected reduction of wasteful investment in redistributing rents in a society. In the last section, the theory was put to the test by examining whether it could be used to formulate an objective test that could inform the framers ex ante whether entrenching certain provision is justified.

The criterion proposed can help us ex post measure the justifiability of eternity clauses; however, it does not inform us on the determinants of the introduction of such constraints. Subsequently, further research is needed towards that direction. Having a theory through which to set a benchmark, it is possible for future research to measure to what extent this benchmark is used or to what extent framers conduct such a calculus before they decide upon which provisions to entrench. Only then, can we formulate expectation on the extent to which rational framers take into consideration the justifiability of the amendment constraint in their decision to include eternity clauses in the constitution.

Acknowledgements I would like to thank Prof. Richard Albert, Prof. Stefan Voigt, Stephan Michel, Jerg Gutmann, Tobias Hlobil and all the participants of the Workshop on Unamendable Constitutional Provisions, Koc University, Istanbul, 9 June 2015 for their valuable comments and feedback.

References

Abdelaal M (2016) Entrenchment illusion: the curious case of Egypt's constitutional entrenchment clause. Chicago-Kent J Int Comp Law 16(1):1

Acemoglu D, Robinson JA (2005) Economic origins of dictatorship and democracy. Cambridge University Press, Cambridge

Acemoglu D, Johnson S, Robinson JA (2005) Institutions as a fundamental cause of long-run growth. In: Aghion P, Durlauf SN (eds) Handbook of economic growth. Elsevier, New York

Ackerman BA (1993) We the people. Belknap Press of Harvard University Press, Cambridge

Ahmed DI, Gouda M (2015) Measuring constitutional Islamization: The Islamic constitutions index. Hastings Int Comp Law Rev 38(1):1

Akerlof GA (1970) The market for "Lemons": quality uncertainty and the market mechanism. Q J Econ 84(3):488

Albert R (2010) Constitutional handcuffs. Ariz State Law J 42(1):663

Albert R (2013) The expressive function of constitutional amendment rules. McGill Law J 59 (2):225

Albert R (2014a) The structure of constitutional amendment rules. Wake For Law Rev 49:913

Albert R (2014b) Constitutional disuse or desuetude: the case of Article V. Boston Univ Law Rev 94:1029

Albert R (2015a) The difficulty of constitutional amendment in Canada. Alberta Law Rev 53(1):85

Albert R (2015b) Amending constitutional amendment rules. Int J Const Law 13(1):655

Albert R (2015c) How unwritten constitutional norms change written constitutions. Dublin Univ Law J 38(2):387

Alesina A, Perotti R (1996) Income distribution, political instability, and investment. Eur Econ Rev 40(6):1203

Beard CA (1913) An economic interpretation of the constitution of the United States. Macmillan, Basingstoke

Boudreaux DJ, Pritchard AC (1993–1994) Rewriting the constitution: an economic analysis of the constitutional amendment process. Fordham Law Rev 62(1):111

Brennan G, Buchanan JM (1985) Reason of rules—constitutional political economy. Cambridge University Press, Cambridge

Brewer DJ (1968) An independent judiciary as the salvation of the nation. In: Annals of America: Proceedings of the New York Bar Association, vol 11 (originally published 1893)

Buchanan JM (1980) Efficient rent seeking. In: Buchanan JM, Tollison RD, Tullock G (eds) Toward a theory of the rent-seeking society. Texas A& M University Press, Texas

Buchanan JM (1987) The constitution of economic policy. Am. Econ. Rev. 77(3):243

Buchanan JM, Congleton RD (1998) Politics by principle, not interest: toward nondiscriminatory democracy. Cambridge University Press, Cambridge

Buchanan JM, Tullock G (1962) The calculus of consent. University of Michigan Press, Ann Arbor

Cho IK, Kreps DM (1987) Signaling games and stable equilibria. Q J Econ 102(2):179

Cofones IN, Michel S (2017) Fixing popular participation in constitution-making www.https://papers.ssrn.com/sol3/papers.cfm?abstract_id=2580849. Accessed on 30 June 2018

Congleton RD, Swedenborg B (2006) Democratic constitutional design and public policy: analysis and evidence. MIT Press, Cambridge

Dahrendorf R (1990) Transitions: politics, economics, and liberty. Washington Q 13(3):133

Dellinger W (1983) The legitimacy of constitutional change: rethinking the amendment process. Harvard Law Rev 97(2):386

Dixon R (2011) Constitutional amendment rules: a comparative perspective. In: Ginsburg T, Dixon R (eds) Comparative constitutional law. Edward Elgar Publishing, Cheltenham

Downs GW, Jones MA (2002) Reputation, compliance, and international law. J Learn Sci 31:S95

Eisgruber CL (2009) Constitutional self-government. Harvard University Press, Cambridge

Elkins Z, Ginsburg T, Melton J (2009) The endurance of national constitutions. Cambridge University Press, Cambridge

Elster J (1984) Ulysses and the Sirens: studies in rationality and irrationality. Cambridge University Press, Cambridge

Elster J, Slagstad R (1988) Constitutionalism and democracy. Cambridge University Press, Cambridge

Eskridge WN, Ferejohn J (2001) Super-statutes. Duke Law J 50(5):1215

Fallon RH Jr (2005) Legitimacy and the constitution. Harvard Law Rev 118(6):1787

Friedman A (2011) Dead hand constitutionalism: Honduras and the danger of eternity clauses in new democracies. Mexican Law Rev 4(1):77

Gavison R (2002) What belongs in a constitution? Const Polit Econ 13(1):89

Gerken HK (2007) The hydraulics of constitutional reform: a skeptical response to our undemocratic constitution. Drake Law Rev 55(4):925

Ginsburg T (2002) Economic analysis and the design of constitutional courts. Theor Inquiries Law 3(1):49

Ginsburg T, Versteeg M (2014) Why do countries adopt constitutional review? J Law Econ Organ 30(3):587

Ginsburg T, Elkins Z, Blount J (2009) Does the process of constitution-making matter? Annu Rev Law Soc Sci 5:201

Guzman AT (2008) How international law works: a rational choice theory. Oxford University Press, Oxford

Harberger AC (1959) Using the resources at hand more effectively. Am Econ Rev 49(2):134

Hardin R (2013a) Why a constitution? In: Grofman B, Wittman D (eds) The Federalist papers and the new institutionalism. Algora Publishing, New York

Hardin R (2013b) Why a constitution? In: Galligan DJ, Versteeg M (eds) Social and political foundations of constitutions. Cambridge University Press, Cambridge

Harsanyi JC (1953) Cardinal utility in welfare economics and in the theory of risk-taking. J Polit Econ 61(5):434

Hayek FA (1960) The constitution of liberty. University of Chicago Press, Chicago

Hillman AL (1989) The political economy of protection. Harwood Academic Publishers, Newark

Holmes S (1988) Precommitment and the paradox of democracy. In: Elster J, Slagstad R (eds) Constitutionalism and democracy. Cambridge University Press, Cambridge

Krueger AO (1974) The political economy of the rent-seeking society. Am Econ Rev 64(3):291

Landemore H, Elster J (2012) Collective wisdom: principles and mechanisms. Cambridge University Press, Cambridge

Leininger W (1993) More efficient rent-seeking—a Muenchhausen solution. Public Choice 75 (1):43

Leininger W, Yang CL (1994) Dynamic rent-seeking games. Games Econ Behav 7(3):406

Levinson S (1995) Responding to imperfection: the theory and practice of constitutional amendment. Princeton University Press, Princeton

Lewis DK (1969) Convention: a philosophical study. Harvard University Press, Cambridge

Lutz DS (2006) Principles of constitutional design. Cambridge University Press, Cambridge

Marsteintredet L (2015) The Honduran Supreme Court renders inapplicable unamendable constitutional provisions. ILJCL http://www.iconnectblog.com/2015/05/Marsteintredet-on-Honduras. Accessed on 30 June 2017

McConnell MW (1997) Textualism and the dead hand of the past. George Washington Law Rev 66(5–6):1127

McGuire RA (1988) Constitution making: a rational choice model of the federal convention of 1787. Am J Polit Sci 32(2):483–522

McGuire RA, Ohsfeldt RL (1989) Public choice analysis and the ratification of the constitution. In: Hoffman B, Wittman D (eds) The federalist papers and the new institutionalism. Agathon Press, Bronx, NY

Mueller DC (2003) Public choice III. Cambridge University Press, Cambridge

Müller C (1998) The veil of uncertainty: unveiled. Const Politl Econ 9(1):5

Nitzan S (1994) Modeling rent-seeking contests. Eur J Polit Econ 10(1):41

North DC, Weingast BR (1989) Constitutions and commitment: the evolution of institutions governing public choice in seventeenth-century England. J Econ Hist 49(4):803

Olson M (1965) The logic of collective action. Harvard University Press, Cambridge

Olson M (1982) The rise and decline of nations: economic growth, stagflation, and social rigidities. Yale University Press, New Haven

Olson M (1993) Dictatorship, democracy, and development. A Pol Sc Rev 87(3):567

Ordeshook PC (1992) Constitutional stability. Const Polit Econ 3(2):137

Ordeshook PC (2002) Are 'Western' constitutions relevant to anything other than the countries they serve. Const Polit Econ 13(1):3

Ostrom V, Allen B (2007) The political theory of a compound Republic: designing the American experiment. Lexington Books, Lanham

Posner RA (1975) The social costs of monopoly and regulation. J Polit Econ 83(4):807

Posner EA, Vermeule A (2008) Constitutional showdowns. Univ Pennsylvania Law Rev 156 (4):991

Preuss UK (2011) Implications of eternity clauses: The German experience. Israel Law Rev 44 (3):429

Ramseyer JM (1994) The puzzling (In)dependence of courts: a comparative approach. J Legal Stud 23(2):721

Rasch BE, Congleton RD (2006) Amendment procedures and constitutional stability. In: Congleton RD, Swedenborg B (eds) Democratic constitutional design and public policy: analysis and evidence. MIT Press, Cambridge

Rawls J (1971) A theory of justice. Harvard University Press, Cambridge

Rogoff K (1990) Equilibrium political budget cycles. Am Econ Rev 80(1):21

Roznai Y (2014) Legisprudence limitations on constitutional amendments: reflections on the czech constitutional court's declaration of unconstitutional constitutional act. Vienna J Int Const Law 8(1):29

Roznai Y (2015) Unamendability and the genetic code of the constitution. Eur Rev Public Law 27 (2):775

Roznai Y (2017) Unconstitutional constitutional amendments: the limits of amendment powers. Oxford University Press, Oxford

Roznai Y, Suteu S (2015) Eternal territory? The crimean crisis and Ukraine's territorial integrity as an unamendable principle. German Law J 16(3):542

Rubenfeld J (1997) Moment and the millennium. George Washington Law Rev 66:1127

Ruhl M (2010) Honduras unravels. J Democracy 21(2):93

Russell RH (1993) Constitutional Odyssey: can Canadians become a Sovereign people? University of Toronto Press, Toronto

Schmitt C (2007) Constitutional theory (trans: Seitzer J, first published 1928). Duke University Press, Durham

Schwartz B (2013) American constitutional law. Cambridge University Press, Cambridge

Schwartzberg M (2009) Democracy and legal change. Cambridge University Press, Cambridge

Stigler GJ (1971) The theory of economic regulation. Bell J Econ Manag Sci 2(1):3

Suber P (1990) The paradox of self-amendment: a study of logic, law, omnipotence, and change. Peter Lang Publishing, Bern

Tullock G (1967) The welfare costs of tariffs, monopolies, and theft. West Econ J 5(3):224

Vanberg V, Buchanan JM (1989) Interests and theories in constitutional choice. J Theor Polit 1 (1):49, 54

Voigt S (1999a) Implicit constitutional change—changing the meaning of the constitution without changing the text of the document. Eur J Law Econ 7(3):197

Voigt S (1999b) Breaking with the notion of social contract: constitutions as based on spontaneously Arisen Institutions. Const Polit Econ 10(3):283

Voigt S (2011) Positive constitutional economics II—A survey of recent developments. Public Choice 146(1–2):205

Voigt S (2013) How (Not) to measure institutions. J Inst Econ 9(01):1

Voigt S (2015) Veilonomics: On the use and utility veils in constitutional political economy. In: Imbeau LM, Jacob S (eds) Behind a veil of ignorance? Power and uncertainty in constitutional design. Springer, Berlin

Weintal S (2011) Challenge of reconciling constitutional eternity clauses with popular sovereignty: toward three-track democracy in Israel as a Universal Holistic Constitutional System and Theory. Israel Law Rev 44:449, 456

Wicksell K (1896) Finanztheoretische Untersuchungen: Nebst Darstellung und Kritik des Steuerwesens Schwedens. Verlag Wirtschaft und Finanzen, Stuttgart

Widner J (2007) Constitution writing in post-conflict settings: an overview. William Mary Law Rev 49(5):1513

Wiggins D (1968) On being in the same place at the same time. Philos Rev 77(1):90

Williamson OE (1981) The economics of organization: the transaction cost approach. Am J Sociol 87(3):548

Conventions of Unamendability: Covert Constitutional Unamendability in (Two) Politically Enforced Constitutions

Gert Jan Geertjes and Jerfi Uzman

Abstract Legal scholarship on the unamendability of constitutional provisions tends to focus on legal systems with a strong tradition of judicial review of legislation. Legal systems such as the United Kingdom and The Netherlands, where the constitutionality of laws is a matter for the political branches and not for the courts, are routinely ignored. They do not fit existing perceptions of constitutional unamendability and arguably fall well outside the categories of either explicit or implicit constitutional unamendability. Nonetheless, these 'politically enforced constitutions' still contain mechanisms of unamendability, be it of an informal nature. These take the shape of judicial or institutional disobedience. The doctrine of unconstitutional constitutional amendments thus becomes relevant to a broader range of constitutional systems. However, this type of unamendability requires a more subtle approach. It does not emerge from constitutional provisions, whether explicit or not, but rather occurs in the form of a constitutional convention of unamendability. The question whether parts of the constitution should be regarded as unamendable thus cannot be solely couched in the all-or-nothing terminology of legal rules. Instead, conventions of unamendability, due to their principle-based character, may be subject to changing circumstances and exceptions. Existing literature on constitutional conventions may be used as a model in order to build a framework of analysis for the concept of constitutional unamendability in politically enforced constitutions.

G. J. Geertjes (✉) · J. Uzman
Leiden University Law School, Leiden, The Netherlands
e-mail: j.a.geertjes@law.leidenuniv.nl

J. Uzman
e-mail: j.uzman@law.leidenuniv.nl

© Springer International Publishing AG, part of Springer Nature 2018
R. Albert and B. E. Oder (eds.), *An Unamendable Constitution?*
Ius Gentium: Comparative Perspectives on Law and Justice 68,
https://doi.org/10.1007/978-3-319-95141-6_4

89

1 Introduction

When in 2009 the Swiss people decided to amend their Constitution in order to ban the construction of mosque minarets, the ban was sharply condemned.[1] Critics argued that it was discriminatory and that it violated the freedom of religion as protected by the Swiss Constitution and the European Convention on Human Rights.[2] Not everyone disliked the idea, however. There were serious political calls for a similar ban in countries across Europe.[3] Indeed, the steady rise of populism increasingly seems to generate proposals of constitutional amendment that sit uncomfortably with traditional approaches of constitutionalism. This development fuels the debate on the ability of constitutions to protect themselves against these kind of modifications. This debate is anything but new. It dates almost from the time that man started to contemplate a written constitution.[4] The world's second oldest constitution in existence, the 1814 Constitution of Norway, already featured a prohibition for the constitutional legislature to act against its 'spirit and principles'.[5] Elements of unamendability were, moreover, already to be found in US constitutional law.[6] Since then, the idea has begun its march of victory throughout the world.[7] Nowadays, many constitutional systems in the world are familiar with the so-called 'supraconstitutional' or 'eternity clauses' limiting the powers of constitutional amendment. These limits have recently gained attention.[8] This should come as no surprise. The last decades have witnessed spectacular attempts to change constitutions worldwide and, moreover, an increased willingness on the part of the judiciary to review those attempts. As Roznai has eloquently shown, this development is rapidly turning into a global trend.[9] Indeed, other contributions in this volume illustrate that unamendability is a key issue in many parts of the world.[10] Perhaps the most enigmatic example featuring in contemporary scholarship, comes from India, where the judicial and legislative branches fought a heroic

---

[1]See art. 72–3 of the Swiss Constitution. More generally Peters (2009) and Green (2010), p. 619.

[2]See articles 15 and 8, respectively, of the Swiss Constitution, and articles 9 en 14 of the ECHR.

[3]For instance from Geert Wilders who, at the time lent vital support to the ruling coalition in The Netherlands. See Green (2010), p. 642.

[4]Garlicki and Garlicka (2011), p. 343.

[5]See s 112 of the Norwegian Constitution; Smith (2011), p. 369.

[6]See generally Roznai (2013), pp. 657, 662.

[7]Ibid., p. 665.

[8]See e.g., Wright (1991), p. 741, O'Connell (1999), p. 48, Mazzone (2005), p. 1747, Jacobsohn (2006), p. 460, Gözler (2008), Albert (2009, 2010, p. 663), Barak (2011), p. 321, Bezemek (2011), p. 517, Cariás (2011), Roznai and Yolcu (2012), p. 175, Halmai (2012), p. 182, Roznai (2013), Colón-Ríos (2013), p. 521, (2014), p. 143) and Albert (2014a), p. 181.

[9]Roznai (2013).

[10]See the contributions of Roznai, Hoque, Olcay, Yegen and Masri.

battle over the amendment powers of the latter in the 1960s–1980s.[11] Equally appealing, though possibly not as controversial, is the South African Constitutional Court's decision to declare the newly adopted Constitution for post-apartheid South Africa unconstitutional.[12] The more recent examples come from the European continent, where several constitutional courts have been confronted with bold and potentially far-reaching constitutional change. Some of them, such as the Turkish and the Czech Constitutional Courts, have risen to the challenge, others—like the Hungarian—have acted more carefully, but it is clear that the issue of unamendability and the judicial enforcement thereof is firmly on the European agenda.[13] Surely the same goes for Latin America where the courts have been struggling with roughly the same dilemma.[14]

Constitutional unamendability, in short, seems to be the trend globally. The concept seems to be somewhat out of place, however, in countries, such as the United Kingdom and the Netherlands, where judicial review of legislation is traditionally less common. In 2010, for instance, a prominent Dutch lawyer and cabinet minister argued that there was nothing in the Dutch Constitution preventing a majority from introducing Sharia Law, as long as the correct procedure of amendment were to be followed.[15] Although his remarks sparked a general outcry, legal scholarship, in a rare moment of unanimity, tended to agree.[16] In short, there seem to be important exceptions to the growing global trend of courts curbing the powers of constitutional amendment. To some extent, these exceptions might be explained by the fact that the constitutional structures in most western European democracies are relatively deeply rooted. Constitutional change is seldom of a controversial nature. But rooted or not, the Swiss example mentioned illustrates that this might change. Should we, in such a case, assume that constitutions without unamendability clauses or judicial doctrines of unamendability are irrevocably flawed? Or may there still be hope?

---

[11]See e.g., the 'Three Musketeers' of Indian constitutional litigation: the Supreme Court judgments in *I.C. Golaknath & Ors v. State of Punjab*, AIR 1967 SC 1643 (27 February 1967); *Kesavananda Bharati v. State of Kerala*, AIR 1973 SC 1461 (24 April 1973); *Minerva Mills Ltd. v. Union of India*, AIR 1980 SC 1789 (31 July 1980). For a compelling accounts, see the contribution to this volume by Satya Prateek; Jacobsohn (2006), p. 470, Albert (2014a), p. 22, and Halmai (2012), p. 186.

[12]*Certification of the Constitution of the Republic of South Africa*, 1996 [1996] ZACC 26, 1996 (4) SA 744 (6 September 1996). See Albert (2009), p. 26, and Halmai (2012), p. 190.

[13]Compare e.g.: Constitutional Court of Turkey, E.2008/18, K.2008/116 (5 June 2008); Czech Constitutional Court, Pl. ÚS 27/09 (10 September 2009); Constitutional Court of Hungary, no. 61/2011 (VII. 13) (13 June 2011). For commentary, see: Özbudun (2009), p. 533, Roznai and Yolcu (2012), p. 175, Roznai (2014), p. 29, and Halmai (2012), p. 182. The Turkish example is particularly informative. See on that subject, the contributions in this volume by Tarık Olcay and Oya Yegen.

[14]See Colón-Riós (2013), p. 521, (2014), p. 143, and Bernal (2013), p. 339.

[15]See Otto (2007), p. 137.

[16]Still worse: as we will see, the Dutch Constitution even prohibits the courts to engage in procedural review of the amendment. See article 120 of the Constitution and the *Van den Bergh v. The State* judgment of the Dutch Supreme Court, NJ 1963/248 (27 January 1961).

We argue here that there is. Although there exists a distinct category of constitutions that, by virtue of their cultural and historical roots, falls well outside the scope of the existing doctrine of constitutional unamendability, even these may still include mechanisms that have much in common with what is traditionally understood as constitutional unamendability. This kind of unamendability is, however, of an extremely informal nature. Instead of explicitly prohibiting or disabling legislatures to formally amend the Constitution, the system simply renders amendments, that have already been brought into force, practically ineffective. We call this *covert unamendability*.[17] The agents of this kind of unamendability mechanism are primarily the courts. But contrary to 'regular' types of unamendability that have been identified thus far, they do not necessarily declare amendments unconstitutional or void. Instead, they simply ignore the amendment or find alternative ways of maintaining the old *status quo*. They apply, what we might call, *judicial disobedience,* or rather a convenient form of *judicial deafness*.[18] However, because of its extremely informal nature, this kind of unamendability is not as tough, or subject to the same rules, as regular forms of unamendability. It lacks a clear rule, codified or not, that a particular constitutional concept may not be affected. Instead, this kind of unamendability rather takes the shape of a convention, which perhaps makes it a somewhat more intangible concept, but at the same time renders it particularly useful to politically enforced constitutions where a system of strong-form judicial review of legislation is absent.

In this chapter, we try to illuminate the concept of covert unamendability. We do this by first establishing its place among the different forms of unamendability. To this end, we develop the distinction between, what we tentatively refer to as 'politically' and 'judicially enforced constitutions'. In our view, the scholarly understanding of constitutional unamendability has so far been very much influenced by judicially enforced constitutions. We then proceed by sketching some potential moments of covert unamendability in two largely politically enforced constitutions: the United Kingdom and the Netherlands. The choice for these two systems is motivated by the fact that they typically represent rooted liberal democracies where the constitution is largely considered a political project and in which there is an established tradition of judicial reluctance to interfere with the legislative domain. Moreover, both jurisdictions lack a written constitutional provision declaring parts of the constitution unamendable. We then conclude with some thoughts on the nature and limits of this covert type of unamendability. To that end, we elucidate on the concept of the constitutional convention. However, it should be noted at the outset that we use this concept only as a model to explain the typical features of the type of unamendability we identified. This unamendability itself concerns rules and not conventions. Hence, we speak of *conventions of unamendability*, not of *unamendable conventions*. Moreover, our inquiry is not normative. For a normative

---

[17]We took a leaf here from Voermans (2009), p. 84.

[18]The term *judicial deafness* was used before, see e.g., Patterson (2007), pp. 279, 280.

assessment of the concept of unamendability in general, we refer to the contributions of Roznai, Michel and Cofone, and Pilpilidis in this volume.[19]

2 The Different Forms of Constitutional Unamendability

Before we move on to the usefulness of unamendability doctrine for politically enforced constitutions, let us first clarify our understanding of two central concepts: constitutional unamendability and politically—as opposed to judicially—enforced constitutions. We leave this latter distinction for the next paragraph, and focus here on the concept of unamendability as such. Constitutional unamendability may roughly be defined as the entrenchment of (parts of) a given constitution to such an extent that changing the Constitution is no longer a legal option.[20] When defining 'constitutional' change, one can distinguish between the constitution narrowly defined, as a written document (usually indicated with a capital latter 'C'), or in a larger sense, as a body of rules that together define the system of government, establish its institutions and the mechanisms that are designed to limit government powers.[21] Although comparative legal scholarship on unamendability—for understandable reasons—tends to focus on amendment of the (written) Constitution, the concept is relevant to the entire spectre of the constitution in the wider context. We, therefore, prefer to apply the wide definition of a constitution here, if only, because we argue that unamendability doctrine has some relevance, even for states without a written Constitution, such as the United Kingdom. Moreover, as Albert observed earlier, even in countries that do have a written constitution—such as the United States—large parts of constitutional law cannot be explained solely by reference to the constitutional text.[22]

The next question would be what is to be understood by constitutional 'change'. There are several ways of changing both the meaning and the practical effects of the constitution. In a book on the subject, Melissa Schwartzberg distinguishes statutory and interpretative change, constitutional amendment and revolution.[23] Again, unamendability doctrine usually discusses the (im)possibilities of inserting textual changes to the written Constitution. Since we do not limit ourselves to codified Constitutions, our present definition of change should also be broader. Yet, we limit ourselves to legislative changes. The kind of constitutional change we propose to discuss here, follows from legislative action directed to change either the

---

[19]Yaniv Roznai, 'Necrocracy or Democracy? Assessing Objections to Formal Unamendability'; Stephan Michel and Ignacio Cofone, 'Credible Commitment or Paternalism? The Case of Unamendability'; Konstantinos Pilpilidis, 'A Constitution for Eternity: An Economic Theory of Explicit Unamendability'.

[20]See e.g., Albert (2008), p. 37.

[21]Voermans (2009), p. 86.

[22]Albert (2009), p. 16.

[23]Schwartzberg (2007), pp. 3–8.

Constitution (in a narrow sense) or a statute with constitutional significance or status. In the British context, this would apply, for instance, to the Human Rights Act 1998, the European Communities Act 1972, the Constitutional Reform Act 2005 or the Scotland Act 1998, to name but a few.[24] Furthermore, the kind of amendment we envisage does not transcend the boundary between amendment and total revision discussed elsewhere in this volume.[25]

Constitutional unamendability comes in several forms.[26] We should, therefore, be clear about the type of unamendability we discuss in the present context. Comparative law regularly distinguishes between both procedural and substantive unamendability, and between formal and informal unamendability.[27] Procedural unamendability concerns the situation in which the constitution allows for amendments but forces the constitutional legislature to follow a more or less complicated procedure. Procedural requirements can sometimes render the amendment of the constitution extremely difficult if not practically impossible.[28] *Formal* procedural unamendability flows directly from a procedural restriction that is codified in a constitutional text. *Informal* procedural unamendability, on the other hand, results from the political process.[29] It develops where the procedural threshold required by a formal amendment rule is so high that political actors cannot realistically (even if they could theoretically) meet the amendment requirements.[30] Although the Dutch Constitution, for instance, does not formally prohibit relinquishment of the principle of bicameralism, the recurring debate in the Netherlands about abolishing the First Chamber of Parliament illustrates that in practice it is presently unimaginable to achieve the necessary political consensus needed for amendment.[31] This is exactly what Albert recently coined 'constructive unamendability'.[32] It would be tempting to apply this concept to the two politically enforced constitutions we discuss here but we resist that temptation. As far as we can see, there is no fundamental difference between politically and judicially enforced constitutions with respect to the possible occurrences of informal procedural unamendability. In both cases, this kind of constructive unamendability is largely a matter for the political branches and not for the courts. The situation

---

[24]At the time of finalizing this article, the European Communities Act 1972 is still in force in the UK legal order as a 'constitutional' statute, since the exit of the UK out of the EU has not yet taken place in a legal sense. The Act will only lose its constitutional status as soon as Parliament repeals it.

[25]Compare the chapter of Yaniv Roznai, 'Necrocracy or Democracy? Assessing Objections to Formal Unamendability' (n 19), para 5A.

[26]We use the recently proposed classification by Albert (2014a) 188–189.

[27]See e.g., Garlicki and Garlicka (2011), p. 347.

[28]See for two such examples in Canada and the US, Albert (2014a), p. 181.

[29]See Schwartzberg (2007), p. 13.

[30]Albert (2014a), p. 191.

[31]van den Berg (2006), Andeweg and Irwin (2014), p. 167.

[32]Albert (2014a), p. 191.

arguably is different to *formal* procedural unamendability, but in that case we have no knowledge of any such realistic example in a politically enforced constitution.

Our main focus here is on the substantive branch of unamendability. This branch concerns the subject matter of constitutional amendments. Like its procedural sister, substantive unamendability comes in a formal and an informal version. *Formal substantive limitations* on the powers of constitutional amendment usually operate in the form of explicit clauses (so-called '*Ewigheitsklauseln*' or 'eternity clauses') in a written constitution. Perhaps the most notable example, at least on the European continent, is article 79(3) of the German Basic Law, declaring unlawful, the amendment of a number of provisions in the Basic Law, for instance, with respect to the republican form of the state, its federal structure, the separation of powers and the protection of human dignity. In a similar vein, the Swiss may amend their constitution freely, but not as far as these amendments might contradict mandatory rules of international law.[33] And the Norwegian legislature should do as it pleases as long as its fruits are in line with 'the spirit' and 'the principles embodied in the Constitution'.[34] However, neither the flexible and uncodified constitution of the UK, nor the written Constitution of the Netherlands include such a provision. This is not to say that this would be conceptually impossible for a politically enforced constitution. True, both formal procedural and substantive unamendability clauses are more often than not enforced by constitutional courts.[35] However, the Norwegian example illustrates that there are systems in which it is assumed that the enforcement is primarily a matter for the political actors.[36] Enforcement is then largely a matter of political reality.[37] Having said that, it is submitted that most European 'eternity clauses' are, in any case, coupled with constitutional courts reviewing constitutional amendments.[38] As we will see, no such constitutional court exists in politically enforced constitutions, nor do ordinary courts fill this gap.

The story of constitutional unamendability does not end though, with these so-called *Ewigheitsklauseln*. A number of jurisdictions operate *informal substantive limits* to the amendment power. In these cases, the constitutional text does not, as such, include any explicit provision legitimizing review—whether political or judicial—of constitutional amendments. And yet, there are several jurisdictions where particularly the courts have found unwritten limits to the amendment power,

---

[33]See articles 193(4) and 194(2) of the Swiss Federal Constitution.

[34]See article 112(1) of the Norwegian *Grundlov*.

[35]See Garlicki and Garlicka (2011).

[36]Smith (2011), pp. 384–386.

[37]As Eivind Smith has conveniently shown, the way in which the role of the monarchy in Norway has developed, is probably not in line with the spirit of the Constitution as perceived in 1814. None of the political actors (including the monarchy itself) raised the issue however. The most likely scenario is that the position of the King in Norwegian constitutional law, although initially clearly part of the 'principles embodied by the Constitution', has—by virtue of the changing political landscape—lost this status along the way of history. See Smith (2011).

[38]See e.g., Barak (2011).

based on the so-called 'inner logic' of the constitution.[39] Thus, in a spectacular move, the Indian Supreme Court in a series of cases, ranging from the 1960s into the 1980s, established ultimately that the power to amend the Indian Constitution 'does not include the power to alter the basic structure or framework of the Constitution so as to change its identity'.[40] Basic constitutional features, in the opinion of the Indian Supreme Court, included, amongst others, the form of government, the separation of powers, the essence of fundamental freedoms and the federal character of the Constitution.[41] Should one of these principles be seriously violated, the amendment would be struck down. This 'basic structure doctrine' has been highly influential in a range of legal systems, such as Nepal, Bangladesh, South Africa and, to some extent, Pakistan.[42] Due to its origins as judge-made law, this doctrine is strongly connected to the possibility of judicial review of the amendment power. Although some jurisdictions, such as Pakistan, show that it is still possible for the judiciary to contemplate implicit substantive limits without actually engaging in review itself that situation remains exceptional.[43]

The question we focus on, in this contribution, is whether this mechanism of informal substantive unamendability is likely to occur in the politically enforced constitutions of the UK and the Netherlands. And it is this concept of politically, as opposed to judicially enforced constitutions to which we now turn.

3 Constitutional Amendment and the Role of the Courts

This short survey of the different forms of constitutional unamendability reveals mainly examples drawn from jurisdictions that have some kind of strong-form judicial constitutional review of legislation.[44] This is unsurprising. Most literature on the subject tends to focus on systems where there is a bold judicial culture of reviewing either legislation or even the political process as such. The classic examples come either from countries such as Germany, Turkey and South Africa—where there exists a constitutional court—or from India, the United States or Brazil, countries where the ordinary judiciary, headed by a Supreme Court, assumes the

---

[39]Take for instance the case of Bangladesh, where unamendability was a judicially declared norm until 2011, when an eternal clause was added to the Constitution. See the chapter of Ridwanul Hoque, 'Eternal Provisions in the Constitution of Bangladesh: A Constitution Once and for All?'.

[40]*Kesavananda Bharati v. State of Kerala*, AIR 1973 SC 1461 (24 April 1973). See also: *I.C. Golaknath & Ors v. State of Punjab*, AIR 1967 SC 1643 (27 February 1967); *Indira Nehru Gandhi v. Raj Narain*, AIR 1975 SC 2299 (19 December 1975); *Minerva Mills Ltd. v. Union of India*, AIR 1980 SC 1789 (31 July 1980).

[41]Samanta and Basu (2008), pp. 499, 501.

[42]See Roznai (2013).

[43]Ibid., p. 698.

[44]See on the weak/strong-form review axis: Tushnet (2006), pp. 1225, 1242. Recently in the context of amendment: Colón-Ríos (2014).

power of reviewing parliamentary legislation.[45] Although it is theoretically conceivable for a jurisdiction to recognize judicial review of the constitutionality of amendments without recognizing judicial constitutional review of statutes, in practice the former is always connected to the latter.[46] One might even say that, in terms of the role of the courts, amendment review is a form of judicial review of statutes 'plus'.[47] In the same vein, one may conceptually distinguish between unamendability of the constitution on the one hand, and judicial oversight of limitations to the powers of amendment on the other.[48] But again, it is submitted that this distinction in practice is relatively modest.[49] In any case, legal literature regularly seems to assume the close link between unamendability on the one hand and judicial review on the other.

This strong emphasis on (quasi-)constitutional court litigation poses problems for constitutions, like the British or the Dutch, which contemplate a rather modest role for the courts in enforcing the constitution. This modesty is not necessarily connected to the judicial power to engage in rights review. Both British and Dutch courts engage in rights review of legislation, be it not on the basis of a national bill of rights but of the European Convention on Human Rights (ECHR).[50] Nor is the fact that UK courts lack the power to invalidate primary legislation and have relatively weak remedial powers conclusive as such. It is conceptually possible for a legal system to have a court which is, or considers itself, empowered to review the constitutionality of constitutional amendments, but which cannot itself remedy a possible violation. What unites both systems, however, is their dependency, in large areas of their respective constitutions, on political actors to enforce it. We may call these 'politically enforced constitutions', as opposed to judicially enforced constitutions.

Nevertheless, this raises the question how this 'judicial modesty' should be defined. If we are to make a distinction between judicially and politically enforced constitutions, we are in need of criteria demarcating one from the other. That is no easy task. It should be noted at the outset that the classification of a particular constitution as either one of these poles is not as clear-cut as it would seem. Few systems, if any at all, are either totally politically or judicially enforced. Even in the most classic example of a legal system featuring judicial supremacy there are at least some areas in which there is no significant judicial interference. Equally, the growing judicialization of politics worldwide has affected jurisdictions that, until quite recently, adhered to legislative supremacy.[51] It is far more likely that any

---

[45]See e.g., Gözler (2008).

[46]Barak (2011), p. 321.

[47]Although he does not use this kind of terminology, Colón Ríos seems to depart from a similar line of reasoning. See Colón Ríos (2014).

[48]Jacobsohn (2009), p. 82.

[49]Roznai (2013), p. 661.

[50]See e.g., Kavanagh (2009) and Uzman et al. (2011).

[51]On this trend see e.g., Hirschl (2008), p. 93.

given legal system is at best leaning towards either one of the judicial and political poles. Moreover, any classification based on a single decisive constitutional feature, such as the distinction between weak-form and strong-form systems of judicial review, is likely to fall short.[52] Rather, this classification depends on a range of historical and cultural factors affecting judicial attitudes and powers. Nevertheless, it would be useful to identify a limited set of defining features which may indicate the likelihood of judicial interference with the constitutional amendment power.

So what is essentially characteristic of politically enforced constitutions? It seems to us that courts in this kind of jurisdiction are traditionally reluctant to view the constitution as 'law' but rather see it as a set of political values and rules.[53] Although they can play a role in protecting these values, for instance where individual rights are concerned, they do not regard themselves designated to determine the meaning of the constitution.[54] This does not mean, of course, that it would be unthinkable for courts to express their opinion on a constitutional matter. However, it is commonplace in the 'ideal' politically enforced constitution to assume that it is in the first place up to Parliament to determine its content. Compare this to the approach taken by the US Supreme Court, in which it has repeatedly stressed that it is ultimately for the Court to define the meaning of the Constitution.[55] Similarly, the Federal Constitutional Court in Germany usually assumes that its own interpretations of the *Grundgesetz* are the final say on the matter.[56]

The idea that the courts play a vital role in shaping the constitution also manifests in the willingness of courts to enforce the constitution within the political arena itself. As we said before, there are areas in which the constitution is not usually enforced by the courts, either because the need for judicial interference simply does not arise or because these areas are considered to be non-justiciable.[57] Yet, there are, even here, occasions in which the courts do interfere. This is particularly the case in jurisdictions blessed with a Kelsenian constitutional court. The German *Bundesverfassungsgericht,* for instance, frequently hears complaints that go to the heart of the political process. Illustrative is its ruling on whether the outcome of a vote in the *Bundesrat* was determined constitutionally.[58] Neither did the Court hesitate to decide on the constitutionality of a parliamentary vote of no confidence against the Federal Chancellor.[59] One could argue that such judicial

---

[52]See on this distinction e.g., Tushnet (2006), p. 1242 and Colón-Ríos (2014), p. 143.

[53]See e.g., in the Japanese context Matsui (2011), pp. 1375, 1413 and Albert (2015a), p. 655.

[54]The concept may thus be antithetical to the idea of judicial supremacy as for instance defined by Whittington (2009), p. 7.

[55]See e.g., *Cooper v Aaron*, 358 US 1 (12 September 1958); *City of Boerne v Flores*, 521 US 507 (25 June 1997); Tushnet (1998), p. 945.

[56]See e.g., BverfGE 96, 260 (15 July 1997), para 12.

[57]European Union law provides a possible exception in this regard: see the remarkable case of John Dalli, a European Commissioner who was forced to resign but challenged his resignation in the European Court of Justice. See Case T-562/12 (12 May 2015).

[58]BverfGE 106, 310 (18 December 2002).

[59]BverfGE 114, 121 (25 August 2005).

boldness stems from the idea that, even within the core of the political system, it is for the Court to decide on the content of constitutional rules. But this way of thinking is not confined to the original Kelsenian constitutional court system. It is perfectly imaginable for a Supreme Court to assume the role of political umpire. In 1969, the US Supreme Court, in *Powell v. McCormack*, ruled on the authority of Congress to deny a member-elect, who had been subject to public scandals, his seat in the House.[60] The Court rejected the argument that this was a political question. Although the Constitution expressly allocated the assessment of the Members qualifications to Congress, the Court interpreted 'qualifications' narrowly. According to the Court, this exclusive role only applied to the qualifications enumerated in the Constitution itself. Exclusion on any other ground was beyond Congressional authority. This judgment in many ways reveals the Court's conception of its role as ultimate guardian of the Constitution. As Terrance Sandalow remarked only shortly after the judgment:

> Throughout, the opinion reflects a conception of the Court as the ultimate interpreter and defender of the Constitution. In Marbury v. Madison, the power of the Court to declare Congressional legislation unconstitutional was justified as a necessary incident of the Court's duty to decide cases in conformity to law, including the Constitution as the "supreme law". Powell demonstrates how far the Court has moved from that rationale. [...] The determination of constitutional questions becomes not merely an incident of the exercise of judicial power, but a reason for it.[61]

This is not to say that the US Supreme Court does not, in any way, recognize political questions.[62] The striking difference with politically enforced constitutions is, however, that the latter's legal tradition makes it virtually unimaginable for a court to hear these cases.

Until now, we have been focusing on the different manifestations of judicial supremacy. We do not claim, however, that *any* jurisdiction in which the courts are considered to have the authoritative say on constitutional meaning is also susceptible to constitutional unamendability either in its procedural or its substantive form. The US example makes this clear. Although the Court clearly considers itself supreme, it has, in the past, rejected substantive challenges to several Amendments.[63] In doing so it appears to have refused to recognize the concept of substantive unamendability, although it might be more willing to accept its procedural sister.[64] There are many factors that influence a court's decision whether or not to embrace a particular version of unamendability. Certainly, not the least of

---

[60]395 US 486 (16 June 1969).

[61]Sandalow (1969) 164, 168.

[62]See e.g., Albert (2014b), pp. 1029, 1073, drawing attention to *Coleman v Miller*, 307 US 433, 454 (1939), in which the Court suggested that disputes concerning Article V of the US Constitution are non-justiciable political questions.

[63]Compare the so-called National Prohibition Cases, 253 US 350 (7 June 1920); *Leser v Garnett*, 258 US 130 (27 February 1922). See also Gözler (2008), pp. 79–80.

[64]Albert (2015b).

those factors appear to be the degree of difficulty in amending the Constitution.[65] The fact remains, however, that politically enforced constitutions differ from their judicially enforced counterparts in the sense that they seem to offer far less potential for courts to engage in a direct confrontation with the political branches over issues of constitutional change. Let us now turn to a brief description of two of such constitutional systems.

4 Two Politically Enforced Constitutions: The UK and the Netherlands

Although both the Dutch and the British constitution are, nowadays, acquainted with the concept of judicial review of legislation, their notions of the proper role of the courts are very different from the examples discussed above. In the previous paragraph, we identified the way in which courts regard the constitution, as either a political or a predominantly legal phenomenon, as what crucially separate politically from judicially enforced constitutions. How should we assess the Dutch and the UK constitution in this respect?

4.1 United Kingdom

To begin with, both constitutions traditionally express reluctance, if not downright scepticism, about the political role of the courts. In the UK, this reluctance is directly linked to one of the two pillars of British constitutionalism, the doctrine of parliamentary sovereignty (the other being the rule of law). According to orthodox Diceyan doctrine, sovereignty of Parliament holds that 'Parliament has the right to make or unmake any law whatever' and that 'no person or body is [...] having a right to override or set aside the legislation of Parliament'.[66] This suggests that Parliament cannot enact any higher 'constitutional' law than an 'ordinary' Act of Parliament. If two Acts of Parliament on the same matter contradict with each other, a court having to decide on the validity of both statutes can simply apply the Act which has been passed later in time. The court then simultaneously rules that the earlier adopted Act has been implicitly repealed.[67]

There is just one legal rule which is, neither implicitly or expressly, subject to repeal. That is the doctrine of parliamentary sovereignty itself. Parliamentary sovereignty does not seem to be a matter of statute law, since this doctrine has never been formally entrenched in a codified constitution or in another document with a

---

[65]Albert (2009), pp. 44–46, (2015b) fn 150.

[66]Dicey (1959), pp. 3–4.

[67]*Ellen Street Estates Ltd v Minister of Health* [1934] 1 KB 590 (25 January 1934).

legal status. Neither does the doctrine seem to be simply a matter of common law in the sense of judge-made law, because it would be implausible for a court to bestow unlimited legislative authority to an institution, which is superior to the courts. Parliamentary sovereignty must, therefore, rather be considered as a matter of common law, which the courts have not created, but only recognized as existing and thereupon endorsed.[68] For this reason, Goldsworthy suggests that the sovereignty of Parliament should be described as a matter of 'customary' law, which is different from both common law and statute law in the sense that it cannot be unilaterally changed by Parliament, the courts or another institution.[69] That is not to say, however, that the legislative supremacy of Parliament cannot be abolished. This would happen in the unlikely event that all 'senior officials' of the UK legal system cease to recognize the Parliament as the supreme law-maker of the United Kingdom.[70]

This state of affairs is arguably founded on the idea that law cannot be a substitute for politics.[71] The foundational paradigm of British constitutionalism seems to be that human rights, and the broader constitution at large, cannot be protected beyond the political process. As a result, constitutional issues should be deliberated upon through democratically elected institutions.[72] This justifies the current position of Parliament as the holder of the supreme law-making authority in the United Kingdom. In this regard, it is important to note that although Parliament is not subject to legal restraints, its power has always been considered to be constrained extra legally (i.e. morally and politically), notably by constitutional conventions.[73] In a legal sense, however, there is no institution which could force Parliament to obey these limitations.[74]

Parliamentary supremacy, however, does not seem to be unfettered. It is mitigated by the second pillar of the UK constitution, the rule of law. In the words of Lord Bridge in a 1990 House of Lords case:

> In our society the Rule of Law rests upon twin foundations: the sovereignty of the Queen in Parliament in making the law and the sovereignty of the Queen's courts in interpreting and applying the law.[75]

The courts traditionally smooth constitutionally sensitive legislation by way of interpretation. Before 2000, when the Human Rights Act 1998 (HRA) came into force, they did so on the basis of a presumption that Parliament could not have

---

[68]Goldsworthy (1999), p. 243.

[69]Ibid., p. 242–243.

[70]If the sovereignty of Parliament should be qualified as a matter of law or as political fact is subject to debate. See Wade (1955), pp. 172, 189 and Goldsworthy (2010) 123–126.

[71]Griffith (1979), p. 15.

[72]Bellamy (2011), pp. 86, 92.

[73]See also below, para 6.1.

[74]Goldsworthy (1999), p. 266. See for a critique on his distinction on legal and extra-legal constraints on Parliament's law-making power, Allan (2013), pp. 156–161.

[75]*X v Morgan-Grampian Publishers Ltd* [1991] 1 AC 1 HL (4 April 1990) (Lord Bridge).

intended to legislate contrary to certain common-law rights.[76] Since then, the HRA explicitly empowers courts to interpret legislation 'as far as possible' consistently with the right enshrined in the Act.[77] Even so, it is controversial to what extent the rule of law empowers courts to act as guardians against legislative abuse.[78] Although the courts may try to interpret legislation creatively, they are still not allowed to openly quash Acts of Parliament violating rule of law principles. It is not entirely clear just how far the courts can take common-law presumptions. Courts have, undoubtedly, sometimes used them to frustrate legislative intent in the past.[79] Indeed, there is some force in the argument that there is, in practice, little difference between the practice of invalidation and a bold use of common-law presumptions.[80] Yet, this view is by no means universally shared.[81]

Having said that, it is worth noting that this traditional political conception of the UK constitution has increasingly come under fire.[82] Over the recent decades, UK Parliament has been faced with new legal and political obligations as a result of the recognition of the supremacy of EU law, the devolution of powers to the governments of Scotland, Wales and Northern Ireland and the incorporation of the ECHR by the Human Rights Act. These developments have had both direct and indirect consequences for parliamentary sovereignty as such. Direct, because although it might be argued that Parliament could restore its legislative supremacy by explicitly repealing the legislation recognizing these obligations, that may not be so realistic from a political perspective.[83] Indirect, because particularly the development of European (human rights) law has, together with other global factors, contributed to the judicialization of the UK constitutional structure.[84] As a result, judicial attitude may have changed somewhat over the years. This was illustrated by Lord Hope when he said, in *R (Jackson) v Attorney General,* that:

> Parliamentary sovereignty is no longer, if it ever was, absolute [...] Step by step, gradually but surely, the English principle of the absolute legislative sovereignty of Parliament [...] is being qualified [...] The rule of law enforced by the courts is the ultimate controlling factor on which our constitution is based.[85]

What this teaches us is that parliamentary sovereignty, and with it the distinct 'all the way' political character of the UK constitution, is on a road to uncertainty. However, that should not cloud the fact that parliamentary primacy in shaping the

---

[76]See: Allan (1985).

[77]See Human Rights Act 1998, s 3.

[78]Allan (2001).

[79]See e.g., *Anisminic v FCC* [1969] 2 AC 147, HL (17 December 1968) (pre-HRA) and *R v A* [2001] *UKHL* 25, HL (17 May 2001) (under the HRA).

[80]Allan (1993), p. 267.

[81]See for a critique e.g., Goldsworthy (2008), pp. 277, 302.

[82]See e.g., Barber (2011), p. 144 and Bogdanor (2009), pp. 271–290.

[83]See e.g., Kavanagh (2009), pp. 305–307 and Elliott (2002), p. 340.

[84]These global factors have been frequently described by Hirschl (2006), p. 721.

[85][2005] UKHL 56 (13 October 2005), para 104, 107.

constitution is still its current foundational principle. Nothing makes this clearer perhaps, than Sect. 4 of the Human Rights Act, which was introduced to enable some form of judicial rights review of legislation against ECHR rights while maintaining parliamentary sovereignty.[86] Though courts may not be able to invalidate primary legislation, they can signal their concerns to the political branches. To that end, Sect. 4 empowers them to issue a so-called declaration of incompatibility. Such a declaration is neither binding for the political actors, nor does it affect the validity of the Act in question. It firmly places Parliament at the centre of a dialogue between the courts, the executive and the legislature, about the proper trade-off between rights and public policy.[87] According to at least a substantial part of academic literature in the UK, the last say in this dialogue belongs to Parliament.[88]

In this constitutional climate, it is hardly likely that the courts assume the role as ultimate interpreters of the constitution. This conclusion is strengthened by the fact that the UK courts, unlike their German or American counterparts, are generally unwilling to interfere in the political process itself. Matters of political and legislative procedure are considered non-justiciable.[89] The examples we mentioned in the previous paragraph are thus very unlikely to occur in the UK. This is not to say that they can *never* occur. The trend of judicialization, we mentioned before, provides ample reason for caution. One would perhaps not have expected the Lords of Appeal to accept the 2005 *Jackson* case, which concerned the procedural validity of the Hunting Act 2004. The fact that they did, arguing that the case concerned a question of law which could not, as such, be resolved by Parliament but which— from of rule of law perspective—had to be decided, echoes the reasoning of the US Supreme Court in *Powell*. Yet, unlike the American example, *Jackson* remains relatively exceptional.[90] It remains to be seen whether the traditional British reluctance to interfere with the political process is indeed gradually giving way to judicial constitutionalism.

---

[86]See Young (2009), pp. 10–11.

[87]This is what Aruna Sathanapally calls, the 'dual review model' of dialogue. Interestingly, Sathanapally argues that s. 4 of the HRA did not achieve the true 'dual review' version of dialogue. Sathanapally (2012), pp. 48, 224.

[88]See e.g., Campbell (2001). Admittedly, a different view is quite as influential. See e.g., Feldman (2007).

[89]*Pickin v British Railways Board* [1974] AC 765 HL (30 January 1974).

[90]*R (Jackson) v Attorney General* (2005), para 27 (Lord Bingham). Another, more recent, instance of a case in which a UK court decided on a largely political matter may be *R (Miller) v Secretary of State for Exiting the European Union* [2017] UKSC 5 (24 January 2017). In the *Miller* case, the UK Supreme Court ruled that the UK Government was not allowed to invoke the procedure for withdrawal from the European Union (the so-called Article 50 procedure) without an Act of Parliament allowing the Government to do so. This case could also be seen as a clear example of court interference with the political process. It could be argued that this was a non-justiciable issue, since Parliament itself could also have claimed decision authority on the UK's withdrawal from the EU through political means.

In short, although there are important qualifications, we conclude that the UK constitution—for the time being—is still very much dominated by the political branches of government. Parliamentary sovereignty makes it, in principle, very hard to identify limits to the constitutional powers of the legislature. Notwithstanding their own important role in shaping the constitution, British courts are currently unlikely to engage in a direct confrontation with Parliament.

4.2 The Netherlands

The constitution of the Netherlands similarly seems to have a political character. There are several important differences though. In the first place, the Netherlands, unlike the UK, has a written Constitution. It is clear, however, that this Constitution is far from exhaustive. Indeed one of the hallmarks of Dutch constitutionalism is that there are vast fields of constitutional law that are either not codified or not entirely controlled by the Constitution. The political process is to a large extent regulated by unwritten rules and conventions.[91] Moreover, the bill of rights lacks several important rights, such as the rights to a fair trial and family life. However, the fact that there is a codified Constitution containing a bill of rights does mean that Parliament in the Netherlands is, at least conceptually, not as supreme as its British counterpart.[92] It cannot, in the words of Dicey, 'make or unmake any law whatever'.[93] Its powers are limited by the Constitution. Still, the Netherlands comes relatively close to a concept of parliamentary sovereignty. The Constitution itself reserves the ultimate say on the constitutionality of primary legislation to Parliament. It does so in article 120 of the Constitution, which reads:

The constitutionality of Acts of Parliament and Treaties shall not be reviewed by the courts.

Article 120 is taken to be a clear expression that matters of constitutionality are a political matter, best left for Parliament. Herein lies its relevance for our present inquiry, perhaps even more than in its prohibition of judicial review as such. In real life, the significance of this ban of judicial review is greatly diminished by the fact that the Constitution does allow the courts to review Acts of Parliament against treaty law. It does so in article 94, where it establishes the supremacy of treaty over statutory law. The combination of Article 120 and the Articles 93 and 94 of the Constitution attributes a rather exotic status to regular statute law. On the one hand, the courts cannot review the compatibility of Acts of Parliament with the domestic

---

[91]One of the cornerstones of the constitution at large, the unwritten rule that the government depends parliamentary support is exemplary in this regard.

[92]Uzman et al. (2011), p. 671.

[93]Dicey (1959), pp. 39–40.

Constitution. On the other hand, the courts have developed a rather rich jurisprudence on the basis of international human rights law, notably the ECHR.[94] This has led to a situation in which the relevance of the domestic bill of rights has greatly diminished.

More importantly, however, article 120 is of crucial importance to the way in which both the courts and Parliament define their respective roles. Its significance is thus of a more indirect nature. The Supreme Court of the Netherlands (*Hoge Raad*) has consistently held that article 120 is to be interpreted broadly. It also prohibits, for instance, review of legislation against unwritten legal principles.[95] Moreover, article 120 is also taken to prevent courts from engaging in procedural review of the constitutionality of legislation.[96] Several judgments show the Court's reluctance to interfere with the political process. In the 1999 *Tegelen* judgment, for example, it ruled that questions of legislative procedure and political propriety were matters for Parliament itself to consider.[97] In a similar vein, the Court has consistently refused to issue injunctions requiring the State to produce or withdraw legislation. This, according to the Court, is a political matter from which the courts should steer clear.[98] Even if Dutch courts have a mandate to engage in strong-form review of legislation, it is thus highly unlikely that they would ever interfere with the political process in a way reminiscent of the examples we discussed in the previous paragraph.

So what does this all mean for the role of the courts with regard to constitutional amendments? That is not an easy question in the Dutch context, if only because of the complexity brought about by the combination of articles 120 and 94 of the Constitution. Traditionally, the Dutch constitution is a typical politically enforced constitution in the sense that it prescribes no limitations to the amendment powers of Parliament (in its constitutional capacity) and that it leaves matters of constitutionality to Parliament. Because the written Constitution is amended by an Act of Parliament, it is—according to article 120—Parliament itself who decides whether its amendment complies with the structure of the constitution or with unwritten constitutional principles. But what if such an amendment would violate the European Convention? Article 94 of the Constitution suggests that the courts would then be able to interfere. We do not exclude that possibility, but it would still be unlikely. Quite apart from the question whether article 94 of the Constitution also establishes the supremacy of treaty law over the Constitution, which apart from EU law is not settled until now, Parliament would still be able to withdraw article 94 itself. This is not unthinkable given the fact that Parliament is currently considering

---

[94]Uzman et al. (2011).

[95]See the Court's *Harmonization Act Judgment*, NJ 1989/469 (14 April 1989).

[96]*Van den Bergh v. The State* 1963/248.

[97]*Tegelen v. Limburg*, NJ 2000/160 (19 November 1999).

[98]*Waterpakt v. The State*, NJ 2003/691 (21 March 2003) para 3.5; *The State v. Clara Wichmann Foundation*, NJ 2010/388 (9 April 2010) para 4.6.2.

such an amendment.[99] Such a withdrawal of their mandate to review would not be reviewable by the courts, unless the European Convention or any other international document would warrant domestic judicial review of statutory legislation. That is, however, still not the case.[100]

5 Unamendability in Politically Enforced Constitutions

As we said before, the concept of unamendability seems highly problematic in politically enforced constitutions. Neither the UK nor the Dutch Constitution prescribe any substantive limits to the amendment power of the legislature. The UK has no written constitution and flexibility of the unwritten version is mandated by the principle of sovereignty of parliament. The Netherlands, on the other hand, does operate a written Constitution, but it lacks any specific substantive unamendability clause. As we have seen, this need not be problematic, but neither is there any role for the courts to play in order to establish some kind of 'basic structure doctrine'. The fact that the courts are not allowed to assess either the procedural or the substantive constitutionality of ordinary, let alone constitutional, legislation, sees to that. In both legal systems, it is simply inconceivable that a court should invalidate a constitutional amendment.

That said, it is equally inconceivable that the courts would simply accept a constitutional amendment touching upon the fundamental principles of either of these constitutions. These principles are simply too deeply rooted for that. However, the judicial reaction in such cases would not be one of (direct) *invalidation*, but rather one of 'judicial disobedience' or 'deafness'. Although the courts, in effect, would render the amendment in question benign, this kind of unamendability, if one might call it so, is thus highly indirect. Two examples, drawn from each of the jurisdictions, might serve to illustrate this.[101]

---

[99]See the proposal of Liberal MP Joost Taverne to limit the reviewing power of the courts to subordinate legislation (*Parliamentary Papers* II 2011/12, 33 359, nr 1–3).

[100]See e.g., the European Court's judgment in *James & Ors v United Kingdom*, [1986] ECHR 2, Series A no 98 (21 February 1986): '*Article 13 does not go so far as to guarantee a remedy allowing a Contracting State's laws as such to be challenged before a national authority on the ground of being contrary to the Convention*'.

[101]The phenomenon of judicial disobedience is not exclusive to politically enforced constitutions. It may apply also to 'judicial supremacy systems' too. See, in the context of the United States, for instance the *Slaughter-house cases*, 83 US 36 (14 April 1873), in which the Supreme Court arguably exacerbated the privileges and immunities clause of the 14th Amendment. Relatedly, the enactment of the Religious Freedom Restoration Act in 1993 could be seen as a reaction to *Lyng v. Northwest Indian Cemetery Protective Association*, 485 US 439 (19 April 1988) and *Employment Division v. Smith*, 494 US 872 (17 April 1990), in which the Supreme Court upheld legislation that prohibited activities which were religiously prescribed.

5.1 Judicial Creativity and Deafness in the United Kingdom

As we have mentioned before, the UK system of rights protection is largely shaped by the Human Rights Act 1998. The Act incorporated most of the rights of the European Convention on Human Rights and allowed British courts to review both government and legislative action against those rights. The introduction of the HRA has been considered a constitutional earthquake. It has fundamentally changed the nature of English public law.[102] Before its introduction, the protection of individual freedom belonged largely to the realm of Parliament.[103] That did not always turn out well. In a book in 1990, British scholars Keith Ewing and Conor Gearty conclude that civil liberties are in a state of crisis.[104] The British political system, it emerges particularly in the 1970s and 1980s, is increasingly unable to protect individual freedoms against the security state, against discriminatory majoritarian views and against the brutal exercise of governmental powers against trade unions, hippies and journalists. Indeed, limitations of rights in legislation are often set in extremely broad terms. Because of parliamentary sovereignty, there is little courts can do in such cases.[105]

Thus, from the 1980s onward, there are political calls for an effective bill of rights and a judicial role in protecting those rights. These calls gradually take the shape of a call for the incorporation of the European Convention.[106] But the political system is slow to respond. Too slow for some. This legislative inertia tempts both judges and scholars to contemplate using the common law in order to develop an already existing body of liberties, inspired by the European Convention and the case law of the European Court.[107] However, it need not come that far. Shortly after the new Labour government takes over in 1997, it introduced the bill that ultimately led to the adoption of the Human Rights Act 1998.

The 1998 Act has radically transformed the position of the courts in the UK. Not only were they now empowered to review both acts of government agencies and Parliament against Convention rights, they also took the enactment of the HRA as a clear sign that Parliament had intended them to develop a sturdy approach towards the protection of human rights. This resulted, for instance, in stricter standards of review in administrative law, a rather bold use of their interpretative mandate under the HRA and an extensive dialogue between the UK courts and the European Court of Human Rights.[108] However, the initial success story of the Act turned against it as time progressed. Gradually the judicial protection of human rights came under attack, beginning with a growing dissatisfaction with the case law of the European

---

[102]See e.g., Elliott (2001), p. 197.

[103]Feldman (2002), pp. 70–74.

[104]Ewing and Gearty (1990), p. 255.

[105]See e.g., *R. v. Home Secretary Ex p Brind* [1991] 1 AC 696 (HL).

[106]Besson (2008), p. 40.

[107]See e.g., Laws (1995), p. 72 and Feldman (2009), p. 544.

[108]See Elliott (2001), p. 233 and Kavanagh (2004), p. 259, Kavanagh (2009), pp. 144–164.

Court of Human Rights.[109] This culminated in a, still ongoing, power struggle between Westminster and Strasbourg over prisoner voting.[110] But it did not stop there: the fight against terrorism and the effects of immigration were a powerful incentive for clashes between both the European Court and domestic courts on the one hand, and the government on the other.

This clash has immediate consequences for the HRA. The Act has never gained real popularity. 'The average person does not feel as though he or she owns it'.[111] Already in 2009, the leader of the Conservative Party, David Cameron, indicated that he will 'tear up the Human Rights Act'.[112] Instead, the Conservative government aims at introducing a British Bill of Rights. Moreover, recent proposals indicate that withdrawal of the European Convention, currently the cornerstone of UK fundamental rights law, is a real probability.[113] However, it is far from clear whether the purely domestic bill of rights envisaged by the Conservatives will still encompass judicial review of legislation. The basic idea behind the Conservatives proposals is after all, to limit the judicial role which, in the eyes of most prominent Conservatives, has led to excessive judicial activism.[114] Whether correct or not, for present purposes we assume that abolishment of the HRA will lead to a significant curbing of judicial power in Britain. This assumption is supported both by recent public remarks by prominent members of the Conservative party and by the reactions of judges and scholars to the proposed withdrawal of the HRA.[115] As early as 2010, the then President of the UK Supreme Court, Lord Phillips, indicated in a speech, that the HRA 'is here to stay'.[116]

How would the courts resist such a withdrawal from the European Convention and the possible departure of their mandate of review? As Mark Elliott has noted, one distinct possibility would be the court's renewed attention for the common law as an, admittedly somewhat modest, substitute for both the HRA and the Convention.[117] Indeed, there are signs that the recent discussions on the future of the HRA have prompted the UK Supreme Court to emphasize the role of the common law as a source of fundamental rights.[118] In a fairly recent line of cases, the Supreme Court has underlined the need for appellants to invoke the common law,

---

[109]See e.g., Hoffmann (2009).

[110]See e.g., Fredman (2013), p. 292.

[111]Arnot (2009).

[112]Palmer (2009).

[113]See Bates (2015).

[114]See e.g., Elliott (2013), p. 137.

[115]See e.g., Elliott (2015), p. 1.

[116]Porter and Hirsch (2010). More recently: '*The question is, can we go back? Can we tear up the Human Rights Convention and go back? ...I don't think we can*', Lord Phillips of Worth Matravers in a panel discussion at King's College London, 24 March 2015, report at <http://ukhumanrightsblog.com/2015/05/15/we-cannot-go-back-debating-the-human-rights-act-eva-pils/#more-25964> accessed on 14 July 2017.

[117]Elliott (2015).

[118]Ibid.

rather than the HRA and the Convention.[119] In *Kennedy v. Charity Commission,* Lord Mance, writing for a narrow majority, said:

> Since the passing of the Human Rights Act 1998, there has too often been a tendency to see the law in areas touched on by the Convention solely in terms of the Convention rights. But the Convention rights represent a threshold protection; and, especially in view of the contribution which common lawyers made to the Convention's inception, they may be expected, at least generally even if not always, to reflect and to find their homologue in the common or domestic statute law. [...] In some areas, the common law may go further than the Convention, and in some contexts it may also be inspired by the Convention rights and jurisprudence (the protection of privacy being a notable example). And in time, of course, a synthesis may emerge. But the natural starting point in any dispute is to start with domestic law, and it is certainly not to focus exclusively on the Convention rights, without surveying the wider common law scene. As Toulson LJ also said [...] "The development of the common law did not come to an end on the passing of the Human Rights Act 1998 [...]".[120]

These are not lone swallows. Baroness Hale, the current Deputy President of the Court, has openly suggested that common-law constitutionalism is on the March.[121] Neither should this be regarded as a mere coincidence. According to Mark Elliott:

> It arguably represents a renaissance in this area, as common-law constitutionalism emerges from the shadow of the Human Rights Act. One of the likely implications of this phenomenon may turn out to be that if the HRA ceases to cast any such shadow—by virtue of being repealed at the behest of a future government—the common-law constitutional landscape that is left behind may be remarkably similar to the situation that has obtained during the era of the HRA. Indeed, Kennedy suggests that, at least in some respects, the common law may already go further than corresponding provisions of the Convention.[122]

Should Elliott be correct, then one might argue that the Supreme Court is in effect resisting the kind of amendment of the UK constitution as envisaged by the current government. Why should it do so? Perhaps because the judicial enforcement of European human rights law is so deeply rooted in UK constitutional law, that— in the words of former Supreme court President, Lord Phillips—'we cannot go back'.[123] However, two remarks are in order.

First, unlike the examples mentioned in Sect. 2, this resistance would certainly not take the shape of an invalidation of such an amendment. There is nothing in the UK constitution that prevents Parliament from withdrawing the HRA or from leaving the European Convention.[124] Resistance would rather take the shape of a creative form of judicial disobedience or deafness. If the message of Parliament is

---

[119]See: *Osborn v. Parole Board* [2013] UKSC 61, [2014] AC 1115; *Kennedy v. Charity Commission* [2014] UKSC 20, [2014] 2 WLR 808; *R (Evans) v. Attorney General* [2015] UKSC 21.

[120]UKSC 20, [2014] 2 WLR 808, para 46.

[121]Hale (2014).

[122]Elliott (2014).

[123]See his recent remarks at a conference at King's College London (24 March 2015).

[124]European law, both in the framework of the EU and the Council of Europe, might pose some obstacles, but they do not concern us here.

that the courts should back off, the Supreme Court might choose not to fully understand such a message. But this 'deafness' is of course limited. It cannot pretend that the HRA, and with it its instruments, has not been withdrawn. This kind of judicial disobedience, therefore, needs some creativity: hence, the development of common-law constitutionalism as an alternative. Of course, Parliament can still respond by curbing the common law by statute, but that would, first, be extremely difficult, and would probably provoke a true constitutional crisis. Question is, whether Parliament would truly want to take such a risk.

Our second observation is that any judicial alternative would probably not provide the same degree of protection, the HRA has to offer. Common-law constitutionalism would, in other words, provide some kind of backup, but the possibilities of judicial law-making in this respect are of course limited.[125] This marks a second difference with the examples of constitutional amendability, most notably taken from the case law of the Indian Supreme Court, we mentioned before. Where invalidation would—in most cases—lead to a return to the previous *status quo*, the kind of covert unamendability we have described here only leads to a partial revival.

5.2 Judicial Disobedience in the Netherlands

As an example of covert unamendability in the Netherlands, might serve the case law of the Dutch Supreme Court regarding the principle of legality. In 1879 the Constitution of the Netherlands did not provide sufficient guidance as to the principle of legality. The development of this principle began as early as 1879, in which year the Supreme Court ruled that the government is only allowed to enact *delegated* legislation, i.e. rules with regard to subjects of which the legislative branch has explicitly attributed the regulation to the government.[126] The legislature, however, found that this would not give sufficient leeway to the government. Therefore, it is provided in the 1889 Constitution that the government should have its own powers to enact general rules in the form of an Order-in-council except for general rules that are enforced by penal sanctions.[127]

In two landmark cases, the Supreme Court decided that the Dutch constitution does not only require a legal basis for measures that are enforced by penal sanctions. The first of these cases, *Fluoridering* (Fluoridation), dealt with the decision of a local authority in Amsterdam, which allowed the local water company to add fluoride to tap water of all people in the City in order to promote public health.

---

[125]See Elliott (2015).

[126]*Meerenberg*, W 4330 (13 January 1879).

[127]This follows from the current Article 89(1) and (2) of the Constitution of the Netherlands, which stipulates: 'Orders in council shall be established by Royal Decree.' A Royal Decree is a decree of the government.

The Supreme Court condemned this measure since it did not rely on a basis in an Act of Parliament. The Court deemed a legal basis for this measure necessary since it was of 'such a fundamental nature that it could not be assumed to fall within the scope of the task of the water company without an explicit basis in an Act of Parliament'.[128] The second case, *Methadonbrief* (Methadone Letter), involved the status of a letter issued by a group chief inspectors of public health to all general practitioners, asking to cease to provide methadone to drug addicts.[129] When a chief inspector of the Dutch Health Inspection learned that a doctor did not adhere to this request, he urged the pharmacists in the area to ignore the prescriptions of this doctor. The general practitioner involved challenged the issuance of the methadone letter. As a result, the Court held that this exercise of power could not be permitted, as there is no Act of Parliament attributing the competence to general practitioners to issue guidance as to the way in which they engage in their profession.[130] Although the issuance of letter involved just a request (and not a binding norm), it could, according to the Court, in fact, be equated to the exercise of power that requires a basis in an Act of Parliament in order to be lawful.

This requirement does not stem from the Constitution, which does not require an express legal basis for measures which are not enforced by penal sanctions. The Supreme Court has thus extended the scope of Article 89 of the Constitution by holding that also other measures involving legal or actual exercise of power require a basis in an Act of Parliament. Interestingly, in later years, the legislator generally agreed with the interpretation of the legality principle by the Supreme Court but deemed amendment of Article 89 unnecessary.[131] The legislator opined that the entrenchment of current interpretation of the legality principle by the courts would not have any added value in practice. The extension of the legality principle is, therefore, regarded to be mainly determined by the case law of the Supreme Court. As a result, it is generally agreed that the government does not have a mandate to autonomously issue general binding norms, even though the Constitution of the Netherlands provides that it does have such a mandate.[132]

Again, the example of legality in the dialogue between the Dutch Supreme Court and the constitutional legislature shows that any amendment by the legislature is not as such invalidated by the Court. Concerns are rather converted into an alternative judge-made arrangement. And again, the outcome of this dialogue might not be what either of the branches had envisaged at the outset. Rather, what follows is something of a compromise between the two key players in the discussion.

---

[128]*Fluoridering*, NJ 1973/386 (22 June 1973).

[129]*Methadonbrief*, NJ 1987/898 (27 June 1986).

[130]Ibid. para 3.3.

[131]*Parliamentary Proceeding of the Second Chamber* (*Kamerstukken II*) 1977/78, 15 047 (R 1099), nr 3, 15.

[132]However, some authors still believe that the government may, and perhaps should, make more use of the competence to autonomously issue Orders-in-Council. See, notably, Donner (2013).

6 Constitutional Conventions as a Model

The examples drawn from the UK and the Netherlands mainly serve to teach us two things. First, the absence of either an eternity clause or a judicial 'basic structure doctrine' in both systems does not imply that amendment of the constitution cannot, in practice, be contested. There are informal mechanisms of obstruction that operate as a kind of 'covert principles of unamendability'. One might say that they complement, in a way, the constructive unamendability identified by Albert a year ago.[133] However, the nature of this kind of unamendability is radically different from the regular forms we have touched upon in the first two sections of this chapter. As we have seen, the form of unamendability is not one of invalidation, but rather of judicial creativity and disobedience. But more importantly, perhaps, this judicial creativity cannot always produce the same results, subject as it is to all kinds of political constraints. As we have seen, the end product of judicial disobedience is likely to be some sort of new arrangement, a compromise. Thus, because of its extremely informal nature, covert unamendability may perhaps not be as tough as regular forms of unamendability. What it needs is some kind of model, to help explain its features.

We think this model may be found in the concept of constitutional conventions. Rather than a clear rule, whether written or judge-made, that a particular constitutional concept is unamendable, covert unamendability triggers the emergence of a particular *convention* that the legislature will not abolish or significantly alter a given constitutional arrangement. The enforcement of such a convention—if it may be called so—is, as we have seen, a matter of disobedience on the part of the other branches of government, notably the courts. In order to gain a deeper understanding of this kind of convention, let us first turn to an inquiry in the nature of constitutional conventions in general.

6.1 The Nature of Constitutional Conventions

In politically enforced constitutions, the final word about the application of a particular constitutional provision is not given by the courts, but rather by the political branches, i.e. the legislature and the executive. The power of these branches are primarily curbed in political sense. That is not to say that they will enact any legislation whatever. On the contrary, a political constitution only works well if the legislature adheres to certain self-imposed moral and political constraints, of which many of them are regarded as constitutional conventions.[134] They originate from the constitutional doctrine of the UK, in which context Dicey has referred to them as 'the conventions, understandings, habits or practices' regulating the

---

[133]Albert (2014a).
[134]Goldsworthy (1999), pp. 302–303.

conduct of the several members of the sovereign power and complementing the legal rules of the constitution.[135] The existence of a convention is usually determined by the application of the Jennings test.[136] According to this test, three questions have to be answered:

> First, what are the precedents; secondly, did the actors in the precedents believe that they were bound by a rule; and thirdly, is there a reason for the rule?[137]

Constitutional conventions are thus not mere precedents, nor mere rules, but a combination of both. A mere practice of a particular office holder can develop into a convention from the moment that others increasingly expect him to act in conformity with this practice.[138] The expectation that an institution will continue to follow a practice may have different causes, varying *inter alia* from a settlement about the interpretation of a constitutional principle which two rivals in the constitution may have reached, to a simple need for efficiency in the political process. In this sense, conventions can be compared to the lithograph 'Drawing hands' (1948) by the Dutch artist M.C. Escher, which depicts two hands that draw each other since the precedents simultaneously create the reason for the convention and vice versa.[139] The coexistence of the precedents and the reasons subsequently create the belief among the responsible institutions are bound by the convention, which is the final component of these social rules. From these characteristics, it follows that the actor involved will experience a convention as *prescriptive*.[140]

Constitutional conventions issue a moral dimension to politically enforced constitutions by subjecting the legal supremacy of the political actors to extra-legal (i.e. moral and political) constraints.[141] It is by means of convention, for instance, that the UK Parliament will never pass the 'Abolition of the Democracy Act' or the 'Murder of Blue Babies Act'.[142] Political constitutions can thus only be properly understood if both the legal rules and the applicable conventions surrounding the constitution are also taken into account.

The conventions of the constitution give voice to the way in which institutions deploy their power in practice. Constitutions attribute different tasks and objectives to the different institutions of the state, which are likely to result in tension or

---

[135]Dicey (1959), p. 24.

[136]Jennings (1959), p. 136.

[137]Ibid.

[138]Jaconelli (2005), pp. 149, 168–176.

[139]One precedent may however be enough to constitute a convention, see Jennings (1959), p. 136.

[140]Compare the distinction between 'positive' and 'critical morality'. Those who advance the positive morality view consider conventions as a description of the applicable moral values in the arena of politics, whereas those who promote the critical morality argue that a more critical stance is needed. Only the conventions which ought to be considered as binding should be properly termed so. See Marshall (1986).

[141]Marshall (1986), p. 7.

[142]Stephen (1882), p. 137 and Dicey (1959), p. 81.

disagreement.[143] In this constellation, every institution aims to maintain the authority which it has acquired or may even compete for more power with other institutions.[144] The relationship within and between institutions can, therefore, be seen as a 'domain of continuing tensions', which sometimes may slowly evolve in 'a process of mutual accommodation'.[145] Conventions are the reflection of the settlements which one or more institutions may have reached. The ongoing competition within and between institutions is not regulated by fixed rules. Neither has a pre-eminent body been appointed to settle disputes between institutions. Disputes on the basis of constitutional conventions thus have to be settled in practice. The resulting settlements will necessarily be only temporary since institutions can call each resolution for a constitutional problem continuously into question.[146]

As opposed to law, conventions appear in a great variety of normative standards with a similarly diverging binding force. This is due to the lack of uniformity of constitutional conventions. Moreover, conventions may in all regards be subject to change, including their bindingness. This explains why the content of conventions cannot be judicially determined: only the political institutions which are involved in the convention concerned can determine its meaning and operation.[147] Indeed, the position of the courts may also be subject to the content of a particular convention, which renders the courts to some extent self-interested as to the content of particular conventions.[148] In other words, conventions may not have a role to play *in* the case law of the courts, but they are relevant *for* the courts as political actors themselves.

In default of a body that could settle disputes between institutions, conventions are merely 'self-policing'. The binding force of a convention particularly depends on the inherent values of a convention, which are inherently linked to the ideals and values of a particular constitutional tradition.[149] As was seen before, conventions are based on often conflicting principles as democracy, the rule of law or the independence of the judiciary.[150] The breach of a convention will thus raise a question of principle. Whether the breach of a convention will be regarded as unconstitutional depends on the actual content of the convention involved and on the constitutional value at stake. A breach that can be considered unconstitutional will usually be uttered in the language of 'wrong-doing, of moving the goal posts, of not playing the game, of failing to respect established values, and so on'.[151] Breaches of conventions which do not have to be couched in this terminology may

---

[143]Morton (1991–92), p. 114, 157–158. See also Feldman (2005), pp. 329, 334, (2011), pp. 117, 123.

[144]Morton (1991–92), pp. 165–166.

[145]Ibid., p. 165.

[146]This is particularly peculiar to political constitutions, see Griffith (1979), p. 20.

[147]Dicey (1959) 422–423.

[148]Morton (1991–92), p. 171.

[149]Ibid., p. 169.

[150]Ibid., pp. 173–174.

[151]Ibid., p. 142.

be allowed, for instance, because they preserve another constitutional value, or may point at the end of the operation of a convention.[152] Institutions may be willing to respect those values or not. However, that is not the only relevant aspect which attributes binding force to constitutional conventions. Some conventions may pose an obligation in a political sense. In such a case, political actors will refrain from violating the standards they have set in particular conventions rather than violating these standards on the basis of their short-term personal interests. They may thus bind institutions on the basis that today's minority may become a majority in the future.[153] In many cases, however, the ethical and political reasons for adhering to constitutional conventions cannot be separated, since conventions comprise both precedent and constitutional values.[154]

It is not always simple to determine whether a convention exists.[155] This raises the question whether how much consensus is needed in order to determine that a convention actually exists.[156] Even the (constitutional) legislator does not have a decisive voice about how disagreement between institutions in the political context should be resolved.[157] Admittedly, a statute or a Constitution might stipulate a sort of settlement for a conflict within an institution or between institutions. However, the actual effect of such legislation remains ultimately dependent on its application by the institutions involved. Moreover, conventions are not dependent on legal structures. They can thus be adjusted after a change with regard to the political and/ or normative views of the political institutions involved. The only requirement for change is thus, as opposed to legal or constitutional change, the consent of the institutions involved.

6.2 Constitutional Conventions and Covert Constitutional Unamendability

What does all this teach us with regard to the existence of a possible constitutional convention of unamendability? First that any principle of unamendability in the politically enforced constitutions such as we have identified is not of a binding nature. This is different for both the judicial enforcement of an eternity clause or for a judicial 'basic structure doctrine'. In both cases, the rule of unamendability is, as a matter of doctrine, part of the Constitution and thus shares in its binding force. The fact that conventions of unamendability have no binding force, does not mean that the courts will not enforce this kind of unamendability. If the amendment

---

[152]The definition of principle here is drawn from Dworkin (1977), 22–28.

[153]Jaconelli (2005), p. 176. See also Jaconelli (2015).

[154]Allan (2013), p. 65.

[155]Munro (1975).

[156]Feldman (2013).

[157]Jaconelli (2005), p. 167.

introduced encroaches upon their powers or on the tasks that they were—explicitly or implicitly—assigned by the constitution, they will usually act. It does mean that this enforcement is of a political nature. It will usually be in the form of a political reaction, by using the judicial powers in such a way that the institutional interests are best protected.

As we have seen, ignoring a convention by one institution may induce another institution to ignore some other convention. In the case of court-legislature dialogue, this will usually be the conventions that regulate the proper judicial role in the framework of the separation of powers. An unconventional role by the legislature thus provokes an unconventional judicial role. However, this role is—again—subject to powerful political constraints. The courts, even if they step outside their traditional role, cannot do anything. Thus, the end result of a court-legislature dialogue provoked by the violation of a convention of unamendability will usually end in a new settlement, somewhere in the middle. The flexible nature of conventions then enables all three branches of government to maintain that the new settlement was part of the original convention all along.

Last but not least, the nature of conventions as political and flexible norms on the functioning of institutions, renders the decision to enforce (or not to enforce) a convention of unamendability essentially of a political nature. It is ultimately a judicial assessment of the political gains and losses institutionally, that determines whether the courts will interfere with the legislative decision to amend. In a way, the same kind of balancing will probably take place in the 'regular types' of unamendability review. The Indian or Pakistani Supreme Courts will, no doubt, have had their thoughts on the prudence, in terms of institutional politics, of the decision whether not to interfere with the constitutional amendments they were confronted with. What makes the convention-type of unamendability stand apart though is that this kind of assessment is not a by-product of the judicial decision, but a matter of principle connected to the idea that the convention (and its enforcement) is a more political rather than a legal rule.

7 Concluding Remarks: 'Which in Our Case We Have not Got'?

Some years ago, Professor David Feldman drew a parallel with a poem by Henry Reed—a parody of British army basic training during World War II, which suffered from a lack of equipment at the time—to underline the different nature of the UK constitution as opposed to written constitutions.[158] Addressing his fellow citizens, he described the essentials of a written constitution and finally added: 'Which in Your Case, You Have Not Got'.

---

[158]Feldman (2005).

We have asked ourselves in the introduction of this chapter, whether the same holds true for constitutional unamendability. Whether such a concept is something that inherently belongs to legal systems that have a strong tradition of judicial review. It seems to us that most legal scholars, in painting a picture of the concept of constitutional unamendability, rely rather heavily on legal systems that have installed a constitutional court, or at least a supreme court with strong powers of judicial review. It would be useful, to our mind, to conceptually distinguish between—what we have provisionally coined—politically and judicially enforced constitutions. In the United Kingdom and the Netherlands, the concept of constitutional unamendability seems, at first sight, to be fully out of place. To quote Reed again: 'Which in Our Case We Have Not Got'.

But is that really true? We think not. We have argued that there are mechanisms, both in the UK and in the Netherlands, that mitigate the effects of amendments to the constitution that might be considered at odds with its essential features. These are not formal mechanisms, nor do they make it entirely impossible for legislatures to change the constitution. Rather, they are a covert version of unamendability in the way that they tend to divert the legislative amendment from its original course, towards a more benign settlement. The nature of this kind of unamendability is thus somewhat different from the unamendability that regularly features in comparative constitutional law. It is first and foremost a political exercise, rather than a legal one. In acting as the guardians of the existing constitution, the courts operate, not so much as interpreters or enforcers of that constitution, but as political actors defending their institutional realm.

We have argued that the norm against amendment, in these cases, is not a legal or binding rule but a constitutional convention. It reflects the idea that the legislature will not abolish or significantly alter a given constitutional arrangement. The enforcement of such a convention is a matter of judicial disobedience. It will not always be available or practical. In this, it might conceptually differ from the enforcement of the more well-known forms of unamendability. But eventually, we do not think that this difference will amount to much in practice. Whether law or convention, the enforcement of the idea that some parts of the constitution are 'eternal' is highly problematic and of a political nature.

Our research has, however, been anything but exhausting. It first has been limited to only two constitutional systems. Other politically enforced constitutions, such as those of the Nordic countries and Japan, may have somewhat different features, which may be included in further scholarship on unamendability in politically enforced constitutions. Second, the model of constitutional conventions that we outlined in this chapter could be further refined. Our future efforts should be directed towards a better understanding of the political nature of unamendability. The main objective of our chapter was to show the relevance of unamendability doctrine to politically enforced constitutions. The constitutional convention model might serve an important purpose here, perhaps even far beyond the realm of politically enforced constitutions.

Acknowledgements We are grateful to Richard Albert and Bertil Emrah Oder for the opportunity to present our paper at the Koç University & Boston College Law School ICON-S Workshop on unamendable constitutional provisions. We thank the participants of the workshop and an anonymous peer reviewer for their helpful advice. Naturally, the usual disclaimer applies

References

Albert R (2008) Counterconstitutionalism. Dalhousie Law J 31:37
Albert R (2009) Nonconstitutional amendments. Can J Law Jurisprud 22:5
Albert R (2010) Constitutional handcuffs. Arizona State Law J 43:663
Albert R (2014a) Constructive unamendability in Canada and the United States. Supreme Court Law Rev 67:181
Albert R (2014b) Constitutional disuse or desuetude: the case of article V. Boston U Law Rev 94:1029, 1073
Albert R (2015a) Amending constitutional amendment rules. Int J Const Law 3:655
Albert R (2015b) The unamendable core of the United States constitution. In: Koltay A (ed) Comparative perspectives on the fundamental freedom of expression. Wolters Kluwer
Allan TRS (1985) Legislative supremacy and the rule of law: democracy and constitutionalism. CLJ 44:111
Allan TRS (1993) Law, liberty and justice: The legal foundations of British constitutionalism. OUP, p 267
Allan TRS (2001) Constitutional justice: a liberal theory of justice. OUP
Allan TRS (2013) The Sovereignty of law: freedom, constitution and common law. OUP, pp 156–161
Andeweg RB, Irwin GA (2014) Governance and politics of the Netherlands. Palgrave Macmillan, p 167
Arnot C (2009) Ruling class: interview with Vernon Bogdanor. The Guardian, London, 17 February 2009. https://www.theguardian.com/education/2009/feb/17/vernon-bogdanor. Accessed on 14 July 2017
Barak A (2011) Unconstitutional constitutional amendments. Israel Law Rev 44:321
Barber NW (2011) The afterlife of parliamentary Sovereignty. Int J Const Law 9:144
Bates E (2015) The UK and Strasbourg: a strained relationship—the long view. In: Ziegler KS, Wicks E, Hodson L (eds) The UK and European human rights: a strained relationship? Hart
Bellamy R (2011) Political constitutionalism and the human rights act. Int J Const Law 9:86, 92
Bernal C (2013) Unconstitutional constitutional amendments in the case study of Colombia: an analysis of the justification and meaning of the constitutional replacement doctrine. Int J Const Law 11:339
Besson S (2008) The reception process in Ireland and the United Kingdom. In: Keller H, Stone-Sweet A (eds) A Europe of rights: the impact of the ECHR on national legal systems. OUP, p 40
Bezemek C (2011) Constitutional core(s): amendments, entrenchments, eternities and beyond—Prolegomena to a theory of normative volatility. J Jurisprud 11:517
Bogdanor V (2009) The New British constitution. Hart, pp 271–290
Campbell T (2001) Incorporation through interpretation. In Campbell T, Ewing K, Tomkins A (eds) Sceptical essays on human rights. OUP
Cariás AB (2011) Constitutional courts as positive legislators: a comparative law study. CUP, Chapter 2
Colón-Ríos J (2013) Beyond parliamentary sovereignty and judicial supremacy: the doctrine of implicit limits to constitutional reform in Latin America. Victoria U Wellington Law Rev 44:521

Colón-Ríos J (2014) A new typology of judicial review of legislation. Glob Constitutionalism 3:143

Dicey AV (1959) Introduction to the study of the law of the constitution. Macmillan, pp 3–4

Donner JPH (2013) The principle of legality revisited. In van Roosmalen M et al (eds) Fundamental rights and principles. Intersentia

Dworkin R (1977) Taking rights seriously. Duckworth, pp 22–28

Elliott M (2001) The constitutional foundations of judicial review. Hart, p 197

Elliott M (2002) Parliamentary Sovereignty and the new constitutional order: legislative freedom, political reality and convention. LS 22:340

Elliott M (2013) A Damp Squib in the long grass: the report of the commission on a bill of rights. Europ Human Rights Law Rev 137

Elliott M (2014) Common-law constitutionalism and proportionality in the supreme court. Kennedy v the Charity Commission. http://publiclawforeveryone.com/2014/03/31/common-law-constitutionalism-and-proportionality-in-the-supreme-court-kennedy-v-the-charity-commission/. Accessed on 14 July 2017

Elliott M (2015) Beyond the European convention: human rights and the common law. CLP 68:1

Ewing KD, Gearty CA (1990) Freedom under thatcher: civil liberties in modern Britain. OUP, p 255

Feldman D (2002) Civil liberties and human rights in England and Wales, 2nd ed. OUP, pp 70–74

Feldman D (2005) None, one or several? Perspectives on the UK's constitution. CLJ 64:329, 334

Feldman D (2007) Institutional roles and meanings of compatibility under the human rights act 1998. In: Fenwick H, Masterman R, Phillipson G (eds) Judicial reasoning under the human rights act. CUP

Feldman D (2009) Human rights. In: Blom-Cooper L, Dickson B, Drewry G (eds) The judicial house of lords 1876–2009. OUP, p 544

Feldman D (2011) Which in you case you have not got: constitutionalism at home and abroad. CLP 64:117, 123

Feldman D (2013) Constitutional conventions. In: Qvortrup M (ed) The British constitution: continuity and change. A Festschrift for Vernon Bogdanor. Hart, p 106

Fredman S (2013) From dialogue to deliberation: human rights adjudication and prisoners' rights to vote. PL 292

Garlicki L, Garlicka Z (2011) External review of constitutional amendments? International law as norm of reference. Israel Law Rev 44:343, 343

Goldsworthy J (1999) The Sovereignty of Parliament: history and philosophy. OUP, p 243

Goldsworthy J (2008) Unwritten constitutional principles. In: Huscroft G (ed) Expounding the constitution: essays in constitutional theory. CUP, pp 277, 302

Goldsworthy J (2010) Parliamentary Sovereignty: contemporary debates. CUP, pp 123–126

Gözler K (2008) Judicial review of constitutional amendments. Ekin Press

Green T (2010) The resistance to minarets in Europe. J Church State 52:619

Griffith JAG (1979) The political constitution. MLR 42:15

Hale H (2014) UK constitutionalism on the March? In: Keynote address to the constitutional and administrative law bar association conference. https://www.supremecourt.uk/docs/speech-140712.pdf. Accessed 14 July 2017.

Halmai G (2012) Unconstitutional constitutional amendments: constitutional courts as guardians of the constitution? Constellations 19:182

Hirschl R (2006) The new constitution and the judicialization of pure politics worldwide. Fordham Law Rev 75:721

Hirschl R (2008) The judicialization of mega-politics and the rise of political courts. Annu Rev Political Sci 11:93

Hoffmann L (2009) The Universality of human rights. Judicial Studies Board Annual Lecture, 19 March 2009. http://www.brandeis.edu/ethics/pdfs/internationaljustice/biij/BIIJ2013/hoffmann.pdf. Accessed on 14 July 2017

Jacobsohn G (2006) An unconstitutional constitution? A comparative perspective? Int J Const Law 4:460

Jacobsohn G (2009) Constitutional identity. Harvard University Press, p 82

Jaconelli J (2005) Do constitutional conventions bind? CLJ 64:149, 168–176

Jaconelli J (2015) The proper role for constitutional conventions. DULJ 38:363, 368

Jennings SI (1959) The law and the constitution, 3rd ed. London University Press, p 136

Kavanagh A (2004) The elusive divide between interpretation and legislation under the human rights act 1998. OJLS 24:259

Kavanagh A (2009) Constitutional review under the human rights act. CUP, UK

Laws J (1995) Law and democracy. PL 72

Marshall G (1986) Constitutional conventions: the rules and forms of political accountability. Clarendon Press, pp 10–12

Matsui S (2011) Why is the Japanese supreme court so conservative? Washington U Law Rev 88:1375, 1413

Mazzone J (2005) Unamendments. Iowa Law Rev 90:1747

Morton PA (1991–92) Conventions of the British constitution. Holdsworth Law Rev 15:114, 157–158

Munro CR (1975) Laws and conventions distinguished. LQR 91:218, 222

O'Connell R (1999) Guardians of the constitution: unconstitutional constitutional norms. J Civ Liberties 4:48

Otto JM (2007) The compatibility of Sharia with the rule of law. Fundamental conflict: between civilisations? Within civilisations? Or between scholars?. In: Groen A et al (eds) Knowledge in ferment: dilemmas in science, scholarship and society. Leiden University Press, p 137

Özbudun E (2009) Judicial review of constitutional amendments in Turkey. Europ Publ Law 15:533

Palmer A (2009) Abu Qatada's compensation makes a Mockery of human rights. The daily telegraph. London, 21 February 2009. http://www.telegraph.co.uk/comment/personal-view/4742387/Abu-Qatadas-compensation-makes-a-mockery-of-human-rights.html. Accessed on 14 July 2017

Patterson M (2007) Surely you didn't mean no jurisdiction: why the supreme court's selective hearing in *Hamdan* is good for democracy. Harvard Law Policy Rev 1:279, 280

Peters A (2009) The Swiss Referendum on the Prohibition of Minarets. (EJILTalk) Blog Europ J Int Law. 2 Dec 2009. https://www.ejiltalk.org/the-swiss-referendum-on-the-prohibition-of-minarets/. Accessed on 14 July 2017

Porter H, Hirsch A (2010) The human rights act is here to stay. The Guardian, London, 23 April 2010. https://www.theguardian.com/commentisfree/henryporter/2010/apr/23/human-rights-act-parliamentary-sovereignty. Accessed on 14 July 2017

Roznai Y (2013) Unconstitutional constitutional amendments: the migration and success of a constitutional idea. Am J Comp Law 61:657, 662

Roznai Y (2014) Legisprudence limitations on constitutional amendments? Reflections on the Czech constitutional court's declaration of unconstitutional constitutional act. ICL J 8:8 29

Roznai Y, Yolcu S (2012) An unconstitutional constitutional amendment—The Turkish perspective: a comment on the Turkish constitutional court's headscarf decision. Int J Const Law 10:175

Samanta N, Basu S (2008) Test of basic structure: an analysis. NUJS Law Rev 1:499, 501

Sandalow T (1969) Comment on Powell v MacCormack. UCLA Law Rev 17:164, 168

Sathanapally A (2012) Beyond disagreement. Open remedies in human rights adjudication. OUP, pp 48, 224

Schwartzberg M (2007) Democracy and legal change. CUP, pp 3–8

Smith E (2011) Old and protected? On the "supra-constitutional" clause in the constitution of Norway. Israel L Rev 44:369

Stephen L (1882) The science of ethics. Elder and Co, Smith, p 137

Tushnet M (1998) Two versions of judicial supremacy. William Mary Law Rev 39:945

Tushnet M (2006) Comparative constitutional law. In: Reimann M, Zimmermann R (eds) The Oxford handbook of comparative law. OUP, pp 1225, 1242

Uzman J, Barkhuysen T, van Emmerik ML (2011) The Dutch supreme court: a reluctant positive legislator? In Brewer-Carias AR (ed) Constitutional courts as positive legislators. CUP, the Netherlands

van den Berg JTJ (2006) De Eerste Kamer, of de zin van rivaliteit. Leiden University Press

Voermans W (2009) Constitutional reserves and covert constitutions. Indian J Const Law 3:84

Wade HWR (1955) The basis of legal Sovereignty. CLJ 13:172, 189

Whittington KH (2009) The political foundations of judicial supremacy. Princeton University Press, p 7

Wright G (1991) Could a constitutional amendment be unconstitutional? Loyola Univ Law J 22:741

Young A (2009) Parliamentary Sovereignty and the human rights act. Hart, pp 10–11

Credible Commitment or Paternalism?
The Case of Unamendability

Stephan Michel and Ignacio N. Cofone

Abstract Constitutions have seen an increasing number of unamendable provisions over the last decades. We look at the functional value of unamendable provisions as commitment devices, as they are often described, and present a new theory based on unamendability as drafters' paternalism. We find unamendable provisions to be undesirable commitment devices. The key problems that limit unamendable provisions' desirability relate to preference changes over time and the risk of abuse by self-interested drafters. These problems can be more generally seen as risks of strong entrenchment. We then provide a new, functional perspective for unamendable provisions under a framework of paternalistic policies. In so doing, we take an incentive-based perspective of drafters, which stands in stark contrast to the assumption of drafters losing their self-interest during constitutional moments.

1 Introduction

During the Age of Enlightenment, the political and philosophical idea of democracy gained credibility, becoming the preferred political system of nation states. The rise of constitutionalism, which has been one of the defining features of modern political systems, enjoys a similar level of acceptance. At first glance, constitutionalism and democracy appear to reinforce one another, but there is one area where they stand at a cross: unamendable provisions. By unamendable provisions, or unamendability, we refer to explicit, formal bans of the amendment of constitutional provisions through the normal amendment procedure as established in the constitution. Under the regime of unamendability, the limitless supremacy of the people's collective action (pure democracy) and majoritarianism's limits through

S. Michel (✉)
Institute of Law and Economics, University of Hamburg, Hamburg, Germany
e-mail: stephan.michel@ile-hamburg.de

I. N. Cofone
McGill University Faculty of Law, Montreal, Canada
e-mail: ignacio.cofone@mcgill.ca

© Springer International Publishing AG, part of Springer Nature 2018
R. Albert and B. E. Oder (eds.), *An Unamendable Constitution?*
Ius Gentium: Comparative Perspectives on Law and Justice 68,
https://doi.org/10.1007/978-3-319-95141-6_5

countermajoritarian devices (constitutionalism) stand at odds.[1] One could also see this conflict as affecting the balance between rigidity, as championed by constitutionalism, and flexibility, which is a concept more in line with majoritarianism's supremacy. The importance of considering this balance between rigidity and flexibility when assessing a constitution has been highlighted in the literature.[2] Furthermore, the amendment procedure's flexibility has served as a key design variable in studies on constitutional longevity.[3] Unamendable provisions tilt this balance toward constitutionalism, which is noteworthy given the finding that unamendable provisions are increasingly used in constitution-making.[4]

From a doctrinal point of view, unamendable clauses are puzzling. According to the general principle of *lex posterior derogat priori*, for all contradicting rules on the same hierarchical level, newer rules trump older rules, and yet unamendable provisions are constitutional clauses that can prevent the enactment of newer provisions. How can one justify that a prior decision prevails over a new one under the same hierarchical level?[5]

Moreover, the power to amend a constitution does not fully fit either in the category of a constitutional power, which creates the constitutional order, or in the category of a constituted power, which derives from such constitutional order; the constitutional amending power presents characteristics of both.[6] From this perspective, amending power can be seen as a derived constitutional power, as opposed to an original constitutional power:[7] it holds the power to create constitutional norms, but it is still bound by (mainly procedurally) those very norms. For this reason, although it has been argued that unconstitutional constitutional amendments seem inconceivable from the logic of legal hierarchy,[8] this could possibly occur if the amendment breaches the rules of the original constitutional power that allow for the existence of the derived constitutional power.[9]

Unamendable provisions have been analyzed using two main perspectives. The functional perspective deals with the direct effects of unamendable provisions,

---

[1] Albert (2010), pp. 663, 664.

[2] Roznai (2015a).

[3] Ginsburg et al. (2009a).

[4] More than half of all constitutions that came into force between 1989 and 2013 included provisions which are unamendable, compared to 27% of all constitutions between 1945 and 1988. See Roznai (2015b), pp. 775, 782.

[5] Roznai (2015a), p. 4.

[6] Ibid., pp. 13–14.

[7] Ibid., p. 15.

[8] Preuss (2011), pp. 429, 431.

[9] An interesting application of this theory can be found when discussing the case of the German constitution. The addition of a right to resist by amendment into an article that is protected by unamendability does not make the added clause unamendable as well. For a more detailed discussion of this problem, see Köybasi (2018).

while the expressive perspective focuses on the effects that unamendable provision have through the mere expression of this heightened attention. While recognizing that expressive functions play a key role in explaining the use of unamendable provisions, we focus on a functional perspective.[10]

The functional perspective focuses on drafters' ability to amend a written constitution and to credibly commit themselves *and* future generations to the clauses. This statement is inspired by analyzing various discussions of unamendable provisions that have been presented in the literature from such functional perspective, in particular regarding their feasibility and desirability to serve as commitment devices. Unamendable provisions present a barrier to change the constitution,[11] and given that constitutions are self-enforcing, any barrier to constitutional change requires the commitment to be credible in order to be functional. Elster discusses four potential reasons to use constitutional pre-commitment: overcoming passions and self-interests, overcoming hyperbolic discounting, overcoming strategic time inconsistencies, and ensuring efficiency gains.[12] These four reasons serve as the basis for this analysis.

We introduce a new functional theory of unamendable provisions, moving from the idea of credible commitment to the concept of (selfish) paternalism. From the analysis that follows, it will be conjectured that under the framework of Elster there are no reasons that make the use of unamendable clauses desirable. However, even if they are not seen as desirable from this perspective, they are by no means without effect.

While there is a recognizable expressive function of unamendable clauses, a functional perspective of these clauses that relies on interpreting paternalistic or hegemonic policies, rather than simply focusing on the pre-commitment perspective, provides a better perspective when dealing with their direct effect. Drafters cannot predict the preferences of future generations. This fact highlights the reality that unamendable clauses are a means for drafters to impose their own preferences on future generations. The defining feature and underlying difference between these paternalistic and hegemonic policies solely depend on whether the imposition of these preferences is inherently benevolent or selfish.

---

[10]For a detailed discussion of expressive functions of unamendable provisions, see Albert (2013), p. 225. The idea of the expressive function also relates to the concept of a constitution as a focal point. If certain provisions are highlighted by their unamendability, it will be harder for the future government to transgress them. Given that modern constitutions can be long and include several provisions, this highlighting can be seen as a key condition for the ability of the citizens to coordinate their behavior based on the provision.

[11]Roznai (2015b), p. 778.

[12]Elster (2000).

2 Reasons for Constitutional Pre-commitment

By disallowing the amendment channel, unamendable clauses raise the costs of future options. Modifying a constitution will always come at a lower cost than redrafting the document as a whole. This leads to two questions: how pre-commitment is motivated in social sciences, and whether these motivations are transferrable to unamendable clauses.

At the individual level, pre-commitment is a relevant part of the everyday lives of people and it has been the subject of legal discussions in various fields.[13] Contracts are a typical device to credibly commit in business, and marriages represent commitment devices in the area of love. The concept of pre-commitment, as one can see, is nothing new to evaluate in legal debates.

The concept of pre-commitment can also be used to evaluate collective decisions in which a society as a whole decides to bind itself for future decisions. When considering the concept of a contract as a commitment device, we might distinguish between contracts made between different collective groups and contracts made within a single collective group. International treaties are an example of the first type of contracts. A constitution is often likened to a social contract that commits the members of a society to follow a specified set of rules and, in this way, is an example of the second.[14] The key difference between individual pre-commitment and collective pre-commitment through constitutions is that constitutions, unlike most means of pre-commitment, may bind others, or they may not bind at all.[15] This argument goes back to the paternalism argument mentioned in the introduction.

Collective pre-commitment has the ability, at the same time, to do more and less than individual pre-commitment, depending on the issue at stake. The prime examples are preventing a preference change in the future (where collective pre-commitment can achieve less) and aims different than binding "oneself" (where collective pre-commitment can achieve more). First, since a society is in constant change, (births, deaths, and migration of its members) it undergoes constant preference changes. While an individual might want to maintain a specific set of preferences regardless of changes in experiences, it seems unjust to force younger generations to maintain the preferences of older generations.[16] Second, collective commitment (for example, in the form of a constitution) can also be abused to bind

---

[13]See, for example, Thaler and Sunstein (2003), p. 175, Sunstein and Thaler (2003), p. 1159, Camerer et al. (2003), p. 1211, Ted O'Donoghue and Rabin (2003), p. 186.

[14]The notion of a constitution as a social contract goes back to Hobbes and has fueled the field of constitutional economics following the seminal contribution of Buchanan and Tullock. See Buchanan and Tullock (1962).

[15]Elster (2000).

[16]This argument does not consider cases of "hypothetical consent" of the younger generation: pre-commitment devices that make them better off. The focus of this argument is on pre-commitment that is in line with the preferences of the older ones, but not with the younger ones.

others instead of binding oneself.[17] One example would be constitutional drafters who anticipate that they will not be in the majority once an election under the new constitution takes place. They might put excessive limits on the future government, not to bind themselves, but to bind the other groups that will have the majority in the future.

The analysis of constitutions and their provisions from the viewpoint of constraint theory, and in particular as pre-commitment devices, has been pioneered by Elster. His reasons for collective pre-commitment have been discussed in the introduction. Before linking these reasons to unamendable provisions, it is important to delineate the aims of unamendability in general.

3 Constitutional Pre-commitment and Unamendability

The purposes of unamendable constitutional provisions have been discussed extensively.[18] Examining these purposes, Albert distinguishes between preservative entrenchment, transformational entrenchment, and reconciliatory entrenchment.[19] Preservative entrenchment focuses on the past and aims to prevent the change of a historical situation, irrespective of social or cultural changes. Transformational entrenchment, on the other hand, looks toward the future and is aimed at provisions that facilitate change. The goal of reconciliatory entrenchment is to overcome past conflicts and limit the risk of another round of violence.

Roznai builds on Albert's terminology by creating a taxonomy with five categories. The five categories are preservative, transformative, aspirational, conflictual, and Bricolage.[20]

Preservative provisions aim to enshrine a certain part of the constitution that has already been established in a society. One example of this could be protecting an existing form of government or protecting democracy. This situation is among the most typical of pre-commitment and is also a justification of constitutions from the perspective of commitment in general.[21]

Transformative provisions, on the other hand, aim to install a new institution or a new value set. A bill of rights in a society with a record of human rights violations would be an example for this kind of provision.[22]

---

[17]Elster (2000).

[18]See, for example, Breslin (2009), Albert (2010), Roznai (2015b).

[19]Albert (2010), pp. 666–667.

[20]Roznai (2015b), pp. 787–799.

[21]Constitutions can be seen as devices to formalize certain rules of the society to make them more stable. This argument relates to constitutions as focal points for coordination [see Weingast (1993), p. 286) and constitutions as conventions (see, for example, Ordeshook (1992), p. 137, Hardin (1989)].

[22]Albert (2010), p. 685.

Aspirational provisions—the third category—are similar to transformative provisions, but have a more demanding purpose. These provisions look at past deficiencies in a society and imagine a better society to which the drafters aspire. Both categories aim to establish new conventions in a society. The goal of aspirational provisions, however, is to change existing (formal or informal) institutions through the means of a written constitution, while the goal of transformative provisions is to create entirely new institutions. It has been argued that the goal of aspirational provisions is too difficult since it is less likely that these provisions are adopted given that the very elements of the political system they want to change work against them.[23]

The fourth category, conflictual provisions, concerns provisions that aim to manage conflicts. It has been proposed elsewhere that constitutions are devices for conflict resolution.[24] Typical provisions for this category would include gag rules and amnesties to prevent the resurfacing of previous conflicts.[25] Protecting amnesties through an unamendable provision makes them a more credible commitment toward the conflict's losing side.[26]

The final category, Bricolage, captures the increasing phenomenon of constitutional transplants. Time is the drafters' scarcest resource, and on occasion, they reduce their own drafting costs and use what is at hands. Thus, unamendable provisions can spread via this mechanism from jurisdiction to jurisdiction and be included for no deeper reason other than expediency. What is common among these categories (except for this last category, Bricolage) is that they require the unamendable provision to be a credible commitment to be able to fulfil the declared function.

Interestingly, Roznai's first four categories map neatly onto the four reasons for constitutional pre-commitment described by Elster. Preservative provisions are mainly employed to thwart self-interest and prevent passionate moments from destroying the fundamental framework of the constitution. Transformative and aspirational provisions are put in place to ensure efficiency gains through the new clause as well as to overcome hyperbolic discounting problems of implementation and strategic time inconsistencies. Finally, conflict management through amnesties is a typical example of preventing strategic time inconsistencies. If, for example, continued conflict is still a serious threat, an autocratic elite might be afraid that the majority's promise of an amnesty is rescinded once they step down from power. In this sense, conflict management can work through unamendable provisions.

---

[23]Elster (2000).

[24]Grossman (2004), p. 29.

[25]For a discussion of unamendability as gag rules, see Roznai (2015b), p. 794.

[26]With regard to the similar category of reconciliatory entrenchment in the nomenclature of Albert, it has been argued that amnesties resemble credible commitments towards the loser of a constitutional struggle. See Albert (2010), p. 693.

Since the Roznai's categories are in harmony with the Elster's reasons, it might be useful to go through the four categories again with a specific focus on how one might use this harmony to justify the use of unamendable provisions.

The desire to overcome passions and interests rests on the assumption that a society might make rushed decisions during a time of chaos when passions tend to be exacerbated. In a democracy, it would be difficult to prevent a majority from making decisions in these passionate moments. Constitutional devices can be useful here by offering the means to eliminate options or create delays in the decision-making process allowing for a cooler, more rational decision after the moment of crisis has passed.[27] Furthermore, the supermajorities requirement and a separation of powers are instruments to prevent rushed decisions as well as to limit interest groups' ability to monopolize the decision-making process. Unamendable provisions can be seen as devices to (1) generate delays in the sense that drafting a new constitution takes a longer time than simply amending an existing one, and to (2) eliminate options from a possible set of actions that politicians might take. One example would be protecting basic rights against the passions and interests of a majority through an unamendable provision that guarantees those rights.[28] This device is, for example, used in the German Basic Law, where Article 1, guaranteeing basic rights, is made unamendable by Article 79 paragraph (3).

The second reason Elster discusses is hyperbolic discounting.[29] A typical illustration of hyperbolic discounting might be the introduction of a costly educational reform, which is delayed to a later point in time due to short-term considerations even though the government knows it will be advantageous in the long-run. Once the later point arrives, new short-term considerations might again hinder implementation. A constitution can be used to commit to these long-term aims by including positive rights. Elster goes as far as proposing "perhaps even to entrench them as unamendable rights."[30] However, no constitution has explicitly entrenched healthcare or education through an unamendable provision.[31]

The issue of strategic time inconsistency deals with the credibility of promises made by the future government. Whenever the state has a monopoly of violence, the question arises of how governments can be prevented from abusing this

---

[27]Elster (2000).

[28]Ibid.,

[29]Hyperbolic discounting is an increasing rate of time preference over time so that the distant future is more heavily discounted than the near future.

[30]Elster (2000).

[31]In the Brazilian Constitutional System, the eternity clauses in Article 60 of the Constitution mention only "individual rights and guarantees," but many Brazilian academics interpret that the limitations of Article 60 were meant to include social rights. When faced with constitutional amendments that seemed to touch upon the material limits set in article 60, the Brazilian Supreme Court has intervened discreetly but repeatedly, building a broader set of material limitations to formal amendments that those included by the constitution's drafters. In such a way, social rights, including health and education, were informally entrenched as unamendable.

monopoly in the future without losing the ability to act as impartial enforcers.[32] A typical solution for this dilemma is establishing a separation of powers, to generate checks and balances. Choosing a form of government and a political setup to ensure a separation of powers is a key area in which a constitution can serve as a commitment device against the future abuse of governmental powers. The form of government and the political system's structure are typical cases where unamendable provisions are used.[33]

Finally, another reason for constitutional pre-commitment is to ensure the political process can be carried out more efficiently. A more stable political regime enables a longer time horizon and improves the ability of citizens to engage in long-term activities, such as growth-generating investments. One example for this would be the requirement of supermajorities to change constitutional provisions. As long as no coalition obtains a large majority, citizens can build expectations based on rules that are protected by a supermajority requirement. It is typically the case that some form of supermajority requirement governs the amendment process, either through the percentage of votes in a single chamber or through a form of bicameralism. In Germany, both chambers need to approve a constitutional change with a two-thirds majority according to Article 79 of the Basic Law.[34] An unamendable provision would hence serve to prevent cyclic changes with the hope of increasing stability.

Following the discussion of how unamendable provisions can be linked to the reasons for collective pre-commitment, the next section goes through the four reasons again and analyzes whether unamendable provisions are effective devices to achieve the aforementioned aims of constitutional pre-commitment or whether they have major drawbacks of their own. The next section further discusses the question whether unamendable provisions should be used to commit to a core set of values (in other words, the spirit of a constitution).

4 Desirability of Unamendable Provisions

Recall that the first potential reason to make provisions unamendable is to protect them from the personal interest of subsequent legislatures, as well as from passionate decisions that would be regretted later. Constitutional pre-commitment can be justified to overcome passions and interests that arise in times of normal politics. If citizens, as well as politicians in ordinary times, behave mainly in a

---

[32]This argument goes back to Hobbes. See Hobbes (1651). More recently, this point was brought into focus in a contribution analyzing the Glorious Revolution, see Weingast (1993). The situation has been coined the "Dilemma of the Strong State". See Dreher and Voigt (2011), p. 326.

[33]Roznai (2015b), pp. 784–785.

[34]There is a difference, however, since the article demands an absolute two-thirds majority of the Bundestag and a simple two-thirds majority of the Bundesrat. Of course, the amendment rule does not include all parts of the Basic Law which are included in the eternity clause.

self-interested way, using constitutional devices to bind themselves is also bene-ficial for the citizens in the long-run.[35] Following this reasoning, a majority should not be able to pursue their interest against the minority regarding some especially important provisions. The protection of basic rights[36] and democracy are typical examples for this case. This argument is key to understanding the choice of several countries to make certain provisions unamendable in their post-World War II constitutions.

However, the use of unamendable clauses for this purpose is problematic. First, if we consider the use of unamendable provisions to provide protection from self-interest, one would need impartial drafters to achieve impartial provisions in the first place. While many authors argue that drafters are less self-interested than politicians in normal times,[37] this by no means implies that constitutional drafters do not pursue their personal aims while drafting a constitution. It can be assumed that drafters of constitutions are also, at least partially, motivated by their private interests, and thus cannot be expected to impose selfless clauses. While it is easy to see that this problem is more likely in nondemocratic settings with an unelected constitutional assembly, the case for selfish drafters does not disappear in a rep-resentative, elected assembly. Constitution-making is a rare event, which reduces the possibility for citizens to hold drafters accountable since there is no option to vote them out of office.[38] More generally, the notion that politicians are rational and self-interested is not novel; it is the main foundation for the research field of public choice and political economy.

Historical evidence tends to support the view that drafters are selfish. Historically, personal motives have played a key role, for example, in the drafting of the US constitution.[39] Furthermore, few countries have a political elite that is large enough to prevent drafters from subsequently entering the political arena. Selfish drafters might attempt to improve their future status by using unamendable provisions to raise the future cost of changing provisions. This is particularly problematic if an elite in power abusively inserts an unamendable provision in order to protect itself against the opposition in conflicts with high stakes.[40] It has been argued that an unamendable provision is a tool that allows selfish constitution-makers to install a

---

[35]Albert (2010), p. 699.

[36]Elster (2000).

[37]See, for example, Ackerman (1991), Elster (1995), p. 364.

[38]Referendums as part of the constitution-making process can be seen as one mitigation for this problem. However, the use of simple majority referendums might not be sufficient to constrain drafters, especially in times of crisis. See Michel and Cofone (2017), p. 402.

[39]Beard (1913). While this argument has seen criticism, econometric studies support the initial Beard's claim that drafters' personal motives are the key determinants of the US constitution. See, for example, McGuire and Ohsfeldt (1989), p. 219, McGuire and Ohsfeldt (1986), p. 79, McGuire and Ohsfeldt (1984), p. 509, Heckelman and Dougherty (2013), p. 407.

[40]Preuss (2011), p. 447.

preferred power asymmetry for the majority.[41] In this light, it is doubtful whether the availability of unamendability will make self-interested decisions of politicians more or less likely, taking the drafters' own interests into account.

Regarding passions, times of constitution-making are rarely times of calm and rational reasoning. Moments of constitution-making, in fact, are at an increased risk of being times of heightened passions. In the past 40 years, more than 200 constitutions have been written in times of crisis.[42] This implies that drafters are unlikely to be particularly cool-headed in their decision-making during the drafting process.[43] Therefore, since the process itself is likely to be passionate, it seems incongruous that the moment of drafting is the optimal time to install a device against passions. In the words of Elster, "[i]t is mainly if the framers are impartial *and* know that impartiality may be lacking on future occasions that they will have an incentive to pre-commit themselves. Although this case cannot be excluded... there is no reason to think that it is typical or frequent."[44] Combining the two arguments presented above, one can conclude that drafters are unlikely to act without self-interest and, even if they do so, their passion would be another obstacle to create unamendable provisions that protect from these same passions and interests. It seems doubtful, for these reasons, that drafters can use unamendability as a rational means to control either passion or self-interest.

The second reason to motivate the use of unamendable provisions for pre-commitment is nonstrategic time inconsistency. Discounting payoffs over time means that individuals often have less utility or disutility from distant consequences than from present ones. One relevant reason for this is that waiting is costly, and another relevant reason is that, over time, payoffs present the risk of either disappearing or depreciating. When either of these two effects is strong, they can lead to nonstrategic time inconsistency, which produces a switch in choice among varying delays while maintaining stable preferences.

Regarding the first reason to discount, a large number of studies have shown that people often display self-control problems, which lead them to choices favoring immediate gratification over welfare-enhancing alternatives.[45] This is the classic problem of the dieter. While a person trying to lose weight is perfectly aware that the long-term effects of a salad are welfare-enhancing, the direct gratification of eating the French fries is too tempting to resist. For these cases, pre-commitment is welfare-enhancing, since it eliminates temptation problems hence allowing the agent to choose the welfare-enhancing option, by disallowing him or her to choose the tempting but welfare-decreasing option.

---

[41]Roznai (2015b), p. 779. In a similar vein, it has been argued that the informal unamendability of the Jewish character of Israel and its dominance over other constitutional clauses is used to establish a hierarchy of citizens. See Masri (2018).

[42]Widner (2007), pp. 1513, 1513.

[43]Elster (2000).

[44]Ibid.,

[45]See, for example, O'Donoghue and Rabin (2001), p. 121.

Regarding the second reason to discount, it has been shown that agents who do not face behavioral biases will reverse their choice when the probability of the payoff disappearing is uncertain.[46] For these agents, the welfare-enhancing mechanism, as opposed to pre-commitment, is an increase in flexibility that allows them to update their choice upon the availability of new information.[47]

From this perspective, a pre-commitment device would be useful to solve nonstrategic time inconsistencies in constitutional choice if and only if these inconsistencies are driven by behavioral biases and not by the uncertainty of the future. If changes in social choices are driven by societal preferences that change over time, a pre-commitment device will be welfare-decreasing. This is especially so in the framework of constitutional choice, where commitments are not really self-binding but rather other-binding, given that a constitution's aim is also to commit future generations; the phenomenon of pre-commitment does not easily translate from individual choice to social choice when considering inter-generational concerns.[48] Moreover, future-generation binding seems especially problematic for strong substantive provisions, such as those that are typically subject of unamendability, given that preferences for those provisions are likely to change.[49] In contrast to abstract provisions, the preferences for substantive provisions are more likely to change over time.

From a practical perspective, it has been argued that the risk of binding future generations is only of limited importance given the fact that a constitution's average lifespan is 19 years, which is roughly one generation.[50] Following this line of reasoning, unamendable clauses may be a more fitting name than "eternity" clause, since the average lifespan of a constitution is nowhere near eternal. The problem with this argumentation stems from the effect unamendable clauses have on a constitution's lifespan. If we turn the argument around, the question becomes whether unamendable provisions have an effect on a constitution's lifespan. Looking at the empirical evidence at hand, the closest proxy for a direct effect of unamendability is the effect of the ease of amendment. Empirically, ease of amendment has an inverse U-shaped effect on the constitutional lifespan.[51] Since unamendable provisions tend to take the ease of amendment to one extreme end of this variable, the evidence at least hints at a negative effect of unamendable provisions on constitutional longevity.

---

[46]See, for example, Sozou (1998).

[47]Casari (2009), p. 117.

[48]Even if societal preferences remained stable, which is unlikely, pre-commitment would still be welfare-decreasing as a device to tackle time inconsistencies if they were driven not by temptation but by uncertainty.

[49]Elster (2000).

[50]Roznai (2015a), p. 45.

[51]Ginsburg et al. (2009a), p. 140.

The third reason to use unamendability is to overcome the problem of strategic time inconsistencies, which could potentially be mitigated through the existence of pre-commitment devices. Two main issues to motivate this use can be identified, namely mitigating the dilemma of the strong state and providing credible commitment for regime changes in conflict situations. The dilemma of the strong state was mentioned in the previous section. By binding its own hands through the deliberate creation of a separation of powers, the government can credibly commit not to abuse its own powers. Separation of powers can be instituted in two classical ways, either horizontally (between the executive, legislative and judicial branches) or vertically (through a federal system). Making either an independent judiciary, a presidential or parliamentarian form of government, or a federal system unamendable can strengthen the separation of powers and increase the credibility of the commitment. Thus, unamendable provisions would have an indirect commitment function. Separation of power is a first-level device to design the machinery of government, while making them unamendable is a higher level constraint to the machinery of amending, which reinforces the first-level device.[52]

In other words, unamendable provisions can be seen as a separation of powers done over time. When a certain clause is made unamendable, parts of the political power, namely the power to amend, remains with the original drafters and prevents future governments from using it. This separation of powers over time has the advantage that the commitment is credible, assuming the constitution is enforced and no new constitution comes into action.[53] Using the case of the Weimar Republic in Germany as an example (which had very low requirements for amendment),[54] it becomes clear how this commitment can add to constitutional stability. However, this separation over time has a problem: its effect in times of crisis or in case of substantial changes. While an "orthodox" separation of powers still allows for all powers to act in unison if circumstances require it, a separation of powers over time, such as the one generated by unamendable clauses, is unable to allow for unified action in times of crisis. It has been argued that unamendability acts like a lock on the door, which is effective in normal times but cannot withstand extraordinary force.[55] While vertical and horizontal separation of powers resembles locking a door with more than one key and distributing them among people with different interests, making certain provisions unamendable can be seen as locking the door and throwing the key away.

---

[52]Elster (2000).

[53]Although to a certain extent, the first assumption could be considered sufficient given that if the constitution is enforced then it is substantially more difficult to deviate from the indicated path.

[54]In the Weimar Republic, constitutional amendments could be done by ordinary law-making, which might have motivated the German use of eternity clauses. See Preuss (2011), p. 436. However, it should be noted that the political instability of the Weimar Republic cannot be attributed to the amendment rules, but rather to a specific set of political circumstances. Our argument is that the flexible amendment rules exacerbated the instability of the political system further.

[55]Roznai (2015a), p. 47.

The second issue is using unamendable provisions to make constitutional agreements intended to end conflicts more credibly. Typical examples of this issue are amnesty clauses protecting the former government from prosecution after a regime change and gag rules to prevent existing disputes from worsening. Amnesties are a case where a strategic time inconsistency arises because the opposition to the old government has incentives to agree to an amnesty clause when the threat of conflict still exists, and then renegotiate on their promise once they are in power.[56] Being aware of this risk, the incumbent government might prefer a violent conflict as opposed to stepping down and facing prosecution despite the promise of an amnesty. In this situation, making the promise as an unamendable constitutional provision can increase the promise's credibility and thereby tip the scales to prevent violent conflict. However, this argument only deals with the case of amnesties that are in the interest of all parties. The flipside of making amnesties unamendable is the risk that an autocratic government will use amnesties to absolve themselves from crimes committed during their reign.[57] In this way, they protect themselves in case of a transition by having raised the costs of removing the amnesty, since rewriting a whole constitution is always costlier than amending a single provision.

Even in the aforementioned case where the opposition agrees to provide an amnesty, the victims of the crimes may not be represented by either of the two groups. One can imagine a scenario where two elite groups struggle for power and use an unamendable amnesty even though victims in the general population are strongly opposed. Recognition of these types of risks is one of the reasons why international law tends to disallow amnesties.[58]

---

[56]This renegotiation threat was the case in the aftermath of the democratization of several countries in Latin America after military dictatorships, such as Argentina, Brazil, Chile, and Uruguay. The amnesties lead later on to public unrest and repeated requests from the Interamerican Court of Human Rights and the Interamerican Commission of Human Rights to declare them void retroactively. In Brazil, Chile and Uruguay the provisions are still valid and the renegotiation threat did not materialize, while in Argentina they were declared void by a Supreme Court ruling in 2005. See Legarre (2006), p. 723. The government has incentives to renegotiate only insofar as it has enough power to keep the members of the old political regime under control. This not always happens. In Brazil and Uruguay, the new democratic governments did not have enough power to judge the members of the military regime—but this can change over time. That is why Brazil's "double amnesty" law, which predates the first free democratic elections by over a decade, was not revised until the late 2000s. In Chile, there was some limited renegotiation not by declaring the amnesty invalid but reinterpreting it to judge some members of the old regime. See Linz and Stephan (1996), p. 101. For general considerations of transitional justice, see Kaminski et al. (2006), p. 295, Nalepa (2010).

[57]These self-amendments were once again seen in most dictatorships during the second half of the twentieth century in Latin America. Had these controversial amnesties been made unamendable, the polemic and social unrest that they caused would have been more severe.

[58]The United Nations High Commissioner for Human Rights, for example, has stated: "Under various sources of international law and under United Nations policy, amnesties are impermissible if they: (a) Prevent prosecution of individuals who may be criminally responsible for war crimes, genocide, crimes against humanity or gross violations of human rights, including gender-specific

The rationale for gag rules is to increase the credibility of compromises between conflicting groups by protecting them with unamendability and thereby also silencing future motions to renegotiate them. An interesting example of a gag rule in a different context can be found in the *status quo* rule from 1852 of the Church of the Holy Sepulchre in Jerusalem. The different Christian groups sharing the church would resort to violence in an attempt to obtain more of the exclusive rights for the use of specific parts of the church. The Ottoman ruler at the time fixed the *status quo* and decided that the rule would never be changed in the future, thereby making it effectively unamendable.[59]

The problem with the use of gag rules is twofold. First, both necessary compromises as well as issues where one can find clear winners and losers can be gagged. Using the gag rule in this way might fix a temporary power difference between groups in society and prevent renegotiation, but it might also lead to dangerous differences between de jure and de facto power in the future. Second, silencing an issue does not necessarily help to solve its underlying problems and may even exacerbate it. In the example of the Holy Sepulchre, violent outbreaks due to the underlying conflict have not completely stopped, despite more than 150 years of having the gag rule in place. Altogether, both examples of conflict-solving mechanisms show that they are problematic as commitment devices to overcome strategic time inconsistency.

Finally, unamendable provisions could be used to ensure efficiency gains. This would be done by expanding the time horizon and by preventing the cyclic amending of constitutional provisions following changes in political power.

Cyclic amendment would only be a problem if the shifts in majorities were large enough to fulfil the amendment requirement in the first place, which is typically a two-thirds majority requirement. Even if a society has big swings in its majorities, making provisions unamendable in the constitutional drafting process would either require selfless drafters, which seems to be an unlikely assumption, or simply establish a "first-mover advantage" to the faction which is enjoying the majority during the constitution's drafting, which is not necessarily a more desirable alternative.

It has been shown that the effect of the flexibility of the amendment process on a constitution's longevity follows an inverted U-shape.[60] In other words, constitutions that are very easy or very difficult to amend are more likely to have a shorter

---

violations; (b) Interfere with victims' right to an effective remedy, including reparation; or (c) Restrict victims' and societies' right to know the truth about violations of human rights and humanitarian law.

Moreover, amnesties that seek to restore human rights must be designed with a view to ensuring that they do not restrict the rights restored or in some respects perpetuate the original violations." Office of the United Nations High Commisioner for Human Rights, 'Rule-of-Law Tools for Post-Conflict States' (2009), p. 11.

[59]For a detailed discussion of unamendability from a rent-seeking perspective, see Pilpilidis (2018).

[60]Ginsburg et al. (2009a), p. 140.

lifespan. This empirical observation fits with the theoretical prediction that super-majorities, providing a middle ground for the amendment process between simple majority rules and unamendability, give great stability to a constitution.[61] Therefore, choosing the most extreme version of a difficult amendment procedure, namely unamendability, seems to be a suboptimal measure to increase the time horizon, all other things being equal.[62]

Beyond these potential reasons for commitment outlined by Elster, protection of the constitution's core is yet another motive discussed in the literature about una-mendable constitutions. In other words, unamendable provisions might be considered a credible commitment to a particular set of values. While amendment powers are argued to be implicitly unable to dismantle a democracy,[63] it is unclear how this implicit ban would be enforced and how to distinguish which amendments would constitute a destruction of democracy and which would not. Unamendable provisions might be used to protect the spirit of a constitution, and thus democracy in an explicit way.

The core or spirit of the document is not necessarily at risk from any of the four reasons discussed previously, but might nevertheless be a value that drafters want to commit to. It has even been argued that the main reason to use unamendability is to protect the founding myth of the constitution from change. In other words, una-mendability is the guardian of the constitution's identity.[64] Once this protection fails and the relevant provisions are changed, the society might veer into chaos and possibly civil war.[65]

The upside of protecting a set of core values is that the risk of abusing of the amendment process that destroys constitutionalism or democracy is mitigated, assuming that the constitution is set in a way that these values are included *and* protected by unamendable provisions. From the perspective of normative individualism, this approach leads to problems. The constitution in itself has no inherent value besides the effect it has on the individuals who are living under its' rules. It is important that a society is not seen as just a different individual, but as an aggregation of the individuals living in it.[66] Therefore, protecting the constitution's spirit or integrity is only valuable if it has a positive overall impact on aggregated welfare in society and is not necessarily positive or negative *per se*.

There are, however, two potential downsides when considering the overall impact on the aggregate welfare of a society. The first downside becomes immediately clear, namely that the tool of unamendability can also be used to protect

---

[61]Elster (2000).

[62]One can argue that constitutions that otherwise have a lax amendment procedure could profit from the additional stability through unamendability. Which effect prevails is an empirical question and outside the scope of this contribution.

[63]Roznai (2015a), p. 27.

[64]Preuss (2011), Roznai (2015b), p. 800.

[65]Preuss (2011), p. 445.

[66]Elster (2000).

autocratic values. As an example, a dictatorship oppressing a minority can enshrine constitutional provisions that will perpetually limit the minority's power. This not only justifies the dictatorship oppressing the minority group but also makes it harder for the minority group to find legal channels to challenge the oppression. Constitutions are a part of many different forms of government. It is unclear how to determine which constitutions incorporate a "good" founding spirit and which ones are more on the side of "evil". Autocracies might create constitutions that protect their core values and the sources of their power simply to increase the cost of transitions in case of an uprising against them. It is difficult to see how a government formed by selfish actors can be stopped from using unamendability simply for their own benefit.

Another dangerous downside of using unamendability to protect the core or spirit of a constitution relates to the fact that constitutional bargaining is costly. It is argued that protecting the core set of values is not a problem as long as citizens still have the constitutive power to replace the old constitution with a new one.[67] Now, assuming that most provisions of the old constitution are acceptable to the society, but a change in preferences has made one or more of the "core" provisions unpopular. All citizens would like to change this provision, but to do so they must draft a new constitution. Even if everyone is satisfied with the other parts of the constitution as they are, placing them back on the negotiation table by redrafting the whole constitution opens the door to strategic bargaining.[68] This cost arises because choosing among constitutions can be likened to a scenario called the "Battle of the Sexes" in game theory.[69] Even when all members of society are better off with any possible constitution, each member still ranks the different options in different ways. For example, assume that the old constitution did not include a positive right to work. While left-wing as well as right-wing groups would prefer to have a constitution, the left-wing group would like to include such provisions and the right-wing would prefer to keep the old setting. In this way, costly negotiations due to strategic options would arise. If these negotiating costs are high enough, a society will refrain from drafting a new constitution even if all of its members dislike certain core unamendable values of the current constitution. This argument presents additional support for the classical critique of "dead-hand" constitutionalism and casts some doubts on whether the protection of the constitution's spirit is something beneficial to society.[70]

---

[67]See Roznai (2018).

[68]A good example of the high costs of bargaining in constitution-making is presented by the failed attempt to draft a new constitution in Turkey. For a more detailed examination of the process, see Yegen (2018).

[69]See McAdams (2009), pp. 209, 239–241, Hardin (1989).

[70]An example for the problems of dead-hand constitutionalism can be found in the case of Bangladesh. For details on this case, see Hoque (2018).

5 An Expressive Device with a Functional Effect

The previous section offers arguments that raise reasonable doubt about the desirability of using unamendable provisions simply for what the functional perspective would call credible pre-commitment. It would seem then that the expressive function of unamendability is the main driver of its increased use. However, unamendability's lack of functionality as a commitment device should not be given to mean that it has no effect other than its expressive use.

We have already pointed out that the entrenchment unamendable provisions offer is not absolute since citizens can always decide to draft a new constitution.[71] One might argue that whenever a substantial majority agrees to dispose of an unamendable provision, they will do so by writing a new constitution; this argument seems to reduce the potency of unamendable provisions. However, this reasoning ignores the costs of renegotiation discussed in the previous section. While a large majority might agree on a single provision, its members could still have different preferences for the rest of the constitution. Redrafting the whole constitution would allow every single provision to be negotiated again while amending it avoids this risk. As an example, one could think of a society with two groups, one rich and one poor. The groups might agree to change a provision that is unrelated to their distributional conflict, but if the whole constitution is to be redrafted, both sides would prefer to shift the constitution's balance in this area as well. Knowing that this conflict can be very costly, they might refrain from redrafting in the first place. Therefore, in this scenario, unamendable provisions would have a strong functional effect. This finding leads to the question of what motivates drafters to put them in the constitution in the first place, given that, as it was discussed above, they are not desirable as commitment devices.

We assume that drafters not only care about the expressive effects of unamendable provisions but have a functional aim in mind. Even if one argues that they are mainly in place for their expressive use, looking at the side effects of these expressive clauses can help gain a better understanding of potential underlying reasons for the visible increase in the use of unamendable provisions. To evaluate this functional aim, one has two options: to consider that the drafters are benevolent when writing the clauses and to consider that they are not.

If the drafters are benevolent, we can infer that they will use unamendable provisions paternalistically to improve the welfare of future generations. Using constitutional constraints is self-binding only if the drafters anticipate that future political agents will prefer to be restricted for the same reasons that motivate the drafters to install the unamendable provision in the first place.[72] This argument is particularly relevant for provisions that fall under preservative entrenchment. It has been argued that preservative entrenchment can be compared to an originalist

---

[71]Albert (2010), p. 684.
[72]Elster (2000).

interpretation of the constitution, at least in spirit.[73] Originalism can be argued to incorporate certain paternalistic traits, which also establishes a link between paternalistic policies and preservative entrenchment. In both cases, the will of the drafters dominates subsequent generations, supposedly for their own good.

Transformative entrenchment is another area in which this paternalistic behavior fits well. In this area, drafters may aim to improve the lot for future generations, for example after bad experiences, and move society into a better direction. The post-World War II constitutions of Germany and Italy are good examples to illustrate this argument. Looking back at the failure of their respective authoritarian central states, and to transform their respective societies, Germany drafted a constitution that entrenched federalism (among other provisions), while Italy entrenched republicanism.[74]

However, this behavior might be myopic or at least naïve because it shows a lack of concern for the changing preferences of future generations. If preferences are changing, the use of unamendability would generate problems.[75] Even in the cases of Germany and Italy mentioned above, it is possible that future generations could find different structures of government to be more suitable, even though they would like to maintain other parts of the existing constitution. Failure to change unamendable clauses, resulting from the prohibitive bargaining costs of redrafting the whole constitution as argued above, could exacerbate tensions within the society. The finding that a highly rigid amendment procedure reduces the expected lifespans of constitutions is further support for this tentative claim.[76]

A different option does not require the assumption that drafters are myopic, but rather questions their motives for using unamendable provisions. Assuming that drafters are rational and act strategically, the explanation that compares unamendability to paternalism drafters falls apart. Under the assumption of rationality and self-interest, drafters will only make provisions unamendable if they expect to benefit from it.

We have argued that the standard credible commitment explanations do not sufficiently explain the functional use of unamendable provisions and, therefore, another strategic motive must be used to explain drafters' behavior. Using the analogy of hegemonic preservation regarding the judiciary's increasing power through judicial review of constitutional issues may shed some light on the issue.[77]

---

[73] Albert (2010), p. 687.

[74] It should be noted that a similar argument with regard to the rise of the German Constitutional Court, namely that the Nazi past is the explanation for its large powers, has recently been disputed. See Hailbronner (2014), p. 626.

[75] The idea that social norms and preferences change over time, even substantially so, is hardly contestable. A salient example of this would be slavery, which was considered normal less than two centuries ago, and now is unthinkable in most of the world. Abortion could be considered another example in many countries, and so could marriage between people from different religions, different ethnicities, or the same sex.

[76] Ginsburg et al. (2009a), p. 140.

[77] Hirschl (2004), pp. 71, 90.

On that account, the political elites empower the judiciary to fortify their current political power and to limit the power of standard democratic policy mechanisms to overturn the current political hegemony. In the case of unamendable provisions, the drafters, who can be seen as the current political elite threatened by subsequent changes in political power, aim to secure their preferences by making certain provisions unamendable. Like the hegemonic preferences argument, the key explanatory factor is the protection against the threat of losing political power. Assuming that drafters seek to maintain their preferred provisions in force for as long as possible, one can also explain the seemingly myopic ignorance of a new generations' preference shift. Instead of assuming that drafters are myopic about the shift, this preference shift can be seen as the motivation for them to use una-mendable provisions.

The discussion of constitutional theories versus constitutional interests might shed some light on the two arguments offered above.[78] In one case, the drafters are seen as using a device which, in their own understanding, will be beneficial for posterity. The problem is not constitutional interest, but rather constitutional the-ories which are not aligned with the real workings of the device that they are using. The second case is an example of constitutional interests at work. The drafters, in this case, are fully aware of the way in which the unamendable provision will affect future generations, but their own interest and the benefit they gain from either its expressive or its functional value supersedes their concern for future generations.

We have argued that unamendable provisions are not useful as pre-commitment devices but they might be desirable as paternalistic devices for the drafters. To analyze specific unamendable provisions, it appears to be more fruitful to analyze the motives for using unamendable provisions from this paternalistic perspective rather than through the perspective of credible commitment. When analyzing from the paternalistic perspective, pessimistic assumptions about the motives of drafters appear to be more consistent with reality. While the self-interest of drafters seems to be a natural part of the drafting process, their naivety and myopia appear to be rather constructed to fit a preferred story about impartiality and selflessness that is otherwise rare in politics. The empirical finding that the executive power was involved in the constitution-making process in more than 50% of all constitutions promulgated between 1789 and 2005,[79] seems to support the idea that drafters use unamendable provisions to extend their influence and power to the time after the end of their executive duties, and goes against the idea that drafters are benevolently paternalistic and selfless. This shift in the functional explanation of unamendable provisions would modify the scope in which these provisions are normatively justified.

---

[78]Vanberg and Buchanan (1989), p. 49.

[79]Ginsburg et al. (2009b), pp. 201, 205.

6   Conclusion

This chapter has shown that unamendable provisions are more easily understood when thought of as paternalistic devices rather than as pre-commitment devices. An analysis from this perspective highlights the problems that unamendable provisions face. Specifically, changes in societal preferences over time, constitutional drafters with hegemonic preferences, and abuse by actors who seek impunity for their crimes. From the paternalistic perspective, the drafters' intentions are key to assess the effects of unamendable provisions. The analysis suggests it is more realistic to focus on the dangerous case of selfish drafters rather than on the often-employed view of the selfless drafter.

These results imply that the key problems that lessen the desirability of una-mendable provisions from a functional perspective relate to the change of prefer-ences over time and the risk of abuse by selfish drafters. These problems can be more generally seen as the risks of strong entrenchment and would also apply, to a limited degree, to alternatives such as the entrenchment simulator proposed by Albert.[80] However, limiting the potentially damaging impact of unamendability should not be considered a negligible feature. Further mitigation is offered both by sunset clauses with a duration of less than a generation, as proposed in the entrenchment simulator, and limits on the ability of drafters to hold political office after the drafting process to reduce their self-interest's impact.

Given that unamendable provisions are still strong in our constitutional reality, the question of how to mitigate the potential damage from the aforementioned problematic aspects arises. It has been argued that constitutional courts play a crucial role in this setting.[81] On the one hand, they need to protect the constitution and prevent extra-constitutional actions by citizens but, at the same time, they should arguably protect the right of self-determination.[82] To protect this right, courts could stop enforcing problematic unamendable provisions thereby bringing them into desuetude.[83] However, this behavior would give enormous power to an unelected body.

In addition, there are no clearly established criteria to determine whether an unamendable provision is problematic enough for the courts to interfere. A final determination concerning the degree to which courts might limit the risks we have discussed, and whether that benefit is worth the cost of granting (informal) amendment powers to an unelected group of individuals, goes beyond the scope of

---

[80]Albert (2010), pp. 706–711.

[81]For an analysis of judicial review striking down laws due to unamendability in the case of Turkey, see Olcay (2018).

[82]Preuss (2011), p. 443.

[83]For a more detailed discussion about the theory and implications of constitutional desuetude, see Albert (2014), p. 641. The concept of constitutional desuetude has been the base of an analysis of informal unamendability in the Netherlands and the United Kingdom, see Geertjes and Uzman (2018).

this discussion. It can be said, however, that the courts are one of the key actors when it comes to the (non-)enforcement of unamendability.[84]

References

Ackerman B (1991) We, the people: foundations. Harvard University Press
Albert R (2010) Constitutional handcuffs. Arizona State Law J 42:663
Albert R (2013) The expressive function of constitutional amendment rules. McGill Law J 59:225
Albert R (2014) Constitutional amendment by constitutional desuetude. Am J Comp Law 62:641
Beard CA (1913) An economic interpretation of the constitution of the United States. The Macmillan Company
Breslin B (2009) From words to worlds. The John Hopkins University Press
Buchanan JM, Tullock G (1962) The calculus of consent: logical foundations of constitutional democracy. University of Michigan Press
Camerer C, Issacharoff S, Loewenstein G, O'Donoghue T, Rabin M (2003) Regulation for conservatives: behavioral economics and the case for "asymmetric paternalism". University of Pennsylvania Law Review 151:1211
Casari M (2009) Pre-commitment and flexibility in a time decision experiment. J Risk Uncertainty 38:117
Dreher A, Voigt S (2011) Does membership in international organizations increase governments' credibility? Testing the effects of delegating powers. J Comp Econ 39:326
Elster J (1995) Forces and mechanisms in the constitution-making process. Duke Law J 45:364
Elster J (2000) Ulysses unbound: studies in rationality, precommitment, and constraints. Cambridge University Press
Gárdos-Orosz F (2018) The Role of non-amendable clauses in judicial review of constitutional amendments: theoretical considerations inspired by Hungarian constitutional court case law. In: Albert R, Oder BO (eds) An unconstitutional constitution?—Unamendability in constitutional democracies. Springer
Geertjes GJ, Uzman J (2018) Conventions of unamendability unamendable constitutional law in politically enforced constitutions. In: Albert R, Oder BE (eds) An unconstitutional constitution?—Unamendability in constitutional democracies. Springer
Ginsburg T, Melton J, Elkins Z (2009) The endurance of national constitutions. Cambridge University Press
Ginsburg T, Elkins Z, Blount J (2009) Does the process of constitution-making matter? Annu Rev Law Soc Sci 5:201
Grossman H (2004) Constitution or conflict? Conf Manage Peace Sci 21:29
Hailbronner M (2014) Rethinking the rise of the German constitutional court: from anti-nazism to value formalism. Int J Const Law 12:626
Hardin R (1989) Why a constitution? In: Grofmann B, Wittman D (eds) The federalist papers and the new institutionalism. Agathon Press
Heckelman JC, Dougherty KL (2013) A spatial analysis of delegate voting at the constitutional convention. J Econ Hist 73:407
Hirschl R (2004) The political origins of the new constitutionalism. Indiana J Global Legal Studies 11:71, 90
Hobbes T (1651) Leviathan or the matter, form and power of a commonwealth ecclesiastical and civil (1651)

---

[84]For a discussion of the importance of judicial review for the enforcement of unamendability, see Gárdos-Orosz (2018).

Hoque R (2018) Eternal provisions in the constitution of Bangladesh: a constitution once and for all? In: Albert R, Oder BE (eds) An unconstitutional constitution?—unamendability in constitutional democracies. Springer

Kaminski M, Nalepa M, O'Neill B (2006) Normative and strategic aspects of transitional justice. J Conflict Resolut 50:295

Köybasi S (2018) To amend the 4th paragraph of article 20 of the German basic law in the light of the separation of the original and derived Pouvoir Constituant. In: Albert R, Oder BE (eds) An unconstitutional constitution?—unamendability in constitutional democracies. Springer

Legarre S (2006) Crimes against humanity, reasonableness and the law: the Simon case in the supreme court of Argentina. Chin J Int Law 5:723

Linz J, Stephan A (1996) Problems of democratic transition and consolidation: Southern Europe, South America, and post-communist Europe. John Hopkins University Press, p 101

Masri M (2018, Sep) Unamendability in Israel-a critical perspective. In: Albert R, Oder BE (eds) An unconstitutional constitution?—Unamendability in constitutional democracies. Springer

McAdams RH (2009) Beyond the prisoners' Dilemma : coordination, game theory, and law. South Calif Law R 82:209

McGuire RA, Ohsfeldt RL (1984) Economic interests and the American constitution: a quantitative rehabilitation of Charles A. Beard. J Econ Hist 44:509

McGuire RA, Ohsfeldt RL (1986) An Economic model of voting behavior over specific issues at the constitutional convention of 1787. J Econ Hist 46:79

McGuire RA, Robert L Ohsfeldt (1989) Self-interest, agency theory, and political voting behavior : the ratification of the united states constitution. Am Econ Rev 79:219

Michel S, Cofone IN (2017) Majority rules in constitutional referendums. Kyklos 70:402

Nalepa M (2010) Skeletons in the closet: transitional justice in post-communist Europe. Cambirge University Press

O'Donoghue T, Rabin M (2001) Choice and procrastination. Quart J Econ 116:121

O'Donoghue T, Rabin M (2003) Studying optimal paternalism, illustrated by a model of sin taxes. Am Econ Rev 93:186

Office of the United Nations High Commisioner for Human Rights (2009) Rule-of-law tools for post-conflict states, p 11

Olcay T (2018) Unamendability of amendable clauses: the case of the Turkish constitution. In: Albert R, Oder BE (eds) An unconstitutional constitution?—unamendability in constitutional democracies. Springer

Ordeshook PC (1992) Constitutional stability. Const Polit Econ 3:137

Pilpilidis K (2018) A constitution for eternity. In: Albert R, Oder BE (eds) An unconstitutional constitution?—Unamendability in constitutional democracies. Springer

Preuss UK (2011) The implications of "eternity clauses": the German experience. Israeli Law Rev 44:429, 431

Roznai Y (2015a) Towards a theory of unamendability, vol 3. NYU School of Law, Public law research paper no. 15–12. https://papers.ssrn.com/sol3/papers.cfm?abstract_id=2569292. Accessed 11 July 2017

Roznai Y (2015b) Unamendability and the genetic code of the constitution. Eur Rev Public Law 27:775, 782

Roznai Y (2018) Necroracy or democracy? Assessing objections to formal unamendability. In: Albert R, Oder BE (eds) An unconstitutional constitution?—unamendability in constitutional democracies. Springer

Sozou PD (1998) On hyperbolic discounting and uncertain hazard rates. Proc Roy Soc Biol Sci 265:2015

Sunstein CR, Thaler RH (2003) Libertarian paternalism is not an oxymoron. Univ Chicago Law Rev 70:1159

Thaler RH, Sunstein CR (2003) Libertarian paternalism. Am Econ Rev 93:175

Vanberg V, Buchanan JM (1989) Interests and theories in constitutional choice. J Theor Polit 1:49

Weingast BR (1993) Constitutions as governance structures: the political foundations of secure markets. J Inst Theor Econ 149:286

Widner J (2007) Constitution writing in post-conflict settings: an overview. William Mary Law Rev 49:1513

Yegen O (2018) Debates on unamendable articles: deadlock on Turkey's constitution-making process. In: Albert R, Oder BE (eds) An unconstitutional constitution?—unamendability in constitutional democracies. Springer

Part II
Unamendability Around the World

Constitutional Falsehoods: The Fourth Judges Case and the Basic Structure Doctrine in India

Chintan Chandrachud

Abstract What impact does India's acclaimed "basic structure" doctrine have on the text of the Constitution? Constitutional theorists have long neglected this question in favour of debates surrounding the implications of the doctrine on separation of powers, popular sovereignty and the role of the judiciary in a constitutional democracy. Over the years, the Indian Supreme Court has struck down multiple provisions of the Constitution on basic structure grounds. These provisions have formally remained part of the text, producing constitutional falsehoods—significant disjunctures between text and practice. By considerably extending the contours of the basic structure doctrine, the Indian Supreme Court's decision in the Fourth Judges Case exacerbates the potential for these falsehoods. This chapter considers how these falsehoods have arisen, the attempts to redress them, and what they mean for constitutional interpretation outside of the courts.

1 Introduction

Constitutional law is amongst the first subjects that Indian law students are taught. High school students across the country learn about the Indian Constitution, which is often prescribed in the academic syllabus.[1] Most Indians receive a healthy dose of constitutional invocation in newspaper articles, television debates and political speeches. For someone seeking to understand the nuances of Indian constitutional law, what is the best place to begin? The seemingly obvious answer is India's constitutional text: that is, the codified, master-text of 1949, complete with its amendments and schedules. This unquestioned assumption means that the written

---

[1]See, for eg, Indian Certificate of Secondary Education History and Civics Syllabus <https://www. icsesyllabus.in/class-10/icse-history-civics-class-10-syllabus>; West Bengal State Board Class 10 History Syllabus <http://boards.edurite.com/west%2Bbengal%2Bboard%2Bhistory%2Bclass% 2B10-syllabus%7EbIn-cMB-s1zc.html>.

C. Chandrachud (✉)
Quinn Emanuel Urquhart & Sullivan LLP, London, UK
e-mail: chintan.dc@gmail.com

© Springer International Publishing AG, part of Springer Nature 2018
R. Albert and B. E. Oder (eds.), *An Unamendable Constitution?*
Ius Gentium: Comparative Perspectives on Law and Justice 68,
https://doi.org/10.1007/978-3-319-95141-6_6

149

constitution (and often, the preamble with which it opens) comprises the first and most important reference point for those attempting to grasp Indian constitutional law.

It is well known that every written constitution is supplemented by important unwritten principles: the constitutional law of all nations (whether they have 'big-C' or 'small-C' constitutions)[2] consists of some combination of the written and unwritten. Judges interpret the abstract language of written constitutions,[3] and speak where the text remains silent.[4] As a codified constitution grows older, it forms less and less of the constitutional law of a nation, having been supplemented by judicial decisions and political practice over time.[5] These claims are now relatively uncontroversial in constitutional discourse.

But what happens when a written constitution diverges from the constitutional law to such an extent that it is not just a 'radically incomplete statement' of the higher law,[6] but to go a step further, is positively misleading? The Indian Supreme Court's body of case law on unconstitutional constitutional amendments (otherwise known as the 'basic structure doctrine') raises precisely these questions, for the Court assumed the power to hold provisions that have been incorporated into the constitutional text, following the textually prescribed amendment procedure, as unconstitutional.

Ever since it came into being in 1973, the doctrine has simultaneously become the hero and villain of the Indian constitutional experiment.[7] It raises significant questions involving the separation of powers, popular sovereignty and the role of the judiciary in a constitutional democracy. These questions, although important, are not of concern to this chapter. Instead, the chapter considers the less frequently analysed question of the impact of the doctrine on the constitutional text itself.

In its operation over the last four decades, the doctrine has extended the disjunctures between constitutional text and constitutional practice. The outcome is that many constitutional provisions plainly mis-state how the Constitution works in practice. The Indian Supreme Court's decision in the Fourth Judges Case of 2015[8] redefining the basic structure doctrine exacerbates these disjunctures and establishes the potential for more significant disjunctures going forward. The chapter addresses how these disjunctures between text and practice have arisen, the attempts to redress them, and what these disjunctures mean for constitutional interpretation outside of the courts.

---

[2]For this distinction, see Ginsburg et al. (2009), p. 48.

[3]Ginsburg et al. (2007), p. 33.

[4]Nariman (2006), p. 15.

[5]Gardner (2011), p. 162.

[6]Ackerman (2007). pp. 1738, 1744.

[7]For scholarship defending the doctrine, see Krishnaswamy (2009), Kumar (2007), p. 365. For criticism of the doctrine, see Upendra Baxi, 'The Constitutional Quicksands of Kesavananda Bharati and the Twenty-Fifth Amendment' (1974) 1 SCC (Jour) 45; P K Tripathi, 'Kesavananda Bharati v State of Kerala: Who Wins?' (1974) 1 SCC (Jour) 3; Ramachandran (2001).

[8]*Supreme Court Advocates-on-Record Association v Union of India* (2016) 4 SCC 1.

2 The Birth of the Basic Structure Doctrine

The story of the birth of the basic structure doctrine is a familiar one. Yet, it is worth recalling some aspects of that story to frame the discussion that will follow. The Indian Constitution occupies the 'middle ground' in terms of amendment difficulty.[9] Although many provisions of the constitution can be amended based on a two-thirds majority of both Houses of Parliament, amendments to some constitutional provisions concerning federal matters require ratification by the legislatures of at least half of the states. In design terms, this procedure lies somewhere between the spectrum with the United States on one side, and the United Kingdom on the other.

The Constitution, including the chapter on fundamental rights, was amended on close to 25 occasions in the first two decades of its existence. Frequent constitutional amendments by Congress governments gave rise to one of the most politically loaded questions of Indian constitutional law, as courts began considering whether there were any limitations *at all* on Parliament's power to amend the Constitution. Article 13(2) of the Constitution proscribes the state from making 'any law which takes away or abridges the rights conferred' by Part III of the Constitution. The debate over the scope of the amending power was framed in the context of whether the term 'law' in Article 13 also included constitutional amendments. If it did, then that would mean that Parliament lacked the constitutional authority to amend fundamental rights, as it had been doing soon after the Constitution was enacted.[10]

When the Supreme Court was first confronted with this question, it decided that 'law' did not include constitutional amendments, paving the way for Parliament to amend any part of the Constitution, including the chapter on fundamental rights.[11] Thirteen years later, while the Court arrived at the same conclusion, two judges expressed skepticism about its correctness. Justice Hidayatullah said that 'stronger reasons' were required in order to arrive at this decision.[12] Justice Mudholkar, on the other hand, articulated that the Constituent Assembly might have intended to give permanency to the 'basic features of the Constitution'.[13] But he chose not to develop what these 'basic features' of the Constitution were in any detail.

A few years later, the question was referred to a bench of 11 judges of the Supreme Court in *Golak Nath*.[14] Aggrieved by the impact of land reform legislation, several litigants led writ petitions in the Supreme Court. They claimed that such legislation, along with certain constitutional amendments that protected the legislation, should be struck down for breaching their fundamental rights.

---

[9]Khosla (2016), p. 235.

[10]Chandrachud (2017), p. 44.

[11]*Shankari Prasad v. Union of India* [1952] 1 SCR 89.

[12]*Sajjan Singh v. State of Rajasthan*, AIR 1965 SC 845 [49].

[13]*Sajjan Singh v. State of Rajasthan*, AIR 1965 SC 845 [61].

[14]*Golak Nath v. State of Punjab*, AIR 1967 SC 1643.

On this occasion, by a thin majority of 6 to 5, the Supreme Court held that constitutional amendments were 'law' within the purview of Article 13(2), effectively rendering the fundamental rights chapter of the Constitution inviolate. However, the Court applied the doctrine of 'prospective overruling' to soften the blow, and avoid the disruption that they expected would follow the invalidation of existing constitutional amendments and the statutes on which they were based.

In 1973, *Golak Nath* was reconsidered by an unprecedented 13-judge bench of the Supreme Court in *Kesavananda Bharati v State of Kerala*.[15] This case arose out of six writ petitions challenging land redistribution legislation and the constitutional amendments that protected it. Eleven separate opinions were delivered in the case. While there was some controversy about whether any majority opinion is deducible from the case,[16] subsequent judgments of the Supreme Court interpret the judgment in this way: although the term 'law' in Article 13(2) does not include constitutional amendments and that Parliament can amend any part of the Constitution (including Part III), the power of amendment under Article 368 of the Constitution does not include the power to alter, abrogate, or destroy the basic structure of the Constitution.

Thus, the 'basic structure' doctrine (also referred to as the 'basic features' doctrine and the 'essential features' doctrine) postulates that although Parliament may amend any part of the Constitution, an amendment that destroys, alters, or abrogates its basic structure can be struck down as an unconstitutional constitutional amendment. What comprised the basic structure of the Constitution was left open, allowing judges to develop the concept incrementally. As one scholar put it, 'a list of this sort lacks precision, which means that the Supreme Court has in effect deployed itself as official arbiter of what is textually changeable in matters constitutional'.[17]

Kesavananda attracted immediate attention not only for its novel doctrine, but also as an act of astute political craftsmanship. The Court conceded the battle to Indira Gandhi's government by overturning *Golak Nath* and upholding the validity of almost every amendment that was challenged (barring an ouster of judicial review in Article 31C), while also arrogating to itself the power to test the validity of any constitutional amendment enacted going forward.[18] The decision was largely driven by textualist underpinnings, as many of the judges in the majority and minority based their reasoning on the language of the amendment clause.[19] Justice Khanna's influential judgment noted that the word 'amendment' necessarily

---

[15] *Kesavananda Bharati v. State of Kerala* AIR 1973 SC 1461.

[16] Seervai (1996), p. 3114; Andhyarujina (2011), pp. 63–7.

[17] Jacobsohn (2005), p. 140. The following are amongst the principles that have been included within the purview of the basic structure doctrine, in *Kesavananda* and subsequent decisions: the supremacy of the Constitution, secularism, the sovereignty of India, federalism, judicial review, the limited power to amend the Constitution, and free and fair elections.

[18] Pratap Bhanu Mehta makes the point that the deliberate vagueness on what the basic structure doctrine includes was also a demonstration of political dexterity. See Mehta (2005), p. 188.

[19] Chandrachud (2016), p. 81.

implied that the Constitution, post-amendment, would continue to subsist without a loss of identity. In the minority, Justices Ray and Chandrachud relied on the very same language in the amendment clause to argue that no change was beyond the reach of Parliament.

In *Minerva Mills v Union of India*,[20] the Supreme Court decisively shifted to a structuralist interpretation of the Constitution. In a sweeping constitutional amendment, Indira Gandhi's government attempted to overturn the basic structure doctrine by adding a provision to the amendment clause categorically stating that 'no amendment of this Constitution … made or purporting to have been made under this article … shall be called in question in any court on any ground'. To make the position even clearer, the amendment clause also 'declared that there shall be no limitation whatever on the constituent power of Parliament to amend by way of addition, variation or repeal the provisions of this Constitution under this article'.[21]

If the Court persisted with a purely textualist understanding of the basic structure doctrine, this amendment would have been decisive. By clarifying that the word 'amendment' was not restricted to altering the non-essential features of the Constitution, the substratum of the doctrine was effectively eliminated. However, the Court made a critical move in favour of structuralist justifications for the basic structure doctrine,[22] striking down the amendment on the basis that the limited power to amend the Constitution was itself a basic feature, which Parliament had no power to transform into an unlimited amending power. This turned out to be the last concerted effort at uprooting the basic structure doctrine. The Supreme Court signaled that the doctrine was entrenched, and would leave an indelible influence on Indian constitutionalism in the years to come.

3 Basic Structure Review and the Emerging Disjunctures Between Text and Practice

While *Kesavananda* and the cases that followed filled reams of pages and are still amongst the longest appellant decisions in history, they left some important questions about the text of the Constitution unanswered. The Supreme Court was, but naturally, concerned about whether Parliament's power of amendment could be restricted *in principle*. What it did not consider was the mechanics of that restriction. Would the exercise of basic structure review to strike down an amendment merely result in the disapplication of the relevant constitutional provision, or would it eliminate this provision from the statute book altogether?[23] In other words, were

---

[20]*Minerva Mills v Union of India* AIR 1980 SC 1789.

[21]Constitution (Forty-second Amendment) Act 1976, Sect. 55.

[22]Chandrachud (2016), p. 82.

[23]For this distinction, see Waldron (2006), pp. 1346, 1354.

the official publishers of the Constitution meant to be concerned about exercises of basic structure review, or would it suffice to treat such review as an interpretive exercise as any other? Whereas some European constitutional courts possess the power to strike legislation out of the statute book, the trend amongst common law courts is for legislation that is struck down to remain on the statute book, but be inoperative for all practical purposes by virtue of the doctrine of precedent.[24]

It soon became clear that constitutional amendments that were struck down in an exercise of basic structure review would be treated in much the same way as statutes that are struck down for violating constitutional provisions. This was a paradoxical combination of transformative doctrine combined with traditional separation of powers theory. While the Court had the power to declare an amendment invalid and deprive it of any effect, it would not be in a position to remove it from the constitutional text altogether, and restore the text as it existed before the amendment was enacted. The provision could be removed only through legislative repeal, or in the case of the Constitution, a further constitutional amendment removing the relevant amendments from the text. One scholar explains the impact of a judicial strike down succinctly:

> A judicial declaration of the unconstitutionality of a statute has not the effect of either annulling it or repealing it. Repeal assumes the existence of a valid law until the moment of repeal [...] to hold that a judicial declaration of unconstitutionality of a statute is tantamount to nullification of the statute would be to attribute to the court legislative powers.[25]

Naturally, the implications of leaving inoperative provisions in the text of a Constitution, as opposed to a statute, are significantly pronounced. The Constitution animates the popular discourse as no other text, including a 'constitutional statute',[26] does. The text is a reference point—a 'common denominator' and 'historical context'[27]—for debates on issues as diverse as the federal distribution of powers, affirmative action in education and employment, and the protection of the rights of minorities. Citizens read the Constitution in the expectation that it accurately lays down the fundamental rules of the game in the state. Yet, the basic structure doctrine has meant that the Constitution functions *differently* from what the text provides in some cases, or in fact with the *opposite* effect to the text in many others.

In *Kesavananda*, the Court held that any constitutional amendment enacted after the date of the judgment, 24 April 1973, could be challenged on the basis that it violated the basic structure of the Constitution. Between 24 April 1973 and 15

---

[24]Field (1926), pp. 1, 13.

[25]Venkatraman (1960), pp. 401, 406.

[26]See Farrah Ahmed and Adam Perry, 'Constitutional Statutes' Oxford Journal of Legal Studies (advance access).

[27]Powell (1986), pp. 1427, 1429.

October 2015, provisions of constitutional amendments were struck down by the Supreme Court in five cases on the basis that they violated the basic structure of the Constitution.[28]

The first example comes from *Kesavananda* itself. Article 31C was inserted into the Constitution by the 25th Amendment in 1971, at a time approaching the pinnacle of the conflict between the Indira Gandhi government and the courts. It stated that no law effectuating a policy aiming to secure the Directive Principles dealing with property redistribution could be struck down for violating the right to equality, the right to freedom and the (erstwhile) right to property. It also usurped the Court's power to decide whether the law effectuated this policy, by stating that 'no law containing a declaration that it is for giving effect to such policy shall be called in question in any court on the ground that it does not give effect to such policy'. The second half of this provision was struck down on the basis that it gave carte blanche to the legislature to immunize any statute from three essential fundamental rights, by simply including a declaration that it was in furtherance of land redistribution.

The second occasion for striking down a constitutional amendment arose soon after *Kesavananda*. The Congress government had mobilized to amend the Constitution in order to secure the election of Indira Gandhi,[29] who had been unseated by a state High Court for engaging in corrupt practices. The Supreme Court struck down part of the amendment on the basis that it was an attempt at validating a specific election through a declaratory judgment.[30] The Court took issue with the fact that the amendment was an attempt at validating an invalid election, without changing the basis upon which the election was invalid in the first place.

Strike three would also take place soon after, in the *Minera Mills* case described earlier. The Supreme Court struck down an attempt to overturn the basic structure doctrine, by holding that a constrained amending power was itself part of the basic structure of the Constitution.[31] Parliament, a creature of the Constitution, could not amend it in a way that transformed it into its master.[32] The Court also struck down an amendment seeking to immunize legislation advancing directive principles from being challenged on the basis that it violated the rights to equality and freedom.

The next occasion involving the striking down of a constitutional amendment arose a few years later, in *Sambamurthy*.[33] Following the creation of the southern state of Andhra Pradesh, widespread agitations, involving the manner in which

---

[28]Exercises of basic structure review by High Courts are not considered here. In at least one of these instances (*Sakinala Harinath v State of Andhra Pradesh* (1993) 3 ALT 471), the High Court's decision was ultimately confirmed by the Supreme Court.

[29]Constitution (Thirty-ninth Amendment) Act 1975.

[30]*Indira Gandhi v Raj Narain* AIR 1975 SC 2299.

[31]*Minerva Mills v Union of India* AIR 1980 SC 1789.

[32]Palkhivala (1980).

[33]*P. Sambamurthy v State of A.P.* (1987) 1 SCC 362.

education and employment in public services were being addressed, took place across the state. This led to a political settlement in the form of a 'six-point formula' between the Andhra and Telangana regions, which promised balanced development of the state. The formula was operationalized through an amendment to the Constitution.[34]

The formula envisaged the establishment of an Administrative Tribunal to address the grievances of government employees. However, it effectively handed the state government a veto power over the decisions of the Tribunal,[35] by permitting it to 'modify or annul' any of its orders within three months of having been made. The only qualifications upon the exercise of this veto power were that the power would need to be exercised in writing and supported by reasons, and the order exercising the power would be laid before the state legislative body.

The Court struck down the veto power granted to the state government by the constitutional amendment. Justice Bhagwati pinned this decision to the rule of law, which the Court had previously held formed of the basic structure of the Constitution. For the state government to have this sweeping veto power over any decision of the Tribunal, including interim orders, would 'sound the death knell' of the rule of law and enable the government to 'defy the law' and 'get away with it'.[36]

Over a decade elapsed before the next occasion arose for the Supreme Court to strike down another constitutional amendment. Unlike most of the other cases, the Court was considering the validity of a constitutional amendment that was not quite hot off the coals. One element of the sweeping amendments made to the Constitution by Indira Gandhi during the national emergency was the introduction of constitutional provisions for the establishment of tribunals that would lighten the docket of the courts. These provisions ousted the constitutional jurisdiction of the High Courts.

The constitutional amendment ousting the jurisdiction of the High Courts was upheld in early decisions of the Supreme Court.[37] However, in *L Chandra Kumar*,[38] the Court reconsidered whether these provisions were consistent with the basic structure of the Constitution. On this occasion, more than twenty years after the amendments were enacted, the Court arrived at a different answer. It held that judicial review formed part of the basic structure of the Constitution, and a constitutional amendment could not exclude judicial review of the High Courts and Supreme Court. Tribunal members, in the Court's opinion, could not be 'effective

---

[34]Constitution (Thirty-second Amendment) Act 1973.

[35]Jacob (1987), pp. 94, 95.

[36]*P. Sambamurthy v State of A.P.* (1987) 1 SCC 362 [3]. Interestingly, the Court directed the state government to amend a presidential order operationalizing these amendments to take account of its decision. It did not, of course, go so far as to direct Parliament to amend the Constitution itself to eliminate the veto power.

[37]For a comprehensive overview, see Thiruvengadam (2016).

[38]*L. Chandra Kumar v Union of India* (1997) 3 SCC 261.

substitutes for the superior judiciary in discharging the function of constitutional interpretation'.[39] Two discrete provisions of the Constitution were thus struck down.

The Supreme Court came close to striking down another provision of the Constitution introduced by a constitutional amendment in *Kihoto Hollohan*.[40] The Court was considering amendments to the Constitution setting out provisions by which legislators could be disqualified on the basis of defection to other political parties. One of these provisions ousted the jurisdiction of the courts with respect to the disqualification of members. This provision was challenged on two grounds— first, that it required the ratification of state legislatures in order to be effective, and second, that it violated the basic structure of the Constitution.

The majority held that the provision was unconstitutional for failing to secure the ratification of the states, and held it unnecessary to consider whether it also violated the basic features of the Constitution. Two judges indicated that they would have struck down this provision on the basis that for the Speaker of the House to be a final arbiter on questions of disqualification violated the rule of law, which by then was well recognized as a basic feature of the Constitution.[41]

4 The Treatment of Constitutional Falsehoods by Public Officials

Kesavananda and the exercises of basic structure review that followed therefore implied that several provisions of the Constitution remained part of the text, but no longer represented practice or reality. The constitutional text says that no Court has the power to the review a constitutional amendment. The Supreme Court's decision in *Minerva Mills*[42] tells us that is plainly false. The text permits Parliament to exclude the jurisdiction of High Courts to review the validity of decisions of administrative tribunals. Yet, we learn from *L Chandra Kumar*[43] that any such attempt would be cast aside as unconstitutional. The text permits state governments to modify or annul the orders of certain administrative tribunals. The Supreme Court has, by denying state governments this power in practice, held exactly the opposite in *Sambamurthy*.[44]

These falsehoods have not entirely escaped the attention of public officials. In fact, what is equally interesting as the falsehoods themselves is the manner in which they have been addressed at the bureaucratic level. The Ministry of Law and Justice

---

[39]*L. Chandra Kumar v Union of India* (1997) 3 SCC 261 [78].

[40]*Kihoto Hollohan v. Zachilhu*, AIR 1993 SC 412.

[41]*Kihoto Hollohan v. Zachilhu*, AIR 1993 SC 412 [103–110].

[42]*Minerva Mills v Union of India* AIR 1980 SC 1789.

[43]*L. Chandra Kumar v Union of India* (1997) 3 SCC 261.

[44]*P. Sambamurthy v State of A.P.* (1987) 1 SCC 362.

of the Government of India frequently publishes updated versions of the Constitution.[45] Provisions of the Constitution that have been struck down as unconstitutional are generally (but not always)[46] footnoted, with a note indicating that the Supreme Court has declared the relevant provision, or some of its aspects, as 'invalid' or 'unconstitutional and void'.[47]

To be sure, the footnotes themselves, having likely been written by bureaucrats in the Ministry of Law and Justice rather than enacted by a two-thirds majority of both Houses of Parliament, are extra textual commentary appended to the formal text of the Constitution. As a formal matter, they carry as much authoritative value as the 'preface', which is also written by a civil servant, and currently opens with this somewhat bland passage: 'Constitution is a living document, an instrument which makes the government system work. Its flexibility lies in its amendments'.[48] There is no assurance that other published versions of the Constitution will carry this commentary. Indeed, the version published by the 'Constitute Project',[49] and a prominent open access Indian legal website,[50] lack this commentary. Uninitiated readers that turn to these sources for the Indian Constitution would, even if briefly, be misled by the text of the Constitution.

Nevertheless, it is worth noting that to enable the executive to add this commentary to the constitution still leaves it with considerable interpretive authority, especially considering that they publish what is likely to be considered the most 'official' version of the Constitution of India that is available.

This footnoting system seems to follow on from the assumption, explained earlier, that Indian courts lack the power to strike a constitutional amendment out of the master-text. This is the reason for which when publishing the Constitution, the Government adds a footnote to the amended text indicating that it has been struck down, rather than leaving the unamended text intact with a footnoted explanation

---

[45]The latest version, as at 9 November 2015, is available here: <http://lawmin.nic.in/olwing/coi/coi-english/coi-4March2016.pdf>.

[46]The provisions of the Constitution that were struck down in *L Chandrakumar* have not been appropriately footnoted. It is not immediately clear why this provision has been treated differently from others.

[47]These footnotes are in the English and Hindi versions of the Constitution published by the government. For examples from the English version, see footnotes 4 and 6 on page 17, footnote 3 on page 61, footnote 1 on page 63, footnotes 1 and 2 on page 65, footnote 1 on page 108, footnote 5 on page 110, footnotes 3 and 6 on page 111, footnote 3 on page 116, footnote 2 on page 247, footnote 1 on page 259. The *Kihoto Hollohan* judgment, in which the Court struck down an amendment on the basis of a failure to secure state ratification, has been treated in much the same way: see footnote on page 358.

[48]Dr. G. Natayana Raju, Preface to the Constitution of India, <http://lawmin.nic.in/olwing/coi/coi-english/coi-4March2016.pdf>.

[49]See Constitute Project, 'India's Constitution of 1949 with Amendments through 2012', https://www.constituteproject.org/constitution/India_2012.pdf.

[50]Indian Kanoon, 'Constitution of India 1949, <https://indiankanoon.org/doc/237570/>.

that an amendment was unsuccessfully attempted. For the government to do the latter would effectively constitute an illegitimate re-amendment of the text of the Constitution.

These disjunctures between text and practice are only at the tip of the iceberg. Many other questions and concerns would arise were we to consider basic structure review in the context of India's federal system. Each of the Supreme Court and the twenty-four High Courts have the jurisdiction to decide constitutional claims. Although the Supreme Court could have chosen to do so, it did not limit the power of basic structure review unto itself.[51] This means that any of the High Courts can, at least in theory, strike down any constitutional amendment at any time.[52] That decision would apply only within the confines of the state, which would mean that the operative text of the Constitution would look different in different states. The Law Ministry's footnote would presumably need to indicate that a provision has been struck down and is invalid only in its application to, say, Tamil Nadu and not its neighboring states of Kerala, Karnataka and Andhra Pradesh.

The question that is then worth considering is how far this disjuncture between text and practice can go. The basic structure doctrine is generally characterized as a substantive limitation on Parliament's powers to amend the Constitution. But in many ways, the limitations it imposes are procedural. The doctrine simply provides that Parliament cannot, relying on its power to amend the Constitution, change the identity of the Constitution. The Supreme Court has recognized that the doctrine has no application in the world of extraconstitutional change. Where Parliament or a new constituent assembly attempts to replace the existing Constitution with a new one, the 'loss of identity' theory is inapplicable. In fact, the very purpose of a replacement or revision is to *change* the identity of the Constitution.[53] Unlike an attempted change of identity masquerading as an amendment, this would be a transparent attempt at changing identity.

Following on from this proposition, we can arrive at the conclusion that the disjuncture between text and practice remains possible so long as Parliament is purporting to exercise its formal power to amend the Constitution under article 368. If, as the Court contemplated in *Kesavananda*,[54] Parliament attempted to use its amendment power to delete all provisions of the Constitution and the amendment is

---

[51]In *Golak Nath v State of Punjab* AIR 1967 SC 1643, for example, the Supreme Court held that only it (and not the High Courts) would have the power to apply the principle of 'prospective overruling' and that this power should be restricted to constitutional cases.

[52]For an example, see *Sakinala Harinath v State of Andhra Pradesh*, (1993) 3 ALT 471, in which the High Court of Andhra Pradesh struck down Article 323A(2)(d) of the Constitution. This decision was ultimately upheld in *L. Chandra Kumar v Union of India* (1997) 3 SCC 261, discussed earlier.

[53]The somewhat paradoxical outcome is that the basic structure doctrine, at least in theory, does not preclude Parliament from relying on an extra-constitutional procedure for replacing the Constitution that is easier than the procedure set out in the Constitution. It is a moot question how the Supreme Court would react were this situation to arise.

[54]See *Kesavananda Bharati v State of Kerala* AIR 1973 SC 1461, 1490, 1566; Sathe (2007).

struck down, current practice would suggest that the Constitution would be printed as a blank document, with a footnote indicating that the amendment deleting all of its provisions had been struck down. Alternatively, if the amendment replaced all existing constitutional provisions with new ones and was later struck down, the new provisions would remain in the text, carrying a footnote that the amendment inserting them was struck down by the courts.

What would happen if Parliament attempted to amend the procedure for amending the Constitution itself? It is worth recalling that one of the constitutional amendments challenged in *Minerva Mills* involved an alteration to the amendment clause. However, this alteration addressed the question of whether courts had the power to review constitutional amendments, rather than what the procedure was for enacting such amendments in the first place. In that case, it is likely that although the new amending procedure would form part of the Constitution, amendments complying with the new amending procedure (but failing to comply with the old amending procedure) would not be incorporated into the constitutional text.

5   The Fourth Judges Case and the New Basic Structure Doctrine

The Supreme Court's case law on unconstitutional constitutional amendments up to 2015 revealed a few distinctive features. First, although the basic structure doctrine was often applied in reviewing ordinary legislation and other forms of adminis-trative decision-making,[55] it was seldom successfully used to dislodge constitu-tional amendments. The Supreme Court generally struck down 'finality clauses'[56] or discrete provisions of amendments that ousted the jurisdiction of the courts, while at the same time substantially upholding foundational aspects of the amendments.[57]

Second, the Supreme Court defined the basic features of the Constitution at a high level of abstraction, relying on meta-principles such as democracy, the rule of law, judicial review, separation of powers and republicanism. As P K Tripathi described it in an incisive piece published soon after the *Kesavananda* decision, the basic features of the Constitution are 'mostly not concrete provisions of the Constitution, but are, instead, themselves statements of general principles'.[58]

---

[55]Krishnaswamy (2009), p. 42.

[56]Sathe (2007).

[57]The Court had struck down provisions of five constitutional amendments from amongst the sixty-eight constitutional amendments that were enacted between *Kesavananda* and the Fourth Judges Case. These numbers can be misleading, for in each of the five cases the Court struck down discrete provisions, allowing the substance of the amendments to stand. The Fourth Judges Case, which is statistically only one amongst six instances, produced a far more disruptive outcome.

[58]Tripathi (1974), p. 3.

The Court's approach took a turn on 16 October 2015, when it decided what can quite easily be described as amongst its most significant constitutional decisions since the turn of the century. The constitutional text provides that the President (who is advised by the executive) holds the authority to appoint judges of the Supreme Court and High Courts, in consultation with one or more constitutional functionaries, including the Chief Justice of India, Chief Justices of States, Judges of the Supreme Court, Judges of the High Courts and State Governors. Beginning from the 1970s, the Supreme Court decided a series of cases resulting in shifts in the center of gravity for the appointment of judges.

In *Sankalchand Sheth*,[59] the Court interpreted the word 'consultation' literally, suggesting that making appointments would never require the concurrence of the constitutional functionaries that the Constitution required should be consulted. Nevertheless, the Court also warned that the executive should typically accept the recommendations of the Chief Justice of India that arose from this consultation process. A few years later, in what is known as the First Judges Case, the Court effectively held that the power of appointments vested exclusively in the Central Government, and that the opinion of none of the constitutional functionaries consulted would be entitled to primacy.[60]

The Supreme Court radically shifted its position when the question arose again in the Second Judges Case.[61] On this occasion, the Supreme Court held that the opinion of the judiciary would be entitled to primacy in the appointments process. The judgment established the framework for judicial appointments by a 'collegium' of judges, consisting of the Chief Justice and his two most senior colleagues, which would recommend appointments to the Central Government. This framework was modified in the Third Judges Case,[62] in which the Supreme Court expanded the collegium to include the Chief Justice and four senior judges.

The collegium system was subjected to widespread criticism in the months and years after the Second and Third Judges Cases. Scholars and commentators became increasingly concerned that the pendulum had swung too far in favour of the judiciary, and that the appointments process lacked transparency. The Prime Minister Modi government—the first in twenty-five years in which a single party secured a majority of seats in Parliament—attempted to dislodge the status quo. By a unanimous vote, the Constitution was amended to replace the collegium system with an appointments process led by a National Judicial Appointments Commission (NJAC).[63]

The NJAC would consist of six people—the Chief Justice of India, the two most senior judges of the Supreme Court, the federal Law Minister, and two 'eminent persons'. These eminent persons would be nominated for three-year terms by a

---

[59]*Union of India v. Sankalchand Sheth* AIR 1977 SC 2328.

[60]*S P Gupta v President of India* AIR 1982 SC 149.

[61]*Supreme Court Advocates-on-Record Association v Union of India* (1993) 4 SCC 441.

[62]*Special Reference No 1 of 1998* (1998) 7 SCC 739.

[63]Constitution (Ninety-ninth Amendment) Act 2014.

committee consisting of the Chief Justice, the Prime Minister, and the Leader of the Opposition in the Lower House of Parliament. Soon enough, the Supreme Court was tasked with deciding the constitutionality of the amendment.

By a four to one majority, the Supreme Court struck down the constitutional amendment in its entirety.[64] The Court held that the amendment violated the independence of the judiciary, and unlike in previous exertions of the basic structure doctrine, could not be salvaged. The Court's logic was that the inclusion of three non-judicial members in the NAC impacted upon the primacy of the judiciary in the appointments process. The majority noted that the political credentials of the Law Minister and the lack of clarity over who the 'eminent persons' should be would detrimentally impact the independence of the judiciary.

Responding to the government's argument that jurisdictions around the world were establishing appointments commissions to appoint judges, the Court made the simplistic argument that the worldwide trend was towards a greater 'judicialisation' of appointments processes, and the Indian system occupied the most favourable position on the spectrum.[65] The majority also cautioned against an executive led-appointments process, which is closely associated with the excesses during the national emergency declared by Prime Minister Indira Gandhi in the 1970s.

In a dissenting opinion, Justice Chelameswar observed that the Law Minister held only one-sixth of the voting power in the NJAC and that the Minister's membership alone would not undermine judicial independence. He also observed that sufficient safeguards were in place against the possible abuse of power in the appointment of 'eminent persons', and that their appointment would in any event be amenable to judicial review.

Many commentators looked upon the Fourth Judges Case as a straightforward application of existing doctrine. The argument proceeded as follows. The Supreme Court held, in *Kesavananda* and later cases, that constitutional amendments altering the basic structure of the Constitution would be struck down. It was within the Court's provenance to decide what the basic structure doctrine included. The Court accordingly found that the new system of appointing judges altered the basic structure, as the Court understood it.[66]

However, on closer inspection, it transpired that the Fourth Judges Case involved a significant departure from existing doctrine. In earlier cases, the Supreme Court had prescribed a set of meta-principles that formed part of the basic structure of the Constitution. The Court's role was to ensure that these

---

[64]*Supreme Court Advocates-on-Record Association v Union of India* (2016) 4 SCC 1.

[65]Jan Van Zyl Smyt, 'Judicial appointments in the Commonwealth: Is India bucking the trend?' UK Constitutional Law Blog (7 March 2016).

[66]See, for eg, Baxi (2016), pp. 152, 157 ('There has been heavy propaganda against the Supreme Court decision invalidating the amendment and the law. However, it is wrong to say that the Supreme Court denied the plenary powers to amend the Constitution; these survive intact since Kesavananda Bharati v. State of Kerala').

meta-principles were preserved.[67] The Fourth Judges Case took a step further, by not only prescribing what those meta-principles are, but also how they ought to be achieved. As a senior lawyer practicing at the Supreme Court put it:

> 'for the future of the basic structure theory, this judgment opens up frightening possibilities. Now you can forget all about overarching principles. Anything which the judges feel merely affects the independence of the judiciary can be brought in within the basic structure concept'.[68]

For the Court to decide that the independence of the judiciary forms part of the basic structure of the Constitution was quite uncontroversial. The Court's judgment, however, was based on an additional assumption—that primacy of the judiciary in the appointments process is indispensable for the independence of the judiciary and by implication, forms part of the basic structure of the Constitution.[69] This was an ambitious claim. As the dissenting judgment records, there may be alternative means of protecting the independence of the judiciary, and Parliament must have a choice amongst them.

The Fourth Judges Case wasn't simply the latest in a series of cases in which constitutional amendments were struck down since *Kesavananda*. Every case before 2015 involved the striking down of discrete provisions, mostly restricting judicial review. Richard Albert explains that whereas some constitutions follow the framework model in which the constitution is written at a high level of generality, others follow the operational manual model, setting out specific details.[70] Of course, it is possible for constitutions to combine these two models, by including some framework-type provisions and other operational manual-type provisions.

The Fourth Judges Case is the first instance in which the Court has struck down a part of the framework of the Constitution. Rather than striking down a discreet provision addressing the method by which judges are appointed through the NJAC, the Court chose to strike down the appointments regime in its entirety. To be sure, the Court had a range of solutions at its disposal to avoid striking down the amendment as a whole. The Court could have defined 'eminent persons' narrowly, modified the process by which eminent persons were appointed, or offered an exclusive veto power in making appointments to the judges on the committee.[71] Yet, the Court chose the nuclear option for the very first time, vastly transforming the potential of the basic structure doctrine as it is applied to constitutional amendments.

The Fourth Judges Case thus exacerbates the potential for disjunctures between constitutional text and constitutional practice. By deciding that it will not only

---

[67]Some scholars argue that associating the basic structure doctrine with high-level principles is foundational to the idea of the state—see Sudarshan (2005), p. 167.

[68]Raju Ramachandran, 'A Case of Self-Selection: Judicial Accountability and Appointment of Judges', DAKSH Fourth Annual Constitution Day Lecture, Bangalore, 28 November 2015.

[69]Chandrachud (2015a); Abeyratne (2017), pp. 129–130.

[70]Albert (2015), p.387.

[71]Chandrachud (2015b).

interrogate whether prescribed meta-principles have been preserved—but also how they will be preserved—the Supreme Court decisively expanded the scope of basic structure review. This also opens up the possibility of the Court striking down framework-type provisions, as opposed to operational manual provisions, in the future.

A constitutional falsehood for a framework provision is far more disconcerting than for an operational manual provision. It is one thing, for example, for the Constitution to provide that no judicial review is available where it exists in practice. It is quite another for the Constitution to set out what is now a meaningless framework for the appointment of judges to the Supreme Court and High Courts. A casual reader of the Constitution would be misled into believing that judges of the Supreme Court and High Court are appointed by a six-member commission that was never formed.

One of the arguments raised by the Government during the NJAC case was that even if the constitutional amendment were to be struck down, that would not automatically revive the provisions of the Constitution (and the body of case law interpreting it) that it replaced. The argument was cleverly framed, suggesting that the amendment involved two separate steps—the first step of eliminating existing constitutional provisions and the second step of replacing those provisions with a new scheme for appointments. The Court would have none of it, for accepting the government's argument would have effectively established a hiatus on judicial appointments.[72]

This discussion demonstrates that constitutional provisions that no longer form part of the text can, on account of the basic structure doctrine, continue to live outside of the text. To the extent that a constitutional provision is amended and the amendment is itself struck down as unconstitutional, the original unamended provision, which is now no longer formally part of the text, would continue to be 'interpreted' by the courts. A set of textual provisions on judicial appointments now exist as extra-textual rules, and continue to live an afterlife following its repeal.

This is precisely the opposite of what we are often used to seeing in other jurisdictions, where a conventional rule is codified into the constitutional text. In the United States, the conventional two-term limit on the Presidency was codified into the Constitution by a constitutional amendment.[73] In the United Kingdom, the conventional rule that the House of Lords would not oppose money bills passed by the Commons, and that Parliament would not legislate for dominions without their consent, were likewise codified into constitutional statutes.[74]

The obvious implication arising from the fact that the Supreme court lacks the power to strike an amendment out of the statute book is that Parliament may, if it chooses to, repeal a constitutional amendment that has already been struck down. There have been occasions on which amendments that have been struck down were

---

[72]*Supreme Court Advocates-on-Record Association v Union of India* (2016) 4 SCC 1 [251].

[73]Constitution of the United States of America, amendment XXII (ratified 1951).

[74]Parliament Act 1911; Statute of Westminster 1931.

repealed by subsequent governments. Article 329A, which was introduced into the Constitution to protect the political office of Indira Gandhi and was struck down in part by the Supreme Court, was repealed by the Janata government as a relic of the emergency years.[75]

It is unsurprising that political actors in India have not expended the capital to amend the provisions of the Constitution that have been struck down. When constitutional amendments are struck down shortly after they are enacted, a government that disagrees with the Court's decision may be seen as admitting its guilt were it to repeal the constitutional amendment. Moreover, any constitutional amendment requires a two-thirds majority in both Houses of Parliament and demands the mobilization of considerable political capital. Governments would likely wish to expend that capital on other pressing matters. The per-amendment cost of repealing amendments that are struck down would reduce were a government to choose to repeal multiple amendments in one go—in the nature of a 'great repeal bill'[76]—rather than each amendment individually.[77] Third, the government may entertain a small glimmer of hope that an amendment that is struck down by one bench of the Supreme Court is later upheld by a larger bench of the Court.[78] This is an unlikely, but not impossible, eventuality.

These constitutional falsehoods precipitated by the basic structure doctrine have implications for the rule of law. They would likely fail the first principle in Raz's classic account of the rule of law – that laws should be 'prospective, open and clear' and not 'mislead' those who 'desire to be guided by it'.[79] When people realise that the constitution does not mean what it says, this disjuncture also holds the potential of causing a loss of faith in public institutions.[80]

Constitutional falsehoods raise another concern, for they effectively exclude the citizenry from the process of constitutional interpretation. As Tushnet explains, '[t] ext and purpose are the only things to which ordinary people have ready-and-unmediated-access. Everything else—legal doctrine and precedents most obviously,

---

[75]The Janata government also failed in its attempt to amend the amendment clause to provide that the basic structure of the Constitution may only be amended following a referendum. This amendment would invariably have required the amendment or repeal of articles 368(4) and (5). This would nevertheless have been a slightly different situation from the one contemplated here, for these provisions were only struck down in a subsequent decision of the Supreme Court, *Minerva Mills v Union of India* AIR 1980 SC 1789.

[76]I borrow this phrase from the the bill proposed in the United Kingdom to address the UK's departure from the European Union: see Department for Exiting the European Union, 'Legislating for the United Kingdom's withdrawal from the European Union', Cm 9446, March 2017.

[77]The government recently embarked on an exercise of repealing obsolete laws *en masse*. See Shreeja Sen, 'The government's report card on removing outdated laws' *Live Mint* (29 July 2016). The same may be contemplated for constitutional amendments that are struck down.

[78]Larger benches of the Supreme Court bind smaller benches, and a judgment of the Court can only be overruled by a bench of a larger size: see Chandrachud (2016), p. 74.

[79]Raz (1979), p. 214.

[80]Albert (2015), p. 387.

but even original understandings—are the province of legal specialists'.[81] Citizens must, at the least, remain prominent players in the process of constitutional interpretation.

For the most authoritative, open-access source of constitutional law to be misleading is a significant barrier to access. This privileges lawyers, and instills them with even greater responsibility as civic educators.[82] The Constitution 'is not the property of lawyers and judges alone'.[83] The Fourth Judges Case increases the potential for disjunctures between constitutional text and practice, and places a premium on constitutional interpretation outside of the courts.

6 Conclusion

The basic structure doctrine is easily the most widely recognized, widely acclaimed, and widely criticized, aspect of Indian constitutional law. Yet, amongst a rich literature on democracy and the separation of powers, one aspect of the *Kesavananda* case and subsequent decisions remained forgotten. What impact would basic structure review have on the text of the Constitution? Over the years, the Supreme Court has struck down multiple provisions of the Constitution. These provisions have remained part of the text, producing disjunctures between the constitutional text and constitutional practice.

By considerably extending the contours of the basic structure doctrine, the Fourth Judges Case exacerbates the potential for disjunctures between text and practice. Bureaucracies find solutions where constitutional lawyers and judges do not- for the government's published version of the Constitution now contains over a dozen footnotes indicating which provisions of the Constitution have been struck down by the courts. Yet, these footnotes lie outside the text of the Constitution. The constitutional falsehoods precipitated by the basic structure doctrine raise concerns from the rule of law and place a premium on constitutional interpretation outside of the courts. The citizens of each generation must be able to 'figure out what the Constitution's promises mean for themselves'.[84] The continuing application of the basic structure doctrine, à la the Fourth Judges Case, only makes the the marginalization of citizens in the interpretive project increasingly likely.

---

[81]Tushnet (2009a), pp. 1379, 1383.

[82]Tushnet (2009b), pp. 1379, 1393. It is arguable that some of these disjunctures, at least vis-à-vis the amendments that were struck down during the tenure of Indira Gandhi, constitute a sobering reminder *to lawyers* of the excesses of the emergency and majoritarian government. Yet, this is an outcome that is outweighed by the significance of offering citizens the opportunity of interpreting the Constitution.

[83]Raju Ramachandran, 'A Case of Self-Selection: Judicial Accountability and Appointment of Judges', DAKSH Fourth Annual Constitution Day Lecture, Bangalore, 28 November 2015.

[84]Balkin (2009), p. 21.

Acknowledgement I am grateful to Mihika Poddar of the West Bengal National University of Juridical Sciences, Kolkata, for research assistance.

References

Abeyratne R (2017) Upholding judicial supremacy in India: the NJAC judgment in comparative perspective, George Wash Law Rev 49:101, 129–130

Ackerman B (2007) The living constitution (2007) Harvard Law Rev 120:1738, 1744

Albert R (2015) How unwritten constitutional norms change written constitutions. Dublin Univ Law J 38(2):387

Andhyarujina TR (2011) The Kesavananda Bharati case: the untold story of struggle for supremacy by supreme court and parliament, Universal Law Publishing, pp 63–7

Balkin JM (2009) Fidelity to text and principle. In: Balkin JM, Riva BS (eds) The constitution in 2020, Oxford University Press, p 21

Baxi U (2016) Demosprudence and socially responsible/response-able criticism: the njac decision and beyond NUJS Law Rev 9:152, 157

Chandrachud C (2015a) Debating the NJAC judgment of the supreme court of India: three dimensions' UK constitutional law blog, 3 Nov 2015

Chandrachud C (2015b) Interpretive remedies in NJAC case. The Hindu, 31 July 2015, http://www.thehindu.com/opinion/lead/interpretive-remedies-in-njac-case/article7482864.ece

Chandrachud C (2016) Interpretation. In: Choudhry S, Khosla M, Mehta PB (eds) The oxford handbook of the Indian constitution. Oxford University Press

Chandrachud C (2017) Balanced constitutionalism: courts and legislatures in India and the United Kingdom, Oxford University Press, p 44

Field O (1926) Effect of an unconstitutional statute. Indiana Law J 1:1, 13

Gardner J (2011) Can there be a written constitution? Oxford Stud Philos Law 1:162

Ginsburg T, Elkins Z, Melton J (2007) The lifespan of written constitutions, American law and economics association annual meetings working paper 33

Ginsburg T, Elkins Z, Melton J (2009) The endurance of national constitutions. CUP, 48

Seervai HM (1996) Constitutional law of India, 4th edn. N.M. Tripathi, p 3114

Jacob A (1987) Government's power to nullify andhra pradesh administrative tribunal's orders ultra vires the amending power of parliament. J Indian Law Inst 29:94, 95

Jacobsohn GJ (2005) The wheel of law: India's secularism in comparative constitutional context. Princeton, p. 140

Khosla M (2016) Constitutional amendment. In: Choudhry S, Mehta PB (eds) The oxford handbook of the Indian constitution. Oxford University Press, p 235

Krishnaswamy S (2009) Democracy and constitutionalism in India—a study of the basic structure doctrine, Oxford University Press, p 42

Kumar V (2007) Basic structure doctrine of the Indian constitution: doctrine of constitutionally controlled governance. J Indian Law Inst 49:365

Mehta PB (2005) The inner conflict of constitutionalism: judicial review and the basic structure. In: Hassan Z et al (eds) India's living constitution: ideas, practices, controversies. Anthem, p 188

Nariman FS (2006) The silences in our constitutional law. SCC J 15(2)

Palkhivala N (1980) Rekindling the light of the constitution. Indian Express, 16 May 1980

Powell HJ (1986) Parchment matters: a mediation on the constitution as a text. Iowa Law Rev 71:1427, 1429

Ramachandran R (2001) The supreme court and the basic structure doctrine. In: Kirpal BN et al (eds) Supreme but not Infallible: essays in honour of the supreme court of India, Oxford University Press

Raz J (1979) The authority of law: essays on law and morality, Oxford University Press, p 214

Sathe SP (2007) From positivism to structuralism. In: Golsworthy J (ed) Interpreting constitutions: a comparative study, Oxford University Press

Sudarshan R (2005) "Stateness" and "Democracy" in India's constitution'. In: Hassan Z et al (ed) India's living constitution: ideas, practices, controversies, Anthem, p 167

Thiruvengadam AK (2016) Tribunals. In: Choudhry S, Khosla M, Mehta PB (eds) The oxford handbook of the Indian constitution. Oxford University Press

Tripathi PK (1974) Kesavananda bharati v state of Kerala: who wins? SCC J 1:3

Tushnet M (2009a) Citizen as lawyer, lawyer as citizen. William Mary Law Rev 50:1379, 1383

Tushnet M (2009b) Citizen as lawyer, lawyer as citizen. William Mary Law Rev 50:1379, 1393

Venkatraman S (1960) The status of an unconstitutional statute. J Indian Law Inst 2:401, 406

Waldron J (2006) The core of the case against judicial review. Yale Law J 115:1346, 1354

Unamendability in Israel: A Critical Perspective

Mazen Masri

Abstract This chapter explores unamendability in Israel. Even though Israel has no full or formal constitution, and no specific amendment rules, two forms of unamdenability could be identified. The first form is concealed unamendability, which prevents certain kinds of amendments through controlling the composition of the Knesset (the legislature which also has the power to enact and amend constitutional Basic Laws). The second is judicially-introduced unwritten unamendability. Unamendability in both cases aims to protect Israel's definition as a Jewish and democratic state. The chapter will examine both forms of unamendability and the functions they serve, highlighting the expressive and the preservative functions. It will also examine the implications of unamendability for constitutionalism in Israel emphasizing the impact of entrenching particular values such as the Jewish definition and its contribution to creating a hierarchy among the citizenry and the entrenchment of favourable status for certain groups.

1 Introduction

The Israeli case presents a peculiar situation when it comes to unamendability. Israel does not have a full and formal constitution, but rather a number of Basic Laws that the Supreme Court has declared as having constitutional status. There are no formal rules that govern the amendment of Basic Laws, apart from the judicially introduced rule that Basic Laws are to be amended by Basic Laws only, which is

M. Masri (✉)
The City Law School, City, University of London, London, UK
e-mail: mazen.masri.1@city.ac.uk

© Springer International Publishing AG, part of Springer Nature 2018   169
R. Albert and B. E. Oder (eds.), *An Unamendable Constitution?*
Ius Gentium: Comparative Perspectives on Law and Justice 68,
https://doi.org/10.1007/978-3-319-95141-6_7

merely a textual and stylistic requirement.[1] This means that Basic Laws could be, and ordinarily are, amended in the same manner and form as ordinary legislation of the Knesset (the Israeli legislature). Nevertheless, the Supreme Court has stated—albeit *obiter dicta*—that certain aspects of the Basic Laws are unamendable, namely the definition of the state, as stated in some of the Basic Laws,[2] as a Jewish and democratic state.[3] In addition to unwritten unamendability, Basic Law: The Knesset, which has nothing to do with constitutional amendment, introduces unamendability through screening the composition of the Knesset, which is both the legislature and the constituent body. Israel, in this sense, presents a unique case: while it lacks a full and formal constitution or any specific amendment provisions, it has introduced two forms of unamendability: unwritten unamendability through the case law and concealed unamendability through other constitutional provisions. Unamendability in both cases relates only to the values of the state as reflected in the definition.

While the topic of unamendable constitutional provisions and principles is relatively new in Israeli constitutional law, the idea that certain constitutional principles or values are eternal and cannot be questioned—let alone changed—could be traced back to 1965 when the Supreme Court barred a political party from participating in the parliamentary elections for questioning certain 'constitutional facts' which included the Jewish character of the state and its eternality.[4] Since then, and including the most recent discussions of the question of unamendability, the debates focused on the definition of the state and its central values as Jewish and democratic. To fully appreciate the scope, depth and significance of unamendability in the Israeli constitutional order, it should be examined in the context of the definition of the state: it is one manifestation of the significance of this definition and the tensions and contradictions that inhere in it. While the definition helps us understand the context of unamendability in the Israeli constitutional order, unamendability can also help cast light on some features of the Israeli constitutional order and the practical meaning of the definition.

In this chapter, I will explore the two forms of unamendability in Israel, their significance, scope and the functions they serve. I will also examine the implications of the entrenchment of particular values such as the Jewish character of the state for Israeli constitutionalism, bearing in mind the composition of the population (which is only 75% Jewish with 20% being Palestinian Arab).[5] The inquiry into this issue will proceed as follows: in next section, I will examine some aspects of

---

[1]One exception is Basic Law: Freedom of Occupation, which stipulates in section 7 that any amendment should be made through a Basic law.

[2]The definition could be found in Basic Law: Human Dignity and Freedom, Basic Law: Freedom of Occupation, Basic Law: The Knesset.

[3]HCJ 6427/02 *The Movement for the Quality of Governance in Israel v The Knesset* (2006) (unpublished) (Hebrew); HCJ 4908/10 *Bar-On v The Knesset* (2010) (unpublished) (Hebrew).

[4]EA 1/65 *Yerdor v Chairman of the Central Elections Committee for the Sixth Knesset* (1965), IsrSC 19(3) 365 (Hebrew)

[5]Since the focus of this chapter is on Israeli constitutional law, any mention of Palestinians or Palestinian citizens shall refer to those who are Israeli citizens but are Palestinian or Arab by national affiliation. As mentioned they are 20% of the population.

unamendable constitutional provisions. I will draw on the existing debates in the literature to point out the importance of unamendable constitutional provisions highlighting their functional and expressive significance. I will then map out the different forms and layers of unamendability in the constitutional edifice. Section 3 will focus on what I call concealed unademnability.[6] In Sect. 4, I explore unwritten unamendability. In Sect. 5, I will elaborate my arguments about the implications of unadmendability for the constitutional order and democracy, highlighting some of the unique aspects of unamendability in Israel. I will finish off with concluding remarks in Sect. 6.

2 The Meaning and Significance of Unamenable Constitutional Provisions

The idea that certain constitutional principles or certain provisions of the constitution are unamendable is neither new nor rare.[7] Despite its ubiquity, it raises serious theoretical and practical questions related to democracy. In some sense, unamendability represents an acute case of the tension between constitutionalism and democracy where not only certain constitutional principles trump legislation enacted by democratically elected representatives[8] but the very possibility of amending these constitutional principles is not available. Unamendability is, therefore, undemocratic because it denies the people the possibility of changing the constitution democratically.[9] However, some academics, such as Yaniv Roznai in his contribution to this volume, disagree and defend unamendability's compatibility with democracy. This defence primarily relies on the distinction between primary constituent power (the power to constitute or reconstitute a constitutional order) and secondary constituent power (the power amend the constitution). The primary constituent power reflects the will of the people: an expression of the sovereignty of the people who create the constitution and have the power to revise it or recreate it. Secondary constituent power, on the other hand, is limited to amendment and it operates within the limits of the existing constitutional order since it is derived from it. As such, and given the 'derivative' nature of secondary constituent power, it is limited in scope and is always subordinate to primary constituent power. Since unamendability only constrains secondary constituent power and does not preclude a revision of the constitution through the exercise of primary constituent power, supporters of unamendablility defend it as democratic. Irrespective of their democratic credentials, unamendable constitutional provisions or principles serve different functions and purposes in different constitutions, and these functions vary

---

[6]I am grateful to Richard Albert for suggesting this characterization.

[7]Roznai (2016), p. 775.

[8]For the tension between democracy and constitutionalism, see Sultany (2012), p. 371.

[9]See for example, Schwartzberg (2007), Albert (2010), p. 663.

according to the political context. In this section, I will draw on comparative constitutional law and constitutional theory in order to highlight the significance of unamendable constitutional provisions and the different functions such provisions fulfill.

Any discussion of unamendability is essentially a discussion of a special kind of constitutional amendment rules. In addition to their functional role (i.e. amending the constitution to reflect political and social change, and to address any problems or shortcomings),[10] constitutional amendment rules have an essential expressive purpose.[11] As Richard Albert notes, 'amendment rules are *one* of the sites where constitutional designers may express a polity's constitutional values, both to the persons who are nominally or actually bound by its terms, and externally to the larger world.'[12] While this expressive function is part of the general expressive function of constitutions,[13] amendment rules also help identify the hierarchy among the different constitutional values depending on the level of difficulty of adopting an amendment.[14]

The expressive function goes beyond identifying the constitutional principles. The combination of the expressive function with the fact that amendments are the main vehicle for changing the constitutional text help in identifying the most fundamental foundations of the state, and the ultimate location and holder of political power. Albert Venn Dicey has identified this feature as early as 1895. For him, knowing and understanding how a constitution is amended 'is almost equivalent to knowing who is the person or who are the body of persons in whom, under the laws of that State, sovereignty is vested'.[15] Similarly, Sujit Choudhry explains that amendment powers 'stipulate where the ultimate locus of political sovereignty lies, and are the most basic statement of a community's political identity'.[16] Other commentators also make the connection between amendment powers and sovereignty,[17] and relate these powers to constituent power.[18] Indeed, amendment rules are so significant and are intimately related to the fundamentals of the constitutional order that they strike 'at the heart of what it means to be a people who have joined together in a common venture both to define itself as a collective and to build the apparatus of their state'.[19] Amendment rules, therefore, could help identify the contours of 'the people' and who is included and excluded from the political grouping that is thought of to hold sovereignty.

---

[10]Dixon (2011).

[11]Holmes and Sunstein (1995), Albert (2013), p. 225, Roznai (2016).

[12]Albert (2013), p. 229.

[13]Sunstein (1996), p. 2021, Tushnet (1999), p. 1225.

[14]Albert (2013), p. 247.

[15]Dicey (1895), pp. 387–388.

[16]Choudhry (2005), pp. 933, 939.

[17]Klein and Sajo (2012).

[18]Colón-Ríos (2010), p. 199, Troper (2012).

[19]Albert (2009), p. 32.

The expressive function of amendment rules is even more pronounced when it comes to unamendable constitutional provisions or principles. Because of their nature, unamendable provisions combine an expressive function with a communicative one.[20] Accordingly, unamendability denotes a high level of importance and the highest level of constitutional protection in addition to denying the citizenry the choice, or even the very possibility, of changing or redesigning the constitution, leaving extra-constitutional channels—including revolution that totally destroys the constitution—as the only option. It is no surprise, therefore, that unamendable provisions and principles are inherently tied to the narrative of the past and the founding act of the constitutional order. As Ulrich Preuss puts it, 'they define the collective "self" of the polity—the "we the people"'.[21]

The expressive function is not the only relevant function. Constitutional theorists have identified more specific functions that unamendable provisions fulfill. Richard Albert identifies three functions of unamendable provisions: the preservative function, the transformational and the reconciliatory.[22] The most relevant function of unamendability for the purposes of this chapter is the preservative one. As the name implies, it seeks to preserve values or principles that are fundamental to the state.[23] As such, it is focused on the past and tries to freeze certain moments or conceptions related to the founding act, and seeks to bestow on them a sense of eternality. Unamendable provisions or principles that reflect preservative entrenchment are particularly problematic from the point of view of democratic legitimacy. They tie the hands of the citizens and inhibit the potential of developing the constitution in a manner that accounts for social, economic and political changes. This is especially problematic when the entrenched value is one that is particular and contested. It is even more so in the context of divided societies where the entrenched values are meant to congeal certain benefits bestowed upon part of the population only. In reality, this hierarchy that is created by the particular entrenchment translates into hierarchy among the citizenry. Given the entrenchment, the possibility of constitutional change to avoid this hierarchy is significantly diminished.

The transformational function, on the other hand, is forward-looking. Transformational unamendable provisions mark a clear cut from the past, usually one that is mired by injustice, with the view of starting afresh and aspiring to entrench values that would put the state on a new track.[24] These values are generally related to democracy, and principles and institutions that are associated with democracy such as human rights protection. Of course, for the transformation process to happen and to achieve the entrenched values is not just a matter of constitutional text. Equally important, if not more important, is the political will

---

[20]Albert (2010).

[21]Preuss (2011), pp. 429, 445.

[22]Albert (2010).

[23]Ibid, p. 678.

[24]Ibid, p. 685.

among the citizenry and the political actors. The transformation, therefore, should reflect, or at least speak to, the aspirations and ambitions of all citizens, regardless of their backgrounds or affiliations.

The third function that Albert identifies is in some sense related to transitional justice, and aims at diffusing the tension between different ethnic or political groups with a history of conflict and achieving reconciliation between the rival groups.[25]

These functions are not mutually exclusive. Similarly, an unamendable provision does not *always necessarily* reflect basic principles.[26] Nonetheless, the classifications and functions discussed in this section are helpful in understanding the significance of unamendable provisions and principles. Building on these theoretical insights, the next sections will examine the significance of unamendability in Israel focusing mostly on the preservative and expressive functions. Here, I adopt Richard Albert's classification of unamendability along substantive and procedural dimensions in addition to formal and informal dimensions.[27]

3   Concealed Unamendability

Constitutional amendment has never been a contested issue in Israel. Even now, when most commentators and the Supreme Court view the Basic Laws as having constitutional status, it is generally accepted that the project of adopting a full and formal constitution has not materialized yet.[28] Given the incompleteness of the project, and with one exception,[29] there are no express provisions that govern amendment procedures for Basic Laws. The Supreme Court, however, has introduced a technical-textual requirement. In the *Bank Mizrahi* case (the case in which the Supreme Court confirmed the constitutional status of Basic Laws and declared them as a partial constitution), the leading opinion of then Chief Justice Barak laid down some rules regarding the amendment of Basic Laws.[30] Since the Basic Laws were to have a higher status than ordinary legislation, it was also decided—contrary to past practice—that Basic Laws could be amended by a Basic Law only. Explaining his 'two hats' theory, Barak asserted that the Knesset 'wears' two hats: under one hat it acts as a constituent body, and under the other it acts as a legislature. Wearing the constituent body hat, the Knesset can amend a Basic Law while

---

[25]Ibid, p. 693.

[26]Roznai (2016).

[27]Albert (2014), pp. 181, 189.

[28]It is not clear if and when this project will be completed. It is not seen as a priority in the current political climate.

[29]Basic Law: Freedom of Occupation.

[30]CA 6821/93 *Bank Mizrahi HaMe'ouha v Migdal Kfar Shitofui* (1995), IsrSC 49 (2) 221 (Hebrew).

exercising constituent power,[31] and not by using its legislative authority. As such, 'ordinary' legislation cannot amend 'constitutional' Basic Laws because of its inferiority in the normative hierarchy. But this judicially introduced requirement relates only to the title of the amending act. Apart from that, and subject to any special majority clauses,[32] there are no specific provisions that deal with the enactment or amendment of Basic Laws as such. The same rules and procedures that apply for ordinary legislation apply to Basic Laws. No special majority or special quorum are required, and indeed, as in the case of Basic Law: Freedom of Occupation, a handful of Members of Knesset (MK) could adopt or amend a Basic Law.

While there are no formal unamendability provisions in any Basic Law, section 7A of Basic Law: The Knesset restricts the right to participate in parliamentary elections in a manner that makes certain constitutional amendments impossible. This provision, together with other instruments which also introduce similar barriers, make certain changes almost impossible as a matter of process. But it is not purely procedural. As will be discussed below, all of these entrenchment methods are open about the objective to protect the substantive values of 'Jewish and democratic'. This kind of entrenchment is unique in that it does not specifically declare certain provisions or principles unamendable, has nothing to do with constitutional amendment rules, but still, in effect, introduces unamendability by making the prerequisites for the amendment of the entrenched values—a majority in the Knesset—virtually impossible. Its inclusion in a Basic Law bears resemblance to formal entrenchment. However, the fact that the relevant section has nothing to do with amendment rules makes this kind of unamendability difficult to identify. It is concealed: only after a careful examination of rules related to the elections, registration of parties and the internal procedures of the Knesset, only then, this concealed unamendability is possible to identify. This concealed unamendability did not always have proper anchorage in constitutional provisions. In fact, until 1985, it was only based on an amalgam of constitutional theories and principles that the Supreme Court used to justify its decision in the landmark *Yerdor* case.[33]

---

[31]The idea of constituent power could carry a number of meanings and different theorists provide different conceptions of what it means, see Colón-Ríos (2014), p. 306. In the context of Israel, constituent power is generally seen as the power of the Knesset to adopt a constitution.

[32]A number of Basic Laws provide that amendments require a majority of all MKs regardless of the number of MKs who are present at the session. This majority is sixty one members. See for example section 5 of Basic Law: Referendum, and section 44 of Basic Law: The Government. Other Basic Laws limit this requirement to certain provisions. See for example, section 4 of Basic Law: The Knesset. Section 45 of the same Basic Law sets a majority of 80 MKs (two thirds) for amending section 44, which provides that emergency regulations cannot amend or temporarily suspend this Basic Law.

[33]*Yerdor* (see Footnote 4).

3.1   Unamendability in Other Name: The Yerdor Case

The idea that some constitutional principles are not to be changed or questioned even
through democratic means was first adopted by the Supreme Court in 1965 in the
Yerdor case. In this case, the Court confirmed the decision of the Central Elections
Committee to bar a Palestinian political group from participating in parliamentary
elections.[34] The group, known as 'the Socialist List', was affiliated with *Al-Ard*
movement. *Al-Ard* sought to organize the Palestinian minority in Israel along
national lines. The movement viewed the Palestinians in Israel as part of a Palestinian
collective and a broader Arab nation, and called for solving the conflict in a manner
consistent with the right to self-determination of the Palestinian people. The state saw
Al-Ard as a direct challenge to Zionism—the political ideology on which the state
was founded—and as such, a serious threat to the state itself. Consequently, it
systematically and consistently repressed *Al-Ard* and its members. The repression
was so severe that the decision to participate in the elections was in some sense an
attempt to seek refuge in the formalism of the law since all other methods of organizing were frustrated by the state. The group relied on the minimal formal eligibility
requirements for standing in the elections and hoped to gain a seat in the Knesset,
which, in their calculations, would have reduced the pressure on the members.[35]

Despite the lack of any formal statutory authorization to do so, the Central
Elections Committee blocked the candidacy of 'the Socialist List'. This decision was
upheld by the Supreme Court by a majority of two to one. The two majority Justices
agreed that the decision of Central Elections Committee was lawful, but each provided
his own reasoning. Then Chief Justice Agranat explained his decision by referring to
constitutional 'givens' or 'facts' that cannot be questioned by the authorities of the
state, and should be taken into consideration in the process of interpretation, especially
interpretation of constitutional laws. These facts, Agranat wrote, include the fact that
the state was created as a Jewish state, fulfilling the right to self-determination of the
Jewish people, and that this state is eternal.[36] Agranat emphasized that a group whose
political goal is 'to undermine its [the state's] very existence cannot, a priori, have the
right to take part in the process of forming the will of the people and therefore cannot
stand for election in the Knesset elections.'[37] Essentially, Agranat fused the Jewish
character of the state with its very existence and its eternity, and declared any challenge to the Jewish character, even if indirect, as a threat to the state as a whole. To
justify his position, and the apparent contradiction with democracy, Agranat used the
Weimar Republic and the American Civil War as examples of how democracy could
be subverted by groups that rise to power democratically.

The other member of the majority, Justice Sussman, agreed with Agranat, but
also added his own reasoning which was based on natural law. He likened the state

---

[34]By Palestinian I mean Palestinian citizens of Israel, sometimes known as Israeli-Arabs.

[35]Jiryis (1976), Harris (2001), p. 107.

[36]*Yerdor* (see Footnote 4) 387.

[37]Ibid.

to a human, and since a human cannot agree to be killed, a state cannot agree to be destroyed. This reasoning, like Agranat's, presumes that the state and the Jewish identity are inseparable. Borrowing a modified version of Germany's post-war principle of 'militant democracy', Sussman introduced the idea of 'defensive democracy'—a state should not allow subversive groups to undermine democracy by using democratic processes. The minority judge, Justice Chaim Cohen, adhered to the formalistic approach which was dominant at the time: he stated that absent explicit statutory authorisation, the Committee has no power to ban candidates.

The *Yerdor* ruling became one of the main constitutional principles in Israeli law. It signalled that in the direct confrontation between Zionism and the classic liberal conception of the rule of law, Zionism prevailed. Even though the majority tried to provide seemingly democratic justifications by using the idea of 'defensive democracy', the essence of the decision was that democracy is subordinate to the Jewish state. Not only is the Jewish character eternal and unchallengeable, any serious questioning of it will eventually mean losing the right to participate in the elections. Furthermore, the ruling also established some principles as having higher normative status with some commentators at the time arguing that the Court introduced a judge-made 'supra-constitution' and created a feeling of uncertainty about the constitutional structure.[38]

3.2 Formalizing Concealed Unamendability: Section 7A of Basic Law: The Knesset

The foundational principle introduced in *Yerdor* was incorporated into Basic Law: The Knesset. In 1985, the Knesset enacted section 7A of Basic Law: The Knesset which gave the Central Elections Committee the power to ban the participation of any party in the elections if its goals and actions, expressly or by implication, include 'the negation of the existence of the State of Israel as the state of the Jewish people', the negation of its democratic character, and incitement to racism.[39]

---

[38]Guberman (1967), pp. 455, 460. For a more detailed discussion, see Masri (2017).

[39]Section 7A was amended in 2002 to combine the first two grounds into one: the negation of the existence of Israel as a Jewish and democratic state. This was meant to bring it in line with the Basic Laws that were enacted in the early 1990s that used the 'Jewish and democratic'. The 2002 amendment also added new grounds especially tailored for Palestinian candidates—supporting armed conflict by an enemy state or a terror organization. As it stands today, section 7A provides that: A candidates list shall not participate in elections to the Knesset, and a person shall not be a candidate for election to the Knesset, if the goals or actions of the list or the actions of the person, expressly or by implication, include one of the following: (1) negation of the existence of the State of Israel as a Jewish and democratic state; (2) incitement to racism; (3) support for armed struggle by a hostile state or a terrorist organization against the State of Israel. (a1) For the purpose of this section, a candidate who has spent time in an enemy country in the seven years prior to the date of submitting the candidate's list, shall be seen as someone whose actions are considered support for armed struggle against the State of Israel, unless it was proved otherwise.

The section clarified the *Yerdor* rule by explicitly including the negation or rejection of Israel's characterization as the state of the Jewish people as grounds for banning participation in the general elections. Until then, this was only implicit in the reasoning of Chief Justice Agranat in *Yerdor*. The section also added negation of democracy and incitement to racism as grounds for excluding a group from the electoral process as a response to the Court's refusal to ban the participation of the extreme right-wing Jewish group *Kach* in 1984.[40] The grounds for disqualification in section 7A were also incorporated in section 4 of the Parties Law-1992, restricting the registration of political parties on the same grounds. The restrictions were further extended to elections for local and city councils through section 39 of the Local Authorities Law (Elections)-1965.

Since its enactment in 1984, there have been numerous attempts to use section 7A in almost all elections for the Knesset. In most cases, the Central Elections Committee, which is comprised of representatives of political parties and headed by a Supreme Court Justice, approved the disqualification from participation in the elections. The Committee usually targets parties that represent Palestinian citizens or extreme right-wing parties. The opposite trend could be identified at the level of the Supreme Court which took a restrictive approach. It ruled that the interpretation of section 7A should be 'specific, narrow and restricted' and its application should be limited to the most extreme cases.[41] It also imposed a high evidentiary threshold.[42] Given the narrow interpretation and the high evidentiary threshold, it is rare for the Court to uphold the ban. Virtually in all cases, other than the landmark 1965 *Yerdor* case, the Court allowed the candidacy to stand. In most cases, the decision was a split decision, and in all cases the Court did not spare words in expressing its disapproval of, and even contempt for the political ideas, statements or actions.

While section 7A does not necessarily ban Palestinian citizens from the Knesset, it does seek to block the access of certain ideas that seek to challenge the status quo based on universal values. What the section does, to put it in the words of former Chief Justice Meir Shamgar, is to 'screen, in advance, what the image of the Knesset and its elected members will be after the elections'.[43] Since the Knesset is the body that has the power to amend the constitution, the restrictions that section 7A imposes are also restrictions on the scope of amendment and change in the Israeli constitutional order. The restrictions, in effect, block the possibility of certain changes by blocking access to the Knesset. Sharon Weintal is right in describing section 7A as 'an implicit eternity clause'.[44] Not only is it implicit, it is concealed in a provision that does not deal with constitutional amendments.

---

[40]EA 2/84 Neiman (1985).

[41]EA 1/88 Neiman (1988).

[42]EC 11280/02 *Central Elections Committee for the Sixteenth Knesset v Tibi* (2003),IsrSC 57(4) 1 (Hebrew).

[43]HCJ 620/85 *Mi'ari v Speaker of the Knesset* (1987), IsrSC 41(4) 169, 211 (Hebrew).

[44]Weintal (2013, 2014, p. 177).

The central principle that section 7A renders unamendable is the definition of the state as Jewish and democratic. This definition is taken to reflect the core values and principles of the constitutional order. This is hardly surprising given that the state was formed by the Zionist movement for the exercise of self-determination of Jews, and that the Jewish character of the state has been taken for granted since its creation in 1948. The Declaration of the Establishment of the State of Israel emphasizes this character,[45] and so do other statutes and numerous Court decisions.[46] As the Supreme Court has highlighted repeatedly, 'the raison d'etre of the state is being a Jewish state'.[47] But what does the phrase 'Jewish and democratic' mean? This has been addressed in a number Supreme Court decisions.[48] The Court provided a number of core characteristics for both parts of the definition. For the 'democratic' element, the Court stated that the minimal characteristics should include the principle of the sovereignty of the people and periodical elections, in addition to the preservation of the core of fundamental human rights.[49] On the other hand, the core characteristics for a minimalist definition of Israel as a Jewish state

> have a Zionist perspective and a traditional perspective at the same time [...]. At their centre stands the right of every Jew to make aliya [Jewish immigration to Israel] to the State of Israel, that in Israel Jews constitute a majority; Hebrew is the main official language of the state, and its main holidays and symbols reflect the national emergence of the Jewish people, the heritage of Israel is a central component of the state's religious and cultural heritage.[50]

This definition is not merely descriptive: it plays an important role in defining the polity, the public culture, immigration rights, state policies and the scope of protection of constitutional rights. It also mandates that Israel *must* have a Jewish majority. According to former Chief Justice Aharon Barak, the definition has a 'normative constitutional status that is above the law'.[51] Its relevance encompasses the entire Israeli legal system. As Barak has put it, the values of Jewish and democratic are 'standards for the interpretation of the purposes of all Basic Laws'.[52] Consistency with these values is seen as a condition to any restriction on human rights, whether those rights are explicitly protected by a Basic Law or not.

---

[45]Para. 10 of the Declaration states that 'Accordingly we, members of the People's Council, representatives of the Jewish Community of Eretz-Israel and of the Zionist movement, are here assembled on the day of the termination of the British Mandate over Eretz-Israel and, by virtue of our natural and historic right and on the strength of the resolution of the United Nations General Assembly, hereby declare the establishment of a Jewish State in Eretz-Israel to be known as the State of Israel.'

[46]See for example, the Law of Return-1950, and the World Zionist Organization and Jewish Agency Status Law-1952.

[47]Tibi (see Footnote 42) 21.

[48]HCJ 6698/96 *Ka'dan v Land Administration of Israel* (2000), IsrSC 54 (1) 258 (Hebrew); ibid.

[49]Tibi (see Footnote 42) 23.

[50]Ibid, p. 22.

[51]Barak (2004), p. 83.

[52]Ibid.

The definition also affects the interpretation of legal texts in general. Similarly, as discussed earlier, the definition also plays a major role in defining the scope of the right to political participation. The Supreme Court balances the consistent emphasis on the Jewish character by stating that it does not mean discrimination against non-Jews. The Court has ruled that Israel 'is a Jewish state in which minorities live, including the Arab minority. Everyone who belongs to these minorities enjoys full equal rights'.[53] It also pointed out that 'equality of rights between humans in Israel, whatever their religion or national belonging is, is derived from the values of the state as a Jewish and democratic state'.[54] While this commitment to equality is to be noted, the repeated emphasis on the Jewish character and essence, and the practical meaning of the definition, in reality translate into favourable treatment for Jews. It is, therefore, hard to reconcile this commitment to equality with the Jewish character and the rulings of the Supreme Court.[55]

3.3   Rules of Procedures of the Knesset

Concealed unamendability is not only limited to the laws and Basic Laws that are related to elections. The internal rules governing the work of the Knesset add more barriers to constitutional changes related to the Jewish character of the state. According to section 75(e) of the Rules of Procedure (formerly, section 134), '[a] private members' bill shall be brought for the approval of the Knesset Presidium. The Knesset Presidium shall not approve a bill that in its opinion denies the existence of the State of Israel as the state of the Jewish People, or is racist in its essence.' The Rules of Procedure also introduce general obligations to act in a manner consistent with the definition. A Member of the Knesset, according to the 'General Principles' section of the Rules, 'shall fulfill his position out of loyalty to the fundamental principles of the State of Israel as a Jewish and democratic state' [section 1A(1)]. Similar principles also apply to members of all-party parliamentary groups that promote certain issues or interest. According to section 138(g), such groups shall not be allowed to function if their goals or activities, explicitly or implicitly, include 'the denial of the existence of the State of Israel as a Jewish and democratic State.'

While the Rules of Procedure are not on the same normative level as legislation or Basic Laws, they are, nonetheless, part of the broader constitutional order that sets the limits to what kind of legislation, including Basic Laws, can even be debated, let alone enacted. While these arrangements can be changed by a simple majority, the existence of a provision like section 75(e) functions as a further

---

[53]*Ka'dan* (see Footnote 48) 282.

[54]Ibid.

[55]Jabareen (2002), Masri (2013), p. 309, Masri (2017), Sultany (2017).

obstacle that would block any legislative proposal from being debated if it does not conform to the Jewishness of the state.

4 Unwritten Unamendability: Constituent Power and Its Limits

Even though the barrier presented by Basic Law: The Knesset is a significant form of entrenchment, especially when added to the near impossibility of achieving a majority for a constitutional amendment that would change the constitutional definition, the Supreme Court and academics have weighed in on the question of the limits of constitutional amendments. The Supreme Court has essentially adopted an unwritten unamendability rule regarding the definition of the state.

It has been widely accepted, since the *Bank Mizrahi* decision in 1995, that the Knesset, representing the people, can exercise constituent power and adopt constitutional norms in the form of Basic Laws. The Court's confirmation of the Knesset's constituent power settled the discussion on the question of the constitutional status of the Basic Laws, but it raised the question of the limits of the power of the Knesset as a constituent body. This question was discussed in the academic literature before it was addressed by the Supreme Court, and the discussions expressed a clear inclination in favour of accepting limits on constituent power. Three views are of relevance here. When former Chief Justice Barak was at the early stages of developing his 'two hats' theory, he suggested that as a constituent body the Knesset can bind itself.[56] Regarding the particular question of unamendability, he did not express a clear position, but raised this issue by way of rhetorical questions, as he did in *La'or Movement* case,[57] or by seemingly neutral reference to the *Yerdor* decision and the decision of the Supreme Court of India in *Kesavananda Bharati v. State of Kerala,* and German cases stating that even the constitutional order as a whole has to conform to certain constitutional values, as he did in *Bank Mizrahi* and in his extra-judicial writing.[58] Later on, and as will be discussed below, Barak adopted a clearer position: the power of the Knesset as a constituent body is limited by the fundamental values of the state as Jewish and democratic. Claude Klein, influenced by continental European constitutional theories, distinguished between original constituent power (*pouvoir constituent originaire*) and derived constituent power (*pouvoir constituent institute*).[59] Applying this approach to Israel, Klein argued that when the Knesset enacts a new Basic Law dealing with a new issue, it exercises original constituent power, and when it amends an existing Basic Law, it exercises derived constituent power—or

---

[56]Barak (1994), p. 43.
[57]HCJ 142/89 *La'or Movement v Speaker of the Knesset* (1990), IsrSC 44(3) 529 (Hebrew).
[58]*Bank Mizrahi* (see Footnote 30) 394; Barak (1994), pp. 566–567.
[59]Klein (1978, p. 203, 1993, p. 123, 1997, p. 341).

amending power. The latter form of constituent power is limited in its scope compared to the former. Ariel Bendor adopted the original/amending distinction, but applied it differently: he argued that only the People's Council of 1948 (the representative body that represented the Jewish community in Palestine on the eve of the creation of the state), which adopted the Declaration of the Establishment of the State, is the body that can exercise original constituent power.[60] When the Knesset exercises constituent power, it only exercises derived constituent power, and this power is limited by the values of the Declaration, mainly, the Jewish character and the democratic mode of governance.

It was only a matter of time until the Supreme Court weighed in on the matter. While none of the cases that reached the Supreme Court required a positive determination on this issue, the Supreme Court did address it a number of times. The discussions, almost all of them *obiter dicta* and incidental to the matters discussed, reflect an inclination among the Justices that the Knesset is not omnipotent when acting in its constituent capacity, and that there are some principles that limit its powers. The most pronounced discussion of this issue was in the case of *The Movement for the Quality of Governance in Israel v. The Knesset.*[61] In this case, the Supreme Court upheld, albeit reluctantly, the constitutionality of a law that deferred mandatory military service for ultra-orthodox yeshiva students.[62] This law, known also as the '*Tal* law', was meant to regulate the military service of ultra-orthodox students who were exempt from such service since the creation of the state. In practice, deferral meant exemption from service. Since this exemption is not granted to other sectors of (the Jewish) society, the law was challenged for violating equality. The majority in the Supreme Court found that there is evidence of infringement on equality but they upheld its constitutionality. More interesting for our purposes was the debate between then Chief Justice Aharon Barak and the lone dissenter, his deputy then, Michel Chechin.

Deputy Chief Justice Chechin relied on social contract theory in his dissenting opinion which held that the law was unconstitutional. He asserted that all states are based on some foundational social contract.[63] Some of the contents of this contract are reflected in the constitution or in legislation, but others, despite their importance, are not. But this does not mean that they are not basic values of the legal system. These basic values could be summoned to directly dictate certain outcomes during extraordinary situations.[64] Chechin viewed the exemption from service as violating three basics: the Jewish character, democracy and equality.[65] He linked the Jewishness of the state to the security threats it faces: without a strong army,

---

[60]Bendor (2000).

[61]*The Movement* (see Footnote 3).

[62]Yeshivas are Jewish religious schools for adult males.

[63]*The Movement* (see Footnote 3) [9] (Chechin J).

[64]Ibid [10]–[11] (Chechin J).

[65]Ibid. [12] (Chechin J).

there can be no Jewish state. A collective exemption from military service, therefore, is a violation of the 'Jewish' values as well as a violation of equality.

Barak agreed in principle but disapproved of going as far as the social contract and the basic values before exhausting other avenues of constitutional examination. Barak's main critique was that the examination of the constitutionality of legislation should proceed according to the Basic Laws by examining the protected rights and the 'limitation clauses' which provide the proportionality tests. The latter include an assessment of the impugned legislation against the basic values of the system.[66] But as a matter of principle, Barak agreed that

> 'there is room for the view that a statute or a Basic Law that negates the character of Israel as a Jewish and democratic state is not constitutional. The people, the sovereign, did not authorize our Knesset to do so. The Knesset was authorized to act within the framework of the basic principles of the regime. It was not authorized to annul them. This case before us does not fall within that narrow frame'.[67]

The fact that this discussion was *obiter dicta* does not detract from its importance. Both the majority and the minority agreed on the principle that some constitutional amendments may be unconstitutional and that the Court has the power to declare them invalid. This position found more support in later case law. In *Bar-On v The Knesset,* Barak's successor as Chief Justice, Dorit Beinisch, expressed her support for the doctrine of unconstitutional constitutional amendment and was of the view that 'the courts in Israel have recognized the existence of principles that cannot be changed. Our Basic Laws have also laid down the central constitutional principle—and it is doubtful that it could be changed—that relates to the Jewish and democratic character of the state'.[68] Beinisch, citing an academic article by Barak,[69] qualified her position explaining that the situation in Israel is not fully ripe for the doctrine's application in a broad manner; since the constitution is still evolving, the doctrine should only be applied in a narrow manner and be limited to the Jewish and democratic character of the state.

In his later extra-judicial writing, Barak anchored this position in the Declaration of the Establishment of the State of Israel. The Declaration 'authorized' the adoption of a constitution, and as the authorizing text, it sets the Jewish and democratic values as the limits of this authorization.[70] Even though the Declaration does not mention the word democracy, Barak read it into the Declaration. This kind of anchoring distinguishes unwritten unamendability in this case from other forms of unwritten unamendability. Richard Albert suggests a theory that derives

---

[66]The 'limitation clause' is section 7 of Basic Law: Human Dignity and Freedom, which provides that 'There shall be no violation of rights under this Basic Law except by a law befitting the values of the State of Israel, enacted for a proper purpose, and to an extent no greater than is required.'

[67]*The Movement* (see Footnote 3) [74] (Barak CJ).

[68]*Bar-On* (see Footnote 3) [33] (Beinisch CJ).

[69]The article appeared in English as Barak (2011, p. 321).

[70]Ibid.

unwritten unamendability from constitutional convention.[71] Applying this under-standing to Canada and Japan, he derives unwritten unamendability from political norms that are based on customs or practices that political actors have acquiesced with, and that are not judicially enforceable. In the case of Israel, however, unwritten unamendability has stronger roots that go beyond constitutional con-vention that develops over time. More importantly, the Jewish and democratic values of the state are enforceable in courts and are not necessarily seen as polit-ically agreed on by all political actors. Palestinians are generally opposed to the 'Jewish' values as central constitutional values, for these reflect Zionist principles that give preference to the Jewish majority. Many conservative, especially religious political parties, are also opposed to the 'democratic' elements of these values.

Unwritten unamendability here is an added and more powerful layer of pro-tection that could protect the Jewish and democratic values in the event that the first layer of protection—Basic Law: The Knesset–fails in its function to screen in advance the composition of the Knesset. Unwritten unamendability also protects section 7A of the Basic Law from amendment. The section is not entrenched, and could, in theory, be amended with a simple majority. However, an amendment repealing the section, or removing the power to disqualify parties or individuals for the 'negation of the existence of the State of Israel as a Jewish and democratic state', could arguably be declared an unconstitutional amendment for it could be seen as a violation of the values as reflected by the Jewish and democratic definition.

5 Unamendability in Israel: Implications for Constitutionalism and Democracy

The myriad forms of entrenchment of the 'Jewish and democratic' definition dis-cussed in the previous parts may give the impression that constitutional change is imminent and that the Knesset is about to vote for change in the near future. This scenario is far from being probable. The Jewish definition is strongly within the national consensus among (Jewish) Israelis. The Palestinian citizens who are negatively impacted by the definition are only 20% of the general population, and their representatives occupy 13 out of 120 seats in the Knesset. While their per-centage in the population is slowly increasing, this growth is not expected to threaten the Jewish majority. A situation whereby such a change is possible in a democratic way will inevitably be preceded by fundamental changes to the state and society. The entrenchment mechanisms are not expected to be of any use in the near future. However, the examination of unadmendablity in this context provides some insights into Israeli constitutionalism. Similarly, the Israeli case is one that can

---

[71]Albert (2015, p. 655).

enrich our understanding of unamendability, and demonstrate how unamendability could be introduced in different forms to deepen certain understandings of the constitutional order and to preserve existing divides and privileges.

5.1 Unamendability in Context: The Israeli Constitutional Order

Unamendability in Israel should be viewed in the context of the constitutional order and the events and circumstances that prevailed at the time the state was established. The creation of the state as a Jewish state in 1948 came mainly as a result of the efforts of the Zionist movement which were facilitated by one of the great powers at the time, the British Empire. The Zionist movement aimed at creating a state with a Jewish majority in an area where the majority of the population was Arab. This meant an inevitable conflict between the new settlers and the native population.[72] This conflict came to a head with the 1948 war, as a result of which the majority of the Palestinians were expelled or were forced to flee from the area that became Israel and effectively creating the Jewish majority.[73] However, the state population was not purely Jewish—12% of the population were native Palestinians. While those were eventually given Israeli citizenship, until today they suffer from discrimination in almost all aspects of life.[74] The state, in reality, oscillated between two poles: the pole of universality expected from a modern state which should be built on citizenship rights, democracy, and the rule of law, and the pole of ethnic/religious state that aims to consolidate and preserve a solid ethnic/religious majority among its citizens.

This oscillation finds its expression in the definition of the state which combines the universal element (democracy) with the particular ethnic/religious element (Jewishness). The outcome of the oscillation between these two poles, however, is not neutral, for the Jewish definition is given more weight. The founding ideologies and the constituent narrative are preserved, and are part of the fundamental principles of the state. They are visible in almost every facet of the constitutional order: they play a role in immigration laws and policies, in political participation, in legislation and legal interpretation, in the process of constitution making and amendment, and in the process of judicial review. Of course, this strong presence is

---

[72]The idea that the Israeli–Palestinian conflict should be seen and studied as a colonial conflict between settlers and natives was first discussed in the academic literature in the 1960s and 1970s. This approach has gain more momentum and increased interest since the late 1990s. See for example, Sayeg (1965), Rodinson (1973), Said (1979) Zureik (1979), Shafir (1996), Veracini (2006), Piterberg (2008), Shalhoub-Kevorkian (2015). This view however is vigorously challenged by other writers, see Aaronsohn (1996), p. 214, Dershowitz (2003), Gavison (2003), Rubenstein and Yakobson (2009).

[73]Morris (2004), Pappe (2006).

[74]For a summary of these policy area, see Hesketh (2011), see also Masri (2017).

reflected in laws and policies that are favourable for Jewish citizens and discriminatory or even racist for the Palestinian citizens.[75]

This context helps explain the significance of the expressive function of unamendability. Not only are the values expressed in the definition foundational, they also present an image of the state that the current generation cannot even envision changing, and in effect ban any change. The expressive function is accentuated by two other factors. The first factor is the fact that Israel does not have a formal and complete constitution, nor does it have any special constitutional amendment rules, but still has unamendable principles. Essentially, this means that the (Jewish) Israeli society is unwilling or unable to reach a consensus on a formal constitution, but can only agree (and express the view) that it should be within the limits of 'Jewish and democratic'. The second is the fact that, as mentioned above, the likelihood that the Knesset would vote to amend the definition is so remote or even impossible, even without recourse to section 7A of Basic Law: The Knesset. The near impossibility of such an amendment highlights the expressive role of unamendability. It has to do more with declaring values and ideology rather than pre-empting possible risks.

5.2   Unamendability and the Hierarchy of Values and Norms

Unamendability is another site where we can see the tension and the oscillation between the universal and the particular. The entrenchment of the 'Jewish and democratic' definition is in effect the entrenchment of two combined values, the Jewish character and democracy. The Jewish character is particular; it is legally defined in the Law of Return-1950 in ethnic and religious terms,[76] and this definition and the question of 'who is a Jew' have been the subject of multiple cases which highlighted the particular aspects.[77] The particularity also extends to the social and political understanding of the term. Democracy on the other hand is a universal value, and its protection also means protection of the right of the population as a whole to participate in governing itself. Despite attempts at reconciling the two elements, the particularism of the Jewish character is generally the dominant element, whether in matters related to symbols and aesthetics, or laws, rights and policies.[78] Unamendability in this context is meant to protect both parts of the definition from change through *a democratic process*. There are good reasons why

---

[75]For a database of discriminatory laws in Israel see, 'Discriminatory Laws in Israel', Adalah, www.adalah.org/en/law/index.

[76]Section 4B of *The Law of Return-1950* provides: 'For the purpose of this law, "a Jew"—a person who was born of a Jewish mother, or has converted to Judaism, and is not a member of any other religion'.

[77]HCJ 72/62 *Raufeisen v Minister of Interior* (1962), IsrSC 13, 2430 (Hebrew); HCJ 58/68 *Schalit v Minister of Interior* (1970), IsrSC 23 (2) 477 (Hebrew). See also Masri (2017).

[78]Jabareen (2002), Masri (2013).

this protection should extend to democracy: it is a universal value and its constitutional entrenchment, even if there is a fleeting majority that wants to change it, refers back to democracy as the foundational principle at the heart of the constitutional order. It does not extinguish the will of the people. On the contrary, it establishes popular sovereignty as the source of the authority of the state. On the other hand, unamendability also means that the Jewish definition, cannot be changed democratically. The Jewish character is not a matter of democratic agreement, but an axiomatic given that cannot be changed or even questioned using democratic processes. This situates the Jewish character above democracy creating a hierarchy among the fundamental values.

This position could be countered using the justification that is generally invoked to defend the democratic pedigree of unamendability: the distinction between secondary and primary constituent power. In his spirited defence of unamendability, Yaniv Roznai argues, *inter alia*, that unamendability may foreclose constitutional amendments based on secondary constituent power, and this foreclosure is justified because it gives expression to the will of the people who adopted unamendability when they exercised primary constituent power.[79] Unamendability, however, does not block the option of exercising primary constituent power, where all values could be revised or reformed, including unamendable provisions or values. According to this line of reasoning, as long as the people have the option to exercise its primary constituent power, then the undemocratic objection to unamendability does not stand or is at least significantly weakened.

At least three objections could be raised against this position. First, this argument pre-supposes that the existing constitution, which contains the unamendable provisions, was adopted in a democratic manner, which is not always the case.[80] If the existing constitution cannot pass the democratic legitimacy test, then this defence of unamendability fails. The second objection is related to the manner and form of exercising primary constituent power. While the distinction between primary and secondary constituent power is neat in theory, the reality and the practice are much more complicated since there is no one formula, template or agreed upon standards or procedures that could be followed. Indeed, one of the main attributes of primary constituent power is that it is generally thought of as extra-constitutional and extra-legal. The lack of processes, institutions, standards or models readily available for exercising primary constituent power makes the idea more complex to translate into practical reality. The requirement to overcome all of these barriers provides for a very high threshold for change. A third objection, is related to legality: most theorists see the exercise of primary constituent power as something that precedes the constitution and, therefore, necessarily outside legality. Exercising primary constituent power to change or remove unamendable provisions or principles means

---

[79]Yaniv Roznai, 'Necrocracy or Democracy? Assessing Objections to Constitutional Unamendability' in this volume.

[80]See for example the Turkish Constitution which was adopted in the aftermath of a military coup d'etat, as described by Oya Yegen and Tarik Olcay in their contribution to this volume.

breaking away from law. But until this revision happens, those who are opposed to the values that are protected by unamendability and act to change them are in some sense outside the realm of legality. In Israel, this is not merely a theoretical concern and a number of examples demonstrate how being outside the realm of legality can easily translate into repressive practices. A statutory amendment from 2011 is a case in point: according to section 3A(1) of the Foundations of the Budget Law (Amendment No. 40) (Reduction of Budget or Support Because of Activity Against Principles of the State)–2011, the Minister of Finance is empowered to reduce funding to a publicly funded body if it makes any expenditure that could be seen as a negation of the existence of the state as a Jewish and democratic state. These powers are, in all but name, powers to impose a criminal penalty in the form of a fine.[81] Outright criminalisation of statements rejecting the 'Jewish and democratic' definition was proposed in a private member bill in 2009.[82] In the same vein, the secret service (GSS or SHABAK) characterizes as 'subversive' any activity that seeks 'to change the basic values of the state and annul its democratic character or Jewish character', and is authorized by the Attorney General to use surveillance and enforcement powers against such 'subversive' activities.[83] Even if there is no clear break with legality, unamendable clauses, as Ulrich Preuss notes, split the constitution into two levels: one that represents constitutional legality and another that embodies the values and principles of the eternity clause which are seen as more important and more fundamental.[84] This split between legality and super-legality is a source of concern for Preuss since the super-legality of the constitution could be used to overrule its legality.

5.3   Unamendability: The Particular v. the Universal

The distinction between the particular and the universal values in the context of unamendability is important. The entrenchment of universal values and principles that are meant to be for the benefit of the general population, especially values that are related to democracy, human dignity and some aspects of human rights, could be defended and justified as intrinsic to democracy. This argument does not stand for particularistic values. The Supreme Court Justices who introduced the unwritten unamendability glossed over this distinction when they sought to draw support for

---

[81] A petition to the Supreme Court challenging the constitutionality of this statute was dismissed in 2012, see HCJ 3429/11 *The Alumni of the Arab Orthodox High School in Haifa v Minister of Finance* (2012) (Hebrew).

[82] Penal Law Bill (Amendment-The Prohibition of Publicising Incitement to Negate the Existence of the State of Israel as a Jewish and Democratic State)-2009.

[83] Letter from the Attorney General's Office to Adalah (20 May 2007), in *Adalah Newsletter* (May 2007) 36, https://web.archive.org/web/20120303210907/, http://www.adalah.org/newsletter/eng/may07/5.php (Hebrew).

[84] Preuss (2011).

their position from comparative law. Barak, for example, writing extra judicially in an article where he reaffirmed his view that any constitutional change cannot violate the heart of democracy and 'Israel's existence as a Jewish state or the minimum requirements for that character',[85] examined the applicability of unamendable constitutional provisions in Turkey, India, Austria, Germany, US, Ireland and Brazil. In *Bar-On*, Beinisch mentioned Turkey and the Czech Republic.[86] Anchoring this position on the unamendability of the Jewish and democratic definition in comparative literature is disingenuous. Almost all of the cases of unconstitutional constitutional amendments mentioned dealt with universal principles such as democracy, human dignity, and the republican form of governance. Some refer to broader principles like 'the basic structure of the constitution' as in India, but none of them are as particular as in the case of Israel.

While Barak and Beinisch have no problem in seeing the definition of the state and its minimum requirements as demarcating the borders of possible constitutional amendments, Sharon Weintal is aware of the tension in holding a particular value such as the Jewish character as unamendable. He acknowledges that this creates tension with popular sovereignty and suggests that such clauses or principles should be interpreted narrowly.[87] He nonetheless accepts that certain founding values, particular as they may be, may be unamendable provided that such arrangements could be changed using what he calls 'three track democracy'.[88] However, Weintal's acknowledgement of the difficulties that unamendability creates in the Israeli context does not stop him from accepting the legitimacy and or even desirability of the current situation where the particular values are dominant. For example, he endorses a constitutional review mechanism based on compatibility with the foundational basic principles to block changes to legislation that contradicts those principles.[89]

Combining universal and particular values and designating these values as unamendable in effect raises these values to a level which is supra-constitutional. But the universalism of democracy does not necessarily counterbalance the particularism of the Jewish definition. The constitutional order is more favourable for those who associate with this particular value; those who do not associate with the particular value are excluded as constitutional actors. Echoes of such exclusion could be heard in Ulrich Preuss' discomfort with some aspects of eternity clauses. As discussed in the previous section, Preuss is concerned about the split between legality and super-legality that unamendability creates because of the possible use

---

[85]Barak (2011), p. 340.

[86]*Bar-On* (see Footnote 3).

[87]Weintal (2011), p. 449, 494.

[88]Under this paradigm the decision making process is divided to three tracks: normal (legislative) politics, constitutional politics, and revolutionary constitutional politics. Entrenched values could not be changed under the first two tracks, but the third track is for him the appropriate track to deal with entrenchment. The third track involves creating a special process and a special ad hoc body to crystallize the new collective will under the supervision of the courts.

[89]Weintal (2014), p. 194.

of super-legality to overrule legality.[90] Unamendability could be used by ruling elites who can 'identify their values and interests with the identity of the polity as a whole and exclude nonconformist and dissenting segments of society as enemies of the constitution, by accusing them of intending to challenge the existential values of the polity and ultimately the existence of the polity itself'.[91] It could be used to identify 'enemies who have a status of less than full citizenship'.[92] Indeed, it seems that the unamendable principles in Israel that highlight the Jewish character 'define the collective "self" of the polity—the "we the people"', as Preuss put it, to the exclusion of 20% of the population.[93] Essentially, the entrenchment of the particular values in this way creates classes of citizenship. It also opens the door and legitimizes the use of coercive state power to repress those who do not agree with the entrenched values. This is exceptionally problematic when those who are subject to these coercive powers are also a distinct national minority.

6   Conclusions

Unamendability has never occupied the centre stage of constitutional debates in Israel. The reasons for this are obvious: the existing constitutional arrangements are seen as partial only and fall short of a full constitution, and they lack provisions about constitutional amendments. This, however, was not a barrier to introducing two forms of unamendability: concealed unamendability, which is the result of restrictions on who can stand for elections, and unwritten unamendability, introduced by the Supreme Court and supported by academic opinion. The state's definition as 'Jewish and democratic' is the red line that no constitutional change could cross. Echoes of this position, which was established clearly in the case law, resonate throughout the legal system, especially when it comes to political participation and the process of legislation. This position is unique in that it determines what could not be changed in the constitution before having a full constitution with amending rules. Equally unique (and more problematic) is the fact that those who support it are not concerned about its implications, especially when it comes to the hierarchy between democracy and the Jewish character, and the extent to which this hierarchy translates into hierarchy among the citizenry.

The situation in Israel presents a good case study of both the expressive and the preservative functions of unamendable clauses and principles and the tension with democracy. The unamendable 'Jewish and democratic' values declare their superiority over other norms and announce that they cannot be changed through democratic ways, and in essence put the Jewish character above democracy.

---

[90]Preuss (2011).

[91]Ibid, p. 447.

[92]Ibid.

[93]Ibid, p. 445.

Equally important is the preservative function. Whether through section 7A of Basic Law: The Knesset and its role in blocking any potential change before it materializes, or through the Rules of Procedure of the Knesset which play a similar role, the preservative impetus is clear to see. Equally clear is the fact that the entrenched values are meant to congeal certain benefits bestowed on part of the population only, that is, full membership in the polity. Since the probability that such change could happen through the existing mechanism is almost non-existent, this preservative function ends up further supporting and amplifying the expressive role.

This analysis of unamendability in Israel shows some of the negative aspects of unamendability and its potential instrumentalization to introduce hierarchy among the citizenry and to entrench a special and favourable status for certain groups at the expense of others. Unamendability in this context also raises questions about the constitutional order itself and its democratic credentials, for it is not clear whether 'the people'–which according to the Supreme Court is the political unit that holds sovereignty and authorizes making and changing the constitution includes the entire collective of citizens.[94] Are the Palestinian citizens part of this unit given the hierarchy that unamendability contributes to? Could they be part of 'the people' when the constitutional order a priori informs them that they cannot even try to change it to remove one of the sources of their legal inferiority? These questions that arise from examining unamendability in Israeli constitutional law highlight the importance of context. Any examination of unamendable provisions or principles should always be situated in the social, political and economic context, for in many cases, unamendability goes beyond mere technicalities and could have a profound impact on state, society and individuals.

Acknowledgements I would like to thank the participants of the 'Workshop on Unamendable Constitutional Provisions' for their comments and feedback. Special thanks to Richard Albert and Bertil Emrah Oder for organizing the workshop, to Esra Ozcan and Zeynep Kocer for helping host the workshop, and to Yaniv Roznai for thorough and very helpful comments.

References

Aaronsohn R (1996) Settlement in Eretz Israel: a colonial enterprise? "Critical" scholarship and historical geography. Israel Stud 1(2):214
Albert R (2009) Nonconstitutional amendments. Can J Law Jurisprud 22:5, 32
Albert R (2010) Constitutional handcuffs. Arizona State Law J 42:663
Albert R (2013) The expressive function of constitutional amendment rules. McGill Law J 59 (2):225
Albert R (2014) Constructive unamendability in Canada and the United States. Supreme Court Law Rev 67:181, 189
Albert R (2015) Amending constitutional amendment rules. Int J Const Law 13(3):655
Barak A (1994) Interpretation in law. Nevo Publishing, New York (Hebrew)
Barak A (2004) A Judge in a democratic society. Nevo Publishing, New York (Hebrew)

---

[94]Masri (2017).

Barak A (2011) Unconstitutional constitutional amendments. Israel Law Rev 44:321

Bendor A (2000) The legal status of the basic laws. In: Barak A, Berenson C (eds) Berenson book, vol 2. Nevo Publishing, New York (Hebrew)

Choudhry S (2005) Old imperial dilemmas and the new nation-building: constitutive constitutional politics in multinational polities. Connecticut Law Rev 37:933, 939

Colón-Ríos J (2010) The legitimacy of the juridical: constituent power, democracy and the limits of constitutional reform. Osgoode Hall Law J 48:199

Colón-Ríos J (2014) Five conceptions of constituent power. Law Q Rev 130:306

Dershowitz A (2003) The case for Israel. Wiley, Hoboken

Dicey AV (1895) Constitutional revision. Law Q Rev 11:387, 388

Dixon R (2011) Constitutional amendment rules: a comparative perspective. In: Ginsburg T, Dixon R (eds) Comparative constitutional law. Edward Elgar, Cheltenham

Gavison R (2003) The Jews' Right to statehood: a defense. Azure 15:70

Guberman S (1967) Israel's supra-constitution. Israel Law Rev 2:445, 460

Harris R (2001) Jewish democracy and Arab politics: Al-Ard movement at the Supreme Court. Plileem 10:107

Hesketh K (2011) The inequality report: the Palestinian Arab minority in Israel. Adalah, Israel. http://adalah.org/upfiles/2011/Adalah_The_Inequality_Report_March_2011.pdf

Holmes S, Sunstein C (1995) The politics of constitutional revision in Eastern Europe. In: Levinson S (ed) Responding to imperfection: the theory and practice of constitutional amendment. Princeton University Press, Princeton

Jabareen H (2002) The future of Arab citizenship in Israel: Jewish-Zionist time in a place with No Palestinian memory. In: Levy D, Weiss Y (eds) Challenging ethnic citizenship. Berghahen Books, New York

Jiryis S (1976) The Arabs in Israel. Monthly Review Press, New York

Klein C (1978) Is there a need for an amending power theory? Israel Law Rev 12:303

Klein C (1993) Basic law: human dignity and freedom: an initial normative assessment. HaMishpat 1:123 (Hebrew)

Klein C (1997) After the Bank Mizrahi decision: constituent power through the mirror of the Supreme Court. Mishpatim 28:341 (Hebrew)

Klein C, Sajo A (2012) Constitution-making: process and substance. In: Rosenfeld M, Sajo A (eds) The Oxford handbook of comparative constitutional law. Oxford University Press, Oxford

Masri M (2013) Love suspended: demography, comparative law, and Palestinian couples in the Israeli Supreme Court. Soc Legal Stud 22(3):309

Masri M (2017) The dynamics of exclusionary constitutionalism: Israel as a Jewish and democratic State. Hart Publishing, Oxford

Minister of Finance (2012) The Alumni of the Arab Orthodox High School in Haifa (Hebrew)

Morris B (2004) The birth of the Palestinian refugee problem revisited, 2nd edn. Cambridge University Press, Cambridge

Neiman (1985) Chairman of the central elections committee for the Eleventh Knesset. IsrSC 39 (2):225 (Hebrew)

Neiman (1988) Chairman of the central elections committee for the Twelfth Knesset. IsrSC 42 (4):177, 187 (Hebrew)

Pappe I (2006) The ethnic cleansing of Palestine. One World, London

Piterberg G (2008) The returns of Zionism: myths, politics and scholarship in Israel. Verso, Memphis

Preuss U (2011) The implications of "eternity clauses": The German experience. Israel law Rev 44:429, 445

Rodinson M (1973) Israel: a Colonial Settler state?. Pathfinder, New Delhi

Roznai Y (2016) Unamendability and the genetic code of the constitution. Eur Rev Public Law 27 (2):775

Rubenstein A, Yakobson A (2009) Israel and family of nations. Routledge, London

Said E (1979) The question of Palestine. Times Books, New York

Sayeg F (1965) Zionist colonialism in Palestine. Research Center—Palestine Liberation Organization, Beirut

Schwartzberg M (2007) Democracy and legal change. Cambridge University Press, Cambridge

Shafir S (1996) Land labour and the origins of the Israeli-Palestinian conflict, 1882–1914, updated edn. California University Press, California

Shalhoub-Kevorkian N (2015) Security theology, surveillance and the politics of fear. Cambridge University Press, Cambridge

Sultany N (2012) The state of progressive constitutional theory: the paradox of constitutional democracy and the project of political justification. Harvard Civ Rights-Civ Liberties Law Rev 47(2):371

Sultany N (2017) The legal structure of subordination: The Palestinian minority and Israeli law. In: Rouhana N (ed) Israel and its Palestinian citizens: ethnic privileges in the Jewish state. Cambridge University Press, Cambridge

Sunstein C (1996) On the expressive function of law. Univ Pennsylvania Law Rev 144(5):2021

Troper M (2012) Sovereignty. In: Rosenfeld M, Sajo A (eds) The Oxford handbook of comparative constitutional law. Oxford University Press, Oxford

Tushnet M (1999) The possibilities of comparative constitutional law. Yale Law J 108(6):1225

Veracini L (2006) Israel and Settler society. Pluto Press, London

Weintal S (2011) The challenge of reconciling constitutional eternity clauses with popular sovereignty: toward three-track democracy in Israel as a Universal Holistic Constitutional System and Theory. Israel Law Rev 44:449, 494

Weintal S (2013) The inherent authority of judges in a three-track democracy to recognise unenumerated constitutional rights: the Israeli story of a Judicial Mission with no ammunition. In: Sapir G, Barak-Erez D, Barak A (eds) Israeli constitutional law in the making. Hart Publishing, Oxford

Weintal S (2014) Judicial limitation clause: on the appropriate scope of protection for abstract constitutional principles. Moznei Mishpat 9:177 (Hebrew)

Zureik E (1979) The Palestinians in Israel: a study in internal colonialism. Routldge & Kegan Paul, Abingdon

Eternal Provisions in the Constitution of Bangladesh: A Constitution Once and for All?

Ridwanul Hoque

Abstract Many modern constitutions today contain what is called eternity clauses (also known as constitutional entrenchment), which make one or more constitutional provisions unamendable. The Constitution of the People's Republic of Bangladesh (hereafter 'the Constitution') originally did not enact any such eternity clause. An eternity clause, however, has been entrenched in 2011 through the 15th amendment to the Constitution. Long before the enactment of the eternity clause, the Supreme Court of Bangladesh in a 1989 famous decision established the basic structure doctrine or the idea of 'unconstitutional constitutional amendment', ruling that Parliament lacks authority to amend the Constitution in a way that would destroy its basic structure. By invoking the basic structure doctrine, the Supreme Court has so far struck down 4 out of 16 constitutional amendments with finality. After the Court handed down its annulment decision in May 2011 invalidating the 13th amendment, the Constitution was amended to enact, among others, an extraordinarily wide eternity clause, article 7B. With this, Bangladesh became the second country in South Asia, after Afghanistan, to have constitutional entrenchment.

1 Introduction

Many modern constitutions today contain what is called eternity clauses (also known as constitutional entrenchment), which make one or more constitutional provisions unamendable.[1] The Constitution of the People's Republic of Bangladesh

---

[1]For example, the German Basic Law of 1949 makes federalism, democracy and socialist Republican character of the State unamendable, while the Turkish Constitution of 1982 declares secularism to be a permanent provision. See, especially, article 79(3), to be read with articles 1 and 20, of the German Basic Law. See Tomuschat and Currie (2010).

R. Hoque (✉)
University of Dhaka, Dhaka, Bangladesh
e-mail: ridwandulaw@gmail.com

© Springer International Publishing AG, part of Springer Nature 2018
R. Albert and B. E. Oder (eds.), *An Unamendable Constitution?*
Ius Gentium: Comparative Perspectives on Law and Justice 68,
https://doi.org/10.1007/978-3-319-95141-6_8

(hereafter 'the Constitution)[2] originally did not enact any such eternity clause. An eternity clause, however, has been entrenched in 2011 through the 15th amendment to the Constitution.[3] Long before the enactment of the eternity clause, the Supreme Court of Bangladesh[4] in a 1989 famous decision established the basic structure doctrine or the idea of 'unconstitutional constitutional amendment', ruling that Parliament lacks authority to amend the Constitution in a way that would destroy its basic structure.[5] By invoking the basic structure doctrine, the Supreme Court has so far struck down 4 out of 16 constitutional amendments with finality.[6] After the Court handed down its annulment decision in May 2011 invalidating the 13th amendment,[7] the Constitution was amended to enact, among others, an extraordinarily wide eternity clause, article 7B.[8] With this, Bangladesh became the second country in South Asia, after Afghanistan,[9] to have constitutional entrenchment.[10]

---

[2]Adopted on 4 November 1972, the Constitution came into force on 16 December 1972. There is a dearth of literature on the history of Bangladesh's constitution-making. For a recent politico-historical account, see Hossain (2013), Chap. 9. For an early account, see Huq (1973). See further n 21.

[3]The Constitution (Fifteenth Amendment) Act 2011 (Act No XIV of 2011) (hereafter '15th amendment').

[4]The Supreme Court comprises two divisions, the High Court Division (hereafter 'HCD') and the Appellate Division. The Appellate Division hears appeals from any order, judgment, or decree of the HCD, which has the original jurisdiction of judicial review. The president appoints the chief justice and other judges. Judges are traditionally appointed first as additional judges to the HCD for two years. See, respectively, articles 95 and 98, and 102 and 103 of the Constitution.

[5](1989) BLD (Special) (AD) 1 (AD = Appellate Division).

[6]In a fifth annulment decision, the HCD on 5 May 2016 struck down the 16th amendment that restored an original provision providing for removal of the Supreme Court judges pursuant to a resolution of Parliament. See *Asaduzzaman Siddiqui v. Bangladesh*, Writ Petition No. 9989 of 2014, HCD. The judgment is available at: <http://supremecourt.gov.bd/resources/documents/ 783957_WP9989of2014.pdf>. For a commentary, see Hoque (2016a). This decision was endorsed by the Appellate Division on 3 July 2017 (*Bangladesh v Asaduzzaman Siddiqui* (2017) CLR (AD) (Spl. 1) where the government's petition for review is currently pending. See further n 141.

[7]See the Constitution (Thirteenth Amendment) Act 1996 (Act No. I of 1996), which introduced the Non-party Caretaker Government system. See Hoque (2013, 2015).

[8]As in Bangladesh, eternity clauses via constitutional amendments have been enacted in Belgium, Cambodia, Columbia, France, Guatemala, Indonesia, Peru and Romania.

[9]See art 149 of the Constitution of Afghanistan of 2004 that makes the state religion clause unamendable.

[10]Contrast the Pakistani Constitution of 1973 (art 239(5)-(6)) that bars judicial review of constitutional amendments and confirms that there is no limitation whatever on Parliament's amending power. On the other hand, the Constitution of India specially protects the amendment rule and a few other important provisions, providing that their amendment, in addition to requiring votes of a two-thirds majority of members of Parliament present, will also require the ratification by not less than a half of the State legislatures (art 368). Exceptionally, article 82(5) of the Sri Lankan Constitution of 1978 authorizes the repeal and replacement of the whole Constitution, but it (art 83) also requires a referendum for the amendment of certain basic provisions including the referendum and state religion clauses. See also the Constitution of the Kingdom of Bhutan 2008 (art 33(9)) and the Constitution of the Republic of Maldives 2008 (art 267) that both contain referendum requirements and prohibit amendments during a state of emergency.

Unlike other constitutions that have entrenched provisions, Bangladesh's Constitution does not specify any principles or fundamental cores that are impervious to amendment rules but rather catalogues a lengthy list of 'provisions' as unalterable. Article 7B makes unamendable the following: the preamble (that contains four 'high ideals' of the State), all fundamental principles of state policy, all fundamental rights provisions, and 'the provisions of articles relating to the basic structures'. It seems that the eternity clause, interpreted literally, renders almost the whole of the Constitution unamendable. It is not yet fully known what motivated the legislature to import such a wide clause that seems to bind the hands of the future generations tight regarding constitutional change or improvement. It is, however, not difficult to presume that it was the fierce political disagreement on the question of national identity principles that acted as a key motivating factor for entrenching those principles by shielding them, through an unamendability rule, against any future change. Extension of the unamendability rule to an unusually long list of provisions, however, logically leaves a question of whether the eternity clause seeks to consolidate democratic values or is anti-democratic itself.

In the 16th amendment decision, the Appellate Division has already imported a further broad meaning of article 7B to invalidate that amendment (see n 6). It is nevertheless too early to assess the likely impact of such a broad-based eternity clause on constitutional politics and adjudication, especially with regard to the Supreme Court's role in interpreting a constitutional amendment in the light of principles of constitutionalism. The difficulty, in this regard, is also somewhat linked with the emergency-type scenario attendant to the enactment of article 7B in the sense that this fundamental change in the Constitution has been brought about by a parliament during the time of what can be called an 'elected' but largely unrepresentative post-2014 government.[11]

The design of the Bangladeshi eternity clause seems to be a stark deviation from global practises of designing constitutional entrenchment clauses that generally seek to protect identity principles of the State such as federalism, republicanism,

---

[11]To provide a detailed account of this is beyond the scope of this chapter. It may be briefly noted that the 5 January 2014 general elections were held in the aftermath of an unresolved political crisis concerning the mode of election-time government. The election witnessed the lowest turnout in history and was virtually a one-party election as the major opposition parties boycotted it altogether. Candidates in 153 seats (out of 300 seats to be elected) were declared 'elected' without contestation, and a party whose candidates, despite their withdrawal from the elections, were declared elected later joined the current Cabinet. Unprecedentedly, that party has also been officially appointed as the opposition in Parliament. In effect, therefore, there is no opposition in the current parliament.

official religion and secularism.[12] By contrast, Bangladesh's extremely broad eternity clause has virtually made a very large part of the Constitution unamendable. This, it is argued, has effectively turned the country's constitution from a living instrument to one that has become almost permanent, thereby retarding the sovereignty of people. This chapter will examine the legality and legitimacy of this type of all-embracing constitutional entrenchment, analyzing its likely political and legal implications in the light of constitutional theories concerning popular sovereignty and judicial role vis-à-vis constitutional changes.

Following this introduction, the present chapter describes the amendment rule of the Constitution (article 142) and briefly charts out its development. The third section provides an account of the founding values of the nation and considers their political development. The objective, here, is to shed some light on the politics of determining or changing the State's identity principles, which have been the subject matter of confrontational politics and hence repeated constitutional amendments. Next, the chapter analyzes the development of the theory of unconstitutional constitutional amendments by the Supreme Court of Bangladesh, investigating, especially, how the Court contributed to the crystallization of fundamental constitutional cores. These analyses form the background for the fifth section, which examines the legitimacy and implications of Bangladesh's eternity clause.

2 Amendment Rules of the Constitution of Bangladesh

Article 142 of the Constitution, embodying the amendment rules, in its original form provided a general, quasi-rigid procedure for the amendment of 'any provision' thereof by a two-thirds majority of Parliament. The original article 142 had been amended several times during the period from 1973 to 1991. Article 142's original form has been recently restored, albeit not fully, by the 15th amendment.[13] The existing provisions of article 142 are as follows:

142. Notwithstanding anything contained in this Constitution –

(a) any provision thereof may be amended by way of addition, alteration, substitution or repeal by Act of Parliament:

Provided that –

(i) [...];
(ii) no such Bill shall be presented to the President for assent unless it is passed by the votes of not less than two-thirds of the total number of members of Parliament;

---

[12]Jacobsohn (2011a). For a brief account of practises of designing amendment rules, see generally Dixon (2011). Beyond entrenching the cores, eternity clauses also aim at preserving fundamental principles of constitutionalism such as human dignity, rule of law, constitutional supremacy, individual liberties and separation of powers. See Roznai (2013), p. 657, and (2016). For a critical summary of works on forms and limitations of amendment rules, see Colon-Rios (2015).

[13]The Constitution (Fifteenth Amendment) Act 2011, s. 42.

(b) when a Bill passed as aforesaid is presented to the President for his assent he shall, within the period of seven days after the Bill is presented to him assent to the Bill, and if he fails so to do he shall be deemed to have assented to it on the expiration of that period.

Before embarking upon the politics of fixing and re-fixing the fundamental cores of the Constitution through amendments, it is pertinent to have a view of the trajectory of the amendment rules. Article 142 was first amended in 1973, not to curtail but rather to increase Parliament's amendment power regarding the fundamental rights provisions. Article 26(2) of the Constitution provided that the State 'shall not make any law inconsistent with any [fundamental rights] provisions.' This left open the question of whether a constitutional amendment could validly enact such a law incompatible with fundamental rights. In this context, the 2nd amendment amended both articles 142 and 26, making it clear that the above limitation on the legislative power would not apply to a constitutional amendment.[14]

A normatively substantial change to the amendment rules came in 1978 when the first military government introduced a two-tiered amendment procedure. This was achieved, ironically, by amending the Constitution extra-constitutionally.[15] This made certain fundamental provisions of the Constitution subject to a more demanding procedure of public ratification through referendum.[16] It was provided that any amendment of the preamble and article 8, which together contained the constitutional fundamentals, and a few other articles including article 142 would have to be endorsed by a referendum.

In the early months of post-1990 democratic transition, the above-protected provisions became the subject matter of a political contestation between the government and then the opposition party, the Awami League, which was against the retention of referendum as part of the amending mechanism.[17] Ultimately, however, the 12th amendment of 1991, which returned the country to a parliamentary form of democracy, retained the two-tiered amendment procedure but shortened the list of harder-to-amend provisions.[18] Protected provisions that were amendable after an affirming referendum were: preamble that contained the four fundamental cores of the Constitution, article 8 (the normative status of the four (amended) fundamental principles), article 56 (parliamentary nature of government), and article 142

---

[14]See the Constitution (Second Amendment) Act 1973 (Act No. XXIV of 1973), ss 2 and 7 (inserting clause (3) to art 26, and clause (2) to the then art 142).

[15]The amendment was made by way of issuing the Second Martial Law Proclamation Order No. IV of 1978. This extra-constitutional amendment was later validated by the 5th amendment. See n 49.

[16]A new clause (1A) was inserted to art 142 that provided as follows: '... when a Bill ... which provides for the amendment of the Preamble or any provisions of articles 5, 8, 48, 56, 58, 80, 92A or this article, is presented to the President for assent, the President, shall, within the period of seven days after the Bill is presented to him, cause to be referred to a referendum the question whether the Bill should or should not be assented to'.

[17]Choudhury (1995), pp. 82–84.

[18]See the Constitution (Twelfth Amendment) Act 1991 (Act No. XVIII of 1991).

(amendment rules). On the other hand, the provisions that were now taken off from the referendum requirement were: the mode of electing the President (article 48), the tenure of Cabinet ministers (article 58), and the legislative procedure (article 80).

Twenty years later, this two-tiered amendment procedure has been done away with in 2011 via the 15th amendment, which controversially amended the amendment rule without the support of a referendum.[19] Although the 15th amendment omitted the referendum mechanism for the amendment of certain protected provisions, it inserted an even more rigorous limitation on Parliament's amending power by introducing an eternity clause, which is the subject of analyses below.

3 Founding Values and the Development of the Idea of Unamendable Provisions

If anything in any given constitution should deserve continuity and hence protection from amendment, it is the constitutional identity or the fundamental cores of the constitution.[20] When Bangladesh's Constitution was being drafted and debated,[21] the framers' minds were fully fresh with memories of scourge and savage of the country's liberation war of 1971 and of the causes for which the people had been struggling for many years.[22] This awareness is reflected, among other things, in the second paragraph of the preamble of the Constitution regarding the national constitutional vision, which states as follows:

---

[19] A potential argument for not referring the Fifteenth Amendment Bill to referendum was probably that the Court in the meantime invalidated the 5th amendment that constitutionalized the referendum requirement (see n 16). This argument is hardly sustainable as the referendum mechanism for the amendment of certain provisions including article 142 was re-enacted by the 12th amendment.

[20] On the concept of constitutional identity, see generally Jacobsohn (2011b), and Rosenfeld (2012, 2010). The development of the concept of constitutional identity is credited with the German Constitutional Court in the early 1950s, which, however, began much earlier in the 1870s. See Polzin (2016). See also the *Southwest Case* (1951) 1 BverfGE 14. On how to identify and constitute national constitutional identity, see Grewe (2013), and Tushnet (2010).

[21] The Constitution of Bangladesh was drafted by a thirty-four-member Drafting Committee of the Constituent Assembly that was constituted with 403 elected representatives of the people who were elected in the 1970–71 elections for provincial and central legislative assemblies of erstwhile Pakistan from which Bangladesh became independent in 1971. See also Hossain (2013) n 2. For the Constituent Assembly Debates, now see Halim (2015).

[22] See generally Ahmed (1994), Hossain (2013), and Muhith (1992). On the history of Bangladesh's emergence, see further Anisuzzaman (1993), Baxter (1984), Chowdhury (1972), and Sisson and Rose (1990).

> Pledging that the high ideals of nationalism, socialism, democracy and secularism, which inspired our heroic people to dedicate themselves to, and our brave martyrs to sacrifice their lives in, the national liberation struggle, shall be the fundamental principles of the Constitution.

In effect, the very drafting process began with guidance from the Constituent Assembly regarding the general principles on which the new Constitution was to be based. By a resolution, the Assembly declared that the 'high ideals of nationalism, socialism, democracy and secularism' would be the fundamental principles of the Constitution. The Drafting Committee ultimately instilled[23] these four ideals into the Constitution as the newly emerged nation's identity principles or the founding values.[24] Article 8 of the Constitution provided that these four constitutional fundamentals,[25] together with the principles derived from them,[26] shall constitute the fundamental principles of state policy as well as the bases of legislation, the interpretation of law and the Constitution, and the actions of the State and its citizens. In addition, *popular sovereignty* and *the constitutional supremacy* are also fortressed as basic features of the Constitution in article 7.[27]

The political and historical contexts in which Bangladesh emerged as a sovereign nation state after having fought a bloody war confirm the founding fathers' intention to give to the above-mentioned principles an entrenched status. In this regard, it is pertinent to cite a noted constitutional scholar who aptly observed with regard to the post-1975 demolition of the principle of secularism as follows:

---

[23]Hossain (2013), p. 140 and at 144 he writes: 'Our efforts, in the Constitution Drafting Committee, had been directed towards, as faithfully as possible, preparing a draft [...] by working out specific provisions on the basis of four principles'.

[24]The meaning and scope of the principles of nationalism, socialism, democracy and secularism were described in, respectively, arts 9, 10, 11 and 12 of the original Constitution of 1972.

[25]It is interesting to note that two pre-Constitution constituent instruments impliedly recognized *democracy* and *popular sovereignty* as founding values. See the Provisional Constitution of Bangladesh Order 1972 (11 January 1972), which spoke about 'the manifest aspiration of the people of Bangladesh that a parliamentary democracy shall function in Bangladesh'; and the Proclamation of Independence Order 1972 (10 April 1972; with effect from 26 March 1971, the Constituent Assembly), which cited the will of the people as the 'supreme' will.

[26]These principles are set out in Part III (arts 8 to 25) of the Constitution.

[27]Article 7 states that '[a]ll powers in the Republic belong to the people' and that '[the] Constitution is, as the solemn expression of the will of the people, the supreme law of the Republic, and if any other law is inconsistent with this Constitution that other law shall, to the extent of the inconsistency, be void'. In a 1975 case, *Md. Shoib v Government of Bangladesh* (1975) 27 DLR (HCD) 315, Justice Bhattacharya described popular sovereignty and constitutional supremacy as a 'basic concept' of constitutionalism: '[T]he Constitution ... is the [s]upreme law of the Republic and all powers of the Republic and their exercise shall be effected only under, and by the authority of, the Constitution. This is a basic concept on which the modern states have been built up.' It seems, therefore, that *Md. Shoib* is kind of a post-Independence precursor to the basic structure doctrine that was established in 1989 in Bangladesh. See also *Sahar Ali v A.R. Chowdhury* (1980) 32 DLR (HCD) 142, in which the HCD famously held that its constitutional supervisory jurisdiction could not be ousted, and thus by implication recognized that judicial constitutional review was a basic feature of the Constitution.

[The Constitution of Bangladesh] has not been imposed upon by any outside power but has originated from a Constituent Assembly that could sit as people's forum only after millions had sacrificed their lives. Those sacrifices were made for a cause, for certain ideals, for certain values which as the sacred will of the people found abode in the Constitution framed by the Constituent Assembly in 1972. Certainly those ideals, and they were first of all ideals of *democracy* and *secularism,* history has the record, formed the basic features of the Constitution of Bangladesh. *They have taken roots from [...] blood of the people. They cannot be changed.*[28]

Since Independence, however, the identity of the Bangladesh State has remained continuously contested. In particular, its cultural Bengali identity and the religious-orientation of the majority Muslims are what have become known as 'contested identities'.[29] Although the country began its journey on a secular basis of nationhood, 'religion soon became an important component'.[30] According to a historical account of Bangladesh's identity formation, there are three streams of political philosophy about national identity: (i) Islamic, (ii) secularism and social-ism and (iii) nationalist (territorial) and democratic philosophy.[31] Again, in view of this narrative, there is a lack of conciliation among these streams. While the extremely right and religion-based forces seek to attain the Islamic philosophy, the Awami League, the party under whose leadership the war of liberation was fought, believed in socialism, secularism and Bengali nationalism. By contrast, the Bangladesh Nationalist Party, a post-1975 political party, is the staunch follower of Islamic ideal/identity and 'Bangladeshi' nationalism as opposed to Bengali nationalism.

In short, the conflict about the national identity of Bangladesh continues to remain unsettled, and the identity discourse is fraught with persistent disagree-ments. The concept of national or constitutional identities in effect remains vague everywhere, especially in a plural, multinational society.[32] As Kabeer puts it, the 'brutal war of liberation was fought in 1971 to defend what Bengali Muslims believed to be their *own distinct national identity*: a fusion of Bengali culture and humanist Islam'.[33] Somewhat similarly, Khondker notes that secularism in Muslim majority Bangladesh has a historical root[34] and 'has never been threatened seri-ously', and 'has a future as long as democratic norms of tolerance and pluralism are strengthened'. Other scholars, however, find a conflict between tradition or culture

---

[28]Alam (1991), pp. 209, 224 (emphasis added).

[29]Bhardwaj (2011).

[30]Mohsin (2004).

[31]Hassan (2004), pp. 185, 189.

[32]On this see, e.g., Faraguna (2016), p. 491. There is a debate regarding whether the constitutional and national identities are two different concepts, or one is subordinate to the other. Here, I have used the two concepts interchangeably. For a view that they mean the same thing, see Besselink (2010), pp. 42–44; Marti (2013) (arguing that 'constitutional identity' also means 'identity of the people themselves'); and Toniatti (2013), esp. pp. 63–67. For a contrasting view, see Rosenfeld (2012), p. 29.

[33]Kabeer (1991) (emphasis added).

[34]Khondker (2010), pp. 185, 188, 201. See also Ahmed (1996), and Anisuzzaman (1993).

and the religiosity of majority Muslims in Bangladesh. Rashiduzzaman, for example, thinks that Islam is an unyielding political identity in Bangladesh that is impossible to ignore, while Karim claims that the placement of secularism in the 1972 Constitution was 'the second contradiction' in the construction of the state identity, after Bengali nationalism.[35]

The framers of the Constitution, by contrast, were cautious in choosing Bangalee nationalism and secularism as fundamental principles. The founding leader of Bangladesh, Bangabandhu Sheikh Mujibur Rahman,[36] was 'aware of the religiosity of the people' himself, and reassured them that secularism did not mean the absence of religion, but that religions could not be used for political ends.[37] This normative meaning of secularism that inspired the drafters is reaffirmed by Dr. Kamal Hossain, the Chairperson of the Constitution Drafting Committee, in these words:

> The principle of secularism that was embodied in the Constitution was very carefully worded so as to make clear that it did not stand for hostility to religion. The constitution-makers were fully conscious that the majority of the [Bangalee] people were practising Muslims. The principle of secularism, as spelt out in the Constitution, was to maintain a separation between the state and religion and to create an environment in which all religious communities could coexist in harmony, free from discrimination and religious intolerance [...].[38]

Indicating the internal connectivity between secularism and Bengali nationalism, Hossain further argues as follows:

> Nationalism represented an assertion by the people of their identity, which evolved during the course of its historical struggle into the right to their language, culture, traditions and history. In declaring independence, the people of Bangladesh had emphasised that they were exercising their right to self-determination to create a nation state. [...] Now that Bangladesh had been established as a nation state, and was recognised as such by the world, their national identity could no longer be questioned.[39]

Hossain, however, acknowledges that the adoption of Bangalee nationalism 'led to smaller ethnic communities, in particular, those living in the Chittagong Hill Tracts, feeling excluded'.[40] Bangladesh is a country of rich pluralism—cultural, ethnic, religious and political. As such, not addressing the issues of ethnic identity and linguistic distinction within the purview of national identity continued to be a

---

[35]Rashiduzzaman (1994), pp. 58–59 and Karim (2015) (arguing that 'one could effectively argue that' the majority Bengali Muslims 'would not favour a secular state', and that 'secularism as a value was not based on a consensus of the population but was imposed from above by the ruling party, the Awami League').

[36]'Bangabandhu', meaning 'Friend of Bengal', was given as a title to the founding leader of Bangladesh by the students in 1969 in the aftermath of a mass upsurge.

[37]Fazal (1999), pp. 190–191. See *Parliamentary Debates* (12 October 1972, Government of Bangladesh, Parliamentary Secretariat 1972) 20.

[38]Hossain (2013), p. 142. See also Hassan (2004) who thinks that the Constitution adopted the principle of secularism in its strongest sense (separation between religion and state affairs).

[39]Hossain (2013), p. 141.

[40]Ibid.

significant source of discontent in the later years. As will be noted below, there has been a kind of mitigation of this problem recently, with the 15th amendment's confirmation that the citizens will be known as 'Bangladeshis' and the people collectively as 'Bangalee' as well as the revival of 'secularism'. These changes have been recently assessed by a leading scholar of legal pluralism with a positive note: 'I read these new developments as a fresh effort to rebalance the kite [of the four founding ideals] of Bangladesh when it comes to minorities of whatever kind'.[41] Indeed, constitutional identities, as Rosenfeld has argued in the US context, 'are dynamic [and are] bound to evolve after they are initially formed'.[42]

Despite the limited ability of constitutional amendment procedures to achieve changes in the domain of constitutional identities and despite their evolutionary character, however, basic tenors of constitutional identities should have an essential degree of permanence for the sake of constitutional durability.[43] It is reasonable, therefore, that once any given constitution identifies its fundamentals, Parliament's power to destroy them becomes curtailed *ipso facto*.[44] Among the leading drafters of the Constitution of Bangladesh were the finest jurists of the country, and they were certainly aware of the idea of supra-constitutional fundamentals that was being developed gradually by the top courts in South Asia at the time.[45] Arguably, therefore, the framers meant the constitutional cores to be durable, although they refrained from entrenching them in the earnest. It is beyond the scope of this chapter to inquire whether the non-entrenchment of the above principles in 1972 was a mere accidental lapse or an act of deliberate pragmatism. Whatever be the case, the entrenchment of constitutional fundamentals was left for the people to attain and manage.

Whether or not for the absence of an eternity clause concerning the constitutional fundamentals or the identity of the State, the higher principles of nationalism, socialism, democracy and secularism became assailed or were completely abandoned not too long after the commencement of the Constitution. In August 1975,

---

[41]Menski (2015), pp. 9, 23.

[42]Rosenfeld (2010), p. 209.

[43]Dixon (2012), p. 1847. On endurance of national constitutions, see Elkins et al. (2009).

[44]See *Jackson v Attorney General* [2006] 1 AC 262 (*per* Lord Steyn) (the UK system has certain 'constitutional fundamentals' that 'even a sovereign Parliament' cannot abolish), quoted in Colon-Rios (2014), pp. 306, 312, n 56. See also *Premier, KwaZulu-Natal v President of the Republic of South Africa* [1996] ZACC 10, in which the South African Constitutional Court remarked in obiter that a constitutional amendment 'radically and fundamentally restructuring and reorganizing the fundamental premises of the Constitution[] might not qualify as an "amendment" at all'. This obiter is somewhat conditioned by *United Democratic Movement v President* [2002] (11) BCLR 1179, in which the Court saw 'little if any scope for challenging the constitutionality of amendments that are passed in accordance with the prescribed procedures'.

[45]In the early 1960s, for example, Pakistani superior courts observed that 'fundamental feature[s] of the constitution' were immune to change. See *M Abdul Huq v Fazlul Quader Chowdhury* (1963) 15 DLR (Dacca) 355; PLD 1963 SC 486. On the other hand, the Indian Supreme Court's decision in *Golaknath v State of Punjab* AIR 1967 SC 1643 can be seen to have inaugurated in India the view that constitutional amendments can be unconstitutional.

the founder of Bangladesh was most brutally assassinated. The assassination of the founding leader was followed by a declaration of martial law, which subjugated the Constitution to military decrees. Quite ironically, however, the assailment of constitutional fundamentals, in particular of the democratic character of the government, first came during the term of the post-1972 constitutional government through the 2nd and 4th amendments of the Constitution. The 2nd amendment introduced provisions for the state of emergency and preventive detention, while the 4th amendment converted the system of parliamentary democracy into a one-party authoritarian rule overnight and made the judiciary a subservient forum.[46] These amendments, especially the 4th amendment, thus drastically changed the basic structure of the Constitution.[47]

The first martial law regime (20 August 1975–9 April 1979) amended the Constitution by issuing military decrees, called proclamations, and began a process of Islamization of the Constitution that 'gained legitimacy in 1977 when Martial Law Administrator Zia[ur] Rahman (1977–81) proclaimed that the secular constitution would now include the words "absolute trust and faith in Almighty Allah"'.[48] Zia amended the preamble and article 8 to replace the fundamental principle of 'secularism' with the principle of 'absolute trust and faith in Almighty Allah', and the principle of 'socialism' with 'socialism meaning economic and social justice'. Zia also replaced Bengali nationalism with Bangladeshi nationalism, proposing the terminology of 'Bangladeshi' to describe citizens of Bangladesh. These changes were later approved and legitimized through the 5th constitutional amendment.[49] On the other hand, the second martial law regime (24 March 1982–11 November 1986) took the task of assailing the principle of secularism to a completion. The second military ruler since Independence, General Ershad (1981–90), got the 8th amendment formally adopted on 7 June 1988 making Islam the official state religion, although with a guarantee that other religions could be practised in peace.[50]

---

[46]See the Constitution (Second Amendment) Act 1973; and the Constitution (Fourth Amendment) Act 1975 (Act No. II of 1975).

[47]Choudhury (1995), p. 45.

[48]Feldman (2001), pp. 1097, 1099.

[49]The Constitution (Fifth Amendment) Act 1979 (Act No. I of 1979). According to one commentator, 5th amendment was an act of Islamization of the Constitution in theory. See Husain (1990), p. 150.

[50]See the Constitution (Eighth Amendment) Act 1988 (Act No XXX of 1988), which enacted article 2A as follows: 'The state religion of the Republic is Islam, but other religions may be practised in peace and harmony in the Republic'. These wordings echoed the language of the Objectives Resolution of 1949 of the Constituent Assembly of Pakistan, which stated that 'adequate provisions shall be made for the minorities to freely profess and practise their religions'. See Murshid (1997), p. 1. General Ershad publicly defended the official status of Islam saying that 'while the distinct identity of the Bengali people lay in their culture, language and geographical entity, independent sovereignty and other spheres of nationalism could only be defined through Islam.' See Kabeer (1991) p. 46 (quoting the Daily Ittefaq, Dhaka, 21 June 1988).

After the introduction of state religion, several civil society organizations, women's organizations, professional bodies and lawyers began a movement against the complete demolition of the secular identity of the State. Several constitutional challenges to the 8th amendment's state religion clause, based on the ground of discrimination against minorities and women, were filed with the High Court Division of the Supreme Court.[51] These events prove that the abandonment of the secularism principle and the embracement of 'political Islam'[52] by the military regimes did not go totally unchallenged.

During the first military regime, an interesting development concerning the amendment rules, especially concerning the idea of entrenched constitutional provisions, occurred. After having done away with 'secularism' and having changed the character of 'nationalism', some provisions including the preamble and article 8 that established the national identity principles were made subject to amendments only after a positive vote in referendum.[53] Howsoever, controversial this referendum provision might be and whatever selfish interest might actually have influenced its introduction, this can certainly be seen to be pointing to the recognition of unamendability of certain basic provisions of the Constitution except through the popular means of referendum.

Bangladesh transited to democracy in 1991 and the Awami League came to power in 1996 through the second post-1990 general elections, but the party did not opt for any restoration of the constitutional fundamentals adopted in 1972. In the meantime, the Supreme Court in two separate decisions struck down the 5th and the 7th constitutional amendments that legitimized, respectively, the first and the second martial law regimes.[54] This judicial intervention effectively meant that the founding values of '[Bangalee] nationalism', 'secularism' and 'socialism' became restored in their original form.

Against such a backdrop, the second post-democratic-transition Awami League government (2009–2014) introduced the 15th amendment which reinstated 'socialism' and 'secularism' and introduced an extensive pool of unamendable provisions, replacing the requirement of referendum for the amendment of certain fundamental provisions. These sweeping changes need to be assessed in the light of a few other changes brought about by the 15th amendment. Interestingly, alongside

---

[51]One writ petition (WP) was filed by a civil society organisation, Nari Pokkha (For Women) (WP No. 1330 of 1988), one by Citizens' Committee for Resisting Communalism and Autocracy (WP No. 1834 of 1988), and the other by Mr. Shakti Das Goswami (WP No. 1177 of 1988). One of these petitions has been recently dismissed by the Court, while the rest are still pending. See Hoque (2016b) and also n 143.

[52]Riaz (2010).

[53]See nn 15–18 and the accompanying text.

[54]See the 5th and 7th amendment cases noted below in nn 85–87. The legitimization was done by inserting protection clauses (respectively paragraphs 18 and 19) into the Fourth Schedule of the Constitution to provide that the laws, proclamations, and regulations made during the martial law regimes would be valid and immune from challenge.

the principle of secularism,[55] the state religion clause has been kept intact albeit with new wordings.[56]

The Bangladesh Nationalist Party (BNP), whose political philosophy is one of Bangladeshi nationalism blended with Islamic tradition and whose founder changed three of the four fundamental constitutional principles, did not consent to the enactment of the 15th amendment. Therefore, it may be argued, in all likelihood the national founding values will continue to remain contested. The fierceness of the possible contestation might, however, be of a lesser degree, in view of the 15th amendment's new compromise between Bangladeshi and Bangalee nationalism and between secularism and the majority Muslims' Islamic identity.[57]

The amended state religion clause now guarantees freedom of other religions for the minorities and imposes a duty on the State to ensure an equal status for those religions. In the context of confrontational politics vis-à-vis the national identity, the coexistence of 'Islam' as state religion with 'secularism', although at first blush it appears contradictory, now seems to offer a uniquely skilled tool to navigate through competing claims of identity. This innovative formula is clearly informed of the pluralist frame of diverse faiths and religions in society. As Menski has insightfully remarked from a plurality-sensitive perspective,

> '[t]here is [...] simply no contradiction in a Muslim-dominated country to have [an] explicit commitment to Islam written into [...] the national Constitution, provided that this same Constitution also contains strong and effective mechanisms for religious and other minorities'.[58]

For the sake of constitutional pluralism and the durability of constitutional identities, as Menski has recently suggested, the relevant actors will have to continually manage the nation's wish kite (*'iccher ghuri'*) of these high ideals.[59] Menski's argument, based on a 'respect for the various differences and hybridities that characterize the nation of Bangladesh [or its identity]', is worth quoting:

> [The fundamental principles of] nationalism, democracy, socialism and secularism, are not only interconnected,[60] but all present continuing complex challenges. [...]. [A] pluralist theoretical perspective [of the constitution and the law] ... [as a method] can help all concerned to understand better to what extent and why the four major elements of the

---

[55]The (Constitution) Fifteenth Amendment Act 2011, s. 4.

[56]Now see art 2A of the Constitution that reads as follows: 'The state religion of the Republic is Islam, but the State shall ensure equal status and equal right in the practice of the Hindu, Buddhist, Christian and other religions'. Further, the amendment (ibid, s 2) added a secular translation of *Bismillah-ar-rahman-ar-rahim* at the beginning of the preamble, namely 'In the name of the Creator, the Merciful', which was first installed by the military regime in November 1977.

[57]For a negative assessment of this balancing, see Halim (2014), p. 83.

[58]Menski (2015), p. 23. For a similar argument, see Billah (2014) (supporting the coexistence of 'state religion' and 'secularism' for 'a politically and constitutionally desirable result').

[59]Menski (2015).

[60]Fascinatingly, this interconnectedness was first explored in a 1973 book on secularism, which until recently remained largely out of sight of scholars and researchers. See Anwar (2015) (arguing that secularism and democracy are the two sides of the same coin).

iccher ghuri have not been secured by now. In view of continuing troubles, the unfortunate foregone conclusion is that all four elements of the national vision remain contested. As this contestation often involves brutal force, rather than constructive discussion and democratic methods, the result is that the nation as a whole does not prosper as much as it might do otherwise. The concluding message is, therefore, that more efforts need to be made by Bangladeshis to learn to live together in a spirit of constructive engagement to facilitate mature national growth.[61]

The following section discusses briefly how the Bangladeshi Supreme Court developed and entrenched the concept of unamendability of fundamental features of the Constitution.

4   The Theory of Unamendability of Basic Structure of the Constitution

The theory of inviolability of basic constitutional structure, the basic structure doctrine, is increasingly gaining hold in other civilian and common-law systems of constitutionalism.[62] For example, in the United Kingdom, where the doctrine of parliamentary sovereignty has the strongest roots, the Supreme Court recently suggested that the UK system has certain 'constitutional fundamentals' that 'even a sovereign Parliament' cannot abolish.[63] Likewise, in Sri Lanka, where the Supreme Court can only review a pre-enactment Bill, the Court found a move to make Buddhism official state religion to be against fundamental premises of the Sri Lankan Constitution, although Buddhism had already had 'the foremost place' in the Sri Lankan constitution.[64]

The basic structure doctrine refers to the idea that certain fundamental cores of any given constitution may never be amended by parliament, which, it is argued, has only a limited amending power and not the 'constituent power' of the people.[65] As such, the judiciary, the organ that is more insulated from politics, should have the legitimate power to 'declare' unlawful, rather than to unmake, any constitutional amendment that destroys the basic structure of the constitution.

---

[61]Menski (2015), p. 9.

[62]The literature on unconstitutional constitutional amendments is quite large. Among noted works with theoretical and comparative focuses are Gözler (2008), Jackson (2013), Jacobsohn (2006), Klug (2015), Krishnaswamy (2009), Rory (1999), Samar (2008), and Roznai (2016).

[63]*Jackson v Attorney General* (2006).

[64]*Re the (Draft) Nineteenth Amendment Bill*, Sri Lankan SC Determination No. 32/2004 (17 December 2004).

[65]*Kesavananda Bharati v State of Kerala* (1973) 4 SCR 225. See also *Minerva Mills Ltd. v Union of India*, AIR 1980 SC 1789. For an account of different conceptions of constituent power, see Colón-Ríos (2014). On constituent power, see further Colón-Ríos (2012), Loughlin and Walker (2007), Somek (2012), Thornhill (2012), and Tushnet (2015). See further Sect. 5.2 below.

As mentioned above, the Constitution of Bangladesh declared four principles as constitutional fundamentals, of which three were modified or substituted by successive post-1975 governments. The rest of the fundamentals, i.e., 'democracy', did not bother the autocratic regimes, because democracy was completely put aside at the time. Against this background and when public movement against autocracy was increasingly mounting, the Supreme Court in a 1989 landmark decision in *Anwar Hossain Chowdhury v Bangladesh*[66] established what is widely known as the basic structure doctrine in South Asia.[67] The decision was handed down in the period following the withdrawal of the second martial law and the 'revival' of the Constitution in 1986.

In this case, the Court invalidated part of the 8th amendment that diffused the Supreme Court's HCD into several regional permanent benches.[68] In the early 1980s, the second martial law regime promulgated a series of regulations deforming the HCD into seven permanent benches, six of them being outside of Dhaka. These changes seemingly stood at odds with the original article 100 of the Constitution that provided for a unitary Supreme Court with two divisions and for its 'permanent seat' in the capital. When this significant change was constitutionalized through the 8th amendment by a parliament of questionable legitimacy,[69] three constitutional challenges were unsuccessfully made at the HCD-level.[70] On appeal, however, the petitioners of the case successfully argued that the unitary character of the Republic was a basic structure of the Constitution, of which the HCD's countrywide judicial power was a part. It was further argued that the impugned innovation was also incompatible with the concepts of judicial independence and separation of powers as the President was given unchecked power over the appointment and transfer of judges. As such, the argument went on, Parliament did not have the authority under the amendment rules to enact the Amendment in question breaching these fundamental features.

---

[66](1989) BLD (Special) (AD) 1. Hearing of this case continued for more than two months, from 19 June to 23 August 1989, and the judgment was handed down on 2 September 1989.

[67]The Constitution did not expressly provide for judicial review of constitutional amendments. From this point of view, some argue that the framers did not intend to establish judicial review of constitutional amendments but rather enacted a UK-style judicial review. See Ahmed (2015); Omar and Hossain (2005) (arguing that the Court's annulment of the 8th amendment was a breach of popular sovereignty). On the Bangladeshi perspective of the basic structure doctrine, see Chowdhury (2014), p. 43, Hoque (2011), pp. 112–119, and Khan (2011a), p. 89 (critiquing judicial review of constitutional amendments as 'judicial tyranny' and dubbing the Supreme Court empowered with this power as 'Leviathan'), Talukder and Chowdhury (2008), p. 161.

[68]The other part of the 8th amendment made Islam the state religion, to which there were constitutional challenges too. See above n 51.

[69]The third parliament that passed the 8th amendment was ingeniously constituted through sham elections in which preselected party people stood and won, and when the military ruler was still the country's President in civilian attire. On electoral fraud and rigging of the 1988 elections, see Akhter (2001), pp. 132–137.

[70]Other two challenges were: *Jalaluddin v Bangladesh* (Civ. Appeal No. 43 of 1988) and *Ibrahim Sheikh v Bangladesh* (Civ. Petition for Leave to Appeal No. 3 of 1989).

In a three-to-one majority judgment,[71] the Appellate Division took the view that Parliament's amendment power is not an 'original', but rather a 'derivative' (derived) constituent power. Putting due emphasis on foundational values of the nation, the plurality Court argued that Parliament's unlimited amending power in the sense of being empowered to demolish the Constitution's basic character would run afoul of the constitutional cores of democracy, rule of law, and constitutional supremacy.[72] In its attempt to stretch out the reasoning,[73] the Court sought to identify the basic structure provisions of the Constitution that were umamendable but could not come to a conclusion as to which they were.[74] Taking a pragmatic approach, Justice M.H. Rahman, who considered 'the rule of law' the most pivotal of basic features, felt it wise to defer the task of identifying the basic structure provisions/principles to the future, observing as follows:

> The doctrine of basic structure is one growing point in the constitutional jurisprudence. It has developed in a climate where the executive, commanding an overwhelming majority in the legislature, gets snap amendments of the Constitution passed without a Green Paper or White Paper, without eliciting any public opinion, without sending the Bill to any select committee, and without giving sufficient time to the members of the Parliament for deliberations on the Bill for amendment.[75]

By contrast, Justice Shahabuddin Ahmed thought that the basic constitutional features were 'clearly identifiable'. His Lordships identified the following eight

---

[71]The only dissenting judge was Afzal J, who, however, conceded (at pp. 212–213 of the judgment) that in the name of amendment 'the Constitution cannot be destroyed'. Compare this obiter with *Pakistan Lawyers' Forum v Federation of Pakistan* PLD 2005 SC 719, in which the Pakistani Supreme Court observed (at para. 56) that 'while there may be a basic structure to the Constitution, and while there may also be limitations on the power of Parliament to make amendments to such basic structures, such limitations are to be ... enforced not by the judiciary [...] but by the body politic [...].' But now see the case noted below in n 128.

[72]Although the Court's reasoning was based on constitutional fundamentals, it was most conspicuously informed and influenced by the famous Indian decision in *Kesavananda Bharati* (n 64) that first authoritatively established in the common-law world the doctrine of basic structure. On this, see, among others, Krishnaswami (2009) and Morgan (1981), p. 307. The doctrine has been recently applied by the Indian Supreme Court in a decision annulling the 99th amendment of the Indian Constitution that gave the executive branch a better role than it previously had in the judicial appointments process. See *the Supreme Court Advocates-on-Record Association v Union of India* (2016) 5 SCC 1 (decision of 16 October 2015).

[73]For criticisms of the Court's reasoning, see Hoque (2011), pp. 114–116 and Kamal (1994), p. 110. An instance of the Court's ambivalent reasoning is to be found in two majority judges' controversial view that a constitutional amendment is not a law within the meaning of art 7(2) of the Constitution that provides that 'any other law' inconsistent with the Constitution would be void. Chowdhury J. (at p. 95), by contrast, observed that the Constitution provided the 'rule of recognition' against which all other laws including an amendment are to be tested. That a Constitution-amending Act is a 'law' under art 7(2) was later established by Justice Kamal in *Kudrat-E-Elahi Panir v Bangladesh* (1992) 44 DLR (AD) 319, 346.

[74]Nor was it necessary for them to provide an exhaustive check list on such a delicate issue. Nevertheless, 'restricting the basic structures of the Constitution to certain fundamental propositions would have strengthened' the Court's reasoning. See Malik (2002), p. 442.

[75](1989) BLD (Special) 1, respectively at 74 and 169.

overlapping 'basic structures': *popular sovereignty; supremacy of the constitution; democracy, Republican Government; unitary character of the State; separation of powers; independence of the judiciary*; and *fundamental rights.*[76]

Interestingly, *Anwar Hossain Chowdhury* had shown inadequate, if any, reflections on the founding values of the Constitution. One of the majority judges, Justice Ahmed, clearly recognized that during martial law regime(s) the fundamental principles of the Constitution were drastically changed,[77] but he offered a self-contradictory and jurisprudentially troubling proposition about the continuing validity of those changes:

> Within a short time came the first Martial Law [by which] the Constitution was badly mauled 10 times. Secularism, one of the Fundamental State Principles, was replaced [...] and socialism was given a different meaning. Supreme Court, one of the symbols of national unity, was bifurcated for about two years and then was restored. All these structural changes were incorporated in and ratified [by] the Constitution (Fifth Amendment) Act, 1979.

> In spite of these vital changes from 1975 [that] destroy[ed] some of the basic structures of the Constitution, nobody challenged them in court after revival of the Constitution; *consequently, they were accepted by the people, and by their acquiescence have become part of the Constitution.*[78]

Equally deficient, on this score, is Justice Rahman's opinion about the foundation principles. He aptly recognized the fundamentality of 'the principles of nationalism, democracy and socialism', but remarked that the 'Preamble [...] now [stood] as an entrenched provision that [could not] be amended by the Parliament alone'.[79] As previously mentioned, the preamble was made an entrenched provision in 1978, but only after 'secularism' was struck out and the three other fundamental principles that Justice Rahman cited were modified. It seems, therefore, that Justice Rahman left unanswered the question of validity of new principles instead of the foundation values.

---

[76]Ibid., p. 156, para 377 ('These are structural pillars of the Constitution and they stand beyond any change by amendatory process'. On the other hand, Justice B.H. Chowdhury (at 60, para. 52) identified the following overlapping principles as basic structures: *sovereignty of the people*; *limited government*; *separation of powers*, *supremacy of the Constitution*, and *'oneness' of the Supreme Court*. Even the opposing counsel and the dissenting judge did not rule out the existence of certain structural pillars. Ibid at 90.

[77]Ibid. 140 and 156, paras. 331 and 377. Justice Ahmed was in effect referring to three fundamentals, secularism, democracy and socialism, when he observed that martial law regime had changed 'secularism and socialism'. He did not mention the status of Bangalee nationalism.

[78]Ibid., p. 140, para. 332 (emphasis added). The idea that unlawful amendments may become part of the constitution because of the failure of someone to challenge them is an overly positivistic view of the law. In *Siddique Ahmed* (2011), the Appellate Division termed this idea as a 'misconceived' one. Justice Ahmed (at p. 140), however, reasoned that 'the fact that basic structures of the Constitution were changed in the past cannot be and is not accepted as a valid ground to answer the challenge to future amendment of this nature'.

[79](1989) BLD (Special) 1, 174, para. 456.

The only dissenting judge, Justice A.T.M. Afzal, noted that 'the changes made in the basic features within a span of 17 years [1972–1989] have been too many and *too fundamental*'.[80] Justice Afzal, in his own words, was trying to show how the organic document of the nation had 'developed and grown in our context in fulfillment of the hopes and aspirations of our people during this brief period of 17 years'.[81] His recognition of all constitutional changes, even though 'too fundamental' or enacted by autocratic regimes, as a reflection of people's 'hopes and aspirations' is an unacceptable denial of the true nature of people's power to change their constitution. It can, however, be said that Justice Afzal recognized the concept of basic constitutional structure, but was willing to relocate the power to amend or sustain the basic features at the hands of Parliament.[82]

Some 20 years after the 1989 decision on parliament's incapacity to amend basic constitutional features, the Supreme Court in 2010 and 2011 declared unconstitutional three more constitutional amendments: the 5th, 7th and 13th amendments.[83] Concerning the constitutionality of the 5th amendment that legitimated the first martial law regime,[84] the Appellate Division by a unanimous decision in *Khondker Delwar Hossain v Bangladesh Italian Marble Works Ltd*[85] largely endorsed the HCD that in 2005 found the changes brought about by the Amendment to be destructive of the Constitution's basic structure.[86] By another unanimous decision in *Siddique Ahmed v Bangladesh*,[87] the Appellate Division struck down the 7th amendment that legitimated the second martial law regime.[88] In both decisions, the Appellate Division emphasized that, by enacting what a parliament cannot legislate,

---

[80]Ibid., p. 209, para. 553 (emphasis added); 'fundamental' here is arguably used in a negative sense.

[81]Ibid.

[82]Ibid. Afzal J. also thought that '[t]oday a basic feature in our Constitution is the Presidential form of government'. This idea too is open to question in that it was Republican 'democracy', and not one of its particular form, that was made a basic feature in 1972.

[83]The Supreme Court in a series of earlier decisions declined to strike down constitutional amendments that reserved seats for women in Parliament. See *Farida Akhter v Bangladesh* (2007) 15 BLT (AD) 206, *Fazle Rabbi v Election Commission* (1992) 44 DLR (HCD) 14, and *Dr. Ahmed Hossain v Bangladesh* (1992) 44 DLR (AD) 109. Further, in at least two famous cases the Supreme Court used the doctrine of basic structure as a substantive normative reference when it enjoined the separation of the junior criminal judiciary from the executive and declared the mandatory death penalty as unconstitutional, arguing in both cases that judicial independence was a basic constitutional feature that could not be dismantled in any manner. See, respectively, *Secretary, Ministry of Finance v Md. Masdar Hossain* (2000) 52 DLR (AD) 82, and *BLAST v Bangladesh* (2010) 30 BLD (HCD) 194 (endorsed by the Appellate Division in its decision of 5 May 2015).

[84]See the text that corresponds to nn 49 and 54.

[85](2010) 62 DLR (AD) 298.

[86]*Bangladesh Italian Marble Works Ltd. v Bangladesh* (2006) BLT (Special) (HCD) 1 (judgment of 29 August 2005). For a brief commentary on this decision, see Hoque (2005).

[87](2013) 65 DLR (AD) 8 (judgment of 15 May 2011), affirming *Siddique Ahmed v Bangladesh* (2011) 63 DLR (HCD) 84.

[88]Constitution (Seventh Amendment) Act 1986 (Act No. 1 of 1986).

the 5th and 7th amendments breached a number of basic features of the Constitution such as democracy, constitutional supremacy, and the rule of law. Specifically, in the *5th Amendment Case*, both Divisions of the Supreme Court reaffirmed that the high ideals of nationalism, socialism, democracy and secularism were non-amendable constitutional fundamentals.[89]

In the third annulment decision in *Abdul Mannan Khan v Bangladesh* (2011), the Appellate Division struck down the 13th amendment that incorporated the system of an apolitical, non-partisan caretaker government in 1996 for the sole purpose of ensuring free and fair general elections within three months of dissolution of parliament.[90] The core of the plurality Court's reasoning was that the system of an 'unelected' government for whatever period was against a basic structure of the Constitution, that is, democracy. I elsewhere argued that this sharply split (4:3) decision was an inappropriate application of the basic structure doctrine and that the misapplication resulted from the Court's constitutional interpretation in exclusion of local political specificities and the compelling purpose of the 13th amendment.[91] For the purpose of this chapter, however, what needs to be stressed is that the *Abdul Mannan Khan* Court reaffirmed the notion of unamendability of the State's democratic character.[92]

5 Bangladesh's Eternal Clauses:[93] a Constitution Once and for All?

The basic structure doctrine or the concept of unamendable constitutional provisions has been entrenched in article 7B of the Constitution through the 15th amendment that in effect sought to remedy the consequences of the judicial invalidation of 5th and 7th amendments. The 5th and 7th amendment decisions[94] were what can be called consequential decisions in that they led to complex

---

[89]In *Siddique Ahmed* (as in n 87 above), the Appellate Division observed that these 'high ideals [were entrenched] both in the Preamble and […] [other] articles of the Constitution so that those fundamental principles […] remain permanent[] as the guiding principles and as the ever-lasting light house for our Republic'.

[90](2012) 64 DLR (AD) 169 (judgment of 10 May 2011) (known as *the Thirteenth Amendment Case*).

[91]Hoque (2013), p. 317. I have further developed this criticism in Hoque (2015), Chap. 9.

[92]In his dissent, Justice M. Imman Ali, above n 90 at 472, commented that the 13th amendment did 'not destroy any basic structures of the Constitution'. See further *M. Saleem Ullah v Bangladesh* (2005) 57 DLR (HCD) 171, in which the HCD held that non-party caretaker government did not breach any basic structure but rather strengthened democracy.

[93]An eternal clause is the one expressly determined to be unamendable. As such, Bangladesh's Constitution contains a very large class of eternal clauses including art 7B, which lists those clauses. Therefore, art 7B is here termed as 'eternity clause', while 'eternal clauses' refers to all clauses that are entrenched.

[94]See above, respectively, nn 85 and 87.

political and constitutional implications. Controversially, they validated certain constitutional changes brought forth during the first and second martial law regimes while striking down as unconstitutional most of the changes by the military regimes. At any rate, however, they largely restored the nation's founding values discussed above.

The Awami League, which was in power at the time of the 5th and 7th amendment decisions, had throughout been against military usurpation of state power and the subversion of the four core principles of the Constitution. In the *5th Amendment Case,* in particular, the Appellate Division made a policy suggestion that parliament might make law to criminalize coups or extra-constitutional usurpations of power.[95] In the wake of this new constitutional development, and given the high status of the top court's policy advice, the Awami League government seemingly found a legitimizing ground from where to proceed toward enacting the 15th amendment. The Amendment reinstated, albeit in a somewhat different form, the four founding values and enacted a provision against extra-constitutional assumption of state power.[96] Arguably concerned with the stability of these significant changes, Parliament also entrenched an unamendability rule.

Set in the above context of the political and judicial development of the idea of unamendable constitutional provisions, the following Section analyses the validity of Bangladesh's eternity clause in the light of the concept of popular sovereignty and judicial role vis-à-vis constitutional amendments.

5.1   The Unwieldy Scope of the Broad Eternity Clause

It is appropriate at this juncture to turn to the content of article 7B, which makes 'basic provisions' of the Constitution unamendable in the following terms:

> 7B. Notwithstanding anything contained in article 142 of the Constitution, the preamble, all articles of Part I, all articles of Part II, subject to the provisions of Part IXA all articles of Part III, and *the provisions of articles relating to the basic structures* of the Constitution *including* article 150 of Part XI shall not be amendable by way of insertion, modification, substitution, repeal or by any other means. (Emphasis added).

If the wordings of the above article are broken down, it will appear that following are the eternal or entrenched provisions:

(i) *the preamble* (which includes the four founding values and other basic concepts of constitutionalism);

---

[95] *5th Amendment Case*, n 85 at 406 (*per* Islam, CJ).

[96] See art 7A of the Constitution (declaring the subversion of, or conspiracy to subvert, the Constitution to be an act of sedition).

(ii) *all articles of Part I* (which [Articles 1 to 7B] contains provisions relating to the Republican character of the state, state religion, state language, concept of constitutional supremacy and the concept of unamendability of basic provisions);

(iii) *all articles of Part II* (which [Articles 8 to 25] provides for fundamental principles of state policy);

(iv) *all articles of Part III* (which [Articles 26 to 47A] entrenches fundamental rights provisions) (*subject to the provisions of Part IXA*);[97]

(v)   *the provisions of articles relating to the basic structures of the Constitution* and

(vi) *article 150* (which in 2011 inserted into Schedules 5th to 7th certain historical speeches and instruments relating to Bangladesh's war of liberation).

Even a quick glance at the above provision would suggest that Article 7B stands at odds with the widely prevalent wisdom of constitutional designs.[98] A function of unamendability rule (or of the amendment rules containing eternal clauses) is to 'express' and entrench core constitutional values.[99] This expressive/entrenchment function seems to be largely absent in this extremely wide eternity clause. Article 7B has, of course, sought to identify and entrench the national identity principles. Its designing, however, is fraught with an extreme level of permanence as the unamendability now covers every single word of the preamble that contains those constitutional cores. In a useful cataloguing of eternity clauses, Friedman has identified three types of such clauses. The first type is 'character of government' clause, the second type is 'spirit or principles' clause, and the third is 'character of the country' clause as in the Turkish and German constitutions.[100] At first blush, Bangladesh's eternity clause seems to be embracing all these three types in a single form. In effect, however, it does not truly pertain to any of them. Rather, it is a *sui generis* eternity clause, extremely susceptible to the question of legitimacy.

Instead of making unamendable only the fundamental constitutional principles and the character of the Republic, Article 7B makes unamendable an unusually long series of provisions, 52 articles in total (arts 1 to 47A, and art 150) that constitute

---

[97] Part IXA, *inter alia,* provides that during a state of emergency certain fundamental rights including the right to move the Court to enforce fundamental rights can be suspended (arts 141B and 141C).

[98] See Dixon (2011). See n 12 and the accompanying text.

[99] Albert (2013), p. 225. For a good example of this type of expressive function of amendment rules, see art 1 of the South African Constitution of 1996 that entrenches certain features (such as democracy, human dignity and equality, non-racialism, supremacy of the constitution, the rule of law, and multiparty system), requiring three-quarter of votes in National Assembly and six votes of the nine provincial delegations in the National Council of Provinces to amend them.

[100] Friedman (2011), p. 80, also discusses the possibility and rate of successes of these varying eternity clauses. On a detailed framework of the classification of eternal clauses, see further Schwartzberg (2007) (the classification is basically based on the degree of permanence of the entrenched provisions and their subject matters). See also Albert (2015) (providing a taxonomy of entrenchment clauses as 'preservative', 'transformational', and 'reconciliatory').

almost a third of the Constitution. Further, making unamendable 'the provisions of articles relating to the basic structures of the Constitution' without defining the basic structures in the first place is far too radical an innovation. This overly fluid reference to basic structure provisions might potentially generate political impasse over the issue of validity of any constitutional amendment not grounded on a consensus. No other constitution in the world, except for a nearly similar case of the Portuguese Constitution,[101] seems to have enacted such an extremely broad eternity clause.

Adding to the complexity, Article 7B has supplied a further gloss to the amendment rule (Article 142) by mentioning certain means of amendment such as 'insertion, modification, substitution, repeal' or 'any other means'. The latter-mentioned phrase, 'any other means', is exceedingly intriguing and vague. It begs a question of whether the Constitution can be amended by 'other means' than those referred to in Article 142 or Article 7B?[102] One might legitimately inquire into whether the drafters had in mind the judicial decisions informally amending the Constitution. If this be the case, has the judicial application of the doctrine of basic structure now become foreclosed, because in such a scenario judicial interpretations might well lead to 'modification' of one or the other provisions mentioned in Article 7B?

If the Article 7B's language is taken literally, it seems to mean that even no improvement of the Constitution with regard to certain major issues would be possible by amendment. This may be explicated a little further by a reference to the unamendability of any of the fundamental constitutional rights as well as the preamble of the Constitution. Instead of the fundamental rights as a whole, it is 'all provisions relating to' fundamental rights that have been made unamendable. Thus, if new fundamental rights such as the right to emergency medical care or the right to education are to be inserted, or, even if the current anti-liberty provision in Article 33 authorizing executive preventive detentions is to be omitted, that would squarely fall within the scope of the eternity clause. Similarly, the much-claimed constitutional recognition of indigenous identity that would entail modification of the nationality clause, when effectuated, would be in conflict with the eternity clause.

This is, however, not to claim that other constitutions have not attempted such a broad-based eternity clause, with the possibility of problematizing improvements of constitutional provisions. The German eternity clause, for example, prohibits an amendment 'affecting', among others, 'the principles' laid down in Article 1.[103] Article 1 proclaims the principle of human dignity and establishes the normative value of human rights enshrined in Articles 2 to 19. One may argue that the term

---

[101]Even the Constitution of the Portuguese Republic (7th revision of 2005), which in its art 288 includes a very long list of eternal clauses such as the 'republican form of government', the 'separation between church and state' and so on, refers to fourteen principles which 'Constitutional revision laws shall [have to] respect'.

[102]Interestingly, art 142 mentions slightly different means than art 7B. Art 142 speaks of 'addition, alteration, substitution, or repeal'.

[103]The Basic Law of Germany, art 79(3).

'affecting' in the German eternity clause provides a very broad template. Usual connotation of this term, however, suggests that the German eternity clause, in fact, prohibits the destruction, and not improvement, of the constitutional fundamental cores. Consider also the Brazilian eternity clause that provides that 'no proposal of amendment shall be considered which is aimed at abolishing' the federative form of State, or 'the separation of the Government Powers' or 'individual rights and guarantees'.[104] In this case, while improvements of individual rights and separation of powers are not arguably prohibited by the unamendability rule, any amendment touching on the open-ended scheme of separation of powers might potentially invite political stalemate or turmoil. Even then, the Brazilian clause only prohibits 'abolition', and not improvement, of separation of powers. Apparently, therefore, the German and Brazilian eternity clauses are strikingly different from Bangladesh's extra-broad eternity clause which, unlike the former, is itself unamendable.

It, therefore, remains a question whether Bangladesh's Parliament, by fore-closing any improvement over so many provisions, at all intended to have such an absurd, dead hand scenario in future. In the famous essential features case of *Kesavananda Bharati v State of Kerala* (1973),[105] the Supreme Court of India was prescient about the possibility of a dead hand constitutionalism scenario through any drastic amendment of the amendment rules. In that case, the Court established that the amendability of the constitution in a basic structure-compliant way is itself an essential constitutional feature. On the entrenched status of the Indian amendment rules, Article 368 of the Indian Constitution, one of the majority judges in *Kesavananda Bharati* forcefully argued as follows:

> Article 368 [...] can itself be amended to make the Constitution completely flexible or extremely rigid and unamendable. If this is so, a political party with a two-third majority in Parliament for a few years could so amend the Constitution as to debar any other party from functioning, establish totalitarianism, enslave the people, and after having effected these purposes make the Constitution unamendable or extremely rigid. This would no doubt invite extra-Constitutional revolution.[106]

Referring to the above comment, one commentator seeks to figure out the likely complex implications of Bangladesh's eternity clause in these words:

> Article 7B virtually makes the Constitution extremely rigid [...]. When [any] particular Constitution becomes rigid, i.e., becomes unamendable, to suit the needs of the day, the only legal option that remains is to frame a new Constitution through a Constituent Assembly. Needless to mention, the present Parliament [of Bangladesh] or any future Parliament has not that authority to do so.[107]

The problem of abusive unamendability rule and its fragility can also be understood through the following question of Tushnet:

---

[104]See the Constitution of the Federative Republic of Brazil 1988, Tittle IV, Section VIII, Article 60, paragraph 4.

[105](1973) 4 SCR 225.

[106]Ibid at 365, para. 309 (*per* Sikri, CJ).

[107]Khan (2011b).

If the people at time-one had the power to place the provision in the constitution and specify that it be unamendable, why should the people at time-two not have the power to amend the provision, through procedures that are functionally equivalent to those used by the people at time-one (even if inconsistent with the procedures the people at time-one specified for altering the constitution)?[108]

As scholars of constitutional designs argue, there are dangers in entrenching unamendable clauses in the constitutions of unstable democracies or the countries that have substantial risks of military coup or unconstitutional regime-change.[109] In the near past, Bangladesh experienced a military-backed emergency government in 2007–8. At present, the country is showing all the symptoms of utterly unstable constitutionalism[110] and is literally thrown into an ever-growing political turmoil and quagmire. A question, therefore, remains whether the Constitution's recent anti-coup protective clause (article 7A) will usher in an effective check against further erosion of political stability or a *coup* in future. It also is a matter to be seen whether an ultra-rigid eternity clause will debar future amendments. After all, constitutional amendments and political attitudes to them are more a matter of 'culture' than institutional restraints.[111] Therefore, any extensive list of eternal clauses in any emerging or unstable democracy is more likely than not to be disobeyed by the amending regime. Portugal offers a notable example of this, where one can see a very controversial and conflicting relationship between their own extensive eternity clause and the regime. Portugal amended its constitution through 'revision' in direct disregard of some of the entrenched provisions in 1989.[112]

5.2 Constitutional Entrenchment V Popular Sovereignty: Legitimacy and Implications of the Eternity Clause

I now turn to the query of whether eternity clauses are undemocratic or whether they reflect a deep respect for the true democratic foundations of constitutionalism.[113] A constitution is an autobiography of a nation,[114] and, therefore, is certain to grow along the line of developments of the nation. Modern constitutionalism presupposes the existence and growth of the constitution as a living organism so that aspirations of the people are reflected and adapted according to the needs of the

---

[108]Tushnet (2015), p. 640.

[109]See, e.g., Friedman (2011).

[110]On the concept of unstable constitutionalism, see generally Tushnet and Khosla (2015).

[111]Ginsburg and Melton (2015), p. 686.

[112]See also a similar instance from Honduras in Landau and Sheppard (2015).

[113]On the relationship between democracy and constitutional unamendability, see, among others, Katz (1996), p. 251 (focusing on the conflict between the desire to preserve constitutional cores and popular sovereignty). See also Abdelaal (2016), pp. 6–15.

[114]Sachs (1990), cited in Hossain (2013), p. 140.

time.[115] As Henkin poignantly remarked, a 'constitution reflecting respect for constitutionalism has to be subject to amendment if it is to reflect the sovereignty of the people contemporaneously, rather than the sovereignty of their ancestors who framed the constitution'.[116] If the constitution is made extremely rigid or largely unamendable, a scenario of dead hand constitutionalism might occur in which the constitution would turn out to be unamendable by the current generation of people irrespective of the 'political feeling' or needs of the time.[117] At the worst, this might lead to deadly political crises or extra-constitutional revolutions.

Bangladesh's unamendability rule, it may be argued, is anything but a true respect for constitutionalism or a real attempt to preserve the basic constitutional foundations. It seems profitable here to dig into the background politics that led to the enactment of article 7B. Generally, 'constitutional amendments in Bangladesh have been used in an instrumentalist way for political expediency which, in turn, gives electoral advantage to the ruling party'.[118] While the 15th amendment generally sets a classic example of abusive exercise of amending power for party interests, art 7B, in particular, is probably a result of micropolitics that quite often keeps the two major parties engaged in conflict and political mud-slinging. The 15th amendment amended article 150 of the Constitution to insert into it three Schedules, 5th to 7th, incorporating certain constituent instruments and historical speeches concerning the Bangladesh liberation struggle including the Declaration of Independence by the founding leader of the country. The Bangladesh Nationalist Party does not recognize the founding leader as the declarant of Independence [119] but rather claims that General Ziaur Rahman, the party's founder, was the one who proclaimed Independence. The author party of the 15th amendment was probably wary of probable deletion of the recognition of the founding leader of the country in future.

By making a large body of constitutional provisions impervious to change by Parliament, Bangladesh's eternity clause has arguably restrained the growth of the Constitution, establishing perhaps a new constitutional doctrine that is claiming infallibility. This undoubtedly is a denial of constitutional political pluralism and the principle of freedom of expression of the people as a collective entity. It is a

---

[115]See Hamilton (1999), cited in Ginsburg and Melton (2015), p. 87 (arguing that a constitution's ability to remedy defects and unintended consequences of texts would make it durable). On the idea of a 'living Constitution' in the sense of developments and changes in constitutional law occurring through constitutional adjudication, see Kavanagh (2003), p. 55, Rehnquist (2006), p. 401, and Strauss (2010). In this chapter, however, the term 'living Constitution' is used to mean, additionally, constitutional changes through formal amendments.

[116]Henkin (1994), p. 10.

[117]Friedman (2011), pp. 77, 79.

[118]Aziz Khan (2015), p. 1.

[119]Against the backdrop of such political confrontation regarding the Declaration of Independence, the matter was dragged to the High Court Division, which in *Dr. M.A. Salam v Bangladesh* (2009) 61 DLR (HCD) 737 held that any publication claiming that Major Ziaur Rahman first declared independence of the country, being incompatible with the Proclamation of Independence Order 1972, is unconstitutional.

matter of great debate whether a parliament having possessed only a derived constituent power, as opposed to the primary constituent power,[120] can legitimately enact such a broad unamendability rule that would incapacitate the people even to make improvements to constitutionalism. It can be argued that Bangladesh Parliament has in the exercise of its 'constituted' power exceeded its authority in enacting an all-embracing eternity clause. Clearly, that was enacted 'by a Parliament holding no greater power than any future Parliament'.[121] In curtailing the amendment power of future parliament, the Parliament enacting the eternity clause has 'acted like a Constituent Assembly, not as a Parliament equal in status and power with any future Parliament'.[122]

Needless to say, the challenge of modern constitutionalism is to reconcile constitutional eternity clauses with popular sovereignty.[123] While popular sovereignty calls for the people's power to amend their constitution to adapt to social and political demands, constitutionalism requires that the founding values of a nation should be secured against unwarranted changes by an overweening majority.[124] A constitution which leaves 'the door open to every kind of change [can] not perform its functions, since the function of a constitution is to ensure stable progress, and certain types of changes are incompatible with progress'.[125] In any democracy, there is an inherent tension between the concepts of 'popular sovereignty' and 'constitutional supremacy'. The internal connectivity between them is quite delicate and subtle. The concept of constitutional supremacy not only heralds the supremacy of any given constitution but also denies any supervening supremacy (or sovereignty) of any particular organ of the State. The concept also refers to the inviolability of certain supra-constitutional norms whether or not they are given any expression in the text. By contrast, the concept of popular sovereignty

---

[120]See Loughlin (2013), p. 18 (arguing that the 'original' and 'derived' constituent power divide is a misconceived idea, because, constituent power is not engaged only at the founding moment but continues to function within an established regime as an expression of the open and dynamic aspects of constitutional ordering). For a similar view, see Tushnet (2015), p. 654 (arguing that the 'originary' constituent power is exercised every time an otherwise unconstitutional transformation of the constitutional order is successful, and that it may take place through the ordinary amendment rule or through extra-legal means). For a distinction between primary and secondary constituent power, proposing a limit on Parliament's amending power see, among others, Roznai (2015, 2017). For an argument of coherent approach to the nature of amending power, see Klein (1978), p. 202, Lutz (1994), p. 355, and Thornhill (2012).

[121]Aziz Khan (2015).

[122]Ibid.

[123]Weintal (2011), p. 449, Barber (2016), p. 325, and Katz (1996).

[124]As Justice Shahabuddin Ahmed in *Anwar Hossain Chowdhury*, above n 66 at 156, remarked, 'the doctrine of bar to change of basic structure is an effective guarantee against frequent amendments of the Constitution in sectarian or party interest'.

[125]Dickinson (1987), cited in Paraas Diwan and Piyushi Diwan 11. It is perhaps from this perspective that some scholars see an unassailable 'fundamental core' in the US Constitution that lacks any express constitutional entrenchment. See Albert (2015) (arguing that the first amendment rights may be regarded as informally unamendable); and Rosen (1991), p. 1073 (arguing that an amendment to the US Constitution violating the freedom of speech would be unconstitutional).

acknowledges the power of the people, at least in theory, to enact anything with regard to their polity. Within that power resides the 'constituent' or revolutionary power to replace the whole existing constitutional order. This power, therefore, potentially brings the two concepts into a scenario of ever-present tension. Further, since parliaments in representative democracies exercise the State power on behalf of the people, they often claim 'parliamentary sovereignty' in the sense of having a capacity to enact any law or constitutional amendment that is not subject to reversal by courts. That such a notion of wide power is no more compatible with the principles of modern constitutionalism is obvious, but the debates surrounding it persist.

Therefore, if the concept of constitutional supremacy were to have an upper claim, constitutional entrenchment of certain fundamental cores is perhaps 'the most powerful tool for constitutionalism to impose limitations on the sovereignty of people [or parliament]'.[126] In the just cited sense of 'sovereignty of people', however, popular sovereignty and parliamentary sovereignty are quite indistinguishable to a significant extent. The concept of constitutional supremacy would nonetheless give 'the sovereignty of people' a primacy over 'the sovereignty of parliament'. In other words, parliament's amending power is an expression of the 'constituted power', 'which is a power created and established by the constitutional text itself', whereas the constituent power 'is actually the power of the people to consent to create a constitution'.[127] A parliament representing the people is, therefore, not authorized to amend the constitution to the level that is amendable only by the people exercising their original constituent power. It is worth referencing to a recent, unusual debate in the Pakistani Supreme Court during the hearing of petitions challenging the 18th and 21st amendments of the Pakistani Constitution involving, respectively, procedures for appointment of superior court judges and the establishment of military courts to try crimes of terrorism.[128] The judges asked the counsel whether 'state religion', a foundational principle of their constitution, could be replaced with 'secularism' by a parliament with the commanding political party with unequivocal support, in its manifesto, to secularism. Leading counsels argued that only a Constituent Assembly could make changes of that scale in the constitution. For our purpose, here, this argument may be taken to

---

[126]Abdelaal (2016), pp. 1, 8–9.

[127]Ibid., p. 36.

[128]On this, see 'Can Islamic Republic of Pakistan be a Secular State?' *The Hindu* (New Delhi, 6 May 2015) <http://www.thehindu.com/news/international/pak-court-debates-possibility-of-secular-state/article7173516.ece>. See the Supreme Court's majority decision of 5 August 2015 in the Constitutional Petition No. 12 of 2010, accepting the concept of unamendability of basic structure of the constitution. See Rizvi (2015). See also a Kenyan case, *Njoya v AG* [2004] 4 LRC 559, 593, in which the Court of Appeal held that Parliament's amendment power did not extend to a power to wholly abrogate the existing Constitution. See further a Venezuelan case of 1999, cited in Colón-Ríos (2012), p. 79–80, in which the Venezuelan Supreme Court held that 'the constitutional amendment rule applied only to the government and not to the people in the exercise of their constituent power, which included the ability to alter the constitutional regime through extra-constitutional means'.

lend support to the view that derivative constituent power cannot enact an extremely broad unamendability clause without incurring the question of legitimacy.

As noted briefly above, constitutional unamendability rule by itself is riddled with the problem of democratic legitimacy.[129] As Katz argued, entrenchment clauses are incompatible with the notion of 'popular control of the government'.[130] For Katz, all provisions in a constitution are amendable, although certain clauses involving fundamental principles may be made subject to a harder and 'more deliberative amending procedure than ordinary constitutional amendments'.[131] Despite the fact that the eternity clauses have become a phenomenon of modern constitutionalism, they in effect put 'handcuffs' on the citizens' amendment liberty.[132] For Albert, '[t]o withhold from citizens the power of constitutional amendment is to withhold more than a mere procedural right. It is to hijack their most basic of all democratic rights. Nothing is more democratically objectionable than dispossessing citizens of the power to rewrite the charter governing the boundary separating the citizen from the state, and citizens from themselves'.[133]

Quite simply, therefore, the eternalization of a lengthy list of constitutional clauses would arguably be an affront, or 'an imminent threat', to the constituent power of the people.[134] Thus, constitutional eternity clauses are legitimate only to the extent that they express and preserve the higher values of constitutionalism moored in any given constitutional order. The extent of an eternity clause both presupposes and should be predicated upon a theory of inviolability of the essential constitutional cores, established by the people on whose behalf the legislature exercises a secondary constituent power.[135] Constitutional unamendability rule, whether entrenched in the eternity clause or is normatively applied by the constitutional court, must not and in fact does not foreclose parliament's secondary constituent power. Its function should essentially be the guarantee of constitutional durability, not the impairment of constitutional progress. It should only prevent parliament's overtaking of primary constituent power and ensure that constitutional

---

[129]In academic discourse, the necessity and legitimacy of entrenchment clauses are a matter of intense debate. While some scholars tend to regard constitutional entrenchment as an effective tool to preserve the state identity, others consider the idea anti-democratic. For a middle-course argument, see Barber (2016) arguing that entrenchment sometimes brings benefits but also presents hazards.

[130]Katz (1996).

[131]Ibid., p. 252.

[132]Albert (2010), p. 663.

[133]Ibid., p. 663.

[134]Abdelaal (2016), p. 9.

[135]It is important to note that the argument of 'essential constitutional cores' should not be considered a reflection of state-centric theorizing of constitutional order that is now seen to be insufficient in a postmodern context. This idea indeed points to a supra-state, supra-constitutional normative structure characteristically bound to any given nation.

amendments are not irreconcilably incompatible with the identity of the constitution or its essential cores.[136]

I will now briefly take up the issue of likely implications of the Bangladeshi eternity clause, which, as indicated, holds seeds of discontent for constitutional politics with the possibility of its being used as fuel to the country's unstable constitutionalism. In view of the curtailment of future parliaments' authority to amend a wide number of constitutional provisions, the political actors will more likely than not take the issue of legitimacy of the eternity clause to the superior courts. Given the selfish party motivations underlying the past amendments,[137] there is also a strong likelihood that politicians, in future, will make use of the amending power to frustrate the current unamendability rule.

Arguably, in any country whose eternal constitutional clauses are not strongly tied with the national identity, and where political consensus amongst the competing actors often remains absent, the interested party politics is most likely to maneuver with, or totally disregard, the amendment rules—a scenario which might give birth to extreme politicization of the judiciary or/and judicialization of politics.[138] Either way, it may be argued, Bangladesh's eternity clause will be of intriguing implications for the judiciary especially with regard to its role in reviewing any constitutional amendments. As the establishment of 'a large part of the nation's law as no longer subject to easy amendment by Parliament becomes [...] an admission of failure of the much-cherished democratic principle of Parliamentary Sovereignty',[139] this posits the judges in a unique place within the constitutional order to manage the tension between the entrenched provisions and constitutional developments. Further, given that the representative organ of the State might tend to usurp the people's constituent power, the higher principle of constitutional supremacy requires and legitimates the judicial application of the basic structure doctrine.[140]

---

[136]In the Bangladeshi context, I elsewhere argued that the extraordinary judicial review power vis-à-vis constitutional amendments should be exercised extremely rarely and only for preserving the 'identity of the State'. See Hoque (2013). See also Talukder and Chowdhury (2008), who, in the context of the then entrenched provisions that required referendum for change, argued that amendments passed through referendum ought to be immune from judicial review. See further Collett (2010), p. 327, Dixon and Landau (2015), p. 606 (arguing that judges should apply basic structure doctrine only when they perceive serious threats to the democratic order, and that they should justify those threats by surveying transnational practises and experiences).

[137]See Aziz Khan (2015). A general source on politics of constitutional amendments in Bangladesh is Akhter (2016).

[138]This has recently happened in Honduras in an unprecedented way. The Honduran Constitution limited presidential terms and made the prohibition of reelection an unamendable clause. In a 2015 decision that is seen as an instance of 'abusive constitutionalism by judiciary', the Constitutional Chamber of Honduras declared inapplicable a series of original constitutional provisions that prohibited presidential reelection. See Landau and Sheppard (2015). On the concept of abusive constitutionalism, see Landau (2013), p. 189 (defining it as the use of the tools of constitutional change such as amendment rules or judicial review to undermine democracy).

[139]Menski (2015), p. 27.

[140]See Dellinger (1983), p. 386 (arguing, in the US context, that judicial involvement in the amendment process is necessary to legitimate constitutional changes).

The judicial role here is, however, innately complex. There are apparently two sources of this complexity. First, the unamendable provisions in the Bangladeshi Constitution are co-extant with the basic structure doctrine at the hands of the Supreme Court. In any likely basic structure challenge, therefore, arguments might be made either that the Court's power to annul any constitutional amendments is now completely foreclosed by art 7B, or that it applies only to amendments implicating provisions that are not mentioned in that article.[141] Second, the 15th amendment that introduced the eternity clause reinstated the founding constitutional values in a way that apparently seems to be internally conflicting. This would facilitate the emergence of difficult questions for the Court to resolve. Consider, for example, the case of 'secularism' as an identity principle sitting along 'Islam' as the state religion. What would be the Court's approach to the task of fathoming the extent and meaning of 'state religion'?[142] How would it reconcile the seemingly irreconcilable principles of secularism and state religion? Undoubtedly, these would be some difficult questions of sociopolitical and institutional ramifications for the Court to handle. In any decision involving the 'basic provisions' of the Constitution, therefore, both the meaning and the modification by the Court of the eternity clause would likely be implicated since art 7B makes the nation's founding values unamendable in any manner.[143]

---

[141]Interestingly, in a recent post-article 7B decision concerning the constitutionality of the Constitution (Sixteenth Amendment) Act 2014 (Act No. XIII of 2014) that brought back an original provision for the removal of judges pursuant to a resolution of Parliament on the ground of proved judicial misconduct, the HCD eschewed these questions. In striking down the 16th amendment, the Court referenced art 7B only in passing, saying that an amendment against the Constitution's basic structure would be unconstitutional. The decision, now on appeal, is deeply problematic in that it had in effect invalidated an original constitutional scheme. In the Appellate Division, however, Justice Ali (at pp. 229–230 of the judgment noted in n 6 above) commented that "the force" of article 7B "would appear to be open to question" as it purports to bind the people of the future.

[142]It is interesting to note that, before the Constitution's revival of the principle of 'secularism', that is, when the 'state religion' alone remained an entrenched provision, there was an implied acknowledgement of the state religion clause's basic structure-incompatibility in M. Saleem Ullah v Bangladesh (2005) 57 DLR (HCD) 171, para 67, in which Awlad Ali J. remarked that the constitutionalization of the principle of 'absolute faith in the Almighty Allah' was destructive of one of its basic structural pillars. In the same way, the Appellate Division in the 5th Amendment Case, n 85 at 367, remarked that the principle of 'absolute trust and faith in the Almighty Allah' was inconsistent with the secular identity of the State. The comparative reader interested in how the Indian superior courts dealt with the meaning of 'secularism' under the Indian Constitution that does not have a state religion clause might see Alam (2009), p. 29, and Bhambhri (2008), Padhy (2008), and Mahmood (2008), p. 755.

[143]In March 2016, the Court studiously escaped an encounter with these questions by summarily dismissing a revived challenge to the state religion clause. The challenge was originally lodged by 15 citizens some 23 years ago on 9 June 1988. See the HCD's order of 28 March 2016 in Kemaluddin Hossain (later Sirajul Islam Chowdhury) and others v Bangladesh, WP No. 1834 of 1988. For a commentary on this decision see Hoque (2016b).

6 Conclusion

This chapter explores the issues of democratic legitimacy and deficiency in the Bangladeshi eternity clause. As indicated above, the reasons for its enactment are more 'political' than constitutional. Moreover, the subject matters of constitutional entrenchment, apart from being deceptively wide, were not the outcomes of democratic deliberations and consensus. Specifically, as argued above, the Bangladeshi eternity clause has arguably turned the Constitution of the country into a largely unamendable document, thereby substantially de-constructing two most basic of constitutional cores: constitutional supremacy and popular sovereignty.

The success and efficacy of entrenchment rules usually depend on whether 'there is a connection between the reason for entrenchment, the manner of entrenchment adopted, and the area of law entrenched'.[144] The connection between these essential attributes of an eternity clause is clearly absent in the Bangladeshi one. This deficiency, coupled with the exceedingly wide scope of this eternity clause, might cause it to incur disobedience or might give vent to political instability. Having become ultra-rigid, it might potentially prevent even political deliberations on the question of national identity principles or constitutional basics.

This chapter argues that the all-embracing Bangladeshi eternity clause is almost certain to yield complex implications for national politics and constitutional adjudication. While it remains to be seen how the superior courts and the political actors would navigate and manage the unintended consequences of the country's unpragmatic eternity clause, a probable way-out might be to accord unamendability only to the fundamental constitutional cores. This chapter accordingly endorses the legitimacy of entrenching the fundamental cores,[145] and notes at the same time the danger of enlarging the folder of the eternity clause unwieldily.

Acknowledgements I gratefully acknowledge Werner Menski's helpful comments on an earlier draft. I also thank the anonymous reviewer for the most helpful comments that helped me improve the content of this work. I sincerely thank Tashmia Sabera for her superb research assistance and Emraan Azad for bringing to my notice some important materials.

---

[144]Barber (2016), p. 2.

[145]Bangladesh's article 7B, despite its creeping limitations, can, therefore, be regarded as an acknowledgement of the presence of a 'higher law beyond state law' and a reflection of increasing legal-plurality-consciousness, not just in theory but also in constitutional practise. The plurality-consciousness, however, has not been demonstrated pragmatically. I thank Professor Werner Menski for drawing my attention to this aspect of the eternity clause.

References

Abdelaal M (2016) Entrenchment illusion: the curious case of Egypt's constitutional entrenchment clause. Chicago-Kent J Int Comp Law 16(2):1

Ahmed AFS (1994) Bengali nationalism and the emergence of Bangladesh: an introductory outline. International Centre for Bengal Studies

Ahmed R (1996) The Bengal muslims 1871–1906: a quest for identity, 2nd edn. OUP

Ahmed K (2015) The supreme court's power of judicial review in Bangladesh: a critical evaluation. Accessed 17 April 2015

Akhter MY (2001) Electoral corruption in Bangladesh. Ashgate, pp 132–137

Akhter S (2016) Amendments to the constitution of Bangladesh 1973–2011: background, politics and impacts. Unpublished MPhil Thesis, University of Dhaka, Department of Political Science 2016

Alam S (1991) The state-religion amendment to the constitution of Bangladesh: a critique. Verfassung und Recht in Übersee (Law and Politics in Africa, Asia, and Latin America) 24(2):209, 224

Alam MM (2009) Constructing secularism: separating 'religion' and 'state' under the Indian constitution. Aust J Asian Law 11(1):29

Albert R (2010) Constitutional handcuffs. Arizona State Law J 42:663

Albert R (2013) The expressive function of constitutional amendment rules. McGill Law J 59(2):225

Albert R (2015) The unamendable core of the United States constitution. In: Koltay A (ed) Comparative perspectives on the fundamental freedom of expression. Wolters Kluwer

Anisuzzaman (1993) Creativity, reality and identity. International Centre for Bengal Studies

Anwar A (2015) The future of secularism. In: Anwar A (ed) Secularism (first published 1973). BDNews24 Publishing Limited

Aziz Khan A (2015) The politics of constitutional amendments in Bangladesh: the case of the non-political caretaker government. Int Rev Law 9:1, 1

Barber NW (2016) Why Entrench? Int J Const Law 14(2):325

Baxter C (1984) Bangladesh: a new nation in an old setting. Westview Press

Besselink LFM (2010) National and constitutional identity before and after Lisbon. Utrecht Law Rev 6(3):36, 42–44

Bhambhri CP (2008) Secular state in a hyper-religious society: the role of the judiciary. In: Dua BD, Saxena R, Singh MP (eds) Indian judiciary and politics: the changing landscape. Manohar

Bhardwaj SK (2011) Contesting identities in Bangladesh: a study of secular and religious frontiers. Asia Research Centre Working Paper No. 36, 2011, LSE, London. http://www.lse.ac.uk/asiaResearchCentre/_files/ARCWP36-Bhardwaj.pdf. Accessed 3 Jul 2016

Billah SMM (2014) Can "secularism" and "state religion" go together? In: Rahman M, Ullah MR (eds) Human rights and religion. Empowerment through Law of the Common People

Choudhury D (1995) Constitutional developments in Bangladesh: stresses and strains. University Press Limited, pp 82–84

Chowdhury SR (1972) The genesis of Bangladesh. Asia Publishing House

Chowdhury R (2014) The doctrine of basic structure in Bangladesh: from "Calf-path" to *Matryoshka* Dolls. Bangladesh J Law 14(1 & 2):43

Collett TS (2010) Judicial independence and accountability in an age of unconstitutional constitutional amendments. Loyola Univ Chicago Law J 4(2):327

Colon-Rios JI (2014) Five conceptions of constituent power. LQR 130:306, 312

Colon-Rios JI (2015) Introduction: the forms and limits of constitutional amendments. Int J Const Law 13(3):567

Colón-Ríos JI (2012) Weak constitutionalism: democratic legitimacy and the question of constituent power. Routledge

Dellinger W (1983) The legitimacy of constitutional change: rethinking the amendment process. Harvard Law Rev 97(2):386

Dickinson J (1987) Cited in Paraas Diwan and Piyushi Diwan, Amending power and constitutional amendments. Deep and Deep Publications

Dixon R (2011) Constitutional amendment rules: a comparative perspective. In: Ginsburg T, Dixon R (eds) Comparative constitutional law. Edward Elgar Publishing

Dixon R (2012) Amending constitutional identity. Cardozo Law Rev 33(5):1847

Dixon R, Landau D (2015) Transnational constitutionalism and a limited doctrine of unconstitutional constitutional amendment. Int J Const Law 13(3):606

Elkins Z, Ginsburg T, Melton J (2009) The endurance of national constitutions. CUP

Faraguna P (2016) Taking constitutional identities away from the courts. Brooklyn J Int Law 41(2):491

Fazal T (1999) Religion and language in the formation of nationhood in Pakistan and Bangladesh. Sociol Bull 48(1 and 2):175, 190–191

Feldman S (2001) Exploring theories of patriarchy: a perspective from contemporary Bangladesh. Signs J Women Culture Soc 26(4):1097, 1099

Friedman A (2011) Dead hand constitutionalism: the danger of eternity clauses in new democracies. Mexican Law Rev 4(1):77, 79

Ginsburg T, Melton J (2015) Does the constitutional amendment rule matter at all? Amendment cultures and the challenges of measuring amendment difficulty. Int J Const L 13(3):686

Gözler K (2008) Judicial review of constitutional amendments: a comparative study. Ekin Press

Grewe C (2013) Methods of identification of national constitutional identity. In: Arnaiz AS, Llivinia CA (eds) National constitutional identity and European Integration. Intersentia

Halim MA (2014) The fifteenth amendment to the constitution: concerns and perils of constitutionalism in Bangladesh. Counsel Law J 2(1):83

Halim MA (ed) (2015) The constituent assembly debates. CCB Foundation

Hamilton A (1999) The Federalist No. 85. In: Rossiter C (ed) The Federalist papers: Alexander Hamilton, James Madison, John Jay (first published 1778). Mentor

Hassan MT (2004) Constitution of Bangladesh, politics and nationality: a philosophical analysis (in Bangla). Chittagong Univ J Law 9:185, 189

Henkin L (1994) Constitutions and the elements of constitutionalism. Occasional Paper Series, Columbia University Center for the Study of Human Rights

Hoque R (2005) On Coup d' Etat, constitutionalism, and the need to break the subtle bondage with alien legal thought: a reply to Omar and Hossain. The Daily Star (Law & Our Rights). Dhaka, 29 October 2005

Hoque R (2011) Judicial activism in Bangladesh: a golden mean approach. Cambridge Scholars Publishing, pp 112–119

Hoque R (2013) Constitutionalism and the judiciary in Bangladesh. In: Khilnani S, Raghavan V, Thiruvengadam AK (eds) Comparative constitutionalism in South Asia. OUP, p 317

Hoque R (2015) Judicialization of politics in Bangladesh: pragmatism, legitimacy and consequences. In: Tushnet M, Khosla M (eds) Unstable constitutionalism: law and politics in South Asia. CUP

Hoque R (2016a) Can the court invalidate an original provision of the constitution? Univ Asia Pacific J Law Policy 2:13

Hoque R (2016b) Constitutional challenge to the state religion status of Islam in Bangladesh: back to square one? Int J Const L Blog. http://www.iconnectblog.com/2016/05/islam-in-bangladesh. Accessed 27 May 2016

Hossain K (2013) Bangladesh: Quest for freedom and justice. University Press Limited, Chapter 9

Huq AF (1973) Constitution-making in Bangladesh. Pacific Affairs 46(1):59

Husain SA (1990) Islamic fundamentalism in Bangladesh: internal variables and external inputs. In: Ahmed R (ed) Religion, nationalism and politics in Bangladesh. South Asian Publishers, p 150

Jackson VC (2013) Unconstitutional constitutional amendments: a window into constitutional theory and transnational constitutionalism. In: Bäuerle M, Dann P, Wallrabenstein A (eds) Demokratie-Perspektiven: Festschrift für Brun-Otto Bryde zum 70. Mohr Siebeck GmbH

Jacobsohn GJ (2006) An unconstitutional constitution? A comparative perspective. Int J Const L 4(3):460

Jacobsohn GJ (2011a) The formation of constitutional identities. In: Ginsburg T, Dixon R (eds) Comparative constitutional law. Edward Elgar Publishing

Jacobsohn GJ (2011b) Constitutional identity. Harvard University Press

Kabeer N (1991) The quest for national identity: women, islam, and the state. Feminist Rev 37:38, 55

Kamal M (1994) Bangladesh constitution: trends and issues. Dhaka University Press

Karim L (2015) In search of an identity: the rise of political Islam and Bangladeshi Nationalism. http://web.uvic.ca/~anp/Public/posish_pap/Karim.pdf. Accessed 6 May 2015

Katz E (1996) On amending constitutions: the legality and legitimacy of constitutional entrenchment. Colum J Law Soc Prob 29:251

Kavanagh A (2003) The idea of a living constitution. Canad J & Law Juris 16:55

Khan S (2011a) Leviathan and the supreme court: an essay on the "basic structure" doctrine. Stamford J Law 2:89

Khan BU (2011b) 15th amendment and some issues. In: The Daily Star (Law & Our Rights), Dhaka, 1 August 2011

Khondker HH (2010) The curious case of secularism in Bangladesh: what is the relevance for the muslim majority democracies? Totalitarian Movements & Polit Religions 11(2):185, 188, 201

Klein C (1978) Is there a need for an amending power theory? Israeli Law Rev 13:202

Klug H (2015) Constitutional amendments. Annual Rev Law Soc Sci 11:95

Krishnaswamy S (2009) Democracy and constitutionalism in India: a study of the basic structure doctrine. OUP

Landau D (2013) Abusive constitutionalism. UC Davis Law Rev 47:189

Landau D, Sheppard B (2015) The Honduran constitutional Chamber's decision erasing presidential term limits: abusive constitutionalism by judiciary? Int J Const Law Blog. http://www.iconnectblog.com/2015/05/the-honduran-constitutional-chambers-decision-erasing-presidential-term-limits-abusive-constitutionalism-by-judiciary. Accessed May 2015

Loughlin M (2013) The concept of constituent power. Critical Analysis of Law Workshop, University of Toronto, 15 January 2013, p 18. http://www.law.utoronto.ca/utfl_file/count/users/mdubber/CAL/12-13/Loughlin-Paper-Constituent%20Power.pdf

Loughlin M, Walker N (eds) (2007) The paradox of constitutionalism: constituent power and constitutional form. OUP

Lutz DS (1994) Toward a theory of constitutional amendment. Am Pol Sci Rev 88(2)

Mahmood T (2008) Religion, law, and judiciary in modern India. Brigham Young Univ Law Rev 3:755

Malik S (2002) Laws of Bangladesh. Chowdhury AM, Alam F (eds) Bangladesh: on the threshold of the twenty-first century. Asiatic Society of Bangladesh, p 442

Marti JL (2013) Two different ideas of constitutional identity: Identity of the constitution v. identity of the people. In: Arnaiz AS, Llivinia CA (eds) National constitutional identity and European integration. Intersentia, Cambridge

Menski WF (2015) Bangladesh in 2015: challenges of the *Iccher Ghuri* for learning to live together. Univ Asia Pacific J Law Policy 1(1):9, 23

Mohsin A (2004) Religion, politics and security: the case of Bangladesh. In: Limaye SP, Malik M, Wirsing RG (eds) Religious radicalism and security in South Asia. Asia-Pacific Center for Security Studies

Morgan DG (1981) The Indian "essential features" case. ICLQ 30(2):307

Muhith AMA (1992) Bangladesh: emergence of a nation. University Press Limited

Murshid TM (1997) State, nation, identity: the quest for legitimacy in Bangladesh. J South Asian Stud 20(2):1

Omar I, Hossain Z (2005) Coup d' Etat, constitution and legal continuity. The Daily Star (Law and Our Rights). Dhaka, 17, 28 September 2005

Padhy S (2008) Secularism and justice: a review of Indian Supreme Court judgments. In: Dua BD, Rekha S, and Singh MP (eds) Indian judiciary and politics: the changing landscape. Manohar, New Delhi

Polzin M (2016) Constitutional identity, unconstitutional amendments and the idea of constituent power: the development of the doctrine of constitutional identity in German constitutional law. Int J Const Law 14(2):411

Rashiduzzaman M (1994) Islam, muslim identity and nationalism in Bangladesh. J South Asian Middle East Stud 18(1):36, 58–59

Rehnquist WH (2006) The notion of a living constitution (first published 1976). Harvard J Law Public Policy 29(2):401

Riaz A (2010) God willing: the politics of islamism in Bangladesh. In: Riaz A, Christine Fair C (eds) Political islam and governance in Bangladesh (first published 2004). Routledge

Rizvi M (2015) South Asian constitutional convergence revisited: Pakistan and the basic structure doctrine. Int J Const Law Blog. http://www.iconnectblog.com/2015/09/south-asian-constitutional-convergence-revisited-pakistan-and-the-basic-structure-doctrine. Accessed 18 Sept 2015

Rory O (1999) Guardian of the constitution: unconstitutional constitutional norms. J Civ Lib 4:48

Rosen J (1991) Was the flag burning amendment unconstitutional? Yale Law J 100(4):1073

Rosenfeld M (2010) Constitutional identity. In: Rosenfeld M, Sajo A (eds) The Oxford handbook of comparative constitutional law. OUP

Rosenfeld M (2012) The identity of the constitutional subject: selfhood, citizenship, culture and community. Routledge, London

Roznai Y (2013) Unconstitutional constitutional amendments: the migration and success of a constitutional idea. AJCL 61:657

Roznai Y (2015) Towards a theory of unamendability. NYU School of Law Public Law Research Paper 515, 24 February 2015

Roznai Y (2016) Unamendability and the genetic code of the constitution. Europ Rev Public Law 28(1):775

Roznai Y (2017) Unconstitutional constitutional amendments: the limits of amendment powers. OUP

Sachs A (1990) Protecting human rights in a New South Africa. OUP

Samar VJ (2008) Can a constitutional amendment be unconstitutional? Oklahoma City Univ Law Rev 33(3):667

Schwartzberg M (2007) Democracy and legal change. CUP

Sisson R, Rose LE (1990) War and secession: Pakistan, India, and the creation of Bangladesh. University of California Press

Somek A (2012) Constituent power in national and transnational contexts. Transnational Leg Theor 3:31

Strauss DA (2010) The living constitution. OUP

Talukder MJU, Chowdhury MJA (2008) Determining the province of judicial review: a re-evaluation of "basic structure" of the constitution of Bangladesh. Metrop Univ J 2(2):161

Thornhill C (2012) Contemporary constitutionalism and the dialectic of constituent power. Glob Constitutionalism 1:369

Tomuschat C, Currie DP (2010) The basic law for the Federal Republic of Germany. Juris GmbH

Toniatti R (2013) Sovereignty lost, constitutional identity regained. In: Arnaiz AS, Llivinia CA (eds) National constitutional identity and European integration. Intersentia, Cambridge

Tushnet M (2010) How do constitutions constitute constitutional identity? Int J Const Law 8(3):671

Tushnet M (2015) Peasants with pitchforks, and toilers with twitter: constitutional revolutions and the constituent power. Int J Const Law 13(3):639

Weintal S (2011) The challenge of reconciling constitutional eternity clauses with popular sovereignty: toward three-track democracy in Israel as a universal holistic constitutional system and theory. Israel Law Rev 44(3):449

Unamendability as a Judicial Discovery? Inductive Learning Lessons from Hungary

Fruzsina Gárdos-Orosz

Abstract The chapter argues that, if we understand constitutionalism as a legal concept, the unamendability of certain constitutional norms becomes party independent of explicit constitutional declarations. The Hungarian case explains that unamendability can be justified as a judicial discovery even when the constitution does not adopt explicit rules on unamendability. Moreover, even if there is no explicit rule in the constitutional text or even if there is no explicit declaration of unamendability in constitutional court case law, legal interpretation methods help to argue that some sort of unamendability is a basic feature of constitutionalism awaiting its legitimate judicial discovery. In analysing the Hungarian example, while bearing in mind the comparative and the theoretical context of the discussion, I arrive at the inductive conclusion that unamendability might belong to the nature of legal constitutionalism. Turning a rule of law democracy into an autocracy, e.g., by constitutional amendments is not a valid legal solution in most constitutional democracies regardless of whether their constitution contains eternity or other entrenchment clauses or not. This is so because, in a rule of law democracy, a living constitution is partly a judicial construction and, in applying a legal doctrine, one finds normative requirements applicable to fundamental constitutional changes. I argue that these requirements can validly be enforced by the guardians of the constitution.

1 Introduction

'All constitutions—or at least some provisions of constitutions—contain values of choice. Parts of these are fundamental values that define the identity of the constitution. Parts of these values are unamendable even if this prohibition is not incorporated explicitly in the text. These are unamendable because the source of the

F. Gárdos-Orosz (✉)
Hungarian Academy of Sciences, Center for Social Sciences,
Institute of Legal Studies, Budapest, Hungary
e-mail: fruzsina.orosz@gmail.com

© Springer International Publishing AG, part of Springer Nature 2018
R. Albert and B. E. Oder (eds.), *An Unamendable Constitution?*
Ius Gentium: Comparative Perspectives on Law and Justice 68,
https://doi.org/10.1007/978-3-319-95141-6_9

231

amending power is in the constitution, it is derived from it, therefore it is not empowered to eliminate essential parts of it.'[1] 'The amendment of the constitution cannot ruin the constitution itself'.[2] 'For ruining the constitution a revolution is needed when the old constitution dies'.[3]

The idea of inherent unamendability is mentioned not only in often cited case law, but also in mainstream, well-known constitutional doctrine: 'Amending the constitution must stay within the constitutional framework, this competence is based on the constitution and it cannot override it. This competence cannot involve the adoption of a new constitution …'.[4]

In modern constitutions, the stability of constitutions is often guaranteed by eternity[5] or other entrenchment clauses.[6] These provisions provide some sort of an obstacle to fundamental amendments to constitutions by stating, in their strictest form, that one or more provisions are unamendable. If the prohibition is final, we talk about eternity clauses (*Ewigkeitsklausel*), and many jurisdictions show examples for this.[7] In Europe, the constitutions of Germany, Italy and France are typical models for other European constitutions, which explicitly limit or exclude amendments of certain provisions. The said states experienced the harm, which totalitarian regimes cause to the individual, society and the state. The preventive function of such unamendability in these states and others copying them leaves no room for doubt,[8] although unamendability is firmly rebutted on the level of constitutional theory.[9] Unamendable provisions on the republican form of government, on the protection of fundamental rights or on territorial integrity, give the

---

[1]András Bragyova, 'Vannak-e megváltoztathatatlan normák az Alkotmányban?' (Are There Unamendable Norms in the Constitution?) in Bragyova (2003). This study is based on an article published in Hungarian, co-authored by András Bragyova: Bragyova and Gárdos-Orosz (2016). Throughout the text I indicate where I refer to his ideas. I profited greatly from his comments on the text and from his recommendations on literature. I also thank for the precious comments of Gábor Halmai on the text and Zoltán Szente for the never-ending discussions on the topic. The manuscript was closed in August 2016, therefore it does not discuss the important decision 22/2016. (XII. 5.) CC of the Constitutional Court that finally declared a certain understanding of unamendability of the Fundamental Law. This fact, however, might strengthen the importance of my argument in the Hungarian constitutional law.

[2]"*The power to 'amend' the Constitution was not intended to include the power to destroy it.*" Marbury (1919), p. 225, 232.

[3]Hormasji "Homi" Servai (1996), p. 3109. For the *Keshavanda Bhavati* case, see Granville (1999), 260 ff.

[4]Schmitt (1928), p. 16.

[5]See all eternity clauses of the world in the Appendix of Roznai (2016).

[6]This chapter does not differentiate between entrenched and entrenchment provisions. For an explanation, see Albert (2010a), p. 706.

[7]The most famous amongst them is Article 79(3) of the German Basic Law.

[8]This is also elaborated by the German Federal Constitutional Court in its Decision BVerfGE 30, 1. See also Küpper (2004), p. 273. For the function of unamendable clauses within the broader context of constitutional change, see Albert (2010b) or Roznai (2013), p. 706.

[9]The arguments and counterarguments are collected by Yaniv Roznai, 'Necrocracy or Democracy: Assessing Objections to Constitutional Unamendability', in this volume.

impression of legal certainty and the inviolability on the basis of the constitutional order.[10] Richard Albert validly points out that the expressive function of unamendability which affects significantly the constitutional culture of values is a leading function of unamendability in practice.[11] Unamendability demonstrates that there are core provisions in constitutions[12] which cannot be amended despite the will of the overwhelming majority. Research on implicit unamendability is about finding this core, the unamendable provisions of a constitutional design by way of judicial interpretation, by legal methodology.[13] The Indian Supreme Court was the first to discover implicit unamendability rooted in the basic structure of the constitution. The doctrine of unconstitutional constitutional amendments has spread the world over and attracted promoters amongst constitutional judges of the world.[14]

Although unamendability has become increasingly fashionable in new constitutionalism,[15] most of the older and many of the new constitutions still do not contain such explicit provisions. This is the case with the 2011 Hungarian Fundamental Law, the newest constitution of the EU. When discussing such a contemporary constitution, one might argue that the fact that a fundamental law does not contain provisions qualified as unamendable shows the clear intention of the framers of the Fundamental Law to exclude unamendability. The question remains, however, whether it is possible at all to create a stable constitutional democracy in the twenty-first century with a completely amendable constitution. I shall take the Hungarian example and shall show different ways of legal reasoning to justify a certain degree of unamendability in the Hungarian constitutional system. I conclude that this experience might lead to the general conclusion that all constitutions must have at least one unamendable norm.[16]

---

[10]Romania's constitution offers nice examples of all kinds of explicit unamendability. Géza Kilény, a former judge of the Hungarian Constitutional Court, claims that unamendable clauses have a sacred function, that they incorporate the value of constitutionalism. Cf. Kilényi (1996), p. 117 with Jacobsohn (2006), p. 460.

[11]Albert (2013), p. 280, 281.

[12]The term 'unamendable core' is used by Richard Albert in his 'The Unamendable Core of the United States Constitution' in András (2015), p. 13.

[13]I use "judicial discovery" rather than "judicial construction" in the title of my chapter, but I do use the two terms in the text interchangeably. Although "judicial construction" is widely used in constitutional law discussions, I believe that "discovery" might be better in this case. Judges in Hungary usually do not create new constructions, but explain what the constitution already contains. The method is further explained and applied in Yaniv Roznai, 'Towards a theory of unamendability' NYU Public Law and Legal Theory Working Papers. Paper 515. 15. Judicial interpretation is not used exclusively by the judiciary. All state actors or all social science may use legal methods. However, the judiciary is responsible for both using this method and developing it.

[14]Colombia, the Czech Republic, etc., are often points of reference in this discussion. Roznai (2014), p. 29, Halmai (2015), p. 951. On the Colombian constitutional replacement doctrine, see ibid, pp. 960–962. On his arguing with Roznai with regard to the Czech case, see ibid, p. 964.

[15]Hein (2015).

[16]I use the expression "norm", because I take into account constitutional provisions, rules, principles, values, state ambitions and interpretation standards when I examine the unamendability of certain norms.

2 Case Law of the Hungarian Constitutional Court on Unamendability

2.1 Circumstances

In Hungary, a one party alliance won a two-thirds majority in Parliament both in 2010 and in 2014. They adopted a new Fundamental Law in 2011, it entered into force in 2012, and was modified six times up to August 2016.[17] The adoption of the new text was based on the former Constitution of Hungary, on Act XX of 1949 on the Constitution of the Republic of Hungary (Constitution). This Constitution was significantly amended in its merits during the democratic transition of 1989/1990, and so scholars in constitutional law teach about this amended Constitution as a substantively new Constitution of the democratic transition. The Preamble of the Constitution declared that 'In order to facilitate a peaceful political transition to a constitutional state, establish a multiparty system, parliamentary democracy and a social market economy, the Parliament of the Republic of Hungary hereby establishes the following text as the Constitution of the Republic of Hungary, until the Republic's new Constitution is adopted'. Point 2 of the Closing and Miscellaneous Provisions demonstrates that the adoption of the Fundamental Law was based on the former Constitution: 'The Parliament shall adopt this Fundamental Law according to point a) of subsection (3) of Sect. 19 and subsection (3) of Sect. 24 of Act XX of 1949." This section of the Constitution states that "Within its sphere of authority, the Parliament shall adopt the Constitution of the Republic of Hungary'. According to Article 24(1) of the Fundamental Law, 'the Constitutional Court shall be the principal organ for the protection of the Fundamental Law'. I shall base many of my arguments presented bellow on these provisions of the constitutional text.

Neither the Constitution nor the Fundamental Law contains explicit, eternal or temporary unamendable provisions. In majority decision, the Hungarian Constitutional Court has never declared definitively that a constitutional amendment can violate the Constitution; it rather held the opposite in its early decisions of the 90s, and consequently further on. It has never found that certain provisions of the Constitution are unamendable. However, during the past 25 years, since the democratic transition, since its establishment, it has discussed these issues several

---

[17]See criticism in Sonnevend et al. (2015), pp. 33–110. Between 2010 and 2011, the two-thirds majority also amended the 1949 Constitution several times. The first amendment after 2010, e.g., introduced a radical reduction of the number of members of Parliament, and changed the legal status of government officials. The Parliament changed the composition of the parliamentary commission nominating judges to the Constitutional Court. The fourth amendment in 2010 changed the rules regulating public service media. The sixth amendment after 2010 created the necessary conditions for retroactively taxing certain payments. The seventh amendment, e.g., changed the rules regulating legislation and public prosecution. One amendment limited the powers of the Constitutional Court in cases in which the acts to be supervised are related to state finance.

times. As both the composition and the competence of the Hungarian Constitutional Court changed over the years, the conclusions it reached slightly differ. After 2010, when the two-thirds parliamentary majority started amending the Constitution with great intensity, partly to reflect the political challenges of the day, partly to give a different (illiberal) shape to the constitutional order,[18] the discussion about unamendability and the related question of unconstitutional constitutional amendments became heated.[19]

The Hungarian Constitutional Court took important steps towards finding the unamendable core of the Constitution and towards justifying the competence of soft substantive reviews of constitutional amendments. In the end, however—after the Fourth Amendment of the Fundamental Law in 2013, which amended the text of the Fundamental Law regarding the review of amendments[20] explicitly excluding substantive review from the scope of revision—the Constitutional Court turned back to a very limited competence of procedural review (explicitly allowed by the new constitutional text). This might as well implicate the absence of unamendable provisions.[21] My thesis is, however, that, in spite of the present majority view of the Constitutional Court, there is unamendability in the Hungarian Constitution and this unamendability can be found and should be enforced by the Hungarian Constitutional Court within its competence.

In this part, I shall first explain the history of the domestic struggle of the Constitutional Court, and then describe a doctrinal framework to understand implicit unamendability in the Hungarian Constitution. This is followed by a

---

[18]Antal (2013), pp. 48–70. See also Vincze (2015). Gábor Halmai explains in detail these amendments in Halmai (2015), p. 979.

[19]Gárdos-Orosz and Szente (2015).

[20]Article 2 of the Fourth Amendment to the Hungarian Fundamental Law "The Speaker of Parliament shall sign the adopted Act within five days and send it to the President of the Republic. The President of the Republic shall sign the Act within five days of receiving it and order its publication. If Parliament has sent the Act to the Constitutional Court for an examination of its conformity with the Fundamental Law pursuant to paragraph (2), the Speaker of Parliament may only sign and send it to the President of the Republic if the Constitutional Court has not found any violation of the Fundamental Law. (4) If the President of the Republic considers an Act or any of its provisions to be contrary to the Fundamental Law, and no examination pursuant to paragraph (2) has been conducted, he or she shall send the Act to the Constitutional Court for an examination of its conformity with the Fundamental Law. The following provision replaces Article S(3) of the Fundamental Law: (3) The Speaker of the House signs the Fundamental Law and amendments to the Fundamental Law, and sends these to the President of the Republic for signature. The President of the Republic signs the Fundamental Law or amendments to the Fundamental Law into law within five days of receiving these, and orders their publication in the Official Gazette. If the President of the Republic decides that the Parliament violated the procedural requirements defined in the Fundamental Law when it adopted the Fundamental Law or its amendment, the President of the Republic sends these to the Constitutional Court for review. If the Constitutional Court does not declare any violation of the procedural requirements, the President of the Republic immediately signs the Fundamental Law or its amendment into law".

[21]See the opinion of a former constitutional court judge Vörös (2014), p. 1.

justification of substantive constitutional reviews of unconstitutional amendments.[22] The Hungarian example, however, shows that, although there are good arguments in constitutional law for justifying implicit unamendability and its protection by constitutional review, the constitutional limitations on state power are sometimes, unfortunately, less effectively enforced by rational legal arguments than with well-functioning constitutional conventions[23] and with a developed constitutional culture.[24]

2.2 Assessment of Unamendability Between 1990 and 2010 in Constitutional Court Case Law

After the transition, the newly established Hungarian Constitutional Court had very high legitimacy.[25] The Court created the principle of the so-called 'invisible constitution', which led to the development of the detailed norms of the Hungarian constitutional order. This is where basic principles and the discussion about unamendability first appeared.[26]

In Hungary, a simple two-thirds majority of all the members of Parliament is required to adopt and also to amend the Constitution. This rule is identical in both the Constitution and the Fundamental Law.[27]

That the Constitution itself is a democratic value and that, therefore, none of its provisions should be explicitly unamendable was the majority opinion of the Constitutional Court after the democratic transition of 1989–1990. The Hungarian Constitutional Court declared several times that there is no hierarchy between the provisions of the Constitution and that none of the provisions are unamendable. Although already in 1990, in the decision on abolishing the death penalty, the Constitutional Court said that human life interpreted together with human dignity is

---

[22]My basic standpoints on a theoretical level are very similar to the understanding of Roznai (2016).

[23]On the effectiveness of conventions regarding implicit unamendability, see Gert Jan Geertjes and Jerfi Uzman, 'Conventions of Unamendability: Unamendable Constitutional Law in Politically Enforced Constitutions', in this volume.

[24]The lack of constitutional culture which makes institutions function is often criticised in Hungary, although the first president of the Constitutional Court argues that the Constitutional Court managed to develop this culture in the nineties. Sólyom (2015a), p. 5.

[25]On the former system of constitutional adjudication in English, see Brunner (1992), pp. 535–553.

[26]Sólyom (2014), p. 1. Although the Hungarian Fundamental Law significantly modified the competencies of the Constitutional Court and the role of the different constitutional institutions in constitutional adjudication, the powers of the Hungarian Constitutional Court remained very strong. The freshest account of this is published by the former President of the Constitutional Court and former President of the Republic of Hungary, Sólyom (2015b), p. 705.

[27]Article S(2) of the Fundamental Law: "For the adoption of a new Fundamental Law or any amendment thereof, the votes of two-thirds of all Members of Parliament shall be required".

the basic value of our constitutional order, this finding led neither to the establishment of a basic structure doctrine as in India, nor to a basic order of fundamental values as in Germany. Certain rights as the freedom of expression or the right to human dignity were acknowledged as the sources of other fundamental rights, but the general value of one provision, however, could not be measured against another in the text. Although in its case law the Constitutional Court gave elevated importance to certain provisions, this has never meant either a concrete or an abstract order of values or unamendability. Although in a decision from 2007[28] the Constitutional Court did use the notion of value order of the Constitution, this concept did not have further implications in case law.[29]

In Hungarian legal literature, it is commonly accepted that the constituent power forms the basis of constitutional democracy, although it is not a part of it much like the way that other state actors are not.[30] However, the scope and immunity of this power and its relation to sovereignty have often been debated.[31] The Constitution, as well as the Fundamental Law, differentiates between the competence of the Parliament to adopt the Constitution and the competence to amend it. One group of scholars argue that this solution proves that both competencies are given to a two-thirds majority of the Parliament, which accordingly means that there is no feature that would distinguish between the constituent power and the amending power in Hungary.[32] The other group of scholars interprets the same constitutional solution as proof of separation between the constituent power and the derived amending power, as the two competencies and the two functions are mentioned separately in the text of the Constitution.[33] The Constitutional Court did not arrive at an explicit decision on this fundamental question when it reviewed the constitutional amendments adopted between 1990 and 2010, although a decision on this issue is essential to be able to make comprehensive decisions on the matter.[34] Although there is no explicit verdict on this problem, the decisions of the Constitutional Court suggest that the majority of judges either overlook this problem or do not find the distinction between the constituent power and the amending power important. In sum, although it is a key issue of interpretation as clearly demonstrated by Roznai[35] and many others, we cannot find much direction in the practice of the Hungarian Constitutional Court.

---

[28]Decision 47/2007. (VII. 3.) CC on the hierarchy of norms ABH 2007 620.

[29]See Tóth (2009), pp. 197–200.

[30]Petrétei (2009), p. 187.

[31]The legal ground for the debate is Article 1 a) of the Fundamental Law, which states that the Parliament adopts and modifies the Fundamental Law of Hungary, and Article S(1) of the Fundamental Law, which states that the President of the Republic, the Government, any parliamentary committee or any Member of Parliament may submit a proposal for the adoption of a new Fundamental Law or for an amendment of the Fundamental Law.

[32]Takács (2011), p. 58, 64, Fröhlich and Csink (2012), p. 424, Szente (2013), p. 11, 18.

[33]Drinóczi (2015), p. 361.

[34]András Bragyova's dissenting opinion in Decision 61/2011. (VII. 13.) CC.

[35]Roznai (2014), pp. 15–22.

The Hungarian Constitutional Court was first faced with the problem of judicial review of constitutional amendments already in its fourth year of existence after the transition of 1989–1990. A 1994 Constitutional Court decision,[36] in which the Constitutional Court refused to have competence for a substantial review of amendments, was adhered to in its main lines of argument by the Hungarian Constitutional Court until 2011. Criticism was also not very loud at the time because the constitutional amendments were more or less in conformity with the Constitution and, what is more, both legal practitioners and the academia were more or less satisfied with the major directions of Hungary's constitutional development. The Constitutional Court argued that the Constitution conferred power to the Constitutional Court solely to review ordinary legislation, and amendments to the Constitution do not qualify as ordinary legislation in this sense.[37] The Constitutional Court stressed that there is no rule in the Constitution that would prohibit another rule from being modified or repealed[38] and, in the Constitutional Court's interpretation, the Constitution contained no explicitly or implicitly unamendable provisions.

In its early jurisprudence, the Constitutional Court also declared that amendments belong to the competence of the constituent power and that the text of an amendment will become part of the Constitution regardless of its substance.[39] The Constitutional Court usually assessed the question of its competence as a classic issue of the separation of powers.[40] This was the starting point of development.

2.3 Scope and Enforcement After 2010

Although the debate on the necessity of entrenchment, on the necessity of implementing eternity clauses should have been more intense during the drafting of the Fundamental Law in 2010–2011,[41] the Fundamental Law contains neither an explicit rule nor any orientation concerning the same.

Decision 61/2011 (VII.12) of the Constitutional Court was the first to react to the fact that the Parliament codified with a constitutional amendment the possibility of levying a tax which was previously held to be unconstitutional by the Constitutional Court. The Court decided that the Parliament using the Fundamental Law to serve its political interest of the day was highly problematic. It signalised that, from the

---

[36]Decision 293/B/1994. CC, ABH 1994. 362.

[37]For a summary, see Decision 1260/B/1997 of the Hungarian Constitutional Court, ABH 1998, 816, 819–826.

[38]Decision 39/1996 (IX. 25.) CC, ABH 134, 138.

[39]Decision 293/B/1994 CC, ABH 1994. 362.

[40]Stumpf (2014), p. 229.

[41]Jakab, András. *Az új Alaptörvény keletkezése és gyakorlati következményei* (The genesis of the new Fundamental Law and its practical consequences) (HVG-ORAC 2011).

standpoint of the rule of law, the stability of law and the constitutional order, such conduct is not acceptable. The Court found the way of forming constitutional order by such amendments problematic, primarily because it weakens the democratic legitimacy of the Fundamental Law given that there is no wide social consensus on each and every provision of the Fundamental Law.[42] However, this strong opinion of the Constitutional Court remained *obiter dictum* as, according to a majority decision the Constitutional court, it is not authorised to conduct a substantive review of amendments of the Fundamental Law. With this argument, the *ratio decidendi* basically reinforced the previous standpoint of the Constitutional Court. One slight novelty of the case was, however, that the Court clearly emphasised that, within its competence, it would review whether the Parliament satisfied all procedural requirements. Although from 1990 onwards, the Constitutional Court's view that it is not competent to review whether amendments were adopted in conformity with the procedural rules worded in the Constitution was almost unanimous, as this question was renegotiated on a case-by-case basis and not settled clearly in the constitutional text, it seemed to be important for the Constitutional Court to emphasise this competence again.

As a signal to the amending power, this decision affirmed that the *jus cogens* of international law, the common principles of constitutional heritage and international law accepted by the Hungarian State, are obligatory for the 'constituent power' as well. The Court, in the same part of the decision, concluded that the separation of powers has a primary role in the Hungarian constitutional order and that the Constitutional Court must respect the limits of its competence. Stepping into the shoes of either the legislative power or of the constituent power is not acceptable.[43] This decision made it clear that the Constitutional Court tackled amendments as acts of the constituent power, and not as acts of the amending power. The Court did not differentiate between original and derived constituent power either.

The reasoning of this decision shows that, in 2011, the separation of powers and deference are still the leading approaches to the question of review. Reading this decision, we must take it for granted that, according to the Court, amendments represent the will of the constituent power and that, therefore, they cannot be reviewed by the Court, although this will has boundaries with regard to merits. There is, however, a contradiction: if the constituent power and the amending power have the same status, it is not that easy to justify the substantive limits of amendments.[44] The struggle of the Court and the tensions, the contradictions in the

---

[42]Decision 61/2011. (VII. 13.) of the Constitutional Court, Reasoning V/1.

[43]For a commentary on the Decision, see Halmai (2012), pp. 182, 200–202.

[44]I believe, however, that this is not impossible. I made an attempt to describe a possible reasoning in Fruzsina Gárdos-Orosz, 'Az alkotmánymódosítasok alkotmányossági felülvizsgálata: elméleti koncepciók, nemzetközi trendek es magyar kérdések' (Judicial review of constitutional amendments in Hungary) in Gárdos-Orosz and Szente (2015), see further Fröhlich Johanna, 'Az alkotmány zártsága és ellentmondás-mentessége—az alkotmánymódosítások felülvizsgálatának lehetőségei és határai' (The coherent constitution and the limits of the judicial review of amendments) in Gárdos-Orosz and Szente (2015).

decision are caused by its doctrinal deficiencies. In a situation in which the Guardian of the Constitution feels that it is necessary to send signals to the Parliament's two-thirds majority, a clear and consequent legal interpretation would probably have been more useful in defence of the constitutional order.[45]

A long year later, after the Fundamental Law of Hungary entered into force on 1 January 2012, Decision 45/2012 (XII.29) of the Constitutional Court ruled that the part on the transition from a Communist dictatorship to a democracy (in the Preamble), many articles of the Transitional Provisions of the Fundamental Law of Hungary, and a separate act adopted in a constitutional amendment procedure on 31 December 2011 are all contrary to the Fundamental Law of Hungary. The Constitutional Court annulled these provisions with a retroactive force as of the date of their promulgation. The Constitutional Court articulated that it is not possible to amend the Constitution with another piece of legislation outside the Fundamental Law even if the legislator calls it a part of the Fundamental Law. This way, the legislator takes the competence of the assumed constituent power, violates the separation of powers and makes it impossible for the Constitutional Court to conduct a substantive review on that piece of legislation.[46] The decision of the Constitutional Court, however, stayed within the limits of procedural, formal reasoning, and did not take into account the content of the relevant Transitional Provisions.[47] In this decision, however, the Constitutional Court *obiter dictum*, with the aim of signalling, emphasised again that constitutional amendments should conform not only to procedural rules but also to the basic founding principles of the rule of law democracy constituted in the Fundamental Law.

However, following this decision, the two-thirds majority of the Parliament made it clear that it has the intention to amend the Fundamental Law in a normal amendment procedure, with the content of the amendment being more or less the same. By the fourth amendment to the Fundamental Law in 2013, the two-thirds majority implemented similar or identical rules in the text of the Fundamental Law that had earlier been struck down by the Constitutional Court on both procedural and substantive grounds as part of ordinary legislation. This time, the Parliament observed the standard amendment procedure rules.[48]

A contradiction in judicial intention could here again be emphasised because, although the Constitutional Court declared the amendment null and void on procedural grounds emphasising that it is not competent to review it substantively, it signalled that the limits of constitutional amendments are not only procedural, but

---

[45]For a detailed analysis of this case in English completely in line with my opinion, see Halmai (2012), pp. 21–34.

[46]Decision 45/2012. (XII. 29.) of the Constitutional Court, Reasoning [111]. The text relies on a translation found on the website of the Constitutional Court.

[47]For criticism of the Decision and its assessment, see Halmai (2015), pp. 978–980.

[48]Examine the provisions adopted by the Fourth Amendment with regard to their merits annulled earlier by the Constructional Court due to their unconstitutionality. Bánkuti et al. (2013), pp. 61–64.

also substantive. The Court referred to unamendable inherent value standards that must be met by constitutional amendments.

In the next cornerstone decision on unamendability—more specifically, in Decision 12/2013 (V.24) CC—the Constitutional Court reviewed the constitutionality of the Fourth Amendment of the Fundamental Law. The Fourth Amendment introduced a significant change in the constitutional order of Hungary and was criticised by many both national and international constitutionalists.[49]

The Fundamental Rights Commissioner filed a petition with the Court for review of the constitutionality of certain provisions of the Fourth Amendment to the Fundamental Law. The Commissioner argued mostly on formal, procedural grounds, but he also claimed that, in addition to the narrow interpretation of the violation of procedural requirements for the adoption of the amendment, the amendment is unconstitutional in a broader sense because it creates a discrepancy within the Fundamental Law itself. Amendments which generate incoherence within the Fundamental Law cannot be incorporated in it. In his opinion, the coherence of the Fundamental Law was clearly violated by the Fourth Amendment because it explicitly contradicted previous Constitutional Court decisions.[50]

The Constitutional Court further stated that, under Article 24(5) of the Fundamental Law, the Court may only review the Fundamental Law and amendments to it for conformity with the procedural requirements laid down in the Fundamental Law with respect to their adoption and enactment (in the case of procedural error). The Court highlighted the limits of such competence. It also added that it would not extend its powers to review the Constitution and new norms amending it without express and explicit authorisation in the constitutional text.[51] The Constitutional Court emphasised that carrying out a substantive review is beyond its competence because the new provisions in the Fourth Amendment to the Fundamental Law explicitly prohibit substantive reviews.[52]

---

[49]Opinion 720/2013 of the Venice Commission on the Fourth Amendment to the Fundamental Law of Hungary available at: http://www.venice.coe.int/webforms/documents/default.aspx?pdffile=CDL-AD(2013)012-e.

[50]Decision 12/2013 (V.24) of the Constitutional Court, Reasoning [9]–[11].

[51]Decision 12/2013 (V.24) of the Constitutional Court, Reasoning [30], [36]–[37], [43].

[52]Article S) of the Fundamental Law contains the following procedural constraints: "The President of the Republic, the Government, any parliamentary committee or any Member of Parliament may submit a proposal for the adoption of a new Fundamental Law or for any amendment to the Fundamental Law. For the adoption of a new Fundamental Law or any amendment thereof, the votes of two-thirds of all Members of Parliament shall be required." The Fourth Amendment to the Fundamental Law made it explicit that, under Article 24(5), "The Constitutional Court may only review the Fundamental Law and any amendment thereof for conformity with the procedural requirements laid down in the Fundamental Law with respect to its adoption and promulgation. Such a review may be initiated by: the President of the Republic in respect of the Fundamental Law and an/any amendment thereof, if adopted but not yet published; the Government, a quarter of the Members of Parliament, the President of the Curia, the Supreme Prosecutor or the Commissioner for Fundamental Rights within thirty days of publication." A translation of the Fourth Amendment is available in English at: http://lapa.princeton.edu/hosteddocs/hungary/Fourth %20Amendment%20to%20the%20FL%20-Eng%20Corrected.pdf.

However, the Court added to these arguments that, when interpreting the Fundamental Law in the future, it will also take into consideration the obligations that Hungary has undertaken in the international treaties it signed or those that follow from EU membership, along with the generally acknowledged rules of international law, and the basic principles and values reflected in them. It stated that these rules constitute a unified system of values which are not to be disregarded in the course of adopting a constitution, adopting amendments or in the course of constitutional review.[53]

These arguments carry doctrinal problems equally to the former decisions I have mentioned. While interpreting the decision, we may observe that the Constitutional Court mentions substantive limits applicable to amendments. These limits are connected to Article E[54] and Article Q[55] of the Fundamental Law, which render the Hungarian constitutional order a part of the EU legal system and part of the international legal world. These limits seem to be interpreted as part of a certain European value system. Although the Constitutional Court is certainly very definitive in eliminating the idea of unamendability from Hungarian constitutional law, when it talks about certain limits to formal constitutional changes, about the constrains created by judicial interpretation, it is, in fact, creating unamendability as a judicial discovery. It is rational enough, as I shall explain in the next subchapter, that if certain limits are constructed by the judiciary, the amending power is no longer unlimited. If it is not unlimited, the judicial interpretation of certain constitutional provisions will constitute a burden on change. Principles, such as general respect for the fundamental values of EU law and adopted international law, must take root in the national constitution. If the Constitutional Court states that constitutional reviews will respect these values, it practically constitutes some sort of unamendability.[56] In other words, by having preserved its competence for the "coherent interpretation" of the Fundamental Law, the Constitutional Court declared that its duties are not limited to identifying the text of the Constitution and to interpreting it according to the original intent of the constituent power, and that they will rule in each and every case by autonomously interpreting[57] the provisions of the Fundamental Law.[58]

One might, therefore, conclude that, although the Fundamental Law does not contain unamendable provisions and although the Fundamental Law since 2013

---

[53]Decision 12/2013. (V.24) of the Constitutional Court, Reasoning [30], [36]–[37], [43].

[54]Article E of the Fundamental Law: "In order to achieve the highest possible measure of freedom, well-being and security for the peoples of Europe, Hungary shall contribute to the achievement of European unity".

[55]Article Q of the Fundamental Law: "In order to establish and maintain peace and security, and to achieve the sustainable development of humanity, Hungary shall strive to cooperate with all the peoples and countries of the world".

[56]See Erdős (2011), p. 54.

[57]Interpretation as the "act of will" and interpretation "based on knowledge" according to the theory of Ricardo Guastini, see Troper (2003), pp. 99–103.

[58]See also Lóránt and Johanna (2013).

explicitly limits the right of the Constitutional Court to review amendments on a substantive basis, the Constitutional Court, by way of interpretation, deducted the right from the Fundamental Law to construct limitations to amendments. Limitations to formal constitutional change mean unamendability.[59]

Although, as I have shown above, the case law of the Constitutional Court has not been too elaborative on doctrinal grounds relating to the mentioned limits of change,[60] in the next part of this chapter, I shall try to explain in detail how unamendability could be reconstructed by interpreting the Fundamental Law of Hungary.

3 Implicit Unamendability in the Fundamental Law of Hungary Discovered by Applying Different Legal Methods

I argue, on the pages that follow that the struggle of the Hungarian Constitutional Court suggests that some sort of unamendability belongs to the nature of a constitutional order, even when a constitution does not contain unamendable provisions. In the following part of my chapter, I shall try to near Hungarian unamendability using the legal methods of judicial interpretation. I shall examine in more depth the ways that these said limits on constitutional amendments could be justified. As a result of this examination, inspired by the argumentation of Judge András Bragyova, I discover several constitutional principles and one concrete unamendable provision in the Fundamental Law.

3.1 The Discovery of Unamendability by Purposive Interpretation

The unamendability of a constitution cannot be explained without taking a stand on how I understand the constitution. When I talk about the Constitution of Hungary in this text, I refer to the Constitution as the supreme law that defines the validity of all the norms of the legal system, the Constitution included.[61] Although adopting a

---

[59]I have constructed this narrative for the purposes of my explaining unamendability. However, such a conclusion might be premature, as the decisions of the Constitutional Court are often inconsistent in Hungary and the current Constitutional Court (of 2016) is even more reserved with regard to controlling parliamentary majority. See, e.g., Szente (2016), p. 123. It is quite likely that the *obiter dictum* desires of the former Constitutional Court will fall on deaf ears.

[60]For a discussion of related case law of the Hungarian Constitutional Court, see Zeller (2013), p. 307.

[61]Kelsen (1967), pp. 35–50.

constitution (the constitutional moment) is undoubtedly a political act,[62] constitutional democracy in Hungary, after the transition of 1989–1990, was based on the concept of legal constitutionalism.[63] The Austrian–German heritage of public law[64] had had a very strong effect on the Hungarian constitutional transition of 1989–1990, and the political elite followed the Hungarian Constitutional Court's view on a legally normative constitution.[65] In this Kelsenian concept, a constitution contains legal norms at the top of a legal system that legally defines the validity of the legal system. This approach was widely accepted not only by the members of the Constitutional Court but also by political actors and most constitutional law scholar. This approach was anticipated as a new level of constitutional development, where a limited government and the protection of fundamental rights are central values.[66] The review power of the Constitutional Court being strong and the activism of lawyers forming a judicial body were also widely accepted by both the political elite and legal scholars because, according to this concept, the constitution can only be part of a normative order if it is interpreted and enforced by the state through constitutional adjudication. Amendments to a constitution are also part of this socially constructed normative order.[67]

A constitution as a special norm contains provisions on the possibility and the limits of its own amendment.[68] These provisions are very special, and the creator of these rules, the constituent power, ceases to exist at the very moment of the adoption of a constitution.[69] Agreeing with Alf Ross, one can suppose that, since the constitutional moment, the final source of law is in the system.[70] Similarly: the source of the legitimacy of a constitutional state is neither with the people nor with the constituted state, but rather in a balanced relation between the normative order, as the ideal of constitutionalism, and governmental action.[71]

In modern constitutions, it is usually the people or the nation[72] who are entitled to be the source of power, but whichever it is, it is the constitution that normatively makes them bear this nature. Without a normative constitution, we cannot identify the source of state power and the limits of government, and we are also not capable of describing the limits of constitutional change, and unable to define

---

[62]András (2012), pp. 18, 30–32.

[63]On the basic differences between the concept of legal and political constitution and constitutionalism, see Bellamy (2007) and Ackerman (2001).

[64]Boulanger (2006), Halmai (2007).

[65]See Sólyom (2014), pp. 717–719.

[66]This mainstream approach was, however, criticised by some in the early nineties and later. One of the critics is now a member of the Constitutional Court. Pokol (2005).

[67]von Wright (1963).

[68]This opinion is affirmed by the Constitutional Court in its decision on a referendum on a constitutional amendment 25/1999. (VII. 7.) CC, ABH, 1999, 251, 261.

[69]This is in line with Beaud (1994), p. 455.

[70]Ross (1929), p. 309: "Das System ist die letzte Rechtsquelle".

[71]Loughlin (2014a), p. 218, 222.

[72]This double formula is found in both the French and the Spanish constitutions (Art. 3. ill. 1. (2)).

unamendability. The normative nature of the constitution implies that the rules on amending the constitution and the limits thereof are open to interpretation.

Depending on their interpretation, constitutional amendments can be of two types. One type is when an amendment does not ruin the meaning of the original provisions but rather complements them. The other is when a new provision is contradictory to the old ones, and so they cannot be valid at the same time. These are unconstitutional constitutional amendments. Whether a new provision belongs to the first or the second category can be decided only by interpretation. Is it, however, possible for a constitutional amendment to be unconstitutional?

Hungarian scholars often argue that the concept of unconstitutional constitutional amendment is not sound, because the sovereignty of the people is unlimited and unique as stated in Article B) paragraph (3) of the Fundamental Law: "The source of public power shall be the people." As "Article 1(2) a) of the Fundamental Law declares that the Parliament shall adopt and modify the Fundamental Law of Hungary", the constitution-making power and the amending power is, therefore, unlimited. This logically implies that there can be no contradiction between the provisions of a constitution, because a later amendment simply either completes or overrules the former rules should we interpret them together. Unconstitutionality is, therefore—nonsense.[73] Furthermore, neither international nor EU legislation can constitute a limit to constitutional change, given that the Constitution is the source of the binding force of both international and EU law.

I shall argue against this interpretation on the basis of the Fundamental Law and in line with other Hungarian scholars.[74] I claim that this view confuses the notion of sovereignty with the notion of the constituent power. Popular sovereignty itself is a highly debated concept in modern constitutional thought and is definitely very far from empowering a concrete ensemble of people.[75]

Amending a constitution in a procedure established by the constitution itself is far from being an act of an unlimited and unique sovereign. Sovereignty forms a constant part of each democratic order, while the existence of the constituent power is limited to the constitutional moments of constitutional democracies. The constitution itself creates a normative ground for the will of the people (constituent power) in order for the constitution to gain legitimacy. The logic of popular sovereignty as a construction of political thought is, on the other hand, that the people as the source of state power are always present in state administration, which makes the government always limited and representatives of the people never completely independent. The constituent power is unlimited at a constitutional moment, while the constitutional concept of popular sovereignty does not mean the

---

[73]This view is strongly represented in legal scholarship. See, e.g., Zoltán Szente, 'Az "alkotmányellenes alkotmánymódosítás" és az alkotmánymódosítások bírósági felülvizsgálatának dogmatikai problémái a magyar alkotmányjogban' (Unconstitutional constitutional amendments and the problems of justification) in Gárdos-Orosz and Szente (2015).

[74]Chronowski (2015), and Sonnevend (2015).

[75]Jakab (2016), pp. 92–99.

concrete, unlimited exercise of the power of the people during the lifetime of a democratic order.[76]

In Hungary, the 1989–1990 democratic transition and the above mentioned general amendment to Act XX of the 1949 Constitution of the Republic of Hungary was certainly a constitutional moment. A socialist constitution became the constitution of a rule of law democracy. I further argue that the Fundamental Law of 2011 was not born in a constitutional moment, and that it was not an act of the constituent power, but a general amendment to the Constitution although adopted in the form of a new text. As I have already mentioned when citing the provisions of the Fundamental Law, the Fundamental Law itself finds its grounds in the Constitution when it declares that the adoption of the new Constitution is the fulfilment of the requirement of the Constitution to adopt a new text which is necessary to finalise the democratic transition.[77]

Because of this specificity, the special circumstances of the adoption of the Fundamental Law, the fact that, from a legal point of view, the adoption was not an original constitution-making process, I shall argue that the new Constitution, the Fundamental Law, cannot contradict the unamendable provisions of the former Constitution. Accordingly, the question is whether there was any unamendability in the former Constitution the force of which was binding for the new Constitution, the Fundamental Law.

Although my approach is purely doctrinal in this text and I do not evaluate constitutional change, I should explain here that originally, in 2011, the constitutional two-thirds majority did not have outstandingly revolutionary constitutional thoughts, and that, in spite of important criticisms of certain parts of the text,[78] many acclaimed scholars qualified the Fundamental Law as a consolidated version of the former Constitution.[79]

I must mention another doctrinal argument so as to buttress the dependent nature of the Fundamental Law. The argument, in a normative sense, says that one constitution cannot bind a subsequent constitution. If a new constitution is created according to the rules of a former constitution as it happened in Hungary, the new constitution cannot be the result of an original constitution-making process.

I argue that, first of all, the old Constitution set limits to the new Fundamental Law in its Preamble. The Fundamental Law is embedded in the constitutional transition of 1989–1990. The legal relation between the old and the new constitutions is—continuity. The Preamble of the Constitution is often referred to by

---

[76]Loughlin (2014b), p. 218.

[77]In its closing provisions, the Fundamental Law declares that the Parliament adopts the Fundamental Law on the basis of Act XX of the 1949 Constitution of the Republic of Hungary § 19 (3) a) and § 24 (3).

[78]Opinion of the Venice Commission on the New Constitution of Hungary http://www.venice.coe. int/webforms/documents/default.aspx?pdffile=CDL-AD(2011)016-e; or Marco Dani, 'The partisan constitution and the corrosion of European constitutional culture', *LEQS* Paper No. 68/2013 http:// www.lse.ac.uk/europeanInstitute/LEQS%20Discussion%20Paper%20Series/LEQSPaper68.pdf.

[79]Jakab and Sonnevend (2013), Küpper (2013) Wirtschaft und Recht in Osteuropa 3.

politicians and scholars alike as proof of the temporary and transitory nature of the Constitution of the transition.[80] It declares (again) that "in order to facilitate a peaceful political transition to a constitutional state, to establish a multiparty system, parliamentary democracy and a social market economy, the Parliament of the Republic of Hungary hereby establishes the following text as the Constitution of the Republic of Hungary until the country's new Constitution is adopted."

According to the Preamble, the Constitution was created to reach a certain level of constitutional democracy. The transition was, therefore, not just any transition, but a transition with well-defined aims and values.[81] According to the Constitution, the text of the Constitution was created in order to reach a certain level of development of constitutional democracy by requiring the adoption of a new constitution based on the said fundamental values. This was the original intention of the constituent power of 1989–1990.

The level of development that had to be reached can be defined by four constitutional requirements: multiparty system, parliamentary democracy, rule of law and social market economy.[82] Are these provisions of the Preamble amendable by a simple procedure of adoption of a new constitution within the competence of the Parliament granted by Article 19(3)(a) of the Constitution ("the Parliament adopts the Constitution of the Republic of Hungary")? Or does this represent a substantive, unamendable requirement that cannot be overruled by the Fundamental Law as a derived constitutional act? Besides the above-mentioned values, is the republican form of government also binding on a general constitutional amendment if it is based on the Preamble of the former Constitution?

A purposive interpretation suggests that, if the new constitution is adopted on the basis of the former constitution referring both to the transitory nature of the former constitution and the aims of the democratic transition so as to create a new constitution, the essence of the purpose of the new democratic constitutionalism cannot be transformed. This does not mean the duty to observe the same understanding of the said value statements, but rather that these are unamendable in a sense that cannot be eliminated, completely overruled within the same constitutional order.

A multiparty democracy and the republic were already immediately established with the transition, but the other values are constantly changing in Hungary's constitutional democracy. These are never completely settled, and their implementation requires the state's ongoing efforts.

I do not analyse here the rule of law index of Hungary after 2012. Many works published also in English show in great detail the deficiencies of Hungary's constitutional democracy.[83] My aim here is modest. I wish to argue that these values

---

[80]The temporary nature of the Constitution is based on the Preamble. This formulation on the nature of the old and the new Constitution is similar to the one in *Grundgezetz* § 149.

[81]Chronowski (2012), p. 111.

[82]The reasoning behind this can be found in Point 5 of András Bragyova's dissenting opinion to the Constitutional Court's Decision 61/2011.

[83]Vörös (2015), p. 173, Bánkuti et al. (2012).

are implicitly unamendable because the Fundamental Law itself defined its origins in the Preamble and in certain provisions of the former Constitution, thus making these substantive and procedural provisions binding for the complex amendment that created the Fundamental Law. But, will they be binding forever?

3.2 The Discovery of Unamendability by Structural Approach

Some constitutional provisions remain binding on constitutional change forever within the same constitutional system. This is a logical outcome if we accept the approach of Alf Ross or Martin Loughlin cited above. If we accept that a constitutional democracy is an order, a system, and that the legitimacy of the constitutional democracy is in the system, we must follow the argument that the entire system must have a guiding rule. If there was no such rule, we would be talking about anarchy and not about a constitutional order. Introducing the case law of the Hungarian Constitutional Court, I have argued that judicial interpretation in Hungary tends to accept that the amending power is limited because the judicial interpretation that will finally lead to the implementation of the disputed provisions will take into account the entire system. None of the constitutional provisions have a separate meaning, all are interpreted jointly. So what exactly is unamendable, which provision?

The Hungarian Constitutional Court does not tell us. The 2014 decision of the Czech Constitutional Court on striking down the constitutional amendment on the new definition of the House of Representatives was heavily criticised, because the content of unamendability that it referred to was (undefined and) open (to interpretation), thus allowing judicial interpretation to define constitutional violations on a case-by-case basis.[84]

The Hungarian coherent interpretation, the basic structure or the constitutional identity arguments are limited in competence. They cannot tell precisely in advance and *in abstracto* what will amount to be unconstitutional in a future case.[85] All they recognise is the nature of constitutionalism, a fight against arbitrariness, against state capture, against undue influence by courts, empowering judicial interpretation with setting limits in concrete cases through the application of the constitutional text. These concepts believe in structures, such as communication, balance, cooperation, negotiated values and structured procedures.

---

[84]Preuss (2016), p. 134.

[85]For criticism and a misuse of this structural approach, cf. the Bangladeshi case see Ridwanul Hoque, 'Eternal Provisions in the Bangladeshi Constitution, A Constitution Once and For All?' in this volume.

Legal interpretation is regarded as yet another procedure to secure justice in a constitutional democracy.[86] It is in line with the original purpose of modern legal interpretation.[87]

Within the concept of legal constitutionalism, when the constitution is part of the normative order like in Hungary, unamendability is perceived as a special pillar of the constitutional construction. If the unamendable norm is amended, all the other norms in the constitution become invalid, the construction collapses.

A coherent, structural interpretation, therefore, primarily helps to avoid this scenario by finding the pillars of the construction. The entire construction must have at least one pillar. Constitutional courts make sure that this pillar remains stable, and invalidate all acts of amendment that try to eliminate it.

It is pure logic that unamendability also applies to the amendment of unamendability rules, otherwise the constitutional construction is not safe.[88] These rules can be both explicit and implicit in a constitution. I shall present a concrete, implicitly unamendable provision of the Hungarian Fundamental Law in the next subchapter.

3.3 Unamendability by Textual Interpretation

I have shown so far, through analysis, that the Hungarian Fundamental Law has unamendable norms according to certain rules of interpretation. I argue here that, as far as the basic provisions of the Fundamental Law on fundamental rights protection are concerned, discovering their unamendability based on a purely textual interpretation of the provision is even less problematic. Since this idea is not the mainstream position in Hungarian legal thought,[89] it needs further clarification. Article 1(1) of the Fundamental Law rules that 'the inviolable and inalienable fundamental rights of Man shall be respected. It shall be the primary obligation of the State to protect these rights'. In paragraph (2), we read that 'Hungary shall recognise the fundamental individual and collective rights of Man'.

This provision is very similar, almost identical in terms of its merits, to the one of the former Constitution expressed in Article 8(1). As András Bragyova already explained in his study in 2003 and his thesis can be applied for understanding the Fundamental Law, there are several essential declarations in these provisions that back up their unamendability.[90] These provisions have three main elements: (1) the

---

[86]Rawls (1996), p. 239.

[87]J. Zoltán Tóth, 'A dogmatikai, a logikai és a jogirodalmi értelmezés a magyar felsőbírósági gyakorlatban' (The doctrinal, the logical interpretation and the use of legal scholarship in the interpretation of Hungarian supreme judicial bodies) MTA Law Working Papers 17/2015, http://jog.tk.mta.hu/uploads/files/mtalwp/2015_17_toth.pdf.

[88]Albert (2015), p. 655.

[89]Jakab and Szente (2009), p. 563. Decision 12/2013. (V. 24.) CC, Part V. 2.1.

[90]Bragyova (2003), p. 65.

provision in the Fundamental Law talks about 'the right of Man', (2) these rights are 'inviolable and inalienable', and (3) Hungary 'recognises these individual and collective rights'.

That human rights, called fundamental rights in the text of the Fundamental Law, are inviolable and inalienable comes not only from copying the text of international treaties but also from the philosophy of human rights. This defines the constitutional nature and the source of validity of these human rights. Inalienable means that the Fundamental Law and the State cannot take these rights away; these are, by nature, immune to state capture. The Constitution prohibits, itself included, the violation of these rights. Therefore, an elimination of these provisions would invalidate the Constitution itself, since a constitutional amendment is validly not capable of eliminating binding rules, which are binding on the amendment as well. Should this happen and should nobody invalidate the amendment, the constitutional system becomes invalid as a whole. (I shall talk about the unamendable nature of constitutional review related to this argument in the next point of this subchapter.)

We can argue that paragraph (3) of the same provision of the Fundamental Law is a necessary consequence of this interpretation. It says that a 'fundamental right may only be restricted in order to allow the exercise of another fundamental right or to protect a constitutional value, to the extent that is absolutely necessary, proportionately to the objective pursued, and respecting the essential content of such a fundamental right'.

This *Wesensgehaltgarantie* also applies to constitutional amendments with regard to fundamental rights, because this basic constitutional guarantee is, by textual interpretation, immune to constitutional change. Even if the Constitution were changed so as to disregard human rights, human rights would continue to exist. In other words, according to the Hungarian Fundamental Law, the 'essential content of fundamental rights' cannot be further derogated by the State. These are unamendable by the national Constitution.

The third element of this provision of the Fundamental Law states that Hungary 'recognises' these rights. The wording of the provision suggests that these rights are not part of positive law, but exist independently. This independence means that it is not the national Constitution which describes the content of these rights, but that they are developed independently. Accordingly, it is also possible that a new right or a different understanding of a right becomes part of the Constitution, and Hungary shall recognise this. This is what recognition is in the Fundamental Law. Thus, these norms have a dual status: (1) they are part of the Fundamental Law as fundamental rights and (2) they are also valid independently of the Constitution.

I believe that the Constitutional Court's Decision 12/2013 (V.24) CC explains the above in detail, emphasising the need to accept the international *ius cogens* in any situation, independently of the national Constitution.[91]

This does not, however, mean that the amending power cannot carry out constitutional change concerning these provisions. Quite the contrary, these provisions

---

[91]Reasoning [48].

on fundamental rights can also be changed by amendments. The guarantee of unamendability requires solely that the essence of these provisions be taken in due account when amending the Constitution. I conclude, in line with Bragyova, that the Hungarian case is very similar to the German one regarding its outcome, although the Fundamental Law does not say so explicitly.[92]

3.4 Unamendability by Logical Interpretation

Following Judge András Bragyova's concurring opinion,[93] I must finally highlight one of the strangest constitutional amendments in Hungary since 2010 in order to demonstrate a further point of unamendability.

I argue that, once it is established, constitutional review as such is unamendable in legal constitutionalism. Once a constitution implements constitutional review, in case of conflict, the instrument of constitutional review is of ultimate necessity to tell if a piece of law is contradictory to the constitution or not. There is no validity without a potential review. It is necessary to accept, based on pure logic, that constitutional review as such cannot, accordingly, be validly eliminated from the constitutional order.

In Hungary, the Constitutional Court is empowered to review and strike down all pieces of law that do not conform with the Fundamental Law. However, Article 37 (4) of the Hungarian Fundamental Law reads that 'As long as the level of state debt exceeds half of the Gross Domestic Product, the Constitutional Court may, within its competence, pursuant to points (b) to (e) of paragraph (2) of Article 24, review Acts on the central budget, on the implementation of the budget, on central taxes, on duties and on contributions, on customs duties, and on central conditions for local taxes as to their conformity with the Fundamental Law exclusively in connection with the rights to life and human dignity, to the protection of personal data, to freedom of thought, conscience and religion, or in connection with the rights related to Hungarian citizenship, and it may annul these Acts only for the violation of these rights. The Constitutional Court shall have the right to annul without restriction Acts governing the above matters if the procedural requirements laid down in the Fundamental Law for the enactment and publication of such Acts has not been observed'.

Already in 2010, the Hungarian amending power limited the competencies of the Constitutional Court in response to the Constitutional Court's uncomfortable decisions. Since then, as has above been described, the legislative power is free to implement any unconstitutional law in the field of financial legislation, because no state body is empowered to judge the validity of these acts. The size of this black

---

[92]Bragyova (2003), p. 80.

[93]His arguments on constitutional change are very similar to Suber (1990).

hole depends on the interpretation of the Constitutional Court, but the black hole most certainly cannot be completely eliminated by judicial interpretation.[94]

This example explains that, in a constitutional system, where validity depends on a judicial interpretation of the constitution as part of the normative legal order, the provision on constitutional review is an unamendable part of the constitution, because otherwise the validity of the legal system becomes obscure and undefined, and this opens the door to arbitrariness.

4 Juridical Review of Unconstitutional Constitutional Amendments

I repeat here that, in its Decision 12/2013 (V.24) CC, the Constitutional Court states that, under Article 24(5) of the Fundamental Law, the Court may only review the Fundamental Law and amendments to it for conformity with the procedural requirements laid down in the Fundamental Law with respect to its adoption and enactment (in cases of procedural error). This wording obviously encompasses proponents of bills, the legislative process, the two-thirds adoption process, provisions with regard to the designation of acts, and the rules of signature and enactment. In sum, the observance of the provisions of the Fundamental Law is required for the amendment to be valid. I pose the following question here: what else does the Fundamental Law require or, rather, what is included in the above-mentioned criteria?

I have argued elsewhere that the arguments of political philosophy might make it possible to justify the review of constitutional amendments. It is easier to do this justification if we accept—what I accept in this chapter revising my earlier standpoint—that the original constituent power can be differentiated from the amending power. I claimed, however, that this justification may be possible even for those who cannot be convinced about the said differentiation.[95] I also concluded that the Hungarian case law uses famous foreign examples to show the stability of the Constitution and to substantively reply to the constant amendments of the Constitution and later to the Fundamental Law after 2010, but the decisions are not clear.[96] Here, the necessary comparative context is already provided by my learned colleagues,[97] and so I prefer to argue that again a legal method of interpretation is capable of verifying that the Hungarian Constitutional Court—and I believe in the general force of this interpretation—has the right and the constitutional duty to substantively review constitutional amendments upon petition. My argument is based on the notions of formal, procedural validity and competence.

---

[94]The rights listed in the Article can hardly be violated by a financial act.

[95]Gárdos-Orosz (2015).

[96]Gárdos-Orosz (2015), pp. 97–111.

[97]Halmai (2012), pp. 182–203.

Article 24 of the Fundamental Law gives competence to the Constitutional Court to review any piece of legislation for conformity with the Fundamental Law. However, Article 25(5)—adopted by the Fourth Amendment to the Fundamental Law in 2013—declares that "the Constitutional Court may only review the Fundamental Law and any amendment thereof for conformity with the procedural requirements laid down in the Fundamental Law with respect to its adoption and promulgation. Such a review may be initiated by the President of the Republic in respect of the Fundamental Law and any amendment thereof, if adopted but not yet published, or by the Government, a quarter of the Members of Parliament, the President of the Curia, the Supreme Prosecutor or the Commissioner for Fundamental Rights within thirty days of publication."

On first reading, we see that there is an explicit desire formulated in the Fundamental Law that amendments shall be reviewed only on procedural grounds. On second reading, however, the situation is more complex than this. What amounts to be a procedural requirement?

Procedure has different understandings in legal doctrine. Both rules on competence and rules on procedure are necessary so as to be able to adopt a certain amendment irrespective of its substance. There is no procedure without competence. Rules on competence could therefore be interpreted as procedural requirements. As has earlier been argued, amending provisions not being able to contradict the unamendable parts of a constitution can be justified. The amending power does not have competence for these amendments. If we accept that the constitution has unamendable parts as I have argued above, the Fundamental Law allowing for quasi-substantive reviews of amendments can be justified if the petition claims that the amending provisions violate the unamendable core issues of the Hungarian Fundamental Law. Procedural guarantees might equal substantive guarantees with regard to the protection of the Constitution, because the amending power does not have competence to violate the unamendable parts of the Constitution due to a lack of competence. Moreover, the reviewing competence is hardly possible without reviewing the substance.[98]

5 Concluding Remarks

Many argue that the *Ewigkeitsklausel* or implicit unamendability as judicial discovery is not eternal because law as a social construct cannot be eternal, the constituent power cannot burden future generations.[99] What is more, as Ackerman

---

[98]My suggestion is similar to the one applied in Colombian case law. See, e.g., Yepes (2007), p. 51–54.

[99]Bentham (1843), p. 403.

points out, constitutions sometimes change independently of changes in the text of a constitution, and these changes are sometimes more significant than the formal amendments.[100] What is then the relevance of our discussion?

Constructing formal or informal unamendability means that, within one constitutional system, it is not possible to amend the constitution either by constitutional amendment or by interpretation, by denying the nature of constitutional democracy. The validity of a formal amendment or the validity of a constitutional interpretation is a normative issue in a rule of law democracy. I have argued in this chapter that normativity, in this sense, means that previously agreed and settled legal rules apply both to constitutional amendments and their judicial interpretation.

Naturally, unamendable norms are unamendable only from the point of view of a normative legal order, they are unamendable only in law and by law, their status belongs to a given constitutional order created by society for ensuring stability, democracy and freedom, limited government and fundamental rights protection. A given constitutional order is over if its unamendable norms change. As a result, a new order is created.[101]

In Hungarian legal literature, it is András Bragyova, a former judge of the Constitutional Court, who formulated the most convincing arguments that justify the unamendability of certain provisions of the Hungarian Constitution and the Hungarian Fundamental Law, although neither includes unamendable provisions explicitly. He expressed this view not only in legal scholarship but in his concurring and dissenting opinions in Constitutional Court case law. However, despite the analysed case law of the Hungarian Constitutional Court, and despite the Hungarian constitutional doctrine explained above, implicit unamendability has neither been acknowledged nor accepted politically so far, and so, in order to avoid conflict, the Constitutional Court itself tends to deny itself its competence to give constitutional balance to the amending power.

But all Members of the European Union should know the limits of amendability of their own constitutions. Intense disputes have emerged on the topic of unamendability with regard to the limits of transfer of state sovereignty to the European Union. The absolute limits of such transfers lie in the unamendable norms or in the otherwise defined unamendability of the constitutions of the Member States. Pure political consensus, for example, cannot consent to certain EU developments if they are in contradiction with the unamendable parts of a constitution.[102]

---

[100]Ackerman (1998).

[101]One of the most highly acclaimed political scientists in Hungary claims that, in Hungary, a new political regime has been created, and that this is not only because of the text and the intention of the new Fundamental Law, but also because of a political change, because of a change in the political narrative on some of the major rules of constitutional democracy. András Körösényi, 'A magyar demokrácia három szakasza és az Orbán-rezsim' (Three periods of the Hungarian democracy: The Orbán regime) in Körösényi (2015).

[102]BVerfG, Urteil des Zweiten Senats vom 30. Juni 2009—2 BvE 2/08—Rn. (1-421), http://www.bverfg.de/e/es20090630_2bve000208.html. BVerfGE, 123, 267 (2009). For more about this problem, see Bragyova (2003), p. 76, Albert (2016), p. 297.

The unamendability of a single provision of a single national constitution alone can influence the limits of EU law because the consent of all the Member States is necessary to be able to amend the EU 'constitutional' order.

What are the consequences of this interpretation for the Hungarian constitutional order? So far, both the amending power, the two-thirds majority of the Parliament and the Constitutional Court agree that procedural reviews of constitutional amendments are unavoidable so as to check whether an amendment has been adopted at all. If the Fundamental Law has unamendable norms, and I have argued in line with Judge Bragyova that there are norms and principles that are unamendable, the judicial protection of the Fundamental Law must include protection against the violation of these unamendable norms. I have argued here that Article I paragraphs (1) and (2) of the Fundamental Law contain unamendable norms, and that, furthermore, a different type of unamendability can also be discovered by judicial methods of interpretation. The principles of democratic constitutionalism stipulated during the democratic transition of 1989–1990 in the Preamble of the former Constitution, such as multiparty democracy, rule of law, social market economy and parliamentary democracy, can be regarded as such unamendable norms. In addition, the principles of coherent (rational, logical) legal interpretation, the protection of the basic structure, and the constitutional order of values may be regarded as judicial innovations of the Hungarian Constitutional Court that could lead, through judicial application, to a formal checks and balances constitutional change with the purpose of protecting the democratically settled constitutional order.[103]

References

Ackerman B (1998) We the people, vol II. Transformations, Belknap
Ackerman B (2001) We the people. Foundations 1. Harvard University Press
Albert R (2010a) Constitutional handcuffs. Boston college law school research paper no. 225, p 706
Albert R (2010b) Nonconstitutional Amendments. Boston college law school research paper no. 187. 9
Albert R (2013) The expressive function of constitutional amendment rules. McGill Law J 59: 225–281
Albert R (2015) Amending constitutional amendment rules. Int J Const Law 13:655
Albert R (2016) Constitutional limits to european integration. Int J Const Law 14:297
András L (2012) 'Szükség van-e írott alkotmányra?' (Do we need a written constitution?). In: András J, András K (eds) Alkotmányozás Magyarországon és máshol. Politika-tudományi és alkotmányjogi megközelítések. (Budapest MTA TK Politikatudományi Intézet—Új Mandátum Könyvkiadó) vol 18, pp 30–32
András K (ed) (2015) Comparative perspectives on the fundamental freedom of expression Complex, p 13

---

[103]On the pitfalls of Hungary's constitutional democracy, see the analyses of, e.g., Vörös (2014, 2015), p. 173 and Kukorelli (2014), Tóth (2015), pp. 129–158.

Antal A (2013) Politikai és jogi alkotmányozás Magyarországon: political and judicial constitution making in hungary, Politikatudományi Szemle 22:48–70

Bánkuti M et al (2013, April) Amicus brief for the venice commission on the fourth amendment to the fundamental law of hungary. pp 61–64, available at: http://fundamentum.hu/sites/default/files/amicus_brief_on_the_fourth_amendment.pdf

Bánkuti M, Halmai G, Kim Laine S (2012) From separation of powers to a government without checks. In: Tóth GA (ed) Constitution for a disunited nation. On Hungary's 2011 fundamental law, CEU Press

Beaud O (1994) La Puissance de l'Etat, PUF, p 455

Bellamy R (2007) Political constitutionalism: a republican defence of the constitutionality of democracy. Cambridge

Bentham J (1843) The book of fallacies. In: Bowring J (ed) The works of Jeremy Bentham, vol II, The Fallacy of Irrevocable Laws, p 403

Boulanger C (2006) Europeanisation through judicial activism: the hungarian constitutional court's legitimacy and the return to Europe. In: Sadurski W, Czarnota A, Krygier M (eds) Spreading democracy and the rule of law? Springer

Bragyova A (ed) (2003) Holló András 60. Születésnapjára, Bíbor Kiadó, p 65

Bragyova A, Gárdos-Orosz F (2016) Vannak-e megváltoztathatatlan normák az Alaptörvényben, Are There Unamendable Rights in the Fundamental Law? Állam- és Jogtudomány 57:35

Brunner G (1992) Development of a constitutional judiciary in eastern Europe. Rev Central East Eur Law 6:535–553

Chronowski N (2012) The new hungarian fundamental law in the light of the European union's normative values numéro spéciale. RevueEst Europa 89(1):111

Chronowski N (2015) The fundamental law within the network of multilevel European constitutionalism. In: Szente Z, Zsuzsanna F, Mandák F (eds) Challenges and pitfalls in the recent hungarian constitutional development, L'Harmattan

Erdős C (2011) Az alkotmány stabilitásának aktuális kérdései. In: The stability of the constitution, vol 1, Diskurzus, p 54

Drinóczi T (2015) Újra az alkotmányozó, az alkotmánymódosító hatalomról és az alkotmányellenes alkotmánymódosításról—az Alaptörvény alapján, The constituent power and the amending power revisited by the fundamental law. Jogtudományi Közlöny 70:361

Fröhlich J, Csink L (2012) Topics of hungarian constitutionalism. TvCR 3:424

Gárdos-Orosz F (2015) Judicial review of constitutional amendments: a theoretical approach. In: Burazin L, Gardašević Ð, Sardo A (eds) Law and state, classical paradigms and novel proposals, Peter Lang

Gárdos-Orosz F, Szente Z (eds) (2015) Alkotmányozás és alkotmányjogi változások Európában és Magyarországon, Constitution making and constitutional change in Europe and in hungary, Nemzeti Közszolgálati Egyetem Part III

Granville A (1999) Working a democratic constitution, OUP

Halmai G (2007) The transformation of hungarian constitutional law from 1985 to 2005. In: Jakab A, Takács P, Tatham AF (eds) The transformation of the hungarian legal order 1985–2005, Kluwer Law International

Halmai G (2012) Unconstitutional constitutional amendments? constitutional courts as guardians of the constitution? Constellations 182(19):200–202

Halmai G (2015) Judicial review of constitutional amendments and new constitutions in comparative perspective. Wake Forest L Rev 50:951

Hein M (2015) Eternity clauses: never say never. Katapult, 4 May 2015, http://katapult-magazin.de/en/artikel/article-katapult/fulltext/never-say-never/

Jacobsohn GJ (2006) An unconstitutional constitution? a comparative perspective. Int J Con L 3 (1):460

Jakab A (2016) European constitutional language, CCUP, pp 92–99

Jakab A, Sonnevend P (2013) Continuity with deficiencies: the new basic law of hungary. European Const Law Rev 9:102

Jakab A, Szente Z (2009) Az Országgyűlés hatáskörei (Competences of the parliament). In: Jakab A (ed) Az Alkotmány kommentárja, Századvég, vol 118, p 563

Kelsen H (1967) Pure theory of law. University of California Press, Max Knight tr, pp 35–50

Kilényi G (1996) Az alaptörvény stabilitását szolgáló garanciák a külföldi alkotmányokban és nálunk, (Guarantees of the Stability of the Fundamental Law in Foreign Constitutions and in Hungary). Jogtudományi Közlöny 51:117

Körösényi A (ed) (2015) A magyar politikai rendszer—negyedszázad után. Osiris

Kukorelli I (2014) Magyarországot saját alkotmánya nélkül kormányozni nem lehet (Hungary can not be governed without a constitution). Méry Ratio Kiadó

Küpper H (2004) Az alkotmánymódosítás alkotmánybírósági kontrollja Magyarországon és Németországban, Constitutional review of constitutional amendments in germany and hungary, Jogtudományi Közlöny, 59:273

Küpper H (2013)\Ungarns neues Grundgesetz von 2011 und seine Änderungen

Lóránt C, Johanna F (2013) A régiek óvatossága: Megjegyzések az Alaptörvény negyedik módosításának javaslata kapcsán, Wisdom of the elderly: thoughts concerning the fourth amendment to the fundamental law. Pázmány law working paper 1. 2013. http:// d18wh0wf8v71m4.cloudfront.net/docs/wp/2013/2013-1-csl-fj.pdf

Loughlin M (2014a) The concept of constituent power. European J Polit Theor 24:218, 222

Loughlin M (2014b) The concept of constituent power. European J Polit Theor 13:218

Marbury WL (1919) The limitations upon the amending power. Harvard Law Rev 33:225, 232

Petrétei J (2009) Az alkotmányos demokrácia alapintézményei, Basic institutions of constitutional democracy, Dialóg-Campus, p 187

Pokol B (2005) Aktivizmus és alkotmánybíróság (Activism and constitutional court). In: Kurtán S, Sándor P, Vass L (eds) Magyarország politikai évkönyve, DKMKKA

Preuss O (2016) Eternity clause as a clever instrument. Lessons from the Czech case law. Acta Juridica Hungarica. Hungarian J Legal Stud 57:134

Rawls J (1996) Political liberalism, 2nd edn. Columbia University Press, p 239

Ross A (1929) Theorie der Rechtsquellen (F. Deuticke), p 309

Roznai Y (2013) Unconstitutional constitutional amendments: the migration and success of a constitutional idea. Am J Comp Law 61:657

Roznai Y (2014) Legisprudence limitations on constitutional amendments? Reflections on the czech constitutional court's declaration of unconstitutional constitutional act. Vienna J Int Const Law 8:29

Roznai Y (2016) Unconstitutional constitutional amendments: the limits of amendment powers, OUP

Schmitt C (1928) Verfassungslehre, Duncker & Humblot, p 16

Servai HM (1996) Constitutional law of India, 4th edn, vol 3. New Delhi, p 3109

Sólyom L (2015a) The rise and decline of constitutional culture in hungary. In: von Bogdándy A, Sonnevend P (eds) Constitutional crisis in the European constitutional area, vol 5. Hart

Sólyom L (2015b) Das ungarische Verfassungsgericht. In: von Bogdándy A, Grabenwarter C, Huber PM (eds) Handbuch jus publicum Europaeum: verfassungsbarkeit in Europa: institutionen, vol VI, Beck, p 705

Sólyom L (2014) Normahierarchia az alkotmányban. Hierarchy of Norms in the Constitution, vol 7, Közjogi Szemle, p 1

Sonnevend P (2015) The role of international law in preserving constitutional values in Hungary— the case of the Hungarian Fundamental Law with International Law. In: Szente Z, Zsuzsanna F, Mandák F (eds) Challenges and pitfalls in the recent hungarian constitutional development. L'Harmattan

Sonnevend P, Jakab A, Csink L (2015) The constitution as an instrument of everyday party politics: the basic law of Hungary. In: von Bogdándy A, Sonnevend P (eds) Constitutional crisis in the European constitutional area, Hart, pp 33–110

Stumpf I (2014) Rule of law, division of powers, constitutionalism. Hungarian J Leg Stud Acta Juridica Hungarica 55:299

Suber P (1990) The paradox of self-amendment: a study of law. Logic, Omnipotence and change, Peter Lang

Szente Z (2013) Az Alkotmánybíróság döntése a Magyarország Alaptörvényének Átmeneti rendelkezése alkotmányosságáról, Decision of the constitutional court on the constitutionality of the transitional provisions of the fundamental law of hungary. Jogesetek Magyarázata JEMA 4:11, 18

Szente Z (2016) The political orientation of the members of the hungarian constitutional court between 2010 and 2014. Const Stud 1:123

Takács P (2011) Az alkotmány legitimitása, Legitimacy of the constitution. Alkotmánybírósági Szemle 2:58, 64

Tóth GA (2009) Túl a szövegen: értekezés a Magyar alkotmányról (Beyond the text: a study on the Hungarian constitution), Osiris, pp197–200

Tóth GA (2015) Hungary's constitutional transformation from a central-european comparative perspective. In: Glaser H (ed) Norms, interests, and values: conflict and consent in the constitutional basic order. Nomos, Baden-Baden, pp 129–158

Troper M (2003) The logic of justification of judicial review. Int J Const Law 99–103

Vincze A (2015) Wrestling with constitutionalism: the supermajority and the hungarian constitutional court. ICL J 86(4):979

von Wright Georg H (1963) Norm and action. Routledge & Kegan Paul 116 ff., 189 ff

Vörös I (2014) The constitutional landscape after the fourth and fifth amendments of the hungarian fundamental law. Hung J Legal Stud Acta Juridica Hungarica 56(1)

Vörös I (2015) Hungary's constitutional evolution during the last 25 years: Südosteuropa. J Politics Soc 63:173

Yepes RU (2007) Judicialization of politics in Colombia: cases, merits and risks. Int J Human Rights 49:51–54

Zeller J (2013) Nicht so beständig… Die jüngsten Novellen des Grundgesetzes Ungarns im Kontext der Entscheidungen des Vergfassungsgerichts. Osteuropa Recht 3:307

Amending the Unamendable: The Case of Article 20 of the German Basic Law

Serkan Köybaşı

Abstract The power which has the right to approve a constitutional norm is called *pouvoir constituant*. The original *pouvoir constituant* which drafts a new constitution is hierarchically higher than the derived one which has only the right to amend an existing constitution in the framework allowed by the original one. In other words, parliaments who want to amend the constitutions are limited by the unamendable provisions. In 1968, Parliament of Germany added the 4th paragraph (which provides German citizens the right to resist any person seeking to abolish the constitutional order) to Article 20 which had been rendered unamendable by the Article 79 of the Basic Law of Germany during the drafting process in 1949. Consequently, although this newly added paragraph is present in an unamendable article, any derived *pouvoir constituant* can amend, change or annul it because it is not approved by an original *pouvoir constituant*.

1 Introduction

One of the main objections concerning the legal value of unamendable provisions within constitutions is that parliaments which represent the will of the nation should not be bound by certain rules adopted by preceding powers. This paper aims to bring a critique to this specific point of view which claims that due to the principles of national sovereignty and democracy, the nation which elects the parliament is sovereign and therefore its representatives are boundless.

Additionally, according to this view, constitutional amendments cannot be annulled because, even if it is considered as derived, the parliament is a *pouvoir constituant* and thus there is no hierarchical difference between it and the original *pouvoir constituant* who drafts and approves the constitution for first time.

S. Köybaşı (✉)
Law Faculty, Bahçeşehir University, Istanbul, Turkey
e-mail: serkan.koybasi@law.bau.edu.tr

© Springer International Publishing AG, part of Springer Nature 2018
R. Albert and B. E. Oder (eds.), *An Unamendable Constitution?*
Ius Gentium: Comparative Perspectives on Law and Justice 68,
https://doi.org/10.1007/978-3-319-95141-6_10

259

Therefore, a hierarchically equal *pouvoir constituant* should not have the right to bind its successor and even if there are some binding rules in the constitution approved by the original *pouvoir constituant*, the successor has the right to repeal them.

Of course, the fact that undemocratic limitations on elected representatives put in place via unamendable provisions adopted by undemocratic original *pouvoir constituants* is a specific problem that needs to be addressed.[1] Therefore, those who defend the aforementioned ideas[2] does not lack some justification. However, such suggestions stem from an archaic and majoritarian reading of democracy. Modern democracy has surmounted the majoritarian democracy of Jean-Jacques Rousseau. Specifically, after having experienced numerous emergencies, especially after the World War II, modern democracy accepts that one of its core pillars is limitation of governments by the adoption of checks and balances systems.

2 The Source of the Separation of the Original and Derived Pouvoir Constituant

Taking into consideration that the difference between the original and derived *pouvoir constituant* remains at the center of the dispute, therefore, these concepts deserve some preliminary consideration.

2.1 The Relation Between the Pouvoir Constituant and Unamendable Provisions

The most important effect of the prohibition to amend some of the articles of the constitution is the determination of the limits of the derived *pouvoir constituant*, because the unamendable articles define the area which remains out of reach from this type of power. Some authors defend that, due to the limitless aspect of the *pouvoir constituant*, the power to amend the constitution should not be called "constituent", but should be considered as only an amending power.[3]

The concept of *pouvoir constituant* has several effects on the legal value of the unamendable provisions of a constitution. It can be said that the legal value of

---

[1]One of the most obvious examples of this kind of undemocratic limitations is the Article 3 of the 1982 Constitution of Turkey concerning the capital, national anthem, flag and unity of the state and the nation. The political will which has established the article as an unamendable provision belongs to the *junta* which lead the *coup d'état* of September 12, 1980.

[2]For some examples see among others: Barthelemy and Duez (1993), p. 231; Özbudun (2013), pp. 180–181; Paine (1984), p. 41.

[3]Beaud (1994), pp. 314–315.

unamendable provisions depends on the context in which the act to constitute is accepted and on the specific limits of the parliament.

2.1.1 What Is the Pouvoir Constituant?

The special quality of constitutions obliges such texts to be drafted by organs which have some form of special political power. These organs which correspond to one of the components of sovereignty are called *"pouvoir constituant"*.[4] In other words, the *pouvoir constituant*, in general, is the power which is equipped with the right to draft a new constitution or to amend the existing constitution. In a nutshell, the power which approves a constitutional norm is called a *pouvoir constituant*.

Very few concepts in the field of philosophy of law has been treated as much as the concept of *pouvoir constituant*. The theory of the *pouvoir constituant* was formulized with the emergence of written constitutions and especially during the American and French Revolutions. Consequently, it can be said that the concept is a product of the 18th century. As most authors accept, the source of the theory of the *pouvoir constituant* is the pre-French Revolution brochure written by Emmanuel Sieyes, called *Qu'est-ce que le Tiers Etat?* (What is the Third State?).[5] The most important result of the formulation of the theory is the separation between the constituent power and the constituted one.

The national representation, one of the indispensable principles for the nation-state, was announced by Sieyès in his booklet published in 1789. Göztepe defends that by describing the bourgeoisie as the pillar of the state and the nation itself, the author generated the final transition from popular sovereignty to national sovereignty.[6]

However, soon after this transition, in this newly established order, a new problem emerged: How to make the derived *pouvoir constituant* respect the constitution written by the original *pouvoir constituant*. With the aim of solving this question, in his speech during the debate of the 3rd Year Constitution in 1795, Sieyes suggested to establish a *Jurie Constitutionnaire* which would guarantee the protection of the constitution. He argued that the constitution as the projection of

---

[4]Turpin (1992), p. 81.

[5]Klein (1996), pp. 7–8.

[6]Ece Göztepe, 'Anayasa Yargısı ve Demokrasi' (2012) Toplum ve Bilim 123, 48. I agree in general with Göztepe. I would argue that the transition was not from popular sovereignty itself but from the idea. Because, in Rousseau's system of popular sovereignty which is a modern version of direct democracy from the Greek city-state of Athens, the public has the right to be directly part of the government. But this system never was put into effect because right after the French Revolution, the bourgeoisie "stole" the Revolution from the populace and established a representative system based on Sieyès' ideas. Indeed, the abstract concepts of "nation" and "national representation" are created by Sieyès with the aim of supporting the monarchy against Rousseau's dangerous thoughts on giving sovereignty to the people. They actually pour out meaning from democracy and give the right to govern not to the general population but to a certain elite group of the society.

the will of the sovereign nation draws the limits and authority of the powers which come into existence through it and, therefore, the representatives of the people should act in conformity with this basic will of the nation who remains the real holder of sovereignty. This suggestion was however not adopted due to the strong wind supporting the idea of the supremacy of the parliament after the Revolution.

In France, the parliament-oriented view is still reflected within the jurisprudence of the Constitutional Council. In one case the Council said that it is not its duty to check the constitutionality of constitutional amendments.[7] In this decision the Council claimed that it had no authority provided by the constitution. While the Council claimed that it had to base its decision strictly on positive constitutional norms, in the background, the persistence of the idea of the supremacy of the parliament from the French Revolution and the equality of the power to amend the constitution and the original *pouvoir constituant* can be felt.[8] In fact, with this decision, the Council adopted an interpretation according to which it suggested that there is no separation between the two *pouvoir constituants*; in other words, they are actually the same.

On the other hand, the possibility to determine some legal limits to constitutional amendments requires a separation between the power to draft the constitution and the power to amend it. Schmitt alleges that, even when there is no unamendable provision in a constitution, the derived *pouvoir constituant* cannot change its essence and therefore, if there is an article in the constitution which prohibits the amendment of some of the provisions, it means nothing else than the approval of the difference between the constitutional amendment and the total abrogation of the constitution.[9] In other words, there is an important difference between the power equipped with the right to amend the constitution and the power which has the right to abolish it. Thus, the former cannot have, at the same time, the right to abolish it which essentially belongs only to the latter.

In fact, the theory of the principle on the separation of these two powers which emerged during the French Revolution is based on the organic separation and the logical difference between the power which drafts the constitution and the organs created by it. Thus, a higher and extraordinary power is established on the top of the ordinary legislative, executive and judiciary powers. The main aims of the former are to create, to manage and to stay out of them. This is the principle which should be called the principle of the separation of the constituting power from the constituted powers.[10]

---

[7]Case no. 2003-469 (23 March 2003), §3, http://www.conseil-constitutionnel.fr/conseil-constitu tionnel/francais/les-decisions/2003/2003-469-dc/decision-n-2003-469-dc-du-26-mars-2003.857.html. Accessed 28 July 2016.

[8]du Loû (2003), p. 731.

[9]Schmitt (2008), p. 244.

[10]de Malberg (1920), pp. 509–510.

2.1.2 Who Is the Sovereign?

The question that we face at this point concerns the identity of the sovereign. Is the sovereign "the nation" which hypothetically exists eternally and which implements its will via elections and representatives or "a founding people" who concretely existed in a definite time and place and who, even though they do not live anymore, as a sovereign wrote the constitution without any limitation?

For Lavroff, this separation between the original *pouvoir constituant* which is used directly by the sovereign and the derived *pouvoir constituant* which is formed by the constitution and bound by the powers and procedural limitations determined under it, is justified due to the duty of the organs created by the sovereign to show respect to its will. If this separation is not accepted, it would correspond to ignoring the powers of the sovereign and indeed, to cutting off the relevant powers from its body in favor of representatives.[11] Consequently, suggesting that the derived *pouvoir constituant* is not bound by unamendable provisions would mean to ignore the existence of an original *pouvoir constituant*.

On the contrary, the dominantly accepted theory on this issue in the United States is that the original and derived *pouvoir constituants* are completely different concepts. Americans, from the foundation of their country onwards, think that it is only the constitution of the United States which is a product of the general will and they see the Congress as a secondary organ founded by the constitution, and not like a parliament which represents the national will. This perception is at such a point that ordinary laws are considered as not the result of the will of the people (nor the nation) but only of the will of the members of the legislative organ. Thereby, Americans have separated strictly the founding power from the power to legislate and put the latter under the sovereignty of the constitution. As a consequence, in the United States, the legislative organ has no authority to solely amend the constitution.[12]

Klein cites Carré de Malberg who calls this situation as the "American difference" and sees it as a result of the double separation of the constituent power from the legislative organ: Legislative organ cannot have the power to constitute and the convention (constituent power) cannot have the right to legislate. Therefore, Klein suggests that according to American mentality the convention is situated out of the legal order: It is only the convention which can propose a constitution or amend it.[13] Consequently, it means that these two powers are strictly different at the point of their formation and function. In parallel, Roznai defends that the space of decision-making (that of the fundamental principles of the polity) is reserved solely for "the people",[14] which means that it is only the founding people, as the sovereign, who has the right to decide what the founding principles of the state are.

---

[11]Lavroff (1995), pp. 99–100, cited by: Gözler (1997), p. 189.

[12]de Malberg (1931), p. 109.

[13]Klein (1996), p. 33.

[14]Roznai (2015), p. 5.

2.2 Challenging the Quality of Being "Constituent" of the Derived Pouvoir Constituant

We have elaborated on the source of the difference between the original and derived *pouvoir constituants* above. However, some authors claim that there is a bigger separation between these powers than a simple "difference".

2.2.1 "Constituent" versus "Constituted"

Schmitt thinks that it is not right to qualify the power limited and constituted by constitutional articles which has only the power to amend the unessential provisions of a constitution as a "*pouvoir constituant*". In his influential work, Theory of the Constitution, he writes that

> the authority to amend the constitutional laws,[15] like the other powers which stem from the constitutional laws, is an authority determined by law and thus, principally limited. It cannot go beyond the framework drawn by the constitutional order which is also the reason for its existence.[16]

Therefore he suggests that the power to amend the constitution is not a constituent, but only a constituted power.

In the same direction, Beaud underlines that qualification of both an unlimited power and a power limited by the absolute power as constituent is contradictory. They do not have the same nature. Therefore, to classify them within the same category and to accept a relative separation instead of an absolute one are results of a logical mistake.[17] Beaud suggests that authors who accept that these two powers have different natures but who also use the adjective "constituent" for both of them are not loyal to their own separation.[18]

From the point of view of Dérosier, the *pouvoir constituant* can only be original. For him, the power to amend the constitution should not be called as "constituent", but simply as an "amending power". Moreover, the author claims that the original *pouvoir constituant* is not a legal term but a political one, because during its existence it still drafts the constitution which means that at the specific instant a legal order does not yet exist. Therefore, the life of the original *pouvoir constituant* occurs in a time period before the foundation of the legal system.[19]

Murswiek also claims that the constitution is established by the *pouvoir constituant* and that the legislative organ which amends the constitution is just one of the constituted state organs. For the author

---

[15]For Schmitt, the provisions which are not essential in a constitution.
[16]Schmitt (2008), p. 236.
[17]Beaud (1993), p 15.
[18]Beaud (1994), p. 315.
[19]Dérosier (2008), pp. 785–795.

the drafter of the constitution and the legislator which amends the constitution are, not only organically different, but also functionally different subjects. There is a hierarchical relationship between these two subjects: The legislator which amends the constitution, as a constituted state organ depends on the constitution and obtains its authority from it within a determined framework.[20]

As a result of this hierarchical positioning, unamendable provisions are the limits to the power to amend the constitution designated by the original *pouvoir constituant* and therefore they can be amended or repealed only by another original *pouvoir constituant*. If the power to amend the constitution tries to amend or repeal the unamendable provisions, it would trespass the limits of its authority.

Burdeau claims that, by its nature the power to amend the constitution cannot seize what belongs to the original *pouvoir constituant*:

> The pouvoir constituant still exists with all of its essential authorities and in the normative hierarchy stays above the constituted power to amend the constitution. The substitution of the original pouvoir constituant by the amending power is unthinkable because it would mean a contradiction in adjecto.[21]

In other words, in this case, a type of power in a lower level would suggest becoming another power in a higher level, yet this cannot be possible because the higher power still exists.

In summary, the quality of being "constituent" for the power to amend the constitution which is usually called derived *pouvoir constituant* is controversial. Ironically, in the light of this ambiguity, the separation between the provisions which provide the essence of the constitution and the rest of them becomes clearer. In contradiction with the positivist approach, there is a qualitative difference between unamendable articles and other articles of constitutions. As a consequence of this difference, while the original *pouvoir constituant* is an unlimited power which drafts the constitution and which has the right to establish unamendable provisions within it, the derived *pouvoir constituant* is a limited power equipped by the right to amend only the amendable articles in conformity with the procedural rules foreseen within the constitution.

To elaborate on this thesis and to understand why the last sentence of the Article 20 of the German Basic Law is amendable, the descriptions and limits of the original and the derived *pouvoir constituants* should be analyzed in further detail, especially in light of the unamendable provisions.

2.2.2 The Original Pouvoir Constituant in Terms of the Unamendable Provisions

As mentioned previously, the term "original *pouvoir constituant*" is one of the most controversial and dealt subjects of the constitutional law theory. Beside its

---

[20]Murswiek (2008), p. 3, cited by: Sağlam (2010), p. 575.
[21]Burdeau (1950), p. 209, cited by: Beaud (1993), p. 16.

importance, this is a natural result from the never-ending debate on whether the term is discrete and non-legal. The limits of the original *pouvoir constituant* can vary from one definition to another. In light of this, and subsequent to summarizing the various existing views on the definition and the limits of the term, I will elaborate on my own view and put forward the justification on why the "original *pouvoir constituant*" should be considered the one and the only power which has an authority to create unamendable constitutional provisions.

The Definition of the Original Pouvoir Constituant

There are various definitions of the term original *pouvoir constituant*. There are as many common points between these definitions as differences. Consequently, we will limit ourselves to the relatively important ones that we come across within the constitutional law doctrine.

The constituent power gains the adjective "original" only in very few circumstances. The most common of these circumstances, as accepted in doctrine, is during the emergence of a new state. In this case, it's accepted that there exists an *ex nihilo* situation. As an example for this situation, one may mention the institutionalization of a personal government, gaining of independence or the annulation of the former legal order after a revolution or a *coup d'état*.[22] In other words, the original *pouvoir constituant* is the power which cannot be bound by any pre-existing rules or limits, which has established a state and which grants it legal and political statutes and which drafts a brand new constitution or rewrites the existing one. This type of power is autonomous and independent.[23] It does not have to show respect to any of the pre-existing method or limitation to write a constitutional norm because a *tabula rasa* situation exists.[24]

In democratic countries, the power of the original *pouvoir constituant* is used by the people or an assembly selected by the people. According to this, people have the power to build their own legal and political order without being bound by any constitutional norm.

Of course history contains many examples of non-democratic forms of original *pouvoir constituant*. In such cases, allegations by the *power* that it has acted "on behalf of the people" or because of "the call of the people" are methods of legitimization. However, only the acts of an original *pouvoir constituant* and not the political discourse adopted by it can determine whether it is legitimate or not. Moreover, it is arguable that there is a close link between the binding nature of unamendable provisions and the democratic quality of the original *pouvoir constituant*. But this subject is outside the scope of this limited paper.

---

[22]Turpin (1992), p. 81.

[23]Kubalı (1971), p. 96.

[24]Robert (2003), p. 362.

The Quality of Being Pre-law Order of the Original Pouvoir Constituant

Democratic or not, the original *pouvoir constituant* is a de facto, first hand and autonomous power. It takes its authority not from some other power, but relies only on itself.[25] Therefore, the state of being *ideo-motris* which qualifies sovereignty in Duguit's theory may also describe the original *pouvoir constituant*. In Duguit's mind, sovereignty is a will which can be defined only by itself and which has a quality peculiar to and only to itself. The only reason which can make it move is a reason that it finds in itself.[26] It can easily be seen that this judgement is in harmony with the idea that in constitutional law the unique and real sovereign is the original *pouvoir constituant*.

In other words, the constituent power which writes a new constitution after an interruption in the old legal order because of the emergence of a new state or because of a revolution or a *coup d'état* is called "original *pouvoir constituant*". And thus, this power takes root not from the legal order, but from politics.[27]

Schmitt describes the *pouvoir constituant* as

> the political will of the power or the authority which has the right to decide concretely and comprehensively on the type and form of the political entity, in other words, to identify entirely the existence of the political unity.[28]

Consequently, the original *pouvoir constituant*[29] not only drafts the new constitution but also "identifies" it as the instrument through which political unity can exist.

From a positivist point of view, the original *pouvoir constituant* depends on the hypothesis that while the new legal order is being created, the older one has disappeared or that there is a legal vacuum.[30] This time period can also be called an *interregnum* during which there is no definitive legal order. Therefore, the original *pouvoir constituant* is a "pre-law order". In other words, the original *pouvoir constituant* which has a de facto quality[31] due to not depending on any pre-existing law or constitution, has no legal quality; it is outside of law.[32]

Moreover, for some positivist writers, the constitutions drafted and approved by an original *pouvoir constituant* which emerges right after revolutions or *coup d'état*'s have no legal value because revolutions and *coup d'état*'s are forced acts

---

[25]Gözler (1997), p. 27.

[26]Duguit (2005), pp. 383–385.

[27]Beaud (1993), p. 14.

[28]Schmitt (2008), pp. 211–212.

[29]It should be remembered that Schmitt ignored the existence of such a concept as derived *pouvoir constituant*. For him, there was only one constituent power which is what we call the original *pouvoir constituant*.

[30]Teziç (2012), p. 156.

[31]Kubalı (1971), pp. 98–99.

[32]de Malberg (1922), pp. 496–497.

lacking legal basis.[33] In other words, such writers think that the non-legal quality of the original *pouvoirs constituants* causes the loss of the legal value of the constitution in force. But in this case, we face an important paradox: If it is only the original *pouvoir constituant* which has the right to draft a new constitution as we claim, and if it is accepted that due to the pre-law quality of the original *pouvoir constituants*, the constitutions which are drafted by them don't have any legal value, and consequently almost all of the constitutions on earth could be considered as invalid.

There can be only one explanation to this paradox: Drafting and approving a brand new constitution without an interruption in the judicial system, like we have seen in the examples of Switzerland in 1999 and Hungary in 2010. Some can also argue the drafting process of the Spanish Constitution of 1978 and the South African Constitution of 1996 as examples to the drafting processes without an *interregnum*. Correspondingly, some suggest that these last two examples correspond to an essential change in the political and legal system to the level of "emergence of a new country". Finally, with regards to the first two examples, it is still disputable whether an original *pouvoir constituant* can exist as a part of the legal order in the light of the theory discussed above.

The idea in which the original *pouvoir constituant* is situated in the legal order suggests that during the original constituent act the dominant conception of law among the citizens transforms and consequently, the legal content of the actual system becomes vacant and all of the mechanisms of the new order depend on the newly established order brought by the revolution.[34] In other words, the old order has been terminated but without leaving a vacuum, the new order has been automatically established. Some authors include in this argument the transitions from one constitutional order to another one,[35] as was seen in South Africa during the transition from *apartheid* to a democratic regime through a process of drafting a new constitution in the first part of the 1990-s.

From a different point of view, some argue that even with the continuity of the actual constitution it is possible that an original *pouvoir constituant* emerges. But for this to take place, we must face a real constitutional break and the democratically established unamendable provisions must be amended with the aim of establishing a new legal order which, at the same time, would require a democratic referendum on this issue. To this respect, Beaud calls the constitutional amendment to the 1958 Constitution of France in 1962 which transformed the political regime from a parliamentarian one to a semi-presidential regime as an act of the original *pouvoir constituant*[36] because a regime change can only be established by a founding act. This would also mean that Beaud supports the possibility of the emergence of an original *pouvoir constituant* within law.

---

[33]Kubalı (1971), p. 99.

[34]Teziç (2012), p. 158.

[35]Klein (1996), p. 18.

[36]Beaud (1994), pp. 383–384.

When we look at the jurisprudence concerning this last issue, we see that the Constitutional Council of France rejected to annul the constitutional amendment of 1962 which was full of procedural problems. The Council based its decision on the existence of a referendum. Besides lacking any positive provision in the constitution which gave the Council the authority to check the constitutionality of constitutional amendments, the Council confirmed that any norm approved by a referendum cannot be annulled because in referendums the sovereign emerges and of course, there cannot be an organ higher than the sovereign which could annul its acts.[37] In France, this stand of the Constitutional Council has been supported by most of the authors, including even those who support a control of constitutionality of constitutional amendments.[38]

3 The Privilege of the Will of the Founders and the Impotence of the Derived *Pouvoir Constituant*: The Example of the 4th Paragraph of Article 20 of the German Basic Law

The will of the original *pouvoir constituant*, due to its superiority to any other will, is sovereign and thus, it is the only power to determine the unamendable provisions. Consequently, the reason for the derived *pouvoir constituants'* inability to violate the unamendable provisions of the Constitution stems from the respect which must be shown to the original *pouvoir constituant*.

3.1 The Source of the Hierarchy Between the Original and Derived Pouvoir Constituants

The original *pouvoir constituant* is in a different, higher and privileged level than the derived *pouvoir constituants* which succeeds it. Therefore, it's normal and possible that it has a right to bind them.

3.1.1 The Special Qualities of the Original Pouvoir Constituant

Schmitt distinguishes strictly the power who writes the constitution for the first time from the powers whose existence depends on the constitution. He believes that the

---

[37]Case no. 62-20 DC, 6 November 1962.
[38]Renoux and de Villiers (1994), p. 624.

pouvoir constituant[39] is used in the execution of the founding decision and the concretization of this decision can be left to national assemblies or to some other institutions. But, he adds that the *pouvoir constituant* cannot be transferred, delegated, incorporated or consumed. Schmitt assumes that this power exists virtually till the end of time[40] in conjunction with the other power (to amend the constitution) and prevails over all of the ancient constitutions and actual constitutional provisions.[41]

As it is clearly seen, Schmitt defends that the original *pouvoir constituant* does not disappear after having completed the duty of writing the constitution and that, instead, it stays alive permanently alongside the derived one. In case of accepting Schmitt's view, it is automatically accepted that the original *pouvoir constituant* and the power to amend the constitution which is called derived *pouvoir constituant* in this paper cannot exist at the same level because, theoretically, there cannot be two sovereigns at the same time within the same country. Thus, if the original *pouvoir constituant* is the sovereign, the derived one is not; the latter depends on former.

In other words, the will who writes the constitution is not an ordinary *pouvoir constituant* but it is different than any other constituent power. On the other hand, there cannot be any supremacy between derived *pouvoirs constituants*. They are all at the same level. Therefore, any act done by a derived *pouvoir constituant* can be amended or annulled by one of its successors. But the founders' will has established the basic principles of the new country and has established the legality of the derived *pouvoirs constituants*. Consequently, it has the right to order them to act within the limits which are determined by the unamendable provisions. The principles within the constitution cannot be split from one another. All as a whole bind anybody who wants to act in conformity of the constitution.[42]

Beaud objects to this idea of continuity. He defends that constituent sovereignty expires and dies with the termination of the founding act. Beaud thinks that the constitution cannot be amended nor annulled by an amendment procedure or another act of founding. As a fruit of human will, it becomes institutionalized. But the impossibility to be changed shows that the founding act has always a revolutionary and non-legal character. Therefore, constituent sovereignty is a tool which aims for the stability of the constitution and thus, of the sovereignty of the people.[43]

---

[39]As it's mentioned before, Schmitt does not accept the existence of such a concept like "derived" *pouvoir constituant*. Therefore, from his point of view, there is only one *pouvoir constituant* and this is the power who writes the constitution for the first time. For Schmitt, what we call as derived *pouvoir constituant* is just a limited power to amend the constitution and it has no right to "constitute". Schmitt (2008), pp. 211–212.

[40]It would be better to understand this "end of time" as "the collapse of the country" which is created by the relevant constitution.

[41]Schmitt (2008), p. 229.

[42]Klein (1996), p. 205.

[43]Beaud (1994), p. 455.

At this point, it should be mentioned that, what is described as unamendable by Beau is the total annulation of the constitution. The provisions other than unamendable ones can definitely be amended and even annulled. The important thing is to avoid the violation of the essence of the constitution and—if there are some—the amendment of the provisions or principles described as unamendable by the original *pouvoir constituant*.

3.1.2 Derived Pouvoir Constituant's Duty to Show Respect to the Founders' Will

Although Sieyes established in his theory the foundation for the supremacy of the parliament, in his book *Fragments Politiques*, he spoke of putting a curb on the majorities' passion in parliaments. Sieyes, who split-off the general will and the will of the majority, emphasized the threat of the latter becoming a tyranny. He equated the separation of powers with the constitution which is in a higher position than any law accepted in the parliament by a simple majority.[44]

Right after the revolution, in July 21–22, 1789, Sieyes talked about the difference between the original and derived *pouvoir constituant*. In his speech, he described the original as independent from all rules and as the greatest and the most important one used by the nation. For Sieyes the constituent power was nothing else than the national will. Consequently, public forces called "constituted powers" were bound by the constitution because their existences depended on it. Within this framework, the function of the constitution is to order and limit the constituted powers in order to protect individual freedoms.[45]

At this point, the famous French author Carré de Malberg deserves to be mentioned because he found such a difference in the foundation of the constitutional order in the United States. From his point of view, in the United States, while they were creating the constitutional order the sovereign constituent people not only isolated some of the rules from the functional space of the legislative organ, but also took the necessary measures to bind and limit its legislative capacity. Thus, from the American point of view, the constituent power and the legislative organ not only have different qualities but also different natures and consequently they are strictly separated from one another.[46]

This view is supported by some contemporary authors too. For example Beaud mentions that the people who write the constitution are the only power which has the quality of being "sovereign" and because there cannot be a determined—and consequently limited—"sovereign" in the constitution, this sovereign people should be considered superior than the constitution.[47] Therefore, the people who write the

---

[44]Sieyes (1999), pp. 492–493.
[45]Sieyes (1989), pp. 1004–1018.
[46]de Malberg (1931), p. 110.
[47]Beaud (1993), p. 37.

constitution, through their sovereignty, are able to determine some limits for the powers, including the derived *pouvoir constituant*, which will succeed them. Correspondingly, the duty of the latter is to respect the rules put by the sovereign power because it owes its own existence to it.

3.1.3 Derived Pouvoir Constituant's Duty to Show Respect to the Unamendable Provisions

According to the idea that the derived the *pouvoir constituant* is a limited power, the process of amending the constitution is also a limited authority. The necessity to have limits for the amending power is accepted first by the doctrine, before relevant decisions have been adopted by the constitutional courts.[48] For example Duverger argued that the limits to amend the constitution bind the amending power because the latter should respect the constitution which it stems from.[49] In the same direction, Gözler defends that derived *pouvoir constituant* should comply with the limits foreseen within the constitution by the original one, if it does not, the former would destroy its own source and creator. According to legal logic, no power could do this. Otherwise, we would be letting it violate the constitution.[50] And in this case, it becomes a de facto power and we can no longer call it derived *pouvoir constituant*.

In fact, at the beginning of the twentieth century, Esmein was already arguing that the parliament should not be considered as a sovereign power. Although he admitted that the French National Assembly is a *pouvoir constituant*, he defended that this power should only be used within the limits and conditions determined by the constitution. Except for its delegated powers, the National Assembly had neither title nor authority.[51] Therefore, the derived *pouvoir constituant* is a political power which has to act within the boundaries drawn by the constitution. In other words, it is bound by the constitution, by its letter and soul. The power to amend is not absolute but limited.[52] But it is still *constituant* because it has the right and power to amend and annul some of the articles of the constitution. But in doing this, it cannot go beyond the authority given by the constitution. Consequently, the derived *pouvoir constituant* is bound by positive law and thus, it is not sovereign.[53]

---

[48]Beaud (1993), p. 14.
[49]Duverger (1948), p. 195.
[50]Gözler (1997), p. 92.
[51]Esmein (1909), pp. 980–981.
[52]Kubalı (1971), p. 101.
[53]Beaud (1993), p. 16.

3.2 The Impossibility for the Derived **Pouvoir Constituant** to Create an Unamendable Provision

One of the results of the above mentioned ideas is that the only power which has the right to determine some unamendable provisions in the constitution is the original *pouvoir constituant*. The derived *pouvoir constituants*, as their name implies, are derived from the original one and because they stay hierarchically in a lower level, they should respect the sovereignty of the higher one and have to comply with the boundaries determined by it. As it is seen clearly, due to the *raison d'être* of the unamendable provisions, there has to be a hierarchical difference between the power which determines the unamendable provisions and the one which has to comply with them. At this point, the question is whether the derived *pouvoir constituant* which cannot amend or annul the existing unamendable provisions can determine an unamendable provision or principle or not.

3.2.1 The Counter-arguments Which Follows the Misleading Example of the 4th Paragraph of Article 20 of the German Basic Law

Özbudun, without any reasoning, defends that the 4th article of the 1982 Constitution of Turkey which renders the first three articles unamendable can be amended by the derived *pouvoir constituant* in order to determine new amending limits.[54] Onar supports him by giving the example of the amendment of the unamendable 20th article of the 1949 Constitution of the Federal Republic of Germany in 1968 and accepts that in addition to the 4th article of Turkish constitution new unamendable articles can be proclaimed.[55]

If we look closer to Onar's example, Article 79 paragraph 3 of the Constitution of the Federal Republic of Germany, the Basic Law, determines the unamendable articles and principles within the German constitutional order. Known as the *Ewigkeitsklausel* (eternity clause), Article 79 paragraph 3 protects the basic principles of the constitution from any amendment. The provision was introduced by the framers of the 1949 Constitution in order to prevent Germany from slipping back into dictatorship through the use of legal measures as was the case with the Weimar Constitution.[56] The prohibition of amendment established by this article, which has been included within the constitutional order of the Basic Law by the original *pouvoir constituant*, covers the federal structure of the German state and the basic principles established in Articles 1 and 20.

---

[54]Özbudun (2013), p. 175.

[55]Onar (1993), p. 18.

[56]Gallagher (2012), p. 2. For an adverse view see: Hailbronner (2014), pp. 628–634.

At the beginning, Article 20 of the Basic Law as enacted in 1949 was as follows:

II THE FEDERATION AND THE LÄNDER

Article 20 (Basic principles of state order).

(1) The Federal Republic of Germany is a democratic and social Federal state.

(2) All state authority emanates from the people. It is exercised by the people by means of elections and voting and by separate legislative, executive and judicial organs.

(3) Legislation is subject to the constitutional order; the executive and the judiciary are bound by the law.

In 1968, the German Parliament adopted the 17th amendment to the Basic Law. This amendment aimed to bring regulation for internal states of emergency which would grant sufficient guarantees to the Three Western Allied Powers (United Kingdom, France and United States of America) so that they could give up emergency rights reserved in Article 5 paragraph 2 of the Convention on relations between the Three Powers and the Federal Republic of Germany[57] for the protection of the security of their armed forces stationed in West Germany. Because of the federal constitutional structure and, more importantly, the disastrous experiences of emergency powers under the Weimar Constitution of the German Reich, the State of Emergency Amendment of 1968 prohibited internal use of armed forces in general[58] and with the aim of becoming a member of the United Nations[59] wanted to prove that Germany was a democratic country in an irreversible way by adding the 4th paragraph to the Article 20. The title of the article was thus extended too to include also the right to resist.

Beside the other amendments, the paragraph inserted to the Article 20 is as follows:

(4) All Germans shall have the right to resist any person seeking to abolish this constitutional order, should no other remedy be possible.

It is politically understandable why the German Parliament was trying its best to be a part of the United Nations Organization and of the democratic world in general, and wanted to give a guarantee to the allied powers about their democratic will and to foresee citizens' right to resist as a security measures. In this perspective, as Roznai remarks, unamendability could be viewed as a tool forestalling the possibility of a democracy's self-destruction.[60]

However, was this amendment justified or even valid in in a legal context? At this point, the questions were (1) whether this amendment is a violation of

---

[57]For the "Germany Treaty" see http://www.cvce.eu/content/publication/2003/10/1/b1885d93-c91a-4fa7-80bd-e1d3b3171b87/publishable_en.pdf.

[58]Khan and Zöckler (1992), p. 168.

[59]Federal Republic of Germany became a full member of the United Nations Organization in 1973, just 5 years after from this amendment.

[60]Roznai (2015), p. 8.

Article 79 paragraph 3 and (2) is this paragraph inserted by the derived *pouvoir constituant* of 1968 binding on the successor derived *pouvoir constituants?*

3.2.2 The Judicial Value of the 4th Paragraph of Article 20 of the German Basic Law

When we look at Article 79 paragraph 3 more closely, we see that it prohibits only the restriction of the content of the unamendable provisions and not their extension. The relevant paragraph is as follows:

(3) An amendment of this Basic Law affecting the division of the Federation into Länder, the participation in principle of the Länder in legislation, or the basic principles laid down in Articles 1 and 20, is inadmissible.

The original word in this paragraph in German translated to English as "affecting" is "*berührt*". The verb *berühren* means also to touch. In this case, to insert new paragraphs to the existing articles would not affect or touch the other paragraphs of the relevant article. In the same direction, Grimm argues that to violate the prohibition in the Article 79 paragraph 3, the content of the Articles 1 and 20 should be repealed or diminished.[61] Therefore, of course, the constitutional amendment in 1968, amended the article but did not change the already existing content of article 20 of the German Basic Law. It inserted a new paragraph while the rest of the article which constitutes the will of the original *pouvoir constituant* is still there and has stayed unchanged. Consequently, the problem here stems from the usage of the term "unamendable" in English instead of "unchangeable" or "eternity clause" like Germans does in order to describe the limits of the derived *pouvoir constituant*. So the answer to the first question is "no"; there is no violation of the Article 79 paragraph 3.

On the other hand, this provision which includes the right to resist, even if inserted into an unamendable article of the German Basic Law, by reason of being added to Article 20 by a derived *pouvoir constituant*, does not have any binding effect for the other derived *pouvoir constituants* which are hierarchically at the equal level.[62] In this sense, it does not matter what was and is the purpose of the paragraph. As Michel and Cofone categorize, some of the unamendable provisions, described as preservative provisions, aim to enshrine a certain part of the constitution that has already been established in a society,[63] like the right to resist to authoritarian governments for the German society which witnessed the destruction brought by the national-socialist movement under the leadership of Adolf Hitler. Therefore, the 4th paragraph of Article 20 aims to protect democracy. But, while the goal of the parliament by determining this amendment unamendable is very

---

[61]Grimm (2010), p. 34.

[62]For an adverse view, see: Gárdos-Orosz (2015), p. 1.

[63]Michel and Cofone (2015), p. 6.

positive, from a technical point of view, it cannot be considered valuable. If we let parliaments add some new unamendable articles to the constitutions, the German Parliament or another one can at some point in time adopt undemocratic articles and declare them unamendable which with the aim of binding future generations.

One can reach this conclusion from another perspective: Judicial review of constitutional amendments. While reviewing the constitutional amendment laws, constitutional courts act as the representative of the founding people and thus possess the authority of the original *pouvoir constituant*. Consequently, constitutional courts may arrive at a comparison between the will of "the founding people" as a superior legal norm and the present will of the political majority as expressed by the constitutional amending power.[64] But in the case of paragraph 4, there is no superiority between the two wills of the political majorities. The political majority of 1968 and of today are hierarchically at the same level. Therefore, the German Constitutional Court doesn't have the theoretical basis to review a constitutional amendment which amends or annuls the 4th paragraph of Article 20.

Consequently, there is no "new" unamendable provision inserted to the Constitution of the Federal Republic of Germany in 1968. There is only an addition to the end of the eternity clause as a paragraph which can be amended or even repealed by the German Parliament any time. From this point forward, the protection rendered by the Article 79 paragraph 3 shall not include the new 4th paragraph of the Article 20 because the latter is not a result of the original *pouvoir constituant*'s will and the derived *pouvoir constituant* does not have the power to constitute at the same level as the sovereign. So, the answer to the second question above is still no: The 4th paragraph of the Article 20 is not binding on the actual German Parliament. Bundestag and Bundesrat can amend and repeal it without any constitutional violation.

3.2.3 Another Misleading Counter-Argument: The Declaration of the Republic in France

An exception-like example to the impossibility for the derived *pouvoir constituant* to accept an unamendable provision should be mentioned at this point. Additionally, this example is far older than the others and consists of the constitutional amendment in 1884 to the French Constitutional Laws.[65] When we look at the background of this amendment, we see that at this time in France, there was a high tension between the republicans and the monarchists. After the general elections in 1881 and the elections for the Senate, the republicans had obtained a majority in both of the chambers. With the support of this new situation, the republicans wanted to block a return to the monarchy and in August 14, 1884 adopted a constitutional amendment according to which the republican form of the

---

[64]Roznai (2015), p. 9.

[65]In 1884, there were three constitutional laws which were in effect all together.

government was declared as unamendable and the royal family members were banned from holding presidential office.

With the insertion of the unamendable provision to the constitutional laws by a functioning parliament whose status was a derived *pouvoir constituant* came under fire. First, Duguit attacked this amendment by saying that the provision was voted by a national assembly which had the power to amend the constitution, thus, it could be amended or repealed by another national assembly which had the power to amend the constitution. Duguit defended that, as a consequence, taking into consideration that during the existence of the relevant provision the national assembly could not change the form of the government, and the needed to be done was to remove the new provision. Once it was repealed, the form of the government could be amended in a very constitutional way.[66] In other words, taking into consideration the general principle of public law which states that "a regulation accepted by an organ can be amended by another organ at the same level", he defended that, even though the provision was an "unamendable provision", a regulation inserted to the constitution by a derived *pouvoir constituant* could be amended by another derived *pouvoir constituant*.

We know that this provision is still in effect as an unamendable provision within the Constitution of France of 1958 as Article 89 paragraph 5. This means that the provision remained unamended since 1884 till today and, moreover, it became a state tradition. Beaud has an explanation for this situation. He believes that, the constitutional bills of 1875 which were in effect in 1884 did not constitute a real constitution because they were not describing a definitive regime for France. But the amendments approved in 1884 banned any amendment on the subject of the republican form of the regime, brought the prohibition for the royal family from seeking presidential office and regulated the aristocratic structure of the Senate and thus prompted some legal results. The author argues that this amendment included two orders. The first was binding for future parliaments due to the constituent power's decision and the limitation of its powers. Contrary to what most of the authors argue, he defends that no derived *pouvoir constituant* can amend the republican form of the government within the constitutional processes and therefore, hereafter, the reconstruction of the monarchy can only become true via a revolution. The second order was that the amendments in 1884 rendered the constitutional laws of 1875 a real constitution. Therefore, Beaud thinks that the amendment in 1884 should be considered as the act of the original *pouvoir constituant* of the 3rd Republic.[67] In other words, Beaud claims that the National Assembly which approved the amendment in 1884 was not a derived *pouvoir constituant*, but an original *pouvoir constituant* because it gave birth to a brand new state.

In this case, we should accept that a derived *pouvoir constituant*, by its own will, declared itself an original *pouvoir constituant*. However, taking into consideration

---

[66]Duguit (1994), pp. 370–371.
[67]Beaud (1994), pp. 382–383.

that since no organ can declare on its own itself a higher organ than it is, therefore, Beaud's thesis is unacceptable.

So, why didn't any future French parliament amend this "unamendable provision" which was in reality amendable? The answer is simple: Because they did not want to. After this amendment the monarchists could not win any majority in the National Assembly until the next constitution's approval in 1946. And the drafters of the latter decided to keep the republican form of the government as an unamendable article[68] and thereafter it truly became an unamendable provision because it was now determined by the only sovereign power which is the original *pouvoir constituant*.

4 Conclusion

In modern constitutional democracies, unamendable provisions in constitutions can serve as guarantees for fundamental human rights and for the democracy against majorities in the parliaments. To recognize their legal value and to say that they bind the parliaments leads us necessarily to the acceptance of a separation between a higher will than the will of the majorities in the parliament. The main quality of the higher will is to bind the legislative organ and limit it on the issue of constitutional amendments. The essential provisions of constitutions such as fundamental right and freedoms or the political regime on which the country is based upon are protected against probable violations from parliamentarian majorities. The organ which establishes the state and, therefore, has the right to determine its basis is called original *pouvoir constituant* and the other organ which can only amend those provisions open to amendments is called the derived *pouvoir constituant*.

The amendment of an unamendable provision by a parliamentarian act would provoke inevitably a violation of this hierarchy because in this case the power to amend would mount up the constitution and this would mean getting out of the established legal order. Therefore, in my opinion, the organ which amends the unamendable provision of a constitution cannot be accepted as an in-law power. But despite of this fact, such a case should not provoke by itself a legal interruption.

The method of the amendment of the Constitution of 1958 of France in 1962 can be used as an example to the in-law original *pouvoir constituant*. In this case the amendment did not change unamendable article of the constitution.[69] Instead, the process of referendum was used to achieve the amendment, and was afforded force following jurisprudence of the Constitutional Council of France which can be considered as a leading process for unamendable provisions' amendments.

---

[68]Article 95.

[69]Article 89/5: "The republican form of the government shall not be subject to any amendment".

On the other hand, in contrast with this example, adding a new paragraph via a constitutional amendment to the unamendable article of the Basic Law of Germany in 1968 shall not be recognized as an act of the original *pouvoir constituant*. Independent from the content of the relevant paragraph which should be accepted as an improvement for the protection of the democratic regime in Germany, this amendment was done by the ordinary process of a constitutional amendment and has no power to bind the future derived *pouvoir constituants* because it is not a product of the will of the founding power but of the majority of the regular parliament. This means that there is no hierarchical difference between that parliament and future parliaments which could have the ambition to change or annul this paragraph. But this doesn't mean that Bundestag and Bundesrat have to change and annul it. Like the constitutional amendment in 1884 to the French Constitutional Laws of 1875, which added the so-called unamendable provisions for protection of the republican form of government and which has not been annulled since then and consequently becoming a real unamendable provision in the Constitution of 1946, paragraph 4 of Article 20 to the German Basic Law can survive without any amendment till it becomes a real unamendable provision if the future original *pouvoir constituant* which would draft a new constitution decides so. Until such a development, the 4th paragraph of Article 20 will stay as an amendable provision inside an unamendable article.

References

Barthelemy J, Duez P (1993) Traité de Droit Constitutionnel. Dalloz, Paris, p 231

Beaud O (1994) La Puissance de l'Etat. PUF, Paris

Beaud O (1993) Maastricht et la Théorie Constitutionnelle (1ere partie)—La Nécessaire et Inévitable Distinction entre le Pouvoir Constituant et le Pouvoir de Révision Constitutionnelle, no 39. Les Petites Affiches, 31 Mar 1993

Beaud O (1993) Le Souverain. Pouvoirs 67:37

Burdeau G (1950) Traité de Science Politique, vol III. LGDJ, Paris, p 209

Duguit L (1994) Traité de Droit Constitutionnel. In: Beaud O (ed) La Puissance De l'Etat, vol IV, 3rd edn. PUF, Paris, pp 370–371

Duguit L (2005) Egemenlik ve Özgürlük. In: Akal CB (ed) Devlet Kuramı. Dost, Ankara, pp 383–385

Duverger M (1948) Manuel de Droit Constitutionnel et de Science Politique, 5th edn. PUF, Paris, p195

Dérosier J-P (2008) Enquête sur la Limite Constitutionnelle: du Concept à la Notion. In: Revue Française de Droit Constitutionnel, no 76, pp. 785–795

Esmein A (1909) Elements de Droit Constitutionnel Français et Comparé, 5th edn. Sirey, Paris, pp 980–981

Gallagher SCP (2012) Euro Crisis: Challenges to the ESM Treaty and the Fiscal Compact Treaty before the German constitutional court. Working paper, p 2, 30 Aug 2012. http://www.iiea.com/publications/challenges-to-the-esm-treaty-and-the-fiscal-compact-treaty-before-the-german-constitutional-court

Grimm D (2010) The basic law at 60—identity and change. Ger Law J 11(1):34

Gárdos-Orosz F (2015) Unamendable Constitutional Provisions and Judicial Review. Paper presented in Koç University in workshop on unamendable constitutional provisions, p 1, 9 June 2015

Gözler K (1997) Le Pouvoir de Révision Constitutionnelle, vol I. Presses Universitaires de Septentrion, Villeneuve d'Ascq

Hailbronner M (2014) Rethinking the rise of the German constitutional court: from Anti-Nazism to value formalism. Int J Const Law 12(3):628–634

Khan DE, Zöckler M (1992) Germans to the front? or le Malade Imaginaire. Eur J Int Law 3:168. http://www.ejil.org/pdfs/3/1/1174.pdf

Klein C (1996) Théorie et Pratique du Pouvoir Constituant. PUF, Paris

Kubalı HN (1971) Anayasa Hukuku Dersleri: Genel Esaslar ve Siyasî Rejimler. İstanbul Üniversitesi Yayınları, İstanbul

Lavroff DG (1995) Le Droit Constitutionnel de la Ve République. Dalloz, Paris, pp 99–100

Michel S, Cofone IN (2015) Credible Commitment or Paternalism? The Case of Unamendability. Paper presented in Koç University in workshop on unamendable constitutional provisions, p 6, 9 June 2015

Murswiek D (2008) Ungeschriebene Ewigkeitsgarantien in Verfassungen. Unpublished paper presented in Bilkent University, Ankara, p 3, 10 Nov 2008. http://www.jura.uni-freiburg.de/institute/ioeffr3/forschung/papers/murswiek/ewigkeitsgarantie

Onar E (1993) 1982 Anayasası'nda Anayasayı Değiştirme Sorunu. Ankara Üniversitesi Hukuk Fakültesi Yayınları, Ankara, p 18

Paine T (1984) Rights of Man. Viking Penguin, New Jersey, p 41

Renoux TS, de Villiers M (1994) Code Constitutionnel. Litec, Paris, p 624

Robert J (2003) La Forme Républicaine du Gouvernement. Revue du Droit Public 2:362

Roznai Y (2015) Necrocracy or democracy. Paper presented in Koç University in workshop on unamendable constitutional provisions, 9 June 2015

Sağlam F (2010) Anayasa ve Değişmez Kurallar. In: Prof. Dr Tunçer Karamustafaoğlu'na Armağan. Adalet Yayınevi, Ankara, p 575

Schmitt C (2008) Théorie de la Constitution, 1st edn. PUF, Paris

Sieyes E (1999) Des Manuscrits de Sieyes, 1773–1799. Honoré Champion, Paris, pp 492–493

Sieyes E (1989) Motion sur la Vérification des Pouvoirs. In: Furet F, Halevi R (eds) Orateurs de la Révolution Française I—Les Constituants. Gallimard, Bruges, pp 1004–1018

Teziç E (2012) Anayasa Hukuku (Genel Esaslar), 15th edn. Beta, Istanbul

Teziç E (2012) Anayasa Hukuku (Genel Esaslar), 15th edn. Beta, Istanbul, p 158

Turpin D (1992) Droit Constitutionnel. PUF, Paris, p 81

de Malberg RC (1920) Contribution à la Théorie Générale de l'Etat Spécialement d'après les Données Fournies par le Droit Constitutionnel Français, vol II. Librairie du Receuil Sirey, Paris, pp 509–510

de Malberg RC (1922) Contribution à la Théorie Générale de l'Etat Spécialement d'après les Données Fournies par le Droit Constitutionnel Français, vol II. Librairie du Receuil Sirey, Paris, pp 496–497

de Malberg RC (1931) La Loi Expression de la Volonté Générale—Etude sur le Concept de la Loi dans la Constitution de 1875, Librairie du Receuil Sirey, Paris

du Loû DMD (2003) Le Pouvoir Constituant Dérivé Reste Souverain. Revue du Droit Public 3:731

Özbudun E (2013) Türk Anayasa Hukuku, 14th edn. Ankara, Yetkin Yayınları, pp 180–181

Özbudun E (2013) Türk Anayasa Hukuku, 14th edn. Yetkin, Ankara, p 175

Debating Unamendability: Deadlock in Turkey's Constitution-Making Process

Oya Yegen

Abstract Constitutional Conciliation Commission (Anayasa Uzlaşma Komisyonu —AUK) of Turkey, established after the 2011 general elections but called off after the commission could not overcome an impasse on a number of issues, was nevertheless a significant experience in Turkey's constitutional development. One of the issues that led to the deadlock in the commission was the controversy over unamendable articles. A point of divide among the four parties that made up the commission was whether the new constitution would maintain the eternal clauses of the present constitution that entrench the republic form of the state, its characteristics, and its language or whether it would not include any irrevocable articles. Except the republic's first constitution of 1921, the three constitutions of modern Turkey included unamendable constitutional provisions, which had previously led to political and constitutional controversies. The subject of unamendable articles was one of the last issues that the commission discussed before the 25 months of enterprise was dissolved. This article traces the evolution of unamendable articles in Turkish constitutions, examines the political parties' proposals for the draft constitution and analyzes the debates conducted within AUK. It concludes that members of the AUK held irreconcilable positions with respect to unamendability and unamendable articles, which contributed to the breakdown of the negotiations.

Modern constitutions are harder to change than other legal texts. Entrenchment clauses, "eternity clauses" exist in 59 constitutions of 193 constitutions of the world, making up 30.6% of all.[1] Turkey is one of those cases. The country's recent attempt at drafting a new constitution, among other constitutional issues brought about a renewed discussion about the unamandable articles: Does an ordinary parliament have the power to change the unamendable articles in the process of

---

[1]Hein (2015).

O. Yegen (✉)
Sabancı Unversity, Istanbul, Turkey
e-mail: zoyayegen@sabanciuniv.edu

© Springer International Publishing AG, part of Springer Nature 2018
R. Albert and B. E. Oder (eds.), *An Unamendable Constitution?*
Ius Gentium: Comparative Perspectives on Law and Justice 68,
https://doi.org/10.1007/978-3-319-95141-6_11

making a new constitution? Will the new constitution maintain these clauses? If so, would that mean that it is actually a new text? Will the provision of unamendability be maintained? What will be the content of these clauses? The study examines the debate conducted by the members of the Constitutional Conciliation Commission (*Anayasa Uzlaşma Komisyonu*, AUK) regarding the unamendable articles on the form, characteristics, and the symbols of the Turkish state as defined in the 1982 Constitution and the unamendability article that entrenches these articles.

"Are these on record? Because in the future these will be discussed from constitutional law perspective" says Süheyl Batum, during one of the commissions session. True, the minutes of the commission offers an excellent opportunity to examine the practical and normative considerations that arise regarding unamendability. A point of divide among the four parties that made up the commission was whether the new constitution would maintain the eternal clauses of the present constitution that entrench the Republic form of the state, its characteristics, and its language or whether breaking with tradition, the new constitution would not include any irrevocable articles. The debate took place in two different time periods during the latter stages of the commission.[2] First stage was in April 2013 and April 17 was the first date the entrenchment clause was exhaustively debated without getting any consensus. The second stage was in late August 2013 where for three days (August 21, 26, and 27), the commission discussed the substance of articles regarding the form, characteristics, and the symbols of the Turkish state as well as the unamendability. As the section on these debates demonstrate, a central question regarding the technical amendability of these clauses, i.e., the debate over original constituent power and derived constituent power clouded the debate over the substance of these articles.

In this chapter, I trace the use of unamendable articles in Turkish constitutions with a special emphasis on the present ones, examine the political parties' proposals, and analyze the debates conducted at the AUK. The chapter begins with a historical account of Turkey's piecemeal constitutional change, starting off with Turkey's 1982 Constitution, the amendments introduced to the constitution, and amendment-making procedures adopted by Turkey so far. The second section discusses in detail the question of unamendability in Turkish constitutional history that legally and politically has led to conflicts at times. The third part examines Turkey's constitution-making after the 2011 general elections and offers some insights about its shortcomings. The fourth section examines the issue of unamendable provision, whether from a legal point it is possible to change the unamendable articles, whether the new constitution is to have unamendable articles, and how the substance of these articles (formerly unamendable or still unamendable) is to be formulated. I argue that parties held irreconcilable positions with respect to unamendable articles, which contributed to the breakdown of the negotiations.

---

[2]The issue of unamendable articles do come up rarely outside of these dates because the members of the commission decided to follow a roadmap in which these contentious issues were deliberately postponed to latter stages of drafting.

1   The 1982 Constitution and Its Discontents

Turkey's 1982 Constitution drafted under military rule, has since its birth been under criticism from different sectors of the Turkish society. The criticism is directed at the nondeliberative, noninclusive, and top-down method of adopting the constitution as well as its authoritarian content.[3] The text was the result of a bicameral Constituent Assembly[4] in which one chamber was the National Security Council (NSC), composed of the five top generals that had led the military takeover on September 12, 1980.[5] The second chamber, the "civilian" chamber called the Consultative Assembly was made up of 160 members that were directly or indirectly appointed by the NSC.[6] The draft prepared by the Consultative Assembly could be amended or rejected by the NSC and there was no mechanism to resolve the differences between the two chambers.[7] A nation-wide referendum was supervised under the extraordinary conditions of the military regime at the time. The NSC prohibited the campaign of "no" vote and the General Kenan Evren embarked upon an intensive campaign of propaganda for the new constitution. Transparent envelopes were used violating the secret ballot principle.[8] Ratified by a public referendum (91.37%), the constitution also confirmed the presidency of Evren for the next 7 years.[9] Unlike the process that had led to the 1961 Constitution, which had tasked the NUC with overseeing the drafting of another text in the event that the public vetoed the first one, there was no clear understanding of the course of action that the military rulers of NSC would take in the event that the draft was rejected in the plebiscite. It was understood that the "no" would only prolong the military rule.

Prepared and ratified under dubious conditions, the constitution in terms of substance was also nondemocratic. Convinced that the political crisis leading up to

---

[3]Yazıcı (2001), pp. 22–32 and 36–40.

[4]The Law on Constituent Assembly (June 30, 1981) charged the assembly with drafting the electoral law, political parties law and took on legislative functions. Özbudun (2005), pp. 19–50.

[5]It was headed by General Kenan Evren, then the Chief of General Staff and also included the commanders of the army, navy, air force and gendarmerie.

[6]The previous Turkish constitution, the Constitution of 1961 was also a direct result of military intervention and was prepared under military influence. However, in terms of its adoption process the 1961 Constitution is considered more "representative". The House of Representatives of the 1960–1961 period included opposition parties and other institutions while the Consultative Assembly of the 1981–1982 period members of all political parties were prohibited from becoming members.

[7]During the 1960–1961 period, National Unity Committee (NUC) the military committee that executed the takeover did not have such absolute power over the House of Representatives Özbudun and Gençkaya (2009), p. 20.

[8]Özpek (2012), p. 153.

[9]Provisional Article 1, 1982 Constitution of Turkey, Law no 2709. The permanent formula for electing the president was via the parliament indirectly. Evren's presidency deviated from this as he was elected directly by the referendum.

the coup was heightened by the weaknesses of the 1961 Constitution, namely the weak authority of the executive branch, strong checks and balances, and elaborative rights and freedoms; the drafters of the 1982 Constitution set out to "rectify" these areas. It empowered the executive branch, established a number of nonmajoritarian institutions, and allowed restrictions on fundamental rights and freedoms under vaguely defined conditions. Although some of the institutions set up by the 1982 Constitution existed under the previous framework, such as the National Security Council and the Constitutional Court, their composition and function had been altered in the new text to fortify the established structure against any future change.

Yazıcı, a long-time critic of the 1982 Constitution points out to aspects of the constitution that may prompt political crisis. These include an empowered office of presidency with vast appointive powers in a parliamentary system which lead to two-tiered executive branch that is prone to deadlocks; a politicized Constitutional Court whose members are appointed solely by the president and acts as a mechanism of *tutelage*; and a guardian role for the armed forces that demonstrate a deep distrust toward civilian politicians.[10]

Despite these authoritarian aspects and lack of legitimacy, the constitution until 1995 has been well espoused by the right-wing conservative governments.[11] However, with the prospect of European Union membership, Turkey has gone through amendments that to a certain extent democratized the fundamental rights and liberties and liberalized the political system.[12] The following section gives a short account of amendments and amendment-making procedures pursued by different governments of Turkey.

1.1 Constitutional Change Process of Turkey

1.1.1 Constitutional Amendments

Before AUK had been established the 1982 Constitution of Turkey had been amended 17 times with changes affecting 113 articles.[13] The 1987 amendment lowered the voting age, changed the constitutional amendment procedure, increased the number of the members of the Turkish Grand National Assembly (TGNA), and

---

[10]Yazıcı (2001), p. 6. As a result of constitutional overhaul that transformed Turkey's parliamentary system to an executive dominated presidential system with weak checks and balances in April 2017, such criticisms have lost their relevance.

[11]Göztepe and Çelebi (2012), p. 17. As the authors point out, an exception to this was the demand expressed by former prime minister and later former president Turgut Özal to change the parliamentary system and adopt presidential system, p. 18.

[12]Cengiz (2014), p. 682.

[13]The 2008 constitutional amendment regarding the principle of equality (Article 10) and right to education (Article 42) was annulled by the Turkish Constitutional Court. If one includes this revoked amendment, the parliament has actually passed 18 amendments. See Roznai and Yolcu (2012), p. 175.

via referendum eliminated the provision than banned former politicians from practicing politics.[14] An attempt to change the constitution to have early local elections was defeated via referendum in 1988. The 1993 amendments abolished the state monopoly on radio and television broadcasting. The 1995 amendments, a product of intense negotiation, resulted in significant changes that eliminated the rationale for the 1980 coup from the preamble; eliminated the bans on political activities of trade unions, associations, foundations, cooperatives, and public professional organizations; allowed for cooperation between these organizations and political parties; increased the number of members of the TGNA; lowered the voting age further to 18; provided for right to vote to Turkish citizens living abroad; provided for the right to unionize for civil servants; lowered the age to become a member of the political party; allowed the instructors and students of higher education institutions to become members of political parties; allowed political parties to establish women and youth branches, foundations, and organizations outside of Turkey; and changed the conditions where one loses membership to TGNA and changed the consequences to members of an outlawed political party.[15] The 1999 amendment reorganized the functions and composition of State Security Courts and eliminated military judges from these courts. Another amendment in 1999 allowed for the privatization of public enterprises and made concession contracts arbitrable.[16]

The 2001 constitutional amendments were the most comprehensive ones.[17] As a result of these, 33 articles and the preamble were modified. The bulk of these amendments were on fundamental rights and freedoms.[18] It eliminated the general restrictions on rights and freedoms; improved political and civil rights; enlarged the scope of social and economic rights; shortened the pretrial detention; eliminated the phrase of "language prohibited by law"; restricted the death penalty to time of war and for crimes of terrorism; increased the quorum for political party prohibition cases, clarified the conditions of anti-constitutional activities and provided for gradual punishment system for political parties; altered the composition of the National Security Council to give numerical majority to civilians and highlighted the institution's advisory nature and eliminated the ban on Constitutional Court's power to review the laws passed under the military regime.[19]

The 2002 amendments changed the clause that prevented Recep Tayyip Erdoğan's election to the parliament and provided for an interim election. This amendment deviated from others as it catered to one individual and did not have democratization, liberalization or EU-conditionality motivation. The 2004 amendments were nevertheless another important moment of comprehensive

---

[14]The following synopsis is based on the summary provided Özbudun (2005), pp. 27–30 and Özbudun and Gençkaya (2009).

[15]For more on the process of the 1995 amendment-making, see Doğanay (2007), p. 388.

[16]See Özbudun and Gençkaya (2009), pp. 31–72.

[17]Gönenç (2004), p. 89, Yüksel (2007), p. 153.

[18]Özbudun (1993–2004), p. 179.

[19]Yüksel (2007).

constitutional change where the EU process was the "leading force".[20] The amendments eliminated all references to death penalty in the constitution; permitted affirmative action for women; abolished state security court; allowed for extradition of Turkish citizens in cases of offense under the International Criminal Court jurisdiction; eliminated the Chief of Military Staff's right to appoint a member of the Board of Higher Education; allowed for Court of Account's auditing of the Armed Forces; and most significantly established that international agreements take precedence in case of conflicts between international agreements and domestic law concerning fundamental rights and liberties. An amendment in 2005 reorganized the Supreme Board of Radio and Television (RTÜK); another one in 2005 expanded the parliamentary supervision of over the government budget. A 2006 amendment lowered the minimum age of holding public office.

Starting with the crisis over the election of a new president, the 2007 and 2008 witnessed constitutional amendments that were reactions to immediate constitutional crises.[21] Approved by a popular referendum the 2007 constitutional amendment allowed for direct presidential election, shortened the legislative period to 4 years and established the quorum needed for parliamentary decisions as one-third of elected members.[22] The early general elections, the Constitutional Court's review of the amendments, the parliamentary election of the new president and the concurrent referendum for the 2007 amendments led to a discrepancy, which was resolved by another constitutional amendment in October 2007.[23] While the AKP-initiated debate on fully revamping the constitution was ongoing, AKP and MHP agreed on another constitutional change on two articles regarding the principle of equality (Article 10) and the right to education (Article 42). The 2008 constitutional amendments intended to abolish the headscarf ban for female university students was annulled by the Constitutional Court on the grounds that it violated the unamendable principle of secularism.

The AKP-supported constitutional amendment package, like the 2007 amendments, because of partisan deadlock, was taken to a referendum. While the most important provisions of the amendment were related to composition and appointment structure of the Constitutional Court (AYM) and the High Council of Judges and Prosecutors (HSYK), these were embedded in a 26-article package that seemingly bolstered rights and liberties and rule of law.[24] These included the introduction of the office of Ombudsman and the individual complaint mechanism; strengthening rights of children and other disadvantaged groups; establishing a separate secretariat and budget for HSYK; increasing the quorum of Constitutional Court in party prohibition and review of constitutionality of constitutional

---

[20]Coşkun (2013), p. 95.

[21]Özbudun and Gençkaya (2009), pp. 97–103. See also Uran (2010), p. 2.

[22]Atikcan and Öge (2012).

[23]AKP during this period asked a group of scholars to draft a new constitution. Özbudun and Gençkaya (2009), pp. 104–106.

[24]Coşkun (2013), p. 109.

amendment cases; strengthening the right of collective bargaining for civil servants; introduced new rights such as personal data protection and right to become members of different labor unions at the same time, allowing judicial monitoring of the Supreme Military Council's decisions and ending the judicial immunity of the 1980 coup-makers.[25] The seventeenth amendment of the constitution that took place in 2011 regarding the disciplinary process of sports federations was the final change introduced to the 1982 Constitution before the AUK was established.

1.1.2 Amendment-Making Procedures

The amendments listed above introduced wide-ranging changes to the constitution in different subject areas. The procedure of amendment-making displayed differences that can be explained by parliamentary arithmetic and the political context.[26] We observe that three methods were adopted during different periods. One is the reliance on ad hoc conciliation commissions; inter-party committee for the 1995 amendments; and the accord committee for the 2001 amendments.[27] We observe that these took place during coalition governments in times of "highly fragmented and polarized legislation", and in the case of 2001 ones, amidst an economic crisis.[28] However, these remain as constitutional amendments that made the most comprehensive overhaul of the constitution, making up 13.6% of all amendments in the 1995 and 28.2% in 2001.[29] Emphasizing consensus-building approach, these ad hoc bodies were "purely political", not subject to the regular rules and procedures of the parliament.[30] Although these broad inter-party agreements have not been easy

---

[25]In response to the petition of a group of members of the parliament, the Constitutional Court reviewed the constitutional amendment package and annulled for the provision that limited judges and prosecutors "to vote for only one candidate" on the account that it was a violation of rule of law, which is one of the principles stated in the unamendable articles. However, the court refused to review the package as a whole on formal grounds. See Tarık Olcay, "Unamendability of Amendable Clauses: The Case of the Turkish Constitution" in this volume.

[26]Parliamentary arithmetic alone cannot explain the variance in procedure especially during the dominant party (AKP) period. Between 2007 and 2011, when the AKP broke the pattern of inter-party compromise tradition of 1990s and 2001, it had increased its electoral support but the percentage of parliamentary seats of AKP had become smaller. See Arato and Tombus (2013). During the making of 2004 amendments, AKP had almost two-thirds of parliamentary seats to amend the constitution, but received the support of opposition parties. However, later, when AKP pushed through the 2010 amendments via a referendum, it had less parliamentary seats (less than three-fifths).

[27]According to Doğanay, it is not possible to simply consider the 1995 amendments a result of EU influence. It would be better "described as a general undertaking shaped by the will of the Turkish parliament itself since we cannot talk about clearly defined and dictated standards of democratization of the EU before the Helsinki summit", Doğanay (2007), p. 389. EU standards played a much crucial role in 2001, see Gönenç (2004), p. 109.

[28]Kalaycıoğlu (2011), p. 265.

[29]Ibid, pp. 269–270.

[30]Oder (2012), p. 82.

and were strategically necessary, they were able to achieve multiparty consensus that could transcend partisan politics.[31] The adoption of consensual procedures even in the face of staunch opposition from veto actors of the regime had become important precedents for Turkey's recent record of parliamentary process of constitution-making.[32]

A second method has been unilateral action during the single-party governments. These constitutional amendments such as the 2004, 2007, and the 2010 instances of constitutional change have been pursued under the direction of the major political party. Without engaging in deliberation and consultation, these constitutional changes have adopted "ruling-party constitutionalism" in order to address political issues of higher significance.[33] A third method has been engaging in alliances with the opposition parties such as the case in 2002 when CHP provided support and 2008 amendment (ultimately annulled) when MHP provided support. Having achieved consensus without due deliberation, this type of "alliance-building con-stitutionalism" dealt with politically sensitive issues.[34]

Of the 17 amendments introduced to the constitution, 11 took place during the post-2002 period when AKP formed a single-party government. However, the two-thirds of the total articles changed did so before AKP rose to power.[35]

1.2 Criticism Toward the Turkish Constitution

Considering the constitution as an "obstacle" to democracy, Tanör emphasizes the structural problems related to the way the constitution organizes the relationship between the state and society and individuals.[36] Although the aforementioned amendments, especially the 1995, 2001, and 2004 amendment packages, aimed to respond to criticism directed at the democratic deficits of the constitution, they remained insufficient as they failed to systematically overhaul the text. Its critics argue "these reforms have not been able to completely liquidate the authoritarian, tutelary, and illiberal features of the Constitution, itself a product of a military coup".[37] Thus, both in terms of content and the origin, the constitution remained a thorny issue by the time AUK was established.

---

[31]Özbudun (1993–2004).

[32]Arato (2010a), p. 476.

[33]Oder (2014).

[34]Ibid. See also Oder (2012) for a comparative anlaysis of constitutional amendments packages that amended or abrogated a signjficiant portion of the 1982 Constitution, from the perspective of EU impact.

[35]Kalaycıoğlu (2011), p. 268.

[36]Tanör (2012), p. 168.

[37]Özbudun (2005), p. 30.

Merely considered as partial reforms, the amendments passed till then had not achieved much with regard to Kurdish minority rights.[38] The constitution maintains the clause on Turkish citizenship (Article 66), which stipulates that "Everybody bound to the Turkish state through the bond of citizenship is a Turk". Moreover, the unamendable provision of Article 3 recognizes Turkish as the language of the state rather than the official language of the Turkish state. The centralized administrative system and lack of right to education in mother tongue remain among the demands of the Kurdish citizens. In recent decades, Turkey had become more "politically and culturally polarized" along religious and ethnic lines,[39] and demand for constitutional adaptation to respond to these new dynamics had become more pronounced.

Although the constitution was partially reconstructed, the idea of making a new constitution remained popular. A survey conducted before the 2010 referendum on constitutional amendments found out that 49.5% of the respondents were not content with the 1982 Constitution and 43.5% reported that a new constitution is needed regardless of the outcome of the impending referendum.[40] Over the years, civil society organizations, academicians, think tanks and other platforms produced proposals of constitutional change, partial and total, and promoted constitutional replacement.[41] The support for a new constitution increased despite the piecemeal constitutional change. According to surveys conducted by TEPAV the ratio of respondents who declared that a new constitution is needed increased from 41 to 69% from 2008 to 2011.[42] However, a central question regarding the procedure of making a new constitution remained unresolved.[43] As the next sections demonstrates, although there was agreement around the need for a "new and civilian constitution-making," there were certain uncertainties regarding the procedure of making a new constitution. The unamendable provisions of the 1982 Constitution contextualized within the broader question of original versus derived constituent power remained unresolved amongst constitutional law scholars and political elites.

---

[38]Cengiz (2014), p. 8. Language restrictions for speech and press (Article 26 and 28 that banned "language prohibited by law" without specifying Kurdish) are amended in 2001.

[39]Keyman (2012).

[40]The results of the survey conducted by A&G research company and TEPAV (Economic Policy Research Foundation of Turkey) is reported in Levent Gönenç, 'Towards a Participatory Constitution Making Process in Turkey' (*TEPAV Policy Note*, January 2011) <http://www.tepav. org.tr/upload/files/1296466407-8.Towards_a_Participatory_Constitution_Making_Process_in_ Turkey.pdf>.

[41]For a detailed discussion of different proposals, see Erdem and Heper (2011). A major criticism directed at this study is that it fails to include the 2009 draft prepared by DİSK—Confederation of Revolutionary Workers Unions Devrimci İşçi Sendikaları Konfederasyonu, in Turkish. See Göztepe and Çelebi (2012), p. 18.

[42]"Social Demand Grows for a New Constitution," *(TEPAV*, 2 March 2011) <http://www.tepav. org.tr/en/haberler/s/1982>.

[43]The next section summarizes different positions promoted by civil society organizations, academicians, think tanks, and other platforms.

2   The Unamendable Amendments and Its Discontents

Under the 1924 and 1961 Constitutions of Turkey, the only irrevocable provision was the republican form of the state.[44] The 1982 constitution has expanded the scope of unamendability and included two other articles that define the character-istics and symbols of the Turkish state.[45] However, the controversy over una-mendability in Turkish constitutional law stems not necessarily from the articles but from the Turkish Constitutional Court's reliance on them to engage in substantial review of constitutional amendments despite an express prohibition of substantial review of amendments.[46] Unlike the implicit limitations expressed by the "Doctrine of Basic Structure" in India, in Turkey the unamendable articles provide for explicit limitations on the amendment powers. However, the fact that the Constitutional Court in Turkey deploys the unamendable articles to move beyond a procedural review of constitutional amendments indicates that the unamendable articles also have been interpreted to provide implicit limitations on the entirety of the constitution.

The Constitutional Court of Turkey, first established under the 1961 Constitution, since its inception has been an assertive actor that challenges gov-ernmental laws and constitutional amendments.[47] The original 1961 Constitution did not have a provision on the judicial review of constitutional amendments.[48] The omission has led the Constitutional Court to assume such authority and review the

---

[44]The 1924 Constitution's Article 104 regarding the amendment-making rules, forbid an amendment to Article 1 of the Constitution stating the form of the government as a republic. After the 1945 amendment that reinstated the constitution after translating it to modern Turkish, the article also added that such an amendment cannot be proposed. The 1961 Constitution's Article 9 similarly stipulated that "the provision of the constitution establishing the form of the state as a republic shall not be amended nor shall any such proposal be made". See Onar (1993) for more information on unamendable clauses in 1924 and 1961 Constitutions.

[45]It is important to highlight that the decision to expand the scope of the unamendable provisions was taken by the National Security Council—the chamber made up of coup organizers. The draft prepared by the Consultative Assembly, the civilian chamber had only included the republican form of state as the irrevocable provision of the constitution and against the possibility of double amendment, self-entrenched the unamendability clause. See Onar (1993), p. 11 and Köybaşı (2013), pp. 334–335.

[46]See Özbudun (2009), p. 533, and Olcay, "Unamendability of Amendable Clauses: The Case of the Turkish Constitution" in this volume. As Olcay rightfully points out, "the practical importance of the question of unamendability in the Turkish Constitutions has not been regarding textual changes to the unamendable provisions themselves, but rather on amendments to normally amendable provisions".

[47]Belge (2006), p. 653.

[48]Gözler (2008).

1969[49] and 1970 amendments with respect to both form and substance.[50] The court's judicial review of the 1970 amendment was the first instance in which the court declared itself competent to review constitutional amendments' compatibility with the unamendable article of the 1961 Constitution regarding the republican form of the state as protected by Article 9.[51] In addition, the Court adopted a wider interpretation of the concept of "republican form of state" to include the characteristics of the Turkish Republic, such as the rule of law, secularism, social state, and democracy.[52] Although in this particular decision, the Court did not find incompatibility with "the republican form of the state" in the 1970 amendment that postponed senate elections for a year, it was a notable case of court's broad interpretation of its power.

In response, an amendment that explicitly prohibits the Constitutional Court from reviewing the substantial constitutionality of constitutional amendments passed in 1971. Despite the restriction to review the constitutionality of constitutional amendments with respect to their form, the court did make five decisions that reviewed amendments with respect to substance, while claiming that they were exercising procedural review.[53] The court argued that these constitutional amendments violated Article 9 which prohibited amending the republican form of the state and as Roznai and Yolcu acknowledge "the Constitutional Court brought in substantive review through the back door".[54] It was within this context that the 1982 Constitution broadened the scope of unamendable articles but limited the Constitutional Court's power to review to form; however, this time explicitly outlining what is included in the formal review: requisite majorities for the proposal and in the ballot, and the prohibition on debates under urgent procedure.

The 1982 Constitution of Turkey describes the principal characteristics of the state in the first three articles.[55] Article 1 establishes that "The State of Turkey is a Republic". Article 2 describes and lists the characteristics of the state as "a democratic, secular, and social state governed by rule of law, within the notions of

---

[49]The 1969 amendment (November 6, 1969) was annulled on procedural grounds (Decision of June 16, 1970, No. 1970/31). The court rejected the application (Decision of April 3, 1971, No. 1971/37) for annulment with regards to form and substance in the 1970 amendment (April 17, 1970). See Olcay in this volume.

[50]Decision of June 16, 1970, No. 1970/31 and Decision of April 3, 1971, No. 1971/37. See Gözler (2008).

[51]During the debates on the 1961 Constitution, the speaker of the House of Representatives specifically argued against inclusion of characteristics of the state among unamendable provisions. Onar (1993), p. 10.

[52]Gözler (2008), pp. 95–97.

[53]Decision of April 15, 1975, No. 1975/87; Decisions of March 23, 1976, No. 1976/1963 and October 12, 1976, No. 1976/46; Decision of January 28, 1977, No. 1977/4; Decision of September 27, 1977, No. 1977/117. See Gözler (2008), pp. 42–45 and Olcay in this volume.

[54]Roznai and Yolcu (2012), p. 196.

[55]See Yayla (1983), p. 133.

public peace, national solidarity and justice, respecting human rights, loyal to the nationalism of Atatürk, and based on the fundamental tenets set forth in the preamble".[56] Article 3 enumerates its symbols and declares, "The State of Turkey, with its territory and nation, is an indivisible entity. Its language is Turkey. Its flag, the form of which is prescribed by the relevant law, is composed of a white crescent and star on a red background. Its national anthem is the 'Independence March'. Its capital is Ankara". Finally Article 4, protects these provisions and states that these shall not be amended, nor shall their amendment be proposed". However, the unamendability clause itself is not self-entrenched.[57] With respect to the powers of the Constitutional Court, it is authorized to examine whether the formal requirements for constitutional amendments, as listed in the Constitution (Article 148), have been fulfilled.

Until the controversial ruling of the Constitutional Court in 2008, the court rejected three requests for substantive review, once in 1987 and twice in 2007.[58] However, with the 2008 decision, the Court declared that the two constitutional amendments regarding the principle of equality (Article 10) and the right to education (Article 42) that aimed to end the headscarf ban for female university, were unconstitutional because they were contrary to the characteristics of the republic as provided in the unamendable Article 2 of the Constitution.[59] The 2008 decision of the Constitutional Court is also significant for the fact that the Court in its reasoning stipulated that, Article 4 because it was made by the original constituent power and if amended it would render the unamendable articles meaningless, is itself also unamendable.[60] In a separate 2010 decision, it further clarified its position vis-à-vis the unamendability article and explained that Article 4, as the assurance of the first three unamendable articles has innate unamendable quality.[61] Constitutional Court's decision, in a way, brought to a halt the debate among constitutional scholars whether through a double amendment procedure it was possible to circumvent the existing entrenchment of the constitution. Because the unamendability clause (Article 4) itself was not self-entrenched against amendment, some have argued that through a two-stage procedure, it was possible to first repeal the unamendability provision prohibiting the first three articles' amendment, and then amend the formerly unamendable articles. Constitutional Court in its decisions clarified that Article 4 was tacitly self-entrenched.

---

[56]For a discussion of these characteristics, see Tanör (2012), pp. 151–152 and Özbudun (2005), p. 31.

[57]According to Albert, this presents as a "design flaw" as the unamendable provisions are susceptible to double amendment. See Albert (2015), pp. 7–8.

[58]See Özbudun (2014), p. 33.

[59]Roznai and Yolcu (2012). Also Özbudun (2008b).

[60]Decision June 5, 2008, E. 2008/16; K. 2008/116, Resmi Gazete 22.10.2008 no 27032. Sevinç (2012), p. 10.

[61]Decision July 7, 2010 E. 2010/49.

After the Turkish Constitutional Court invalidated the 2008 amendments, despite the preclusion against substantial review, it became another rallying point for the critics of the 1982 Constitution.[62] Venice Commission referred to the broad conceptualization of the characteristics of the Turkish Republic in the unamendable provisions as problematic because it has become "basis for the review of constitutional amendments in a manner that has no parallel in other European states."[63] Through the utilization of unamendable articles, constitutional change has become a significant matter of political contention between political parties.[64] However, the discontent is not limited to the Constitutional Court's reliance on these articles to assume substantive review power. Different partial and total proposals produced by civil society organization reveal that none call for maintaining the 1982 Constitution's eternal clauses in their entirety.

Turkish Industrialists and Businessmen Association's (TÜSİAD)[65] 1992 report before the 1991 elections recommended a constitutional amendment that would limit unamendability to the principle of Republican state before the ordinary parliament embarks upon a project of drafting a new constitution. The report also advised that the vague notions stated under Article 2, such as "public peace" and "national solidarity" are eliminated, and ideological provisions such as "nationalism of Atatürk" are removed and reference to "fundamental tenets set forth in preamble" that are difficult to identify and agree upon is abolished. The TÜSİAD report also changed the provision on language, to "official language" under Article 3. The Union of Chambers and Commodity Exchanges of Turkey (TOBB) 2000 report maintains the Article 4, the intangibility clause prohibiting amendment but makes subtle changes to first three articles.[66] Turkish Union of Bar Associations (TBB) 2001 study maintains the unamendability clause protecting the first three articles but provides for it under article 184 of its proposal. The content of the second article is changed to fortify commitment to human rights. TBB's 2007 study actually expands the scope of unamendable articles and includes a fourth article that stipulates that "sovereignty belongs to people" among irrevocable articles. The 2007 constitutional study headed by Professor Dr. Ergun Özbudun and prepared at the request of AKP do not include the unamendability provision but does change the content of the Article 2 to eliminate "public peace" and "national solidarity and

---

[62]Özbudun (2008a).

[63]Buquicchio (2010).

[64]Yüksel (2007), p. 356.

[65]Türk Sanayicileri ve İşadamları Derneği in Turkish. Its report before the 1991 elections have maintained the view that the ordinary parliament has the authority to draft a new constitution. The report, prepared by nine constitutional law scholars refer to Turkey's 1924 Constitution as a precedent for such authority where the parliamentary Constitutional Commission prepared a draft that was ratified without a public referendum. Bülent Tanör, one of the drafters of this report, argues in his book that to deny that the ordinary parliaments cannot make a new constitution would be to make the claim that only in the aftermath of revolutions and through the establishment of "constituent assembly" a new constitution can be drafted. See Tanör (2012), pp. 172–173.

[66]Yazıcı (2001), p. 58.

justice" notions, but not "nationalism of Atatürk" and embraces the notion of "based on human rights" rather than the 1982 Constitution's weak provision that says "respecting human rights".[67]

These reports and constitutional draft studies do share some common features. First, all proposed changes to unamendable articles of the 1982 Constitution. Second, all texts referred above do eliminate "public peace" and "national solidarity and justice" notions from the second article on characteristics of the Republic. Third, all drafts do change the provision from "state language" to "state's official language" under Article 3.[68] It is important to note that proposals for constitutional change are not limited to these drafts. By the time Turkey embarked on a constitutional change effort in 2011, the fate of unamendable articles under a possible new framework was unknown.

3 The Failed Process of Constitutional-Making in Turkey

Turkey after going through "gradual, never completed, yet highly significant packages of constitutional changes" entered a constitution-making process in 2011.[69] The constitutional crisis of 2007 over the election of a new president, party closure case against the AKP and the Constitutional Court's unconstitutional constitutional amendment decision in 2008, AKP began to favor a unilateral approach with regards to constitutional change.[70] But it is also important to note that a conciliatory approach was attempted with no avail couple of times before AKP-backed constitutional amendments. In 2008, Köksal Topsal, the President of the TGNA sent out letters to the chairmen of all political parties calling to set up commission to discuss constitution, parliamentary by-laws and EU harmonization legislation. However, it had failed because CHP, the main opposition party, did not respond to it.[71] President Abdullah Gül also made such an attempt to establish a reconciliation among political parties, which was also unsuccessful. AKP moved on with a package of twenty-six articles that were approved in a referendum on September 12, 2010.[72] However, the intensely polarized atmosphere of the

---

[67]See also Yüksel (2007),pp. 357–363.

[68]Yazıcı (2001), p. 60.

[69]Arato (2010a), p. 476.

[70]In early 2007, the ruling AKP government asked a group of experts to draft a new constitution, criticized for both its content and the unilateral process of drafting. Discussed above, the draft constitution was set aside. See Table 1 for the timeline of events in Baburoglu and Göker (2014), p. 374. See also Yüksel (2007).

[71]'Turkey's main opposition CHP rules out compromise over constitution' (Hürriyet Daily News, 16 February 2009) <http://www.hurriyet.com.tr/english/domestic/11015880.asp>.

[72]Arato (2010b), p. 345. See also Yüksel (2007), p. 351.

referendum did not quell the constitutional debate, rather with the approaching general elections, the topic of a new and "civilian" constitution became the chief issue.[73] Despite an overwhelming victory for AKP, the party failed to get the two-thirds of the seats in the Parliament, which would have made it possible for it to unilaterally draft and ratify a constitution.[74]

Despite achieving a landslide victory, AKP lacked the constitutional mandate to unilaterally draft a new constitution. However, all political parties that had campaigned for a new constitution during the general elections, after the results also reiterated their positions. Thus, the idea of a broad-based participatory committee became a possibility. AKP had won 50% of the votes (327 seats), CHP won 26% (135 seats), MHP 13% (53 seats), the independents, running under the banner of EDOB,[75] and supported by the pro-Kurdish BDP received 6.5% of the votes (35 seats). Proponents of an ordinary parliament drafting a new constitution argued that the parliament, despite the exclusionary electoral law with a 10% threshold, had 95% representation of Turkish voters.[76]

AKP proposed the idea of establishing a committee to draft a new constitution. With the initiative of the presidency of the parliament, Constitutional Conciliation Commission (AUK), with equal representation from four parties represented in the parliament was formed in the late 2011.[77] Regardless of the distribution of the seats in the parliament, the Justice and Development Party (AKP), Republican People's Party (CHP), Nationalist Movement Party (MHP), and Peace and Democracy Party (BDP) were given equal representation of three members in the commission.[78] The commission, distinct from the standing committees of the Grand National Assembly of Turkey (TBMM), was established as an *ad hoc* commission that prepared its own working principles.[79] It was a "purely political body" that was not subject to the regular rules and principles of the Parliament.[80] The "elite-driven process" was within an institutional framework that was based on limited consultation, but nevertheless, was carried out with success previously in 1995 and 2001.[81] The most important aspect of the working principles, 15 articles in total, was that the

---

[73]Besides the criticism directed at the 1982 Constitution, one of the main contentions of proponents of new constitution is that "none of the three Republican Constitutions (those of 1924, 1961, and 1982) was made by a freely chosen and broadly representative constituent assembly through inter-party negotiations and compromises", see Özbudun (2012), p. 39.

[74]Cengiz and Hoffmann (2012), p. 255.

[75]Labor, Democracy and Freedom Bloc, Emek Demokrasi ve Özgürlük Blogu, in Turkish.

[76]Considering that the voter turnout in the 2011 elections was 87.6%, in the new parliament 83.14% of the Turkish electorate is represented. Barın (2014), p. XXIV.

[77]Arato and Tombus (2013).

[78]The four political parties that have groups in the parliament were asked to identify three deputies by October 11, 2012 to join the commission.

[79]Turkey had relied on a similar model of establishing an ad hoc conciliation commission during the two successful amendment-making processes of 1995 and 2001.

[80]Oder (2014), p. 137.

[81]Ibid.

decisions would be taken in consensus with all the political parties.[82] Before the deliberations began, the commission until May 4, 2012 listened to the inputs of social organizations including 42 political parties, universities and other institutions, 39 professional associations and unions, 79 nongovernmental organizations, foundations and platforms[83] in three sub-committees.[84] The commission also called for individuals and civil society organizations to communicate their views via the website set up for the constitution,[85] post mail, and e-mail and received inputs from 64 thousand people, including 440 civil society organizations.[86] In addition to these, meetings were held in different provinces of Turkey and surveys were conducted to collect citizen opinions, which provided an opportunity for people to directly voice their opinions.[87]

From the beginning, the commission's work was not embraced by all sectors of the society. On the one hand, some maintained that the parliament lacked the authority to enact a new constitution. Similarly the ad-hoc nature of the commission, with no legal basis in the constitution or in rules of procedures of the parliament led to claims that it lacked legal authority.[88] Those concerned with the representativeness of the commission, referred to the high threshold of the Turkish electoral system (10%) that have led to the parliament in power and called for a specifically established Constituent Assembly that would have ultimate representativeness of all social clusters of Turkish society.[89] Also, those critical of ordinary legislators working as constitution-makers raised the issue that daily politics would

---

[82]For the Working Methods of the Constitutional Conciliation Commission, see TBMM Anayasalar Sitesi <http://yenianayasa.tbmm.gov.tr/calismaesaslari.aspx>.

[83]The platforms are not legal entities.

[84]Mumcu (2013), Uçum and Genç (2012). Constitution Platform organized conferences that brought together civil society actors with regular citizens and was conceived to be a medium for public deliberation, Baburoğlu and Göker (2014).

[85]The website set up for the constitution was available at https://yenianayasa.tbmm.gov.tr/default. aspx but has been renamed. Documents are preserved at TBMM Anayasalar Sitesi. For proceedings, see Komisyon Tutanaklari https://anayasa.tbmm.gov.tr/tutanak.aspx.

[86]Mumcu (2013) and Uçum and Genç (2012).

[87]Examples of these include the meetings of New Constitution Platform, Federation of the Civil Servant Associations, Turkish Union of Chambers and Commodity Exchanges (TOBB), and Economic Policy Research Foundation of Turkey (TEPAV) and the survey of Memur-Sen. See Uçum and Genç (2012).

[88]A related criticism is that the parliamentary permanent Constitutional Commission and the General Assembly are the legal authorities to refer to for constitutional change. However, such political committees have been used successfully for partial constitutional change in 1995 and 2001.

[89]According to Ginsburg, Elkins, and Blount, constituent legislatures, legislatures that also function as constitution-making bodies are more commonly observed (by itself and together with other actors) than constituent assemblies (by itself and together with other actors). See Ginsburg et al. (2009), p. 201.

muddle the constitution-making process.[90] For this substantially political process, there was no prior effort to build trust among political parties that could help alleviate their strong opposition to each other's positions. Also, there was no declaration of principles or a document that highlighted the significance of the process.[91] Although the commission had equal representation from political parties, in terms of representation of gender, it fell short. On the other hand, those who were not critical of the parliament's authority to draft a new constitution were skeptical of the working of the commission. One criticism directed at the commission was that it functioned in an undemocratic political climate where there are tacit and explicit obstacles to freedom of expression. Without first addressing these, the public opinion would be limited in its capacity. Another criticism was directed at the unanimity decision-making rule of the commission. In an atmosphere of political polarization where the political parties have firmly embedded "red lines", the requirement of achieving absolute consensus made the new constitution unattainable. The procedural principles were also limited in detail and failed to provide the imperative legal rules that could facilitate consensus-building.[92] The lack of openness of the commission's work was another point of concern.[93] In terms of inclusiveness, one major impediment is the overall illiberality of discourse in Turkey when it comes to contentious issues. The fact that the commission received abundance of opinions and suggestions from civil society did not automatically translate into civil society involvement in the process. The commission chose not to disclose the input of civil society. A much lively constitutional debate could have been accomplished, had there been free access to different proposals.[94] Having accumulated a wide range of proposals from different sectors of the society, the commission failed to to prepare a text of principles that would have guided the drafting process. The members of the commission worked in harmony for the initial months of the commission, unfazed by the polarizing political rhetoric of daily politics.[95] Part of this was because the commission postponed the discussion of more contentious issues such as the unamendable articles, native-language education, the issue of decentralization and local governance, the Preamble, and

---

[90]In the literature, there is a general skepticism against ordinary legislatures functioning as constitution-making bodies, see Elster (2006). A legislator that is elected to represent a constituency and presumably its local interests may not have the qualities that one might look for as a constitution-maker. Also, it is assumed that a legislature when designing the structure of government may choose to empower the parliament. Ginsburg, Elkins and Blount test this institutional self-interest but do not find support that legislative-centered processes are more likely than constituent assemblies to aggrandize the legislative branch. See Ginsburg et al. (2009), p. 213.

[91]Oder (2014), p. 138.

[92]Ibid.

[93]Uçum and Genç (2012).

[94]Cengiz (2014).

[95]Bozkurt (2012).

citizenship to latter dates.[96] Essentially working in a highly flexible setting without effective deadlines, participants pursued their narrow interests, engaging in negotiation but not deliberation that can overcome differences. The commission that aimed to finish the drafting in three months could not do so after 18 months of work.[97] The next section will outline the main points of contention during the drafting process regarding the unamendable article.

4   The Debate on Unamendable Articles

Before the commission held its first meeting, Cemil Çiçek, President of the Parliament and the chair of the constitutional process held a structured session that brought together professors of constitutional and public law and discussed the method of making a new constitution.[98] A central issue of the debate among the scholars was the question of whether the parliament possessed the constituent power to make a new constitution or if it was limited to amending power to revise the constitution. Hence, whether the process would lead to a new constitution or a thorough revision was from the beginning a central debate. Participants were divided into two camps between those who argued that the Parliament had the power to totally revise the constitution and those who argued that only a constituent assembly could change the constitution in its entirety.

Centered around the distinction between primary constituent power and derived constituent power, the participants of the meeting also raised the issue of unamendable articles with regard to this matter. The scholars that maintained that an ordinary legislative (derived) power lacked the power to make a new constitution without first there being a "legal (constitutional) loophole" were in the minority. Challenging the necessity of a new constitution, Professor Canikoğlu raised the question of whether the conditions that demand the birth of the authority of constituent power were present. Arguing that a "legal (constitutional) loophole" is absent, she maintained the impossibility of the parliament to claim the authority of constituent power and warned that a constitution born from such legal uncertainty would suffer from legitimacy problems in the future. Reasoning that only if the conditions that necessitate the abrogation of the 1982 Constitution exists, then it would be possible to proceed with making a new constitution; she highlighted that it would require to endow the Parliament with the authority of constitute power via a legislation that would allow it to function as a constituent assembly elected by a

---

[96]It was decided beforehand that the commission would begin their work on less contentious issues and those deemed most controversial would be referred to party leaders. Hayatsever (2012).

[97]See Oder (2014) for a thorough analysis of the failed process.

[98]For a full list of participants and the minutes of the meeting held on September 19, 2011 see TBMM Yeni Anayasa Internet Sitesi <http://yenianayasa.tbmm.gov.tr/docs/anayasa-hukukculari-ile-toplanti.pdf>.

popular vote. Absent these conditions, it would not be possible to replace the constitution. The minority that argued in favor of a constitutional convention stressed that only such an inclusive and pluralistic process could bring together different societal forces and provide the institutional framework for deliberation.[99] On the other hand, scholars that argued that the ordinary assembly has the power to make a new constitution referred to the absence of a constitutional prohibition against such an endeavor.

More than one-third of the professors specifically raised the issue of unamendable articles and considered whether they pose an obstacle to drafting a new constitution and whether in this new constitution they should be maintained. A controversial matter was the question of how an ordinary parliament that lacks constituent power and possibly utilizing the existing constitution's mechanism for amendment, could remove or alter the unamendable articles. The majority of the professors that argued in favor of maintaining the unamendable articles asserted that it was the essence of these articles that needed to be safeguarded, meaning the principles of the republic and not the articles in their entirety.[100] Professor Gören considered it to be a deceitful and unlawful act for the derived constituent power, the parliament, to change the unamendable articles. However, he argued that it could be possible to make refinements on these articles, provided that the core remains unaltered. Stressing the importance of legal continuity, Gören argued that the principles outlined in these articles have remained constant since the 1924 Constitution and their unamendability is a prohibition against the annihilation of the Constitution's identity and the legal foundational order. Only by safeguarding these principles, Gören argued, it would be possible to prevent the manifestation of contestation and societal tension.

Eleven of the 24 professors that attended the meeting called for a preliminary legislation or a document of understanding that would strengthen the legal base of the ordinary parliament's power to write a new constitution. Suggestions included adding a provision to the article regulating the amendment-making process (Article 175) that would clarify the constituent power of the parliament or allow for the election of a constituent assembly, issuing a legislation or a memorandum of understanding that would clarify the roadmap of making a new constitution. Although this was the main focus of the meeting of professors, their suggestions were not incorporated and as the next paragraphs reveal, the commission began to work without a legal framework. The status of unamendable articles in light of a constitutional replacement process remained unresolved.

A thorough review of civil society organization's inputs regarding unamendable articles is beyond the scope of this study. However, reports published elsewhere indicate that some of the civil society organizations were in favor of maintaining the

---

[99]Oder (2014), p. 137.
[100]Kentel et al. (2012).

three unamendable articles of the current constitution, while most agreed that the first three articles could be kept provided that the clause prohibiting their amendment (Article 4) do not necessarily remain.[101]

The commission began to work without resolving the debate on whether the Turkish parliament or the AUK had the original constituent power to write a new constitution in the first place and whether it could do so in consideration of unamendable articles of the 1982 Constitution. It was also not clear whether the draft that would be ultimately produced by the commission would rely on the amendment-making rule of the constitution (Article 175) and/or public referendum. TESEV-the chief think tank of Turkey, early on recognized that "the most fundamental obstacle before the progression of the new constitutional process consists of the "irrevocable provisions" of the Constitution".[102] Thus, they recommended to address this issue and "to add a clause to the new constitution that sets out the rules for enacting the new constitution and states that a public referendum would be held to pass the new constitution, irrespective of the results of the parliamentary vote; or for the current Parliament to draft and pass a bill to legally define the terms of making a new constitution".[103] However, such calls from academicians and civil society actors were disregarded and the commission embarked upon drafting without clarifying these crucial legal points. The proposal, supported by CHP, to first issue an understanding of "the new constitution's spirit and philosophy" was not embraced by the commission. The idea was to have the parties agreed on a number of constitutional principles before the commission embarked upon the process. However, the commission moved forward without establishing such a document of understanding.[104] Moreover, recognizing that the preamble and the general principles, including the unamendable articles of the 1982 Constitution regarding the form, characteristics and the symbols of the state and the unamendability clause would be the most difficult to reconcile, the commission decided to leave that section to latter dates.[105]

Thus, it was only in April 2013 that the commission began to deliberate about the unamendable articles of the 1982 Constitution. Note that this was after the AUK's self-imposed deadline at the end of March had passed.[106] The political parties' proposals submitted before the deliberations began, indicated their different positions regarding the first three articles and the fourth article on

---

[101]According to TESEV's report, a small segment of these civil society organizations (such as KAMU-SEN) also are against the idea of drafting a new constitution. Uçum and Genç (2012).

[102]Ibid.

[103]Ibid.

[104]In South Africa, the political parties had established such an understanding of constitutional principles before they held the elections for a constituent assembly.

[105]Cumhuriyet 'Anayasada kriz önlendi', (Cumhuriyet, 9 May 2012) http://www.cumhuriyet.com.tr/haber/diger/341104/Anayasada_kriz_otelendi.html.

[106]The original tentative deadline was the end of 2012. Radikal 'Anayasa'da Kader Günü' (Radikal, 1 April 2013) <http://www.radikal.com.tr/turkiye/anayasada_kader_gunu-1127494>.

unamendability.[107] The right-wing nationalist party MHP did not propose any change of any kind in the first four articles. Both AKP and BDP did not have any provision on unamendability. The AKP's proposal maintained the gist of the first three articles but did introduce changes,[108] the CHP proposed some minor changes regarding the wording[109] and the BDP's proposal offered the most comprehensive change.[110] The main discussion on the issue of unamendability took place on April 17, 2013[111] and after it was understood that the consensus could not be reached, the commission moved onto next articles. By the time, the commission held its session on "unamendable articles" of the 1982 Constitution, it had agreed on 59 articles.[112] However, none of these included the difficult topics such as citizenship and mother language. Thus, when the commission began to deliberate the unamendable articles for the second time (on August 21, 26, and 27), the unamendable articles were the first on the agenda of a package of articles that includes the first three articles of the constitution, Article 4 (the unamendability provision) the definition of citizenship, and the right to education in mother language. It is important to note that the commission was dissolved in late November 2013.

Next the debate that took place over these four days will be analyzed to identify the points raised by members of different parties, trace whether arguments evolved

---

[107]To review political parties' proposals, see Yeni Anayasa TBMM <http://yenianayasa.tbmm. gov.tr/siyasipartiteklifleri.aspx>. Also see Barın (2014), pp. 7–14 for a comparison of the 1982 articles, AKP, CHP, MHP and BDP proposals and each of their final proposals and in cases where consensus is reached, the agreed provision of the commission.

[108]Regarding Article 2, AKP proposed to eliminate "public peace" and "national solidarity and justice", "loyal to the nationalism of Atatürk," and "based on the fundamental tenets set forth in the preamble" and strengthen the human rights provision by replacing "respecting human rights" with "based on human right". Regarding Article 3, AKP changed the provision on language, from "state language" to "official language" and instead of stating ""The State of Turkey, with its territory and nation, is an indivisible entity", AKP proposes "The State of Turkey is an invisible entity as a territory and nation".

[109]Regarding Article 2, CHP proposed only a subtle change to replace "respecting human rights" with "based on human right". CHP proposal did not introduce any changes to Article 3.

[110]BDP proposal did not include the Article 1, which proclaims, "Turkish state is a Republic,"— the rationale being that the phrase "Turkish Republic" is stated in the following provisions. BDP's proposal for Article 2 highlights that the Turkish Republic recognizes plurality and maintains impartiality. It also adds that the administrative structure of the state is based on the principle of decentralization and the state's territorial integrity is inviolable. BDP's maintains the symbols of the state as it is dictated in the 1982 Constitution but expands the provision on language to include that state's official language is Turkish, all citizens have a duty and a right to learn the official language, regional parliaments may decide to use a second official language, everyone in their private life and relations with public offices have the right to use their mother tongue along with the official language, and the state is obliged to respect, protect and ensure that all languages that make up the cultural heritage of the country is used and developed.

[111]The members of the commission do deliver their opinions on unamendable articles before that date (April 17, 2013) as well. However those sessions such as on March 18, April 8, and April 16 were not specifically conceived to be on these issues.

[112]The commission had discussed and written down 113 articles with reservations.

as a result of negotiation and determine to what extent the issue of unamendability interacted with other matters of drafting a new constitution.

On the one hand, the members of the commission debated whether they had the power to change the unamendable articles of the constitution; as some formulated whether they had the original constituent power or were limited to derived constituent power. On the other hand, the content of these clauses were debated. The earlier sessions (specifically April 17 and August 21, 2013) centered around the issue of unamendability. However, the issue also appeared even when the commission moved onto discussing the substance of the general principles of the state (the first three articles). Instead of going chronologically, the analysis here summarizes and highlights some of the points raised by the members of the AUK. AKP from the beginning advocated that the new constitution should not have any unamendable articles and the fact that the current constitution had them was not a legal obstacle for drafting a new constitution. Ahmet Iyimaya's early statement that if needed, the 1982 Constitution can be abrogated was not raised once the commission began to seriously discuss these articles. AKP maintained two points regarding the legal implications of unamendable articles in the existing text and whether they propose an obstacle. First, AKP argued that the parliament has the original constituent power because the question of 'who has the constituent power' is determined by the end result, i.e., whoever made the constitution has the constituent power. Second, AKP representative Mustafa Şentop made a compelling argument, which CHP representative Rıza Türmen also found credible and useful to overcome the issue of unamendability. According to Şentop, the wording of the unamendability clause (Article 4) is such that it does not offer an absolute prohibition. Article 4 prohibits the amendment of "the characteristics of the Republic in Article 2," it does not prohibit amending the entire article. Thus, Şentop reasons that Article 2 can be amended to eliminate vague and nonlegal provisions that do not necessarily fall under "the characteristics of the Republic". According to him, even if the argument is made that the parliament does not have the original constituent power to make a new constitution (by replacing the unamendable articles), it does have the power to amend Article 2 as long as the substance of the article remains.

Some constitutional law scholars, also embrace the argument that Article 4 does not actually offer an absolute entrenchment but that it allows for change in the wording and expression, provided that its attributions regarding the characteristics of the Republic remain unaltered.[113] Thus, an ordinary parliament that does not claim to possess original constituent power could also make such changes to its wording. For instance, according to Yazıcı, changing the wording from "respecting human rights" to "based on human rights" would only strengthen the commitment

---

[113]For example, according to Sevinç, Article 4 does not require maintaining the first three articles verbatim. He argues that the article allows for changing the wording in order to introduce expressions to strengthen it, as long as the core of the articles are maintained. This solution, according to Sevinç, can provide for a more liberal reading of the unamendability clause and work around the Constitutional Court's decision that Article 4 is indeed, although tacitly, self-entrenched. See, Sevinç (2012), p. 36. Also see Yazıcı (2001), pp. 60–61, for a similar reading of the article.

to human rights. The constitutional law professor also holds the view that "public peace, national solidarity, and justice" define the "state respectful of human rights", rather than the state per se.[114] Professor Gören, during the structured meeting between the public law professors and Speaker of the Parliament before the commission began its deliberations, also argued that it is possible to introduce some modifications to Article 2, provided that these do not infringe upon the characteristics of the republic.[115] However, others disagree. For instance, according to Kemal Gözler, each of these statements defines one characteristic of the state.[116] Rıza Türmen ponders why the drafters of the 1982 Constitution did not simply said that Article 4 prohibits Article 1, 2, and 3 and asks whether it is possible that the unamendability clause offers not an absolute entrenchment but a qualified one. Another question that Rıza Türmen brings to the table is whether the prohibition against Article 2 also covers the preamble- because Article 2's definition of the republic includes the phrase "based on the fundamental tenets set forth in the preamble". According to Ahmet Iyimaya, the answer is positive and the preamble through that provision must also be unamendable. However, according to Süheyl Batum, the preamble is outside the scope of unamendability. It is a rather interesting point raised by Türmen since the preamble was amended before in 1995 and 2001.

Şentop makes a similar argument regarding the unamendability of Article 3, defining the symbols of the state—including the language.[117] According to Şentop, unamendability clause does not prohibit Article 3 in its entirety, but its provisions and thus allows changes to its wording- therefore it is possible to change the wording to "official language is Turkish".[118] Besides these points, AKP representatives make references to Constitutional Court's past decisions based on the unamendability clause. In essence, raising the "enhancing judiciary's power objection" that Roznai defines, AKP argues that judicial enforcement of unamendability has historically led to political problems and Constitutional Court's assumption of political and ideological judicial review.[119] Moreover, AKP

---

[114]Additionally Yazıcı argues that these notions (public peace, national solidarity and justice) do not have the same legal weight as "democratic, secular and social state", Yazıcı (2001), p. 62.

[115]See explanations by Professor Zafer Gören during the meeting held on September 19, 2011 at TBMM Yeni Anayasa Internet Sitesi <http://yenianayasa.tbmm.gov.tr/docs/anayasa-hukukcular iile-toplanti.pdf>. p. 17.

[116]Ibid, p. 61.

[117]Another argument raised by Şentop is that the unamendability clause does not offer full protection against amendment. He draws a scenario where an amendment to Article 2 is passed in the parliament with the approval of 500 deputies, where the president does not take it to Constitutional Court for review and there is not enough members of the TGNA to take it to Constitutional Court. Then the Article 4 will not be able to protect the unamendable clauses. August 21, 2013 minutes.

[118]See Professor Gören's similar reasoning during the meeting held on September 19, 2011 at TBMM Yeni Anayasa Internet Sitesi <http://yenianayasa.tbmm.gov.tr/docs/anayasa-hukukcula riile-toplanti.pdf>. p. 17.

[119]The argument raised by AKP representatives fall under what Roznai summarizes as "enhancing judiciary's power objection". See Roznai' s article in this volume for more on the subordination objection raised against unamendability.

members question why even after the drafters of unamendable articles have left this earth the clauses must remain, raising the "dead hand" objection[120]; argue that unamendability may become problematic when new principles arise or the existing ones become void and contend that the provisions of the current unamendable articles are internalized, thus do not need entrenchment since we can trust the people who have embraced and internalized them. Another argument that AKP puts forward in favor of eliminating unamendability in the new constitution is what Roznai describes as "the revolutionary or forcible objection".[121] According to Professor Yusuf Şevki Hakyemez, AKP's consultant, denying the TGNA the power to draft a new constitution because it does not have original constituent power and because the existing constitution includes unamendable articles, incite recourse to extra-constitutional means.[122] AKP members also bring forward "the limited effectiveness of unamendability" argument,[123] providing a scenario where an amendment is introduced to Article 2 or 3, with a high majority in the parliament and since the Constitutional Court does not carry ex officio review, if nobody authorized by the constitution to apply for annulment do not take the matter to the court and time lapses for application, the Constitutional Court fails to provide juridical oversight over unamendability.[124] Finally, a point raised by an AKP member holds that constitutions are not sacred texts that can protect, through unamendability, a country's social structure.

AKP members do not rely on "undemocratic objection",[125] which rests on the argument that unamendability clauses 'deny citizens the democratic right to amend their own constitution and in so doing divest them for the basic sovereign rights of popular choice and continuing self-definition'.[126] A rather strong objection, the reason that AKP members' and similarly BDP members' decision not to raise the "undemocratic objection" is most probably because they do not want to perpetuate the suspicion that these two parties actually may prefer to change the foundational principles and symbols of the republic, if they are not immunized against amendment.

---

[120]See Roznai's article in this volume for more on "dead hand" objection.

[121]See Roznai's article in this volume for more on the revolutionary or forcible objection raised against unamendability.

[122]Professor Hakyemez's argument (April 17, 2013) rests on a report by TÜSİAD published in 1991 and also includes reference to TGNA's prior experience, in 1924, in drafting a new constitution.

[123]See Roznai's article in this volume for more on the limited effectiveness of unamendability argument.

[124]According to Article 149, access to apply for annulment is granted to the largest opposition parliamentary group and one- fifth of the members of Parliament as well as the president and the prime minister. The right to apply for annulment lapses sixty day after publication of the contested law in the Official Gazette, Article 150.

[125]See Roznai's article in this volume for more on the undemocratic objection raised against unamendability.

[126]Albert (2010), pp. 664, 667.

There are differences among the positions of CHP representatives. Atilla Kart gives examples of other countries that do have unamendability but argues that while it is possible to do some improvement and strengthening with the first three articles, their unamendability must be protected. Rıza Türmen, for instance, believes there can be consensus on the issue of unamendability. However, from the beginning of the debate on unamendable articles, the fellow representative Süheyl Batum argues that only the amendment mechanism outlined in the constitution can be used and every article of the constitution can be changed and replaced except the una-mendable article because the commission is exercising derived constituent power. His argument rests on several, sometimes contradictory points. He argues that the external interference of the prime minister to the constitution-making process and his declaration that if the other parties reject the presidential system, AKP plans to introduce its own amendment has made the original constituent power argument meaningless. He reasons that a commission that cannot agree on the constitution's provisions regarding the executive, legislative and judiciary branch is only able to offer a partial constitutional change and as such, there is no original constituent power. He contends that AKP is planning to take the amendments agreed so far to a referendum and thus what the commission is engaging in is an exercise of derived constituent power.[127] He also anticipates that the real intention is to be able to amend the first three articles one day and that is why AKP (and BDP) are against unamendability. Batum insists on the distinction between original and derived constituent power. On August 26th meeting, he warns against double amendment/ two-stage process, where first the parliament amends the unamendability clause and then the unamendable articles. Able to convince his fellow representatives from the party, CHP members decide to withdraw back their proposal to introduce changes to first three articles, as long as there is no consensus on the issue of unamend-ability. CHP establishes unamendability as its "red line"—a matter it refuses to derogate from under any circumstances.

MHP from the beginning argues that the unamendability must be maintained (as well as the substance of these articles). Their argument rests on the contention that what the commission is tasked to do is to draft a constitution for an established state, and not to establish a new state, and thus the unamendable articles as well as unamendability must be maintained. A second argument provided by MHP is that the political parties during their electoral campaign (the 2011 general elections) did not elaborate on the content of "the new constitution", did not express their posi-tions on the unamendable clause, and hence do not have original constituent power. The normative argument MHP makes in favor of maintaining unamendability rests on the fear that Turkey may face a threat to its integrity and the unamendability clause protects the foundational philosophy of the Turkish state.

---

[127]Related to this, Batum argues that AKP is under some type of mandate from Abdullah Öcalan and Murat Karayılan (leaders of PKK—the outlawed Kurdistan Workers' Party) to pass the amendments as quickly as possible.

BDP, like AKP also advocates that there should be no unamendability clause in the future constitution. BDP representative Meral Daniş Beştaş believes that the distinction between original and derived constituent power is theoretical and the parliament has the optimum representativeness. Bengi Yıldız argues that unamendability is outmoded, constitutions are not sacred and inserting unamendability only puts handcuffs on the future generations. A point raised by BDP members several times is that if the military regime can make the claim of constituent power, so can a parliament freely elected. BDP is especially troubled about the fact that it was the National Security Council (NSC), the chamber made up of coup organizers that decided to expand the scope of unamendable provisions when the Consultative Assembly, the civilian chamber had only included the republican form of state as the irrevocable article. A point that is also raised by AKP members with reference to "five generals", insinuating the members of the NSC, is that coup-makers have attempted to rule for generations to come. Against this reliance on unamendable provisions as "paternalistic devices" that the generals planted based on the belief that the republic was under threat, BDP and AKP argue that maintaining the unamendability provision convey the impression that trust cannot be placed on the public and its representatives and only the coup-makers may provide the most solid shield against threats to the republic.[128]

A careful review of the debate on unamendability that took place in Turkey's Constitutional Conciliation Commission (AUK) reveals that although it was quite technical, as the BDP member Meral Daniş Beştaş recognized, arguments were fundamentally based on political identities, ideologies and perspectives.[129] After discussing unamendability for two days (April 17 and August 21, 2013) and not reaching consensus, the commission decided to move onto the substance of the articles. Immediately the commission achieved consensus on Article 1 on the republican form of the state. For the next two days, the commission discussed Article 2 and 3, however, because the issue of unamendability was unresolved, the discussion revolved around that issue as well. The debate on substance did not proceed as a negotiation but with each member clinging to their party positions. The debates also deviated from the content to other general issues, debating the question of ethnicity, nation-state, the history of Kurds, the history of the republic and presidential system, reflecting how politicized the issue of unamendability is in the Turkish context. For instance, the debate on Article 2 (August 26, 2013) focused on the presidential system proposal of AKP. The second and third sessions revolved around the question of whether there is a foundational philosophy of the state, and if there is, what it is, and quickly moved to issues of ethnicity and race. The members of the commission exhausted the debate without reaching consensus. Across all political parties, members engaged in backward-looking arguments such as the

---

[128]Stephan Michel and Ignacio N. Cofone "Credible Commitment Or Paternalism? The Case Of Unamendability" in this volume.

[129]Özgür Sevgi Göral, one of the consultants to the commission, argues on August 27, 2013 that the unamendability is not an issue where there is an established scientific view, as positivists claim and adds that the scientific judgment does include political opinion.

Constitutional Court's controversial decisions to review constitutional amendments' compatibility with the unamendable article; the TGNA's experience of drafting a constitution (the 1924 Constitution); the insertion of Article 2 and 3 by the National Security Members; the experience of the Independence War and the fear of history repeating itself; with references to Ottoman Empire and recent history of the Middle East. The weight of history, exemplary or alarming directed the nature of the debates.

As a result of the shortcomings of the working methods with respect to consensus and trust-building, every day political tensions are reflected in these debates.[130] The scheduled meeting to discuss Article 3 (August 27, 2013) witnessed a heated debate between members of AKP and CHP regarding CHP's member Batum's objection to article on "right to travel" that had previously achieved consensus among the commission member. Lack of a clear roadmap and essentially no deadlines allowed for an open-ended process in which it became possible to resume deliberations on articles already agreed-on, which are outside of the scope of the meetings. Another shortcoming of the commission that vitiated the debate on the substance of these articles is the lack of detail in principles and working methods of the commission. Absence of clear rules regarding the consultants position in the commission, led to agitated exchanges between consultant Yavuz Atar, and MHP member Oktay Öztürk and CHP member Süheyl Batum.

The issue of trust arises in different contexts. For instance, during the April 17th meeting MHP argued that if there is an agreement on the form, characteristics and the symbols of the Turkish state, then others need to inspire confidence and agree to not change the unamendable articles of the 1982 Constitution. AKP members, on the other hand, argued that there is no need to entrench articles, it is important to place trust on the public. CHP members (most notably Batum) fear several scenarios regarding the presidential system and partial revision of the constitution through a referendum. The lack of trust precludes the members from making compromises.

In the end, the commission is not able to reach a consensus on unamendability—whether to maintain it; if so, to entrench which articles and with respect to Article 2 there is no consensus on its substance. However, with regards to Article 3 AKP, CHP and MHP agree to preserve it as it is in the constitution. AKP withdraws its proposal to change the language of the provision from "Its language is Turkish" to "Its official language is Turkish". AKP member Iyimaya resolves that regardless of what it says, the state does not have a "special" language and in any case the title of the articles says "official language". AKP's compromise rests on the understanding that both expressions can possibly be interpreted the same.

The debates reveal that MHP and BDP maintain their original positions regarding both the issue of unamendability and the substance of the current constitution's unamendable articles. CHP members' position changed. Although CHP was initially in favor of making wording improvements to first three articles,

---

[130]Oder (2014), p. 139.

provided that the unamendability clause remained intact later they reverse their position and become against any change regarding the first four articles. Although CHP makes the argument that AKP is using unamendability issue as a bargaining chip for the presidential system, which has been the single most contentious issue brought to the table by the ruling party, the difference in opinions within CHP are also noteworthy. AKP also changes its position, it agrees to Article 3's current formulation. BDP, at the final hour of the debate during the closing remarks states that provided that they can agree on the principles of the state, they would be willing to negotiate including the general issue of unamendability. Thus, the commission makes a full circle to the issue of unamendability without reaching any consensus on the matter.

5 Conclusion

The 2011–2013 experience of the AUK was an exercise in constitution-making that remained as an exercise. For scholars, its minutes offer a great insight but remains as such. It is easy to argue that it was destined to fail when the participating political actors had such divergent positions and were clinging to their red lines in an institutional design that did not foster trust-building. Absence of a dispute-resolution process when the debates hit deadlocks, provided the ammunition to hold onto political parties' initial policy preferences.[131] The requirement to have absolute agreement between four parties also made the dynamic less flexible. Political parties did not gradually converge on polarizing issues such as citizenship, education in mother tongue, decentralization and presidential system but instead insisted on their own proposals. The ruling-party's insistence on a shift to presidential system inhibited the rest of the commission from engaging in meaningful participation when they anticipated such transformation would take place in any case. However, a detailed look into the minutes on the unamendability issue reveals that the failure to clearly define the procedure of making a new constitution, not having a guideline on the unamendability clause of the 1982 Constitution and not establishing an understanding of the spirit of the new constitution, has played a significant role in complicating the process. Questions exhaustively discussed remained unresolved: Is it possible to change the unamendable articles? If so, how? Will the new constitution maintain an unamendability clause? If so, which articles will be protected from amendment?

The commission did agree on articles that are relatively easy to "reconcile", most related to basic rights and freedoms. However, the members of the commission could not agree on most contentious issues of Turkey related to Kurdish issue, the relation between state and religion and the form of government—specifically AKP's insistence to switch from the parliamentary system. True, it was not simply

---

[131]Oder (2014), p. 139.

the impasse over unamandable articles that led to the dissolution of the commission. In addition to major contestation regarding a shift to presidential system advocated by the AKP, the realpolitik of the upcoming elections also made it unlikely that the political parties could reach consensus. According to Article 15 of the Working Methods, the commission was to be repealed if any of the political parties withdrew from the table. With the local elections in March 2014 and the presidential elections in August 2014 and unable to move forward, the commission reached a deadlock and was incapable of overcoming it. The ruling party, AKP, which would later espouse a unilateral approach to constitutional change, withdrew from the table. Sharing the development that the commission had reached an impasse, Cemil Çiçek- the president of the commission announced that it was time to conclude the work of the body. After years of disagreement among constitutional law professors of Turkey regarding unamendability, politicians proved that they also could not settle it.

References

Albert R (2010) Constitutional handcuffs. Ariz St L 42:664, 667
Albert R (2015) Amending constitutional amendment rules. Int J Const Law 13:7, 8
Arato A (2010a) Democratic constitution-making and unfreezing the Turkish process. J Philos Soc Crit 36:476
Arato A (2010b) The constitutional reform proposal of the Turkish Government: the return of majority imposition. Constellations 17:345
Arato A, Tombus E (2013) Learning from success, learning from failure: South Africa, Hungary, Turkey and Egypt. J Philos Soc Crit 39:427–441
Atikcan EO, Öge K (2012) Referendum campaigns in polarized societies: the case of Turkey. Turk Stud 13:449–470
Baburoglu ON, Göker GZ (2014) Going large scale: the polling conference process for participatory constitution making in Turkey. Act Res 12:374
Barın T (2014) Türkiye'nin Yeni Anayasa Arayışı: 2011–2013 TBMM Anayasa Uzlaşma Komisyonu Tecrübesi, 1st edn. On İki Levha Yayıncılık, Istanbul
Belge C (2006) Friends of the court: The Republican Alliance and selective activism of the constitutional court of Turkey. Law Soc Rev 40:653
Bozkurt G (2012) Turkish PM's sincerity test in the new constitution. Hürriyet Daily News, http://www.hurriyetdailynews.com/turkish-pms-sincerity-test-in-the-new-constitution.aspx?pageID=238&nID=16853&NewsCatID=342. Accessed on 26 Mar 2012
Buquicchio (2010) Keynote speech: democratization process in Turkey in light of the new constitution, 'Turkey in Europe' Conference, Istanbul November 2010. http://www.venice.coe.int/Newsletter/NEWSLETTER_2010_04/8_Speech_TUR_EN.html
Cengiz F (2014) The future of democratic reform in Turkey: constitutional moment or constitutional process? Gov Oppos 49:682
Cengiz F, Hoffmann L (2012) The 2011 general elections in Turkey: potential implications on domestic and international politics in the shadow of a discourse change? Parliam Aff 65:255
Coşkun V (2013) Constitutional amendments under the justice and development party rule. Insight Turk 15:95
Doğanay U (2007) The Turkish parliament on democracy. Parliam Aff 60:388

Elster J (2006) Legislatures as constituent assemblies. In: Bauman RW, Kahana T (eds) The least examined branch: the role of legislatures in the constitutional state. Cambridge University Press, Cambridge

Erdem FH, Heper Y (2011) Türkiye Cumhuriyeti Anayasaları ve Anayasa Önerileri (Madde Karşılaştırmalı), 1st edn. SETA Yayınları XV, Istanbul

Ginsburg T, Elkins Z, Blount J (2009) Does the process of constitution-making matter? Annu Rev Law Soc Sci 5:201

Gönenç L (2004) The 2001 amendments to the 1982 Constitution of Turkey. Ankara L Rev 1:89

Gözler K (2008) Judicial review of constitutional amendments: a comparative study. Ekin Press, Bursa

Göztepe E, Çelebi A (2012) Demokratik Anayasa: Görüşler ve Öneriler, 1st edn. Metis, Canada

Hayatsever H (2012) Panel for new charter starts landmark duty in Turkey. Hürriyet Daily News, http://www.hurriyetdailynews.com/panel-for-new-charter-starts-landmark-duty-in-turkey.aspx? pageID=238&nid=19568. Accessed on 30 Apr 2012

Hein M (2015) Eternity clauses: never say never. Katapult Cartography and Social Science Magazine (2015). http://katapult-magazin.de/en/artikel/article-katapult/fulltext/never-say-never/. Accessed on 4 May 2015

Kalaycıoğlu E (2011) The Turkish–EU Odyssey and political regime change in Turkey. S Eur Soc Polit 16:265

Kentel F, Köker L, Genc O (2012) Making of a new constitution in Turkey: Monitoring Report October 2011–January 2012. TESEV, http://tesev.org.tr/Upload/Publication/f100d8f6-928b-4c32-8a1a-428305e0755e/12366ENGanayasaizleme1_10_07_12.pdf. Accessed on 29 Feb 2012

Keyman F (2012) Turkey's new constitution: transformation, democratization, and living together. E-International Relations. http://ipc.sabanciuniv.edu/wp-content/uploads/2012/08/TurkeysNew Constitution_TransformationDemocratizationandLivingTogether1.pdf. Accessed on 25 July 2012

Köybaşı S (2013) Anayasalarda Değişmez Maddelerin Teorisi ve Pratiği. DPhil thesis, Galatasaray Universitesi, December 2013, pp 334–335

Mumcu O (2013) Anayasa Uzlaşma Komisyonu: Kısa bir değerlendirme notu. TEPAV http:// www.tepav.org.tr/tr/blog/s/3717#_ftn2. Accessed on 9 Jan 2013

Oder BE (2012) Turkish constitutional transformation and the EU: Europeanisation towards constitutionalism? In: Nas C, Özer Y (eds) Turkey and the European Union, process of Europeanisation. Ashgate, Farnham

Oder BE (2014) The much-awaited and deeply controversial constitutional process: learning from Turkey's failed process. In 2013 Conference Notifications "Themes of conflict in Middle Eastern democracies: a comparative perspective from Turkey and Israel" 2014. Friedrich Ebert Stiftung & The Van Leer Jerusalem Institute & Kadir Has University Middle East and Africa Research Center, December 2014, Istanbul, 136

Onar E (1993) 1982 Anayasasında Anayasayı Değiştirme Sorunu. Ankara Üniversitesi, Ankara

Özbudun E (1993–2004) Democratization reforms in Turkey. Turk Stud 8:179

Özbudun E (2005) Constitutional law. In: Ansay T, Wallace D (eds) Introduction to Turkish law, 2nd edn. Kluwer Law International, The Netherlands

Özbudun E (2008a) Reasoning for headscarf decision: new constitution is now a must. Today's Zaman, 16 November 2008

Özbudun E (2008b) AYM'nin 5.6.2008 tarih, 2008/16 esas, 2008/116 karar sayılı iptal gerekçesi üzerine değerlendirme. Milliyet Blog. http://blog.milliyet.com.tr/aym-nin-5-6-2008-tarih–2008-16-esas–2008-116-karar-sayili-iptal-gerekcesi-uzerine-degerlendirme/Blog/?BlogNo= 139547. Accessed on 22 Oct 2008

Özbudun E (2009) Judicial review of constitutional amendments in Turkey. Eur Pub L 15:533

Özbudun E (2012) Turkey's search for a new constitution. Insight Turk 14:39

Özbudun E (2014) Türkiye'de Demokratikleşme Süreci Anayasa Yapımı ve Anayasa Yargısı. Bilgi Üniversitesi Yayınları, Istanbul

Özbudun E, Gençkaya OF (2009) Democratization and the politics of constitution-making in Turkey, 1st edn. Central European University Press, Budapest

Özpek BB (2012) Constitution-making in Turkey after the 2011 elections. Turk Stud 13:153

Roznai Y, Yolcu S (2012) An unconstitutional constitutional amendment. The Turkish perspective: a comment on the Turkish constitutional court's headscarf decision. Int J Const Law 10:175

Sevinç M (2012) Anayasaların doğumu: TBMM yeni bir anayasa yapabilir mi? Toplum ve Bilim 123:10

Tanör B (2012) İki Anayasa 1961–1982, 4th edn, vol 12. Levha, p. 168

Uçum M, Genç O (October 2012) Yeni Anayasa Sürecini İzleme Raporu Şubat 2012-Haziran 2012. TESEV, http://tesev.org.tr/wp-content/uploads/2015/11/Yeni_Anayasa_Surecini_Izleme_Raporu_2_Subat_Haziran_2012.pdf. Accessed 5 May 2015

Uran P (2010) Turkey's hasty constitutional amendment devoid of rational basis: from a political crisis to a governmental system change. J Polit Law 3:2

Yayla Y (1983) 1982 Anayasasına Göre Devletin Özü. Idare Hukuku ve Ilimleri Dergisi 1:133

Yazıcı S (2001) Yeni Bir Anayasa Hazırlığı ve Türkiye: Seçkinlikten Toplum Sözleşmesine, 2nd edn. Bilgi Üniversitesi Yayınları, Istanbul

Yüksel S (2007) Constitutional changes of Turkey in 2001 under the framework of the EU adaptation process. Annales XXXIX 56:153

The Unamendability of Amendable Clauses: The Case of the Turkish Constitution

Tarik Olcay

Abstract Although it has not been constitutionally empowered to do so, the Turkish Constitutional Court has exercised substantive review of constitutional amendments under three different constitutional settings, striking down amendments to the normally amendable provisions of the Turkish constitution. In doing so, it relied upon the unamendability clauses. The Court created an intra-constitutional hierarchy based on the unamendable clauses and exercised substantive review of constitutional amendments to check whether amendments violated the principles laid down in the unamendable clauses. This chapter looks at whether this judicial practice of identifying a constitutional core and exercising substantive review of constitutional amendments on this basis can find a justification in Carl Schmitt's distinction of the *constitution* and *constitutional laws*. In the first part, it argues that while Schmitt's distinction, which is based on democratic decisionism, might justify the Court's reasoning that there are limits to constitutional amendment; his understanding of the guardian of the constitution is incompatible with the judicial oversight of the constituent decision. What makes Schmitt's radical democratic constitutional theory consistent is his conception of the popularly elected head of state as the guardian of the constitution. Such conceptual justification of constitutional unamendability is not compatible with judicial review of constitutional amendments. In the second part, the chapter analyses all of the unamendability cases the Turkish Constitutional Court has decided and explains the Court's arguments with regard to its authority over constitutional amendments. The chapter concludes by explaining that even if a Schmittian account of the constitution is adopted, the unamendability clause in the Turkish constitution remains a merely political and not a judicial check on the constitutional amendment power.

T. Olcay (✉)
School of Law, University of Glasgow, Glasgow, UK
e-mail: tarikolcay@gmail.com

© Springer International Publishing AG, part of Springer Nature 2018
R. Albert and B. E. Oder (eds.), *An Unamendable Constitution?*
Ius Gentium: Comparative Perspectives on Law and Justice 68,
https://doi.org/10.1007/978-3-319-95141-6_12

313

1 Introduction

Two relatively recent judgments of the Turkish Constitutional Court (TCC),[1] in which the Court invalidated two constitutional amendments on the grounds that they violated the unamendable clauses of the Turkish constitution, marked the revival of Turkey's long-simmering constitutional amendment saga. While the Court's reasoning as to its authority to review constitutional amendments and its interpretation of the constitutional principle of secularism in the 2008 judgment were questioned by many,[2] some even contended that the court's judgments were nonsensical and needed to be deemed null and void ab initio,[3] whereas others diagnosed the court with paranoid schizophrenia when it comes to the protection of the founding principles of the republic.[4]

The text of the Turkish constitution explicitly limits the TCC's authority over constitutional amendments. Article 148 of the constitution restricts the Court's authority to review constitutional amendments only to procedural grounds, specifying in detail the criteria for procedural review. Consequently, commentators have regarded the TCC's expansive interpretation of its authority as ultra vires, and they accused the Court of trying to act as the constituent power.[5]

Prima facie accounts of these cases indeed indicate a usurpation of authority by the TCC, when one takes into consideration the detailed provision of the constitution regarding the Court's authority to review constitutional amendments. Still, it remains unclear whether the Court's judgments can be justified by adopting a certain understanding of constitutional theory that would create a hierarchy among constitutional norms and appoint the constitutional court as the arbiter of disputes stemming from this stratification. In other words, it is worth seeking an answer to the question whether it is possible to identify a theoretical framework in which the reasoning of the Turkish Constitutional Court can be reasonably accommodated.

In this chapter, I attempt to demonstrate how Carl Schmitt's constitutional theory, which argues for unamendability, eventually does not serve to justify the TCC's oversight of the limits on constitutional amendment. First, I discuss how Schmitt's theory explains the value of constitutional norms and a hierarchy within the constitution, along with his understanding of the positive concept of

---

[1]E. 2008/16, K. 2008/116, 5 June 2008, 45/2 AYMKD 1195–1253; E. 2010/49, K. 2010/87, 7 July 2010, 47/2 AYMKD 1069–1237.

[2]See Özbudun (2009), p. 533, Saygılı (2010), p. 127, Roznai and Yolcu (2012), p. 175, Can (2013), pp. 271–292.

[3]Can (2013), pp. 261–269.

[4]Saygılı (2010), pp. 135–139.

[5]Zühtü Arslan, who has been appointed as a member of the Turkish Constitutional Court in 2012 and has been elected as its president in February 2015, had written following the headscarf decision of 2008 that the TCC acted as a 'positive constitution-maker', rather than a 'negative legislator' in Kelsen's terms, and borrowing the term from Alec Stone Sweet, called the judgment a 'juridical *coup d'état*'. See Arslan (2009), p. 9. For Alec Stone Sweet on the concept of juridical *coup d'état*, see Sweet (2007), p. 10.

constitution, constituent power and the guardian of the constitution. Then, I summarise the TCC's interpretation of the unamendability clauses and its authority to review the constitutionality of constitutional amendments in 15 cases under three different constitutional settings. Lastly, I look at the TCC's reasoning in terms of Schmitt's constitutional theory and discuss to what extent the TCC's interpretation can be explained with it. I conclude that while the application of Schmitt's constitutional theory conveniently creates a constitutional core and a hierarchy between the unamendable and amendable provisions, casting the TCC as the arbiter of constitutionality of constitutional amendments still cannot be justified when the political nature of Schmitt's concept of constitution and Schmitt's concept of the guardian of the constitution are taken into account. This reading is in conformity with the view that the unamendability clause can be provided in a constitution to create *political accountability*, rather than a legal one, especially when the judicial review of constitutional amendments is strictly limited to procedural review or prohibited altogether.

2 A Theory of Constitutional Stratification

2.1 Why Carl Schmitt?

Constitutional unamendability is a contentious issue. Arguing for it is even more so. Richard Albert likens unamendability clauses to 'throwing away the key to unlock the handcuffs that constitutions attach to the wrists of citizens'.[6] Clearly, a proponent of unamendability needs to address how this 'throwing away' can be justified, or convincingly demonstrate how the keys are to be fetched.

Carl Schmitt's constitutional theory provides a powerful set of tools for those seeking a theory of limitations on constitutional amendments. His theory eventually suggests that the very concept of constitution intrinsically includes limitations to its amendment by the institutions it creates and authorises. Therefore, regardless of whether there are explicit substantive or procedural limitations on amending a constitution, there are always certain implicit limits to constitutional amendment. This conclusion is based on his positive concept of constitution, a constitution as a fundamental political decision, and his concept of constituent power, the political subject of this political decision. Schmitt criticises the normativist idea that the constitution is 'nothing but a statute that is more difficult to amend'.[7] For him, the constitution is rather an existentialist statement of a political unity. Therefore, it is necessary in a democratic society to hold this constituent decision above ordinary politics and protect it against contingent democratic, especially parliamentary, majorities. Today, in practice, this protection is generally provided by judicial

---

[6]Albert (2010), pp. 663, 667.
[7]Schmitt (1996), p. 48. For the translation of parts of this work, see Vinx (2015).

bodies which uphold constitutional fundamentals over constitutional amendments. However, while Schmitt was a proponent of substantive limits on constitutional change, he was a strong critic of constitutional adjudication in general, and thus was not sympathetic to the idea that constitutional judiciary should be the guardian of the constitution. In what follows, I explain Schmitt's understanding of the constitution and how it responds to the problem of the limits on constitutional amendment before shortly sketching his answer to the question of who the guardian of the constitution should be.

2.2   The Positive Concept of Constitution

Carl Schmitt's understanding of the concept of constitution is contrary to that of a normativist account. According to Hans Kelsen, who was Schmitt's normativist adversary, the normative legal order cannot be based upon something outside of itself. For him, norms can only be derived from norms.[8] This means that their validity can only be based upon some other (hierarchically superior) norms, and that no political or moral values can be the reason for their validity. A norm is only valid if it can be traced back to the presupposed *Grundnorm*, which is the logical presupposition that the first constitution is valid, and validity has nothing to do with the content of the norms.[9] Schmitt, however, opposes the closed normative order and bases the entire legal order on a political decision that is taken outside the sphere of legality. As Lindahl notes, for Schmitt, 'a political concept of constitution precedes its legal notion, both chronologically and conceptually: prior to "having" a legal constitution, a state *is* a constitution, a *status*: the "concrete aggregate state of political unity and social order". This existential status, not a basic norm, grounds the validity of a constitution.'[10]

In *Constitutional Theory*, rejecting the relative and ideal concepts of constitution, Carl Schmitt adopts what he calls the positive concept of the constitution before looking into various problems of constitutional theory.[11]

The understanding that the constitution is a set of individual laws, without any substantive distinction among its contents, which is the normativist account of constitution, is what Schmitt calls the relative concept of constitution.[12] For Schmitt, the fact that constitutions include fundamental provisions such as the first paragraph of Article 1 of the Weimar Constitution reading 'The German Reich is a republic', and at the same time materially rather trivial provisions like Article 129 stating 'civil servants are secure in their personal effects' shows that the normativist

---

[8]Kelsen (1957), p. 279.
[9]Kelsen (2001), p. 198.
[10]Lindahl (2007), p. 13.
[11]Schmitt (2008), p. 96.
[12]Ibid., p. 67. Also, see Loughlin (2010), p. 214.

approach relegates genuinely fundamental provisions to the level of constitutional law detail.[13] This relativisation of the constitution, therefore, results in 'the losing of the concept of *the* constitution in the concept of individual constitutional *law*'.[14] Schmitt, thus, rejects the relative concept of constitution that reduces the constitution to a collection of written laws contained in a constitutional text, as it fails to distinguish between the fundamental and the trivial. Schmitt further rebuffs the idea that defines constitution merely as a statute with a special amendment procedure. He argues that amendment provisions in the constitution—Article 76 in the Weimar Constitution—are not mere constitutional laws as otherwise, they would be subject to change under conditions they establish and would be prone to eliminating themselves.[15]

Schmitt also opposes what he calls the ideal concept of constitution, which is a constitution with a particular desired content, as there will always be disagreement as to the ideal form of the constitution depending on the opinions of different parties.[16] Schmitt says that 'there are just as many possible concepts of constitution as there are political principles and convictions' and concepts like freedom, justice, public order and security can be defined differently according to what ideal is adopted.[17] He acknowledges that the dominant understanding in his day had been the liberal ideal of constitution that stipulates a written constitution that creates a system of guarantees of bourgeois freedom and the separation of powers, yet he rejects that this (or any other ideal of the constitution) can explain the 'entire state constitution', as it falls short to address the political component of the constitution, which contains 'the positive decision over the form of political existence'.[18]

Eventually, according to Schmitt, 'a concept of the constitution is only possible when one distinguishes constitution and constitutional law'.[19] Under this distinction, the constitution originates from the act of constituent power, in which it is established by a political will, whereas 'constitutional laws are valid ... on the basis of the constitution and presuppose a constitution'.[20] What follows ultimately from this distinction is that the authorities and procedures that make and change the constitution and constitutional laws are substantially different, and there is a clear hierarchy between the two, the former establishing the authority of the latter. The positive constitution, thus, is basically a model containing the basic features of the political organisation of the polity. In contrast with Kelsen's vacuous *Grundnorm*, which is devoid of substantive content and merely denotes the presupposition that

---

[13]Schmitt (2008), pp. 67–68.

[14]Ibid., p. 71.

[15]Ibid., p. 74.

[16]Ibid., pp. 89–90.

[17]Ibid., p. 90.

[18]Ibid., p. 93.

[19]Ibid., p. 75.

[20]Ibid., p. 76.

the first constitution is valid,[21] Schmitt's positive constitution contains fundamental preferences of the constituent power to determine the basics of the constitution. It denotes, therefore, 'the core constitutional identity of a democratic political order'.[22] The elements of the constitutional order, accordingly, are understood in light of this 'core', and 'constitutional laws' are merely the institutionalisation tools for 'the constitution'.

Distinguishing the constitution and constitutional laws are significant in the sense that it requires a stratified understanding of constitutional norms—usually within the same document that is containing the constitutional provisions, i.e. the text of the constitution—in which some of these norms are hierarchically superior to others, and consequently more difficult to change. Schmitt deals with the problem of constitutional change by making a distinction between the constitution-making power and the authority to amend (revise) constitutional laws. For him, 'the constitution-making power is the political will, whose power or authority is capable of making the concrete, comprehensive decision over the type and form of its own political existence',[23] whereas the authority for constitutional amendments can be exercised only if 'the identity and continuity of the constitution as an entirety is preserved'.[24] Following Sieyès' distinction of constituent and constituted powers,[25] he regards the constitution-making authority as the constituent power and the amending authority as a constituted power. This distinction is of vital importance when identifying the limits of constitutional change by constituted authorities (constitutional revision).

Schmitt mentions five types of constitutional change: (i) constitutional annihilation, which is the abolition of the existing constitution and the underlying constitution-making power; (ii) constitutional elimination, which is the abolition of the existing constitution but retaining the underlying constitution-making power; (iii) constitutional revision, denoting a change in the text of the previously valid (individual) constitutional laws; (iv) statutory constitutional violation, which is the infringement of constitutional provisions without effecting their validity; (v) constitutional suspension, the temporary setting aside of single or multiple constitutional provisions.[26] He subsequently draws the boundaries of the authority for constitutional amendments as relating only to constitutional revisions (iii) and rules out the other four, as their exercise requires a different kind of authority (not a constitutional, i.e. constituted one).[27] Therefore, the constitution can only be amended by making revisions to constitutional laws in a way that respects the core of the constitution, i.e. the positive constitution.

---

[21]Kelsen (1992), pp. 59–60.

[22]Kalyvas (2008), p. 139.

[23]Schmitt (2008), p. 125.

[24]Ibid., p. 150.

[25]Sieyès (2003), p. 136.

[26]Schmitt (2008), pp. 147–148.

[27]Ibid., (2008), pp. 150–158.

What does this theory tell us about the constitutionality of constitutional amendments? Can it be argued, under this understanding of the constitution, that matters dealing with the essential characteristics of a polity in the text of the constitution, or a preamble explaining the motivation of the constitution-making power, make up the positive constitution, regardless of their level of entrenchment within the text of the constitution, or even within the legal system as a whole? Is it possible to extract the positive constitution from the text of the constitution? If there are relatively more strongly entrenched constitutional provisions in the text of the constitution, e.g. unamendable clauses, are these the definitive tools in making sense of the positive constitution? It is possible to find direct answers in Schmitt's writings to some of these questions.

Schmitt clearly regards preambles of constitutions as part of the positive constitution. He criticises the pre-war approach in Germany that regarded the preamble 'mere proclamations', 'mere statements' or 'commonplaces'.[28] For him, elements of the preamble were among what constituted the substance of the Weimar constitution. Consequently, it was superior to the trivial constitutional laws.

For Schmitt, in terms of identifying its character, it seems that the existence of a prohibition of a particular constitutional change in the form of an explicit constitutional provision is unimportant, as he holds that such prohibitions are 'only a matter of confirmation of the distinction of constitutional revision and the elimination of the constitution'.[29] It is evident from this that the positive constitution is not necessarily limited to the text of the constitution. Therefore, it is more of a substantive account than a formally definitive one as to what makes up the positive constitution and what remains merely as constitutional laws. In other words, the constitution as the political decision does not necessarily consist solely of the unamendable provisions. Nonetheless, the confirmation by the constitution-making power shows that unamendable provisions are at least part of the positive constitution.

2.3 The Guardian of the Constitution

The substantive constitutional core that the democratic decisionist account of the concept of constitution establishes brings about another important question. If there is a constituent decision that limits people's authority to revise their constitution,

---

[28]Ibid., p. 78. Schmitt writes that democracy, one of the most fundamental political decisions in the Weimar Constitution, found its expression in the preamble. See ibid., p. 77. This is striking as the preambles of the Turkish constitutions included many vague principles and ideological statements and the unamendable Article 2 of the 1982 Constitution even makes a reference to the 'fundamental principles' in the preamble by stipulating 'the Republic of Turkey is ... based on the fundamental tenets set forth in the preamble'. On reference to the preamble in the Turkish context, see Sects. 3.2 and 3.3.

[29]Ibid., p. 152.

by what means are these limits to be observed and can there be a constitutional watchdog that oversees the sustainment of this fundamental decision? Especially as the recent trend shows that courts' involvement in the constitutional review of constitutional amendments is increasing, the question of 'who ought to be the guardian of the constitution' needs to be addressed. Looking at this question allows us to identify the actors involved in the tension between the constituent decision and the will of the constituted. Just as Kelsen's and Schmitt's conceptions of the constitution are in conflict, their ideas and exchange on how the constitution is to be protected (or upheld) point to contrasting institutional settings, and help us understand what they regard as worthy of protection in a constitution.

I should, however, note that the question of how the constitution should be protected and whether courts have democratic credentials to exercise (or assume) such guardianship role is one of the central questions of constitutional theory and is far from confined to the Kelsen-Schmitt debate. Contemporary positions range from arguing that constitutional review lacks democratic legitimacy[30] to providing robust democratic justifications[31] of constitutional review. However, my focus on the Kelsen-Schmitt debate is due to the TCC's assumption of the guardianship of the constitution through a Schmittian decisionist interpretation of the constitutional fundamentals.

In the absence of a constitutional court during the Weimar era, Kelsen advocated centralised constitutional adjudication and argued that the constitution needed to be guarded by a constitutional court.[32] He emphasised the importance of 'the legality of laws' and contended that constitutionality was the means to achieve this.[33] His argument is based on the theory of the hierarchy of norms, which stipulates that the law consists of norms at hierarchical levels, norms at each level deriving their validity from the next superior level of norms. In every step, though decreasing in scope as norms are substantively more specific in the inferior sets of the hierarchy, there is discretion involved in any norm-making. The constitution, sitting at the top of the domestic legal hierarchy, binds the legislator, but still gives it a relatively wide discretion to create laws. To make sure legislation is made in accordance with the higher level norm that is the constitution, and just as any other discretionary legal norm-making is subject to judicial review, Kelsen argued that legislation should also be subject to judicial review in the form of constitutional adjudication. This is what, for Kelsen, guaranteed the constitutionality of laws.[34]

---

[30]See Waldron (2006), p. 1346, Bellamy (2007), pp. 26–48. These accounts, however, are very different to that of Schmitt's as they are largely defences of parliamentary democracy, whereas, as explained below, Schmitt was a critic of parliamentary democracy as well as judicial review of legislation.

[31]Dworkin (1996), pp. 15–38, Ely (1980), Raz (2009), pp. 361–364, Habermas (1996), pp. 238–244.

[32]Kelsen (2015), pp. 22–78.

[33]Ibid., pp. 22–25.

[34]Ibid., p. 25.

Kelsen also argued that constitutional review of legislation was particularly significant in democratic polities. He saw the essence of democracy 'in the continuing compromise between the different parts of the people that are represented in parliament by the majority and the minority', and contended that *constitutionality* ensured this state of affairs.[35] As constitutional adjudication is the instrument that guarantees *constitutionality*, it is an important element of democratic republics in pursuit of the effective protection of minorities against the potential oppression of the majority rule.[36]

One might be inclined to think that Schmitt's positive concept of constitution and his definition of constituent power also would require a system of judicial review in order to protect, not the minorities, but the constituent power's fundamental political decision against the acts of constituted powers. In this way, such a judicial body would adopt the constituent choice as the reference norm for constitutionality and review the compatibility of the acts of the legislature, including constitutional revisions, vis-à-vis this set of core commitments. However, Schmitt forcefully opposes constitutional adjudication. In his attack on constitutional adjudication in *Der Hüter der Verfassung*, he states that while the call for a constitutional court as the guardian of the constitution is a call for a neutral guardian, this is in fact impossible. The constitutional court would be yet another political actor as 'no amount of judicial procedure could veil the fact that such a ... constitutional court would be a highly political authority, endowed with a competence of constitutional legislation'.[37] Furthermore, Schmitt contends that constitutional adjudication, when directed against a parliament and not a monarch— as was the case at the turn of the century—would fail to meet the requirements of the democratic principle. Raising the democratic objection, he insists that it would not be legitimate to 'transfer such powers to an aristocracy of the robe'.[38] Schmitt further defines adjudication as merely 'the decision of a "case" on the "basis of a statute"',[39] and warns that formalism regarding any decision of the judiciary would eventually result in the judiciary's decisions becoming norms and making the constitution.[40] Granting a constitutional court the authoritative interpretation of the positive constitution would mean hijacking the constituent power of the people. Therefore, for him, it is not democratically legitimate for the judges to exercise such power. In other words, Schmitt's account of democratic decisionism[41] requires limits to constitutional change while at the same time dismissing the idea of judicial mechanisms creating and overseeing these limits.

---

[35]Ibid., pp. 71–72.

[36]Ibid.

[37]Schmitt (1996), p. 155.

[38]Ibid.

[39]Ibid., p. 37.

[40]Ibid., p. 38.

[41]Democratic decisionism is 'a theory according to which the people remain completely at liberty to change the political order without having to appeal to ultimate moral, religious or philosophical foundations' see Müller (2003), p. 128.

For Schmitt, it is solely for the people as the holder of the constituent power to interpret the constitution and resolve constitutional conflicts: 'Every genuine constitutional conflict, which involves the foundations of the comprehensive political decision itself, can, consequently, only be decided through the will of the constitution-making power itself.'[42] This means that even the people, when not *acting as* the constituent power, cannot alter the fundamental political decisions or make different ones.

Who, then, should oversee the positive constitution, which needs to be protected against contingent parliamentary majorities?[43] This question is crucial, as for Schmitt, deciding in case of disagreement is definitive as to the exercise of sovereignty.[44] Therefore, the question of the preservation and fulfilment of the positive constitution is as significant as the distinction of constitution and constitutional laws. As noted earlier, the widespread practice is the courts' creation, identification and upholding of the fundamental constitutional values.[45]

Schmitt, however, famously advocated the popularly elected head of the executive to be the guardian of the constitution. Note here that what Schmitt envisages the guardian of the constitution protecting is not the rights entrenched in the constitution or the rule of law principle as would be the case with liberal constitutionalists.[46] Building upon his positive concept of constitution, he seeks a guardian to protect the concrete order and the political unity of the whole people, and in the case of the Weimar constitution, the whole German people.

It is important to remember that Schmitt is a staunch critic of parliamentarianism and parliamentary pluralism as he found these destructive to the state.[47] His point being the realisation of the will of the people in a democracy yet acknowledging that representation is inevitable in the twentieth century polities, Schmitt argues that the parliament is destined to either

"become [...] incapable of reaching a majority and of acting due to its immanent pluralism" or "the momentary majority employs all legal possibilities as instruments and means of the protection of its own hold on power, that it abuses the time during which it possesses the power in the state in all directions, and, above all, that it attempts to restrict as far as possible the [principle of equal] chance of its most powerful and dangerous opponent to do the same".[48]

---

[42]Schmitt (2008), p. 126.

[43]Schmitt (1985), (1996), pp. 73–91.

[44]Schmitt (2005), p. 6.

[45]The Indian Supreme Court's creation of the basic structure doctrine is the typical example. On the basic structure doctrine, See Chandrachud C (2017). The Indian example has been a model for many other jurisdictions. See Roznai (2013), pp. 657, 690–699.

[46]For instance, John Rawls advocated that the Supreme Court of the USA should invalidate constitutional amendments violating what he calls 'constitutional essentials' in the USA constitution. According to Rawls, basically, constitutional essentials include the fundamental principles as to the political process and basic political rights. See Rawls (2005), p. 232.

[47]Schmitt (1996), p. 131.

[48]Ibid., p. 89.

He further criticises the identification of democracy with liberalism and parliamentarianism, and argues that the institution of parliament is no more democratic than a dictatorship in the name of the people. In *The Crisis of Parliamentary Democracy,* he attacks the notion that 'the *ratio* of the parliament rests [...] in a process of confrontation of differences and opinions, from which the real political will results'.[49] He does not see why *ratio* (or reason) is to be found in parliamentarians and concludes that the idea of truth inherent in this conception corresponds merely to the 'function of the eternal competition of opinions'.[50] He contends that 'discussion' cannot be the foundation of democracy.[51] He believes that parliaments do not have the capacity to resolve political conflicts as, instead of deciding, they *discuss.* Considering this 'empty and trivial formality'[52] inherent in parliamentarianism, which is not fit to sustain political unity, and the need for the protection of the *actually* democratic foundational will, Schmitt puts forward a constitutional guardian. The guardian of the constitution, for him, therefore, is essentially meant to protect the people's constituent choice against contingent parliamentary majorities.

In his study of the Weimar constitution, Schmitt states that the nature of the powers granted to the President[53] creates a neutral authority that is in immediate connection with the whole of the state, and equipped with effective competences for the active protection of the constitution.[54] Neutrality of this post is critical in the sense that it preserves the continuity of the state against the war of interests in the parliament and institutional divisions within the state. What is crucial here for the guardian of the constitution is that it has 'the opportunity to connect itself immediately to the unified will of the German people and to act as the guardian and preserver of the constitutional unity and wholeness of the German people'.[55] Schmitt's solution to the problem of overseeing the positive constitution, thus, in Andrew Arato's words, is that 'only a power like the president of the republic, armed with an extraordinary jurisdiction like that of Article 48 [regulating emergency powers of the president] could stop a formally legal revolution against the constitution. Such a revolution would not be stopped by declaring amendments unconstitutional but by eliminating the political force that is willing and capable of

---

[49]Schmitt (1985), p. 34.

[50]Ibid., p. 56.

[51]Ibid., p. 15.

[52]Ibid., p. 50.

[53]'Both the relatively static and permanent aspects of the presidency (election for seven years, difficulty of recall, independence from changing parliamentary majorities) as well as the character of the president's competences (the powers under article 45 and 46 of the constitution of the Reich, the dissolution of the Reichstag under article 25 and the initiation of a popular referendum under article 73 of the constitution of the Reich, the preparation and promulgation of statutes under article 70, federal execution and protection of the constitution in accordance with article 48)'. See Schmitt (1996), p. 158.

[54]Ibid.

[55]Ibid., p. 159.

enacting it.'[56] It is, therefore, a political force that would neutralise the threat of unconstitutional amendments to the positive constitution, not a judicial one. Yet, it must be kept in mind that this oversight concerns a potential 'formally legal revolution' and not changes occurring extra-constitutionally. To refer back to Schmitt's five-fold categorisation of constitutional changes, the guardian of the constitution thus protects the constitution against constitutional revisions that in fact amount to constitutional annihilation, constitutional elimination, statutory constitutional violation or constitutional suspension. These four types of change happening without the guise of formally proper constitutional revision are outside the scope of the guardianship of the constitution.

Although Schmitt portrayed such a guardian of the constitution, he did not place it above the constitution, nor did he consider it the sovereign.[57] The presidency as the guardian of the constitution, for Schmitt, is a constituted office, bound by constitutional limits as to the goals it can legitimately pursue.[58] Also, the fact that the president's dictatorial powers as stipulated by Article 48 of the Weimar Constitution can only be exercised as long as the Weimar Constitution is still in force means that this specific authority is dependent on the sovereignty of the constitution. Consequently, while Schmitt thinks the president is equipped with such extensive extraordinary powers, he remains coherent by not placing the president above the constitution and not deeming it the sovereign dictator. He endows these upon the people as the constituent power.

3   Constitutional Unamendability in Turkey

The problem of unconstitutional constitutional amendments in Turkey stems from the fact that the unamendability clauses in the Turkish constitutions have been drafted in a way that seeks to preserve the provisions *in* the protected clauses. Unamendability clauses in the Turkish constitutions, including the current Article 4,[59] have forbidden the amending *of* the provisions they stipulate, not any amendment *affecting* these provisions. Yet, to this day, the practical importance of the question of unamendability in the Turkish constitutions has not been regarding textual changes to the unamendable provisions themselves, but rather on amendments to normally amendable provisions.[60]

---

[56]Arato (2011), pp. 324, 336–337.

[57]Schmitt (2013), p. 208.

[58]Vinx (2016), pp. 34–49.

[59]The text of this current unamendability clause is as follows:

   Article 4—The provision of Article 1 regarding the form of the State being a Republic, the characteristics of the Republic in Article 2, and the provisions of Article 3 shall not be amended, nor shall their amendment be proposed.

[60]A recent exception is the debate on the revocation of the unamendable clauses in the context of writing a new constitution in the Constitution Reconciliation Committee, which was set up in 2011

Throughout Turkish constitutional history, the judicial enforcement of una-mendability emerged as an issue with regard to attempts to amend normally amendable clauses, rather than the unamendable ones.[61] In the practice of the TCC, we witness the extension of the effect of the unamendability clause to amendments that the clause does not, in fact, protect from change. The Court's argument is that amendments to normally amendable clauses may hollow out the fundamentals of the constitution and can thus violate the unamendability clause. Hence, we face the conundrum of the unamendability of amendable clauses.

Constitutional amendment as a specific legal procedure in Turkish constitu-tionalism is historically significant, as the Republic of Turkey was founded in 1923 with a constitutional amendment to the 1921 Constitution.[62] A year later, the 1924 Constitution marked the first unamendable provision in Turkish constitutional history. Article 102 of the constitution explicitly prohibited any amendment pro-posals to Article 1 specifying the form of the state as a republic. During the period the 1924 Constitution was in place, no attempts for such a proposal have been made. Moreover, there was no authorised body to exercise constitutionality review of laws during that period. There were several attempts to exercise decentralised constitutionality review by first instance courts, with two bills in this regard failing in Parliament.[63] Therefore, the unamendability of Article 1 remained a political question during this period, rather than a legal one.

The history of the judicial review of constitutional amendments by the TCC is analysed in four phases below. While (i) initially the 1961 Constitution did not include any explicit provisions in this regard, following the Court's activist approach to constitutional amendments, (ii) Parliament amended the constitution in 1971 and empowered the Court to review constitutional amendments, albeit on formal grounds only. While the TCC admitted that it could no longer exercise substantive review of constitutional amendments, it insisted on exercising it under the guise of formal review. In order to prevent this practice, (iii) the 1982 Constitution specifically provided the criteria for formal review, and until 2008 the

---

to write a new constitution but failed to produce a full draft and dissolved by the end of 2013. This was not a judicial but a parliamentary debate. For a study of this debate in the Committee, see Yegen (this volume).

[61]There have been, however, two amendments in 1995 and 2001 to the Preamble of the 1982 Constitution, the fundamental principles in which are regarded as unamendable based on the reference to it in the unamendable Article 2. Article 2 stipulates that the state is 'based on the fundamental tenets set forth in the Preamble' and as Article 4 prohibits amendments to the 'characteristics of the Republic' found in Article 2, the fundamental principles found in the Preamble are regarded to be included in the unamendability protection. These two amendments to the Preamble mainly aimed to remove the remarks that justified the military coup of 1980, as well as to relatively tone down the chauvinistic language of the Preamble. In any event, the amend-ments were not challenged before the Constitutional Court and did not prove to be contentious from the perspective of constitutional unamendability. On these amendments, see Oder (2009), pp. 264–266.

[62]Law No 364 dated 29 October 1923.

[63]Onar (2003), pp. 165–195.

Court abided by this restriction. Finally, (iv) the Court again adopted its post-1971 amendment attitude after 2008 and reviewed the constitutionality of two amendments substantively.

3.1 The Early Activism of the TCC (1962–1971)

Originally, there were no specific provisions regarding the judicial review of constitutional amendments in the 1961 Constitution. The newly established constitutional court's power to exercise constitutionality review was limited to laws and the rules of procedure of Parliament.[64] However, the TCC deemed itself competent to review and invalidate constitutional amendments, and exercised its authority accordingly.

The first amendment to the 1961 Constitution was made in 1969, and the TCC invalidated it a year later. Yet, an earlier decision gave hints as to what would follow, where the TCC interpreted in *obiter dictum* the meaning of Article 155[65] of the 1961 Constitution, which regulated constitutional amendments. In this decision, after stating that the provisions of the constitution are amendable, except for the one specifying the form of the state as a republic, the Court introduced a vague set of extra limitations. According to the Court, amendments should 'be in line with the spirit of the constitution' and 'raise the Turkish society to a more advanced level of civilisation'. The constitutional amendment power, therefore, does not provide for 'the realisation of purposes of causing regression to the Turkish society, destroying fundamental rights and freedoms and the principle of the rule of law, in a word, taking away the Essence of the 1961 Constitution.'[66]

The only explicit limitations on the constitutional amendment power in the 1961 Constitution were the amendment procedures to be followed in Parliament, and the unamendability of the form of the state as a republic.[67] Despite this framework, in this decision, the TCC introduced a new set of limitations by rendering the spirit of the constitution, the advancement of the Turkish society, the preservation of fundamental rights and freedoms, and the principle of the rule of law, as criteria for the validity of constitutional amendments. Furthermore, while not explicitly granting

---

[64]The relevant provision is as follows: Article 147—The Constitutional Court shall review the constitutionality of laws and the rules of procedure of the Turkish Grand National Assembly.

[65]Article 155—Proposals for the amendment of the Constitution may be submitted in writing by at least one-third majority of the plenary session of the Grand National Assembly of Turkey, but may not be debated under urgency. An amendment proposal shall be adopted by a two-thirds majority vote of the plenary session of each legislative body. Outside of the requirements of paragraph 1, the debate and adoption of proposals for the amendment of the Constitution are subject to the provision governing the debate and enactment of laws.

[66]E. 1963/173, K. 1965/40, 26 September 1965, 4 AYMKD 329 (my translation).

[67]Article 9—The provision of the Constitution establishing the form of the State as a Republic shall not be amended nor shall its amendment be proposed.

itself the authority to exercise constitutional review of constitutional amendments, the Court signalled that it might actually do so.

Five years later, Parliament enacted the first constitutional amendment to the 1961 Constitution, removing the political rights restrictions on some politicians of the pre-1960 *coup d'état* government.[68] The Workers Party of Turkey (*Türkiye İşçi Partisi*) (*TİP*), the then main opposition party, took the constitutional amendment to the TCC claiming its unconstitutionality. This was the first time a constitutional amendment had been brought before the Court. After interpreting the constitution in a way that empowers the TCC to exercise constitutionality review of constitutional amendments, it invalidated the amendment on procedural grounds.[69] As regards its jurisdiction, the Court stated that a constitutional amendment is, in its form, a law, and since the constitution empowers the TCC to exercise constitutionality review of laws, constitutional amendments stand no exception to it. Constitutional amendments failing to satisfy the procedural criteria set out in the constitution accordingly, should be invalidated.[70] Furthermore, according to the Court, the unamendability clause regarding the form of the state as a republic poses a substantive limitation to the constitutional amendment power, and not only for amendments to the unamendable Article 1 itself, as 'what is deemed unamendable is not the word 'Republic', but the Republican regime with its characteristics as stipulated in the Constitution', and thus 'no law amending the principles of the 1961 Constitution or *by way of amending other provisions of the constitution directly or indirectly aimed at amending these characteristics* may be proposed or adopted [emphasis added]'.[71] In its formal review, the Court decided that the constitutional amendment was unconstitutional, as the required majority of two-thirds for the approval of the bill was observed only in the voting of the entire bill at the end, whereas it should have been observed in the voting of all individual articles. It did not exercise substantive review in this instance.[72]

Two months before this decision was given, Parliament adopted another constitutional amendment, which extended the terms of some members of the Senate.[73] Again, the *TİP* petitioned the TCC to invalidate the constitutional amendment. Repeating its recent reasoning, the Court deemed itself competent to exercise both formal and substantive review of constitutional amendments, yet this time it decided the amendment was constitutional.[74] In this decision, the Court sketched the framework of limitations on constitutional amendments as follows:

> The constitutional order has such fundamental institutions and rules of rights and duties, that if they are subordinated to provisions contrary to the necessities of contemporary

---

[68]Law No 1188 dated 12 November 1969.

[69]E. 1970/1, K. 1970/31, 16 June 1970, 8 AYMKD 313–340.

[70]Ibid., p. 322.

[71]Ibid., p. 323 (my translation).

[72]Ibid., pp. 330–332.

[73]Law No 1254 dated 17 April 1970.

[74]E. 1970/41, K. 1971/37, 13 April 1971, 9 AYMKD 416–449.

civilisation, it could result in a trauma to the order as a whole [...]. The form of the state being a republic is a poetry of principles with its fundamental institutions and rules of rights and duties. Thus it results from the explicit provisions and the spirit and philosophy of the Constitution that constitutional amendments erasing or rendering impracticable the form of the state as a republic, cannot be made [...]. It should not be presumed that provisions other than the provision on the form of the state are amendable by the legislative organ without any conditions [...]. It is in line with the Constitution that the Constitutional Court, exercising the powers vested by Article 147, protects the Constitution against the sovereignty of the majority.[75]

Although in this instance the Court did not find the amendment unconstitutional, it insisted that there are certain criteria that represent the 'spirit and philosophy of the constitution', and no amendment infringing them could be made. It should be noted that while the Court referred to limitations to the amendment power, it refrained from specifying any principles, other than vague terms such as 'the necessities of contemporary civilisation'.

The decisions of the TCC in this period have been praised by scholars defending the notion that the distinction between the original and derived constituent powers has practical consequences as to the limits on constitutional amendments. Derived constituent power is bound by the spirit of the constitution,[76] this argument went, and cannot make amendments that fall outside of the political preference of the original constituent power.[77] Therefore, for them, the TCC was right to review the constitutionality of constitutional amendments by interpreting Article 9 broadly. Moreover, it has been intrepidly suggested that the TCC is the guardian of the constitution and the constitutional order, as can be observed in the oath members of the TCC take when they are appointed to the bench.[78] However, the Court's practice received much wider criticism than appreciation.[79] For instance, Özbudun argued that this practice has been defended either by accepting that there are supra-constitutional legal norms or by assuming that there is a hierarchy of norms within the constitution. He concluded that since there was no norm in the positive Turkish constitutional law regarding these, the TCC's decisions were

---

[75]Ibid., pp. 428–429 (my translation).

[76]Kubalı (1971), p. 102 cited in Gözler (1999), pp. 227–228, Serim (1977), pp. 33, 34.

[77]Serozan (1972), pp. 135, 138.

[78]See Erdal (2008), pp. 165, 181. Erdal refers to the oath in the later law in his article. In the Law on the Constitutional Court at that time, the oath was as follows (Law No 44 dated 22 April 1962, Art 10/2): 'I vow upon my honour to protect the Constitution of the Republic of Turkey, which finds it *true guarantee in the hearts and wills of the Turkish citizens*; and to carry out my duty rightly, impartially, and with respecting righteousness, and by only observing the orders of my conscience. [emphasis added]' (my translation). The emphasised clause is borrowed into this law from the Preamble of 1961 Constitution. I think this oath rather signals the prioritisation of democratic choices to judicial decisions.

[79]See Eroğul (1974), pp. 164–168, Özbudun (2010), p. 174, Onar (2003), pp. 141–142, Turhan (1976), pp. 63, 99.

questionable.[80] Still, it has been widely accepted that the TCC had the authority to review the procedural regularity of constitutional amendments, as it had that of ordinary legislation.[81]

3.2 Substantive Review under the Guise of Formal Review (1971–1982)

As a response[82] to this practice, Parliament limited the TCC's authority to review constitutional amendments only on a formal basis by amending Article 147 of the 1961 Constitution.[83] It is worth noting that Parliament stated in the Reasons of this amendment that constitutional amendments are technically not 'laws', but 'constitutions'.[84] This means that the TCC's authority to review the constitutionally specified acts of the legislature does not necessarily include the acts of Parliament acting as the derived constituent power (constitutional amendment power). With this amendment, however, it has been authorised to do so, but only on formal grounds.

In 1975, the TCC again invalidated a clause in a constitutional amendment.[85] The constitutional amendment in question introduced an exception to Article 138 which stipulated that the majority of the members of military courts should be qualified judges. The amendment provided that in the event of war, this condition was not required.[86] In its discussion regarding its authority to review constitutional amendments, the Court conceded that it could no longer exercise substantive review, yet concluded that the formal review included a *proposability test* under Article 9. The reasoning of the Court was that Article 9 consisted of two elements, namely the principle of unamendability, and the prohibition to propose amendments. According to the Court, since provisions regarding the proposal of laws are

---

[80]Özbudun (2010), p. 174.

[81]Onar (2003), p. 138, Eroğul (1974), p. 164.

[82]Özbudun (2010), p. 175, Can (2013), p. 158. The spokesperson for the Constitution and Justice Committee in the Senate expressed that the reason for this amendment was to limit the TCC's authority to formal review of constitutional amendments as to the regularity of the specific proposal, debate, and approval terms. See Cumhuriyet Senatosu Tutanak Dergisi, Cilt 67, 115. Birleşim, 14 September 1971, 505 www.tbmm.gov.tr/tutanaklar/TUTANAK/CS__/t10/c067/cs__10067115.pdf.

[83]Law No 1488 dated 20 September 1971.

[84]Can argues that this shows the TCC's earlier conclusion that constitutional amendments are 'laws' is legally and politically invalid, whereas Gözler emphasises that the Court's reasoning regarding its interpretation of the term 'law' can be criticised, but as the decisions of the Court are binding, their validity cannot be challenged. See Can (2013), pp. 159–160, Gözler (2008), p. 24.

[85]E. 1973/19, K. 1975/87, 15 April 1975, 13 AYMKD 403–478.

[86]Law No 1699 dated 15 March 1973, Art 4.

rules regarding the procedure, the provision prohibiting the proposal is just another such rule. As the constitution at that time empowered the TCC to exercise only formal review of constitutional amendments, in its formal review, the Court concluded that it was competent to review the amendment with regard to the unamendability provision. Moreover, this formal review included the test of conformity to the characteristics of the republic as stipulated in Article 2[87] and the Preamble, because according to the Court, what Article 9 protects is not the word 'Republic', but the republican regime with these characteristics. As a result, the TCC ruled that the amendment provision in question violated Article 9 because it was not in conformity with the characteristic of the republic that it is built upon human rights as stipulated in Article 2 and the Preamble.

One year later, the TCC reviewed another constitutional amendment, which provided that the compensation to be paid to the property owner in expropriation would be calculated not in terms of its real value, but on the basis of tax returns.[88] While the TCC found this amendment constitutional, in doing so, it did exercise substantive review disguised as formal review. In this decision, the Court ruled that the amendment did not infringe upon the essence of the right to property 'when the ideal of social justice is taken into account'.[89]

In another case, the TCC reviewed the same constitutional amendment and an ordinary law in one judgment.[90] While the Court decided there was no ground for a judgment as the provisions had been already annulled, it applied the same procedure and review criteria to a constitutional amendment and an ordinary law under the same file. Clearly, the Court was of the opinion that ordinary laws and constitutional amendments were subject to the same constitutional review procedures and criteria.

The TCC invalidated two more constitutional amendments in this period. It invalidated the provisions that made it impossible to legally challenge the decisions of the High Council of Judges and the High Council of Prosecutors. In both decisions, the Court followed its practice of applying Article 9 as a limitation on constitutional amendments beyond Article 1. In the first case,[91] the TCC stated that the inability to exercise the right to legal remedies against the decisions of the High Council of Judges was in conflict with the principle that the state is built upon

---

[87]Article 2—The Republic of Turkey is a national, democratic, secular and social State governed by rule of law, based upon human rights and the fundamental tenets set forth in the Preamble.

[88]E. 1975/167, K. 1976/19, 23 March 1976, 14 AYMKD 118–160.

[89]With a slightly different composition, the TCC reviewed the very same constitutional amendment again in less than 7 months and invalidated it. Following its rationale regarding Article 9 being a formal rule with the prohibition on proposal, the Court exercised formal review as including the proposability test, and concluded this time that the amendment was unconstitutional, as it infringed upon the essence of the right to property, the principle of equality, and the principle of democratic state governed with the rule of law. See E. 1976/38, K. 1976/46, 12 October 1976, 14 AYMKD 252–286.

[90]E. 1976/26, K. 1976/47, 12 October 1976, 14 AYMKD 287–300.

[91]E. 1976/43, K. 1977/4, 27 January 1977, 15 AYMKD 106–131.

human rights, the principle of the rule of law as specified by Article 2, and the principle of equality, which is a fundamental principle of the rule of law. The Court concluded that such violations by constitutional amendments are impermissible under Article 9. In the second case, regarding the decisions of the High Council of Prosecutors,[92] the Court referred to the first case and annulled the provision on the same grounds.

Further, in this period, in a case regarding *Sayıştay* (The Court of Accounts), the TCC implied in *obiter dictum* that there is a hierarchy among the provisions of the constitution:

> It should be kept in mind that while constitutional norms are of the same value, it is necessary and natural to prioritise the principles regarding the fundamental institutions of the State against other norms when interpreting any norm.[93]

While a few Turkish scholars[94] were of the opinion that there is a hierarchy among the constitutional provisions and that provisions regarding the principles governing the state should be prioritised over the other provisions, the TCC's practice in this period has been widely disapproved of. The broad interpretation of the concept of 'republic' in Article 1 and the Court's reliance on vague terms and the characteristics of the republic have been considered as excessive limitations, since any constitutional amendment could be directly or indirectly linked with the concepts of 'human rights', 'national, democratic, secular and social state', and the principles in the preamble.[95] The counter-majoritarian argument was also put forward following these decisions of the Court, as this practice meant that 15 judges' interpretation of the basic characteristics of the Republic would frustrate the ability of citizens to amend the constitution through their elected representatives.[96]

---

[92]E. 1977/82, K. 1977/117, 27 September 1977, 15 AYMKD 444–464.

[93]E. 1972/56, K. 1973/11, 6 March 1973, 11 AYMKD 141 (my translation).

[94]Coşkun San wrote a detailed account of why the constitutional amendment power is substantively limited. He argued that the constitutional amendment power is conceptually limited and cannot amend the constitution in a way that destroys the constitutional amendment rules, unamendable clauses, fundamental rights and freedoms, political rights and parliament, separation of powers and supra-constitutional limits. See San (1974), pp. 77–89. On the Turkish cases, see Tosun (1978), p. 21, Serim (1977).

[95]Onar (2003), p. 146. Özbudun criticises the Court's approach for four reasons. Firstly, since it is only the republican form of the state that is protected in Article 9, it was a mistake to also include the characteristics of the republic as protected principles, as the constituent power would have expressly stated it had it wished to include them. Secondly, it is impossible to avoid substantive review when deciding whether a constitutional amendment is in line with the characteristics of the republic. Thirdly, the meanings of the enumerated characteristics of the republic are so vague that the Court has too wide a discretion. Lastly, in times of struggle between constitutional courts and the majority of the people, experience shows that the authority of the former is at the risk of being taken away. See Özbudun (2010), pp. 177–178. Also, for a critical account of unamendability with a wide scope in the context of the Bangladeshi constitution, see Hoque (this volume).

[96]Turhan (1976), p. 100.

3.3 Restrained Formal Review (1982–2008)

As the 1971 amendments had no significant effect on the jurisprudence of the TCC, the drafters of Turkey's current 1982 Constitution regulated the constitutional review of constitutional amendments in a most specific manner. Following the model of the amended 1961 Constitution, the 1982 Constitution restricts the TCC's authority to review constitutional amendments only to formal grounds, but it also specifies in detail what the criteria for formal review are. The relevant clauses in Article 148, entitled 'Functions and Powers' (of the TCC) read as follows:

> The Constitutional Court shall examine the constitutionality, in respect of both form and substance, of laws, decrees having the force of law and the Rules of Procedure of the Grand National Assembly of Turkey, and decide on individual applications. Constitutional amendments shall be examined and verified *only with regard to their form* … the verification of constitutional amendments shall be *restricted to consideration of whether the requisite majorities were obtained for the proposal and in the ballot, and whether the prohibition on debates under expedited procedure was observed* [emphases added].

While restricting the authority of the TCC, it should be noted that, with Article 4, the constitution-makers extended the unamendable clauses and included along with Article 1, which stipulated the form of the state as a republic, Articles 2 and 3, which are entitled 'Characteristics of the Republic', and 'Integrity, official language, flag, national anthem, and the capital of the State' respectively[97]:

> The provision of Article 1 regarding the form of the State being a Republic, the characteristics of the Republic in Article 2, and the provisions of Article 3 shall not be amended, nor shall their amendment be proposed.

In 1987, the first constitutional amendment after 1982 that the TCC reviewed provided for a referendum for the lifting of the political rights restrictions on some politicians.[98] The unconstitutionality claim concerned the drafting of the law, in which the first paragraph made the necessary amendment, yet the second paragraph stipulated it to be put to a referendum. With the adoption of the amendment, according to the claim, the constitution had been amended and the referendum clause was unconstitutional, as the constitutional procedure for constitutional amendments had already been fulfilled. The TCC dismissed this request for invalidation by clearly stating that its authority is limited to the review of whether the majorities for proposal and the voting were obtained and that the prohibition of expedited procedure was observed.[99]

---

[97]Extension of the scope of unamendability while simultaneously restricting the TCC's authority over constitutional amendments has been regarded by many as an incoherence. See Onar (2003), pp. 156–164. Indeed, this seems to be an incoherency from a legal constitutionalist perspective, but as touched upon below, unamendability clauses without a judicial guarantee may be justified in terms of political constitutionalism.

[98]Law No 3361 dated 17 May 1987.

[99]E. 1987/9, K. 1987/15, 18 June 1987, 23 AYMKD 282–294.

Until 2007, twelve more amendments have been made to the 1982 Constitution, but none of them were taken to the TCC. In 2007, two constitutional amendments were taken to the TCC with requests for annulment.

The first amendment included the reduction of the legislative term from 5 to 4 years, the election of the president by popular vote, the introduction of clearer provisions regarding the majorities for quorum and ballot in the meetings of Parliament,[100] and some technical regulations and transitional provisions regarding the election of the president.[101] The claim for unconstitutionality, in this case, which was petitioned jointly by President Sezer and 140 deputies, was on formal grounds. The TCC exercised formal review and decided the amendment was adopted in line with the required procedure, thus constitutionally.[102]

The second amendment brought before the TCC in 2007 was regarding changes to the constitutional amendments made with Law No. 5678, which were then pending for a referendum.[103] This amendment sought to remove the provisional clauses in the pending amendment allowing the popular election of the next president and provided for still another parliamentary presidential election. Again, the TCC stated that it could only review constitutional amendments for the observance of the required majorities for proposal and voting, and of the prohibition of expedited procedure.[104]

In none of these three cases were there claims of unconstitutionality on the grounds that the amendments were in conflict with the unamendable clauses. The claims were regarding procedural and formal aspects of the amendments, but the TCC strictly conformed to the restrictions on its authority to review constitutional amendments as specified by Article 148 of the constitution.

3.4 The Activist Comeback in 2008

2008 witnessed the TCC's sharp return to its post-1971 judicial activism. On 9 February 2008, Parliament enacted Law No. 5735 on Amending Some Provisions of the Constitution of the Republic of Turkey. The amendment included an additional paragraph to the article on equality and another to the right to education.[105]

---

[100]This was deemed necessary as a result of the TCC's striking down the presidential election in the Turkish Parliament in 2007. See Özbudun (2014), pp. 299–300.

[101]Law No 5678 dated 31 May 2007.

[102]E. 2007/72, K. 2007/68, 5 July 2007, 44/2 AYMKD 1053–1108.

[103]Law No 5697 dated 16 October 2007.

[104]E. 2007/99, K. 2007/86, 27 November 2007, 45/1 AYMKD 429–456.

[105]The text of the amendment was as follows: Article 1—The phrase 'and in benefiting from all kinds of public services' is added after the phrase 'in all their proceedings' in Paragraph four of Article 10 of the Constitution of the Republic of Turkey dated 7.11.1982 and with Law No. 2709. Article 2—The following paragraph is added after Paragraph six of Article 42 of the Constitution of the Republic of Turkey. 'No one can be deprived of the right to higher education due to any

'For a long time some female students have not been able to enjoy the right to education in universities due to their outfit covering their heads' and 'in order to bring up generations free in thinking, free in conscience, free in understanding, and due to the principle of equality before law, persons should not face discrimination on any grounds in the utilisation of the right to higher education', the General Reasons for this amendment stated.[106] After the constitutional amendment came into force, the Republican People's Party (*Cumhuriyet Halk Partisi*) (*CHP*), the main opposition party, petitioned the TCC to annul the amendment on the grounds that it was in conflict with the unamendable provisions of the constitution.

Once more, the TCC exercised substantive review of the constitutional amendment, disguised as formal review.[107] In this decision, famously known as the Headscarf Decision, the Court first made a distinction between the original constituent power and derived constituent power, as to the legal position of Parliament to make constitutional amendments. The Court defined the original constituent power as follows:

> Original constituent power is the constitution-making will that specifies the fundamentals of the new legal order in the case of an interruption in the political regime of a certain country. In participatory, deliberative and reconciliatory democracies, it is the people that holds the original constituent power.[108]

According to the Court, once a new constitution is made by the original constituent power, it is the source of legitimacy of the authorities of all state organs, including Parliament in its capacity to make constitutional amendments following Article 175, which regulates amendments to the constitution. Article 175 grants Parliament the authority to make constitutional amendments, and the Court states that Parliament is able to make constitutional amendments following Article 175 only within the limits imposed by the constitution.

The TCC then referred to Article 4 of the constitution, which stipulates that the provisions of Articles 1, 2 and 3 are unamendable. The Court interpreted this amendment prohibition in a way that constitutional amendments must be in line with the 'fundamental preference that is embodied in the first three articles of the constitution'.[109] As for the TCC's authority over constitutional amendments, Article 148 reads, '... the verification of constitutional amendments shall be restricted to consideration of whether the requisite majorities were obtained for the proposal and in the ballot, and whether the prohibition on debates under expedited

---

reason other than expressly written in the law. The limits of the exercise of this right shall be determined by law.' Article 3—This Act shall come into force on the date of its promulgation and voted in whole if put to referendum.

[106]General Reasons for this amendment can be reached at www2.tbmm.gov.tr/d23/2/2-0141.pdf. accessed 1 August 2016.

[107]E. 2008/16, K. 2008/116, 5 June 2008, 45/2 AYMKD 1195–1253.

[108]Ibid., p. 1231 (my translation).

[109]Ibid., p. 1232 (my translation).

procedure was observed'. According to the Court, the review of the requisite majorities condition for the proposal included reviewing whether a 'valid proposal' had been made.[110] The Court, therefore, concluded that a parliamentary act amending the first three articles or amending other articles affecting the first three articles, as they fail to be proposed constitutionally, needed to be invalidated.

After creating this framework for the constitutionality test of the formal review, the Court went on to review the substance of the amendment vis-à-vis the unamendable clauses, and ruled it unconstitutional, since it found that the amendment violated the unamendable principle of secularism.[111]

While the Headscarf Decision of 2008 was the only example of the TCC's activist approach regarding the review of constitutional amendments during the era of the 1982 Constitution, it took only 2 years for the Court to repeat its interpretation regarding the limits on constitutional change and its authority to review constitutional amendments.[112] In March 2010, the deputies of the ruling Justice and Development Party (Adalet ve Kalkınma Partisi) (AKP) proposed Law No. 5982, a democratisation package in the form of a constitutional amendment, which was later adopted by a referendum on 12 September 2010. The constitutional amendment package included 26 articles reforming various principles and institutions in the constitution, ranging from the compositions and authorities of the High Council of Judges and Prosecutors (HSYK) and the TCC to social rights and protection of personal data, as well as creating the institutions of ombudsman and constitutional complaint.[113] After the enactment of the amendment in Parliament, but before the referendum took place, the deputies of the CHP petitioned the TCC to annul the

---

[110]A linguistic explanation must be made here. In Turkish, the clause in Article 148 reads 'teklif ve oylama çoğunluğuna ve ivedilikle görüşülemeyeceği şartına uyulup uyulmadığı', which includes three elements as the criteria for formal propriety: (i) teklif çoğunluğu (majority for proposal), (ii) oylama çoğunluğu (majority for voting), (iii) ivedilikle görüşülemeyeceği (not to be debated under expedited procedure). The TCC interprets 'teklif ve oylama çoğunluğu' not as 'the majority for proposal and voting', but as 'the proposal, and the majority of voting', therefore applying the regularity of proposal as an extra criterion. While Oder thinks this reasoning of the Court is at odds with Article 148, she argues that the systematic and teleological interpretations of the constitution support the Court's practice, when the lex specialis nature and the objective telos of the unamendability clause are considered. See Oder (2010), p. 54. On Oder's cautious justification for the judicial enforceability of Article 4, see Sect. 4 of this chapter below.

[111]For the discussion of the substantive review in this decision, which is left out here as it is out of the scope of this chapter, see Özbudun (2014), pp. 304–306, Roznai and Yolcu (2012), pp. 202–206, Jacobsohn (2010), pp. 327–337, Hirschl (2010), pp. 157–159, Can (2013), pp. 287–292. For a test of the TCC's rationale in the Headscarf Decision by Hans Kelsen's Grundnorm and HLA Hart's rule of recognition, see Acar (2009), p. 141.

[112]E. 2010/49, K. 2010/87, 7 July 2010, 47/2 AYMKD 1069–1237.

[113]For an overview of this constitutional amendment package, see Gönenç (2010).

amendment on the grounds that it is not in conformity with the unamendable provisions of the constitution.

In this case, the TCC repeated its reasoning in the Headscarf Decision regarding the limits to constitutional amendments, and further defined the limits more specifically, adding that 'the substantive review of constitutional amendments must be regarding and limited to whether the principles which are unamendable and which their amendments cannot be proposed have been directly or indirectly destroyed or emptied of their content and rendered meaningless'.[114]

In the substantive review, the Court found a conflict with the principle of 'a democratic state [...] governed by the rule of law' and declared unconstitutional only the voting procedures to the *HSYK* and the TCC, and the provisions allowing the president to appoint political science and economics academics or senior executives to the *HSYK*. In terms of substantive review, the result was relatively minor. However, the TCC clearly insisted on its reasoning regarding the limits on constitutional change, and expressly stated that it also exercises substantive review of constitutional amendments.

The decisions of 2008 and 2010 have been regarded by most as clear instances of ultra vires,[115] and by one scholar as 'the final example of the paranoid schizophrenic state of the Court, when the subject matter is the protection of Kemalist ideology'.[116] According to these criticisms, the historical fact that the gradual restriction of the TCC's authority to review constitutional amendments should mean that it must not exercise substantive review whatsoever. Furthermore, it has been suggested that the institutions of state are deemed incompetent unless they are authorised by the constitution, the rules providing for state authority are exceptional, and thus cannot be interpreted in ways that extend the scope of authority.[117]

The Venice Commission in its *Report on Constitutional Amendment* has also criticised the TCC's interpretation of the unamendable provisions in the Headscarf Decision.[118] The Commission concluded, 'unamendable provisions and principles should be interpreted and applied narrowly'.[119]

In a more recent decision,[120] the TCC rejected applications by 70 deputies to invalidate a constitutional amendment selectively lifting parliamentary

---

[114]E. 2010/49 (2010) 1155 (my translation).

[115]Roznai and Yolcu (2012), pp. 197–198, Özbudun (2009), p. 537, Can (2013), pp. 278–287, Abdulhakimoğulları and Baykan (2012), pp. 17, 32, Aydın (2010), pp. 215, 238, Köker (2010), pp. 328, 335.

[116]Saygılı (2010), p. 136. Kemalism is the founding ideology of the Republic of Turkey, named after Mustafa Kemal Atatürk, the founder of the Republic. See Tunçay (2016).

[117]Köker (2010), p. 335.

[118]European Commission for Democracy Through Law (Venice Commission), 'Report on Constitutional Amendment' CDL-AD(2010)001, para 234 www.venice.coe.int/webforms/documents/default.aspx?pdffile=CDL-AD(2010)001-e. 1 August 2016.

[119]Ibid., para 250.

[120]E. 2016/54, K. 2016/117, 3 June 2016 http://kararlaryeni.anayasa.gov.tr/Uploads/2016-117.doc. Accessed 1 August 2016.

immunity.[121] The applications were made by individual deputies[122] who argued, *inter alia*, that all acts lifting parliamentary immunity, including constitutional amendments, are subject to review under Article 85 of the Constitution.[123] The Court rejected this argument and held that it is only authorised to review constitutional amendments according to the procedure set out in Article 148. Importantly, the Court, moving away from its jurisprudence of 2008 and 2010 decisions, stated in *obiter dictum* in this *unanimous* decision that constitutional amendments cannot be reviewed with regard to their substance but only with regard to their form, and that this is limited to the review of whether the requisite majorities were obtained for the proposal and in the ballot, and whether the prohibition on debates under expedited procedure was observed.[124] This is especially striking as two judges, Osman Alifeyyaz Paksüt and Serdar Özgüldür, who argued for review under Article 4 in 2008 and 2010, joined the majority opinion in this case to abandon their earlier position.[125]

4 A Political Clause of Unamendability

As I explained, in three different constitutional settings, the Turkish Constitutional Court managed to find a way to invalidate constitutional amendments on the grounds that they violated the unamendability clause. In doing so, it made use of several arguments in different cases, ranging from arguments on the nature of

---

[121]For the English translation of this law amending the constitution, see European Commission for Democracy Through Law (Venice Commission), 'Turkey Law No. 6718 Constitutional Amendment as to Lifting Parliamentary Immunity' CDL-REF(2016)056 www.venice.coe.int/webforms/documents/default.aspx?pdffile=CDL-REF(2016)056-e. Accessed 1 October 2016.

[122]The reason why a case under Article 148 could not be brought before the Constitutional Court was that the total number of deputies sought to challenge the amendment fell short of 110, as Kemal Kılıçdaroğlu, leader of the main opposition party CHP, urged his party's deputies not to sign a petition challenging the amendment's constitutionality. See 'Rift in CHP over lifting parliamentary immunities widens' *Hürriyet Daily News* (9 June 2016). www.hurriyetdailynews.com/rift-in-chp-over-lifting-parliamentary-immunities-widens.aspx?pageID=238&nID=100309&NewsCatID=338. Accessed 1 August 2016.

[123]Article 85—(As amended on July 23, 1995; Act No. 4121) If the parliamentary immunity of a deputy has been lifted or if the loss of membership has been decided according to the first, third or fourth paragraphs of Article 84, the deputy in question or another deputy may, within seven days from the date of the decision of the Plenary, appeal to the Constitutional Court, for the decision to be annulled on the grounds that it is contrary to the Constitution, law or the Rules of Procedure. The Constitutional Court shall make the final decision on the appeal within fifteen days.

[124]E. 2016/54 (2016) para 11.

[125]This amendment was specifically aimed at the deputies of the mainly Kurdish HDP (People's Democratic Party), as was later demonstrated by the detainment and arrest of the co-chairpersons and other deputies of the HDP from November 2016 onwards. The political contexts of the cases and the accompanying shift in the legal stances of the judges tell a story about 'the spirit of the Turkish constitution'. On the problematic nature of this amendment, see Acar (2016).

constitutional amendments to the definition of constituent power and the scope of the unamendability clause. In an attempt to look for a justification for the Court's lines of reasoning, one might resort to Carl Schmitt's positive concept of constitution. In doing so, one realises that the Court's understanding of the concept of constitution through a duality of acts of original and derived constituent powers bears a resemblance to Schmitt's distinction of the constitution and constitutional laws. Now, the concept of derived constituent power does not sound Schmittian at all. Indeed, for Schmitt, it is a fundamental error to regard a constitutionally regulated authority a *pouvoir constituant*.[126] However, the TCC's usage of the term 'derived constituent power' is not to stress that it is a *pouvoir constituant* per se, as the Turkish equivalent of constituent power (*kurucu iktidar*) in legal scholarship simply corresponds to law-making at the constitutional level.[127] By establishing this distinction, the Court simply tries to create a core within the constitution, untouchable by any power, save for the people directly acting as the sovereign. In the Headscarf Decision, the TCC states that the original constituent power specifies the fundamentals of the legal order, and in a democratic system, this power belongs to the people.[128] Therefore, presumably unwittingly, the TCC adopts Schmitt's distinction of changing the constitution by the constituent power and changing constitutional laws by the constitutional amendment power.

In the first era of the TCC's review of constitutional amendments, when there were no specific provisions in the Turkish constitution as to the constitutional review of constitutional amendments, the Court made the arguments that constitutional amendments may not be contrary to 'the spirit of the constitution' and 'the fundamental values of the constitutional order', and that they cannot violate 'the characteristics of the republic', as the amendment of the republican form of the state was prohibited. This understanding of the constitution with intrinsic limits to its amendment is based on a view that there is a fundamental political preference that needs to be guarded against contingent majorities, which corresponds to Schmitt's idea of the positive constitution.

Another argument the TCC made while the judicial review of constitutional amendments was not expressly provided for in the constitution was that constitutional amendments were acts of ordinary legislation, and thus would be regarded as 'laws' and subject to the same review constraints and procedures (formally and substantively). This was an implicit reference to the distinction of constituent power and constitutional amendment power, where the Court regarded itself competent to determine whether the constitutional amendment in question was in line with the

---

[126]Schmitt (2008), p. 146.

[127]Joel Colón-Ríos writes that Schmitt would probably regard this widespread distinction especially in the French and Latin American doctrine a conceptual confusion. See Colón-Ríos (2011), p. 381.

[128]For a defence of unamendability based on this distinction named slightly differently as primary and secondary constituent powers, see Roznai (this volume). Roznai argues that unamendability is 'the ultimate expression of *democracy*', as it protects the choices of the more fundamental political power, i.e. the primary constituent power.

spirit of the constitution and whether it was a progressive undertaking that would not cause regress to the Turkish society, presumably referring to the founding Kemalist principles. In this way, the Court made Schmitt's distinction of the constitution and constitutional laws, only with a different label.

The TCC's argument in justifying its review of constitutional amendments that it protects the constitution against the sovereignty of the majority illuminates the function it accords itself when taken together with the fact that the Court has not been a liberal institution that promoted rights since its establishment.[129] Mostly in party closure and constitutional amendment cases, the TCC has a record of protecting the constitution's political ideology over rights.[130] Therefore, the TCC has *functionally* been the guardian of the constitution in the Schmittian sense, as it protected the constituent choice entrenched in the constitution against the democratic will to amend the constitution. Having said that, it cannot be regarded as a Schmittian guardian of the constitution *institutionally*, as Schmitt opposes granting the protection of the constitution to judicial bodies, as they lack democratic credentials by nature.

The TCC's interpretation of the unamendability clause (Article 4) in the constitution as a legal limitation on the constitutional amendment power is a contentious one. In the constitutional amendment case of 2010, the TCC clearly expressed the scope of Article 4 and how it limits the constitutional amendment power. The substantive review of constitutional amendments, the Court argued, would be as to whether they *directly* or *indirectly* destroyed or emptied the content of the unamendable principles, and thus rendered them meaningless. Consequently, the TCC attached to Article 4 an effect stretching over the whole constitution. The Court created a test for constitutional amendments to any provision of the constitution to see whether they compromise the republican form of the state, the national, democratic, secular and social characteristics of the state, the principles of the rule of law and human rights, and perhaps even the arguably chauvinistic 'fundamental tenets set forth in the preamble', as referred to in the unamendable Article 2.

While the legal significance of Article 4 is far from settled in Turkish constitutional scholarship,[131] many argue that the lack of the TCC's authority to review

---

[129]For a study of the TCC's ideology-based paradigm through its jurisprudence on political rights, see Arslan (2002), p. 9. On how the TCC's judicial activism has played out with regard to the protection of human rights, see Hakyemez (2009).

[130]These two practices of the Turkish Constitutional Court are among the clearest examples of the militant democracy practice in Turkey. See Oder (2009), Hakyemez (2000).

[131]When the then Speaker of the Turkish Parliament Cemil Çiçek convened a meeting of constitutional law professors in Turkey in 2011 to consult them regarding the establishment of the Constitution Reconciliation Committee which would draft a new constitution, the value of the unamendability clause was a central theme in the meeting. The (legal) significance of Article 4 surfaced in the debate regarding whether the Turkish parliament could make a completely new constitution or what it set out to do would be a major constitutional amendment. Article 4 was regarded in the meeting by most academics as not an obstacle in making major constitutional changes. Participants agreed the principles it made unamendable should be protected in essence, but most argued that they could be amended to make the wording better and the principles clearer.

constitutional amendments substantively deprives Article 4 of a legal sanction.[132] Some others are, however, more reluctant in denying legal enforceability to the unamendability clause. Oder, for instance, suggests an original justification for a cautious substantive judicial review of amendments under the present constitutional setting. While criticising the TCC's textual twist in Article 148 in 2008 and 2010 decisions explained above, she argues that what the purpose of the existence of unamendable clauses that incorporate the basic constitutional values requires overrides what the textual interpretation of Article 148 requires.[133] Still, She adds the caveat that the Court should leave a greater margin of political discretion to the constitutional amendment power than it would do to ordinary legislation.[134]

Lastly, many scholars have also argued for the double amendment procedure, i.e. since Article 4 does not prohibit its own amendment, it is permissible to amend the unamendability clause first, and then amend the first three articles.[135] This formalist approach, however, does not sufficiently address the question of why Article 4 exists at all. An attempt to both argue that Article 4 is legally amendable and that it serves the idea of constitutionalism, can be done through a political understanding of the constitutional provision. The first step of the double amendment procedure, namely the parliamentary procedure and debate on amending Article 4, would still serve constitutionalist purposes, compared to the non-existence of such a norm at all. Indeed, the constituent choice of entrenching unamendable clauses and simultaneously preventing the judiciary from enforcing this unamendability shows that the unamendability clause is rather addressed to the political actors, creating political accountability. The making of this constituent choice can also be strikingly seen in the Constituent Assembly's debates. As the unamendability clause was debated in the making of the 1982 Constitution in the Advisory Council, when a deputy asked, 'what if the unamendability clause prohibiting the amendment of the republican form of the state is amended?', the speaker of the Advisory Council's Constitution Committee replied 'our dear friend should not worry, we 45 million (then Turkey's population) would oppose this!'.[136] The unamendability clause in the Turkish constitution, therefore, seems to carry the characteristics of a political check rather than a legal one.

It is worth noting that Articles 1, 2 and 3 were seen to be respected for political reasons rather than because of a legal force attached to Article 4. See TBMM, *TBMM Başkanı Cemil Çiçek Başkanlığında Anayasa Hukuku Profesörleri ile Toplantı* (Ankara, 19 September 2011).

[132]Özbudun (2010), pp. 181–182, Kaboğlu (2017), p. 352, Erdoğan (2005), p. 308.

[133]Oder (2010), pp. 53–54.

[134]Ibid., p. 55.

[135]Onar (2003), pp. 19–20, Özbudun (2010), p. 173, Tanör (2013), p. 160.

[136]Onar (2003), pp. 164–165.

5   Concluding Remarks

The Turkish Constitutional Court's judicial activism in constitutional amendment cases blended with its extension of the scope of the unamendability clauses faced wide and occasionally harsh criticism. The orthodox normativist viewpoint interprets the unamendability clause much more narrowly, as well as rejecting outright the Court's authority to review constitutional amendments. However, if Carl Schmitt's positive concept of constitution is adopted for the sake of argument, it can rightly be argued that the constitutional amendment power should not be regarded as competent to harm or destroy the values and principles that are regarded as the content of the positive constitution. Therefore, Schmitt's distinction between the constitution and constitutional laws is but one theory that could justify the Court's argument in this respect. Yet, Schmitt does not regard the judiciary as the legitimate body to protect the democratic fundamental decision, which makes up the positive constitution, against contingent democratic majorities. For him, this authority for oversight belongs exclusively to the popularly elected head of the executive.

Recall that the drafters of the 1982 Constitution chose to considerably expand the scope of unamendability not only to the characteristics of the republic, but also to include the integrity, official language, flag, national anthem, and capital of the state. At the same time, they regulated the Constitutional Court's authority over constitutional amendments in a most specific manner by restricting it to three criteria of procedural technicality. Consequently, it is safe to say that Article 4 is a limitation on the constitutional amendment power without a binding force in the legal sense. It is rather a political check on the Turkish parliament—just as it was in the 1924 Constitution, where the republican form of the state was unamendable but there was no mechanism prescribed for the judicial review of any legislation.

Acknowledgements I would like to thank the participants of the Unamendable Constitutional Provisions workshop at Koç University, and in particular Richard Albert for serving as the discussant for the earlier workshop draft of this chapter with invaluable comments and suggestions, and Bertil Emrah Oder and the anonymous reviewer for written comments. I am grateful to Asli Ozcelik and Thomas Raine for their help and suggestions.

References

Abdulhakimoğulları E, Baykan M (2012) Anayasa Değişikliklerinin Yargısal Denetimi. Ankara Barosu Dergisi 70:17
Acar A (2009) Tension in the Turkish constitutional democracy: legal theory, constitutional review and democracy. Ankara Law Rev 6:141
Acar A (2016) De-constitutionalism in Turkey? Int J Const Law Blog, 19 May 2016. http://www.iconnectblog.com/2016/05/deconstitutionalism-in-Turkey. Accessed 1 Aug 2016
Albert R (2010) Constitutional handcuffs. Ariz State Law J 42:663
Arato A (2011) Multi-track constitutionalism beyond Carl Schmitt. Constellations 18:324
Arslan Z (2002) Conflicting paradigms: political rights in the Turkish Constitutional Court. Critique Crit Middle Eastern Stud 11:9

Arslan Z (2009) Başörtüsü, AK Parti ve Laiklik: Anayasa Mahkemesinden İki Karar Bir Gerekçe. SETA

Aydın M (2010) 1982 Anayasasına Göre Anayasa Değişikliklerinin Şekil Bakımından Denetimi. Gazi Üniversitesi Hukuk Fakültesi Dergisi 14:215

Bellamy R (2007) Political constitutionalism: a republican defence of the constitutionality of democracy. Cambridge University Press, Cambridge

Can O (2013) Kurucu İktidar. Alfa, pp 271–292

Chandrachud C (2017) Constitutional Falsehoods: The Fourth Judges Case and the Basic Structure Doctrine in India. In: Richard A, Bertil E O (eds) An Unconstitutional Constitution? Unamendability in Constitutional Democracies (Springer, Forthcoming). Available at SSRN: www.https://ssrn.com/abstract=3031280.

Colón-Riós J (2011) Carl Schmitt and constituent power in Latin American courts: the cases of Venezuela and Colombia. Constellations 18:381

Dworkin R (1996) Freedom's law: the moral reading of the American constitution. Oxford University Press, Oxford

Ely JH (1980) Democracy and distrust: a theory of judicial review. Harvard University Press, USA

Erdal M (2008) Anayasa Kurallarının Kademelendirilmesi Sorunu. Türkiye Barolar Birliği Dergisi 76:165

Erdoğan M (2005) Anayasa Hukuku. Orion

Eroğul C (1974) Anayasayı Değiştirme Sorunu. AÜSBF

Gönenç L (2010) 2010 proposed constitutional amendments to the 1982 constitution of Turkey (TEPAV Evaluation Note, September 2010). www.tepav.org.tr/upload/files/1284468699-0.2010_Proposed_Constitutional_Amendments_to_the_1982_Constitution_of_Turkey.pdf

Gözler K (1999) Anayasa Normlarının Geçerliliği Sorunu. Ekin

Gözler K (2008) Judicial review of constitutional amendments: a comparative study. Ekin

Habermas J (1996) Between facts and norms. MIT Press, USA

Hakyemez YŞ (2000) Militan Demokrasi Anlayışı ve 1982 Anayasası. Seçkin

Hakyemez YŞ (2009) Anayasa Mahkemesinin Yargısal Aktivizmi ve İnsan Hakları Anlayışı. Yetkin

Hirschl R (2010) Constitutional theocracy. Harvard University Press, USA

Hoque R (this volume) Eternal provisions in the constitution of Bangladesh: a constitution once and for all?

Jacobsohn GJ (2010) Constitutional identity. Harvard University Press, USA

Kaboğlu İÖ (2017) Anayasa Hukuku Dersleri (Genel Esaslar). Legal, p 352

Kalyvas A (2008) Democracy and the politics of the extraordinary: Max Weber, Carl Schmitt, and Hannah Arendt. Cambridge University Press, Cambridge

Kelsen H (1957) The pure theory of law and analytical jurisprudence. In: Kelsen H (ed) What is justice? Justice, law, and politics in the mirror of science. University of California Press, USA

Kelsen H (1992) Introduction to the problems of legal theory (trans: Paulson BL, Paulson SL). Clarendon

Kelsen H (2001) Pure theory of law (trans: Knight M). University of California Press, USA

Kelsen H (2015) In: Vinx L (ed) The guardian of the constitution: Hans Kelsen and Carl Schmitt on the limits of constitutional law. Cambridge University Press, Cambridge

Köker L (2010) Turkey's political-constitutional crisis: an assessment of the role of the constitutional court. Constellations 17:328

Kubalı HN (1971) Anayasa Hukuku Dersleri: Genel Esaslar ve Siyasi Rejimler. İÜHY

Lindahl H (2007) Constituent power and reflexive identity: towards an ontology of collective selfhood. In: Loughlin M, Walker N (eds) The paradox of constitutionalism: constituent power and constitutional form. Oxford University Press, Oxford

Loughlin M (2010) The foundations of public law. Oxford University Press, Oxford

Müller JW (2003) A dangerous mind: Carl Schmitt in post-war European thought. Yale University Press, USA

Oder BE (2009) 'Turkey'. In: Thiel M (ed) The 'Militant Democracy' principle in modern democracies. Ashgate, UK

Oder BE (2010) Anayasa Yargısında Yorum Yöntemleri. Beta

Onar E (2003) Kanunların Anayasaya Uygunluğunun Siyasal ve Yargısal Denetimi ve Yargısal Denetim Alanında Ülkemizde Öncüler. Ankara

Özbudun E (2009) Judicial review of constitutional amendments in Turkey. Eur Public Law 15:533

Özbudun E (2010) Türk Anayasa Hukuku. Yetkin

Özbudun E (2014) Democracy, tutelarism, and the search for a new constitution. In: Rodríguez C et al (eds) Turkey's democratization process. Routledge, London, pp 299–300

Rawls J (2005) Political liberalism. Columbia University Press, USA, p 232

Raz J (2009) Between authority and interpretation: on the theory of law and practical reason. Oxford University Press, Oxford

Roznai Y (2013) Unconstitutional constitutional amendments—the migration and success of a constitutional idea. Am J Comp Law 61:657

Roznai Y (this volume) Necrocracy or democracy? Assessing Objections to Formal Unamendability

Roznai Y, Yolcu S (2012) An unconstitutional constitutional amendment—The Turkish perspective: a comment on the Turkish Constitutional Court's headscarf decision. Int J Const Law 10:175

San C (1974) Anayasa Değişiklikleri ve Anayasa Gelişmeleri. AİTİA

Saygılı A (2010) What is behind the headscarf ruling of the Turkish Constitutional Court? Turk Stud 11:127

Schmitt C (1985) The crisis of parliamentary democracy (trans: Kennedy E). MIT Press, USA

Schmitt C (1996) Der Hüter der Verfassung. Duncker & Humblot, Germany

Schmitt C (2005) Political theology: four chapters on the concept of sovereignty. University of Chicago Press, USA

Schmitt C (2008) Constitutional theory (trans: Seitzer J). Duke University, USA

Schmitt C (2013) Dictatorship (trans: Hoelzl M, Ward G). Polity, UK

Serim E (1977) Anayasayı Değiştirme Sorunu. Ankara Barosu Dergisi 34:33

Serozan R (1972) Anayasayı Değiştirme Yetkisinin Sınırları. İstanbul Üniversitesi Hukuk Fakültesi Mecmuası 37:135

Sieyès EJ (2003) What is the third estate? In: Sieyès EJ (ed) Political writings including the debate between Sieyès and Tom Paine in 1791 (trans: Sonenscher M). Hackett, UK

Sweet AS (2007) The juridical Coup d'Etat and the problem of authority. Ger Law J 8:10

Tanör B (2013) İki Anayasa: 1961–1982. XII Levha

Tosun Ö (1978) Anayasanın Anayasaya Aykırılığı Sorunu Hakkında Anayasa Mahkemesi Kararları. Ceza Hukuku ve Kriminoloji Dergisi 1:21

Tunçay M (2016) 'Kemalism'. The oxford encyclopedia of the Islamic world. Oxford Islamic studies online www.oxfordislamicstudies.com/article/opr/t236/e0440. Accessed 1 Aug 2016

Turhan M (1976) Anayasaya Aykırı Anayasa Değişiklikleri. Ankara Üniversitesi Hukuk Fakültesi Dergisi 33:63

Vinx L (2015) The guardian of the constitution: Hans Kelsen and Carl Schmitt on the limits of constitutional law. Cambridge University Press, Cambridge

Vinx L (2016) Carl Schmitt and the problem of constitutional guardianship. In: Arvidsson M, Brännström L, Minkkinen P (eds) The contemporary relevance of Carl Schmitt: law, politics, theology. Routledge, London

Waldron J (2006) The core of the case against judicial review. Yale Law J 115:1346

Yegen O (this volume) Debates on unamendable articles: deadlock on Turkey's constitution-making process

Brazil in the Context of the Debate Over Unamendability in Latin America

Juliano Zaiden Benvindo

Abstract Unamendability appears to be a contradictory concept in Latin America. Though the rate among its countries varies strongly and the pace of constitutional replacements has waned in the last years, Latin America has long been portrayed as the region where changing the constitution is a common pattern. This paper will explore how this debate has taken place in Brazil, a major player in Latin America whose constitutionalism has been rather underexplored, though unamendability has long been regarded as a logical concept in its constitutionalism. Brazil is an interesting example since it has inscribed far-reaching unamendable provisions in its Constitution and has struck down constitutional amendments through judicial review in some relevant cases. Moreover, the fact that it had set out unamendable clauses in the constitutional text has not prevented its Supreme Court and the constitutional literature from going further in interpreting the scope of such clauses, expanding thereby the very concept of unamendability.

1 Introduction

Unamendability appears to be quite a contradictory concept in Latin America, where constitutional change has long been a natural feature of its many constitutionalisms. Though the rate among its countries varies strongly,[1] and the pace of constitutional replacements waned in the last years,[2] Latin America has long been portrayed as the region in the globe where the idea of changing the constitution, either by amending or replacing it, is a common pattern.[3] As Detlef Nolte counted, "in the period between 1978 and 2010, 350 constitutional amendments have been passed in Latin America, and the annual rate of amendments has increased in most of the countries in the region

---

[1]Nolte and Schilling-Vacaflor (2012).
[2]Negretto (2012), pp. 752–753.
[3]Nolte and Schilling-Vacaflor (2012), p. 753.

J. Z. Benvindo (✉)
University of Brasília, Brasília, Brazil
e-mail: juliano@unb.br

© Springer International Publishing AG, part of Springer Nature 2018
R. Albert and B. E. Oder (eds.), *An Unamendable Constitution?*
Ius Gentium: Comparative Perspectives on Law and Justice 68,
https://doi.org/10.1007/978-3-319-95141-6_13

345

in the decade 2000–2009 compared to 1990."[4] In such a context, the prospect that any particular constitutional provision is not prone to amendment appears to be quite a challenge. Countries like Brazil and Mexico, in particular, where the amendment rate clearly places them among the champions in the world[5] (Brazil has already amended its 1988 Constitution more than 100 times, while Mexico has surpassed the mark of 700 amendments to its 1917 Constitution),[6] may interpret flexibility as a fundamental principle of its constitutional culture and a way of making their Constitutions more resilient to replacement. Other countries, such as Argentina, where for an amendment to pass a convention must be called,[7] the very concept of amendment quite merges with that of revision, and such a rigidity could better explain why the 1853 Argentinean Constitution, as last revised in 1994, has since not been amended. In this case, it is as if the very concept of unamendability, due to the rigidity of the Argentinean constitutional framework, has become a practical effect at least in the last 20 and few years. Other Latin American countries, in their turn, do not differ from the average amendment rate in the world. Indeed, as Gabriel Negretto argues, "the mean number of amendments is significantly higher in western Europe than in Latin America."[8]

Unamendability is, therefore, a much more complex concept when confronted with the varying constitutional frameworks and cultures in Latin America. There is not a single pattern of how amendments are undertaken in the distinct countries in the region, some using this mechanism quite routinely, others practically avoiding it, and most using it in not very different ways from many other countries in the globe. It is no wonder that also the way courts have dealt with such a concept varies across the region. Unamendability tends to play a more visible role as a normative concept in countries where there is no unamendable clause in their constitutions or where the hypotheses for formal unamendability are not broad enough to reach distinct situations. In countries where unamendability is inscribed in the constitutional text and those provisions are vague, open, and far-reaching, there is, at least in principle, a formal barrier to such changes, so the appeal to unamendability as a normative and abstract concept, at first sight, seems less necessary. In both circumstances, the role of Supreme Courts in exerting judicial review of constitutional amendments, though not a condition,[9] has become a more prominent feature of contemporary constitutionalism. Especially in countries where Supreme Courts have gained strength[10] in the form of declaring the unconstitutionality of an amendment based on either explicit or implicit unamendability, the debate over the limits of the judiciary in some sensitive matters or the encroachment on political

---

[4]Nolte (2008).

[5]See Ginsburg and Melton (2015), p. 686, 689.

[6]See Pou-Giménez and Pozas-Loyo (2018).

[7]Constitution of the Argentine Nation, Article 30.

[8]Negretto (2012), p. 753.

[9]See Roznai (2017) (arguing that "the recognition of implicit unamendability does not necessarily carry with it judicial review of constitutional amendments").

[10]See Tushnet (2003), pp. 2781–2782.

affairs has also gained momentum. In Latin America, this symptom has been visibly felt as, first, supreme courts have become more powerful and socially trusted as a legitimate body for determining the boundaries of constitutional change,[11] and, second, constitutionalism has itself been increasingly regarded as the needed counterpart of a successful democracy.

In the comparative constitutional literature, whenever the debate over una-mendability appears, the most cited and studied examples in Latin America come from Colombia, whose Constitutional Court has become the most acclaimed constitutional court in the region. Manuel José Cepeda Espinosa and David Landau, for instance, argue that "few if any courts in the world have had such a profound impact on different spheres of society and public policy."[12] One such impact is its far-reaching interpretation of the concept of unamendability even in the absence of any explicit unamendable provision in Colombia's 1991 Constitution. The Colombian Constitutional Court has largely been praised, along with the Indian Supreme Court, as the one that has best developed the concept of unconstitutional constitutional amendments and has deployed it quite frequently.[13] The so-called "substitution of the constitution doctrine" is based, among others, on the premise that "the power to amend the constitution does not imply the power to replace it, but only to modify it."[14] It would be then a way to "protect the constitutional democracy against a merely majoritarian account of democratic procedures."[15] The Constitutional Court has applied it to the distinct circumstances,[16] the most famous of which is the decision that declared unconstitutional a call for a referendum allowing President Alvaro Uribe to be reelected for the third consecutive term.[17] In that decision, the Court stated that such a reelection "would involve a breakdown of the constitutional order and would substitute various definite axes of the 1991 Constitution."[18] Its frequent application, however, has raised some controversy over the limits of the Constitutional Court, and scholars have argued that the Court has, in some circumstances, used it to defend vested interests[19] or to strike down "ordinary exercises of the amendment power."[20]

Though Colombia is certainly a rich source, other countries in Latin America have also provided relevant contributions to the subject. The comparative constitutional literature, however, has practically overlooked those other Latin American

---

[11]See Helmke and Ríos-Figueroa (2011) (contending that "Constitutional courts have taken on a pivotal political role throughout the region").

[12]Espinosa and Landau (2017).

[13]Ibid., p. 328.

[14]Bernal (2013), p. 339, 340.

[15]Ramirez-Cleves (2016), p. 213.

[16]Bernal (2013), pp. 341–346.

[17]Colombian Constitutional Court, Decision C-141, 2010.

[18]Colombian Constitutional Court, Decision C-141, 2010, as translated by Manuel José Cepeda Espinosa and David Landau in Espinosa and Landau (2017), p. 358.

[19]See Sarria (2016).

[20]Dixon and Landau (2015), p. 620.

realities,[21] following the natural trend of concentrating on the same countries whenever a new topic gains ground.[22] This paper will explore how this debate has taken place in Brazil, a major player in Latin America whose constitutionalism has been rather underexplored, though unamendability has long been interpreted as a logical concept in its constitutionalism and been deployed in distinct cases by its Supreme Court. Brazil, as many countries in Latin America, is a young democracy whose past was marked by severe instabilities and constitutional changes. It has endured a civil–military dictatorship from 1964 to 1985 and, in 1988, a new democratic and largely participative Constitution was drafted, which boosted a reconfiguration of the relationship among the three branches. In particular, the Supreme Court has since gradually gained the presence as a central player not only in typical activities of constitutional courts, such as exerting the judicial review and serving as a check on the other powers, but also in sensitive political matters. If, in the period right after the transition to democracy, the STF was still a very self-restrained court, much having to do with the legacy of the military dictatorship,[23] over the years of democratic life, its participation in defining the limits of activity of the other branches has become much more visible. The judicial review of constitutional amendments—and, thereby, the adoption of the very concept of unamendability—has been regarded as a natural consequence of its role as guardian of the Constitution.

This paper will fill this gap by presenting a country which, unlike Colombia, has inscribed, in its 1988 Constitution, broad and far-reaching unamendable provisions. While Colombia, for example, had to build a new theoretical concept based on the premise that "the power to amend the constitution does not imply the power to replace it, but only to modify it,"[24] Brazil could directly make reference to one of its unamendable provisions to strike down a constitutional amendment. However, the fact that it had explicitly set out those unamendable clauses in the constitutional text has not prevented its Supreme Court and the constitutional literature from going much further in interpreting the scope of such amendments. The debate over the extension of those amendments, especially the one that protects "individual rights and guarantees,"[25] has been remarkably fruitful. Moreover, the way the Supreme Court has dealt with such unamendable provisions has shown a gradual, though still self-restrained, behavior toward a more active role in shielding the Constitution from changes by parliament. This paper will explore how this debate has taken place in the Brazilian constitutional literature and how the Supreme Court has dealt with such a concept in its decisions. It will conclude by asking whether and to which extent, as a rising influential Supreme Court, unamendability may function as a general concept to expand its powers even further.

---

[21]One important exception is Roznai (2017).

[22]See Hirschl (2014) (arguing that "selection biases abound" in the comparative constitutional literature).

[23]See Koerner (2013), pp. 69–85.

[24]Bernal (2013), p. 340.

[25]Constitution of the Federative Republic of Brazil, Article 60, §4, IV.

2   The Debate Over Unamendable Clauses in the Brazilian Constitutional Literature

Unamendability in Brazil is a concept that, at first sight, seems to require a less abstract approach as a mechanism to defend the Constitution from changes in its core principles. The argument in favor of implicit unamendability, which, as Yaniv Roznai puts it, "entails the idea that even in the absence of explicit limitations on the amendment power, there are certain principles which are beyond the reach of the constitutional amender,"[26] would apparently not have much reason to gain ground in Brazil due to a prosaic reason: The 1988 Brazilian Constitution sets out very vague and far-reaching unamendable provisions, which can effortlessly be used as the primary argument to strike down a constitutional amendment. Article 60, §4, of the 1988 Constitution defines that "no proposal of amendment shall be considered which is aimed at abolishing: I—the federative form of State; II—the direct, secret, universal and periodic vote; III—the separation of the Government Powers; IV—individual rights and guarantees." Particularly for "individual rights and guarantees," the doctrinal understanding is that it at least entails the whole Article 5 of the Constitution, which in its 78 clauses, is comprehensive enough to protect those principles normally associated with the concept of implicit unamendability.

As a young democracy after 21 years of civil–military dictatorship, it sounds logical that, better than putting much faith in implicit unamendable clauses, those core principles should be entrenched in the constitutional text, easing thereby possible political tensions the Supreme Court could suffer to strike down a constitutional amendment. Brazil followed, in this regard, a similar path to Portugal's, whose 1976 Constitution has one of world's broadest set of unamendable clauses.[27] The Portuguese Constitution features, in Article 288, 14 unamendable clauses, ranging from common explicit clauses such as "the republican form of government" and "universal, direct, secret, and periodical suffrage" to very unusual ones, such as "the existence of economic plans within the framework of a mixed economy" or "the rights of workers, workers committees, and trade unions." Like the Brazilian Constitution, it was also the outcome of transition from a dictatorial period—the so-called "Estado Novo," which ruled the country for 41 years and only ended with the Carnation Revolution in 1974,[28] and was aimed at establishing a new democratic moment.[29] Brazil's Constitution inherited somehow the programmatic feature

---

[26]See Roznai (2017), p. 70.

[27]Roznai (2017), p. 36 (mentioning that "the only countries with similarly detailed and unique unamendable provisions are those that were formerly Portuguese colonies").

[28]See Chilcote et al. (2015).

[29]Yaniv Roznai will call such a feature of Brazilian constitutionalism aspirational and transformative. According to him, "The unamendable provision in the Brazilian Constitution, which reflects an aspirational character, can also be characterized as transformative, since it was adopted as a direct response to the former military dictatorship." Roznai (2017), p. 32.

of the Portuguese Constitution, though in a more measured and less detail-oriented way. One such contribution is the protection to the "rights, freedoms, and safeguards of the citizens" (Art. 288, c, of the Portuguese Constitution) and the "individual rights and guarantees" (Art. 60, §4, IV, of the Brazilian Constitution). It is worth noticing that this provision was absent in the previous Brazilian Constitutions, whose unamendable clauses limited to the protection of the republican federal form of government or the equal representation of the States in the Senate.[30]

It is natural that such comprehensive unamendable clauses would spark interesting debates over the legitimacy of the constituent power to impose limits on the sovereignty of the people to change the Constitution whenever they see fit. In a comparable manner, also in Brazil, the well-known clash between Madisonians and Jeffersonians on why and how the constitution should bind the future[31] has had some resonance. As elsewhere, the argument that "without tying their own hands, the people will have no hands"[32] has been central for Brazilian democracy. No wonder that this paradox has also extended to whom or which institution has the last say in setting the limits of the will of the people, a consequence that reflects on the rising role of Supreme Courts. If the people have limits to change the Constitution, how far can Supreme Courts go to exert control over their will? By explicitly laying down unamendable clauses in the Constitution, as is the case of Brazil, this endeavor has seemingly some backing by the original constituent power, but, even so, such general and broad clauses are ripe for divergent interpretations and for questions on whether the Supreme Court has overstepped the boundaries of its duty of protecting the Constitution.

Rodrigo Brandão, a professor of constitutional law at the State University of Rio de Janeiro, for example, brings some relevant insights about this conflict between the limits of the secondary constituent power[33] and the will of people. According to him, there are serious difficulties in democratically justifying such limits in view of the supermajorities needed to pass a constitutional amendment, in particular when it comes to defend privileges some minorities have entrenched in the constitutional text as unamendable (he calls it the "constitutional entrenchment of privileges").[34] The second point is that those "constitutional principles are marked by high semantic abstraction and moral density,"[35] which not only largely extends the judge's freedom of interpretation but also may clash with the moral disagreement of

---

[30]See Constitutions of Brazil of 1891 (Art. 90, §4), 1934 (Art. 178, §5), 1946 (Art. 217, §6), 1967 (Art. 47, §1).

[31]See Holmes (1988), pp. 199–221.

[32]Holmes (1988), p. 231.

[33]See Roznai (2017), p. 123 ("While the aforementioned primary constituent power is a true power that rests with 'the people', the secondary constituent power, namely the amendment power vested in a constitutional organ, is an authority. It is an empowered legal competence that is established by the constitution, but it may be limited by it.").

[34]See Brandão (2007), p. 9.

[35]Ibid.

any pluralistic society (the so-called countermajoritarian difficulty).[36] In any case—
he argues—the democratic feature of the Constituent Assembly of 1987–1988[37]
created a legitimate barrier for the secondary constituent power as long as, particularly in the 1988 Brazilian Constitution, the rather flexible framework for
constitutional amendments (the threshold is the approval of 3/5 of the members of
the two Houses in two readings)[38] and the absence of any plebiscitary mechanism
has "a lower deliberative quality than the one presented at the National Constituent
Assembly."[39] He defends, therefore, a more proactive role of the Supreme Court in
exerting the judicial review of constitutional amendments, particularly in view of
the "Brazilian constitutional model and experience," the risk of National Congress
or the Executive branch "to incorporate, in practice, the popular sovereignty," and,
finally, "essential values such as human dignity would be left to the adventurism of
political groups."[40]

This favorable point of view of the Supreme Court in defending the Constitution
from the "adventurism" of political groups that could undermine the democratic
values entrenched by the Constituent Assembly is, however, not consensual.
Scholars who have historically been placed in the very conservative spectrum of
constitutional law, and, in particular, those who had, in the past, contributed with
some legal justifications for the civil–military dictatorship (1964–1985) could not
easily cope with the very concept of unamendability. One such scholar is Manoel
Gonçalves Ferreira Filho, a professor of constitutional law at the University of São
Paulo who is famous, among others, for writing the book "A Democracia
Possível"[41] (The Possible Democracy)—a clear attempt to justify the authoritarian
military government. In 1995, he wrote the article titled "Significação e Alcance das
'Cláusulas Pétreas'" (Meaning and Reach of Petrous Clauses), in which he argues
that those unamendable provisions do not have the power to "petrify" the legal
system.[42] His argument is structured in the following premises: (a) the legal doctrine of the constituent power is unrealistic in view of the many exceptional ways
constitutions have been drafted in history[43]; (b) "constitutions do not follow a social
pact..., but replace previous organizations..., which are the 'material constitutions'"[44]; (c) "there is no intrinsic superiority—derived from the democratic
legitimacy—of those, the constituent-representatives, from those, the ordinary
representatives[45];" and (d) the constitution is the supreme law that the

---

[36]Ibid., pp. 9–10.

[37]See Barbosa (2012).

[38]See Constitution of the Federal Republic of Brazil, Article 60, Paragraph 2.

[39]Brandão (2007), p. 16.

[40]Ibid., p. 18.

[41]Ferreira Filho (1976).

[42]Ferreira Filho (1995), p. 11.

[43]Ibid., p. 12.

[44]Ibid., p. 13.

[45]Ibid.

representatives of the people must respect, but "by reason of a convention… whose nature is not metaphysics."[46] He concludes that "if the original constituent power cannot give a solid basis for the unamendable clauses, much less can do so the derived power."[47]

Yet, he, based on Carl Schmitt, contends that there is an essential core "that is out of reach by the power of reform,"[48] the question lying in identifying which contents are part of this fundamental core, whose protection is nonetheless political. Therefore, in practical terms, those unamendable provisions are as such untouchable "as long as they are in force."[49] For Ferreira Filho, those unamendable provisions can be "modified or abolished,"[50] an argument originating from the so-called "double revision thesis," strongly advocated by the Portuguese constitutional scholar Jorge Miranda[51] in light of all those extensive set of unamendable clauses inscribed in the 1976 Portuguese Constitution. According to this thesis, in order to change an unamendable provision, it suffices to revoke or amend the constitutional norm that sets out the distinct hypotheses of unamendable provisions. For Miranda, these "are constitutional norms as any other and can be themselves subject of reform, with the inherent consequences."[52] Since those constitutional norms are themselves not among the hypotheses of unamendability, they could thereby be amended and revoked. For Ferreira Filho, moreover, any appeal to an abstract and implicit concept of unamendability to protect such provisions has no basis at all:

> This thesis is only founded on the argument that it would be a fraud to the Constitution to admit the suppression of the 'petrous clause'. But this would stand if the Constitution had inscribed, among the 'petrous clauses', the procedure for constitutional change it enshrined… Otherwise, it is a gratuitous statement, or that it is only based on the appeal to implicit clauses, because these are up for grabs for all tastes.[53]

In the case of the 1988 Brazilian Constitution, this would mean revoking any of those clauses of Article 60, §4, laying thereby the groundwork for amending, for instance, an individual right as set out in Article 5. He contends, moreover, that Article 60, §4 only forbids proposals of amendment that are aimed at "abolishing" any of those four clauses, not the ones aimed at modifying or regulating them.[54] As would be the typical argument by someone who interpreted the Brazilian transition to democracy as a continuation of the so-called "revolutionary cycle" of the

---

[46]Ibid.
[47]Ibid.
[48]Ibid., p. 14.
[49]Ibid.
[50]Ibid.
[51]See Miranda (2002).
[52]Ibid., p. 416.
[53]Ferreira Filho (1995), p. 15.
[54]Ibid., p. 16.

civil–military dictatorship,[55] Ferreira Filho ends his paper by sustaining a very controversial argument. For him, since the 1988 Constitution was the outcome of a constitutional amendment to the 1967/69 Constitution (Constitutional Amendment n. 26/85),[56] those unamendable provisions are, in fact, not originally from the primary constituent power, but from the secondary constituent power: "the 'petrous clauses' in force came out from a constitutional reform and are the work of the derived constituent power. What the derived power establishes, the derived power can change."[57] Of course, based on these arguments, there would be no reason whatsoever to authorize the Supreme Court to exert the judicial review of consti-tutional amendments. In the end, after all, the unamendable provisions (in the Brazilian case, according to Ferreira Filho, not even a product of the primary constituent power, like the whole 1988 Constitution) are no different from any other constitutional provision. And, if there exists any obstacle, there is no prohibition to change Article 60, §4, which would then authorize changes in any of those four unamendable clauses.

Virgílio Afonso da Silva, also a professor at the University of São Paulo, pro-vided a very direct argument against Ferreira Filho's main claims. For him, even though it sounds logical that, once revoked or modified Article 60, §4, those unamendable provisions would lose this quality, Ferreira Filho's thesis is "weak."[58] What is beneath that claim, according to Silva, is nothing other than the non-acceptance of the so-called *implicit limits*.[59] His defense of the existence of implicit limits lies in the premise that "if a competence derives from a higher authority, it seems logical that its limits can be modified only by this higher authority, but *never by the derived authority*."[60] Furthermore, Ferreira Filho's claim that the 1988 Constitution is the result of a simple constitutional amendment to the prior Constitution, and, as such, a Constitution drafted by the secondary constituent power does not stand up to scrutiny. As he clearly points out: "this change to the constitution from 1969—by means of which a new constitution was created—cannot be understood as mere product of a constitutional amendment, but as a *political solution* in order to break with the illegitimate constitutional order of that time."[61] Virgílio Afonso da Silva shares the understanding of many other scholars[62] who contend that very moment was indeed a rupture with the past, and thereby there is no other possible conclusion than calling that amendment an "act of

---

[55]For a discussion of distinct interpretations of the Brazilian transition to democracy, see Benvindo (2017), pp. 332–357. See also Barbosa (2012).

[56]See Ferreira Filho (1985), pp. 129–145.

[57]Ferreira Filho (1995), p. 16.

[58]Da Silva (2004), p. 459.

[59]Ibid.

[60]Ibid., p. 460.

[61]Ibid., p. 468.

[62]See Barbosa (2012), p. 211, Paixão (2014), p. 415, (2015), pp. 89–105.

usurpation,"[63] because, logically speaking, that amendment could not "convene an Assembly to *destroy* the constitution that should be amended."[64]

Therefore, in contrast to those who defend the "double revision thesis," most Brazilian constitutional scholars have sustained that the rules regulating the procedure for constitutional amendment cannot be modified in a way that would make it more flexible.[65] The same is true for Article 60, §4, since it also imposes limits on the secondary constituent power. Despite that, Brazil has a long history of attempts to soften the rules for constitutional amendment through the so-called "constitutional revisions,"[66] aimed at reforming a specific subject, such as the political system, the tax system, or any other disputed topic that would demand a massive support of Congress to have it passed. Unlike the general provision regulating the procedure for constitutional amendment, these "constitutional revisions" would set up a temporary and particular fast-track procedure—normally requiring only the absolute majority of the members of Congress in a unicameral session—to make changes on a set of specific provisions of the constitutional text. The Proposals for Constitutional Amendment with such a purpose, nonetheless, have all failed up until now,[67] and, though the Brazilian Constitution has already been amended more than one hundred times, those changes have been the outcome of the regular procedure for constitutional amendment as originally set out in the 1988 Constitution. This signals that constitutional thresholds and institutional constraints may have so far worked quite well against proposals aimed at breaching the pre-commitments undertaken by the primary constituent power.[68] If this outcome has to do with the theory of implicit unamendable clauses, it is hard to conclude, but some scholars have clearly pointed out that the secondary constituent power has no

---

[63]Da Silva (2004), p. 469.

[64]Ibid., p. 468.

[65]See Sampaio (1995), pp. 95–108, Silva (2005), Horta (2010), Sarlet (2003), pp. 78–97.

[66]The Brazilian Constitution and the constitutional doctrine in Brazil have used the concept of "constitutional revision" in a distinct way from the general understanding in comparative constitutional law. In Brazil, it is normally used to indicate a change in the constitutional order as a result of a "fast-track" procedure of constitutional amendment that is normally less rigid than the regular one.

[67]See Proposta de Emenda à Constituição n. 25 (Sen. Humberto Lucena, DCN2, 11 de maio de 1995, p. 8026); Proposta de Emenda à Constituição n. 30 (Sen. Sérgio Machado, DCN2, de 19 de maio de 1995, p. 8480); Proposta de Emenda à Constituição n. 62, Dep. Saulo Queiroz, DCN1, de 7 Junho de 1995, p. 12404); Proposta de Emenda à Constituição n. 463/1997 (Dep. Inocêcio Oliveira, DCD, de 4 de Junho de 1997, p. 14551); Proposta de Emenda à Constituição n. 478/1997 (Dep. Inocêcio Oliveira, DCD, de 23 de outubro de 1997, p. 24819); Proposta de Emenda à Constituição n. 554/1997 (Dep. Miro Teixeira, DCD, de 13 de dezembro de 1997, p. 41684); Proposta de Emenda à Constituição n. 71 (Sen. Delcídio do Amaral, DSF, de 3 de setembro de 2003, p. 26040; Proposta de Emenda à Constituição n. 157 (Dep. Luiz Carlos Santos, DCD de 26 de setembro de 2003, p. 50457); Proposta de Emenda à Constituição n. 193 (Dep. Flávio Dino, DCD, 11 de dezembro de 2007, p. 65361).

[68]See Benvindo (2018).

legitimacy to make such changes, in particular, in view of the overly democratic moment of the Constituent Assembly of 1988.[69]

More controversial, though, is the extent of those unamendable provisions in the Brazilian constitutionalism. For example, based on the social core of the Constitution, part of the constitutional literature has long contended[70] that also the extensive list of social rights—and not merely the individual rights and guarantees, as set out in Article 60, §4, IV—is also protected by unamendability. Ingo Wolfgang Sarlet, a constitutional professor at the Pontifical Catholic University of Rio Grande do Sul, may be the one who more widely advanced such a thesis. In a paper titled *Os Direitos Fundamentais Sociais como "Cláusulas Pétreas"* (*The Social Fundamental Rights as "Petrous Clauses"*), he claims that the 1988 Constitution visibly enshrines the premise of Brazil being not only democratic, but also a social welfare state, as defined in Articles 1 and 3.[71] "There is no doubt that the social welfare state principle as well as the social fundamental rights integrate the essential elements, that is, the identity of our Constitution." As a consequence—he says—those "social rights (as well as the fundamental principles) could be regarded—even though not expressly set out in the list of unamendable clauses—as authentic implicit material limits on constitutional reform."[72]

Indeed, this expansive understanding of the unamendable clauses of the Brazilian Constitution has recently gained strength during the discussion of the Constitutional Amendment n. 95/2016,[73] which curbs annual growth of public spending by adjusting it only to the previous year's inflation rate during a period of twenty years (though this methodology could be revised after a period of ten years). The so-called "new fiscal regime" sparked various controversies among scholars and policymakers. Some praised this measure as it would restore confidence in Brazil that would translate into sustainable public policies.[74] Others, however, have

---

[69]See Paixão et al. (2013).

[70]See Sarlet (2003), pp. 78–97, Silva (2000), p. 124.

[71]Article 1. The Federative Republic of Brazil, formed by the indissoluble union of the states and municipalities and of the federal district, is a legal democratic state and is founded on: I—sovereignty; II—citizenship; III—the dignity of the human person; IV—the social values of labor and of the free enterprise; V—political pluralism [...] Article 3. The fundamental objectives of the Federative Republic of Brazil are: I—to build a free, just and solidary society; II—to guarantee national development; III—to eradicate poverty and substandard living conditions and to reduce social and regional inequalities; IV—to promote the well-being of all, without prejudice as to origin, race, sex, color, age, and any other forms of discrimination.

[72]Sarlet (2003), pp. 78–97.

[73]Emenda Constitucional n. 95, de 15 de dezembro de 2016, DOU 16 de dezembro de 2016, p. 2.

[74]See Armando Castelar Pinheiro, "Por que Sim à PEC 241", (*Valor Econômico*, 7 October 2016). http://www.valor.com.br/opiniao/4737903/por-que-sim-pec-241; "PEC do teto não é ótima, mas é o possível neste momento", (*Exame*, 8 October 2016). http://exame.abril.com.br/economia/noticias/pec-do-teto-nao-e-otima-mas-e-o-possivel-neste-momento; "Temer: public policies are unsustainable without spending control", (*BrazilGovNews*, 30 September 2016), http://www.brazilgovnews.gov.br/news/2016/09/temer-public-policies-are-unsustainable-without-spending-control.

argued that such a constitutional amendment would strongly affect the social rights, especially health, education, and social welfare, while not helping to restore economic growth.[75] Marcus Faro de Castro, a professor of economic law at the University of Brasilia, argued that this proposal adopts macroeconomic policies that "in practice... become political expediencies as far as they are perceived as effective by those who benefit from them, and not because they demonstrably embody ideals of justice that society aims to achieve."[76] The Economist, which acknowledged that "austerity could have distributional consequences" and "has been a misguided approach in recent years," pointed out that Brazil is a "special case" that may, however, justify it. But it did so not without first titling the article "there is more than one kind of economic mess to be in."[77]

Beneath this controversy lies the very discussion of the social core of the 1988 Brazilian Constitution as part of its identity, recalling Sarlet's argument of the implicit unamendability of the social welfare principle enshrined in the constitutional text. According to this premise, the "new fiscal regime" would clash with that implicit unamendable clause as long as this policy would evolve in a way that especially those sectors of society more in need would lose in the increasingly competitive share of the now fixed budgetary pie. It is no wonder that scholars have stressed how this amendment will signal a "change in the Brazilian social contract" as it was originally drafted in the 1988 Constitution, a document originated from broad social participation and wherein social rights have best represented the marriage of that constitutional moment with a new democratic impetus after years of dictatorship.[78] Drawing from the Brazilian experience, Richard Albert, for example, also interprets this amendment as a violation of the social core of the Constitution, qualifying it to what he calls "constitutional dismemberment", that is, a change that "seeks deliberately to alter the fundamental rights, structure, or identity of the constitution with recourse to the ordinary rules of constitutional amendment."[79] The very argument that such a modification could affect the identity of the Constitution connects to something more structural than simply the explicit unamendable clauses set out in the Brazilian constitutional text: it would radically alter the foundations of the Brazilian Constitution:

---

[75] See "Economistas lançam documento com críticas à PEC dos gastos púlbicos" (Valor Econômico 10 October, 2016). http://www.valor.com.br/politica/4740633/economistas-lancam-documento-com-criticas-pec-dos-gastos-publicos.

[76] De Castro (2016).

[77] "Brazil and the new old normal: There is more than one kind of economic mess to be in" (The Economist, 12 October 2016). http://www.economist.com/blogs/freeexchange/2016/10/brazil-and-new-old-normal.

[78] See Benvindo (2016).

[79] Albert (2018), p. 82.

The impact of this Public Spending Cap Amendment on the next generation's enjoyment of social rights in Brazil, combined with how directly it undermines the Constitution's founding and continuing commitment to social rights, suggests that it may be more than a simple amendment. Its purposes and effect suggest that it should instead be called a constitutional dismemberment.[80]

As seen, the debate over the unamendable clauses in Brazil goes far beyond one could first expect in view of the open, far-reaching, and vague contents of the four so-called "petrous clauses" of Article 60, §4 of the 1988 Brazilian Constitution. The simple fact that the Constitution has embraced a large set of hypotheses in order to protect the Constitution from changes has not provided a much greater consensus in the constitutional literature. The arguments range from those who defend the so-called "double revision thesis" and even sustain that the 1988 Constitution is nothing other than a simple reform to the previous authoritarian 1967/1969 Constitution to those who extend unamendability to the very social core of the 1988 Constitution or interpret such changes as a clear "dismemberment" of the Constitution. Naturally, constitutional designers should be aware that enshrining principles as unamendable in the constitutional text is just that the tip of the iceberg of a much more complex array of strategies political actors can undertake to transform the constitutional order. The question thus lies in how institutions can better cope with such strategies and how, even in the context of open, vague and far-reaching explicit unamendable clauses, they should behave in view of the many possible interpretations for such clauses. Those explicit unamendable clauses may probably help, for instance, Supreme Courts by providing them with an immediate argument in the circumstance of striking down a constitutional amendment, but it would be naïve to ignore the fact that the text itself is one of the many sources feeding constitutional interpretation. In constitutional democracies, it is expected that Supreme Courts undertake this role of protecting the constitution. Yet, like the argument itself of unamendable provisions—which, regardless whether they are explicit or implicit, raise serious disagreements—the judicial review of constitutional amendments is also controversial.

The next session will discuss how the Brazilian Supreme Court has managed such arguments and this particular role amid its rising presence in Brazilian democracy. Of particular interest is how the Supreme Court has interpreted the extension of the concept of "individual rights and guarantees" (Art. 60, §4, IV). Even though it has long ruled that its role of exerting the judicial review of constitutional amendments derives naturally from its role as guardian of the Constitution, it is worth noticing that it has gradually expanded the scope of this protection to reach a broader dimension of constitutional basic rights.

---

[80]Ibid., p. 42.

3   The Brazilian Supreme Court and the Unamendable Clauses

The Brazilian Supreme Federal Court (STF) consolidated the understanding that it is part of its role as guardian of the Constitution to exert the judicial review of constitutional amendments in 1993, whose basis, however, was already presented in a previous case under the 1967/1969 Constitution.[81] In a decision of October 1980,[82] the STF had already introduced the argument that a proposal for constitutional amendment that violates an unamendable provision—in the case, one that aimed at abolishing the republic—could not even be subject of deliberation in Congress. The case was dismissed, but the argument made explicit that not even a proposal for constitutional amendment could have its proceedings in Congress taken effect if it were in contradiction with the unamendable provisions. The thesis of a prior control over those acts, which the Court currently adopts, was as such introduced:

> In such cases, the unconstitutionality pertains to the very progress of the legislative pro-
> ceedings, and this is because the Constitution does not want - in view of the seriousness of
> these deliberations, if consummated - that it even reaches deliberation, forbidding it
> explicitly. The unconstitutionality, if occurring, already exists before the bill or the proposal
> turns into law or constitutional amendment, because the very proceeding already frontally
> disrespects the Constitution.[83]

Under the 1988 Constitution, a Direct Action of Unconstitutionality[84] (ADI n. 820-3)[85] aimed at questioning the constitutionality of an amendment whose purpose was to anticipate the plebiscite to define the system of government as set out in Article 2 of the Temporary Constitutional Provisions Act[86] led the Court once again to adopt that argument. Though it was also dismissed, Justice Moreira Alves was very direct in defending the role of the Supreme Court for such a matter —and even went further by making a comparison with the United States. He also argued in favor of the Supreme Court exerting this control in cases of not only explicit but also implicit unamendable provisions:

---

[81]There is an even older decision of the Supreme Court issued in 1926 which discussed the constitutional revision of 1926 to the 1891 Constitution. The Court ruled, in the end, favorably to the constitutionality of the revision based on formal grounds, but it left open the possibility of striking down a constitutional amendment if it had violated one of the unamendable provisions of the 1891 Constitution. See STF, HC n. 18.178, Rel. Min. Hermenegildo de Barros.

[82]STF, MS n°. 20.257-DF, Rel. Min. Moreira Alves, DJ 27 de fevereiro de 1981, p. 1304.

[83]Ibid. (Ementa).

[84]The Direct Action of Unconstitutionality is an action aimed at directly questioning the uncon-stitutionality of a federal or state law or normative act directly in the Supreme Federal Court through the abstract and centralized system of judicial review. See Articles 102, I, *a,* and 103 of the 1988 Brazilian Constitution.

[85]STF, ADI n. 829-3-DF, Rel. Min. Moreira Alves, DJ 16 de setembro de 1994, p. 24278.

[86]The constitutional amendment anticipated the plebiscite from September 7, 1993, to April 21, 1993.

There is no doubt that, in view of our constitutional system, this Court has the authority, in diffuse or centralized judicial review, to examine the constitutionality or not of a constitutional amendment, as it happens in the case, which is contested because it violates explicit and implicit unamendable clauses.

Contrary to what has taken place in the United States of America, where the Supreme Court - as the Attorney-General of the Union well registered and manifested - has hesitated to acknowledge questions of such a nature because it understands that it is often a political question, immune thereby to judicial review, in Brazil, the Supreme Federal Court has long sustained its authority for the judgment of such matters.

The Supreme Court would finally strike down a constitutional amendment in the Direct Action of Unconstitutionality n. 939 in 1993.[87] The case originated from a constitutional amendment aimed at authorizing the Union to implement a tribute on financial transactions in the same year of its approval by Congress. The main claim was that the so-called IPMF (*Imposto sobre Movimentação ou Transmissão de Valores e de Créditos e Direitos de Natureza Financeira*) would be in direct clash with Article 150, III, *b,* of the Constitution, which clearly forbids any member of the federation from "[collecting] tributes... in the same fiscal year in which the law which instituted or increased such tributes was published."

Though not in Article 5 of the Constitution, the Supreme Court interpreted that this provision was also covered by the protection of unamendability since this is an individual right of the taxpayer. Such a broader interpretation derived from Article 5, §2, which says that "the rights and guarantees expressed in this Constitution do not exclude others deriving from the regime and from the principles adopted by it, or from the international treaties in which the Federative Republic of Brazil is a party." Its final ruling had the following content:

1. A Constitutional amendment, emerging then from the derivative constituent power, when in violation of the original Constitution, can be declared unconstitutional by the Supreme Federal Court, whose essential role is to guard the Constitution [...]. 2. The constitutional Amendment n. 3, of March 3rd, 1993, which, in Article 2, authorized the Union to institute the IPMF, committed the vicious of unconstitutionality when it set out, in paragraph 2 of this Article, that, as regards to the tribute, Article 150, III, b and VI, of the Constitution does not apply, because, in doing so, it violated the following principles and immutable provisions (just them, not others): 1 - the principle of anteriority, which is an individual guarantee of taxpayers [...].

The scope of the expression "individual rights and guarantees" among the hypotheses of unamendable clauses has been used as an important parameter to strike down distinct constitutional amendments, though the controversy on its reach has been permanent in the constitutional literature.[88] The Supreme Court, however, has progressively, though sparingly, adopted the thesis that such protection extends to distinct circumstances that are not immediately derived from the vast list of individual rights and guarantees of Article 5 of the 1988 Constitution, as the precedent on ADI 939 demonstrates. In the last years, it has, for instance, applied

---

[87]STF, ADI n. 939, Rel. Min. Sydney Sanches, DJ 05 de janeiro de 1994.

[88]See previous session. See also Brandão (2007), pp. 19–30.

this concept to hypotheses such as changes in (a) the maximum term for the members of the federation to pay their debts by virtue of court decisions (Art. 100)[89]; (b) how the social contributions should be collected (Art. 195, §6)[90]; (c) the principle of ex-post-facto electoral rule (Art. 16)[91]; and (d) the social security contribution of federal, state and municipal public servants since a new tax would impose a discriminatory treatment among them.[92]

The Court has not yet ruled on a possible extension of such concept to also embrace social rights, as part of the constitutional literature has defended,[93] but, indirectly, one could argue it did so in a case related to women's rights to maternity leave.[94] A constitutional amendment which altered the social security system[95] defined "the maximum limit for the amount of benefits of the general social security scheme referred to in Article 201 of the Federal Constitution" to R$ 1.200,00, adjustable... "to the end that its real value is permanently maintained...". The Brazilian Socialist Party (PSB) filed a Direct Action of Unconstitutionality[96] arguing that that provision would affect the maternity leave since it would set a cap on the maximum amount a woman could earn during the exercise of her right. The Supreme Court argued that constitutional amendment should be then interpreted as if it did not apply to the maternity leave, because this would create a "discrimination the Constitution sought to combat when it prohibited the difference in wages, in the performance of duties or in hiring criteria based on sex (Art. 7, XXX, of the 1988 Constitution)."[97] Yet, the final argument connected such a prohibition to the individual right to equality (Art. 5, I), which is an explicit unamendable clause: a "prohibition which, in essence, is an outcome of the principle of equal rights between men and women as set out in Article 5, I, of the Federal Constitution."[98]

Noticeably, the concept of "individual rights and guarantees" set out in Article 60, §4, IV has been the primary source for the rising empowerment of the Brazilian Supreme Court to exert the judicial review of constitutional amendments. Though it has not yet directly applied it to circumstances that would allow for an even greater scope of that protection as to explicitly reach social rights, it has gradually laid the groundwork for a potential turning point in this direction. The Supreme Court has indeed stated that it should keep open the reach of the unamendable clauses in the best way to protect the "principles" of the Constitution, without, nonetheless, explaining much further what such "principles" would effectively entail. Justice

---

[89]STF, ADI n. 2.362, Rel. Min. Ayres Britto, DJe 19 de maio de 2011.

[90]STF, ADI n. 2.666, Rel. Min. Ellen Gracie, DJ 6 de dezembro de 2002.

[91]STF, ADI n. 3865, Rel. Min. Ellen Gracie, DJ 10 de agosto de 2006.

[92]STF, ADI n. 3.105, Rel. Cezar Peluso, DJ 18 de fevereiro de 2005.

[93]See previous session.

[94]See Brandão (2010), pp. 134–135.

[95]Emenda Constitucional n. 20, de 15 de dezembro de 1998.

[96]STF, ADI n. 1946, Rel. Min. Sydney Sanches, DJ 16 de maio de 2003.

[97]Ibid.

[98]Ibid.

Gilmar Mendes, in this regard, for example, argued that "the effective content of 'eternity guarantees' can only be obtained through an hermeneutic effort", which, as a matter of fact, is the "only activity [that] can reveal the constitutional principles which, though not expressly embraced by the unamendable clauses, carry a narrow link with the principles protected by them and thus covered by the immutability guarantee therefrom."[99] It is clear from such words that the Supreme Court has strategically left open the space for an even far-reaching scope of unamendable clauses, whose "principles", grasped from a systematic interpretation of the constitutional text, can be both explicit or implicit. The question is, however, how far the Supreme Court can go in the protection of such core "principles" those unamendable provisions may embrace.

4 Conclusion

All these circumstances add to the conclusion that, despite the existence of explicit unamendable provisions, their constraint on the Supreme Court is relatively limited, which can, instead, use such openness to extend their scope to new situations as its power increases. It can do so without the burden of strongly justifying it on even greater abstract concepts normally associated with the doctrine of implicit unamendable clauses.[100] This is particularly true in cases like the Brazilian Constitution, whose contents originating from those unamendable clauses are open enough to the most divergent interpretations and controversies, while serving both as a guidance and an enabler of a more active behavior of the Supreme Court. Up until now, though, the Supreme Court has acted quite self-restrained in this matter, not following much of the claims the constitutional literature has raised in favor of a larger protection of rights, such as social rights. The balance between unamendability and constitutional change will be a difficult task for a Supreme Court still striving to position itself as an effective guardian of the Constitution amid many vested interests in the Brazilian society.[101] On the other hand, nonetheless, those cases clearly point out that it has increasingly made use of its power to declare null and void constitutional amendments without even raising doubts on the legitimacy of such a task, interpreting it as an evident consequence of its very existence. There is no coincidence between this role and the rising power of the Supreme Court as a central institutional player in Brazilian democracy. Both are, in fact, parts of the same phenomenon.

---

[99]STF, ADPF n. 33-MC, Rel. Min. Gilmar Mendes, DJ 7 de dezembro de 2005.

[100]See Roznai (2017).

[101]See Costa and Benvindo (2014) (showing how the Brazilian Supreme Court, despite the discourse of protection of basic rights, has felt short of expectations, at least in the centralized system of judicial review).

The Brazilian experience, where the Supreme Court has long decided in favor of its power to strike down constitutional amendments when in violation of the original constitutional provisions, is thus a relevant and rich source for comparative constitutional literature. Though largely unknown and underexplored, the distinct nuances of the debates over unamendability have sparked in Brazil show that the very existence of a set of unamendable clauses in the Constitution, rather than having narrowed the Supreme Court's margin of appreciation, has expanded it even further. The doctrine of implicit constitutional unamendability pervades every single interpretation of such broad and far-reaching unconstitutional clauses of Article 60, §4, of the 1988 Constitution, usually under the label of "core constitutional principles" to be protected. The distinction between explicit and implicit unamendable provisions, especially in unamendable provisions like the ones in Brazil, is, therefore, much less pronounced. Like in Colombia, where the "substitution of the constitution" doctrine is based on the premise that any constitutional change that is detrimental to the fundamental principles of the constitution is not an amendment, but a new constitution,[102] in Brazil any amendment that affects those "core principles" beneath the explicit unamendable provisions are also interpreted as an attack on the constitution. In both cases, the Supreme Court, in Brazil, and the Constitutional Court, in Colombia, have established themselves as the logical authority to strike down a constitutional amendment which violates a "core principle" of the constitution. The distinction is that, in Brazil, the Supreme Court will justify it by making reference to at least one of those explicit unamendable provisions.

In the end, unamendability is such a strong normative concept that, regardless of whether it is implicit or explicit, it will be there as a call for the Supreme Court's final say, especially in times of their rising political influence. Its application is then much more a matter of how and to which extent the Supreme Court is willing to exert such a role, and how and to which extent the society at large is prone to accepting its Supreme Court's rising authority over its constitutionalism. The constitutional literature has defended that the "invalidation of constitutional amendments should be a remedy of last resort"[103] and be "limited in scope,"[104] the question thus lying if, with such an incentive, Supreme Courts will not be tempted to go much further, especially when there are such open clauses as in the Brazilian Constitution.[105] Up until now, the Brazilian Supreme Court appears to be using it with relative restraint, but, as this paper aimed to prove, it will not be the existence of explicit unamendable provisions that will prevent it from using it to enhance even further its powers.[106]

---

[102]See Espinosa and Landau (2017), p. 340.

[103]Roznai (2017), p. 225.

[104]Dixon and Landau (2015), p. 606.

[105]See Mendes (2005), p. 461.

[106]See Dixon and Landau (2015), p. 620 (showing the dangers of the doctrine of unconstitutional constitutional amendments being applied, in Colombia and India, to cases that were nothing other than "ordinary exercise of the amendment power").

References

Albert R (2018) Constitutional amendment and dismemberment. Yale J Int Law 43:2, 82

Barbosa LAA (2012) História Constitucional Brasileira: Mudança Constitucional, Autoritarismo e Democracia no Brasil Pós-1964. Biblioteca Digital da Câmara dos Deputados, Rome

Benvindo JZ (2016) Preservationist Constitutional Amendments and the Rise of Antipolitics in Brazil. Int J Const L Blog. http://www.iconnectblog.com/2016/10/preservationist-constitutional-amendments-and-the-ris-of-antipolitics-in-brazil/. 26 Oct 2016

Benvindo JZ (2017) The forgotten people in Brazilian constitutionalism: revisiting behavior strategic analyses of regime transitions. Int J Const Law 15:332–357

Benvindo JZ (2018) Constitutional moments and constitutional thresholds in Brazil: mass protests and the "Performative Meaning" of constitutionalism. In: Albert R, Bernal C, Benvindo J (eds) Constitutional Change and Transformation in Latin America. Hart

Bernal C (2013) Unconstitutional constitutional amendments in the case study of Colombia: an analysis of the justification and meaning of the constitutional replacement doctrine. Int J Const Law 11:339, 340

Brandão R (2007) Direitos Fundamentais, Cláusulas Pétreas e Democracia: Uma Proposta de Justificação e de Aplicação do art. 60, §4°, IV da CF/88. Revista Eletrônica de Direito do Estado (REDE), Salvador, Instituto Brasileiro de Direito Público 1:9

Brandão R (2010) A Proteção dos "Direitos e Garantias Individuais" em face de Emendas Constitucionais à luz da Jurisprudência do STF. Revista Carioca de Direito 1:134–135

Chilcote RH et al (2015) Transitions from dictatorship to democracy: comparative studies of Spain, Portugal and Greece. Routledge, UK

Costa AA, Benvindo JZ (2014) A Quem Interessa o Controle de Constitucionalidade? O Descompasso entre a Teoria e a Prática na Defesa dos Direitos Fundamentais. Soc Sci Res Netw. http://dx.doi.org/10.2139/ssrn.2509541

Da Silva VA (2004) A fossilised constitution. Ratio Juris 17:454, 459

De Castro MF (2016) A PEC 241 e os Juristas Direito-Economia-Sociedade. Economia Legal. https://economialegal.wordpress.com/2016/10/12/a-pec-241-e-os-juristas/. 12 Oct 2016

Dixon R, Landau D (2015) Transnational constitutionalism and a limited doctrine of unconstitutional constitutional amendment. Int J Const Law 13: 606, 620

Espinosa MJC, Landau D (2017) Colombian constitutional law, vol 1. Oxford University Press, Oxford

Ferreira Filho MG (1976) A Democracia Possível. Saraiva, Brazil

Ferreira Filho MG (1985) Nova Perspectiva do Processo Constitucional. Revista Brasileira de Estudos Políticos 60/61:129–145

Ferreira Filho MG (1995) Significação e Alcance das "Cláusulas Pétreas". Revista de Direito Administrativo 202:11

Ginsburg T, Melton J (2015) Does the constitutional amendment rule matter at all? Amendment cultures and the challenges of measuring amendment difficulty. Int J Const Law 13:686, 689

Helmke G, Ríos-Figueroa J (2011) Introduction: courts in Latin America. In: Helmke G, Ríos-Figueroa J (eds) Courts in Latin America, vol 21. Cambridge University Press, Cambridge

Hirschl R (2014) Comparative matters: the renaissance of comparative constitutional law, vol 4. Oxford University Press, Oxford

Holmes S (1988) Precommitment and the paradox of democracy. In: Elster J, Slagstad R (eds) Constitutionalism and democracy. Cambridge University Press, Cambridge, pp 199–221

Horta RM (2010) Direito Constitucional. Del Rey

Koerner A (2013) Ativismo Judicial? Jurisprudência Constitucional e Política no STF Pós-88. Novos Estudos CEBRAP 96:69–85

Mendes CH (2005) Judicial review of constitutional amendments in the Brazilian supreme court. Florida J Int Law 17:449, 461

Miranda J (2002) Teoria do Estado e da Constituição. Forense, Rio de Janeiro

Negretto G (2012) Replacing and amending constitutions: the logic of constitutional change in Latin America. Law Soc Rev 45:749, 752–753

Nolte D (2008) Constitutional change in Latin America: power politics or symbolic politics? In: ECPR Joint Sessions, Rennes, France, vol 7

Nolte D, Schilling-Vacaflor A (2012) 'Introduction: The Times they are a Changing': constitutional transformations in Latin America since the 1990s. In: Schilling-Vacaflor A, Nolte D (eds) New constitutionalism in Latin America promises and practices, vol 8. Routledge, UK

Paixão C (2014) Autonomia, Democracia e Poder Constituinte: Disputas Conceituais na Experiência Constitucional Brasileira (1964–2014). Quad Fiorentini 43:415

Paixão C (2015) Past and future of authoritarian regimes: constitution, transition to democracy and amnesty in Brazil and Chile. J Const Hist 30:89–105

Paixão C et al (2013) Constituinte Exclusiva: Inconstitucional e Ilegítima. Consultor Jurídico. http://www.conjur.com.br/2013-jun-27/proposta-constituinte-exclusiva-inconstitucional-ilegitima?imprimir=1. 27 June 2013

Pou-Giménez F, Pozas-Loyo A (2018) The paradox of Mexican constitutional hyper-reformism: enabling peaceful transition while blocking democratic consolidation. In: Albert R, Bernal C, Benvindo J (eds) Constitutional change and transformation in Latin America (Hart, forthcoming)

Ramirez-Cleves GA (2016) The unconstitutionality of constitutional amendments in Colombia: the tension between majoritarian democracy and constitutional democracy. In: Bustamante T, Fernandes Gonçalves B (eds) Democratizing constitutional law. Law and philosophy. Springer, Berlin, p 213

Roznai Y (2017) Unconstitutional constitutional amendments. Oxford University Press, Oxford

Sampaio NS (1995) O Poder de Reforma Constitucional. Nova Alvorada, pp 95–108

Sarlet IW (2003) Os Direitos Fundamentais Sociais como "Cláusulas Pétreas". Cadernos de Direito 3:78–97

Sarria MC (2016) The unconstitutional constitutional amendment doctrine and the reform of the judiciary in Colombia. Int J Const L Blog. http://www.iconnectblog.com/2016/09/the-uncon stitutional-constitutional-amendment-doctrine-and-the-reform-of-the-judiciary-in-colombia/. 1 Sept 2016

Silva GJC (2000) Os Limites da Reforma Constitucional. Renovar, Mumbai, p 124

Silva JA (2005) Curso de Direito Constitucional Positivo. Malheiros, p 68

Tushnet M (2003) Alternative forms of judicial review. Mich Law Rev 101:2781–2782

Unamendable Constitutional Provisions and the European Common Constitutional Heritage: A Comparison Among Three Waves of Constitutionalism

Valentina Rita Scotti

Abstract When debating which constitutional values are shared among European countries, scholars increasingly refer to the European Common Constitutional Heritage, which is a common set of values defined through their constitutional evolution and thanks to the role played by supranational regional organizations, such as the Council of Europe (CoE) and the European Union (EU). This essay discusses the interplay between said common heritage and the unamendable provisions in constitutions approved in Italy and Germany after World War II and in Romania and Czech Republic after the fall of the Berlin Wall. Given that European values crossed continental borders thanks to regional forms of cooperation, this essay also analyzes the Constitutions of Morocco and Tunisia in order to understand whether the unamendable constitutional provisions of each country, introduced after the so-called Arab Spring, have been influenced by and are consistent with the European Common Constitutional Heritage.

1 Introduction

The role of constitutional unamendability is at the center of a long-lasting debate, which became evident during the drafting of the U.S. Constitution. Thomas Jefferson affirmed that each generation should have the right to choose its own Constitution,[1] while James Madison thought that frequently recurring to people might reduce the authority of the government and its role in providing stability.[2] The latter position seemed to succeed and, henceforward, constitutional framers

---

[1]On the possible objection to unamendability, see, in this book, the contribution of Yaniv Rosnai, 'Necrocracy or Democracy? Assessing Objections to Formal Unamendability'.
[2]On the U.S. debate, see Sunstein (2009), pp. 1–16.

V. R. Scotti (✉)
Department of Political Science, LUISS University of Rome, Rome, Italy
e-mail: vrscotti1@gmail.com

© Springer International Publishing AG, part of Springer Nature 2018
R. Albert and B. E. Oder (eds.), *An Unamendable Constitution?*
Ius Gentium: Comparative Perspectives on Law and Justice 68,
https://doi.org/10.1007/978-3-319-95141-6_14

365

from all over the world have progressively defined specific extraordinary procedures for constitutional amendment, whose complexity varies from one constitution to another.[3] Some constitutional provisions, however, are considered unamendable.

This idea of unamendability was consolidated for the first time in France, when the 1875 Constitutional Law introduced Article 8, Section 3, and made the republican form of government unamendable. Since then, and through the different waves of constitutionalism,[4] constitutional framers have considered some principles fundamental for the social pact constitutions represent[5] and have, thus, explicitly deemed these principles as perpetual. Consequently, such principles can only be amended through that *extra ordinem* activity represented by the exercise of the *pouvoir constituant*,[6] drawing a distinction between primary and secondary constituent power.[7] Through unamendable provisions, framers may entrench a constitutional culture, thereby preventing that occasional—but numerically significant—majorities use amendment procedures (secondary constituent power) to change the pillars of the Constitution. This reserves the power to modify unamendable provisions for extraordinary representatives "free from any prior constitutional restrictions or procedures"[8] (primary constituent power), should their social relevance change.

---

[3]See Klein and Sajò (2012), p. 437; Roznai (2013), p. 657.

[4]In this essay, waves of constitutionalism are modeled after the waves of democratization proposed in Huntington (1991), pp. 35–48, basing on the assumption that the mere approval of a Charter is not enough to envisage a regime change and that it should be coupled with the protection, in the Constitution, of freedoms, liberties, and democratic values. According to this assumption, Huntington stated that the first wave occurred from 1828 to 1926, the second one from 1943 to 1962, and the third one from 1974 to 1990; therefore, the 2011 Northern African wave may be considered as a fourth wave. The same chronologic criterion has been used in this essay to define the waves of constitutionalism.

[5]This idea remounted to Benjamin Constant's speculations, according to which people's sovereignty does not include the possibility of the dissolution of its fundamentals. On the need to protect the core values enshrined in constitutional texts, see Fusaro and Oliver (2011).

[6]The origin of this notion of *pouvoir constituant* (constituent power) may be traced back to the *Abbé* Emmanuel Joseph Sieyés, who, speaking in front of the French National Assembly in 1789, stated that "*une Constitution suppose avant tout un pouvoir constituant*". Being this power an expression of the will of the Nation, it is not bound by any limit deriving from positive law, instead of the constituted power. Sieyés (1789), p. 18.

[7]Roznai (in this book). This distinction recalls the French doctrine one between *pouvoir constituant institué* and *pouvoir constituant dérivé*. See Burdeau et al. (1993), p. 356.

[8]See Roznai (2014), p. 86. For a critical vision on the attitude of framers toward the introduction of unamendable clauses, and more generally on their approach to constitutional drafting, see S Michel, IN Cofone, 'Credible Commitment or Paternalism? The Case of Unamendability', in this book.

Meanwhile, the power to adapt and vivify the constitutional culture resides in the hands of judges,[9] which are called to interpret the provisions on unamendability.[10]

In some cases, judges safeguard core constitutional values by affirming the existence of implicit limits to amendability. These implicit limits are derived from rights and principles that existed before constituent moments,[11] which Charters merely recognize, and from a "basic structure"[12] of the Constitution.

These core principles have also been recognized at the supranational level. In Europe, for instance, they have taken the form of a constitutional common ground, namely, the European Common Constitutional Heritage. The Council of Europe's soft power and the European Union's conditionality have led this Heritage to cross European borders and become a debated element in the Southern Mediterranean area, particularly during the constitution-making processes started in 2011. There, the European Heritage mingled with the Islamic and African ones, each codified in specific Charters and through supranational organizations,[13] making the comparison between unamendable provisions even more interesting.

Following an expressive perspective,[14] this essay will analyze the relationship between the European Common Constitutional Heritage and the unamendable clauses provided by national constitutions in different constitutional waves. This essay is divided into three parts. The first discusses Italy and Germany's post-World War II constitutional experiences. The second part discusses the postcommunist Constitutions of Romania and the Czech Republic. Finally, the third part of this essay discusses the Constitutions approved after the so-called Arab Spring in Tunisia and Morocco, which are examples of the aforementioned cross-border influence of the European Heritage. Some concluding remarks try to answer the following questions: Does the entrenchment of values through unamendable constitutional provisions change from one wave of constitutionalism to another? Does judicial interpretation modify the understanding of constitutional values? Does the European Common Constitutional Heritage influence the definition of values entrenched through unamendable provisions?

---

[9]For a deeper reasoning on the role of constitutional culture, see Albert (2008), p. 15.

[10]On the role Courts may play in providing a sort of unamendability even in countries where it is not constitutionally declared, see, in this book, GJ Geertjes, J Uzman, 'Conventions of Unamendability. Unamendable Constitutional Law in Politically Enforced Constitutions'.

[11]The idea of the existence of supra-constitutional laws originated in France and then spread all over Europe. For an in-depth analysis of the debate in France, see Arné (1993), p. 460. For non-French scholars who debated on the point, see Schmitt (2004), Schmitt (2008).

[12]This definition has been introduced by the Supreme Court of India in the case *Kesavananda Bharati v. State of Kerala*, AIR 197 SC 1461 (24 April 1973). For further information, see Abraham (2000), p. 195, Andhyarujina (2012).

[13]See Alicino and Gradoli (2013).

[14]Albert (2013), p. 225.

2 The European Common Constitutional Heritage

Because the European Common Constitutional Heritage calls into question national, political, religious, and ideological elements, a complex study is necessary to find a suitable definition for it. In a few words, the European Common Constitutional Heritage represents the inner sense of the European identity. It is worth noting, however, that the European Common Constitutional Heritage cannot be conceived as the mere sum of CoE or EU members' identities, which are themselves difficult to define as the changes European society undergoes cause these identities to evolve. Sometimes, the European Common Constitutional Heritage reflects the aspirations of European countries more than the goals they have already achieved.

According to some scholars, identity is constructed to find a valuable past justifying present decisions, as "one essential element of statesmanship is inventing a glorious tradition to continue".[15] Considering the Latin etymology of the noun "invention" (from *invenio*, which means "to find"), it is possible to affirm that Europe has invented a glorious constitutional tradition. It began in England, with the 1215 *Magna Charta* and subsequent Charters recognizing the people's rights and framing the King's powers. It then flourished with the 1789 French Declaration, which stated that the protection of rights and the separation of powers represented the main and essential aim of any constitution (Article 16). Henceforward, constitutions affirmed as fountain sources, the Kelsenian *Grundnorm*,[16] where the fundamental tenets of people's sovereignty, rule of law, separation of powers, and protection of human rights are entrenched.[17] During the first wave of constitutionalism between 1828 and 1926, the Weimar Constitution (1919) made democracy and people's sovereignty the centerpieces of all the aspects of the country's institutional life,[18] making it one of the great masterpieces of European Constitutionalism. The legal framework this Charter introduced, however, led to Germany's instability. During the constitution-making processes European countries underwent after World War II, the elements that had weakened the Weimarian system and allowed for the ascendance of National Socialism (e.g., extreme proportionality, lack of judicial review, and constitutional flexibility) became essential during the debates of constitutional framers from the second wave of constitutionalism. In the meantime, while States engaged in the approval of Charters and Declarations to protect fundamental rights at the international level (e.g., the 1948 UN Declaration), European integration took its first steps. The attempt to overcome the atrocities of dictatorships by defining forms of cooperation followed two different but parallel paths. On one side, the establishment of the Council of Europe (May 5, 1949) led to the approval of the European Convention for the Protection of

---

[15] See Murphy (1995), p. 167.

[16] See Kelsen (1967).

[17] This is the sense of modern constitutionalism according McIlwain (1940).

[18] On the content and the relevance of this Constitution, see Mortati (1946).

Human Rights and Fundamental Freedoms—ECHR (1950)—and to its system of rights' adjudication. On the other side, the ECSC Treaty (Paris, 1951) and the ECC Treaty (Rome, 1957) started the European Communities economic integration, which evolved into an integrated eco-financial system that also protected rights and freedoms, currently known as the European Union.

After the fall of the Berlin Wall in 1989, the third wave of constitutionalism began with the overturning of the dictatorships in Portugal, Greece, and Spain. It concluded with the approval of liberal democratic constitutions in Central and Eastern European countries, which joined Western Europe in the construction of the European Heritage after the difficult and bloody communist regimes.

Hence, the identity of Europe and its heritage for future generations has mainly been built on the negation of elements of the past (the *ancien régime*, the XX century authoritarianisms, the communist regimes)[19] and the progressive integration of European countries through international cooperation. In the 1970s, the EU Court of Justice highlighted for the first time the existence of constitutional traditions common to the Member States,[20] representing a sort of unwritten bill of rights.[21] Since then, the main pillars of the European Common Constitutional Heritage started to be debated constantly. The pillars emerged as conditions for joining the EU as a member and were finally individuated by the so-called Copenhagen criteria[22]: democracy and respect of rights and of the rule of law, market economy, accountable and transparent institutions, and decision-making processes.[23]

CoE also played a relevant role by intervening in the definition of a continentally accepted catalogue of rights, which EU also wants to adopt, as demonstrated by the aim expressed in EU Treaty of Lisbon (2009) but, in 2016, still controversial and difficult to realize.[24] Furthermore, CoE's institutions discussed the interplay between the European Common Constitutional Heritage and national constitutional traditions. As the distinguished Antonio La Pergola, President of the Commission for Democracy through Law (known as the Venice Commission), stated in 1996, this common heritage is "interwoven with the threads of domestic

---

[19]See Rosenfeld and Sajo (2012).

[20]The Court referred to the common constitutional tradition for the first time in its case law in case 4/73 *J Nold KG v. EC Commission* [1974] ECR 491, 507.

[21]See C-11/70 *Internationale Handelsgesellschaft mbH v. Einfurt und Vorratsstelle fur Getreide und Futtermittel* [1979] ECR 1125.

[22]Even though the rules on conditionality were actually defined at the 1993 Copenhagen Council, the relevance of the respect of such principles for being a EU member became evident since the accession negotiations of Spain, when the *Birkelbach Report*, issued in January 1962, preconized the link between democracy and accession.

[23]The possibility that this identity may be linked to the evolution of specific religious tradition is still controversial. It suffices to remind the debate during the drafting of the European Constitution on the reference to the Judaic-Christian roots of Europe or the controversial decisions of the Court of Strasburg in cases concerning religious symbols (see, i.e., *Lautsi and Others v. Italy* App no. 30814/06 (ECtHR 18 March 2011).

[24]On the EU ratification of ECHR, see Schütze (2012), pp. 410–418.

constitutionalism"[25] and does not represent a superimposition, but rather a recognition of the fact that all the European Constitutions tend to protect the same values. The constant dialogue between national and supranational courts demonstrates such interplay. In the CoE context, for example, it passed through the recognition of the margin of appreciations of the States.[26] In the EU context, it evolved through the so-called counter-limits theory.[27]

Furthermore, the European Common Constitutional Heritage could not merely be considered another denomination of European Constitutional Law, given the differences in their content. The latter is composed of CoE and EU aquis, each of them enforceable in front of a competent Court. The former, on the other hand, represents a set of values, even progressively enshrined in the Law, which is derived from the philosophic elaboration of European thinkers and the history of the "Old Continent".[28] This history led to the existence of specific elements that characterize the European Heritage, which partially overlaps with the values of so-called global constitutionalism. In fact, Europe directed global attention to human rights by giving prominence to social rights, which are protected by the CoE's European Social Charter and by the EU's Charter of the Fundamental Social Rights of Workers (1989). The understanding of rights as based on the sanctity of human dignity also provides for another distinctive element of European Heritage: the total abrogation of the death penalty.[29] Furthermore, fundamental rights are intended to provide individuals with a secure and safe place, where social justice, equality, and solidarity are considered the leading principles and where the development of new technologies and modernization primarily serve the scope of eradicating poverty and granting environmental protection and sustainable development.[30] Another fundamental element that characterizes European Heritage concerns the idea of democracy, assigning a specific role to local entities, even in non-federal European States. In fact, CoE provided a Congress of Local and Regional Authorities (1957) to allow for periodical meetings among them on specific issues. At the EU level, the Committee of the Regions (1994) provided a specific advisory body for EU institutions, which allowed for the participation of local entities in the decision-making process. Finally, local entities' importance has

---

[25]Proceedings of the Conference, *The Constitutional Heritage of Europe*, Montpellier, 22–23 November 1996 (Council of Europe Publishing 1997).

[26]See Arai and Arai-Takahashi (2002).

[27]For references in the legal doctrine, see, among many others, Slaughter et al. (1998).

[28]See Rousseau (1997), p. 57.

[29]The abolition of death penalty is mainly due to the strong engagement of the Council of Europe, which passed the Protocols no 6 (1983) and no 13 (2002), and to the case law of the Strasburg Court (see, i.e., *Al-Saadoon and Mufdhi v. United Kingdom* App no 61498/08 (ECtHR, 2 March 2010).

[30]In their later formulation, all these principles and aims have been summarized in the Preamble of the EU Treaty.

been highlighted in the European Charter of local self-government passed in 1985 by CoE members and has been recalled in EU treaties.[31]

As previously mentioned, this European Common Constitutional Heritage does not always represent a consolidated aquis, but rather is sometimes constituted by the common aims of European States. Among these aims, there is also, in the words of the Treaty of Lisbon, the promotion of European values and the contribution to the establishment of peace and security (Article 3, Section 5). For these reasons, the EU's attention toward Mediterranean countries increased after the EU expanded to Central and Eastern Europe in 2004. The EU debated the meaning and content of the Heritage with these countries, distinguishing between the negotiations with candidate States and those with non-European neighboring countries.[32] Turkey, which is not the topic of this essay, the most well-known case of Heritage discussions with a negotiating candidate. The second category mainly includes North African countries, which have been considered partners of the European Neighboring Policy since its establishment in 2004. Furthermore, these countries were involved in a policy specifically devised for the Mediterranean area. The same was launched in 1995 with the Barcelona Process and eventually evolved into the Union for the Mediterranean in 2008. Pursuant to these policies, the EU established economic relations with Mediterranean countries and, thus, introduced shared European principles of respect for democracy and the rule of law.[33] Recognizing that a dialogue regarding shared values had existed for centuries, these policies facilitated partnerships focused on cultural exchanges in order to implement said shared values. The CoE, with the assistance of the Venice Commission on a consultative role, developed activities specifically for these countries. This has been, for instance, the case with Morocco and Tunisia—members of the Commission since 2007 and 2010, respectively. Both countries have been experiencing an intervention since 2011 while undergoing their respective constitution-making processes. In these instances, the experts of the Venice Commission tried to help North African framers by underlining the constitutional provisions that best evidenced reliance upon the rule of law, democratic principles, and protection of human rights. The result was not the importation of the European model, but rather a merging of local traditions with the European Common Constitutional Heritage, consistent with the sentiment that had already been expressed in La Pergola's speech. This means that despite the controversial situations in Hungary and Ukraine, the Common Constitutional Heritage is generally affirmed in Europe. By contrast, the consolidation of the values of democracy, pluralism, human rights, and rule of law, however, is still ongoing in North African neighboring countries. These are the main reasons why the analysis of which unamendable provisions these

---

[31]See Articles 4 and 5 of the Treaty of Lisbon and its Protocol no 2 on subsidiarity.

[32]See Morlino and Magen (2004), p. 5.

[33]It has to be admitted that, for long time, these policies did not prove their effectiveness as EU considered Northern African countries governed by autocrats, such Ben Ali's Tunisia or Mubarak's Egypt, as liable partners, not to say of the controversial relations established with Libya during the Gaddafi's regime.

countries choose to protect is particularly relevant when trying to understand whether and how a Common Constitutional Heritage is spreading.

In fact, Europe proved to have a specific identity when it comes to understanding unamendability. Europe's understanding differs from that of the U.S. for example, because constitutional courts are afforded the power to strike down unconstitutional constitutional amendments (i.e., those constitutional reforms that comply with provided procedures but contravene core constitutional values).[34] In other words, unelected bodies as Courts may intervene in the amending procedures in order to safeguard fundamental values[35] despite the U.S.'s concept of democracy being based upon popular sovereignty. This is clear *a contrario* evidence of the existence of a European identity.

The Venice Commission made some considerations when discussing the commonalities between the unamendable clauses of CoE members' Constitutions. It highlighted that Constitutions approved after turmoil usually provide these clauses for the purposes of protecting democracy and rights and consolidating a constitutional culture based on the European identity. As previously mentioned, this identity is not immutable and the Commission urged the States for "a restrictive and careful approach to the interpretation and the application of unamendable provisions"[36] in order to let principles such as democracy, federalism, and rights evolve, as it had already happened to them between the XIX and the XX century. Even if amending unamendable clauses is a possibility, the Commission highlighted the huge responsibility placed on the Courts, which should carefully consider the sociopolitical and historical context in which the amendment proposals take place.

3   Unamendability in Post-World War II Constitutions: The Cases of Italy and Germany

In Europe, post-World War II constituent moments were characterized by the attempt to avoid the establishment of new authoritarianisms through written, rigid, and democratic constitutions. Said constitutions included instruments of self-protection, such as the establishment of Constitutional Courts with the power to annul unconstitutional laws and amending procedures to protect Legislatures' role in modifying the fundamental Charter. In some constitution-making processes, some unamendability clauses were included, shielding some provisions from any possible modification.

---

[34]For an overview on how the idea of unamendability of some provisions affirmed in Europe, see Roznai (2013), p. 657.

[35]On this distinction, see S Holmes, CR Sunstein, 'The Politics of Constitutional Revision in Eastern Europe', in Levinson (1995).

[36]See Venice Commission (2010).

The cases of Italy and Germany are relevant in this sense and allow for an interesting comparison in light of the European Common Constitutional Heritage's role. Both cases demonstrate the importance of the long-lasting European constitutional tradition despite the process of supranational integration was just at its beginning. The influence of such a Heritage is evident from the debates in the Constituent Assemblies, particularly when they discussed the definition of the unamendable elements of the constitutional order.

The drafting of the Italian Constitution started after the institutional referendum and the election of the Constituent Assembly on June 2, 1946. It ended with the Assembly's approval on December 22, 1947.[37] The Italian Constitution is deeply influenced by the transitional period that began when the King decided to dismiss Benito Mussolini, leader of the National Fascist Party, from his charge of Prime Minister.[38] This Charter fashioned the new Italian legal system as a constitutional democracy, based on values and principles rooted in republicanism.[39] In order to protect such principles, Article 139 of the Constitution states the unamendability of the republican form of government, mirroring the wording of the coeval French Charter.[40] Like the French framers, the Italian framers aimed at entrenching a constitutional culture able to overcome the Italian society's lack of political homogeneity and establishing a pluralistic democracy to counter the idea of a strong political majority[41] and its possible distortions. These were also the reasons for bicameralism and for a system of institutional counterpowers, such as the vast competences attributed to the Constitutional Court and the establishment of local authorities.

In Germany, the beginning of the constitutional movement was more troubled. At the Potsdam Conference (from July to August 1945), the winning powers of the War (Britain, the U.S., France, and the USSR) decided to divide the country into four zones of influence. This division soon resulted in the polarizing between liberal democracy and popular democracy and two separate constitution-making processes started. In the Soviet zone (German Democratic Republic), a Constitution was approved on October 7, 1949, based on the tenets of a Communist State.[42]

---

[37]Then, the Constitution came into force on January 1, 1948.

[38]Mussolini was appointed as Prime Minister in 1922. The King decided to dismiss him after a sort of vote of non-confidence of the Fascist executive body (*Gran Consiglio*) on July 25, 1943, and appointed as Prime Minister General Pietro Badoglio. He established a new government in Southern Italy, while in the North the Italian Social Republic was established under the guide of Mussolini and the German support. During this period, the legitimacy of the Monarchy was challenged and the will to establish a Republic after the end of the war and the defeat of Nazi Fascism diffused.

[39]See Cheli (2006), pp. 32–33.

[40]Both Article 95 of the 1946 French Constitution and Article 89 of the 1958 one stated the unamendability of republicanism affirming that 'The Republican form of government shall not be the object of any amendment'.

[41]See Crisafulli (1958), p. 188.

[42]See Lanchester (2002), pp. 81–84.

The three other zones were united as the German Federal Republic, whose constitutional framers—feeling the territory halved—approved a text known as Basic Law. In theory, the Basic Law would have been considered the Constitution only once the country was reunited, as it effectively happened in 1990,[43] after the fall of the Berlin Wall. Notwithstanding, it was clear that the Basic Law was only provisional with regard to the geography; the choice for democracy and the rule of law (*Rechtsstaat*, in German) was definitive. These principles were so important that the 1949 German Basic Law declared, at Article 79, the inadmissibility of amendments concerning the division of the Federation in *Länder* and their participation in the legislative process. Additionally, Article 1 declared the inviolability of human dignity. Article 20 further established the democratic and social federal character of Germany, the principle of people's sovereignty, and the Germans' right to resist any attempt to abolish the constitutional order.[44] The reasons for providing such unamendability reside in the aforementioned constitution-making process and in the country's constitutional history[45]; they also seem to reflect the main characteristics of the European Heritage. In fact, the preservation of federalism is considered a tool to safeguard subnational entities' (*Länder*) democratic participation in the legislative process, thereby avoiding the restoration of a dangerous centralism. The unamendability of the provision on human dignity is an attempt to safeguard people from mass violations of human rights—such as the ones perpetrated by the Nazi regime—and denotes a deep understanding of the fundamental right to life. The U. N. Declaration of Human Rights (1948) is a similar declaration at the international level. The German Federal Constitutional Tribunal (GFCT) put forward these considerations in 1967, declaring that the content of the Basic Law and its approach toward the protection of fundamental principles may be

> explained by the historical experience and by the moral-ethical recollection of the past system of National Socialism. The almighty totalitarian state demanded limitless authority over all aspect of social life and, in pursuing its goal, had no regard for individual life. In contrast to this, the Basic Law established a value-oriented order, which puts the individual and his dignity into the very center of all its provisions.[46]

The will to protect democracy, intended not only as a procedural practice, but rather as a set of principles based on the rule of law and on rights' protection, emerges also from the rules on the ban of political parties (Article 21 of the

---

[43]The Unification Treaty, signed by the Federal Republic, the Democratic Republic and the four WWII winning countries on August 31, 1990, legally defined the reunification.

[44]Although Article 79 does not explicitly contain the noun "unamendable", it concretely provides for the ineffectiveness of any amendment attempt. See Albert (2008).

[45]See Fox and Nolte (1995), p. 19. The Authors recall that German framers decided to introduce unamendable clauses being aware that if they were present in the Weimar Constitution, Hitler would have had to violate them, making a sounding difference for German people, traditionally bound by legalistic sentiments.

[46]*Abortion I*, 39 BVerfGE 1 (1975).

Constitution). The ban confirms Germany as a militant democracy, 'one that will defend itself from those who attempt to destroy it or its fundamental values'.[47]

The understanding of such values in both countries is directly connected to the interpretation of unamendable clauses Constitutional Courts provide. In fact, in Italy, the Constitutional Court progressively extended unamendability by affirming it also affects the rights qualified as "inviolable" by the Constitution, along with all the principles enshrining the essence of the supreme values on which the Constitution itself is based. The extent of the protection of rights had been strongly discussed since the drafting in the Constituent Assembly, where the three main ideological groups (Catholics, Socialist-Communist, and Laics) supported different positions. Catholics supported an individualistic idea of the inviolable rights; Socialist-Communists supported a connection of those rights with popular sovereignty; and Laics supported viewing rights according to a natural law perspective. The engagement of the Communist leader Palmiro Togliatti and of the Catholic representative Giuseppe Dossetti, as well as the drafting activity of the Christian Democrat Giorgio La Pira and of the Socialist Lelio Basso, allowed for a compromise that concluded in Article 2 of the Italian Constitution stating:

> The Republic recognizes and guarantees the inviolable rights of the person, as an individual and in the social groups where human personality is expressed. The Republic expects that the fundamental duties of political, economic and social solidarity be fulfilled.[48]

According to this provision, the Italian Constitutional Court affirmed in 1956 that Article 2 recognizes the non-negotiable heritage of human beings.[49] Nonetheless, for a long time, the Court limited its enforceability to the rights explicitly enumerated in the Constitution[50] and, residually, to rights that were not listed but were coessential to those that were listed.[51] During the 1980s, the case law of the Italian Constitutional Court evolved. Article 2 started to be considered a clause foreclosed from values that were not related to the Constitution, but open to new interpretations of its content based on the changing social context.[52] It is up to the constitutional judges to decide, case by case, whether a right may be included among the inviolable ones. The role of the Italian Constitutional Court was not limited to the recognition of inviolable rights as implicitly unamendable given that its case law broadened the limits to amendability following the so-called systematic interpretation. Notably, in 1988, the Court stated that constitutional amendments cannot modify the principles the Constitution explicitly considers as absolute, such as the republican form of the government and those "that, although not expressively

---

[47]*Klass*, 30 BVerfGE 1 (1970).

[48]For further elements on the compromise among the framers of this article, see Baldassarre (1989), p. 11.

[49]Italian Constitutional Court, decision n. 11/1956.

[50]Italian Constitutional Court, decision n. 188/1980.

[51]Italian Constitutional Court, decision n. 98/1979.

[52]For some examples of the Italian case law concerning the introduction of rights through the open interpretation of Article 2, see Guastini (2007), p. 333.

mentioned among those not subject to the principles of constitutional revision, are part of the supreme values on which the Italian Constitution is based".[53]

It is worth noting that the German Federal Constitutional Tribunal (GFCT) has debated the existence of implicit limits to constitutional amendability as well. In 1951, the GFCT considered (and agreed with) the declaration the Bavarian Constitutional Court issued one year before, which stated that:

> there are constitutional principles, which are of so elementary a nature and so much expression of a law that precedes the constitution, that the maker of the constitution himself is bound by them. Other constitutional norms [...] can be void because they conflict with them.[54]

The Tribunal further stated that "Taken as a unit, a constitution reflects certain overarching principles and fundamental decisions to which individual provisions of the Basic Law are subordinate". Two years later, the Tribunal declared that positive constitutional laws might be invalid when transcending the limits of justice.[55] Nevertheless, the more Germany consolidated as a democratic State, the more the Tribunal set aside the natural law theory and started to rely on the principles stated in Article 79, interpreting them extensively.[56] Particularly, the Tribunal seems to have built a vision of the pillar principles of the legal system from the tension between personal and communitarian values. Human dignity and freedom to develop individual personality represent the highest ranked elements conceived as a whole in the right to personality (*Persönlichkeitrecht*); on the top of the hierarchy of the communitarian values, there are the laws of ethics and the liberal democratic legal system.

As previously stated, neither country enjoyed the support of a fully established European integration. Nonetheless, they relied on the already existing European Heritage and represented a source of inspiration for its further evolution. Both Italy and Germany reiterated, despite using different wording, the fundamentality of a system based on democratic institutions and the existence of checks and balances among them. They also used meticulously selected words to underline the State's duty in protecting fundamental rights. In Germany, this duty was considered so fundamental—to the extent of being *unamendable*—since the constitution-making process began; In Italy, an intervention of the Constitutional Court was needed to determine the unamendability of the inviolable rights.

A further consideration is necessary regarding the role of Constitutional Courts in the evolution of the European Common Constitutional Heritage. The GFCT engaged in an intense dialogue with EU institutions on the consistency of the EU

---

[53]See Italian Constitutional Court, decision n. 146/1988.

[54]The Bavarian Court's declaration was issued in the decision 2 VR 65, April 4, 1950. It was quoted in the GFCT's decision *Southwest*, 1 BverfGE, 32 (1951).

[55]See *Equality*, 3 BverfGE 225, 234 1953.

[56]This change in the parameter used by the German Tribunal has been evident in the *Klass* case (30 BVerfGE 1 1970).

Treaties with national constitutional laws and traditions—probably more so than any other European Court. It stated that as long as the protection of rights seems to be higher in Germany than in the rest of the European system, the devolution of powers at the supranational level has to be limited.[57] In Italy, the Constitutional Court dealt with the role of ECHR and with the relations between national constitutional law and European Law. The ECHR, as previously discussed, has been used to give a broader interpretation to the catalogue of fundamental rights by declaring the provisions of the Convention as interposed norms (*norma interposta*), part of the Italian legal order, but always subject to judicial review.[58] As for the relationship with EU Law, the Court, mirroring the German Tribunal, affirmed that

> it is directly enforced by all legal authorities, courts included [...] regardless of whether it infringes or bypasses existing ordinary or even constitutional provisions. The only limit [...] is that European norms always prevail as long as they are not proven to infringe the supreme principles and inviolable rights on which the Italian Constitutional order is based.[59]

This clearly demonstrates that (a) the European Heritage cannot be simplified as an overlap with European Union Law and (b) its evolution continues to be intertwined with national constitutional traditions.

4   After the Fall of the Berlin Wall: The Cases of Romania and the Czech Republic

Since 1989, Central and Eastern Europe had been engaged in a crucial constitution-making moment.

As Elster underlines, all countries involved in this constitutional wave shared common elements: they emerged from communist regimes, which tried to completely strike down their once sturdy constitutional traditions; they coupled the democratic transition with a transition from a central to a market economy; and their national stories had always been intertwined. For these reasons, when the Berlin Wall fell down, the events in one country influenced the neighboring ones in a domino effect,[60] and they all looked at the European Common Constitutional Heritage to find inspiration for their constitution-making processes.

Romania and the Czech Republic are two of the countries involved in this wave of constitutionalism. Their experiences are meaningful because they provide an interesting contrast.

---

[57]*Maastricht-Urteil*, BVerfGE 89, 155, October 12, 1993, and *Lissabon Urteil*, 2 be 2/08, June 30, 2009. On the point, see Preuss (2011), p. 429.

[58]For the decisions of the Italian Constitutional Court declaring ECHR provisions as interposed norms, see decisions n. 347/2007, n. 348/2007, and n. 39/2008.

[59]Fusaro and Oliver (2011).

[60]See Elster (1991), p. 448.

In Romania, the transition was led through a revolutionary and violent regime change, which ended with the execution of dictator Nicolae Ceausescu on December 25, 1989. Then, a transitional council was established under the leadership of the National Salvation Front (NSF), which was strongly tied to the previous communist regime.[61] At the elections for the Constituent Assembly held on May 1990, NSF obtained a relevant majority (355 seats out of 515), and thus could appoint 13 of the 28 members of the Constitutional Committee,[62] thereby influencing the debate regarding the content of the Constitution.[63] Even though it has been considered "the most illiberal constitutional draft presented so far in any Eastern European country, confirming [...] that a 'second transition' may be needed",[64] the Assembly approved the Constitution on November 21, 1991. A popular referendum ratified it on December 8 of that same year.

By contrast, the Czech Republic's transition was peaceful, despite its concurrence with the dissolution of the Czechoslovak Federation[65] (also known as "the Velvet Revolution").[66] In fact, the Parliament of the Federation decided to dissolve the union of these two States[67] beginning on January 1, 1993.[68] Meanwhile, both States began their respective constitution-making processes. On the Czech side, the Parliament elected on June 1992 appointed a constituent Commission, which drafted a Charter reminiscent of the democratic features of the 1920 Czechoslovak Constitution. With an overwhelming majority (172 votes in favor out of 198 voters), the Parliament approved the Constitution on December 16, 1992 and the same went into effect on January 1, 1993, the same day the Federation was officially dissolved. In contrast with the Romanian framers, the Czech framers decided to only include in the Constitution the provisions regarding the institutional functioning of the State, keeping as catalogue of rights the 1991 Charter of Fundamental

---

[61]On the NSF and its role in the transition, see Pasti (1997).

[62]The President of the Committee, Antonie Iorgovan, was formally considered as an independent, but he actually had a communist background and supported political positions close to the NSF.

[63]See Lungu (2002), p. 397.

[64]Elster (1991), p. 463.

[65]The country already existed since the dissolution of the Austro-Hungarian Empire, but the 1920 Constitution organized it as a unitary State without any federal elements. For an overview of Czech constitutional history, see Kuklík (2015).

[66]Probably, this denomination highlighting the peaceful way the transition happened has been invented by the dissident Rita Klimovà, which then became the Czech Ambassador in United States.

[67]On this process, see Elster (1994), p. 10.

[68]Constitutional Act n. 542, November 25, 1992.

Rights and Freedom,[69] which had been approved before the dissolution of the Federation and remained valid.[70]

These two different constitution-making processes led to the approval of very different provisions on unamendability. In Romania, only a few amendments were introduced in 2003 in order to comply with EU membership conditions, despite the text being considered "illiberal" at the time of its approval. On that occasion, the provision on unamendability simply "slipped" from Article 148 to Article 152, in order to leave a placeholder for the provisions on the Euro-Atlantic integration (Title VI) without having to change the content. A new amendment process started in 2012, and it is still ongoing in 2016.[71] Whatever its outcome might be, the clauses on unamendability do not seem to be at the center of the constitutional debate, which would preserve the content of Article 152. Article 152 prohibits the revision of the provisions concerning the national, independent, unitary, and indivisible character of the Romanian State, the republican form of the government, territorial integrity, independence of justice, political pluralism, and official language. It also states that "no revision shall be made if it results in the suppression of the citizens' fundamental rights and freedoms, or of the safeguards thereof" and provides for specific timeframes during which the Constitution cannot be amended, such as during a state of siege or emergency or wartime. It is worth noting that the unamendability concerns the *provisions* on those subjects and not the *principles* they enshrine. In a way, this makes a reform even harder.[72] In the Czech Republic, by contrast, Article 9 of the Constitution declares the general unamendability of the fundamental attributes that characterize the legal system as a democratic one. Nevertheless, the essence of fundamental rights may also be considered protected by an implicit unamendability given that (a) the Charter of Fundamental Rights and Freedom is an integral component of the Constitution (Article 3); and (b) the limitation of fundamental rights cannot breach "the essence and the significance of these rights and freedom" (Article 4)—which are inherent, inalienable, non-prescriptible, and irrepealable (according to Article 2 of the Charter). Therefore, in both Constitutions, the focus of unamendability is on democracy and rights, with a clear attempt to safeguard principles that, though proclaimed, were effectively disregarded by the communist regimes in order to ensure the control of

---

[69]The Czech one may be considered a poly-textual Constitution. It is composed by the text effectively named Constitution and by the mentioned Charter of Rights, but also by the Constitutional Acts connected to the dissolution of Czechoslovak Federation, the Constitutional Acts passed on specific topics (such as those on self-government and on the referendum for the accession to the EU), and the Constitutional Acts defining the national borders.

[70]It must be noted that while the Czech Republic adopted the Charter without any modification, simply stating that it is part of the Constitution, Slovakia integrated it in the Constitution and partially modified its content.

[71]On this amendment process, which affects also the relationship between Romanian legal system and the European Heritage, see Venice Commission (2014).

[72]This approach is not common among European countries. Only Turkey, Greece, and Azerbaijan provide for a similar kind of unamendability of some provisions.

the State by the Party. As in the Italian and German cases, a country's history influences framers' decisions to introduce unamendable clauses for the purpose of protecting values which are perceived as fundamental but that may be put in danger by unexpected choices of future political majorities. In order to protect fundamental values, Romanian and Czech Constitutions established Constitutional Courts, but, in contrast with the Italian and German cases, the analysis should concern the competences attributed to the Courts rather than their activism. In fact, the Romanian Court proved to be less powerful than one would have expected from a Court constitutionally declared as the guarantor of the supremacy of the fundamental law (Article 146). By contrast, the Czech Constitutional Court demonstrated a great authority in assuming powers not explicitly provided by the Constitution. The Romanian Constitutional Court may review bills for constitutional amendment only as a preventive control (a priori), given that it must review all the amendment initiatives before the Parliament begins the procedure to enact them and to submit the text to a compulsory popular referendum. The Constitution, however, provides the Court with a great ability to test the amendment, including its consistency with the core values of the Constitution that the text itself establishes as unamendable.[73] The Court was able to halt amending procedures on property rights in 1996 and 2000[74] because they were inconsistent with the requirements for constitutional revision. Nevertheless, in 2003, the constitutional provisions on the control of constitutional amendment proved to be weak.[75] The Court declared a part of the bill of revision that vastly amended the Constitution in the light of the EU requirements for the accession[76] inconsistent with the unamendable provisions on fundamental rights. Although the Parliament seemed to modify the bill according the Court's decision before approving it, the constitutional amendment has been challenged for unconstitutionality after its entry into force. The Court could not do anything but declare its lack of competence under the a posteriori control of constitutional amendment,[77] confirming that the Romanian Constitution seems to assign the protection of fundamental values to political powers rather than to the Constitutional Court.[78]

Formally, the same weakness seems to affect the Czech Constitutional Court. Article 82 of the Constitution only entitles it to judge and nullify acts that are inconsistent with the Constitution. However, the Court itself broadened its powers

---

[73]For further detail on the procedures for constitutional amendments in Romania, see Valea (2011), p. 91.

[74]Cfr. decision n. 85, September 3, 1996; decision n. 82, April 27, 2000.

[75]The Court intervened in constitutional revision also with the decisions n. 6, July 4, 2007 and n. 799, June 17, 2011, but they were just "notifications" of the unconstitutional elements the Parliament had to modify before to pass the constitutional acts.

[76]See decision n. 148, April 16, 2003.

[77]See decision n. 356, September 23, 2003 and decision n. 285, October 15, 2003.

[78]See Blokker (2013), p. 187.

when determining the unconstitutionality of an act shortening the term of office of the Chamber of Deputies.[79] The Court stated that the act might be declared void starting from the interpretation of Article 9, which has been considered not a mere declaration but an enforceable provision. Thus, the Court affirmed its competence in annulling any constitutional act that violated the essential requirement of a democratic State.[80] This decision to annul a constitutional act that complied with the amending procedures because it infringed upon the main pillars of a democratic State seems to be mainly based on the historical origins of the current Czech legal system. It is evident that the Court wanted to preserve the constitutional guarantees to democracy—which had been strongly infringed during the communist regime—by assigning such a specific and important role to the unamendability clauses.[81] This decision is also relevant because of the Court's reasoning, which showed the existence of a constant debate among constitutional judges on the very complex topic of controlling the constitutionality of the amendments to the fundamental Charter. In fact, the Court strongly relied on the German Tribunal case law interpreting Article 79 of the Basic Law and affirmed that its self-attribution of competence to conduct judicial review in this field is not ultroneous, but in line with the constitutional developments of European democracies.

5 The Arab Uprisings and the Constituent Processes in Tunisia and Morocco

The Arab uprisings, known also as the Arab Spring, began when the Tunisian people started an anti-authoritarian revolt against Zine al-Abidine Ben Ali and the corrupted regime he had built (December 2010). Since then, the main requests of the people, who had been demonstrating on squares and streets for several months, were democracy, social justice, and constitutional reforms. In Morocco, by contrast, reforms had been passed continuously since King Mohamed VI ascended to the throne (1999). Therefore, when the demonstrations began in February 2011, he was able to immediately introduce a constitutional amendment and thus bring peace to the country.

The constitution-making moments of these countries seem particularly interesting to the eyes of a European scholar because, in both cases, framers frequently debated on the reliance of the texts they were drafting with global constitutionalism, and asked for the consultative support of the Venice Commission[82] (although Morocco did not ask for a specific Opinion on the Constitution as Tunisia did). The

---

[79]Constitutional Law n. 195, September 10, 2009.

[80]Czech Constitutional Court, judgment n. Pl. ÚS 27/09, September 10, 2009.

[81]On this decision, see Williams (2011), p. 33.

[82]For a general overview of the role played by the Commission toward these countries, see the Commission web site (http://www.venice.coe.int/WebForms/pages/default.aspx?p=03_ Mediterranean).

Venice Commission broadly recognized the democratizing efforts of framers of both countries, generally underlining how even the unamendable clauses provided in the new Charters were roughly consistent with the European Common Constitutional Heritage. The Commission particularly welcomed the provisions aiming at controlling the "superpower" of one institution—the President of the Republic in Tunisia and the King in Morocco—and the will to introduce stronger means to protect people's rights. At the same time, however, the Commission highlighted the relevancy judges—particularly constitutional ones—were going to have in the future developments of democracy. The Commission underlined how their interpretations of the unamendable clauses should be as narrow as possible, in order to safeguard the will of the framers as well as the will of the people. Furthermore, the Venice Commission warned the framers about the procedures for constitutional amendment, particularly focusing on the risk that the compulsory approval of constitutional amendments through a popular referendum could transform an instrument of democracy into a tool to legitimize authoritarian deviations. The Commission urged for measures stating that the King or the President should submit the constitutional amendment to the Assembly before holding the referendum.

5.1   A New Tunisia: Which Values Need to Be Protected by Unamendable Clauses?

Having achieved its independence from France in 1956, Tunisia adopted its first Constitution in 1959. This text was formally based on the French model of the 1958 Constitution, even though it strongly empowered the President of the Republic. According to the vision of the main power of the State, the procedures for amending the Constitution gave the President a very important role, providing that

> the initiative of revision of the Constitution belongs to the President of the Republic or to one-third at least of the members of the Chamber of Deputies, under reserve that it does not infringe on the Republican form of the State. The President of the Republic can submit the bill of revision of the Constitution to referendum (Article 76).

In the absence of a rule safeguarding some unamendable elements, the whole text was theoretically subject to the President's will to amend it.

When in 2011 the revolts caused the end of the authoritarian regime of Ben Ali,[83] a transitional government was established and a new constitution-making process started.

---

[83]Ben Ali succeeded to Bourguiba, the first President of Tunisia and leader of its independence, in 1987, with the so-called medical coup d'état, allowing him to take the charge of President assuming the incapability for health reasons of the 80 years old Bourguiba.

On October 23, 2011, Tunisians elected the 217 members of the Constituent Assembly, assigning the majority (89 seats) to the representatives of the Islam-inspired party *Ennahda*. The constitution-making process started on February 13, 2012. After a period of bargaining between political forces, and thanks to the mediation of the main labor union and to the strong participation of the civil society, the Constitution was finally approved on January 26, 2014.

As for the provisions on amendability, Article 143 of the Constitution confirmed that the President shares the power of initiative with one-third of the Legislative Assembly and that the amendments initiated by the President shall take precedence. In contrast with the former text, however, the 2014 Constitution provides some clauses on unamendability in Articles 1 and 2. They state that "Tunisia is a free, independent, sovereign State; its religion is Islam, its language is Arabic and its system is republican. This Article might not be amended" (Article 1) and that "Tunisia is a civil State based on citizenship, the will of the people, and the supremacy of law. This Article might not be amended" (Article 2).

Some reflections should be made on the drafting process of these provisions. First, the introduction of an unamendable clause regarding the role of Islam is more than the simple affirmation of a State religion in the Constitution; it shows the significant influence Ennahda has had in the constitution-making process. Furthermore, the content of Article 1 makes difficult for the Constitutional Court to interpret it consistently with (a) the guarantees to the State impartiality as provided in Articles 14 and 15; (b) the principle of civil State affirmed in Article 2; and (c) the provision of Article 146, which states that "the Constitution's provisions shall be understood and interpreted in harmony, as an indissoluble whole". Also, the Venice Commission warned Tunisian framers about the risks this unamendable clause may cause to the legal system in the Opinion delivered in 2013 in connection with the constitutional draft.[84] Although Tunisian authorities informed the Commission of their will to erase this clause from the list of unamendable elements (then provided by Article 141) at the time of the Opinion, the list disappeared from the final version of the Constitution; the unamendable clauses were instead "spread" throughout different articles, but the constitutional role of Islam continued to be unamendable.

Second, an important step forward in the implementation of the protection of human rights has been taken by declaring the unamendability of the content of the catalogue of rights. According to Article 49

> the limitation that can be imposed on the exercise of the rights and freedoms guaranteed in this Constitution will be established by law, *without compromising their essence*. Any such limitation can only be put in place for reasons necessary to a civil and democratic state and with the aim of protecting the rights of others or based on the requirements of public order, national defense, public health or public morals, and provided there is proportionality between these restrictions and the objective sought. Judicial authorities ensure that rights and freedoms are protected from all violations. There can be no amendment to the Constitution that undermines the human rights and freedoms guaranteed in this Constitution.

---

[84]See Venice Commission (2013).

The content of this provision is very relevant in understanding how the European Common Constitutional Heritage has influenced the new Tunisian legal system. The establishment of core rights the State could not limit or infringe, indeed, is in line with several other European countries. Article 49 contains interesting references to the ECHR, such as the proportionality that must exist between limits and rights and the need for this proportionality in a democratic State. Nevertheless, the aforementioned Opinion of the Venice Commission underlined how such a provision is "a fairly widespread unamendability clause", warning the Constitutional Court that its interpretation should take into account the debate in Tunisian society.[85]

Third, Article 75 states that "the Constitution may not be amended to increase the number or the length of presidential terms". This provision is strictly linked to the history of the country during its authoritarian era, when elections were transformed in a sort of plebiscite and the dictator continued to be among the candidates—oftentimes the favorite—because he was able to amend the Charter in order to extend his ability to run for another mandate. The Venice Commission welcomed this provision, considering it a good tool to help democratic consolidation in a country "whose democratic structures and their cultural foundations have not yet been consolidated".[86]

5.2 A Reformist King and the Uprising: The 2011 Moroccan Constitution and Its Unamendable Provisions

After gaining independence from the French Protectorate in 1956, Morocco has always had a monarchic form of government tempered with some forms of constitutionalism. The Constitution approved after independence (1962) tried to frame the role of the King, but it effectively resulted in an excessive and extremist reference to the 1958 French semi-presidential model, which made the King the cornerstone of the institutional system. The amendment introduced in 1970 further strengthened the control of the Crown over the other powers and upon the people, which survived the approval of the new Charters in 1972[87] and in 1992,[88] and the constitutional reform passed in 1996.[89] On the contrary, the ascendance to the throne of Mohamed VI represented a turning point, as he started new reforms at

---

[85]Venice Commission (2013) § 214.

[86]Venice Commission (2013) § 215.

[87]The Charter, "octroyed" by the King, was approved by referendum and had the aim to answer to the request for more popular participation in the institutions.

[88]Even in this case, the Constitution derived from a "concession" of the King, and was later approved by referendum.

[89]The reform originated from the need of change derived from the popular support to the Socialist Party led by Abderrahmane El-Youssefi, returned from the exile in 1995.

the legislative level and was ready to confront the population on the introduction of a deep constitutional amendment when the people began demonstrating on February 20, 2011 and the Arab Spring drew Morocco's interest.

In fact, on March 10, 2011, the King appointed a Consultative Commission for Constitutional Reform, comprised of representatives from the whole spectrum of political parties and civil society, which drafted a constitutional amendment that effectively and completely replaced the Constitution—even auditioning political movements and labor unions, academics, and civil society organizations. Thus, the Council of Ministers approved the draft of the Constitution on June 17 before the presence of the King, who, on the same day, announced that the referendum would be held on July 1, 2011. Although some groups tried to boycott the process, such as the 20 February Movement, the population approved the constitutional amendment with a large majority (98.5% of the voters were in favor) and the King finally promulgated it with the royal decree (*dahir*) n. 1-111-91 of July 29, 2011.

Notwithstanding this constitutional reform, the content of the provisions on unamendability remained unchanged, their main aim being the protection of the monarchy and the role of Islam,[90] which is also the source of legitimacy of the Crown itself. Still, the Constitution put the King at the center of the amending process, as he is its main initiator and fundamental actor[91] (Article 172).

Nevertheless, the current Constitution contains an interesting extension of the unamendable elements, which somehow demonstrates the influence of the European Common Constitutional Heritage. Article 174 states that

No revision may infringe the provision relative to the Muslim religion, on the monarchic form of the State, *on the democratic choice of the nation or on [those] acquired in matters of [the] fundamental rights inscribed in this Constitution.* [emphasis added]

Obviously, a single sentence is not enough to affirm a clear permeation of the European Heritage in Morocco and the opinion of those scholars which still consider it as a hybrid regime[92] have to be taken into account.[93] However, a path has been paved for democratizing the country, given that the constitutional provisions, even those on unamendability, include references to the pillars of global

---

[90]Even changing a bit their wording, constitutional provisions did not change their content: the 1962 Constitution provided that the "monarchic form of state as well as the provisions relating to the Muslim religion may not form the subject of a constitutional amendment" (Article 108); the 1970 Constitution stated that "the royalist system, and provisions relating to Islam, shall not be subject to revision" (Article 100); the 1972 Constitution declared that "neither the State system of monarchy nor the prescriptions related to the religion of Islam may be subject to a constitutional revision" (Article 106); the 1992 Constitution said that "the monarchic form of the State as well as the provisions relating to the Islamic religion cannot be the object of a constitutional revision" (Article 100).

[91]It is noteworthy that the King has always been the sole initiator of constitutional reforms, even though this competence has been assigned also to the Parliament and to the head of government since the 1962 Constitution.

[92]See Morlino (2008), p. 70.

[93]See Biagi (2015).

constitutionalism. Thus, it will be in the hands of the ordinary legislators to implement such provisions and of judges to interpret them according to the contemporary understanding of constitutionalism.

6 Concluding Remarks

Almost diffused among European countries,[94] unamendable provisions may be conceived as a tool for framers to express the culture of the people, their heritage, and their expectations[95] at the constitution-making moment. In other words, they are means to sanctify the fundamental elements of the constitutional culture of a country by avoiding their modifiability through the ordinary amendment procedures. As highlighted, the will to provide a more definitive protection of such core values derives from the history of the countries and from the contexts under which Constitutions have been approved.

Thus, the first question this essay wants to deal with is: Does the entrenchment of values through unamendable constitutional provisions change depending on the wave of constitutionalism being considered? Remembering that waves of constitutionalism have been defined according to a chronologic criterion,[96] it could be noted that belonging to a wave is less relevant than the history of a country for purposes of defining unamendable clauses. In fact, notwithstanding the waves they belong to, the will to preserve the system from the reestablishment of authoritarianisms seems to be the major concern of the European cases considered. At the same time, the drafting of unamendable provisions is strongly linked to the way framers perceived the illegal behaviors of previous autocrats. In Germany, the introduction of unamendable clauses aims at protecting those principles that the flexibility of the Weimar Constitution allowed Nazis to nullify. In Italy, the task was to preserve the institutional choice for the republican form of the government done with the institutional referendum, which demonstrated the will of Italians to definitively foreclose the possibility of any kind of authoritarian power taking over, whether at the hand of a King or a tyrannical President. Furthermore, the Italian Constitution, despite not explicitly declaring their unamendability, proposed a list of "inviolable" rights, reminiscent of the protection of human dignity under the German Basic Law. In Central and Eastern European transitions, unamendable clauses were introduced in the Charters in order to protect human rights from violations such as the ones that had existed under the Communist regimes, and secure the existence of the rule of law, thereby avoiding that Constitutions will be

---

[94]In Europe, unamendable clauses are provided in the Constitutions of Azerbaijan, Belgium, Czech Republic, Cyprus, France, Germany, Italy, Luxemburg, Moldova, Romania, Russia, Turkey, and Ukraine.

[95]On this point, see Haberle (2000), p. 79.

[96]See n 4.

used to arm the State against citizens.[97] Nevertheless, in Romania, the provisions on the control of unconstitutional constitutional amendments strongly safeguard the secondary constituent power by preventing the Constitutional Court from exercising a posteriori control. Meanwhile, in the Czech Republic, the Court self-attributed this kind of competence in the previously discussed 2009 decision regarding the amendment to the Chamber of Deputies' term. Following a different reasoning, unamendable clauses in the current Tunisian and Moroccan Charters continue to protect stability, although sometimes this may grant more protection to the government rather than to fundamental rights, according to a characteristic of Arab Constitutions the doctrine already highlighted.[98] Furthermore, the unamendability of the provisions concerning Islam is controversial and the role of Judiciaries confirms to be, once again, at the center of the future developments of these legal systems.

The role of Judiciaries calls into question the second issue this essay wants to bring to light: Does the judicial interpretation modify the understanding of constitutional values? In fact, judicial interpretation represents the most useful tool to avoid the stagnation of the fountain source, given that, while it may facilitate the preservation of the core elements of Constitutions, it may also limit their adaptability to the current needs of society. As previously stated, in Italy and Germany, Constitutional Courts developed case law that considers the right to personality a fundamental element of the legal system, combining individual dignity and freedom to develop one's own personality in social activities. The case law states that this is a tool for strengthening the will to protect human rights through the Constitution. Thus, the interpretation does not seem to alter the intentions of the framers, but it rather broadens them, enlarging the values that are protected as unamendable. Similarly, in the Czech case, the Constitutional Court intervened in the protection of the basic structure of the Constitution. By contrast, in Romania, the different framers' attitude toward the protection of unamendable elements—which, in a sort of "back to future" game, connects the Romanian system to the constitutionalism based on absolute centralism of the parliamentary sovereignty—weakened the Court and reduced the influence of judicial interpretation in protecting constitutional core values. Nothing can be said, finally, for the constitutional interpretations of Tunisian and Moroccan Courts, as they have yet to interpret the unamendable provisions recent constitution-making processes have yielded. Nevertheless, some auspices may be formulated. As long as these countries continue to be at the center of a dialogue with other democracies and the international support to their democratic consolidation continues despite the attacks threatening their stability, the risk that they will return to an authoritarian regime are fewer. The risks of a constitutional interpretation prone to a backlash that obliterates the achievements of separation of powers and human rights' protections are also lower.

---

[97]Sajò (1996).

[98]See Brown (2002) and Brown (2003).

The last question proposed at the beginning of the essay was: Does the European Common Constitutional Heritage influence the definition of values entrenched through unamendable provisions? As Rosnai notes, "a nation's constitutional identity is defined by the intermingling of universal values with the nation's particularistic history, customs, values and aspiration".[99] The analysis proposed here seems to confirm this premise, highlighting how unamendable constitutional provisions safeguard values that characterize the national identity of a country and the common constitutional heritage. Furthermore, if "the purpose of unamendable clauses is mainly symbolic"[100] (i.e., showing the will of a State to overcome the past and demonstrating the adherence to some specific values), in European countries such values are the result of a shared history and of a common legal path. Nevertheless, at the end of the analysis, it must be noted that these countries did not show clear references to the specific features of the European Heritage in the wording of their Constitution, which are more generally reminiscent of the tenets of global constitutionalism. A more evident influence may be found in the interpretation of the unamendable clauses, when Courts constantly took, and continue to take, into account the understanding of concepts such as democracy and protection of rights as developed in the European continent. As for the two remaining cases of Morocco and Tunisia, even though the implementation of the Constitutions is still ongoing and proving their value will be the real bench, the dialogue with the European Common Constitutional Heritage seems to have represented a useful parameter to affirm the fundamental tenets of the constitutional State.

References

Abraham M (2000) Judicial role in constitutional amendments in India: the basic structure doctrine. In: Andenas M (ed) The creation and amendment of constitutional norms. BIICL, p 195

Albert R (2008) Counterconstitutionalism. Dalhousie Law J 31:15

Albert R (2013) The expressive function of constitutional amendment rules. McGill Law J 59:225

Alicino F, Gradoli M (2013) L'Islam nel XXI secolo e gli international human rights. In: Bonella CD (ed) Tradizioni religiose e tradizioni costituzionali. Carocci

Andhyarujina TR (2012) The Kesavananda Bharati case. The untold story of struggle for supremacy by supreme court and parliament. Universal Law Publishing

Arai Y, Arai-Takahashi Y (eds) (2002) The margin of appreciation doctrine and the principle of proportionality in the jurisprudence of the ECHR. Intersentia

Arné S (1993) Existe-t-il des norms supra-constitutionnelles? Revue du Droit public 2:460

Baldassarre A (1989) Diritti Inviolabili. In: Enciclopedia Giuridica, pp 11

Biagi F (2015) The pilot of a limited change: Mohamed VI and the transition in Morocco. In Frosini J, Biagi F (eds) Political and constitutional transitions in North Africa: actors and factors. Routledge

---

[99]Roznai (in this book), p. 47.

[100]See Elster (1991), p. 447.

Blokker P (2013) Constitution-making in Romania: from reiterative crises to constitutional moment? Rom J Comp Law 2:187

Brown N (2002) Constitution in a non-constitutional world: Arab basic laws and the prospects for accountable governments. SUNY Press

Brown N (2003) Palestinian politics after the Oslo accord: resuming the Arab Palestine. University of California Press

Burdeau G, Hamon F Troper M (1993) Droit constitutionnel. Librairie Générale de Droit et de Jurisprudence, p 356

Cheli E (2006) Lo Stato costituzionale. Radici e prospettive. ESI, pp 32–33

Crisafulli V (1958) Aspetti problematici del sistema parlamentare vigente in Italia. Jus 9:188

Elster J (1991) Constitutionalism in Eastern Europe: an introduction. Univ Chicago Law Rev 58:448

Elster J (1994) Transition, constitution-making and separation in Czechoslovakia. IRIS Working Pap 145:10

Fox GH, Nolte G (1995) Intolerant democracies. Harvard Int Law J 36:19

Fusaro C, Oliver D (2011) Towards a theory of constitutional change. In: Fusaro C, Oliver D (eds) How constitutions change. A comparative study. Bloomsbury Publishing

Guastini R (2007) Esercizi di interpretazione dell'art. 2 Cost. Ragion Pratica 29:333

Haberle P (2000) The constitutional state and its reform requirements. Ratio Juris 13:79

Huntington SP (1991) The third wave: democratization in the late twenty century. University of Oklahoma Press, pp 35–48

Kelsen H (1967) The pure theory of law (trans: German, second edition of 1960). University of California Press

Klein C, Sajò A (2012) Constitution-making: process and substance. In: Rosenfeld M, Sajó A (eds) The oxford handbook of comparative constitutional law. Oxford University Press, p 437

Kuklík J (2015) Czech law in historical contexts. Karolinum Press

Lanchester F (2002) Le Costituzioni tedesche da Francoforte a Bonn. In: Giuffré, pp 81–84

Levinson S (ed) (1995) Responding to imperfection. The theory and practice of constitutional amendment. Princeton University

Lungu I (2002) Romanian constitutional nationalism. Pol Sociol Rev 140:397

McIlwain CH (1940) Constitutionalism: ancient and modern. Cornell University Press

Morlino L (2008) Hybrid regimes or regimes in transition? FRIDE Working Paper, p 70

Morlino L, Magen A (2004) EU rule of law promotion in Romania, Turkey and Serbia-Montenegro: Domestic elites and responsiveness to differentiated external influence. In: Paper for the workshop on 'Promoting Democracy and the Rule of Law: America and European Strategies and Instruments'. Stanford University 4–5 Oct 2004, p 5

Mortati C (1946) La Costituzione di Weimar. Sansoni

Murphy WF (1995) Merlin's memory: the past and future imperfect of the once and future polity. In: Levinson S (ed) Responding to imperfection. The theory and practice of constitutional amendment. Princeton University. p 167

Pasti V (1997) The challenges of transition. Romania in transition. Boulder East European Monographs

Preuss UK (2011) The implication of "eternity clause": the German experience. Isr Law Rev 44:429

Rosenfeld M, Sajó A (eds) (2012) The Oxford handbook of comparative constitutional law. Oxford University Press

Rousseau D (1997) European constitutional heritage: a condition for European constitutional law. Federalist 2:57

Roznai Y (2013) Unconstitutional constitutional amendments. The migration and success of a constitutional idea. Am J Const Law 61:657

Roznai Y (2014) Unconstitutional constitutional amendments: a study of the nature and limits of constitutional amendment power. A thesis submitted to the Department of Law of the London School of Economics and Political Science, p 86

Sajò A (1996) Western rights? Post-communist application. Kluwer Law International

Schmitt C (2004) Legality and legitimacy. Duke University Press

Schmitt (2008) Constitutional theory. Duke University Press, Durham

Schütze R (2012) European constitutional law. Cambridge University Press, pp 410–418

Sieyés EJ (1789) Préliminaire de la Constitution. Reconnaissance et exposition des droits de l'homme, 1st edn. Baudouin, p 18

Slaughter A-M, Sweet AS, Weiler J (eds) (1998) The European court and national courts: Doctrine and Jurisprudence: legal change in its social context. Bloomsbury Publishing

Sunstein CR (2009) A constitution of many minds. Princeton University Press, p 1–16

Valea DC (2011) The Control of constitutionality of the initiatives for the revision of the Romanian constitution. Curentul Juridic 47:91

Venice Commission (2010) Report on constitutional amendment. CDL-AD(2010)001, 19 Jan 2010

Venice Commission (2013) Opinion on the final draft constitution of the republic of Tunisia, 17 Oct 2013, CDL-AD(2013)032

Venice Commission (2014) Opinion on the draft law of Romania, 24 Mar 2014, CDL-AD(2014) 010

Williams K (2011) When a constitutional amendment violates the "substantive core": the czech constitutional court's September 2009 early elections decision. Rev Central Eastern Eur Law 36:33